The Roman Roadside settlement at Westhawk Farm, Ashford, Kent: excavations 1998-9

By Paul Booth, Anne-Marie Bingham and Steve Lawrence

with contributions by

Lindsay Allason-Jones, Steven Allen, R N E Barton, Joanna Bird, Kayt Brown, Dana Challinor, Bethan Charles, H E M Cool, Louise Harrison, Hugo Lamdin-Whymark, Malcolm Lyne, Quita Mould, Sarah Paynter, Ruth Pelling, Mark Robinson, Fiona Roe, Ian Scott, Penelope Walton Rogers, Patricia Wiltshire, Vicky Winton, Annsofie Witkin

Illustrations by

Luke Adams, Peter Lorimer, Sarah Lucas, Lucy Martin, Rosalyn Lorimer

Edited by

Edward Biddulph and Ian Scott

The Roman roadside settlement at Westhawk Farm, Ashford, Kent: excavations 1998-9

Published by Oxford Archaeology as part of the Oxford Archaeology Monograph series

Edited by Edward Biddulph and Ian Scott

For more information visit http://thehumanjourney.net

Figures 1.1, 1.2, 1.3, 1.5 are reproduced from the Ordnance Survey on behalf of the controller of Her Majesty's Stationery Office, © Crown Copyright, AL 100005569

Figure 1.4 British Geological Society. © NERC. All rights reserved

Typeset by Manila Typesetting Company
Printed by Alden Press

isbn   978-0904-220-483

Contents

Contents

List of Figures

List of Plates

List of Tables

Summary

An area of *c* 6 hectares was excavated at Westhawk Farm, Ashford prior to a housing development. Flint artefacts included Lower Palaeolithic as well as Mesolithic and later pieces. The earliest features formed part of a field system probably of middle to late Bronze Age date. Its principal alignment (NE-SW) was followed by that of the Roman road from Canterbury to the Weald, probably established soon after the mid 1st century AD. A second road, from Lympne, formed a junction with the first, around which developed a previously unknown major settlement perhaps 15 hectares in extent. The plan of the focal (junction) area of the settlement was revealed by geophysical survey while the excavation concentrated on its south-west end (Area B).

The settlement was established within a generation of the Roman conquest. A rich cremation burial probably of pre-Conquest date suggests a pre-existing local focus of high status settlement. In Phase 2, the earliest Roman occupation of pre-Flavian date, the Canterbury road was partly defined by roadside ditches, but a feature diverging from this alignment formed an early boundary on the north-west side of the settlement in the vicinity of the road junction. At the south-west margin of the settlement area on the north-west side of the Canterbury road two structures were used in this phase, while south-east of the road at least one settlement unit, probably of agricultural character, was also of pre-Flavian date. A small cemetery was established outside the main north-west settlement boundary very early in the life of the site (Area C).

Phase 3, dated *c* AD 70-150, saw most of the main features of the settlement in place. These included a shrine structure, set in a rectilinear enclosure within a larger open space on the south-east side of the Canterbury road. The north-east side of the open space was defined by a double-ditched enclosure that fronted onto the road. Trackways led from outside the settlement up to the shrine area and domestic/agricultural activity continued in the complex on the south side of this area. On the opposite side of the road from the shrine, overlying the early settlement boundary, an iron-producing workshop housed both smelting and related smithing activities.

This workshop was abandoned early in Phase 4 (AD 150-200), the surrounding area being incorporated within a series of plots set out approximately at right-angles to the line of the Canterbury road. Further south-west another block of five or six rectilinear plots was laid out. These contained a variety of timber structures. South-east of the road, occupation continued in the area south of the shrine complex and two sides of the shrine enclosure were redefined.

The last phase of widespread occupation in the south-west part of the settlement is dated *c* AD 200-250 (Phase 5). Intensive activity continued in some of the south-west roadside plots and a plot on the opposite side of the road also remained in use. South of the shrine area the latest building, still of circular plan, may have been linked with a new iron-working structure north of the shrine. Like the earlier iron working establishment, this structure accommodated both smelting and smithing activities.

Early 4th century deposits in Area B were concentrated in a waterhole beside the Canterbury road. These contained large numbers of redeposited 2nd century coins perhaps from the shrine opposite. The only late 4th century activity in Area B was the apparent removal of a large post which had been a central feature within the shrine complex. Elsewhere, metal-detected finds of early-mid 4th century coins suggest continuing activity within the focal (unexcavated) part of the settlement, but even there such material was scarce. The latest burials in the Area C cemetery were probably of early 4th century date.

Limited activity of 13th century date, possibly indicating adjacent settlement, was located at the extreme southern end of Area B.

The Roman settlement contained areas of contrasting plan - groups of carefully laid out plots interspersed with zones of more 'organic' form. The 20 or so excavated structures were of timber and circular and rectilinear building forms were found side by side throughout the period. The economic emphasis of the settlement was presumably on agriculture and local market functions. Iron production was important, but its scale is such as to suggest that it had only local significance. It is possible, however, that one function of the settlement may have related to the administration of iron production. The finds, amongst which the large pottery assemblage is particularly important, suggest for the most part only modest prosperity.

A striking aspect of the site is the effective cessation of occupation by the mid 3rd century. This pattern is reflected in a considerable number of other rural settlements and a number of the Wealden iron working sites in the region. Its significance remains uncertain.

Acknowledgements

The Oxford Archaeology fieldwork team was led by Steve Lawrence and Anne-Marie Bingham, to whom principally is owed the credit for making the excavation a success. Key team members included Rachel Barton, Dan Bashford, Anthony Beck, Bethan Charles, Phil Chavasse, Peter Crawley, Guy Cockin, Simon Greenslade, Jon Hart, Mark Lacey, Darko Maricevic, Penny Middleton, Stuart Milby, Kirstin Miller, Chris Richardson, Gavin Robinson, Kathelen Sayer, Mike Simms, Mark Steinmetzer, Rosemary Wheeler and Michael Wood. The part played by all the other team members, too numerous to name individually, is also gratefully acknowledged. The project was managed for OA by Paul Booth under the oversight of Bob Williams (head of fieldwork) and Anne Dodd (head of post-excavation). Edward Biddulph and Ian Scott helped bring the report to completion and Paul Backhouse expedited its production.

Ashford Borough Council ensured through the planning process that part of the site was preserved *in situ* with part being excavated in advance of development. Special mention should be made of Michael Hayley, Lois Jarrett and Anthony Slack. Funding for both fieldwork and post-excavation phases of the project was provided very largely by Wilcon Homes, whose role in enabling a large part of the site to remain unaffected by development should also be remembered. Particular thanks are owed to Peter Armfield of Wilcon Homes for much assistance both before and during the fieldwork programme and, once construction was underway, to successive site managers Steve Bray and Bill Shelvey for their cooperation whilst building and archaeological work proceeded in tandem. Steve Bray's prompt action in alerting OA staff to the discovery of burial 9200 merits particular mention.

The role of Kent County Council (KCC) Heritage Section was very important throughout the project, from initiation onwards. Dr John Williams, the county archaeologist, played a lead role in securing the project funding and the case officers once the project was established were Wendy Rogers and Simon Mason. Paul Cuming and Stuart Cakebread kindly provided Sites and Monuments Record data. Richard Hobbs organised the 1998 metal detector survey while attached to KCC as Finds Liaison Officer and his successor Catherine Read co-ordinated the input of metal-detector groups in the subsequent excavation. KCC also provided financial support with regard to the 1999 training excavation. The undergraduate student contributions to the excavation were arranged through the good offices of Professor Rick Jones (Bradford) and Dr Neil Christie (Leicester).

Staff of Ashford Borough Council are thanked for their help in relation to the training programme and also to open days. Dana Goodburn-Brown also helped in this regard. Staff of Ashford Library, particularly Shirley Sheridan, were very supportive of the outreach aspects of the project. The training programme was also generously supported by the Kent Archaeological Society, to whom, with their then President Paul Cannon, thanks are owed. KAS members also provided a register of volunteer excavators (as well as participants in the more formal training programme) and Ted Connell, in particular, did an immense amount of work here, in addition to providing very helpful seminars on the pottery of the region. Further financial support for the training programme came from English Heritage, and Peter Kendal, the regional Inspector of Ancient Monuments, both helped to secure this and gave active encouragement throughout the project. English Heritage also made a very significant contribution to the post-excavation programme by committing staff and facilities to undertake investigative conservation of cremation burial 9200, carried out by Karla Graham, and most particularly to the recording and analysis of the substantial collection of iron slag, in relation to which thanks are owed to David Starley, Justine Bayley and particularly Sarah Paynter. Rob Vernon, then a research student at Sheffield University, carried out a fine-scale magnetometer survey of one of the ironworking areas and kindly made the results of this available.

Other help and information was generously given by a range of individuals and organisations. These include Neil Aldridge, Jeremy Hodgkinson of the Wealden Iron Research Group and Dr Bernard Worssam, who discussed geological matters with a number of members of the project team. Mr Arthur Ruderman kindly provided information of the Westhawk place-name. Ian Greig and Casper Johnson, both then of Archaeology South-East, are thanked for information on Brisley Farm, and Paul Bennett and particularly Keith Parfitt of Canterbury Archaeological Trust (CAT) discussed several aspects of Roman Kent. Jon Rady provided information on CAT sites in south Ashford. Tim Champion gave helpful advice on late Iron Age burials and Martin Millett offered a number of thought provoking suggestions and kindly gave access to a draft of a chapter on Roman Kent. None of those named here or below, however, is responsible for the defects of this report.

The contribution of all the specialists and technical support team, both in-house OA staff and externally based, is gratefully acknowledged. The contributions of the principal specialists were of value well beyond the scope of their individual reports. Hilary Cool would like to thank Nina Crummy for discussing aspects of the Stanway finds in relation to Burial 9200, Vanessa Fell for investigative conservation and the analysis of the metals that are included in the catalogue entries and John Cherry of the British Museum for identifying the 14th century seal. Joanna Bird would like to thank Brenda Dickinson for her comments on a particular samian bowl (no. 10 in the catalogue of decorated samian (see Chapter 6)). Dana Challinor would like to thank Rowena Gale for much help and constructive criticism of a draft of the charcoal report. Sarah Paynter is indebted to Roger Wilkes, at the Centre for Archaeology, who jointly sorted the slag and to Justine Bayley, who jointly undertook the initial slag assessment, as well as to the members of the Wealden Iron Group, in particular Dr Bernard Worssam who shared his expertise on the geology of the Weald and local ores, Dr Tim Smith who provided useful information on ore and slag compositions and Brian Herbert who provided slag samples from other Wealden sites. Penelope Walton Rogers wishes to thank Dr Allan R. Hall, English Heritage Research Fellow, Environmental Archaeology Unit, University of York, for information on botanical evidence from prehistoric Britain.

Last but by no means least it is a pleasure to acknowledge the interest and practical support and participation in the project of many other local people. These include members of the Mid Kent, Romney Marsh, Swale and West Kent metal detector clubs who gave up their time to assist in the 1999 excavations, and the tenant farmer, Mr Reeves. Amongst the local volunteers David Baldwin, David Dixon, Bill Dryland and Adam Stone were particularly regular helpers.

Chapter 1:   Introduction

LOCATION AND SITE CHARACTER

The Roman settlement of Westhawk Farm, Kingsnorth, Ashford, Kent, lies some 3 km south-south-west of the centre of Ashford, with its centre at NGR TR 000399 (Fig. 1.1). Topographically it is located along the north-east – south-west aligned edge of a slight plateau of Cretaceous Wealden Clay, and also extends down its south-eastern side towards the Whitewater Dyke, a tributary stream of the Great Stour. The underlying geology is capped with moderately acidic silty clays. The development site within which the Roman settlement principally lay covered a larger area of some 24.5 ha, divided in two by a major north-east to south-west aligned field boundary which ran along the edge of the plateau mentioned above.

The settlement is situated at the junction of two important Roman roads (Fig. 1.2). The main axis of the settlement is formed by a road (Margary route 130 (1973)) running up from the Weald on a generally WSW-ENE alignment, which adopts a more south-west – north-east line through the settlement before heading down the valley of the Great Stour towards Canterbury, some 25 km away. This is met in the area of the settlement by the road (Margary 131) from Dover and Lympne (the latter only about 13 km distant to the south-east). Previously thought to have formed a crossroads with road 130, it is now clear that road 131 heads north-westwards towards Maidstone, and thence (via Margary 13) to Rochester, from a point some 3 km west of Westhawk Farm in Shadoxhurst parish (Aldridge 1995; 2006).

The situation of the site and its scale as revealed by excavation and geophysical survey justify its description as a nucleated, roadside settlement or 'small town'. This is discussed in detail below, but for simplicity much of the site description and preliminary discussion takes this interpretation as its starting point. For present purposes the term roadside settlement, which carries less semantic baggage (cf Burnham 1993, 101) than 'small town' (with or without the quotation marks), is preferred.

PROJECT BACKGROUND

Prior to the commencement of exploratory work, occasioned by the proposal of a major housing development, and despite the potentially important junction location, there was little evidence in the immediate area, except the find of a single late 1st century cremation burial from the site of Westhawk Farm itself, to indicate the presence of a substantial Roman settlement. The work carried out prior to the determination of the planning application for the site, took the

form of a gradiometer survey undertaken by Geophysical Surveys of Bradford (GSB 1996; 1997; 1998), supplemented by evaluation trenching, principally of the north-western half of the development area, by the Kent Archaeological Rescue Unit (Philp 1997), in part informed by the results of the geophysical survey (Fig. 1.3). The success of the initial gradiometer survey, carried out at the end of 1996, led to expansion of its scope in successive stages, until detailed survey eventually covered some 18 ha. This showed a complex settlement plan based around the major road junction but incorporating numerous other features on several alignments (Fig. 1.6).

The broad chronology of the site was suggested by the evaluation trenching which revealed evidence of occupation, including timber structures, mostly within a date range of AD 70-250. There was only a little evidence for 4th-century activity, in particular. This was subsequently borne out by a controlled metal-detector survey carried out over the site in Spring 1998, which produced a range of material, principally Roman, but with some later items, and one pre-Roman coin (of Epillus). Only 6 out of a total of 87 Roman coins were demonstrably of 4th-century date, a remarkably low proportion had the site seen significant late Roman activity. Superficially, at least, this material confirmed the apparent early Roman emphasis of the site.

After negotiations between Kent County Council, Ashford Borough Council, English Heritage and the developer (Wilcon Homes), it was agreed that the part of the site including the focal area of the settlement as defined by the geophysical survey (Area A, an area of c 10 ha) would be taken out of the development proposal and retained as open space, while the south-western part of the settlement (Area B) would be subject to excavation. Both these areas lay south-east of the major modern boundary mentioned above. Provision was also made for limited excavation on the north-west side of the focal area of the settlement (and north-west of the major modern boundary), principally in order to see if the Roman road to Maidstone could be located here (Area C). Otherwise, it was felt that this area lay largely beyond the limit of the Roman settlement, had produced no significant features in either the geophysical survey or evaluation trenching, and did not justify the expenditure of significant resources upon it. The extent of the site to be examined in whole or part by excavation was approximately 8 ha.

The Oxford Archaeological Unit (now Oxford Archaeology, hereafter OA except in relevant publication references) offered a successful tender to carry out the excavation and subsequent work on a phased

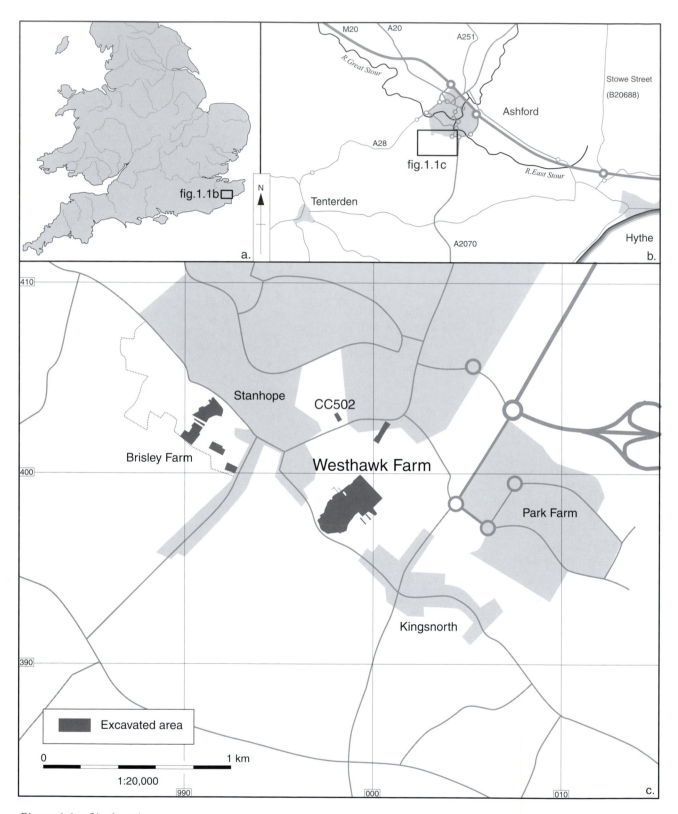

Figure 1.1   Site location.

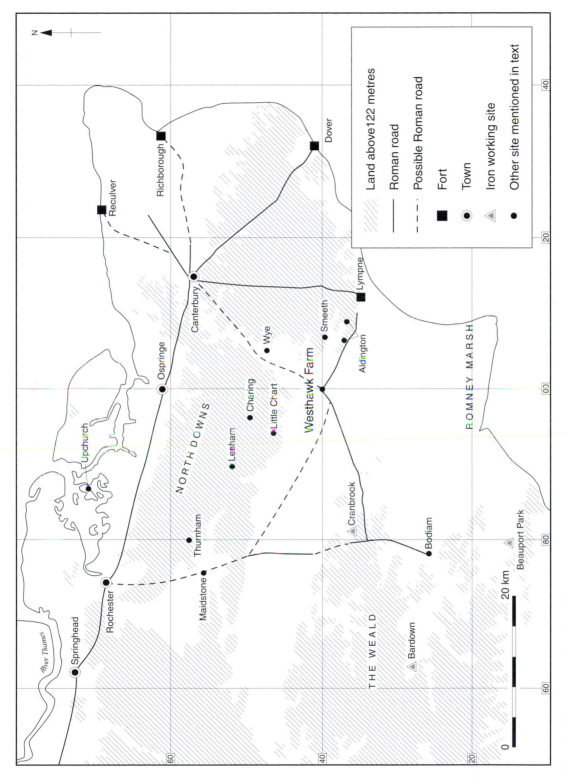

Figure 1.2   Principal Roman roads and settlements in Kent.

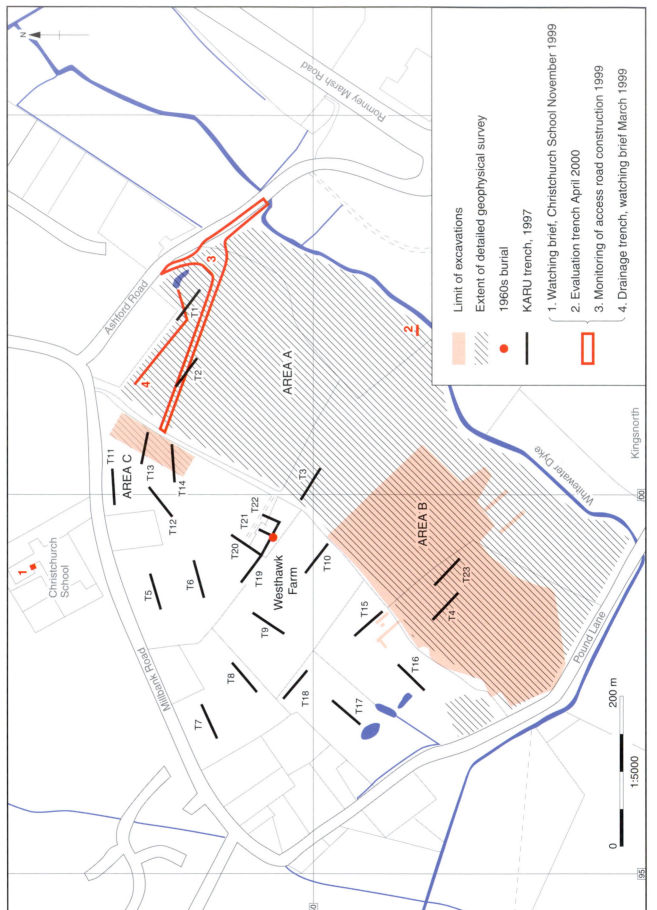

Figure 1.3   Site plan showing extent of detailed geophysical survey and location of evaluation trenches, main excavations and other archaeological observations.

programme, and the first season of excavation was carried out between late August and mid November 1998. The second - and last - season of fieldwork commenced in early July 1999 and was completed in early November of that year. Funding for the project was provided almost entirely by Wilcon Homes, and was administered by the Heritage Conservation team of Kent County Council, who commissioned the work on behalf of Wilcon Homes and also developed the strategic framework for the site's investigation. In the second year the excavation team was supplemented by students from the Universities of Bradford and Leicester and by (mostly local) participants in a training excavation programme put together with support from Kent County Council, the Kent Archaeological Society, English Heritage and Ashford Borough Council. The total excavated area was eventually almost exactly 6 ha. On completion of the basic site archive a programme of post-excavation assessment was carried out between June and December 2000 (OAU 2001) and followed immediately by the commencement of work on the full-scale analysis and reporting of the results of the excavation.

A number of small-scale observations in the Westhawk Farm area were made in the course of and subsequent to the main programme of excavation. These consisted of:

1   A watching brief during limited building work at Christchurch School, Millbank Road (NGR TQ 999 404), just north of the site, unrelated to the main housing development, in November 1999. No archaeological features or finds were revealed.
2   Excavation of a short length of sewer trench adjacent to the Whitewater Dyke at NGR TR 003 398, on behalf of Babtie Group in April 2000. No archaeological features or finds were revealed.
3   Monitoring of construction work for a new access road across Area A in 1999. This was built on a causeway entirely above modern ground level and had no impact on the underlying archaeological deposits.
4   Recording of a drainage trench at the northeastern margin of Area A in March 1999.

Only the last of these provided useful information relating to the Roman settlement, and this is summarised below.

PHYSICAL AND ARCHAEOLOGICAL BACKGROUND

The following brief summary of the physical and archaeological background is focussed on an area within a 10 km radius of Westhawk Farm, with only selected reference to sites and features beyond this.

Geology, Topography and Soils

Kingsnorth and south Ashford lie towards the northern margin of the extensive Weald Clay deposits which constitute the earliest part of the (Cretaceous) geological sequence in this area (Fig. 1.4). To the north the Weald Clay is overlaid by the component deposits of the Lower Greensand, upon which central Ashford is located, in turn succeeded by Gault and the Lower, Middle and Upper Chalk of the North Downs, the last of these being exposed barely 5 km north of Ashford. Locally the Lower Greensands are capped with river gravels and deposits of Head and Head Brickearth, the Brickearth occurring particularly north of Ashford between Kennington and Wye. On the Downs the Upper Chalk is widely overlaid by Clay-with-flints.

The southern margins of all these deposits lie broadly on a WNW-ESE aligned front, cut by the valley of the Great Stour which runs north-north-eastwards from Ashford past Wye as far as Chilham, and then turns north-eastwards in the direction of Canterbury. Significant alluvial deposits are found in places not only in the valley of the Great Stour but also associated with the East Stour and its tributary stream the Whitewater Dyke. Such deposits extend around the east and south margins of the Westhawk Farm complex. They are much wider than would normally be expected in relation to such relatively small streams (Smart *et al.* 1966, 278) and may date to a late stage in the last glaciation (B Worssam, pers. comm.).

The geological sequence of the region gives rise to a series of historical/topographical zones or *pays* (Everitt 1986, 44-5) on the same broad WNW-ESE alignment (Fig. 1.5). From the north these are the Chalk Downland, bordered by the narrow band of Holmesdale and then the slightly wider Chartland zone, giving way to the Weald in the south. Holmesdale corresponds broadly to the underlying Gault Clay, and Chartland to the south lies on the Lower Greensand formation, while the Weald zone lies on the eponymous Clay. Some 8 km north of central Ashford the Downs reach a height of 176 m at Rattle Hall. To the south, the Holmesdale and Chartland zones lie roughly between 50 and 90 m OD, while the Stour valley is lower-lying. Westhawk Farm itself lies at about 40 m OD. The Weald country immediately south of Westhawk Farm is undulating, for the most part ranging between *c* 25 and 45 m OD, with localised higher and lower points (Plate 1.1).

The 'natural' subsoil revealed in the excavation varied distinctly, reflecting the site topography. The strip of land on the highest ground at the plateau edge, lying north-west of the north-east to south-west aligned Roman road, was occupied by a mottled yellowish brown silty clay (perhaps the surface of the Wealden Clay). South-east of the road on land sloping gently down to the Whitewater Dyke, the subsoil comprised an orange brown clayey silt *c* 0.2-1 m thick overlying clay. This deposit contained locally high concentrations of manganese and several palaeolithic flints were recovered from it. Towards the bottom of the slope the subsoil was a relatively homogenous alluvial clay with a low to moderate silt content.

The predominantly silty and/or loamy clay drift soils are characteristic of the Wickham 1 (711e) soil

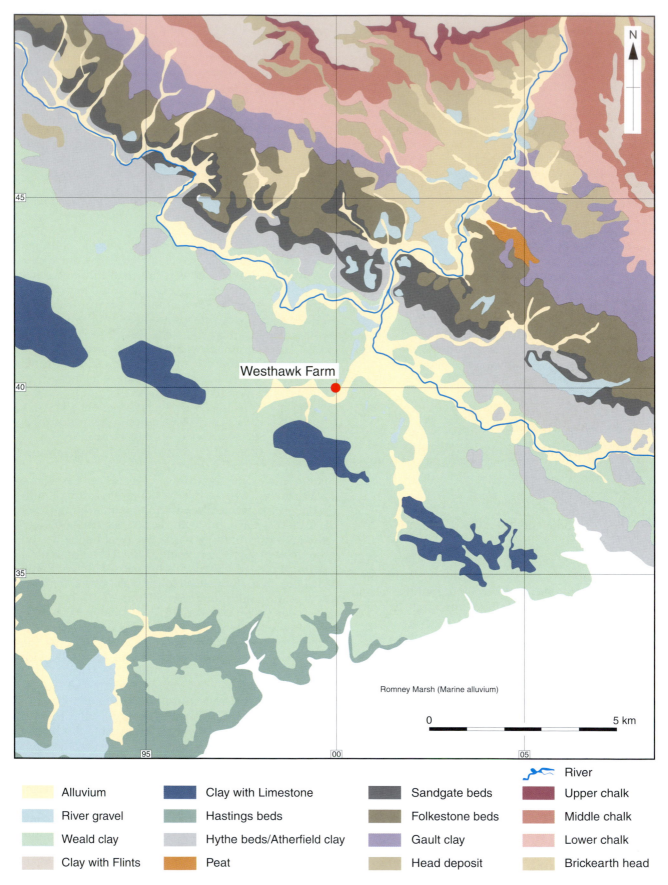

Figure 1.4   Simplified geology map of the Ashford area, centred on Westhawk Farm.

Plate 1.1   General view of the site looking south-west.

association (SSEW 1983). The soils were consistently quite acidic (the specific pH was not recorded), to the extent that bone did not normally survive unless burnt. There was localised survival of bone in unusual conditions such as waterlogged deposits.

Prehistoric

Relatively little earlier prehistoric material has been recorded from the Ashford area. A single Palaeolithic hand-axe was found *c* 3 km NNW of Westhawk Farm and Palaeolithic and Mesolithic flint flakes come from Stanford some 13 km east of Westhawk Farm. Further Mesolithic material is known at Aldington some 9 km to the south-east and at a dozen or so locations within a 10 km radius of Westhawk Farm, but many of these are findspots of individual objects. The most significant Palaeolithic and Mesolithic material in the area comes from Park Farm, a little over 1 km east of Westhawk Farm. Here a few Upper Palaeolithic flints were found, together with very extensive evidence for flintworking in the Mesolithic period (Clark 1996). A small quantity of Neolithic flint is also known from Park Farm.

Neolithic and Bronze Age finds are more common across the area than those of the Palaeolithic and Mesolithic, but they lie largely to the north and east of Westhawk Farm, with very few finds of this date located on the fringes of the Weald to the south and south-west. The Neolithic material again consists almost entirely of finds, some single objects, principally of flint. The Bronze Age evidence is more diverse and includes barrows and ring ditches on the Downs in the north of the area and indications of settlement in the lower lying areas in the vicinity of the lower East Stour. Significant Late Bronze Age settlement evidence comes from Little Stock Farm, just east of Mersham (Glass 1999, 196), and closer to hand from the Waterbrook area south-east of Ashford (Rady 1992, 32). A small but striking concentration of Bronze Age metalwork finds clusters around the Stour Valley in north Ashford.

A broadly similar distribution of sites and finds is observed in the Iron Age, at which time the absence of evidence for activity south and south-west of Westhawk Farm is even more marked than in the Bronze Age. At the same time there is also less evidence for activity on the Downs, though there is a minor concentration of sites and findspots in the vicinity of Wye and on the adjacent higher ground on both sides of the Stour Valley. No major foci of settlement, in the sense of hillforts and/or *oppida*, lie in the area, the nearest being at Canterbury to the north-east and towards Maidstone to the north-west. (For a recent distribution map of hillforts in the region see Hamilton and Manley 2001, 10). The principal concentration of Iron Age sites and finds in the area is in the vicinity of Ashford itself. This is largely a consequence of the increased

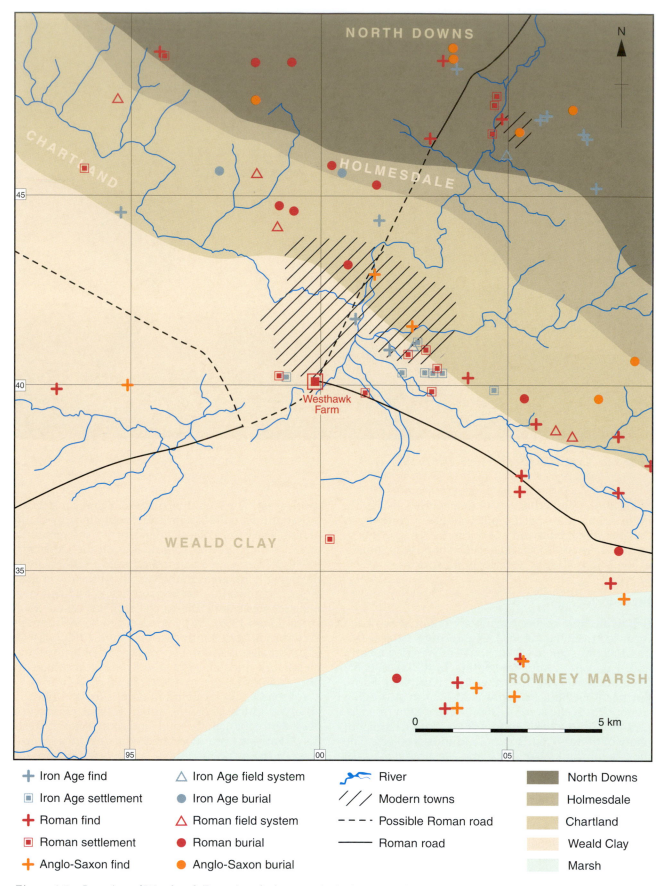

Figure 1.5   Location of Westhawk Farm in relation to principal topographic units and Iron Age, Roman and Anglo-Saxon features in the Ashford area.

volume of archaeological work in the area arising from the major development of Ashford in recent times, particularly on the south and south-east sides of the town, and also reflects the volume of archaeological fieldwork associated with the construction of the Channel Tunnel Rail Link (CTRL; for detailed reports on all the CTRL work see http://ads.ahds.ac.uk/catalogue/projArch/ctrl). However, the new evidence also serves to underline the contrast, in this and other periods, between the desirability of Holmesdale, with its relatively fertile and well-watered soils, and the less tractable Weald Clays to the south-west. Chartland, lying between these zones, is also typically poor ground, though more fertile in the 'central reaches, between the Medway and the Stour' (Everitt 1986, 51).

This recent work has generated considerable evidence for late Iron Age settlement in the immediate vicinity of Westhawk Farm, though much of the evidence, some of it only from evaluation rather than larger scale excavation, has yet to be formally published (Fig. 1.5). Little Stock Farm, east of Mersham, has produced late Iron Age settlement evidence, succeeded by Roman field systems (Glass 1999, 196). A notable concentration of late Iron Age findspots and related features occurs at Sevington, south of the railway line roughly 3 km east of Westhawk Farm (Booth and Everson 1994, 412, 433). The nature of the dating evidence is such, however, that some of these sites could date to the early Roman period rather than (or perhaps as well as) the late Iron Age. A similar situation prevails at Waterbrook Farm just to the south of this area, where ditch systems and associated domestic activity including at least one structure were located by the Canterbury Archaeological Trust (Rady 1996).

The most significant evidence for late Iron Age settlement in the area, however, comes from recent excavations by Archaeology South-East at Brisley Farm, only *c* 600 m west-north-west of Area B at Westhawk Farm. Here there was extensive settlement of later Iron Age date, with which were associated two high status 'warrior' inhumation burials (Johnson 2002).

Roman

As already discussed the site lies at the junction of two major Roman roads which link it to major settlements within the region (Fig. 1.2). To the east these are the ports and military establishments of Lympne and Dover, the former only *c* 13 km distant, while Canterbury, 25 km distant to the north-east, was the tribal capital of the Cantiaci. West of Canterbury, however, significant nucleated settlements ('small towns'/roadside settlements) seem to be confined to the line of Watling Street, leaving the south-western part of Kent apparently without such settlements. Despite the peculiarities of the chronological range of activity at Westhawk Farm it is now clear that this site can be regarded as a major nucleated settlement in a classic road junction location. Maidstone, to the north-west, has also been suggested from time to time as the location of another 'small town' (cf

Wheeler 1932, 98-101; Webster 1975, 59 and 63; but see Detsicas 1983, 78-9; Houliston 1999, 158). While the evidence is not conclusive such an identification is plausible in terms of distribution. Whatever the status of Maidstone, however, the identification of Westhawk Farm as an important centre, certainly at local if not at regional level, is clear.

A range of Roman rural settlement is found around Ashford, though as in earlier periods there is much less evidence for the Wealden area west and particularly south-west of Ashford than for the Stour valley and the area immediately south-west of the Downs (Fig. 1.5). Knowledge of the latter area has again been considerably enhanced by work carried out in connection with the construction of the Channel Tunnel Rail Link (Glass 1999). The most obvious evidence for rural settlement consists of stone buildings, including a bathhouse near Little Chart (Detsicas 1983, 143), a small villa near Charing (ibid., 96-7) and a further villa and another building near Wye (loc. cit.), all to the north of Ashford. Recent finds of building material in Wye indicate the presence of additional structures there, though the character of these is unknown (Sparey-Green 1999). Two more presumed villas are known at Aldington, one close to the Roman road from Lympne *c* 7 km south-east of Westhawk Farm, and another some 2.5 km further east.

Rural settlement types not characterised by stone buildings have only tended to be recognised relatively recently in the area, particularly in work associated with the Channel Tunnel Rail Link and with the expansion of Ashford. Boundary ditches relating to field systems and settlement have been located at several CTRL sites both east and west of Ashford. The most significant settlement site to emerge from this work is that at Bower Road, Smeeth, where several posthole structures were associated with rectilinear enclosures and other features (Diez forthcoming - see below), the majority of activity falling in a late Iron Age to late 2nd century date range. Scattered evidence for Roman activity, again mainly of early Roman date as discussed above, comes from Park Farm, the Boys Hall area and Brisley Farm.

The presence of rural settlements is indicated additionally by the occasional occurrence of burials, almost invariably cremations, at a number of sites in the area. The Ashford area has also produced evidence of iron production in several locations, on such a scale that these are characterised as ironworking sites, rather than as agricultural sites in which iron production was a secondary activity. Such a site is identified at Wye (Bradshaw 1970, 178). The principal focus of iron production in the region, of course, lies in the Weald some distance to the west of Ashford (Cleere and Crossley 1985, 57-86; Hodgkinson 1999).

Post-Roman

Anglo-Saxon material, most either demonstrably or probably associated with early burials, is found in the Ashford area at some eight sites stretching in an arc from Westwell through Wye to Brabourne Lees, with further findspots in Ashford and Willesborough (Fig. 1.5). A number of these finds (including the two last) are, however, only approximately located. A further group of Anglo-Saxon finds, mostly of pottery, is known from an area centred roughly 9 km southeast of Westhawk Farm near Newchurch in Romney Marsh.

The principal historically attested foci of Anglo-Saxon activity in the area were at Wye and at Westwell. Wye lay at the point where the Pilgrims Way and the Downland ridgeway joined to cross the Stour. Having been something of a focus of Roman settlement it became 'an important *villa regalis* [by 762], the *caput* of a Kentish lathe, an early market centre, and a focal point of heathen worship' (Everitt 1986, 86) and in due course the site of a Minster church. Westwell was also an early estate centre, one of a number found on the springline of Holmesdale, and the site of secondary mother-church, a category of churches unlikely to have been minsters themselves but known to have given birth to secondary foundations (ibid, 197).

Archaeologically almost nothing is known of the middle-late Anglo-Saxon period in the area, though recent work at Mersham has produced finds of both these periods as well as 11th-12th century material (Glass 1999, 212-213).

In the area only South Ashford(?) is clearly referred to in the Domesday record, under the name of *Estefort* (*VCH* 1932, 247). It was part of Hugh de Montfort's lands and was held by Maigno. In the time of Edward the Confessor, Turgis had held it from Earl Godwin. South Ashford (?) had land for half a plough, with one in the demesne, and eight acres of meadow. Two villeins (unfree tenants) are recorded, having a plough between them. Two serfs are also recorded. The land was assessed at one sulung (the Kent equivalent to a hide). The land was valued at 30 shillings, compared with 25 shillings when Turgis had held it.

According to Edward Hasted (1797-1801, 588-9), "West Halks" was usually called "West Hawks", and was held by the Manor of Kenardington. The farm gave its name to the Halk family; hawks were present on the family seal. This family, and hence the farm, extend back to at least the 14th century: Sampson de Halk died in AD 1360 (loc.cit.). By the mid-15th century, the Halks family estate had passed to the Taylor family, and had in turn passed to the Clerk family by *c* 1500. By the time Hasted was writing, Westhawk was in the possession of Henry Eaton. Alternative views of the origin of the placename are possible, one being that it is Anglo-Saxon, perhaps meaning 'west corner', with analogous names in Kent including Hawkinge and Hawkhurst (Arthur Ruderman pers comm). The locational description would fit exactly the position of the site at the western end of Ashford parish (see below).

Documents relating to the site of Westhawk Farm, rather than the owning family, are scarce, and a potential 16th-century reference (cf Philp 1997) proved on examination to contain three deeds, two dated 1776 and one 1769, that refer to properties and named fields in the parish of Bexley with no reference to Westhawke Manor (*Ashford Parish Index* ref U.6.T.36, of 1581 'Westhawke Manor'). The recently-demolished farm buildings may have been of early 19th-century date (Philp 1997). They appear on the Kingsnorth tithe map of 1839 (Ref: IR30/17/208) but not on Kent Sheet 3 of the Ordnance Survey one inch to one mile survey, published in 1819 (Harley and O'Donoghue 1975). The latter clearly shows West Hawk on Pound Lane a little to the south-west of the recent site at a location which would correspond with 'Old House Field' as given in the documentation associated with the Kingsnorth tithe map. The mid 19th-century mapping shows a linear pond here (no longer extant) which might suggest that the 'Old House' was moated, like nearby Kingsnorth Court Lodge, barely 300 m distant to the south-west, or Park House (Farm) some 1.5 km to the east.

Both the Kingsnorth tithe map and the Ashford tithe map of 1843 (Ref: IR30/17/12; "Copied and corrected" from an 1818 survey and with the Apportionment book dated 1842) give information on the associated fields at that time. These, including 'Old House Field', were principally pasture, but there was some arable. The field names do not generally provide any hint of the existence of a Roman settlement, but it is notable that the small field immediately south-east of Whitewater Dyke and south-west of the present Ashford Road is called Stone Acre, and that the adjoining field to the south-east, separated from Stone Acre by the Kingsnorth-Ashford road, is called Causeway Field. Both names must refer to the existence of the Roman road from Lympne which runs through them.

The site of Westhawk Farm itself lay in Kingsnorth parish, but the tithe maps and the subsequent 1st Edition Ordnance Survey 6" map (surveyed 1871-2) show that land immediately south-east of the farm buildings, including much of the area of the recent excavations, lay within a narrow south-westerly projection of Ashford parish, the south-westernmost point of which, then (as until recently) situated in the middle of an open field, was marked by a boundary post, the position of which was identified in the excavation of Area B. The correspondence between this projection and the extent of the Roman settlement, while not precise, is generally quite remarkable. While there is no clear evidence to indicate why this should have been the case the only likely explanation is that the area of the Roman settlement, and perhaps in particular the line of the Canterbury road, retained some significance, though the cartographic evidence suggests that the line of the latter through Ashford was no longer known by the mid 19th century.

GEOPHYSICAL SURVEY

The initial gradiometer scan of the site, carried out in 1996 by Geophysical Surveys of Bradford, covered 25 ha in scanning mode while simultaneous detailed survey covered some 4 ha (GSB 1996). Further detailed work was undertaken in 1997 (GSB 1997) and

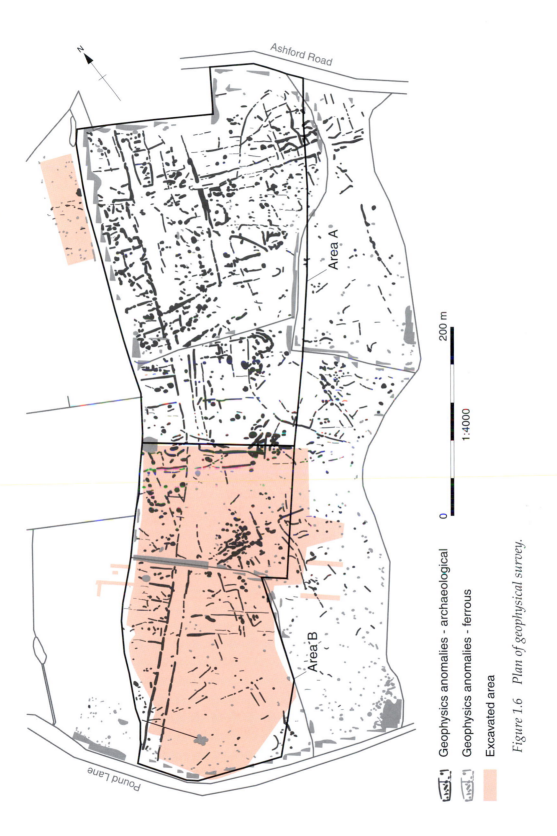

Figure 1.6   Plan of geophysical survey.

Geophysics anomalies - archaeological

Geophysics anomalies - ferrous

Excavated area

Ashford Road

Pound Lane

Area A

Area B

N

0   1:4000   200 m

with additional work in 1998 (GSB 1998) the area subjected to detailed survey was ultimately almost 18 ha (note that Figure 1.6 only shows the extent of detailed survey). The principal features revealed by the survey were linear anomalies, but numerous discrete features were also present, although their interpretation was more problematic.

In outline, the survey showed that the Weald-Canterbury road, defined along much of its length by linear boundaries, formed the axis of a settlement extending along it for a distance of at least *c* 700 m, with the north-east extent of the settlement lying under existing housing beyond the development area. There was a distinct bend in the road alignment at about the midpoint of its detected length. The road from Dover and Lympne was also detected, the two roads meeting at right angles at what was presumably the focal area of the settlement (towards the northern end of the development site). Here there appears to have been a substantial rectilinear open space, defined by ditches which were particularly marked (in the gradiometer survey) at the point where the Dover/Lympne road entered the focal area. There was no sign of a north-westerly continuation of that road towards Maidstone, however. The settlement along the axial road was characterised on its north-west side by ditched plots ranging from *c* 18-30 m in width laid out at right angles to the road alignment. South-east of the road there was more variety of layout, including (from the north-east) the focal ditched zone or possible open space already mentioned, groups of substantial linear features, some of which may have defined a large enclosure, an area where there was no indication of roadside ditches and, at the south-western end, clear definition of the road but little sign of large-scale activity adjacent to it. In the central part of the surveyed area, south-east of the axial road and south of the focal ditched zone, a number of concentrated magnetic anomalies were detected which were interpreted as being associated with ironworking. A number of linear features were noted which did not conform to the general pattern of the site layout. These were of two types; irregular alignments which it was thought could indicate pre-Roman activity, and straighter features, at least one of which is now known to be of early Roman date.

KENT ARCHAEOLOGICAL RESCUE UNIT EVALUATION

The evaluation, undertaken by the Kent Archaeological Rescue Unit on behalf of the then owners of the site, was carried out in March 1997, in the light of information derived from the ongoing programme of geophysical survey. Twenty-three machine trenches were excavated (Fig. 1.3). Five of these were sited within or adjacent to parts of the Roman settlement (as indicated by the geophysical survey) on the south-east side of the axial modern field boundary. The remaining trenches lay north-west of this boundary in areas suggested by geophysical scanning to be largely devoid of archaeological interest. Four of

these trenches were located in and around the site of Westhawk Farm itself in the hope that further evidence relating to the burial found in the 1960s might be revealed. In the event this hope was not realised, and only one trench (Trench 14) of those on the north-west side of the axial field boundary revealed any archaeological features or dating material. This was situated in the area subsequently excavated as Area C (see below). Trenches 1-4 and 23 to the south-east of the boundary all produced Roman features and finds. Trench 3 contained two areas of metalling, one of which was thought likely to be part of the surface of the Weald-Canterbury road, also indicated by roadside ditches. In Trench 4 eight large postholes indicated a substantial timber building identified in the subsequent excavation as Building D.

The assessment of the finds from the evaluation suggested that the settlement was occupied mainly between *c* AD 70 and 250 and that on the basis of 'the absence of masonry buildings, the substantial absence of building materials and the generally poor quality of the artefacts' the settlement, though extensive, was 'of low quality' (Philp 1997, section H; see also Philp 1998).

METAL-DETECTOR SURVEY

The survey, carried out in April 1998, was organised by Richard Hobbs of Kent County Council as part of an initiative to involve local metal-detector users in formal archaeological projects. Members of a number of clubs participated in the survey under the direct supervision of Richard Hobbs and significant objects (as defined in the field) were pinpointed using an EDM, the survey work being done by Peter Guest. The survey covered a wide area of the proposed development site, but concentrated most intensively on the focus of the Roman settlement in Area A. The results were summarised by Hobbs (1998). The finds consisted principally of Roman and later material, of which the coins were the most important. These included one pre-Roman coin (of Epillus), and some 87 Roman coins (see Guest below), the majority of which were of 1st-2nd century date. A summary listing of the most significant non-coin finds is contained in the project archive. Inevitably, much metalwork of relatively recent date and little archaeological interest was recovered.

1998-1999 EXCAVATION

Site Methodology

The excavation was carried out in two seasons, from late August to mid November 1998 and from early July to early November 1999. Topsoil and a subsoil consisting of plough-disturbed horizons, possibly reflecting activity of medieval as well as post-medieval date, were removed by tracked 360° excavators using toothless ditching buckets under direct archaeological supervision. The two deposits were removed separately, and in 1999 in particular the exposed subsoil was subject to systematic scanning by metal detector users before its removal. Metal objects found within this deposit were then located precisely using an EDM, to allow the possibility of relating some of them to underlying, subsequently-excavated features. Topsoil heaps were also scanned with metal detectors. Excavation and on-site recording followed standard Oxford Archaeology procedures.

Preservation

Excavation conditions varied very considerably. The natural subsoil, which ranged from clays and silty clays to a compact silty sand with a high manganese content, particularly in the south-western part of Area B, was relatively poorly-drained both on the valley side as well as on the plateau (Area C) and at times was very wet indeed. A major question that had to be resolved was the extent of the truncation of archaeological deposits. The plough-worked subsoil deposit was variable in preservation and thickness. At the top of the slope in the northern corner of Area B this deposit did not survive at all and the modern topsoil, averaging 0.25-0.28 m in thickness, directly overlay the natural Wealden clay at most points. The subsoil layer increased in depth down the slope, and at its greatest depth, at the south-east corner of Area B, was up to *c* 0.28 m thick below a topsoil averaging *c* 0.35 m in depth. However, while the greater depth of subsoil afforded protection from modern ploughing to the underlying archaeological deposits, damage had already been done to these deposits in the course of formation of the subsoil layer itself. Nevertheless the greatest truncation of the archaeological deposits was clearly towards the top of the slope in the north-west part of Area B and in Area C. The extent of this can be judged in part from the degree of truncation of vessels placed in cremation burials. On the assumption that when placed in the ground the cremation urns were complete vessels and did not project above the contemporary ground surface, it can be estimated that at least 0.15-0.20 m has been lost from burial groups 210 and 220, at the north-eastern margin of Area B, and the extremely poor preservation of a number of the cremation burials in Area C would be consistent with a similar if not a greater depth of truncation. The level of truncation cannot be quantified consistently across the site, but there are no convincing indications that it was ever significantly less than the values proposed here.

As a consequence of plough truncation of the archaeological deposits there was very little *in situ* stratigraphy. For example, there was limited, localised survival of surface or sub-surface material within the corridor of the Weald-Canterbury road. Elsewhere, almost the only significant accumulations of vertical stratigraphy were noted halfway down the valley side in the vicinity of the ironworking structure R at the north-east edge of Area B and in the circular structure P some 90 m to the south-west. In both cases the presence of underlying features with gradually settling fills may have contributed to the survival of deposits associated with the buildings, but it is notable that both structures lay relatively close to the line of a post-medieval field boundary running across the valley slope. It is therefore possible that accumulation of soil adjacent to this boundary afforded a degree of protection from post-medieval ploughing and thus enhanced the preservation of deposits in this area.

Overall, however, areas of surviving stratigraphy were few and very limited in extent. The nature and quality of what has been lost cannot be assessed adequately. Nevertheless it is clear that post-Roman truncation of the site sequence is not the explanation for the relative absence of late Roman activity, since this, had it been present, would still have been reflected in the presence of some cut features and of late Roman finds, and particularly coins, in the topsoil and subsoil. Such material was conspicuously absent.

Despite the variations in preservation it was clear that the surviving features constituted an important sample of the settlement and that the complexity of the remains still necessitated careful consideration of the overall approach to excavation within the resources available. The broad approach decided upon was to reveal as much as possible of the plan of the settlement rather than to concentrate on intensive examination of localised sequences within it. Emphasis was also placed on establishing the chronological framework of the development of the site. Sampling of features was perforce of limited extent in parts of the site, and some discrete features were not examined at all. This approach of 'strip, map and sample' has been developed by Kent County Council's Heritage Conservation team for work in Kent in response to large-scale development activity in the County. A priority is to consider the wider spatial and chronological frameworks both intra- and inter-site, rather than concentrating in detail on more limited areas.

Site sequence

For the most part understanding of the site sequence was based upon the relationships between cut features (Fig. 1.7). These were sufficiently numerous to allow the construction of a phasing scheme for the principal linear elements of the site plan. Groups of related features, or constituent cuts of the same linear feature, were combined (after careful examination to confirm their equivalence) under *group numbers*. The basis of the site sequence is provided by group number matrices, which establish in particular the sequence of the principal linear features on the site - ditches and gullies which formed part of or could be related to the two roadside ditch sequences along the axial Weald-Canterbury road. Establishment of the chronological framework of the site, based on the sequence in Area B, involved consideration of the horizontal as well as the vertical stratigraphic sequence. This resulted in the definition of a series of *phases* within major *periods*. The resulting sequence was then closely correlated with dating evidence provided principally by ceramics and

599750E
139800N

599850E
139750N

	Period 1, Prehistoric
	Period 2, Phase 2: AD 43-70
	Period 2, Phase 3: AD 70-150
	Period 2, Phase 4: AD 150-200
	Period 2, Phase 5: AD 200-250
	Period 2, Phase 6: AD 250-350
	Period 2, Phase 7: AD 350-400
	Period 3, Post Roman

NB: In case of multi-period features,
phase shown is latest, not construction

0   50 m

1:1000

Figure 1.7   Overall plan of excavation in Area B showing all periods/phases

coins to provide at least approximate 'absolute' date ranges for the Roman phases. Discrete features were assigned to these phases, where possible, on the basis of spatial relationships with features of known phase and of independent dating evidence, particularly that of pottery. Some features of course could not be assigned to phases in this way and so do not appear on individual phase plans. Alternatively, features which are only broadly dated may appear on more than one phase plan. Such features might have been in use over an extended time span or have had only a short life within the overall date range of the phases to which they are assigned.

Site narrative

The following narrative presents a highly condensed summary of the information available for the stratigraphic sequence of the site. Much detail is omitted and while the description is as objective as possible it necessarily relies for ease of use upon an interpretative framework developed in part during the fieldwork and refined further during the post-excavation assessment. Justification for the assignment of individual features to a specific phase is not normally presented, though the most problematic points are discussed. More detailed information can be found on the CD-ROM attached to this report, and also in the project archive.

The site description proceeds chronologically as far as possible, but for the Roman period a spatial and chronological approach has been followed, the principal excavated area (Area B) being divided into a number of zones both for ease of reference and to facilitate presentation of the data.

The chronological scheme adopted is as follows:

> Period 1. Prehistoric
> Period 2. Late Iron Age-Roman
> > Phase 1 Late Iron Age-*c* AD 43
> > Phase 2 *c* AD 43-70
> > Phase 3 *c* AD 70-150
> > Phase 4 *c* AD 150-200
> > Phase 5 *c* AD 200-250
> > Phase 6 *c* AD 250-350
> > Phase 7 *c* AD 350-400+
> Period 3. Medieval
> Period 4. Post-medieval and modern

The scheme of phasing within Period 2 has been deliberately left quite broad in view of the character of the archaeological features and the limitations of the dating evidence. Subdivision of individual phases, particularly of Phases 3 and 4, is possible in some parts of the site, and is presented in the site narrative below, but was considered inappropriate for many areas where the phasing of discrete features was largely dependent upon pottery dating. The suggested beginning and end dates for each phase are, of course, only approximate.

Terminology of spatial units

For the purposes of the site narrative as systematic as possible a set of terms has been used to define component zones or distinct topographical or functional components of Area B. These terms are both interpretative as well as descriptive. This is intended to make them more readily comprehensible; justification of the interpretative aspects will be presented in the narrative and subsequent discussion. The principal units of the site narrative for Area B Period 2 are as follows:

1 The axial Weald-Canterbury road (abbreviated to 'the Canterbury road' or 'the road') and its associated ditches.
2 Features north-west of the Canterbury road:
    North-west oblique ditch (an early feature diverging from the road alignment) and related features, superseded by,
    North-west roadside plots defined by linear boundaries (numbered NW1-?NW4);
    North-west undivided roadside area, between the north-west and south-west groups of roadside plots;
    South-west roadside plots defined by linear boundaries (numbered SW1-SW6).
3 Features south-east of the axial road:
    North-east enclosure area, comprising the ditch complexes at the north-east margin of Area B which related to features beyond it;
    The Shrine area, consisting of the whole of the open space within which the shrine enclosure proper was placed;
    South-central settlement area, consisting of the complex sequence of linear boundaries, enclosures and associated structures located at the south margin of the shrine area. These can be defined further as a series of plots (numbered SC1-SC6). An isolated Plot (SE1) fronting onto the Canterbury road is also relevant to the definition of Plots SC1 and SC2. This area includes the 'south trackway', a well-defined north-south trackway running through this complex;
    South peripheral area. The southern margins of the settlement, including burials and a possible mortuary enclosure.

ARCHIVE

The archive is currently held by Oxford Archaeology pending identification of an appropriate repository. A microfilm copy of the archive is held by the NAR at Swindon.

Chapter 2:   Period 1 - From the Palaeolithic to the Bronze Age

INTRODUCTION

Some evidence for activity dating from the Palaeolithic to the Bronze Age was recovered from Westhawk Farm. This comprised in the main worked flint, although some evidence for a pre-Roman field system possibly of Bronze Age date was found.

Some fifteen certain or probable Lower Palaeolithic artefacts were recovered, one from Area C and the remainder from Area B. The condition of these was variable, but some at least were quite sharp, suggesting they had not moved a great distance since deposition. Eight of the objects, including the one from Area C, came from the top of the 'natural' subsoil (contexts 3, 5002 and 7002), six were from Roman deposits and one was from topsoil.

A further topsoil find (SF1, context 1) was a probable Mesolithic tranchet axe, roughly made. Twenty-nine flints from fairly closely adjacent features gully 8087 and ditch 8418 were also dated to the Mesolithic, though the features themselves were Roman, of Phases 5 and 2 respectively.

The remaining flint comprised 155 flints recovered from 84 contexts and was all residual in Roman contexts. They include a further ten isolated finds of probable/possible Mesolithic pieces; the latter are included with the Neolithic and Bronze Age material in Table 2.3. The remainder of the flint spanned the Neolithic to Bronze Age, with the majority of the pieces probably being of Bronze Age date, adding weight to the assumption that the pre-Roman field system (see below) was also of this date. The Neolithic and Bronze Age flint forms a low density spread across the site; no flint was recovered from contemporary features and nor were any concentrations observed. In addition, 101 pieces/828 g of burnt unworked flint was recovered from the site.

PALAEOLITHIC FINDS
by Vicky Winton

Several artefacts thought to be Palaeolithic in age were submitted to the author. Table 2.1 contains a description and interpretation of each of the pieces. The raw material groupings are described below. A consideration of the evidence suggests a general principle of economy in use of raw materials among the Westhawk Farm artefacts, though the artefacts may represent more than one episode of Lower Palaeolithic activity.

Most of the artefacts seem to fall into three main groups reflecting both the raw material and the general condition of the artefacts. These are:

LB (Light Brown)   A relatively coarse grained and heterogeneous raw material that has a yellow or cream patina and Munsell colour chart values of 10YR 7/6 yellow and 2.5Y 8/4 pale yellow.

DB (Dark Brown)   This classification denotes Munsell colour chart values of 7.5YR 5/8 strong brown, 7.5YR 6/6 reddish yellow and 10YR 5/8 yellowish brown for the surface of the artefact and the condition is moderately sharp.

BC (Brown + Cream)   This is good quality (fine textured and homogeneous) flint of 10YR 4/4 dark yellowish brown, 2.5Y 4/4 olive brown in sharp to slightly rolled condition.

In addition in Table 2.1, VWDB stands for Very Weathered Dark Brown and B distinguishes a mid-brown coloured artefact apparently of different raw material from LB and DB. Artefact 776 displays both BC and DB patinas on the apparently ancient surfaces which could suggest a continuum between BC and DB patinas, and further that the two patinas do not distinguish artefacts of different ages.

The assemblage includes handaxes and handaxe trimming flakes showing that the Lower Palaeolithic flint knapping represented at the site involved the production of bifacial handaxes. There are no very large flakes or entirely cortical flakes, which suggests that the earliest stages of stone tool manufacturing process are not represented. The presence of handaxe trimming flakes and handaxes, without significant amounts of other knapping debris, suggests that the assemblage represents a tool kit that was used away from the place where the tools were made.

Differences in patination and condition are put down to differences in local environmental conditions. That the contexts from which artefacts derive provide diverse chemical environments (and thus differences in patination which are not related to age)

Figure 2.1   Period 1: Plan showing distribution of Palaeolithic flint and possible Bronze Age features.

599750E
139800N

9480

10160

10110

10100

8241

10485

10486

9943

9945

10090

10080

599850E
139750N

10120

▲ Location of palaeolithic flints

0

50 m

1:1000

599800
139900

791

8517

10200

1735

599950E
139900N

1640

1130

9590

10140

10130

1820

600050E
139900N

600050E
139800N

Table 2.1   Catalogue of Palaeolithic flint. Pieces marked with an asterisk are illustrated in Fig. 2.2.

Provenance	L (mm)	W (mm)	T (mm)	Raw Material/Patina	Type	Condition	Description and Interpretation
9142 (Fig. 2.2)	72	62	15	DB	Handaxe?	Slightly rolled or weathered with pot-lid fracture surfaces on both faces.	A bifacially worked piece with concentric pattern of flake scars on both faces. Part of a small biface? Lower Palaeolithic age.
9389	75	57	18	BC	Flake	Sharp and slightly patinated with concretion adhering to surface in places.	Relatively large hard hammer struck flake with at least six flake scars one of which is on the ventral surface. Debitage from core reduction or maybe early stage of biface shaping? Lower Palaeolithic age.
3 sf 9 (Fig. 2.2)	97	80	24	LB	Handaxe	Rolled or weathered with refitting broken off tip (recent break) and some dark brown concretions.	Wymer type JK biface (cordate - ovate). Lower Palaeolithic age.
5002 sf 500	66	64	19	BC	Flake	Slightly rolled appearance with numerous patinated frost pits and broken into two major parts by unpatinated thermal fracture.	Relatively large flake that may be debitage from a biface since a bifacially flaked edge is preserved on the butt end of the flake. Perhaps from re-shaping a handaxe during use. Lower Palaeolithic age.
3 sf 246	61	42	12	LB	Part of handaxe?	Sharp-slightly rolled / weathered with extensive unpatinated break surfaces.	Part of a biface (bifacial flaking along one edge) with unpatinated freeze-thaw break surfaces. Lower Palaeolithic age.
7002 sf 1383 (Fig. 2.2)	139	78	36	DB	Biface	Rolled / weathered condition (more so on one face than the other) with some unpatinated damage and two large freeze-thaw break surfaces on the butt area.	A well made pointed biface (Wymer type F). Lower Palaeolithic age.
8242	57	30	8	DB	Flake	Rolled / weathered condition with two patches of concretion adhering to ventral and dorsal surfaces.	Flake with at least eight flake scars on the dorsal surface. Could be from the shaping or re-sharpening or re-shaping of a biface.
7514	42	38	15	VWDB	Flake	Very rolled / weathered and patinated.	Small flake with cortex on distal and two dorsal flake scars. General knapping debris. Lower Palaeolithic age.
7001 (Fig. 2.2)	63	46	14	BC	Biface trimming flake	Slightly rolled or weathered (more so on highest part of dorsal surface). The distal tip is broken off and this break surface is less patinated than the dorsal flake scars (though not unpatinated).	The flake has numerous flake scars on the dorsal surface and platform (which could be the remnants of a bifacial tool edge) and has a thin, arched profile. This flake is in the form of a classic biface trimming flake, which may attest to resharpening of a handaxe during use. Lower Palaeolithic age.
776	20	35	9	BC and UP	Flake	Mint ventral surface, remnants of patinated flaked surface on dorsal and platform	A small transverse flake struck from a patinated artefact. The patination on the dorsal surface is different to that on the platform suggesting differential patination on the artefact from which this flake was struck.
8329	34	53	14	B	Flake	Sharp	A transverse waste flake which is not necessarily of Palaeolithic age.
7002 sf 1332	60	42	11	LB	Flake	Rolled / weathered, lustrous surfaces with a great deal of manganese staining	Flake apparently a by-product of Lower Palaeolithic handaxe manufacture or re-sharpening on the basis of the condition and soft hammer flake scars on the dorsal surface - though the flake itself appears to be hard hammer struck.
7002 sf 1336	47	50	20	LB	Flake	Ventral surface is more rolled or weathered than the dorsal surface. Thick patina with hard lustrous surface and light ochreous colouration. There is a significant break along the left side.	Thick flake - possibly from shaping a pointed biface (since ovate forms would not yield a flake with such steep edges) or re-shaping or re-sharpening a handaxe. Lower Palaeolithic age.
7002 sf 1335	78	40	23	LB	Flake fragment	Slightly rolled / weathered with manganese stains and iron stained striations on ventral and broken edge along left side	A thick flake, which seems to have had 2 flakes struck from the dorsal surface. Thus this artefact might be described as a flaked flake in the sense of Ashton et al., (1991). Lower Palaeolithic age.
7002	91	32	15	DB	Blade	Rolled / weathered and patinated. The ventral surface is more glossy than the dorsal and has some manganese staining	Essentially a waste product from stone tool manufacture, though it may have yielded a single small flake (14 mm long) from the right side. Lower Palaeolithic age.

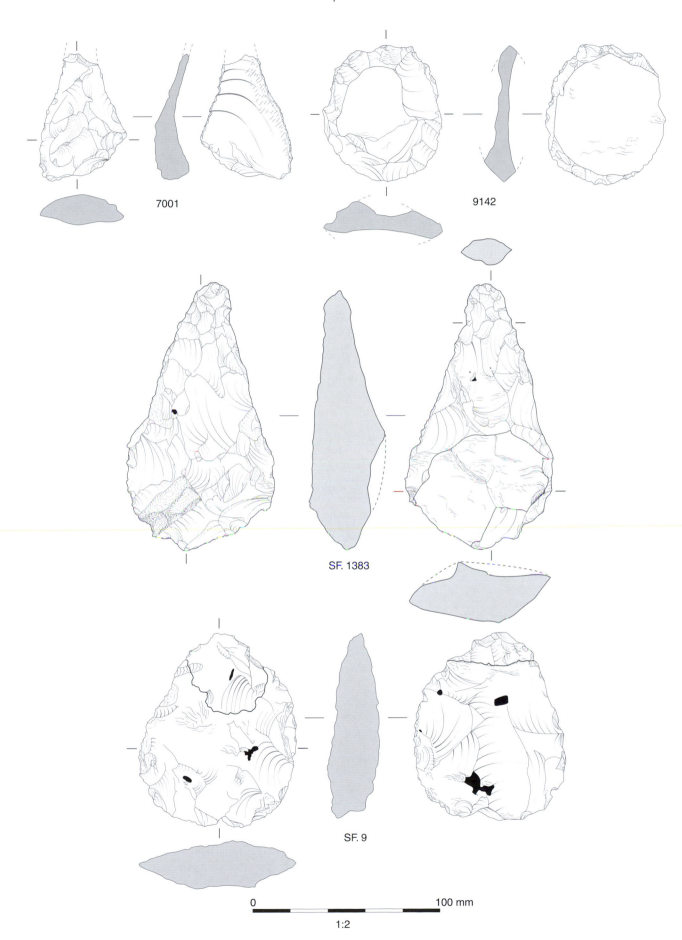

7001

9142

SF. 1383

SF. 9

0   100 mm

1:2

Figure 2.2   Palaeolithic flints.

is suggested by the similarity of patina and condition of a Mesolithic tranchet axe (Sf 1, context) and that of a classic Acheulian handaxe (Fig. 2.2, Sf 9). Differential effects across surfaces of the same artefact are also in evidence. For instance a pointed handaxe from context 7002 (Fig. 2.2, Sf 1383) has more worn flake scar intersections on one face than the other; the handaxe trimming flake from context 7001 (Fig. 2.2, 7001) has more worn flake scar intersections on the most protruding part of the dorsal surface (the area is marked on Fig. 2.2); a blade from context 7002 (not illustrated) has a more glossy ventral surface than dorsal; and a flake (Sf 1336; not illustrated) from the same context has a more weathered ventral surface than dorsal. This suggests that aspects of the same artefact have been affected by different degrees of mechanical and/or chemical weathering. This may have been caused by incorporation into the bed of a watercourse, or by the artefacts having lain exposed on the surface with one face subjected to the elements and the other relatively protected (Roe 1981, 183-4). Further investigation of the 'natural' sediments would be useful in this regard.

In any case, differential patination and weathering on these artefacts lends further support to the argument that the contexts from which they derive did not provide constant, homogeneous conditions and therefore patina and condition are unlikely to fit into an age-delineated pattern.

It could be suggested that the co-occurrence of a pointed handaxe and an ovate form should be interpreted as evidence of two separate episodes of activity (one involving an ovate bearing group of archaic humans and one involving a group who preferred pointed forms). In fact, this need not be the case since it is clear that pointed handaxes and ovates are indeed found together in apparently homogeneous assemblages, even when the assemblage as a whole shows a clear preference for one or the other type. An example of this would be Worthington Smith's site of Round Green, Luton (see illustrations in Roe 1981, 186).

There is perhaps some suggestion of the use of flakes as cores from which to strike small flakes. Artefacts from contexts 7002 (Sf 1335 and no Sf number) and 9389 have flake scars bearing negative bulbs of percussion; that is the flake scars were created after the flake itself was struck from the core or nodule). The sharp edges of the small flakes produced may have been used for cutting, or perhaps the resultant notched edge of the parent flake blank was used. Ashton and McNabb (1996, 201-236) applied the term 'flaked flakes' to artefacts of comparable form recovered from the Lower Gravel and Lower Loam of Swanscombe (see also Ashton *et al.* 1991). In the absence of handaxes, flaked flakes and cores would be described as Clactonian as opposed to Acheulian, on the basis that the Clactonian does not contain handaxes.

In Ashton and McNabb's view there is, however, no reason to suppose that the Clactonian and Acheulian were created by separate groups of people or separate 'cultures'. Rather, they have suggested that the Clactonian and the Acheulian form part of the same continuum of Lower Palaeolithic approaches to tool manufacture. It seems perfectly believable that the people who made the handaxes at Westhawk Farm might also be responsible for the few items that formally appear to have 'Clactonian' affinities. Alternatively, it is possible that these items do not belong to the same assemblage of tools as the either of the handaxes or handaxe trimming flakes.

In conclusion, there is no definite evidence that the Lower Palaeolithic finds from Westhawk Farm belong to a single assemblage. Different handaxe typologies are represented (pointed and ovate), and perhaps different techno-complexes (Clactonian and Acheulian). The condition of the artefacts also varies in terms of patination depth, colour and degree of weathering and/or rolling. However, there does seem to be a general unifying theme of economic use of raw material in the flint-working represented. The lack of large and/or cortical flakes and the presence of handaxe trimming flakes suggest that handaxes were being used and re-sharpened away from the place where they were made. The presence of flaked flakes, in the absence of cores, also suggests that the artefacts were being made and used at some distance from the place where those flakes had originally been struck from cores. The sources of the raw material out of which artefacts were made no doubt had a significant impact on the patterns of artefact manufacture, use and discard. The economy in the use of flint suggested at Westhawk Farm is really only to be expected, given that the site is located some distance away from a plentiful source of flint.

A possible counter-argument might see the lack of large flakes as a product of the depositional environment (ie one which favoured the deposition of smaller clasts) rather than having anything to do distance from source. However, this does not explain why there are two handaxes, which are effectively large and heavy clasts, in natural contexts. Also, there is no good reason why non-cortical flakes or indeed handaxe trimming flakes would be favoured by any natural mechanism of deposition; there are no fully (or even largely) cortical flakes amongst the assemblage and there are several handaxe-trimming flakes. This further suggests that the early stages of tool manufacture were not carried out in the immediate vicinity.

The contexts from which the artefacts derive and their condition suggest some potential for the local 'natural' as a source of *in situ* Palaeolithic material. This might mean that the incorporation of Palaeolithic artefacts into Roman contexts and later ploughsoils is simply the result of the local 'natural' deposits being disturbed. It is also true, however that cases exist where flint artefacts were collected during the Roman period and purposefully put into pits and waterholes. Turner and Wymer (1987) discuss the deliberate placing of over 40 Palaeolithic artefacts (mostly complete handaxes) at the Roman religious site of Ivy Chimneys, Witham, Essex and Roe (1980) reports the occurrence of an Acheulian handaxe in a Roman context from Woolbury in Hampshire. However, both of the Westhawk Farm handaxes were from natural contexts and so seem not to have been purposefully collected during the Roman period.

The Southern Rivers Palaeolithic Project records just three handaxes from the Ashford area: two handaxes recorded in museum collections by Roe and one found in a field approximately 3 km north of Westhawk Farm (Wymer 1993, 143). The Westhawk finds therefore contribute significantly to the body of evidence for local Lower Palaeolithic occupation. Wymer (1999, 91) remarks upon the paucity of Lower Palaeolithic finds in the area of the upper reaches of the Stour, which again emphasises the importance of the Westhawk finds, particularly if they are indicative of a larger assemblage waiting to be unearthed at this locality. The Palaeolithic artefacts from Westhawk Farm no doubt represent incursions of archaic hunter-gatherer peoples into the upper reaches of the Great Stour river system. Many hundreds of Lower Palaeolithic artefacts have been collected from further downstream in terraces 2 and 3 of the Great Stour at Sturry and Fordwich (Wymer 1993, 146-148; Roe 1968, 177-179 and 153). It is possible that the 'natural' deposits from which the Westhawk Farm artefacts derive, are also part of terrace 3 of the Great Stour (see map S2 of the Southern Rivers Palaeolithic Project Report number 2 1992-1993).

MESOLITHIC FLINT
by R N E Barton

An assemblage of 29 flints dating from the Mesolithic was recovered from gully 8087 and ditch 8418, possibly redeposited from a contemporary feature or surface truncated by the gully and ditch. A small number of isolated finds (possibly *c.* 10 flints), may also date from the Mesolithic but are included in Table 2.3 in the Neolithic and Bronze Age flint assemblage.

Context 8088 (fill of gully 8087)

The seventeen flint artefacts in this assemblage consist of 11 flakes, 4 blades, 1 core tablet and 1 piece of shatter. Fourteen of the artefacts are of a brown mottled flint and could derive from the same core reduction sequence, although attempts to refit the assemblage proved negative. The artefacts are in generally sharp condition and only lightly patinated. The presence of cortical surfaces on nine of the artefacts, plus the existence of a core tablet, demonstrates that some parts of the early stages of core reduction are represented in this group. If the artefacts did all come from the same knapping sequence they could have been introduced into the gully fill as a result of waste disposal or site clearance activity or have been part of a flint scatter knapped *in situ*. However, for each of these cases much higher numbers of small flint chips (< 10 mm) would be expected to survive. The absence of such pieces in this assemblage suggests a form of winnowing and implies that the artefacts may have

been incorporated from a nearby surface and not deliberately deposited. Four artefacts show evidence of thermal damage but this does not necessarily mean the local presence of a hearth. The pieces could have been affected by post-depositional burning of the ground's surface (eg brush fires).

The only retouched tool is a flake with direct, semi-abrupt to abrupt retouch along part of its right lateral margin. Although the tool in itself is not particularly diagnostic, it is interesting to note that negative flake scars on its dorsal surface indicate bi-directional removals from an opposed platform core. Combined with features on many of the other artefacts, and assuming the assemblage to be homogeneous, it is likely that this small collection of flints is of Mesolithic age.

Context 8090 (fill of ditch 8418)

Ten artefacts, mainly of debitage, and comprising 5 flakes, 2 blades, 1 bidirectionally crested blade, 1 bladelet and 1 microlith tool (Table 2.2). The assemblage is only lightly patinated and is in fresh condition with minimum signs of post-depositional modification. The most characteristic pieces of debitage in the collection are a crested blade and a plunging blade. The plunging blade is 42 mm long and derives from the edge of an opposed platform core that shows typical bladelet removals. The crested blade is a distinctive piece, which belongs to the preparatory phases of blade core, manufacture (Barton 1997). Also in this group is a broken bladelet (defined as a small blade less than 12 mm wide). All of these pieces can be seen as belonging to a Mesolithic technology.

The only diagnostic tool is a microlith, which can be defined within Clark's type A, as an obliquely blunted point (Clark 1934). The microlith point has direct abrupt retouch on its left side. It is 49 mm long and 13 mm wide, and is fairly thick (5 mm). The flint is a rich brown colour and is in sharp condition. There are some signs of damage (minute step fractures and a snap) on the ventral surface at the proximal tip probably incurred during use and suggestive of drilling (Alison Roberts pers. comm.). Similar damage has also been reported in the past on microliths believed to have been used as arrowheads (Barton 1992).

Context 8093 (fill of ditch 8418)

These are two broken flakes of undiagnostic types. Both flakes display unilinear flake scars on their dorsal surfaces indicating that they were detached from one-platform cores. One of the pieces has direct abrupt retouch developed along part of the break edge. Due to the generally fresh, unpatinated appearance of the flake it is tempting to suppose that the retouch is the result of deliberate manufacture. The artefact also shows a notch at its distal end. It does not conform to any of the major classes of Mesolithic tools; rather it belongs to a miscellaneous category, which is more likely to be of post-Mesolithic type.

Table 2.2   Summary of Mesolithic flint assemblage.

Category Type	Context			Total
	8088	8090	8093	
Flake	10	5	1	16
Blade	4	2		6
Bladelet			1	1
Shatter	1			1
Rejuvenation flake tablet	1			1
Crested blade		1		1
Microlith		1		1
Retouched flake	1		1	2
Total	17	10	2	29
No. burnt flints	4	-	-	4
(%)	(23.5)			(13.8)
No. broken flints	8	6	2	16
(%)	(47.1)	(60)	(100)	(55.2)
No. retouched flints	1	1	1	3
(%)	(5.9)	(10)	(50)	(10.4)

Individual finds

A small number of individual finds (*c* 10 flints) recovered across the site may also date from the Mesolithic. These flints are primarily blades and blade fragments, such as a narrow plunging blade (<12mm wide) from context 8473 which was struck from an opposed platform bladelet core and a narrow bladelet from context 9706 that exhibits heavy platform edge abrasion and traits of soft hammer percussion. Two retouched tools, a possible tranchet axe and an end of blade scraper, also belong to this period. The scraper is at the proximal end of a broken blade. The semi-abrupt, direct retouch only extends across part of the break suggesting the tool was unfinished. The scraper is characterised by a uniform, slightly milky patina that covers the entire piece. The quality of manufacture and size of the blade support (width 20 mm x thickness 7 mm) strongly suggest an early Mesolithic or late Palaeolithic tool type. The possible tranchet axe (SF1) was recovered from the topsoil and is slightly rolled with some unpatinated recent damage. The artefact is quite roughly manufactured and is 123 mm in length.

Due to the problem of identifying individual Mesolithic flints with any degree of confidence the finds are included in Table 2.3 with the Neolithic and Bronze Age flintwork.

NEOLITHIC AND BRONZE AGE FLINT
by H Lamdin-Whymark

The Neolithic and Bronze Age assemblage consists of 155 flints, although this figure includes ten possible Mesolithic flints discussed as individual finds above. The Neolithic and Bronze Age flintwork was spread relatively evenly across the excavated area and none was contained in contemporary features, most being recovered from Roman contexts. Due to the disturbed character and mixed date of the flintwork the assemblage is discussed as a whole with reference to broad technological and typological trends.

Methodology

The artefacts were catalogued according to broad artefact/debitage type, general condition noted and dating attempted where possible. Unworked burnt flint was quantified by fragment count and weight.

Raw Material and Condition

The majority of the flint in the assemblage exhibited abraded cortices, and interiors that varied through light to dark browns and greys. Thermal fractures were a common trait of this flint. This flint probably derived from the superficial gravel and clay with flint deposits present over much of the weald, and was locally available either from surface collection or riverbeds. There were occasional pieces of relatively good quality black flint which may have originated from the chalk, although no thick chalk cortices were found to support this statement.

The condition of the flint was generally poor. Numerous flints exhibited some post-depositional edge damage and a few flints were rolled; several plough nicks were also present. The condition of the flint-work is consistent with having been redeposited.

Assemblage

The assemblage is primarily flake based, although a few blades and blade-like flakes are present. The flint was struck using a mixture of soft and hard hammer percussion, although the latter dominates the assemblage. A number of trimming flakes, including cortical trimming flakes, are present. The cores include both single and multi-platform flake varieties, many of which lack platform preparation and platform edge abrasion. A single platform blade core, with platform edge abrasion, was also present. In addition, a multi-platform flake core, weighing 154 g, was re-used as a hammerstone.

A total of fourteen retouched tools (excluding two Mesolithic forms) were present, accounting for 9.5% of the assemblage. Four of the tools were scrapers, manufactured on thick flakes and all relatively crudely retouched. Other retouched artefacts include a crudely retouched piercer made on a flake, two notched flakes and seven simple edge retouched flakes. One of the notched flakes also exhibited abrupt edge retouch around much of artefact's circumference.

Conclusions

The assemblage includes flintwork with differing technological traits. However, the majority of the material represents the production of flakes and therefore probably dates from the late Neolithic or Bronze Age, although the presence of a small number of Mesolithic flints is noted above, and it is likely that several Neolithic flints are also present. Further refinement of the dating is hindered by a lack of typologically diagnostic artefacts.

The limited number of Neolithic and Bronze Age flints recovered from Westhawk Farm and the ab-

Table 2.3   Summary of the Neolithic and Bronze Age flint assemblage.

Category Type	Total
Flake	104
Blade	9
Blade-like	4
Irregular waste	1
Chip	2
Sieved chips 10-4 mm	6
Rejuvenation flake tablet	1
Thinning flake	1
Core single platform blade core	1
Single platform flake core	1
Multi-platform flake core	5
Keeled non-discoidal flake core	1
Core on a flake	2
End scraper	2
End and side scraper	2
Scraper on a non-flake blank	1
Piercer	1
Notch	2
Retouched flake	7
Tranchet axe	1
Hammerstone	1
Total	155
Total (excluding chips)	147
No. burnt flints (% assemblage excluding chips)	9 (6.1%)
No. broken flints (% assemblage excluding chips)	38 (25.9%)
No. retouched flints (% assemblage excluding chips)	16 (10.9%)
Burnt unworked flint (g)	101 (828)

sence of contemporary features suggest that the assemblage represents a low intensity background spread, an is derived from an occasional presence in the Neolithic and Bronze Age rather than representing a specific activity area, although it is possible some of the flints relate to activity in the possible Bronze Age field system.

POSSIBLE BRONZE AGE FIELD SYSTEM

Later prehistoric activity was indicated by series of shallow ditches or gullies forming part of a probable field system, the orientation of which may conceivably have influenced the Roman road alignment (Fig. 2.1). None of the ditches produced dating evidence, but a Bronze Age date is possible, and perhaps likely (see discussion below). The basis of the system was a north-east to south-west aligned axial ditch, Groups 1640/10100: two ditches running virtually end to end, with distinct terminals in both. The north-east end of 1640, which extended beyond the limit of Area B, had a broad shallow flat based profile, which changed to a more V-shaped profile to the south-west, as seen also in 10100. Both ditches had a characteristic pale grey silt fill. The alignment was continued south-west of the south-west terminal of ditch 10100 by Group 10485. Running parallel to these ditches approximately 36 m to the south-east were segmented ditch Groups 10140/1820, 10130 and 10120.

At right angles to this series of parallel ditches were the remains of a possible division boundary, ditch 9590 orientated north-west to south-east. This was approximately 12 m in length, 1.30 m wide and 0.20 m deep and was also filled by a single deposit of pale grey silt. A similarly aligned length of ditch (1735) lay west of the axial boundary 1640 at the extreme north-east edge of Area B. It survived beneath the line of the Roman Canterbury road, but it is not clear whether it was (coincidentally) coterminous with the limits of the road, in which case it would have been of very similar length to ditch 9590, or whether it was significantly truncated at both ends by Roman roadside features. Some 113 m south-west of 1735 was another short length of north-west to south-east aligned ditch (Group 10200) of similar character. Associated with this was a short length of roughly north-south aligned ditch 8517. This passed through the line of the later road and looked in plan like a continuation of Period 2 Phase 2-3 ditch 8700, but its fill was of the characteristic pale grey silt and suggests that it was prehistoric in origin. A small group of early Roman pottery from this feature was presumably intrusive.

In the south-western part of the site was a north-west to south-east aligned ditch (Group 10110), which terminated approximately 9 m short of Group 10100. Parallel to 10110 was ditch 9480, which then turned to the north-east and continued for 52 m before being completely truncated by the ditch sequence on the north-west side of the Roman road. Running between the roadside ditches was Group 10160, aligned north-west to south-east and extending for 17 m. At the southern end of the site, south-east of ditch 10485, was a series of small segmented ditches aligned north-east to south-west comprising features 10080, 10090, 9943 and 9945. Ditch 10486, which lay between ditch 10485 and the segmented sequence, was on the same alignment. All of the above ditches contained the characteristic pale grey silt fill, with no stratigraphic relationship between them.

A small number of discrete features produced prehistoric pottery. Possible tree-throw pit 8241 was located approximately 16 m south-east of ditch 10100. It was 2.70 m in diameter and 0.18 m deep and was filled by a single grey silt with lenses of orange natural clay throughout. Pit 791, which lay in the north corner of Area B, was up to 2 m across and *c* 0.30 m deep, with steep sides and a flat base. The middle of its three fills, of light grey brown silty clay, contained pottery and charcoal. Posthole 1130 was part of fence line Group 1070, a second phase of boundary for the shrine complex.

Together these features produced 46 sherds (462 g) of pottery, out of a total of 54 sherds (502 g) of such material from the site overall. Some of the sherds were abraded and those in posthole 1130 must be residual. The pottery was all tempered with calcined flint. Feature sherds were lacking but the general character of the material and the thicknesses of many of the sherds are consistent with a middle Bronze Age date; though a later date is possible.

Chapter 3:   Period 2 - Late Iron Age and Roman

PHASE 1, UP TO *c* AD 43

The principal feature assigned to this phase was a single cremation burial adjacent to, but outside, Area C. No excavated feature in Area C was of this date. None of the excavated features in Area B was demonstrably of this date, although a small number of features contained pottery which could suggest a pre-conquest date (including cremation 1261 at the north-east margin of Area B, see below), but none of the features need have been that early.

Burial 9200

The report starts with a description of discovery of the grave; this is followed by a description the burial as found, and interpretation of the layout of the burial and location of the finds, and finally a discussion of the finds. The finds are catalogued in detail in Chapter 8.

Recovery

The burial was located at TQ 99976 40168 and 43.96 m above OD, situated some 40 m due west of the south-west corner of excavated Area C (Fig. 3.1). The burial was revealed on Friday October 8th 1999 in an area adjacent to the Wilcon Homes compound during stripping by contractors for an access driveway to new houses. After exposure, and before OA staff were summoned, parts of the burial were excavated by workmen using hand tools. By the time OA staff arrived cremated bone and fragments of wood and copper alloy objects had been identified and considerable disturbance had occurred. The remaining *in situ* parts of the burial were cleaned and recorded as far as was possible, given the extensively disturbed nature of the remains and the need to clear the site to allow construction work to continue (Plate 3.1).

As seen in the field the approximate dimensions of the disturbed area containing the burial were 1 m x 0.70 m, within which the remains of a wooden box, a wooden stave bucket, a *terra nigra* platter and fragmentary copper-alloy objects including parts of a jug, a bowl, a fluted fragment from a shallow vessel - a *patera* - and several possible fittings, were apparent together with cremated bone (Figs 3.2 and 3.3). The outline of the original cut for the cremation was unclear due to the presence of redeposited clay backfill and the disturbance of the feature by the contractors. Subsequent cleaning and the examination of the deposits already removed showed that at least two distinct fills existed. One was redeposited natural clay around the box and bucket; the other was a compact grey clay silt that sealed the box lid.

As a consequence of the character of the surrounding solid clay natural and clay rich fill, and the evident complexity and fragility of the objects within the burial, what remained of the cremation was lifted in blocks. A small trench was machined around three sides of the remains and the clay cut away from the edges of the feature. The exposed deposits were then cut in two at a point where it was thought that this would cause the minimum amount of damage

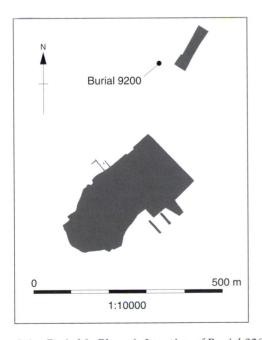

Plate 3.1   Burial 9200 as revealed by contractors' excavation.

Figure 3.1   Period 2: Phase 1. Location of Burial 9200.

N

Burial 9200

0   500 m

1:10000

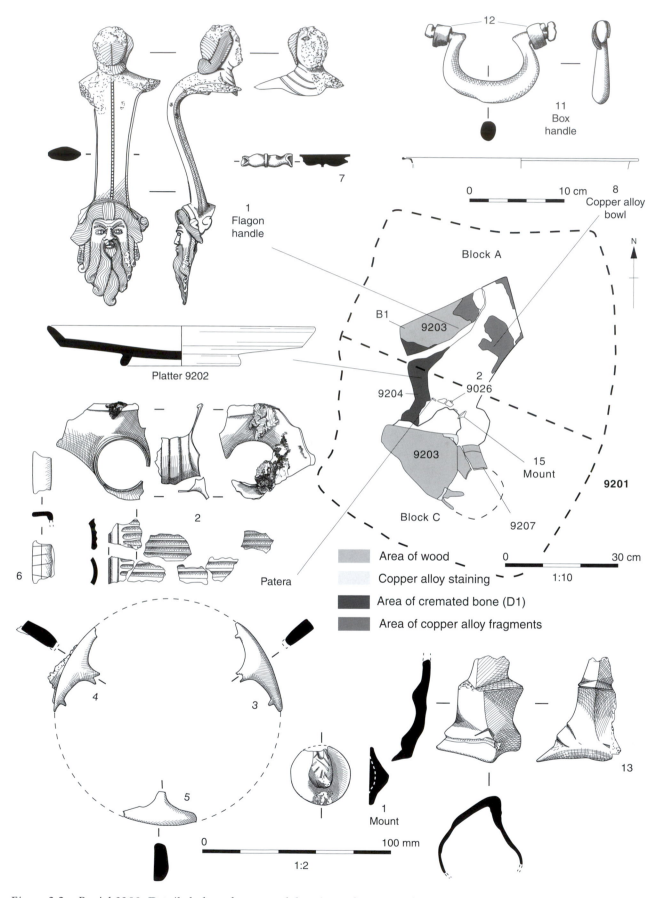

Figure 3.2   *Burial 9200: Detailed plan of grave and drawings of grave goods.*

28

Figure 3.3   Burial 9200: Hypothetical reconstruction of principal identified grave goods.

to the remaining deposits. The two resulting blocks being labelled A (to the north) and C (to the south). All of the soil disturbed by the building contractors was also collected. This fell into two categories: loose soil (mostly grave fill) which was collected in sample buckets, and larger clay lumps of varying size, in some cases still containing fragmentary archaeological material *in situ*, some of which were also assigned individual block numbers. One such large block (B1) measured 0.4 x 0.3 x 0.15 m and included a distinct semi-circular stain of copper alloy. Another (block D1) held the impression of the foot ring of the platter with cremated bone beneath it. Where possible these were related spatially to the archaeologically recorded remains of the burial.

The excavated blocks and the salvaged lumps/ blocks were subsequently dissected under controlled conditions by Karla Graham at the English Heritage Centre for Archaeology at Portsmouth. Full records of this are held in the project archive. In the light of this work and detailed examination of the finds, some of the interpretations made on site were shown, inevitably, to have been mistaken. Despite the careful

work undertaken at Portsmouth, some fundamental aspects of the burial, and much of the detail, remain obscure.

Description of the grave and contents as found

The plan (Fig. 3.2) shows the extent of major disturbance from the contractors' excavation and the principal surviving *in situ* elements in the centre of this area. The original edges of the cremation burial pit (notional cut 9201) had been heavily disturbed by the contractors on site, and only the position of the objects suggested the approximate dimensions of the grave pit. This was possibly, but not certainly, square or rectangular, perhaps roughly 0.55 m x 0.50 m with the probable longer axis approximately north-west to south-east, and perhaps up to 0.30 m deep below the level of the top of the plough-truncated natural subsoil, though none of the recovered soil blocks was greater than *c* 0.20 m in depth.

At the base of the cut at or towards its northern edge were the possible remains of a wooden box (9203) with copper alloy components. Parts of this were recovered in blocks A and B1, but traces of decayed organic material and fragments of copper alloy were observed widely across the feature, though it is unclear if these represent a single object or several different items of broadly similar construction. The north-east corner of the box was relatively well-defined, but disturbance elsewhere makes it impossible to establish its precise dimensions. This question is, however, crucial for interpretation of the burial overall. The principal possibilities are that a small or medium sized box (perhaps up to 320-360 mm x 200-220 mm) aligned NE-SW lay in the northern corner of the grave pit, or that the majority of the identified items lay within the box, which occupied most of the grave pit and on this interpretation might have been up to *c* 450 mm x 350 mm in plan, with the long axis aligned NW-SE. The original height of the box is unknown. The wooden remains were too degraded to allow identification of the species used. Many copper alloy fragments were associated with the decayed organic material, but none survived in a recognisable form. This suggests that the box was decorated and/or reinforced with thin sheet, or indeed that it might have been largely covered with such sheeting.

Interpretation of the layout of the burial and location of the finds

For the purposes of the following description the 'large box' interpretation is followed, but is, of course, speculative. The corollary of this assumption is that most of the identified objects, with the principal exception of the wooden bucket (see below) lay within the box, but it is possible that some were placed on top of it.

The northern corner of the box (9203) may have contained one or more copper alloy objects - presumably vessels of thin metal since the surviving fragments cannot be identified to form. Towards the western corner of the box was the main deposit of cremated bone (9204), which was noted on site as a relatively discrete and coherent deposit. This deposit included cremated fragments of bird, sheep and pig, as well as the human remains of an adult, probably male. The cremated bone was partly overlain by the *terra nigra* platter of Camulodunum form 1 (Fig. 3.2: 9202) with a diameter of *c* 280 mm. Unburnt animal bone and copper alloy fragments were recovered from within the platter. The bones were from a lamb; further fragments, presumably, but not certainly, from the same animal, were amongst the unstratified material from the contractors' excavations grouped as context 9200. The copper alloy was almost certainly from the *patera* (9206; Cool, Chapter 8, Cat. nos 2-5) (Fig. 3.2: 2-5). What is less certain is the relationship between this vessel and the lamb, but the latter may have been placed adjacent to the edge of the box west of the former.

The *patera* can be reconstructed with some confidence, despite its extremely fragmentary nature, on the basis of surviving components of the handle (Cool, Chapter 8, Cat. No. 2) (Fig. 3.2: 2), a rim fragment (Cat. no.6) (Fig. 3.2: 6) and three cast feet (Cat. nos 3-5) (Fig. 3.2: 3-5). Parts of the handle were recorded *in situ* in a location consistent with the positioning of the body of the *patera* above the *terra nigra* platter, though it may be that the components were not attached, since a piece of linen fabric, preserved by corrosion products inside the hollow cast handle, overlapped the edge of the handle attachment in a way that should not have been possible had the handle been attached to the body of the vessel. The vessel has an estimated diameter of *c* 220 mm.

At least two other copper alloy vessels were identified and on the present interpretation of the grave were probably inside the box. The first of these was a jug of which only the highly decorated handle, depicting Silenus, survived (Cool, Chapter 8, Cat. no. 1) (Fig. 3.2: 1). The handle was recovered by the workmen and was not *in situ*. Fluted fragments, initially thought to belong to this vessel, were part of the *patera* 9206 (Cat. no.2) (Fig. 3.2: 2). Sufficient corroded fragments were associated with the jug handle, however, to indicate that this was buried as a complete vessel rather than a detached object.

The other copper alloy vessel was a probable bowl, of which only part of the rim was recognisable in detached soil block B2 (Cool, Chapter 8, Cat. Nos 8-10). This vessel was fairly shallow and may have been either circular or oval in shape, at least *c* 250 mm in diameter, and probably had a drop handle (Cat. no.11) (Fig. 3.2: 11), though this was also an unassociated find.

The principal problem relating to these two vessels is their location. It is likely that both lay towards the north-east side or east corner of the box, and possible that the jug was placed in the bowl. Alternatively, the numbering of block B2 suggests a perceived association with the other B blocks - B1, certainly located on the north-west side of the grave, and the smaller detached block B3 which proved to overlie it. It is possible therefore that B2 also originally joined onto B1, but the complete absence of any traces of cremated bone in B2 does not support this suggestion (unless the bowl in B2 had lain on top of the box rather than within it), so a location further south-east is preferred, albeit tentatively.

Towards the south-east side of the grave were the remains of a stave bucket (9207) (Plate 3.2). Parts of this survived as preserved wood, possibly as a consequence of anaerobic conditions resulting from the bucket having been tightly packed and surrounded with sterile, redeposited natural clay (9208) and perhaps enhanced by the proximity of copper alloy. The surviving fragments, of yew wood (species identification by Mark Robinson), indicated a diameter of about 150 mm. The bucket had been badly damaged before recovery, and the southern edge was completely lost, but large parts of the remains were contained within soil block C1 examined at the English Heritage Centre for Archaeology. In this work 16 fragments of wood were eventually given separate numbers, but it is highly improbable that these represented 16 different staves, many of the fragments

Plate 3.2   Block C1 from Burial 9200.

being very small. The best preserved stave had maximum surviving dimensions of *c* 137 mm x 77 mm recorded at the time of initial examination, while the adjacent stave 2 was 101 mm x 50 mm. It is not clear if the latter dimension was the full width of the stave, but this is possible. At an average width of *c* 77 mm only six or seven staves would have been required in the bucket. It seems likely that most staves were rather narrower than this, but their original number is unknown; an interim assessment identifying nine staves is probably close to the mark, however. The bottom of the bucket did not survive, though its position is indicated by indentations towards the base of some staves. Staining of some of the wood and the presence of copper alloy fragments suggest that the bucket was probably bound with bands of copper alloy sheet.

The bucket had clearly been placed upright in the grave, though by the time of recovery the best preserved staves were leaning to the south-east. The uppermost parts of the bucket, including handle and suspension loops, were completely missing. A copper alloy mount (Cool, Chapter 8, Cat. no. 15; see below) (Fig. 3.2:15), found just north of the bucket, might have come from it.

As already noted a sterile yellow silt-clay (9208), almost indistinguishable from the natural subsoil of this part of the site, was packed in and around the stave bucket. This material was also used to fill the rest of the grave pit, which accounts for the effective invisibility of the edges of the grave cut in its disturbed state. It also supports the interpretation that the bucket lay outside the box, which occupied most of the remainder of the grave pit. The principal fill encountered in and above the area of the box and extending as far as the north-west edge of the bucket was a layer of light grey clay silt (9205) varying between 0.02-0.3 m in depth. This is likely to have represented both the gradual processes of infilling of the box itself as it decayed, as well as the accumulation of material in the hollow above the box at the same time, but there was no meaningful distinction between the character of the soil in these two different contexts.

A number of fragments of copper alloy, only located during examination of the remains of the burial at the Centre for Archaeology, suggest the presence of further objects not referred to here.

Copper alloy artefacts from Burial 9200
by H E M Cool

Interpreting the copious quantities of copper alloy found associated with this burial is fraught with difficulties. The first problem stems from the fact that copper alloy does not survive well at Ashford. Though part of the burial was lifted entire and excavated in the laboratory (report in archive), much of the copper alloy had been reduced to the state of undiagnostic tiny fragments or copper corrosion products. Extensive radiography before laboratory excavation was relatively unhelpful and in only one case revealed any hint of the outline of a vessel. The second problem is that in nearly all cases the most diagnostic pieces had been removed prior to the arrival of the archaeologists and so there are doubts as to where some of them were placed within the burial. This is particularly regrettable as it is clear that the burial contains unusual forms of artefacts and it would have aided interpretation to have known which elements were associated together.

It will be helpful to summarise here what it was thought had been found on site at the time the burial was lifted. It was known that there was a jug as the fine handle (Cool, Chapter 8, Cat. no. 1) (Fig. 3.2: 1) had already been removed. It was assumed that this was associated with a cylindrical fluted object (Cool, Chapter 8, Cat. no. 2) (Fig. 3.2: 2) which was still *in situ* and which was thought to have been the neck of the vessel. A fragment referred to as a possible strainer bowl (see Cat. no. 2) was located a little to the north of this (the precise position being uncertain). There was also thought to be a large bowl as a semi-circle of copper alloy could be seen in one of the blocks removed by the contractors (Cool, Chapter 8, Cat. no 10) and rim fragments (Cool, Chapter 8, Cat. nos 8-10) were also lying loose. The box holding the remains was observed to have had copper alloy fragments scattered with the decayed wood that had formed it, and in one case a distinct corner was preserved. Fragments of copper alloy were also observed on the *terra nigra* platter and it was suggested that this might either be a vessel placed on the platter or have been derived from a vessel alongside the platter, Finally it was also observed that there might be another copper alloy object below the cylindrical fluted object. A wooden bucket was also recognised.

The one vessel that can be identified with certainty is the jug represented by its handle (Cool, Chapter 8, Cat. no. 1) (Fig.3.2: 1). This type of handle is used on jugs with wide trefoil mouths, short necks and wide bodies (Tassinari 1993, type 2112). A jug of this sort with a very similar handle is known from Pompeii (*ibid*, vol. 1, 42, vol. 2, 65, Tav. CV 3 and 4, no. 18763). That has a female bust on the upper attachment with precisely the same hairstyle as seen on the Ashford attachment. The lower attachment of the Pompeii jug has a very similar male bearded face, but little stumps of horns can be seen on the forehead suggesting the figure was intended to be Pan. On the Ashford handle, these are missing and it is likely that the mask was intended to represent Silenus. The body of these jugs was thin and spun out of sheet on a lathe (see Toynbee 1967, 240 for technique), so there need be no surprise that no recognisable pieces of the body survive. In the soil conditions at Ashford, the body can be expected to have fragmented into small undiagnostic pieces.

Jugs of this type are part of the earliest Imperial service of jug and *patera* to which Nuber (1972, 38) has given the name of Hagenow. These were in use during the first half of the 1st century AD, though examples of the jugs are found in contexts that suggest they continued in use into the Flavian period, for example in a rich Flavian burial at Winchester (Toynbee 1967). Though the form has been recovered at Pompeii, it is not common there (Tassinari 1993), suggesting it might not still have been in contemporary use by the time of the eruption in AD 79. There is, therefore, the possibility that the Ashford jug could have been a pre-Conquest import. As well as the example from the Flavian grave at Winchester, another jug of this type was found in the Welwyn-type burial at Standfordbury, Bedfordshire (Stanfordbury A). This jug is a closer parallel for the Ashford jug as the female busts on the upper attachments of both are very similar to each other (Toynbee 1963, 175, plate 130, no. 114). Their lower attachments differ, however, as the Standfordbury example has two comic masks at the base of the handle. Standfordbury A also contained a stamped Gaulish copy of an Arretine cup dated to *c* AD 35-45 (Stead 1967, 47), suggesting the burial may have been made about the time of the Claudian conquest.

The form of the jugs with handles make it clear that the fluted cylindrical object (Cool, Chapter 8, Cat. no. 2) (Fig. 3.2: 2) could not have been part of this vessel. As the catalogue entry shows the fragments from this were collected both on site and during the excavation in the laboratory. The distinctive cast fluting on the fragments and on the broken tip of the piece originally identified on site as part of a possible strainer bowl make it clear that both groups were from the same item. The fragments are consistent with this being the handle of a *patera*; for general form see those from the Welshpool deposit (Boon 1961, fig. 4, nos 2-4). The handles of *paterae* were cast separately and generally had a terminal in the form of the head of a ram or wolf and a shield-like plate or wall at the other end for attachment to the bowl. The ridged appearance on the interior of the plate/cylinder junction of the fluted handle makes it clear that this was not intended to be seen in contrast to the apparently well-finished exterior. The difference in slope above and below the junction with the cylinder is what is to be expected of an attachment for a shallowly sloping bowl, and the finished edges observable on the wall or plate makes it clear that this is indeed an attachment plate rather than a compete vessel wall. *Patera* handles could be cast solid in one piece, but hollow ones are also known, as well as ones which are recorded as being filled with some other material (Waugh and Goodburn 1972, 138 nos 148-9, figs 44-45). It may be noted here that the traces of a linen textile (see below) were inside the handle apart from one fragment that spills out over the broken edge. Whether this was the original filling though is open to question. The position could be the fortuitous result of breakage and perhaps the vessel was placed in the grave wrapped in cloth.

The lack of a terminal is puzzling as it could normally have expected to be cast with the handle even if the latter was hollow. However, the terminal fragments have well-finished edges and clearly if it did have an animal-head terminal it must have been cast separately. As a solid casting some part of it might have been expected to survive even the corrosive soil of Ashford, but there is no recognisable trace of such an item within the copper alloy from the deposit. It has to be assumed therefore that this *patera* was not placed in the grave with a terminal in position.

There are no fragments that can be recognised as being from the body with any certainty. The body would have been cast and probably finished on a lathe, but it would have been thin-walled. The fragments of copper alloy found on the platter did include small convex-curved fragments that had probably originated from a cast vessel wall. There was also one tiny fragment that retained part of an angular moulding very similar to that on the shield-like attachment of the *patera* handle. Given the position of the platter and the planned angle of the fluted part of the handle the evidence would be consistent with the bowl of the *patera* having been placed in the platter with the handle pointing towards the east. The large fragment from the junction of the handle and attachment was only approximately located, but its general position is consistent with the arrangement proposed.

There were many different types of *paterae* in use in the Roman world. The lack of an animal head terminal, the neatly fluted handle with transverse mouldings at either end, the relatively plain attachment shield all suggest the Ashford *patera* may have been of the form that has often been observed in Hagenow services of *paterae* and jugs (Nuber 1972, 39; see for example Taf. 3.1a-b). Unusually for *paterae* these often have three small separately cast feet applied to the base to protect it, rather than the base being raised on an integrally cast foot ring. There are three such feet from the grave (Cool, Chapter 8, Cat. nos 3-5) (Fig. 3.2: 3-5). Two (nos 3 and 5) were found loose on site. The third (no. 4) was excavated from Block B3 in the laboratory, but the original location of this is not known precisely. Given the removal of the platter from the grave by the contractors and the presence of nos. 3 and 5 loose in the items also removed by them, it seems reasonable to suggest that these feet did indeed come from the *patera*. If, as suggested, the *patera* sat in the platter then these solid cast pieces would have been obvious items to have been picked out on first discovery. The outer diameter of the feet would also have been appropriate for a *patera* such as this. It would have been too small for the other bowl known from the burial.

Such *paterae* had horizontally out-turned rims and a single fragment of a rim of the appropriate type was recovered (Cool, Chapter 8, Cat. no. 6) (Fig. 3.2: 6). It was clearly made in a different way from, and has a different profile from, the rim from the large dish in the grave (Cat. nos 8-9, see below), and so could well have come from the *patera*. Its original location is unknown. Finally the small mount (Cool, Chapter 8, Cat. no. 7) (Fig. 3.2: 7) may be considered, though again its original location is unknown. It has corrosion products on the back indicative of having been soldered onto another piece of metal. The cupped ends have a conical aperture of about 4 mm depth.

In overall appearance the piece is very similar to the central part of a swing handle that was attached to a vessel (see den Boesterd 1956, 52, pl VIII, no 170). The recessed ends would be most suitable to anchor the ends of the handle itself. Some Hagenow *paterae* have this sort of swing attachment opposite the handle, and this may explain the function of no. 7.

It seems very likely that the grave contained the classic *patera* and jug combination used for hand washing and for libations, and well known from many sites throughout the Roman world (Nuber 1972; Koster 1997, 74). As already noted in the discussion of the jug handle no. 1, the jugs typical of the Hagenow service have occasionally been found in contexts as late as the Flavian period. The presence of both elements of the service in this grave, however, strongly suggests that the deposition may have been made during the *floruit* of the service. Nuber (1972, 40) notes dates of deposition ranging from the beginning of the 1st century AD to the Claudian period. It may be noted, however, that at least one Hagenow *patera* from a Claudian context was old by the time it was deposited. This was the one placed in the warrior burial at Snailwell, Cambridgeshire (Lethbridge 1952, 33, plates VIa, VII). If the mount no. 7 does indicate the presence of a swing handle, then this would suggest an early date as it is not a feature that has been observed on those placed in the later contexts. The presence of a Hagenow service cannot certainly indicate that the grave was pre-conquest, but the possibility that it may have been is a strong one. The presence of these expensive imported items, probably originating in Campania, also suggests that the deceased was an elite member of his community.

A larger raised bowl is represented by the fragments catalogued as nos. 8 to 10 (Cool, Chapter 8, below). Again given the circumstances of their discovery - in and around Block B and collected loose on site - there is no guarantee that they all belong the same vessel, but all are made from sheet metal, and the rim and base diameters would be consistent with a vessel of *c* 200 mm base diameter with sides sloping out slightly to a rim of *c* 250 mm. The X-radiograph of the base suggests that it *may* have been elliptical rather than circular, perhaps like the elliptical shallow sheet dish found in the Welwyn Garden City burial (Stead 1967, 26, fig. 14) which had a single drop handle. Among the copper alloy collected on site there is an omega-shaped drop handle (Cool, Chapter 8, Cat. no. 11) (Fig. 3.2: 11) and some fragments that clearly served to attach it to something (Cat. no. 12) (Fig. 3.2: 12). It is not known where these fragments came from. One possibility is that they should be viewed as part of the bowl. Both the elliptical bowl and the strainer from Welwyn Garden City (Stead 1967, 23, fig. 12) had single handles, and the footed bowl from an earlier burial at Welwyn may also have had just the single handle (Smith 1912, 16, fig. 11). Presumably they served for hanging these large vessels safely out of the way when not in use. Though there is no proof that the handle and the large bowl were associated here, this seems as least as likely as the possibility that the handle was part of the box fittings, none of which otherwise survive in any recognisable form.

The fragment no.13 (Cool, Chapter 8) (Fig. 3.2:13) was excavated in the laboratory below the position of the *patera* handle. Between the handle and no. 13 another mass of copper alloy was found, the only recognisable part being Cat. no. 14, and it is possible that the two are connected. The interior of no. 13 and the edge of the 'rim' does not appear to have the finish that would be expected if these surfaces were to be seen. The most likely interpretation of it appears to be as a stand, possibly the foot of some composite item. Precisely what this was remains uncertain. Metal furniture feet at this time normally took the form of the feet of felines and stands for little statuettes were normally cubic or cylindrical. None appears to have the complex shape seen here.

The shape and size of the bucket that stood to one side of the wooden box is best understood from the excavation records both on site (see above) and in the laboratory (report in archive). Though in places the wood has survived remarkably well, in no case is it possible reconstruct a complete stave or even (with certainty) the width of a complete stave from the surviving fragments, although a particularly well-preserved fragment from Stave 1 was 77 mm wide on initial recording, and this may have been its complete width. There was a small amount of information about the base as on Stave 6 the finished end of the stave is preserved. On the interior a black organic deposit from another layer of wood runs transversely across this stave and would be consistent with a base plate *c* 22 mm thick with the base of stave projecting *c* 5 mm beyond it. Two fragments of wood (Stave 10 and un-numbered) retain the remains of slots which were probably the seating for the base. No iron fittings were preserved, but one fragment of wood (Stave 16) retains the effects of compression, possibly caused by a band.

It may well be that at least the lower part of the bucket was decorated by copper alloy sheet. In several cases during excavation it was noted that the staves stood on black organic matter. The deposit of this below Stave 4 shows much fragmented copper alloy in the X-radiograph. On the base of Stave 6, preserved as black organic material rather than recognisable wood, there is clearly a deposit of copper alloy corrosion products on the exterior. Though it is possible that this copper alloy was derived from another object on which the bucket stood, the evidence of the iron shanks makes this unlikely. These shanks were found in the lower parts of Staves 15 and 16. Where measurable the shank was 3.5 mm in diameter. A small void close to the end of Stave 2 might have been produced by a similar or slightly smaller shank though no metal is now detectable. Iron nails or rivets are not functionally necessary for coopered buckets (see Morris 1990, 206-21) and a more likely explanation for their presence is that they were present to attach copper alloy plates to the woodwork as was done in the case of the Aylesford bucket (Evans 1890, 360). On that bucket the bottom two copper alloy bands were plain and the upper one was decorated with repoussé reliefs of fantastic animals and decorative scrolls. At Ashford there is no evidence of such decoration, but it may be noted that the excavation of block C1 in which part of the bucket was embedded did produce a few scraps of thin ribbed copper alloy sheet.

It is possible that mount no. 15 (Cool, Chapter 8, Cat. no. 15) (Fig. 3.2:15) may have decorated the bucket. It was lifted separately on site from the area of the bucket and had clearly decorated a wooden object as wood is embedded in the corrosion products. The details of the decoration are a little unclear due to corrosion damage, but they appear to represent a feline face, and it is tempting to wonder whether this might have been the attempt of a native craftsman to depict a lion, a creature often associated in Classical art with funerary items and which was to be adopted later in the 1st century by Romano-British metalworkers (see for example Borrill 1981, 315-6). Equally the mount could have come from the box in which the burial was placed, but as there is only one example this seems less likely. On the caskets decorated by lion-headed studs several are usually used to produce a symmetrical pattern, and the solid nature of this mount makes it unlikely that others would have disappeared entirely through corrosion.

Only the jug handle (Cat. no. 1) now obviously hints at the splendours of the grave furnishings originally provided for this individual. The cremated bones were placed in a wooden casket decorated with copper alloy fittings. At least three copper alloy vessels of some pretension were placed in the grave as well as the *terra nigra* platter, the bucket and possibly some piece of elaborate furniture. It should also be stressed that other items may also have been present, now reduced to unidentifiable fragments and dust. In both block B1 and in the platter deposits of red dust were recovered, for example. These are clearly magnetic and may hint at additional iron fittings. There can be no doubt that the person buried would have been an elite member of his community as the finds place the burial amongst the most richly furnished of the Aylesford-Swarling tradition.

PHASES 2-7, AD 43-400

The report begins with a description of the main road and roadside ditches, which divide the site into blocks. An understanding of road ditches is critical to understanding the overall layout and phasing of the site. This is followed by description and discussion of the evidence of occupation within the blocks defined by the roadside ditches

The Weald to Canterbury Road

The main axis of the Roman settlement within Area B was formed by the Weald to Canterbury road, aligned north-east to south-west. Within the excavation area this extended for 337 m, with a maximum width of 18 m as defined by roadside boundaries, but generally averaging 13 m (Plate 3.3). The roadside boundaries comprised a sequence of ditches, successive

Plate 3.3   Examination of north-west roadside ditch sequence.

phases of which generally encroached slightly upon the area defined by the road itself.

North-west roadside ditches

Phase 2 c AD 43-70

The earliest phase of the ditches on the north-west side of the road consisted of (from the north-east) groups 860, 40, 8700 and 8950 (Fig. 3.4). From the ceramic evidence, it would appear that the ditch was established during Phase 2 of Period 2 and was silting up during the early part of Phase 3 (see Lyne, Chapter 6, Assemblages 4 and 5 for the early fills and 8 and 9 for the later ones).

Ditches 860, 40, 8700 and 8950 represented one continuous ditch, which extended south-westwards through Area B. It originated at the northernmost corner of the area at some distance from the edge of the road as later defined; a short length of a gully (164) in a roadside location at the extreme margin of Area B was assigned tentatively to Phase 2, but its extent must have been very limited. The profile of the earliest ditch in this area varied slightly throughout its 290 m length. As it approached the line of the road from the north, reaching it some 95 m from the north-east baulk of Area

B, the ditch generally ranged from 1.70 m to 2.20 m in width and had 45° sloping sides and a flat base (Fig. 3.5), although about 30 m from the north-east baulk it was more U-shaped in profile with splayed upper edges (Fig. 3.5, section 17). It had an average depth of 0.70 m. The fills were predominantly silt clays, apart from the uppermost deposit, which was a grey-brown silt. None of the deposits within the ditch produced much to signify any specific or intense domestic or industrial activity within the area. Only the upper silts of the ditch in the vicinity of Phase 3 Structure I (Fig. 3.5, section 8) produced evidence of activity, but this consisted of intrusive metalworking debris which had settled into the surface of the earlier ditch.

At the point where the ditch reached the road to follow the north-east to south-west alignment, it was cut by all the later phases (Phases 3-4) of the roadside ditch (Fig. 3.5, section 1049), and had a splayed U-shaped profile. Its average width at this stage was 1.60 m and it ranged from 0.40 m to 0.80 m in depth. As the ditch ran to the south-west the excavated sections illustrate how the roadside ditch sequence moved slightly south-eastwards in successive phases (Fig. 3.6). As well as showing the continuous roadside ditches, the sections also demonstrate the regularity of the gully sequence which defined the south-west group of settlement

8930

B A

8950

9060

0   50 m

1:1000

Figure 3.4   Period 2: Phase 2, c AD 43-70. General plan, plus road surface 9011.

599800E
139900N

860

40

8950

8700

oad
011

8620

SC1

599950E
139900N

8620

9360

SC2

S

9270

10460

SC3

7820

600050E
139900N

600050E
139800N

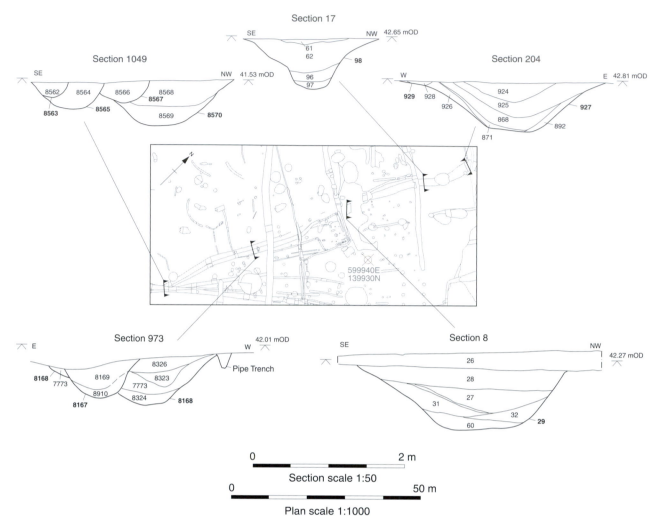

Figure 3.5   Sections of ditches 860, 40 and 8700: Sections 204, 17, 8, 973 (cut 8168), 1049 (cut 8570).

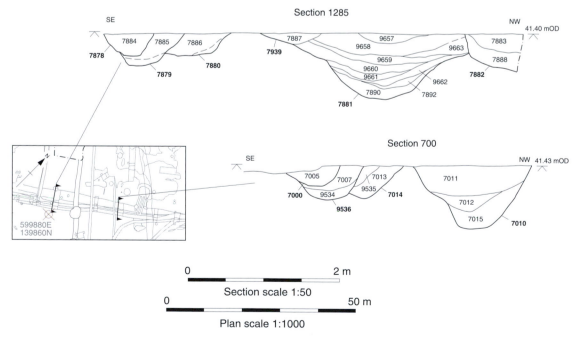

Figure 3.6   Sections of ditch 8950: Sections 700 (cut 7010), 1285 (cut 7881).

plots in Phase 4. These consisted of a continuous rectilinear gully representing the first stage, succeeded by a
north-west/south-east gully and a separate north-east/
south-west gully fronting the road.

As the Phase 2 ditch ran south-westwards towards
the periphery of the settlement the fills became more
homogeneous, comprising in some cases a single clay
silting deposit with very few inclusions, suggesting a
lack of activity to the north-west of the road at this
stage of the roadside ditch sequence (Fig. 3.7).

South-east roadside ditches

Roadside ditches on the south-east of the Canterbury
road were identified in the south-western part of
Area B, but terminated well short of the north-east
margin of the site, at the south-west corner of the
shrine area, where they to the east to define the south
side of the shrine area. Subsequent roadside ditches
characteristically extended further to the north-east,
encroaching a little more into the shrine area with
each successive phase (see below).

Phase 2

The primary phase ditch group 8620 to the south-east
of the road probably ran parallel with the north-western roadside ditch sequence for approximately 195 m.
It is assumed that ditch 8620, and Phase 3 ditch 8670
(see below), extended as far as the south-west limit
of Area B, but evidence for both had been completely
removed by a later (Phase 4) ditch on the same alignment. At the south-west corner of the shrine area ditch
8620 turned south-eastwards away from the road line
for 35 m before returning to the south-west as ditch
group 9060 (Fig. 3.4). At the point where 8620 turned
to the south-west, a further ditch (Group 9360) extended south-eastwards from 8620 for 25 m, and most
likely extended at least as far as a north-south Phase
2 gully 7820 (see Plot SC3 below). The full length of
9360 was not identified as Phase 3 ditch 7850 truncated its south-east end. Ditches 9270 and 9108 possibly combined with 9360, and may also have utilised
later ditch 7850, to form an enclosure fronting onto
the south side of the shrine area (see Plot SC2 below).

Ditch 8620 had an average width of 1.50 m and a
depth of 0.70 m throughout its length and the profile
comprised generally moderately sloping, but irregular sides with a rounded or uneven base. The deposits, which filled this ditch, were very consistent,
comprising a primary yellow-brown silt clay sealed
by a light grey-brown silt (Fig. 3.8, sections 928, 929,
922). This sequence of deposits varied as the ditch
neared the south-eastern part of Area B, where four
distinct fills were identified. These comprised a primary light grey-orange silt clay, overlain by a yellow-
grey silt clay. Sealing these were two clay silting
deposits, the uppermost made up of a fine grey silt
(Fig. 3.8, section 914). These fills produced a modest
quantity of pottery (see Chapter 6, Assemblage 6).

The above sequence of deposits continued in the
south-western return of the first phase ditch 9060, up

to a 9 m stretch of which had two distinct deposits
of charred remains (Fig. 3.8, section 978). These consisted largely of grain, chaff and weeds, indicating
that cereal processing activity was occurring within
the vicinity (see Pelling, Chapter 9). Beyond this area
the south-western end of ditch 9060, up to its terminus, had a more consistent profile with sides sloping moderately to a flat base (Fig. 3.9), and was filled
with three distinct layers of grey silt.

Phase 3

A further stage of definition of the south side of the
shrine area early in Phase 3 was marked by ditch 7850,
which cut the top of Phase 2 ditch 9360. Ditch 7850 did
not extend quite as far as the south-east roadside ditch
sequence at its west end, but ran eastwards for 80 m, before turning to form the western boundary of a north-
south trackway (Fig. 3.10). Ditch 7850 ranged from 1
m to 2.5 m in width, but was on average 2 m wide and
0.65 m deep. Throughout its length it was typically
filled with three distinct deposits and had a consistent
profile of steep sides to a slightly rounded base, giving a broad U-shaped appearance (Fig. 3.11). The recorded deposits generally comprised a primary light
grey clay, overlain by a dark grey clay silt and sealed
by a mid-grey fine silt, although in some cases (eg Fig.
3.11, sections 1073 and 872), a single grey silting fill was
the only deposit identified. There were relatively small
amounts (less than 5%) of charred remains present
within the deposits. Collectively they contained among
other finds a fragment from a blue-green glass bottle
(SF1007), a yellow-green glass fragment (SF1260), a
coin dated AD 69-96 (SF1413; see Guest, Chapter 5, Table 5.5), and a fragment from a lava quern (SF1339; see
Roe, Chapter 5, Cat. no.31). Small find 1007, dated to
the late 1st century, came from the primary clays of the
ditch and the remaining three were all retrieved from
the upper silts. Almost the full length of the ditch was
cut into by later gullies, all representing later boundaries along the same axis; as the ditch extended further
to the east it was sealed by Phase 5 soil spread 7439 associated with Structure P (Fig. 3.11, section 811).

The Phase 3 south-east roadside ditch 8670 presumably followed the same course as Phase 2 ditch 8620,
but extended for a further 5 m to the north-east before
turning roughly to the east to define the next stage of
southern boundary for the shrine area (Fig. 3.10). After a slight break this ditch line was resumed as ditch
9730 which extended for 26 m before turning to the
south-west and continuing as ditch 7840, which cut
ditch 7850 (above). Ditch 8670 had moderately sloping sides, curving slightly to a flat base. With average
dimensions of 1.20 m in width and 0.30 m in depth
it was consistently filled with a single brown-grey
clay silting deposit (Fig. 3.12, section 919). Its continuation, 9730, had a more rounded profile and was
slighter with an average width of 0.70 m width and a
depth of 0.20 m (see Fig. 3.11, section 830). Similarly
this stretch of the ditch was also filled with a single
grey clay silt deposit which produced amongst other
finds a yellow-green glass fragment (SF1375; see

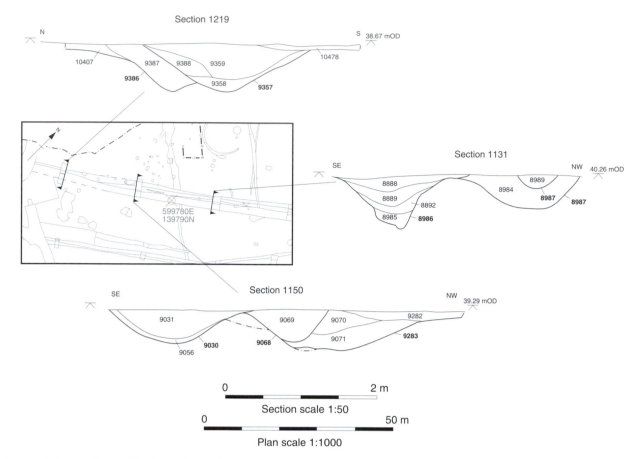

Figure 3.7   *Sections of ditch 8950: Sections 1131 (cut 8987), 1150 (cut 9283), 1219 (cut 9386).*

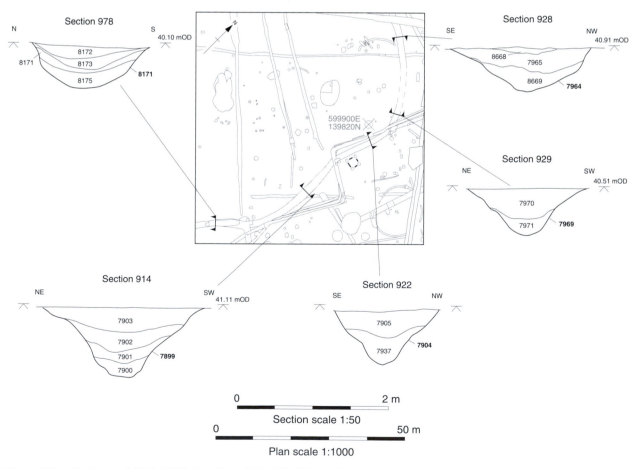

Figure 3.8   *Sections of ditch 8620: Sections 928, 929, 922, 914, 978.*

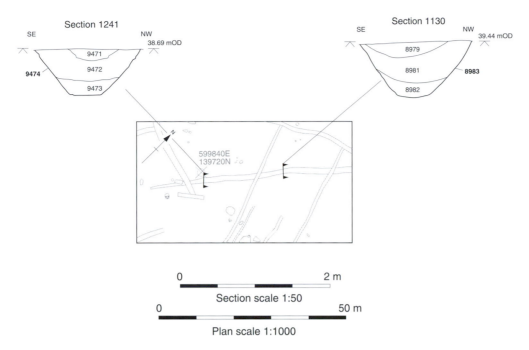

Figure 3.9   Sections of ditch 9060: Sections 1130, 1241.

Cool, Chapter 5, Cat. no. 70). As the south-western return, ditch 7840 extended for 128 m and was filled along its length with a grey-brown clay silt. The profile was also consistent, with moderate to steep sides, a flat base, a width of 0.60 m and a depth of no more than 0.28 m (Fig. 3.12, sections 741, 870, 891, 1014).

Running parallel to 8670/9730 was a series of ditch segments which eventually extended to the western boundary of the north-south trackway. From west to east these consisted of 9490, 7790 and 8140 (Fig. 3.10). Ditch 9490 was filled with a single light brown silting deposit. The profile had moderate sides to a flat base with average dimensions of 0.32 m width and 0.08 m depth (Fig. 3.13, section 732). Ditch 7790 had the same profile (Fig. 3.13, section 746) and was also filled with a single deposit of grey-brown clay silt which produced a blue-green glass fragment from an indented beaker (SF 966; see Cool, Chapter 5, Cat. no.41). This part of the ditch widened to give average measurements of 0.5 m width and 0.15 m depth. The easternmost stretch of the ditch, 8140, had an average width of 0.60 m and a depth of 0.22 m and was filled with a single deposit of light grey clay silt with occasional inclusions of iron slag (Fig. 3.13, section 963).

Phase 4

The Phase 4 roadside ditch followed the same alignment as its predecessors extending to the north-east again for a further 6 m (Fig. 3.14). Ditch 8680 was seen extending from the south-west limit of Area B, cutting into the top of the previous two phases of ditch (Phase 2 ditch 8620 and Phase 3 ditch 8670; see Fig.

3.15, section 994), in most cases removing all trace of them. Ditch 8680 generally had a broad U-shaped profile with a rounded base, but varied locally, in places having a more V-shaped profile with a flat base (Fig. 3.15). Its average dimensions were 1.35 m wide and 0.60 m deep. Throughout its course it was generally filled with three distinct deposits. These comprised a light grey clay primary deposit, a brown-grey clay silt, and an upper fill of grey clay silt, which produced amongst other finds a fragment from the base of a glass vessel (SF1096; see Cool, Chapter 5, Cat. no.66). There was little variation in the character of these deposits, but occasionally there were dump deposits of charred remains. A consistent trait was the moderate level of flint and iron slag present within the secondary and upper deposits which most likely derived from the erosion of the adjacent road surface.

At the south-west corner of the shrine area ditch 8680 turned to the east to define the north side of enclosure SC1. It terminated after 28 m. There was a small break or possible entrance some 2 m wide before the alignment resumed as feature 9500. This continued to extend to the east in the form of gully segments 7780 and 10479. The segments of gully were filled with a single grey silting deposit with occasional inclusions of iron slag and small amounts of charred remains. Gully 9500 had an average width and depth of 0.60 m and 0.14 m (Fig. 3.13, section 732, cut 7145), while the remaining two gullies had average dimensions of 0.47 m width and 0.22 m depth (Fig. 3.16, sections 747, 768). Throughout the length of this phase of gully, a moderate to steep sided, flat based profile was maintained.

599750E
139800N

8930

9280

8950

8730

9170

599850E
139750N

0   50 m

1:1000

Figure 3.10   Period 2: Phase 3, c AD 70-150. General plan.

G

7944

7269

7306

H

8780

8690

8630

8640

1340   1705

1270

796

840

1720

602

K   8670

SC1

9730
9490

SC2

7850

L

7790

7850

1750

Q

7850

8280

SC3/SC4

7740

1721

10400

10380

SC5

8140

M

N

1030

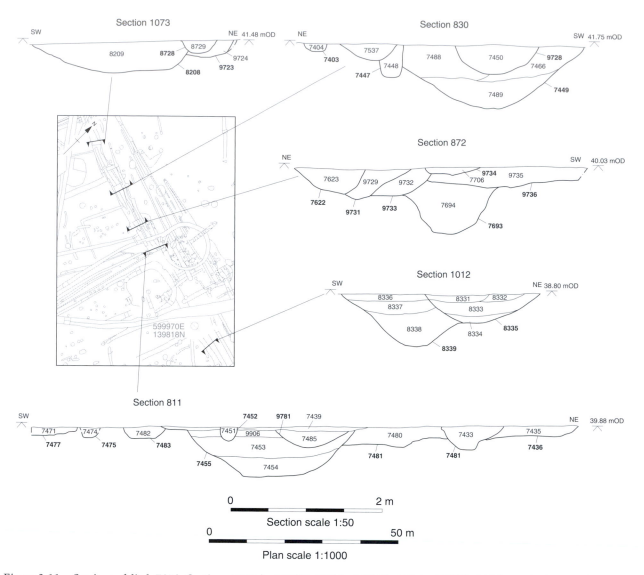

Figure 3.11   Sections of ditch 7850: Sections 1073 (cut 8208), 830 (cut 7449), 872 (cut 7693), 811 (cut 7455), 1012 (cut 8339).

A number of other gullies within this phase were observed either side of 9500 following the same east-west alignment. Gullies 9740, 7800 and 7750/7760 complemented the main boundary, or represented a form of intermediary sub-phase occurring between the main boundary and its predecessor (Fig. 3.14). Gully 9740 was observed for 16 m cutting into the top of Phase 3 ditch 7850. It had moderately sloping sides and a rounded base. As it extended to the east it became progressively deeper, but overall it averaged 0.80 m in width and 0.30 m in depth (See Fig. 3.11, section 830). Gully 7800 was some 36 m long and had steep sides and a flat base (Fig. 3.16, section 745). The western terminal was shallow and ill defined and may not have reflected the original limit of the feature. As 7800 extended to the east the sides sloped more steeply to a rounded base, and the average dimensions were 0.50 m wide and 0.18 m deep. Gullies 7750 and 7760 were cut on the same alignment, 7760 being the later. Both had steep sides and a rounded to flat base (Fig. 3.16, section 1161). 7760 extended for 27 m to end in a rounded terminal to the east while

7750 was only 15 m long. Both ditches were cut by Phase 5 penannular Structure P (Group 7500), and their course to the east was occasionally obscured by spreads of occupation debris. However, in plan, 7750 is likely to have corresponded to 7770 which was seen emerging from the eastern edge of the penannular structure and extending eastwards up to the junction with north-south ditch 8020 (Fig.3.17). All the above mentioned ditches were filled with the same single deposit of light grey clay silt which had occasional inclusions of iron slag, fired clay and charred remains.

A change in the layout to the boundary system south-east of the road was demonstrated by gully 8980/9350. This was truncated by successive phases of gully, but was seen clearly terminating to respect the eastern terminal of roadside ditch 8680 (Fig. 3.14). Gully 8980/9350 originated 10 m south of ditch 9060 and extended to the north in a zig-zag fashion. The southern part of the gully (8980) was 0.7 m wide and 0.25 m deep where its full profile existed. It had a steep-sided flat-bottomed appearance, and was filled with a single deposit of grey silt (Fig. 3.16, section

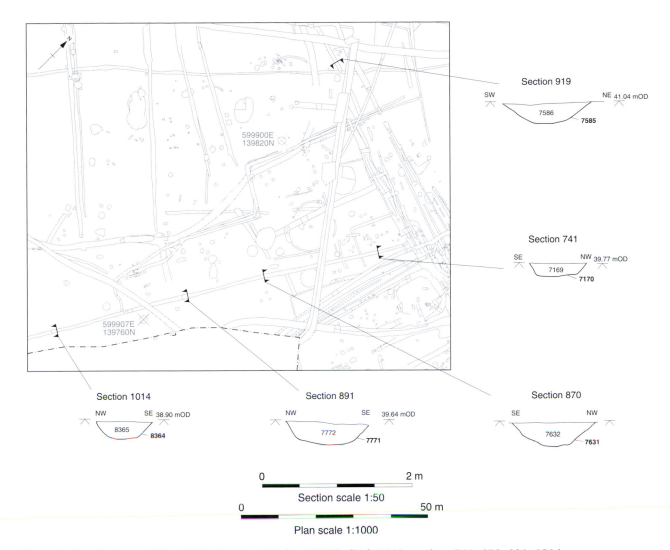

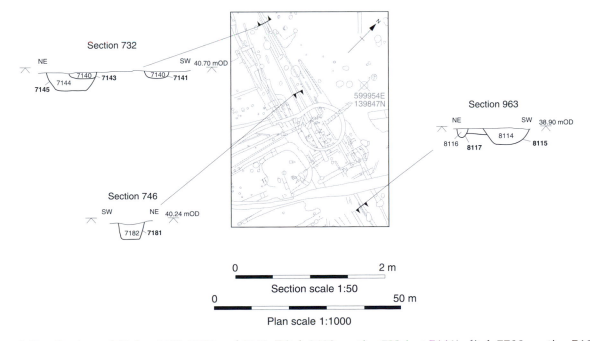

Figure 3.12   Sections of ditch 8670: Section 919 (cut 7585); ditch 7840: sections 741, 870, 891, 1014.

Figure 3.13   Sections of ditches 9490, 7790 and 8140: Ditch 9490: section 732 (cut 7141); ditch 7790: section 746 (cut 7181); ditch 8140: section 963 (cut 8115).

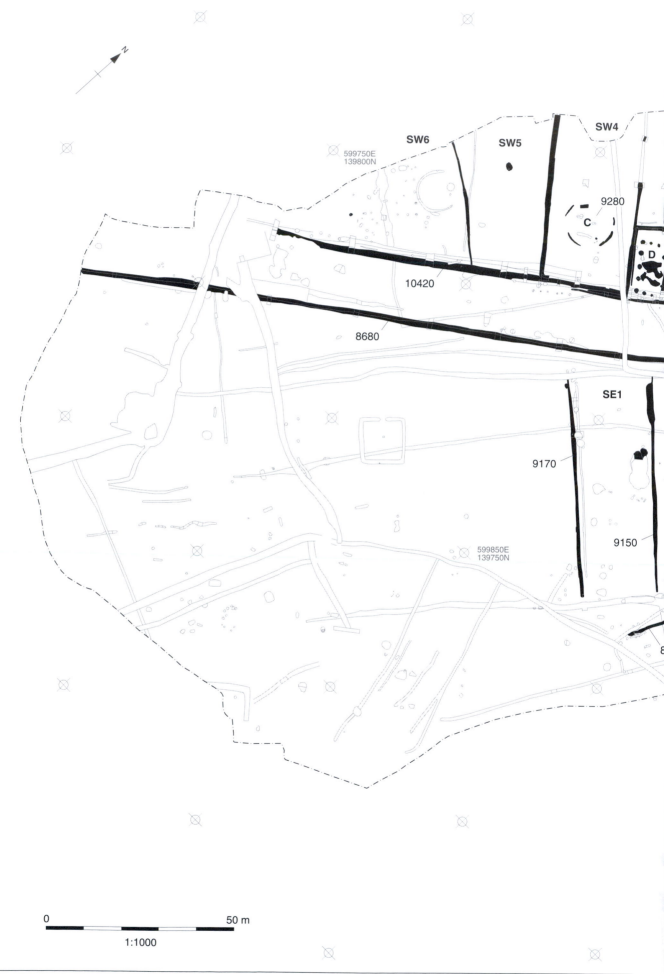

SW6

SW5

SW4

599750E
139800N

9280

C

D

10420

8680

SE1

9170

9150

599850E
139750N

89

0   50 m

1:1000

Figure 3.14   Period 2: Phase 4, c AD 150-200. General plan.

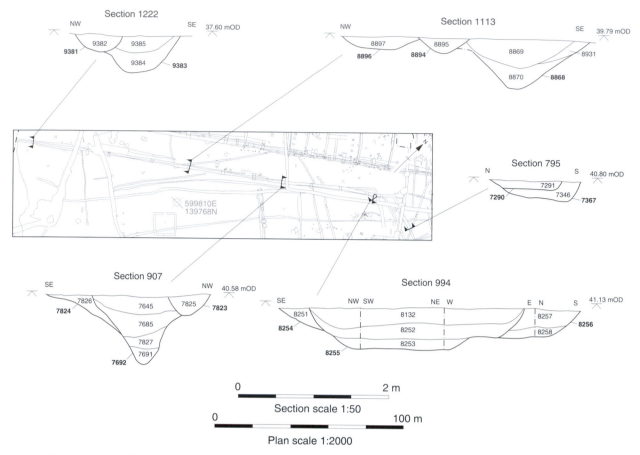

Figure 3.15 Sections of ditch 8680: Sections 1222 (cut 9383), 1113 (cut 8868), 907 (cut 7692), 994 (cut 8255), 795 (cut 7367).

967). As it continued to the north as 9350, the profile remained consistent and the gully was filled with a primary grey clay, in places sealed by an upper grey silting deposit with occasional inclusions of iron slag and sub-rounded flint nodules. Gully 9350 was on average 0.6 m wide and up to 0.26 m deep, and was the earliest in an alignment of three gullies (Fig. 3.16, section 860, cut 7871), which represented the continued use and definition of the same boundary throughout the occupation of the area, with each subsequent phase being positioned further to the north.

Phase 5

Ditches 8850, 8770/8920 and 43/595 clearly formed the latest stage of the roadside ditch sequence. The roadside gully 8850 (Fig. 3.17) extended approximately 143 m from the south-western limits of the site. Along its length it cut into the top of Phase 4 ditch 8680 and finally ended in a well-defined rounded terminal. The gully was filled with dark brown clay silt which was very distinctive in plan, and the profile varied little from moderate to steep sides and a rounded base. The width was between 0.46 and 0.85 m and the depth between

0.23 and 0.35 m (Fig. 3.15). It is possible that the north-eastern end of ditch 8680 survived in part into this phase north of the point at which it was recut by 8850.

Phase 5 saw the first definition of the south-east margin of the road in the vicinity of the shrine, in the form of ditch 43/595 (Fig. 3.17). This feature extended from the north-east edge of Area B for 56 m along the south-east side of the road, until it was totally removed by a large post-medieval field division. The ditch had a rounded profile measuring on average 0.6 m wide and 0.25 m deep, and was mostly filled with a single grey clay silting deposit (Fig. 3 18, section 4), but in the north-east part of the gully this sealed a compact clay layer containing dense sub-rounded flint (Fig. 3.18, section 134). This feature represented a single phase of roadside definition that did not correspond to the sequence on the north-west side of the road, which had at least two phases of roadside definition within Phase 5.

The penultimate phase of gully sequence defining enclosure SC1 was represented by 9340, 8940, 7018 and 7730 (Fig. 3.17). Gully 9340 possibly followed the same alignment as its predecessor 9350/8980, but for part of its probable length the feature was totally removed

48

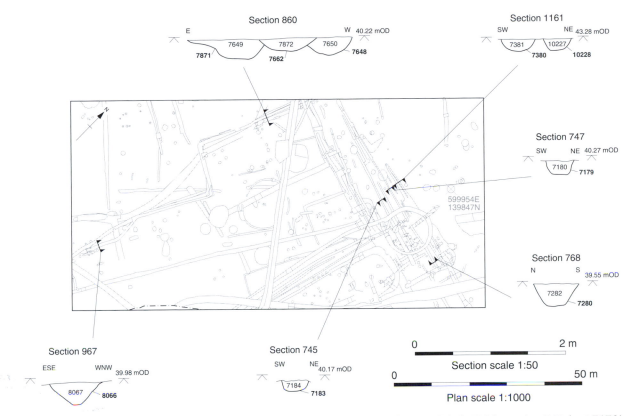

Figure 3.16   Sections of ditches 7780, 10479, 7800, 7750, 7760, 8980 and 9350: Ditch 7780: section 747 (cut 7179); ditch 10479: section 768 (cut 7280); ditch 7800: section 745 (cut 7183); ditch 7750: section 1161 (cut 10228); ditch 7760: section 1161 (cut 7380); ditch 8980: section 967 (cut 8066); ditch 9350: section 860 (cut 7871).

by the next phase of gully and was only seen for a 30 m stretch, extending northwards to a rounded terminal. Gully 9340 was generally 0.55-0.6 m wide, with a maximum depth of 0.2 m and was roughly U-shaped in profile (Fig. 3.18, section 706, cut 7034), occasionally splaying to a slightly rounded V-shaped profile at points along its length. Gully 8940 began 2 m north of the terminal of 9340 and extended for 12 m on a WNW-ESE alignment. It became progressively narrower and shallower as it extended to the west. It was 0.91 m wide and 0.45 m deep at the east end, and only 0.29 m wide and 0.18 m deep at the west end. Primary and secondary deposits of grey silt clay were noted in the east terminal, overlain by a grey clay silt deposit which extended throughout the remaining length of the gully (Fig. 3.18, section 708). Two further segments of gully, 7018 and 7730 (Fig. 3.18, sections 701 and 888) were 8 m and 2 m in length respectively and aligned NE-SW defining the south-eastern edge of the road. Both gullies had steep sides and a flat base, were typically 0.60 m wide and 0.25 m deep, and were filled with the same single deposit of grey clay silt with inclusions of subrounded flint, deriving from the surface of the road.

The last Phase 5 boundary within this sequence was defined by zig-zag gully 8770/8920 (Fig. 3.17).

This originated from the south-east at the junction with Phase 3 ditch 7840, which suggests that the latter boundary was still defined in some way during this phase of settlement. This stage of gully extended on the same alignment as its predecessors, extending northwards for a further 2 m. The average dimensions of the gully were 0.65 m wide and 0.24 m deep, shown in a profile which was consistently steep sided with a flat to slightly rounded base. The northern stretch of the gully was filled with a single brown-grey clay silt which produced notable amounts of iron slag and sub-rounded small stones (Fig. 3.18, section 701, cut 7020; section 707). Towards the southern end of the gully, just beyond the point where it cut into the top of Phase 2 ditch 9060, the fills comprised a primary clay silt overlain by a dump deposit of dark grey clay silt containing a large amount of charred plant remains and fragments of ceramic building material (Fig. 3.18, section 1097).

Of all the phases of gully south-east of the road and defining the south side of the shrine area, it is notable that the Phase 5 features, 8940 and 8770/8920, were the only ones to reflect the exact WNW-ESE axis of the primary phase of rectilinear enclosure around the shrine (group 70 features).

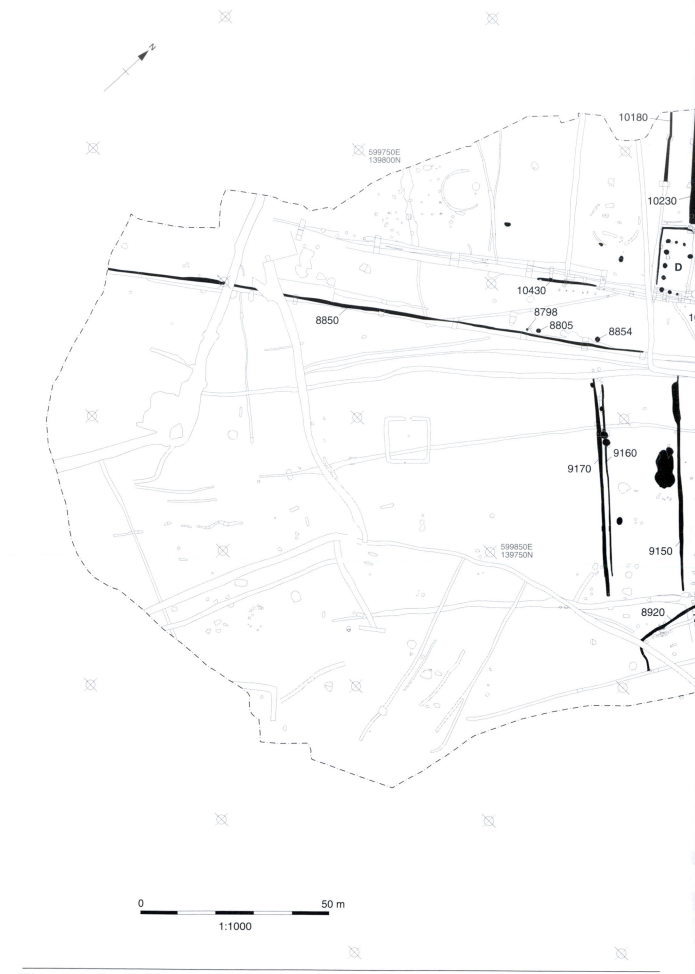

Figure 3.17   Period 2: Phase 5, c AD 200-250. General plan.

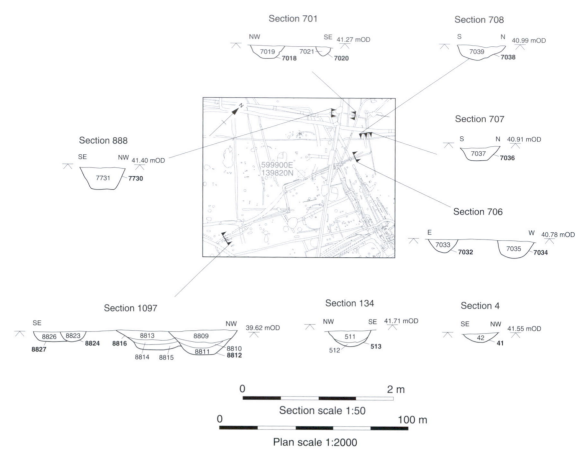

Figure 3.18 Sections of ditches 9340, 8940, 7018, 7730, 8770/8920, and 43/595: Ditch 9340: section 706 (cut 7034); ditch 8940: section 708 (cut 7038); ditch 7018: section 701; ditch 7730: section 888; ditch 8770/8920: sections 707 (cut 7036) and 1097 (cut 8812); ditch 43/595: sections 4 and 134.

Pits

Within the area of the road, directly north-west of the last phase roadside gully (8850), were three pits, possibly all of Phase 5 date. The most north-easterly, 8854, lay opposite the north-eastern end of fenceline 9470 and in line with the south-western boundary of Plot SE1 (see below). This was a well-defined five-sided pit with vertical sides and a flat base, 1.3 m wide and 0.48 m deep. The primary fill was a thin layer of dark brown silt clay with occasional charcoal flecks, sealed by a 0.43 m deep upper fill of dark grey silt clay also with charcoal. Fourteen iron objects were recovered from the pit, eleven of them nails from the uppermost deposit (8855). The other three objects were a handle or tang (SF1465), a possible length of chain (SF1467; see Scott, Chapter 5, Cat. no.18; Fig.5.12) and a triangular plate fragment of uncertain function (SF1471). Other finds from this feature included a piece of copper alloy binding (SF1469; see Cool, Chapter 5, Cat. no.120) and two fragments of blue-green bottle glass (SF1470 and SF1481) dated late 1st to early 3rd century, which came from the uppermost fill. The shape of the pit suggests that it held a wooden post.

Approximately 15 m south-west were pits 8798 and 8805. Pit 8798 was circular with a diameter of 0.7 m and a depth of 0.23 m, steep sides and a rounded base. It was filled with grey-black clay silt containing occasional patches of charcoal. Pit 8805 was also circular, 1.2 m in diameter and 0.26 m deep, with steep near vertical sides and a flat base. Its fill was the same as that of 8798 and produced a fragment of a *denarius* of Caracalla (SF1286, AD 196-211; see Guest, Chapter 5, Table 5.5).

Road surfaces

Almost nothing remained of the road surfaces, presumably owing to plough truncation. The only surviving part of the road comprised three discrete irregular patches, deposit 9011 (Fig. 3.4), which covered an area of approximately 35 sq. m located just north-east of the modern north-west to south-east aligned field boundary which divided Area B into two unequal parts. Layer 9011 was deposited directly on top of the natural Wealden clay, indicating that the topsoil had been removed prior to the laying of 9011; there was no sign of make up or levelling layers to facilitate the construction of the road. Layer 9011 consisted of a mixture of flint and gravel with occasional inclusions of iron slag debris surviving to a maximum depth of 0.15 m. Lenses of silty clay throughout the matrix suggest that it was periodically exposed to flooding or waterlogging, and hint that the deposit may have comprised parts of several successive surfaces which were not otherwise distinguishable, though it is also possible that 9011 represented a form of bedding layer for the metalled surface proper. These deposits were not dated.

South of 9011 were the remains of two parallel wheel ruts which extended for 20 m along the line of the road. These were 1.5 m apart from their external edge, and 1.1 m apart from their internal edge. Both ruts had a maximum depth of 0.05 m and were filled with compacted iron slag and small sub-rounded flint nodules.

Concentrations of gravel and iron slag were noted in the vicinity of the road line within the post-Roman subsoil in the course of removal of this deposit by machine. These suggest that despite its general appearance within the excavated area the road had originally been surfaced for its full length.

North-west oblique ditch area

At the northern limit of the site where Phase 3 ditch 840 met Phase 2 ditch 860, a range of features extending to the south-west indicated domestic and industrial activity.

Phase 3

Ditch 840 (Fig. 3.10), which approached the road from the north-east in the extreme northern corner of Area B, projected the alignment of, and was probably the same feature as, the major settlement boundary ditch encountered at the south-eastern margin of Area C

(see below). Ditch 840 extended for approximately 13 m before it turned to the south-east into a large area of predominantly silt deposits (602), which extended to the north-west margin of the road. Along the north-east to south-west alignment the ditch was filled with a single grey silt, and was on average 1.6 m wide and 0.4 m deep (Fig. 3.19, section 193). As it turned to the south-east it widened to a maximum of 3.4 m (Fig. 3.19, section 174 cut 710), but generally the average dimensions in this stretch were 2 m wide x 0.40 m deep. There were two clay silting fill deposits, both producing appreciable amounts of pottery.

The large area of clay silt deposits into which 840 ran may have represented the fill of a sump for water draining away from the settlement if ditch 840 represented the southern limit of the north-west boundary of the settlement at this time. The drainage would also have been facilitated by ditch 1720 which ran eastwards from 840 and presumably continued into Area A, where, from the evidence provided by the geophysical survey, it would have continued on the alignment of the ditches fronting the north-west side of the road.

There were three different stages of roadside ditch or gully which span the time frame defined by Phase 3, consisting of 8690 and associated gully 8780, 1340/8630 and 1705/8640 and gully 1270. Each stage of ditch radiated from the same point, moving successively clockwise towards the eventual north-east to south-west line of the road (Fig. 3.10).

Ditch 8690 was aligned NNE-SSW and extended for approximately 42 m from its north-east terminal. It varied in width from 1.0 m to 1.20 m, and in depth from 0.30 m to 0.40 m. The profile remained consistent along its length, having a broad U-shaped appearance

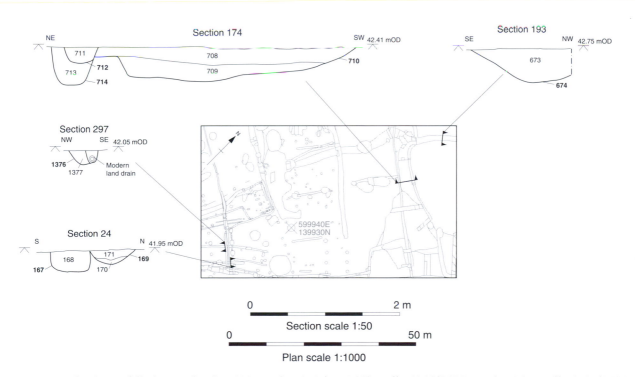

Figure 3.19   Sections of ditch 840: Section 193, section 174 (cut 710); gully 1340/8630: section 297; gully 1705/8640: section 24 (cut 169).

with a slightly shallower slope on its western edge (Fig. 3.5, section 973, cut 8167). A contemporaneous gully, 8780, extended WNW from the western side of 8690 for 13 m (see Possible Plot NW4 below). These ditches represented the earliest stage of activity, pre-dating the division of this area into regular plots during Phase 4. Ditch 8690 is likely to have corresponded with ditches 7939 and 9930 as they extended south-west along the line of the Canterbury road, continuing to the south-western limit of Area B as ditch 10070. A broad correspondence between ditch 8690 and 8960 to the south-west is also possible, however, and the two features produced contemporaneous pottery (see Chapter 6, Assemblage 11), though ditch 8960 was tentatively assigned to Phase 4 (see below).

Ditch 8630/1340 was aligned NE-SW and was approximately 44 m long. It terminated to the north-east, and was truncated by 8640/1705 to the south-west. It had an average width of 1.0 m and an average depth of 0.40 m with the profile varying from a slightly rounded 'V' shape to straight sided with a sharply defined flat base (Fig. 3.19, section 297). The fill of this ditch was consistent throughout its length, comprising a single clay silting deposit with more instances of iron slag in the vicinity of Structure I (Phase 3).

Ditch 8640/1705 and gully 1270 represented the final stage in the sequence of radiating ditches. The former was aligned ENE-WSW and extended for approximately 35 m. It was truncated by waterhole 7329 and also by roadside ditch 8950 to the west, where it met the straighter line of that ditch. Feature 8640/1705 had a maximum width of 0.40 m and a depth of 0.40 m and had a U-shaped profile with a rounded base (Fig. 3.19, section 24). Two grey silting deposits filled the length of the ditch, with the lower having a larger amount of sub-rounded flint and iron slag. Ditch 1270 was located just north-west of the above mentioned ditch and extended a further 9 m eastwards. It had all of the characteristics of 8640/1705, but was conceivably associated with 8630/1340.

North-west roadside plots (Fig. 3.20)

At the northern corner of Area B were a series of divisions which lay north-west of the road, defining plots referenced here (from north-east to south-west) as NW1, NW2 and NW3, with slighter evidence for a further plot, NW4. These plots north-west of the Canterbury road were laid out roughly at right-angles to the road alignment, defined by boundaries aligned approximately north-west to south-east, and were between 11 m and 20 m wide. The group of six south-western plots (see below) were more regularly laid out and were between 17 m and 22 m in width. In all cases each plot had a common boundary with the adjacent plot. The chronology of the north-west roadside plots is slightly uncertain. Plot NW3 was certainly in place in Phase 3, but the evidence for Plots NW1 and NW2 is less clear. The whole group may have been laid out at one time, but their arrangement could have been more piecemeal.

Fronting the road to the south-east of the north-west plot divisions were a series of roadside gullies. At the north-eastern edge of Area B were Phase 4 ditches 1700 and 1690 which combined to form a small three-sided rectilinear 'enclosure' approximately 9 m wide, which must have been broadly contemporary with the north-west plot sequence. The 'enclosure' fronted the road, but its south-eastern boundary was not defined at this stage by a roadside ditch, nor was there any such ditch north-east of the enclosure. Ditch 1700 was a possible re-cut of 1690 and had a different sequence of fills, with a notably higher concentration of charcoal within its upper silting fills. Its maximum depth was 1 m, seen at the junction with 1690. As it turned the corner to the south-east it ended in a distinct terminal 0.50 m deep approximately 2 m short of the edge of the road alignment. Ditch 1690 began at the junction with 1700, extended to the road and continued on the north-east to south-west alignment for 26 m before terminating south-east of waterhole 796. At its south-western terminal ditch 1690 was approximately 0.40 m wide and 0.10 m deep, but it became wider and deeper to the north-east. In the vicinity of Structure J, however, 1690 narrowed sharply from 0.90 m to 0.50 m, and became more shallow, being only 0.12 m deep here. At this point the profile also changed; its rounded shape became more pronounced with sharply sloping sides and a flat base. The ditch was filled with a consistent sequence of light brown silting deposits throughout its length, but there was a notable quantity of charred remains in the deposits south-east of Structure J. These may have been associated with the use of this building.

Phase 4 gully 1685 continued the alignment of 1690 towards the south-west, with a gap of 4 m between their terminals defining an access to waterhole 796. Gully 1685 survived for a length of 13 m and was at least 0.40 m wide, being cut along its length by a later roadside ditch 1680. The gully had a variable profile. It was rounded and approximately 0.10 m deep at its north-east terminal, deepening to 0.40 m at the mid point of the gully. The profile became more angular and flatter based further to the south-west, reaching a steep-sided narrow south-west terminal 0.55 m deep. As with 1690, gully 1685 was filled with a single silting deposit. Two postholes were located north-west of the termini of 1685 and 1690. Posthole 175 had a diameter of 0.90 m and 190 had a diameter of 0.75 m, both were 0.25 m deep with moderate sloping sides and flat bases. Grey-blue silt clay containing occasional charcoal flecking and slag fragments filled both postholes, which may have served to help define access to waterhole 796.

Gully 1685 occupied the same stratigraphic position as 1690 and reflected the same phase of layout. Both features represented the first straightening of the roadside boundary, in contrast to previous phases (Phases 2 and 3) in which the boundary deviated to the north from the road alignment.

Plot NW1

Plot NW1 was bounded by Phase 4 gullies 870 and 850 to the north-east, and by ditch 30 to the south-

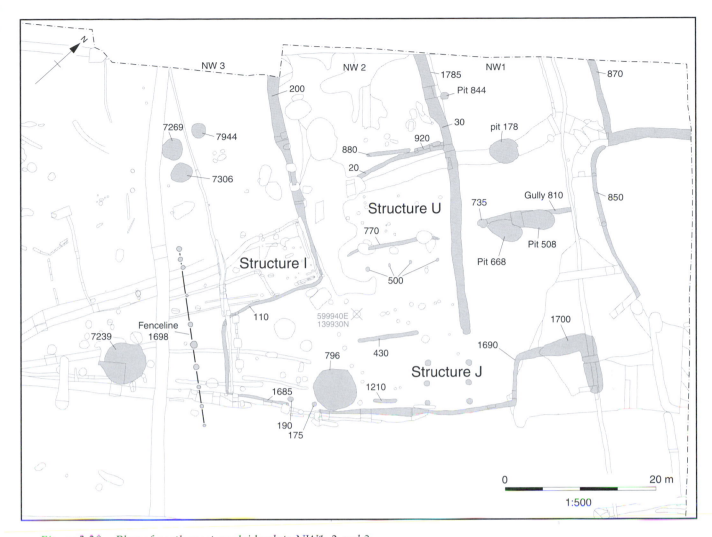

Figure 3.20   Plan of north-west roadside plots NW1, 2 and 3.

west, defining an area 20 m wide and at least 40 m in length (Fig. 3.20).

Gully 850 was located in the northern corner of Area B and followed the north-eastern edge of ditch 840 (Phase 3). Close to the north-western terminus of 850, the south-east end of a similarly NW-SE aligned ditch (870) also cut ditch 840. The common relationship of these features to ditch 840 suggests a degree of association and together gullies 850 and 870 probably formed the north-eastern boundary of Plot NW1, albeit rather irregularly aligned. Gully 850 had moderately sloping sides and a flat base (Fig. 3.19, section 174, cut 712), with a maximum depth of 0.20 m and a consistent width of 0.60-0.70 m. Gully 870 had the same profile and depth and was only marginally wider at 0.86 m (Fig. 3.21, section 165, cut 660). Both gullies were filled with a single deposit of clay silt, with the fill of 850 including small amounts of charred remains.

Approximately 20 m to the south-west was a NW-SE aligned boundary ditch (30), which mirrored the alignment of 870 and 850 and was approximately 38 m in length. This ditch was a later version of ditch 1785 which was on the same alignment, but was only

identified in plan over an 8 m length at the north-west margin of Area B. The average width and depth of ditch 30 was 1.20 m and 0.50 m and it was consistently filled with clay silts throughout its length (Fig. 3.21, sections 5 and 221). Three nails were retrieved from the south-eastern terminal of the ditch and a body fragment from a glass vessel was recovered from its north-western end.

No structures were identified within Plot NW1. It contained principally two Phase 3 pits (178 and 844), a Phase 4 gully (810), and several Phase 5 pits (group 820).

Pit 844, which lay just north-east of ditch 30, cutting through the edge of earlier ditch 1785, was steep sided with a flat base, 1.2 m in diameter and 0.7 m deep (Fig. 3.21, section 221). The base of the pit was filled with three layers of clay silt which possibly derived from the erosion of the feature's edges. A layer of redeposited clay containing large pieces of charcoal sealed these deposits and in turn was overlain by three dark grey silt clays all containing high levels of charcoal flecking. The upper silting deposit also contained many charcoal flecks as well as fragments of burnt clay. Small finds 169-171, 173 and 177, all blue-green glass vessel fragments, were also retrieved from the upper silts. Practically all of the deposits within this pit yielded large amounts of pottery, totalling almost 18 kg (See Chapter 6, Assemblage 17).

Pit 178, 4 m across with steep sloping sides, cut into the top of Phase 2 ditch 860 and was excavated to a depth of 1 m without reaching natural clay. The lowest excavated fill was an orange grey silt clay with sub-rounded flint, producing small amounts of charcoal and a blue-green glass base from a globular vessel (SF19; see Cool, Chapter 5, Cat. no.54). Above this was a layer of grey silt clay containing a large amount of charcoal fragments and a light yellow-brown neck and shoulder from a glass globular jug (SF 13; see Cool, Chapter 5, Cat. no.45). This was overlain by a yellow brown clay silt, which in turn was overlain by a grey clay silt, which contained dense charcoal fragments. The two upper deposits consisted of grey-brown clay silts.

Approximately 6 m south-east of pit 178 was gully 810. Aligned NNE-SSW, at right-angles to the plot boundaries, it was traced for *c* 13 m from its southern terminus, but it is not clear if it extended across ditch 840 as far as the plot boundary gully 850. Gully 810 was cut by the later pits, but where it was not disturbed it had a maximum width and depth of 0.60 m and 0.40 m respectively, and was filled by single grey-brown silt clay along its length.

Three pits cut gully 810. Pit 508 was oval in shape and measured 6.50 m NE-SW and 2.50 m NW-SE, with a depth of 0.50 m. Pit 668 had a diameter of 2.25 m and a depth of 0.45 m. Pit 735, at the southern end of gully 810, was 1.70 m in diameter and 0.28 m deep. All

three pits were filled with grey-brown clay silts containing fragments of fired clay, and collectively they produced nine small finds, consisting largely of nails and further unidentified pieces of iron which possibly derived from the truncated gully. Although pit 668 was cut later than 508, it was clear that the latter was still partially open since a fine grey silt deposit (671) extended across the top of both features (Fig. 3.21, section 166).

Plot NW2

Plot NW2 was bounded by ditch 30 to the north-east and by gully 200 to the south-west (a short segment of this gully was later re-cut as 300), creating an area some 20 m wide by 47 m long (Fig. 3.20).

Within the area created by these boundaries were a number of Phase 4 linear features aligned almost perpendicular to ditch 30. From the north-west these consisted of gully segments 880 and 920, gully 20, gully/beamslot 770, post-row 500 and beamslot 430. Gully segment 1210 to the extreme south-east could also belong to this sequence.

Gully 20, the earliest of these features, lay immediately south-east of gully segments 880 and 920. It was slightly curving in plan and extended up to ditch 30, which cut the gully, suggesting that gully 20 might have been contemporary with ditch 1785, the antecedent of ditch 30. It is possible that gully 20 represented an intermediate phase between the disuse of the Phase 2 settlement boundary ditch 40 and the laying out of boundary 1785. Gully 20 extended 14 m to the south-west where it was masked by soil spread 26 which was associated with Structure I. Gully 20

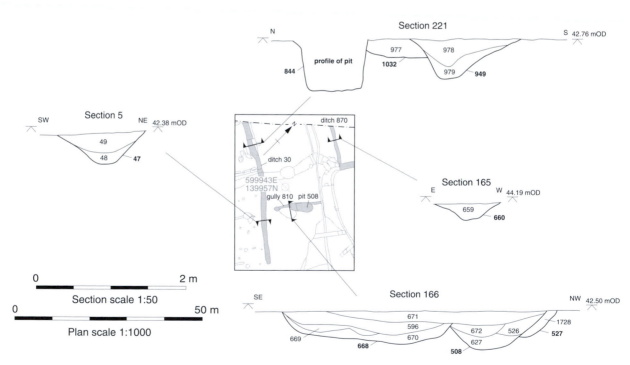

Figure 3.21   Plot NW1: Sections of ditch 870: Section 165; ditch 30: section 221 (cut 949), section 5; ditch 1785: section 221 (cut 1032); pit 668, pit 508 and gully 810 (cut 527): section 166.

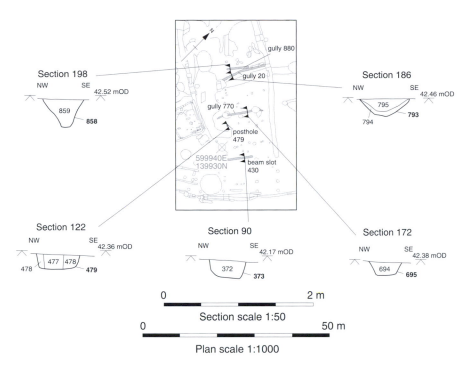

Figure 3.22   Plot NW2: Sections of gullies 880, 20 and 770; beam slot 430, and posthole 479: Sections of gully 880: section 198 (cut 858); gully 20: section 186 (cut 793); gully 770: section 172 (cut 695); beam slot 430: section 90 (cut 373); posthole 479: section 122.

had a maximum width and depth of were 0.70 m and 0.24 m respectively, and had moderate sloping sides to a flat base. Throughout its length it was filled with a yellow-grey silt clay, overlain by an upper grey clay silt deposit, which included occasional sub-rounded flints (Fig. 3.22, section 186).

Structure U

Gullies/slots 880/920, 770 and 430 were spaced at regular 11 m intervals suggesting that they were contemporaneous features within this phase. In view of this, and other similarities of character, it is possible, if perhaps unlikely, that these features, together with posthole group 500, were parts of a structure or structures, but in the absence of other evidence the nature of the structure (tentatively labelled Structure U) is unclear. It is perhaps more likely that these features simply served to subdivide Plot NW2.

Two segments of gully, 880 and 920, 6 m and 4 m long respectively and set almost end to end, were located north-west of earlier gully 20. Gully 880 had an average width and depth of 0.60 m and 0.30 m; 920 had an average width of 0.50 m and an average depth of 0.20 m. Both gullies had a steep V-shaped profile with a flat base, and were filled by a single deposit of silt clay (Fig. 3.22, section 198).

Shallow gully 770 to the south had an average depth of 0.10 m and a width of 0.33 m, cut by shallow pits at either end. It had steep sides and a flat base (Fig. 3.22, section 172) and was most likely a beamslot. A single silt clay deposit was present through-

out its length and contained very little other than two iron nails (SF153 and SF154). At its south-western end this gully cut a small pit (630), the fill of which contained a significant assemblage of charred plant remains. Two metres south-east of, and parallel to, gully 770 was a row of post holes 500.

Post-row 500 consisted of four postholes which extended collectively for a length of 9.3 m. Three of the postholes, which had an average diameter of 0.34 m, contained a single silt clay deposit with occasional sub rounded flint inclusions. The posthole (479) at the south-west end was slightly larger than the others with a diameter of 0.58 m, and was the only one to have a post pipe, some 0.26 m across (Fig. 3.22, section 122). The post pipe deposit was dark grey silt clay, surrounded by a redeposited natural clay packing fill which contained occasional sub angular flint nodules.

South-east of gully 770 and postholes 500 was gully segment 430 (Fig. 3.22, section 90). This had a typical beamslot profile with steep, near vertical sides and a flat base. Average width and depth were 0.30 m and 0.20 m and its single clay silt deposit had the appearance of a single back-filling episode, which contained an appreciable amount of fired clay and iron slag, as well as one iron nail and a glass vessel body fragment.

None of these features extended as far north-east as boundary ditch 30, but had well-defined termini to the north-east and the south-west. Therefore, even though they were cut within the same general phase as ditch 30, there was no stratigraphic relationship between them and the main boundary.

Structure J (Phase 4) (Fig. 3.23)

Structure J, a six post square structure measuring up to 5.6 m square, which fronted the north-west side of the Canterbury road, was located beyond the south-eastern terminal of ditch 30. The north-east side of the structure was aligned of the plot boundary.

The postholes were all very similar, with a maximum diameter of 0.86 m, and a maximum depth of 0.30 m. The two posts fronting the road were filled with a single clay silt deposit with occasional sub rounded flint, and approximately 10% charred plant remains. The four remaining postholes had postpipes. They had an average depth of 0.22 m, and were filled with a clay silt deposit representing the positions of the posts which had diameters measuring between 0.29 and 0.33 m. The postpipe deposits produced a concentration of charred remains, approximately 20%, and were surrounded by clay silt packing fills containing sub-rounded and larger sub-angular flint nodules. A handful of pottery sherds associated with the postholes suggest a late 2nd century *terminus post quem* for the construction of the building (see Chapter 6, Assemblage 30).

Waterhole 796 (Fig. 3.24; Pl. 3.4 and Table 3.1)

Waterhole 796 was a circular feature with an approximate diameter of 5 m and a depth of 4 m. It was located on the line of the boundary between plots NW2 and NW3, at the south-east corner of plot NW2 and the north-east corner of plot NW3 (Fig. 3.24; Plate 3.4). The lowest excavated deposits of the waterhole were dated to Phase 3 and its overall period of use was from Phase 3 to Phase 6. It would have provided

a water supply for Phase 3 structure I, and Phase 4 structure J. The waterhole was excavated in quadrants to a depth of 3 m and the base fills up to a metre deep were investigated with an auger. Each excavated quadrant was issued separate context numbers which were all cross-referenced (see below, and Table 3.1).

The lowest excavated deposit was 1628, a light grey silt at least 0.64 m deep, assigned to Phase 3. The underlying material examined by augur was exactly similar in character and may have represented a sequence of fairly rapid silting. The upper profile of 1628, however, was very irregular and had probably been recut, perhaps to improve access to water. The overlying deposits, a series of waterlogged grey silt clays, were assigned to Phase 4. The earliest of these was 1583 and contained fragments of wood and a twist of withies in a semi-circular shape which could have been used as a rope (SF250; see Allen, Chapter 5, Cat. no. 4; Fig.5.14). Sealing 1583 was a series of layers 1604, 1603, 1596 and 1602, which produced no dating evidence. Layers 1604 and 1603 were very clean deposits. Layer 1596 above them had fragments of wood throughout.

The first deposit with dating material was 1547, a dark grey silt clay, which produced pottery dating to AD 170-200+. It also contained worked wood in the form of several pegs (see Allen, Chapter 5, Cat. nos 2 and 3; Fig.5.14) and five small finds: leather shoes (SF247 and SF251; see Mould, Chapter 5, Cat. nos 1-3; Figs 5.17-15.18), an iron bucket handle fragment (SF248, see Scott, Chapter 5, Cat. no.15; Fig.5.11) and a handle mount (SF253, see Scott, Chapter 5, Cat. no. 16; Fig.5.12), and a fragment from a lava rotary quern (SF249; see Roe, Chapter 5, Cat. no. 16; Fig.5.13).

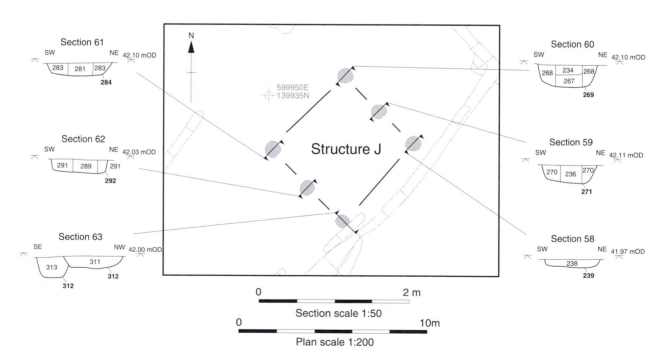

Figure 3.23   Plot NW2: Plan of Structure J and sections of postholes.

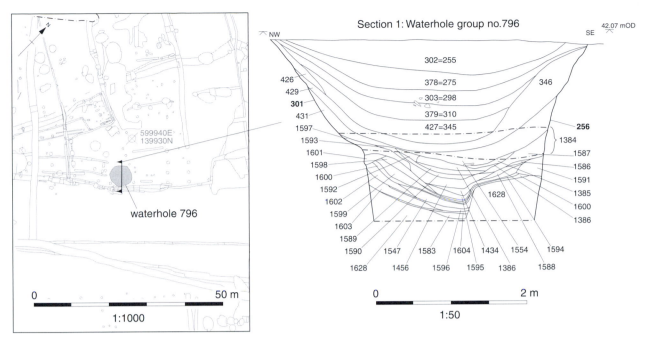

Figure 3.24   Plots NW2/NW3: Section and location of waterhole 796.

Plate 3.4   Excavation of waterhole 796.

Table 3.1   Waterhole 796: Summary of contexts, finds and dating evidence, from the earliest (1628) to the latest fill (302/255/675/707)

Context	Description	Depth	Phase	Finds
1628	light grey silt	0.64 m	3	
1583	grey silt clay, waterlogged	0.1 m	4	wood (incl. withies SF250)
1604		0.04 m	4	
1603		0.16 m	4	
1596		0.08 m	4	wood fragments
1602		0.20 m	4	
1547	dark grey silt	0.16 m	4	pottery AD 170-200+; worked wood (incl handle and pegs); shoes (SF247, SF251); iron bucket handle and mount (SF248, SF253); rotary lava quern (SF249)
1600	dark grey silt	0.08 m	4	
1599	dark grey silt	0.18 m	4	no finds
1594	dark grey silt	0.04 m	4	no finds
1598	dark grey silt	0.12 m	4	no finds
1595	dark grey silt	0.10 m	4	
1591	orange brown silt clays	0.32 m	4	
1601	orange brown silt clays	0.18 m	4	
1597	light grey silt	0.10 m	4	
1434	light grey silt	0.10 m	4	rotary lava quern fragment (SF244)
1593	silty clay		4	
1588	silty clay		4	
1586	silty clay		4	
1456	dark grey clay	0.20 m	4	pottery AD 100-130 (residual); wood; shoe (SF245)
1590	dark green-grey silt clay	0.20 m	4	
1587	mid grey silt clay	0.20 m	4	
1589	dark green-grey silt clay	0.08 m	4	pottery AD 170-230; wood (incl pegs)
1386	green brown silt		4	pottery AD 100-150; wood (incl plank fragment)
1592	green brown silt		4	
1385	green brown silt	0.08 m	4	pottery AD 43-200+
1554*	orange brown clay silt	0.14 m	5	pottery AD 200-250; wood
1384	series of deposits		6	pottery AD 270-300
368	grey orange sand	0.06 m	6	
437/724/346	mid brown silt sand		6	pottery AD 200-270; 1 x coin 2nd century (SF240)
367	blue grey silt clay	0.20 m	6	pottery AD 200-270; iron ring (SF73)
431/1379	light yellow brown sand silt		6	
429/366/1359/1380	dark grey black clay, rich in charred remains. Dumped deposit	0.19 m	6	pottery AD 150-300
428	mid orange brown silt		6	charcoal and fired clay
427/345/758/725	silting deposit	0.52 m	6	pottery AD 200-300; 2 x coins 2nd century (SF217-218); quern fragment (SF198); glass fragment (SF196); 6 x nails
344	grey black clay, charred remains	0.18 m	6	pottery AD 200-270; coin of Gallienus (SF59)
322	light orange yellow clay		6	
379/310/723/739	grey brown silt clay with occasional charcoal flecks, pieces of fired clay and local Ragstone fragments	0.30 m	6	pottery AD 200-300; 29 x coins 2nd to early 3rd century (SF151, SF219-236, SF238-239, SF264-269, SF275-276); glass fragment (SF199); fragment of lead (SF270); iron bracket (SF263) and 7 x nails
303/298/677/726	grey brown silt clay with quantities of large Ragstone blocks	0.24 m	6	pottery AD 200-300; 31 x coins (SF51, SF56-57, SF60-65, SF131-135, SF137-142, SF144-146, SF162-168) mainly 2nd-century but including 3 x 3rd-century radiates (SF51, SF138, SF164) and one 4th-century (SF166); glass bottle frgament (SF136); 2 x nails
378/275/676/720	dark brown clay silt occasional charcoal and fired clay flecking	0.34 m	6	pottery AD 150-350; 2 x 1st-2nd-century coins (SF128-129); 2 x glass bottle fragments (SF125, SF143); lead alloy frgament (SF172)
302/255/675/707	dark brown clay silt with occasional charcoal, fired clay flecking and ceramic building materials		6	pottery AD 200-300; 7 x coins (SF23-24, SF49, SF54, SF58, SF121 SF124) latest dated AD 244-249; 4 x glass fragments (SF120, SF122-123, SF150); decorated lead alloy strip (SF161); 2 x iron objects (SF28, SF50); 5 x nails

* Pottery from contexts with numbers in bold = Pottery assemblage 39.

Overlying 1547 was 1600, another dark grey silt clay layer, and then a series of light grey clay silts, 1599, 1594 and 1598, none of which produced finds. Three deposits (1595, 1591 and 1601) sealed 1598. Layers 1591 and 1601 were orange brown silt clays and represented the weathering and erosion of the feature's edges. Above 1591 and 1601 were two light grey silts (1597 and 1434). A lava rotary quern fragment (SF244, see Roe, Chapter 5, Cat. no. 15; Fig.5.13) came from 1434.

The upper part of the Phase 4 sequence consisted mostly of further silty clays. Deposits 1593 and 1588 were overlain by 1586 and 1456. The latter was a waterlogged dark grey clay layer, which produced pottery - presumably residual - dating to AD 100-130, a leather shoe (SF245; see Mould, Chapter 5, Cat. no. 4; Fig. 5.20), and a piece of unidentified waterlogged wood, which displayed tool marks (see Allen, Chapter 5, Cat. no.1; Fig.5.14). Above 1456, was layer 1590, a dark green-grey silt clay with wood fragments throughout, and 1587, a mid grey silt clay layer. Deposit 1589 sealing 1587 was a dark green-grey silt clay, which again fragments of waterlogged wood, including two pegs, and pottery dating to AD 170-230. Above this deposit lay 1592 and 1386, both green brown silt clays with densely packed fragments of wood. Deposit 1386 also produced pottery dating to AD 100-150 and three larger pieces of waterlogged wood consisting of a plank, a beam which may have been structural, and a piece of unworked wood. The last deposit in the Phase 4 sequence, 1385, was a grey brown silt clay with a concentration of waterlogged wood fragments and pottery dated broadly to AD 43-200+.

A change of character in the fill sequence was indicated by the overlying deposit 1554, an orange brown clay silt with occasional fragments of wood and pottery dating to AD 200-250. This deposit belonged to Phase 5 and may have represented a levelling horizon within the sequence of fills. It was overlain by a series of deposits of Phase 6 date which may simply have accumulated above 1554 or may have been fills of another recut of the waterhole. These deposits, clearly assigned to Phase 6 on the basis of ceramic finds (see Chapter 6, Assemblages 39 and 40), were notable for containing a substantial number of coins, mostly of 2nd-century date. Deposit 1384, which lay at the interface of Phase 4, 5 and 6 fills, incorporated a number of different deposits because poor weather conditions made recording of individual deposits impossible. This layer produced pottery dating to AD 270-300. Finds from 1384 were therefore assigned to Phase 6.

The primary Phase 6 fills were 368, and 437/724/346. Layer 368 was a grey orange silt sand deposit created by water running down the edge of the feature. Layer 437/724/346 was a mid brown silt sand with pottery dating to AD 200-270 and a 2nd-century coin (SF240; see Guest, Chapter 5, Table 5.5).

Above these was 367, a blue grey silt clay with occasional charcoal flecks, containing pottery dated to AD 200-270 and an iron ring (SF73; see Scott, Chap-

ter 5, Cat. no. 19). A light yellow brown sand silt (431/1379) above 367 may have represented redeposited natural originating from the erosion of the edge of the feature. Above layer 431/1379 was a deposit (429/366/1359/1380) that had probably been deliberately dumped. This consisted of a dark grey black clay rich in charred remains, possibly derived from the area of Building I to the north-west. It contained pottery dating to AD 150-300. Above this, were successive silting layers 428 and 427/345/758/725. This latter layer produced pottery dating to AD 200-300 and ten small finds, comprising two 2nd century coins (SF217 and SF218; see Guest, Chapter 5, Table 5.5), a quern fragment (SF198; see Roe, Chapter 5, Cat. no.36), a glass fragment (SF196; see Cool, Chapter 5, Cat. no. 68) and six nails. This was overlain by 344, a deposit of grey black silt clay, which contained a high proportion of charred remains tipped in from the east, and produced pottery dated to AD 200-270 and a coin of Gallienus (SF59; see Guest, Chapter 5, Table 5.5). A light orange yellow clay (322) was located above this around the southern edge of the feature, and was overlain by 379/310/723/739, a grey brown silt clay with occasional flecks of charcoal, small pieces of fired clay and fragments of local Ragstone. This deposit contained pottery dated AD 200-300, and 38 small finds, including 29 coins of 2nd to early 3rd century date (SF151, SF219-236, SF238-239, SF264-269 and SF275-276; see Guest, Chapter 5, Table 5.5) and the remainder consisted of a glass fragment (SF199), a fragment of lead (SF270; see Cool, Chapter 5, Cat. no. 133), an iron bracket (SF263; see Scott, Chapter 5, Cat. no. 23; Fig.5.12) and seven iron nails.

Above this deposit was 303/298/677/726, a grey brown clay silt containing considerable quantities of large Ragstone blocks. This produced pottery dated to AD 200-300 and 34 small finds: two iron nails, a glass bottle fragment (SF136; see Cool, Chapter 5, Cat. no. 62) and 31 coins (SF51, SF56-57, SF60-65, SF131-135, SF137-142, SF144-146 and SF162-168; see Guest, Chapter 5, Table 5.5). The majority of the coins were of 2nd-century date, although there were three 3rd-century radiates (SF51, SF138, SF164) and an issue of AD 316 (SF166), the only 4th-century coin recovered from the excavated areas (see Guest, Chapter 5, Table 5.5). Fill 303/298/677/726 was overlain by 378/275/676/720, a dark brown clay silt with occasional charcoal flecking and fragments of fired clay. The finds included pottery dated broadly to AD 150-350, two glass bottle fragments (SF125 and SF143), a fragment of lead alloy (SF172; see Cool, Chapter 5, Cat. no.131), two 1st- to 2nd-century coins (SF128 and SF129; see Guest, Chapter 5, Table 5.5) and four nails. The uppermost fill was 302/255/675/707, a dark brown clay silt with small amounts of charcoal, fired clay and ceramic building material. This deposit also produced a large quantity of pottery which was dated to AD 200-300 and nineteen small finds. These included four glass fragments (SF120, SF123, SF122, see Cool, Chapter 5, Cat. no. 64, and SF150, see Cool, Chapter 5, Cat. no. 61), a decorated lead alloy strip possibly from a candlestick (SF161, see Cool, Chapter 5, Cat. no. 78;

Fig.5.5), two iron objects (SF 28, see Scott, Chapter 5, Cat. no. 20; Fig.5.12; SF50) and five iron nails. There were seven coins (SF23-24, SF49, SF54, SF58, SF121 and SF124; see Guest, Chapter 5, Table 5.5), the last (and latest) of which was dated AD 244-249.

Plot NW3

Plot NW3 was a 12 m wide area defined by boundary gullies including those relating to the Phase 3 metalworking Structure I (see Fig. 3.25). The plot NW2/NW3 boundary was formed by two north-west to south-east gullies, 300 and 200 (Fig. 3.25, section 25). Gully 200 was the earlier and extended 28 m from the north-west edge of Area B. It had moderately sloping sides and a rounded base and was consistently 0.4 m wide and 0.12 m deep. The fill was a single dark brown silt clay with infrequent charcoal flecks, occasional iron slag fragments and two large iron nails (SF11, SF12). Gully 300, 8.5 m long, was a recut of the east-south-east end of gully 200 and had 45° sloping sides, a rounded base, and ranged in width from 0.2 m to 0.44 m, but was consistently 0.15 m deep. Again the fill was a single dark brown silt clay which produced a *dupondius* of Hadrian (SF10; see Guest, Chapter 5, Table 5.5).

A further gully (110) ran south-south-westwards from the terminus of gully 200, with which it was probably contemporary, for some 15 m before turning south-east to extend to the line of the road, ending at a junction with roadside gully 1685. Gully 110 had steep sides and a flat base with an average width of 0.48 m and a depth of 0.22 m (Fig. 3.25, section 299). Its two fills were a primary orange-brown clay silting deposit overlain by a dark brown clay silt, containing frequent charcoal and small sub-rounded stone and a reasonable quantity of pottery (see Chapter 6, Assemblage 10).

Successive stages of definition of the south-western boundary of Plot NW3 were indicated by gullies 8540, 1400, 8550 and 1410/8530. Many had similar near vertical sided profiles and flat bases (Fig. 3.25, section 300), with the same dimensions and sequence of deposits as noted in gully 110. At its north-west end gully 8540 extended beyond the edge of Area B, and was parallel to 200 and some 12 m from it. Its south-easterly extent is uncertain as it was truncated by later features, but it may have continued as far as the angle of gully 110, although its relationship to that feature is not known. A probable second stage of the plot boundary, a redefinition of its south-eastern half, was represented by ditch 8550 which appeared to terminate before its line was resumed by gully 1400. The latter then extended all the way to the roadside ditch sequence, cutting gully 110. Strictly, however, the relationship between 8550 and 8540 is not known and the latter could have been the later of the two. Immediately south-west of Structure I (see below) the plot boundary was redefined again by gully 1410/8530, with a total length of *c* 9.5 m.

Some 4-5 m south-west of these boundaries and approximately parallel to them was a post-row, group 1698 (see Fig. 3.20), consisting of a series of fourteen postholes 0.4-0.7 m in diameter, and 0.1-0.3 m deep. Not all had post pipes, but where these did occur they measured 0.25-0.3 m in diameter and were filled with a dark brown silt clay, surrounded by an orange-brown silt clay packing with occasional charcoal and slag. The group extended WNW as far as the limit of excavation and also projected slightly south-eastwards into the line of the Canterbury road. It probably represented a late stage of definition of the south-west margin of Plot NW3.

On the same WNW-ESE alignment, but north of gully 1400 was a row of three postholes linked by a narrow gully (1790) extending for 8 m. The postholes of 1790 were rectangular, up to 0.98 m long and 0.48 m deep. They were filled with grey silt clay packing containing sub-angular flint. The post pipes contained dark grey silt with moderate amounts of wood charcoal and had diameters between 0.35 m and 0.5 m. The gully or beamslot extending for 2 m between each post-pit was quite narrow, 0.24 m wide and 0.05 m deep with a vertical sided flat based profile, and was filled with an orange-brown clay silt.

Structure I (Fig. 3.25)

Structure I was a small rectangular enclosure with an internal area of *c* 88 sq. m, situated in the angle formed by the northern plot boundary and its south-south-westward continuation gully 110. The structure was principally of beamslot construction, though these features were discontinuous. Internal features included postholes, but these did not form any particularly coherent pattern, and not all could be closely phased (Figs 3.20 and 3.25).

The structure itself was made up of four beamslots, 1610, 1620, 360, and 1480 which formed a rectangular shape. Feature 1610 was aligned NNE-SSW and formed the 'west' side. It had steep sides and a flat base and was 0.4 m wide and 0.22 m deep (Fig. 3.25, section 341). The primary deposit within this slot was a yellow-brown silt clay, sealed by a dark brown clay silt. Both deposits contained occasional charcoal and slag pieces, as well as small sub-rounded stone. Slot 1620 extended 5 m ESE from the north end of 1610. It was 0.3 m wide and 0.2 m deep and also had near vertical sides and a flat base. Unlike 1610, however, it had a single fill of dark brown silt clay containing small sub-rounded stone, infrequent charcoal flecking, and occasional iron slag fragments (Fig. 3.25, section 25). There was a gap of *c* 2.4 m between the end of 1620 and the presumed north-east corner of the structure, marked by the north-north-east end of slot 360. The latter feature was 2.5 m long, almost vertical-sided with a flat base and was typically 0.4 m wide and 0.2 m deep. Contemporaneous posthole 188, 0.45 m across and 0.22 m deep, was located at the south-south-west terminal of 360 (Fig. 3.25, section 77), but there were no further traces of the 'east' wall to the south of 188. Both the beamslot and the posthole were filled with a grey-dark brown clay silt producing notable amounts of furnace debris. A possible

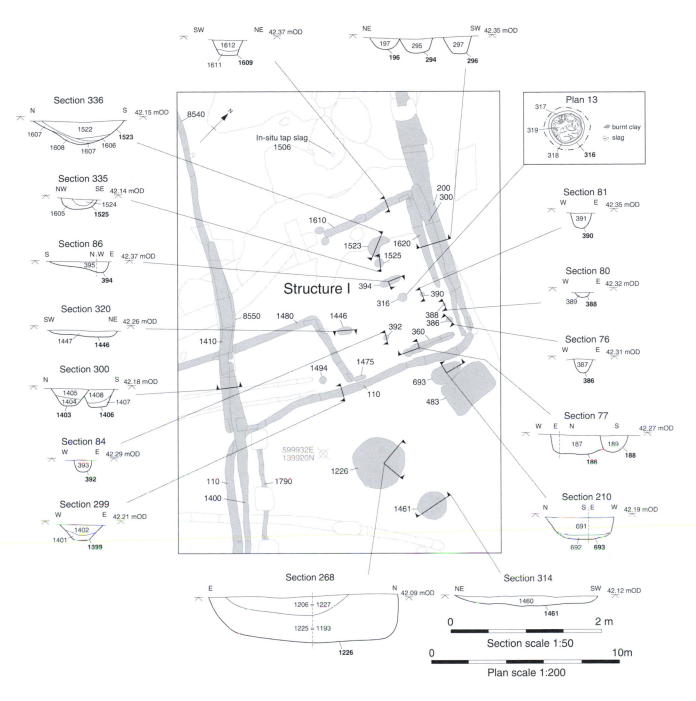

Figure 3.25   Plot NW3: Plan and sections of Structure I and associated features, including sections of beam slots 1620, 1610 and 360; and gullies 110, 200, 300, 1400 and 1410: Beam slot 1620: section 25 (cut 296); beam slot 1610: section 341 (cut 1609); beam slot 360: section 77 (cut 186); gully 110: section 299 (cut 1399); gully 200: section 25 (cut 196); gully 300: section 25 (cut 294); gully 1400: section 300 (cut 1403); gully 1410: section 300 (cut 1406).

'south' wall was indicated by slot 1480. A 4 m length of this feature was aligned almost E-W, not exactly parallel to 1620. It then turned SSW for some 7.5 m. Slot 1480 had steep sides and a flat base with average dimensions of 0.28 m width and 0.1 m depth, and was filled with a deposit similar to the fill of 360.

Internal features of structure I included eight postholes with average dimensions of 0.25 m depth and 0.4 m diameter, although the largest was 0.58 m in diameter. These were all vertical sided with flat to slightly rounded bases, and were filled with a single grey clay silt, containing occasional charcoal (Fig. 3.25, sections 81, 80, 76, 84). A crescent shaped hearth, 1523, was located in the north-west corner of the structure (Fig. 3.25, section 336). This was 1.2 m across and 0.3 m deep with moderately sloping sides and a rounded base. It had a yellow-brown clay lining which was overlain by a charcoal rich deposit, possibly dumped as the clay beneath showed no sign of *in situ* scorching. Above this was an orange-red silt clay made up predominantly from fired clay fragments. The uppermost deposit comprised a dark grey clay silt containing charcoal and a large amount of iron slag (*c* 40% of the deposit). A second internal hearth, 1525, measured 0.46 m in diameter and 0.14 m in depth. This had steep sides and a rounded base and was filled with a primary yellow clay lining, overlain by a dark grey clay silt containing at least 80% wood charcoal (Fig. 3.25, section 335). Pit 316 was 0.48 m across and 0.4 m deep, and contained an upright storage jar with a girth diameter of 0.4 m (Fig. 3.25, plan 13). The pot was held in place by a deposit of light brown silt clay around its edges. As found, the pot was truncated at its maximum girth, and was filled with a grey silt clay containing notable amounts of iron slag and general furnace debris.

External features included two large pits to the east of the structure. Pit 483, adjacent to the north-east corner, was sub-rectangular in shape and measured 2.65 m x 1.7 m x 0.3 m deep. The profile was steep sided to a rounded base. A dark brown clay silt containing charcoal, slag, and small rounded stone in moderate quantities filled the base of the pit. A grey clay silt containing approximately 20% slag and fired clay overlay this. The upper deposit was a light brown clay silt and produced marginally higher quantities of slag, fired clay and wood charcoal. Pit 1226 (Fig. 3.25, section 268), south of 483, was circular with a diameter of 2.55 m and a depth of 0.6 m, with sides sloping at 60° to a flat base. This was filled with a primary grey clay silt which contained a large amount of fired clay and slag with occasional charcoal, sealed by a light grey clay silt which had a slightly lower amount of the same material.

Two smaller pits associated with Structure I were also located within this area. Pit 693 (Fig. 3.25, section 210) lay east of boundary 110 between it and pit 483, was oval in shape and measured 1.6 m by 0.9 m with steep sides and a flat base. A thin deposit of brown-yellow silt clay within the base of the feature was overlain by a brown-orange clay silt, with slag, fired clay and wood charcoal pieces making up about 20% of its composition. Further east, circular pit 1461 (Fig, 3.25, section 314) measured 1.9 m diameter and 0.14 m depth and had moderate sloping sides and a flat to irregular base. It was filled with a single deposit of grey-orange silt clay which produced occasional charcoal flecking and small pieces of iron slag.

Occupation spreads associated with the metal-working process were noted to the west of the structure. Deposit 1627 was very mixed in composition, and measured approximately 8 m by 3.50 m. The eastern part of this spread adjacent to Structure I was predominantly composed of grey silt with discrete patches of wood charcoal. The western area of this deposit had a concentration of wood charcoal and a patch of *in situ* scorching. To the west of this spread was an area that contained possible *in situ* tap slag (1506, Fig. 3.25; see Chapter 7, Structure I) and measured approximately 2 m by 3 m.

Further west again were two large pits, 7944 and 7306, and a small well, 7269 (Fig. 3.20). Only the first of these lay within the plot as defined by the gullies 8540. The other two features lay south of 8540, but between it and the post-row 1698 and it is quite likely that the latter was a fenced boundary that related to an expansion and redefinition of plot NW3.

Pit 7944 (Fig. 3.26, section 1028) was sub-circular, some 1.9 m across and was excavated to 1.2 m without encountering the natural clay. The lowest excavated deposit was a light grey-orange silt clay (8782) which possibly formed through the collapse of the pit edges, or a similar rapid process. Overlying this was a very mixed deposit (8454) consisting of thick lenses of dark grey silt clay and orange-brown silt clay which had been dumped into the centre of the pit. The upper fill (7945) was a grey-orange silt clay which was again very mixed in composition. This contained a substantial amount of charcoal, fired clay and pieces of iron slag.

Pit 7306 (Fig. 3.26, section 774) was 2.5 m in diameter and 1 m deep. It had irregular, but steeply sloping sides and an angled base. The lowest fills were yellow silt clays (7492 and 7446) representing the erosion of the feature's edges. Overlying these were three deposits (7437, 7430 and 7407) of dark grey silt clay all containing notable amounts of charred remains and iron slag. The next five deposits (7427, 7402, 7397, 7396 and 7307) all appeared to have been deliberately placed within the pit. All comprised dark grey-black clay silts, mixed with patches of yellow clay, and all contained large amounts of charcoal, fired clay, iron-working debris, and pottery sherds.

Feature 7269 (Fig. 3.26, section 781) was a relatively small well which was excavated to a depth of 1.8 m without reaching the natural clay. The construction pit, cut on its south-west edge by post-medieval ditch 9020, measured at least 2.7 m in diameter at the surface and was 1.2 m in diameter at the lowest excavated point. The well shaft was 1.1 m across at the surface, but only 0.44 m in diameter at the excavated base. Part of the lining survived, consisting of Ragstone blocks measuring on average 0.3 m by 0.15 m by 0.1 m, bonded together with grey clay. Four courses of stone survived around the south-west side of the shaft, but only occasional stones were present to the north-east. The clay matrix (7535) between the stones and the packing of the construction pit behind them was identical. As this material appeared to form the edge of the well shaft where there were no stones it is possible that the stone lining was only ever partially present, although if so it is hard to see how the lower sides of the shaft could have been kept stable.

The lowest excavated deposit within the well shaft was a very clean grey clay (7523). This was overlain by three layers of grey-brown silt clay (7328, 7327 and 7309) which contained infrequent charcoal and small pieces of iron slag. The three upper deposits (7271, 7308 and 7270) were all dark grey silts containing substantial amounts of iron slag, charcoal and occasional fragments of ceramic building material.

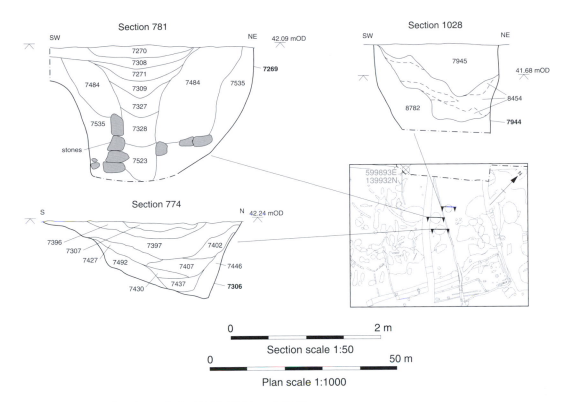

Figure 3.26   Plot NW3: Sections of pits 7306, 7944 and 7269.

Possible Plot NW4 *(Fig. 3.27)*

The possible existence of a fourth plot in this series is hinted at by gully 8780. This was contemporary with gully 8690 which redefined the line of the Phase 2 oblique settlement boundary ditch running approximately south from Structure I in Phase 3. Gully 8780 extended WNW from gully 8690 for 13 m. It was exactly parallel to, and some 18 m from, gully 8540 that defined plot NW3 (Fig. 3.25), giving a projected plot width quite closely comparable to those of NW1 and NW2. There was no further evidence to support this interpretation, however.

North-West Undivided Roadside Area *(Fig. 3.27)*

An undivided zone with a maximum possible width (at the roadside) of some 77 m lay between the two groups of north-west and south-west roadside plots. If the existence of plot NW4 is accepted, then the area was rather smaller. Until Phase 4 this area contained the southern end of the north-west oblique ditch.

Structure H (Phase 3) *(Fig. 3.28)*

A possible structure (labelled H) was located west of the north-west oblique ditch 8700 in the north-eastern part of this area of the site. It comprised three lengths of gully with an average width of 0.40 m and ranging in depth from 0.06 to 0.32 m (Fig. 3.28, section 856, cut 7602; section 796, cut 7371; section 905, cut 7794). A common characteristic of all three gullies

was the presence of a primary deposit of blue-grey clay which seemed to act as a lining. This was sealed by a layer of dark grey silt clay which produced notable amounts of charred remains, a blue-green body fragment from a square glass bottle and a small group of pottery (see Chapter 6, Assemblage 13). The gullies were probably linked with gully 8970 which drained into roadside ditch 8700. The lack of physical continuity between the gully lengths, and the rather irregular nature of their plan, make interpretation difficult. The features could, however, have served as intermittent drains around the south side of a circular building up to *c* 10 m across (this assumes that gully 8780, also assigned to Phase 3, was not exactly contemporary with the structure). No specific structural features survived, however.

Waterhole 7239 *(Fig. 3.27; Table 3.2)*

This feature was located immediately north-west of the Phase 4 roadside ditch group 8590 where it cut Phase 3 features. It had a diameter of 6.50 m at subsoil level, and a total depth of 3.40 m. The top 1.20 m was excavated entirely by hand, while the remainder was excavated by machine, to 38.20 m above OD. The sides of the waterhole sloped at approximately 45° for the first 0.8 m, thereafter the feature was cut more vertically, though had an irregularly rounded base.

The primary fill was 9398, a grey silt clay containing small sub-rounded stones (Table 3.2). A deposit of blue grey clay (9397) overlay this. Overlaying 9397 and extending down the south-western edge and

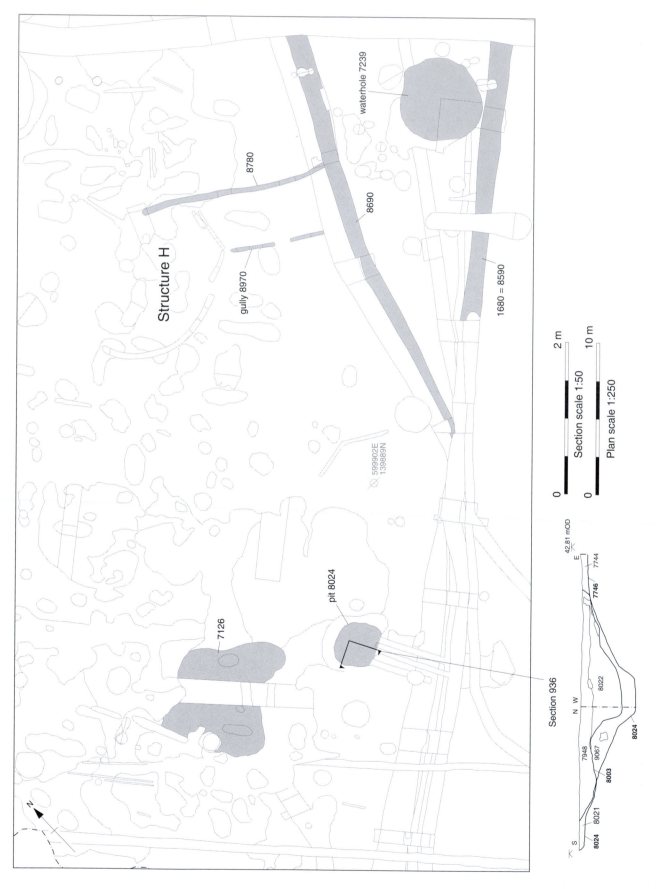

Figure 3.27   Plan of undivided north-west roadside area; section of pit 8024.

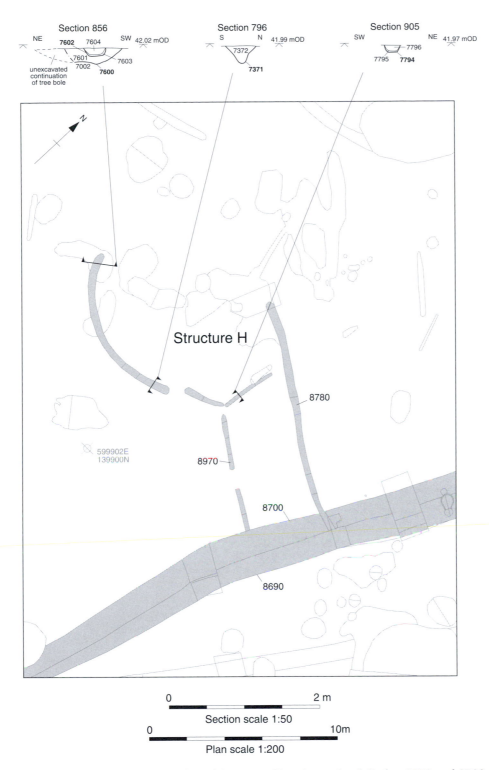

Figure 3.28   Undivided north-west area: Plan of Structure H and associated ditches 8970 and 8780, and sections of curvilinear ditches.

across the base of the feature was an orange grey silt clay 9395/9176. Next came a number of deposits (9396, 9394, 9393, 9392/9197, and 9158) all made up of similar inclusion-free blue grey silt clays. Contexts 9396 and 9392/9197 produced well preserved water-logged timbers. Part of an oak ladder (SF1517; see Allen, Chapter 5, Cat. nos 12-13; Fig.5.15) came from

context 9396 while an object identified as a separate rung from the ladder (SF1516; see Allen, Chapter 5, Cat. no. 10; Fig.5.15) came from context 9392/9197.

Overlying these deposits was 9391 (equivalent to 9154 and 9157), which produced no dating evidence. It was overlain by 9155 the earliest deposit to produce pottery, dated AD 120-160. Three small finds also

Table 3.2   Waterhole 7239: Summary of contexts, finds and dating evidence, from the earliest (9398) to the latest fill (7240)

Context	Description	Depth	Finds
9398	grey silt clay	0.22 m	
9397	blue grey clay	0.10 m	
9395/9176	orange grey silt clay	0.10 m	
9396	blue grey silt clay		waterlogged timbers (incl. oak ladder, SF1517)
9394	blue grey silt clay		
9393	blue grey silt clay		
9392/9197	blue grey silt clay		waterlogged timbers (incl rung from ladder, SF1516)
9158	blue grey silt clay		
9391/9154/9157	brown orange silt clay	0.60 m	
9155	orange grey clay silt		pottery AD 120-160; 1 x coin (illegible *dupondius*); L-shaped iron key (SF1508) and an unidentified iron object (SF1507)
9153/7242	compact grey brown clay with slight iron panning	0.56 m	pottery AD 100-200
7241	orange brown silt clay	0.35 m	pottery AD 120-200; fragment of glass (SF982)
9152/7314	grey brown silt clay. Dumped deposit	0.40 m	pottery late 1st-century
7120	orange brown clay silt	0.24 m	
7243/7251	brown grey clay silt	0.18 m	pottery 2nd-century
7250	dark grey clay silt, much charcoal. Dumped	0.12 m	pottery 1st-2nd century
7249	brown grey clay silt		pottery AD 150-250
7246	brown grey clay silt		pottery AD 100-250; fragments of ceramic building materials; slag
7245	orange brown clay silt	0.06 m	
7248	grey brown clay silt with charcoal	0.16 m	pottery AD 150-200; ceramic building materials
7247	densely packed ceramic building materials in a dark ornage red clay matrix	0.10 m	pottery AD 150-200; ceramic building materials; quern fragment (SF997)
7244	grey clay silt with charcoal	0.30 m	pottery AD 150-275; ceramic building materials; perforated lead sheet (SF998)
7240	light grey clay silt with charcoal	0.38 m	pottery; window glass (SF959)

Waterhole 7239 produced Pottery Assemblage 32, late 2nd-century.

came from this deposit; a possible L-shaped staple of iron (SF1507; see Scott, Chapter 5, Cat. no.26), an L-shaped key (SF1508; see Scott, Chapter 5, Cat. no.11; Fig.5.11) and an illegible *dupondius* (SF1509; see Guest, Chapter 5, Table 5.5). Overlying 9155 was 9153/7242, which produced pottery dated AD 100-200. Fill 7241 above this produced pottery dated AD 120-200 and a fragment of glass (SF982). Context 9152/7314, was next in sequence, and produced late 1st-century pottery. Above 7241 was layer 7120, followed by deposit 7243/7251, which produced 2nd-century pottery. Deposit 7250 was next and contained 1st- to 2nd-century pottery. A brown grey clay silt (7249) above this contained pottery dated to AD 150-200. Next was a thin dumped deposit (7246) which contained fragments of ceramic building material, slag, and pottery dated AD 100-250. Overlying this was 7245, which formed a silting layer that had accumulated within the centre of the feature.

A series of dumped deposits followed, all of which contained relatively large amounts of domestic refuse, in some cases consisting of redeposited debris. Layer 7248 was a grey brown clay silt with charcoal and ceramic building material fragments throughout, as well as pottery dated AD 150-200. Context 7247 on the south-eastern edge of the feature consisted largely of densely packed ceramic building material fragments in a dark orange red clay silt matrix. The pottery was again dated AD 150-200. A quern fragment (SF997)

also came from this deposit. Deposit 7244 was next in the sequence and comprised a grey clay silt with charcoal and fragments of ceramic building material. Pottery from this context was dated AD 150-270; it also produced a perforated fragment of sheet lead (SF998; see Cool, Chapter 5, Cat. no. 127). The uppermost deposit in the feature was 7240, a light grey clay silt with charcoal and ceramic building material inclusions. This produced pottery and a fragment of blue/green cast window glass (SF959; see Cool, Chapter 5, Cat. no.93). Overall the upper fills of the feature contained a substantial pottery assemblage, which suggested a date at the very end of the 2nd century AD for the filling of the feature (see Chapter 6, Assemblage 32).

Pit 8024 (Fig. 8.27)

Pit 8024, placed within Phases 3-4, was located some 42 m south-west of waterhole 7239 and linked with the nearby roadside boundary ditches by three different stages of narrow gully. The pit was sub-circular measuring approximately 3 m in diameter and reaching a depth of 0.73 m. It was re-cut as pit 8003 which had a smaller diameter and the same profile, but was only 0.54 m deep (Fig. 8.27, section 936). The deposits at the base of the pit 8024 were all yellow clays with occasional inclusions of charcoal and iron slag. The upper deposits (8022) consisted of silt clays and produced higher densities of charred remains and iron slag. The predominance of silt clays within the pit suggests that this feature possibly acted as a sump for the drainage of water from the roadside ditches.

Area of soil spreads (Fig. 8.27)

North-west of pit 8024 was a collection of irregular soil spreads and apparently natural hollows which contained deposits of general domestic debris. Of all the soil spreads, 7126/7127 was the most extensive, covering an area approximately 48 sq. m for a depth of 0.04-0.26 m. This produced a largely 2nd-century ceramic assemblage, as well as four blue-green body fragments from a glass vessel, a lead alloy disc (see Cool, Chapter 5, Cat. no. 127) and numerous iron nails.

No coherent features were recorded in this part of the area. One unusual find, however, was a cache of 33 rounded flint pebbles, perhaps slingstones, from context 10239, an amorphous patch of grey silt. This deposit was unfortunately not dated.

Phase 4 roadside boundary ditches

Ditches 8960 and 9520 defined the south-eastern margin of the north-west undivided roadside area in Phase 4. The ditches terminated at their south-west ends respecting the north-east boundary of plot SW1 (see below; Fig. 3.31), which itself consisted of two stages of gully. Both 8960 and 9520 were traced north-eastwards from here for some 35 m, beyond which they were truncated by ditch 1680/8590, also of Phase 4 date. Ditch 8960 was the earlier of the two (and was possibly of Phase 3 date). Where surviving the profile had a flat base with a reasonably sharp, but rounded break to straight sides (Fig. 3.6, section 1285, cut 7880). Ditch 9520, a re-cut, is thought to pre-date ditch 1680/8590, and therefore probably relates to the first stage of plot SW1 boundary (9910/9380). The general width and depth of 9520 were 0.90 m and 0.40 m respectively, and the profile, again where it survived truncation, was steep sided and flat based (Fig. 3.6, section 1285, cut 7879). It produced a group of pottery dating to the second half of the 2nd century (see Chapter 6, Assemblage 18). Ditch 9520 was cut by the second phase of plot SW1 boundary gully (9390/9890) which was of the same phase as roadside ditch 8590.

Phase 4 roadside ditch 1680/8590 extended unbroken for approximately 105 m all the way from Structure J in Plot NW2 up to the north-east corner of Plot SW1 before terminating (Fig. 3.31). It had a consistent profile along its length: moderate sides and a flat base with an average width and depth of 0.7 m and 0.24 m respectively (Fig. 3.6, section 1285, cut 7878). Another consistent characteristic of this ditch was the nature of the fill, which comprised a dark grey clay silting deposit containing a high proportion of rounded gravel flint which presumably had eroded from the adjacent road surfaces, including 9011. The

fills produced a group of pottery of late 2nd-century date (see Chapter 6, Assemblage 19).

Feature 1680/8590 was part of the final major phase of boundary definition north-west of the Canterbury road and was probably contemporary with the second (and final) stage of definition of the boundaries of Plot SW1 (see below).

South-west roadside plots

The south-west roadside plots were all defined by gullies extending from the road at right angles to its alignment (Fig. 3.29). Plots SW1, SW2 and SW3 all had two stages of definition of their boundary gullies, both falling within Phase 4. In each case the first stage of definition consisted of a NW-SE aligned gully which on reaching the roadside ditch alignment turned to the south-west to run along the line of the road. In the second stage of boundary definition of plots SW1-SW3 the side boundary gullies terminated at their south-east ends and were associated with separate segments of gully fronting the road. The fronts of the other plots, SW4, SW5 and SW6, were mostly defined by a single feature, the final Phase 4 roadside ditch 10420.

Ditch 10420 was first seen at the midpoint of the plot SW3 frontage, emerging at the junction with ditch 10270, which subdivided the plot longitudinally (see below). The ditch (Fig. 3.33, section 1432, cut 10305) extended south-west from this point to the south-western margin of Area B, defining the north-west edge of the Canterbury road over this distance. Its north-eastern extent beyond this point is unknown, having been removed by later (Phase 4, second stage) gullies related to plots SW1-SW3. It is possible that 10420 represented a continuous roadside ditch which related to the first stage of the south-west plot gullies, and would therefore be associated with ditch 10060 (fronting Plot SW2) for example. In the area fronting Plots SW3-SW6 ditch 10420 was disturbed by the later modifications to the roadside frontage, but south-west of the plots it constituted the final Phase 4 north-west roadside boundary, undisturbed by later sequences of gully. In this area the ditch had an average width and depth of 1.38 m and 0.56 m respectively, and a profile generally consisting of slightly irregular, but moderately, sloping sides with a rounded to flat base (Fig. 3.30).

The fills of ditch 10420, as examined in the vicinity of the plots, especially close to Structure D in plot SW3, had larger amounts of charred remains which may have been dumped into the partially silted ditch. In this area the fills of the ditch largely consisted of a yellow-brown silt clay sealed by a dark grey-brown silt. The primary fill produced a fragment of a frit melon bead (SF1543; see Cool, Chapter 5, Cat. no. 26), while the upper silts contained a worn *as* of Trajan (AD 98-117) (SF1546; see Guest, Chapter 5, Table 5.5). Further south-west, the ditch fills reflected the lack of any substantial activity, domestic or otherwise, in the surrounding area. These deposits generally comprised a yellow-brown silt clay overlain by a

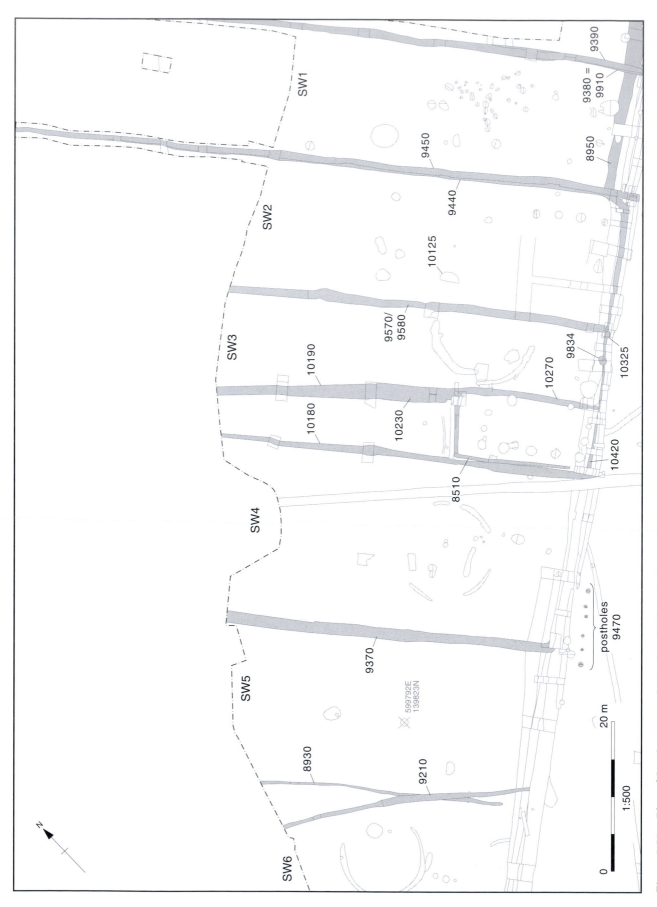

Figure 3.29   Plan of South-west roadside plots SW1, 2, 3, 4, 5 and 6.

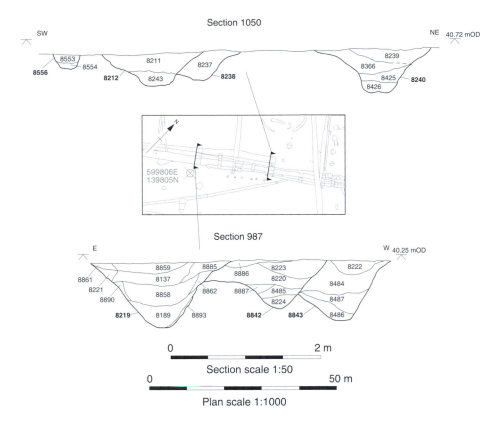

Figure 3.30   Sections of ditch 10420: Section 1050 (cut 8212), section 987 (cut 8219).

grey-brown silt clay and then sealed by a fine grey clay silt, which had built up over a period of time. The only exception to this sequence of deposits was noted in a section excavated along the front of plot SW5. Here a more complex sequence of deposits was noted, consisting largely of clay silts on the edges of the ditch, deriving from the silting of the natural edges and the up-cast from the original excavation slumping back into the ditch.

Plot SW1

The first stage of the Phase 4 gully that formed the north-east boundary of plot SW1 was 9380/9910 (Figs 3.29 and 3.31). This originated at a point beyond the original north-west edge of Area B and extended 68 m south-eastwards to the line of the road before turning to the south-west to define the front of the plot. The gully terminated at the junction with the first stage of the north-east boundary of plot SW2 (gully 9440/10060). The profile of 9380/9910 was most pronounced to the north-west, where it had a sharply defined V-shaped cut. As it turned at a right-angle to run alongside the road its profile changed to fairly straight sides and a flat base (Fig. 3.31, section 1164, cut 9278; section 1132, cut 8969) eventually ending with a rounded terminal. The maximum width and depth were 0.7 and 0.28 m, but the feature became shallower as it turned to the south-west and at its terminal end. The gully had a maximum of two deposits throughout its length, the primary deposit being

a yellow brown silt clay sealed by a deposit of grey silt. The south-west terminal end was filled with a single deposit of light brown silt clay. Pottery from these features included material dating to the first half of the 2nd century as well as later (see Chapter 6, Assemblage 20A).

This first boundary was cut along its length by the second stage of boundary consisting of gullies 9390/9890 and 9900. Gully 9390/9890 was cut on the same alignment as the previous phase, but terminated 5 m after turning to the south-west at the road frontage. There was a break of approximately 2 m to define an entrance to the plot from the road before gully segment 9900 began, extending for 9 m and terminating at the south-west corner of the plot. generally had a broad U-shaped profile (Fig. 3.31, section 855, cut 7565; and section 1164, cut 7561) with a width and depth of 1 m and 0.30 m respectively. Where it turned to the south-west it became narrower and shallower, reaching on average 0.50 m in width and only 0.10 m in depth, although at the south-west terminal the depth increased slightly to 0.20 m. The fill of this gully was consistent along its length and consisted of a grey brown silt clay with a small percentage of charred remains noted along its NW-SE length, and occasional flint nodules present along the NE-SW alignment, possibly deriving from the eroded road surface. Mid 2nd- to mid 3rd-century pottery was also recovered (see Chapter 6, Assemblage 22A). The segment of gully 9900 again had a single deposit of silt clay along its length (Fig. 3.31,

71

section 1132, cut 8938) and produced a fragment of an iron nail.

The latest roadside features specific to plot SW1 were three circular postholes, group 10005, one of which cut the fill of gully 9900. These had an average diameter of 0.6 m and a depth of 0.23 m, with the largest being 0.86 m across (Fig. 3.31, section

939). The profiles were almost vertical sided with flat bases, and the fills consisted of a silt clay packing with Ragstone pieces up to 0.2 m in size, and a dark grey clay silt post pipe fill ranging in diameter between 0.25 m and 0.48 m. It is unclear if these quite substantial postholes formed part of a boundary or, perhaps more likely, a structural feature.

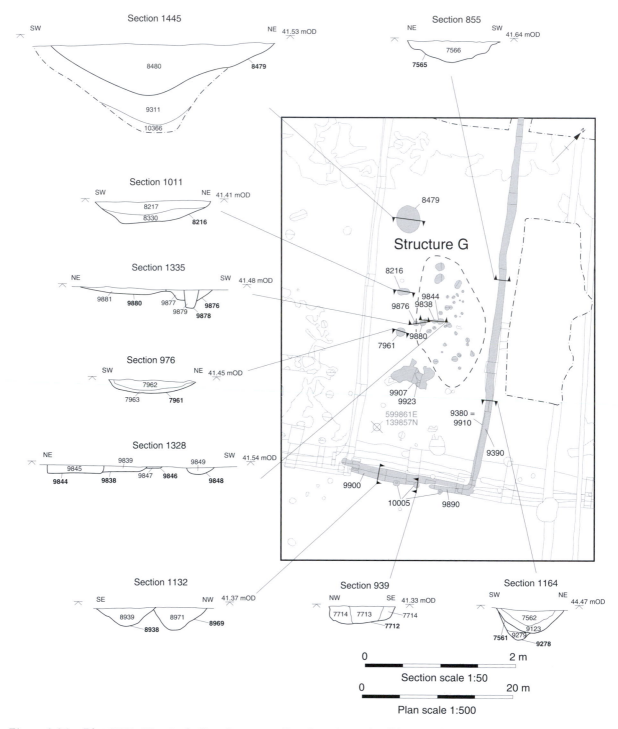

Figure 3.31   Plot SW1: Plan including Structure G and sections of gullies 9380/9910, 9390/9890 and, 9900: Gully 9380/9910: section 1164 (cut 9278), section 1132 (cut 8969); gully 9390/9890: section 855 (cut 7565), section 1164 (cut 7561); gully 9900: section 1132 (cut 8938).

A number of features ranging in date from AD 70-250 were found within the area of Plot SW1. Towards the front of the plot was a series of inter-cutting shallow pits including 9907 and 9923. The former was oval with steep sides and a flat base measuring 2 m across and 0.24 m deep, the latter had similar dimensions, but had shallower sides and an irregular base. Both were filled with a dark grey silt clay, containing occasional charcoal flecking. Two isolated pits, 7961 and 8216, lay further north-west. These were sub-circular and were up to 1.2 m in diameter and 0.19 m deep. Both had irregular bases and sides and were filled with a grey silt clay, which produced a small amount of pottery datable to Phase 3. North-east of these pits was an area of postholes and possible stakeholes. There were 37 of these features within an area of approximately 150 sq. m. No coherent building plan was identified despite careful examination, but it is possible that the evidence was affected by truncation. The features were therefore tentatively grouped as Structure G (Fig. 3.31). A few of the postholes, 9876, 9880, 9838, and 9844, had well-defined profiles with steep sides and flat bases, and measured on average 0.6 m in diameter and 0.1 m deep. They were filled with a dark grey silt clay that contained large amounts of wood charcoal. Posthole 9838 had an iron nail (SF1528) at the base, and 9876 was filled with a packing stone measuring 0.1 m by 0.15 m. Pottery associated with these features was mostly dated late 1st to mid 2nd century (see Chapter 6, Assemblage 29). Further to the north-west was a large pit or waterhole (8479), 3.2 m in diameter and 1.3 m deep. This contained two distinct fills; the earlier was a thick layer of grey silt clay and was sealed by a grey brown clay silting deposit 8480, which produced a possible millstone fragment in millstone grit (SF1491; see Roe, Chapter 5, Cat. no. 38) and pottery datable to Phase 5 (see Chapter 6, Assemblage 38).

Plot SW2 *(Fig. 3.32)*

Plot SW2 mirrored SW1 to the north-east in terms of the sequence of phases (Figs 3.29 and 3.32). Again the primary phase of boundary gully was represented by a continuous rectilinear feature 9440/10060 extending from the north-west and turning to the south-west as it reached the line of the road. This was succeeded by NW-SE aligned gully 9450 and its NE-SW continuation, 10050. Gully 9440 was on average 0.8 m wide and 0.3 m deep and had a U-shaped profile with a flat base (Fig. 3.32, section 1180, cut 10455; section 849, cut 9332). It was approximately 77 m long before it turned to become 10060 (Fig. 3.32, section 1004, cut 8027). There was a single grey-brown silt clay fill present throughout its length, with a progressively higher proportion of charred remains noted in the 25 m stretch nearing the road. As it turned to form the boundary to the roadside (10060) the feature deepened to 0.6 m and widened to 1.3 m with a well-defined flat base and straight sides at an angle of 50°. This reduced again along its south-westerly course to a profile with a flat base and moderate sloping sides,

approximately 0.7 m wide and between 0.2 and 0.3 m deep (Fig. 3.32, section 1004, cut 8027), eventually ending in a rounded terminal at the point of contact with the corner of plot SW3. A primary deposit of grey silt clay was noted intermittently along the length of 10060, sealed consistently by a grey brown silting deposit which produced a notable amount of charred remains (approximately 30%) and some iron slag. These ditches produced pottery mainly dated to the first half of the 2nd century (see Chapter 6, Assemblage 20B).

The second stage plot SW1/SW2 boundary gully 9450 was investigated well beyond the limit of Area B to determine its extent. A machined trench revealed that 9450 extended 36 m beyond the original boundary of Area B before turning to the south-west to define the rear of plot SW2. In total this gave a depth of 83 m from the road frontage, and judging by the consistency of the dimensions of the rectilinear divisions it is possible that this was the length of most of the plots in the SW group. It is notable that there was no north-westerly projection of the rear boundary of the plot to form a comparable rear boundary for plot SW1. Gully 9450 cut into the edge of 9440 along its length and generally had a U-shaped profile with a flat base and ranged from 0.5 m to1 m in width and 0.2 to 0.3 m in depth. It was filled with a single deposit of grey silt clay throughout its length (Fig. 3.32, section 1180, cut 9223; section 849, cut 7567; section 851, cut7571) containing mostly late 2nd-century pottery (see Chapter 6, Assemblage 22B). This gully terminated towards the south-east where it met the line of the road. From this point 10050 ran south-westwards defining the north-west edge of the road for 37 m. The profile varied slightly from straight-sided and flat-based to a more rounded U-shape (Fig. 3.32, section 1004, cut 8312). The width was consistently near to 0.5 m, but the depth fluctuated between 0.08 and 0.3 m. A single distinctive dark grey silt filled 10050 and was clearly visible in plan extending along the line of the road. A notable feature of this deposit was the quantity of large pieces (average 0.05 m) of wood charcoal concentrated in the easternmost 10 m length of the feature. The fill of 10050 also produced sporadic concentrations of fired clay, slag and tap slag as well as a 1st- to 3rd-century blue/green glass body fragment.

Two gully segments, 10040 and 10240, which cut into the top of 10050, represented the final stage of roadside boundary associated with plot SW2 and were assigned to Phase 5. These were on average 0.5 m wide with a surviving depth of 0.05 m and a broad flat base and splayed sides (Fig. 3.32, section 1004, cut 8321; section 1384, cut 10107). Both gullies were filled with a coarse silt-sand clay, which was a distinctive mottled brown-yellow colour, and both ended in well-defined rounded termini, defining a 5 m wide gap giving access to plot SW2 from the Canterbury road.

Within the north-east corner of plot SW2 was a NW-SE aligned row of four substantial postholes, referred to as Structure F. All but one had a silt clay packing fill with flint and stone measuring up to 0.16 m x 0.07 m,

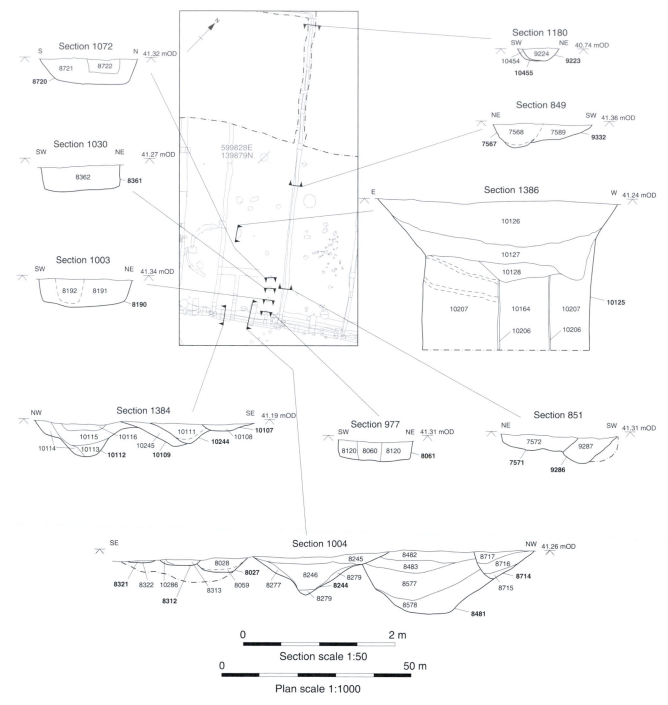

Figure 3.32   Plot SW2: Plan including Structure F, and sections of ditches 10060, 10050; gullies 9440, 9450, 10240 and 10040: Ditch 10060: section 1004 (cut 8027); ditch 10050: section 1004 (cut 8312); gully 9440: section 849 (cut 9332), section 1180 (cut 10455), section 851 (cut 9286); gully 9450: section 1180 (cut 9223), section 849 (cut 7567), section 851, (feature7571); gully 10240: section 1384 (cut 10107); gully 10040: section 1004 (cut 8321).

and a dark grey silt clay which represented the fill of the post void. The packing fills produced pottery of later 2nd-century date (see Chapter 6, Assemblage 33). The diameter of the postholes ranged from 1 m to 1.28 m and the surviving depths reached a maximum of 0.36 m. The diameter of the post voids was on average 0.4 m (Fig. 3.32, sections 1072, 1030, 1003 and 977). The area directly to the south-west was in-

vestigated carefully to examine the possibility that the posts formed part of a larger structure, but no evidence was found. The posts cut the top of Phase 2 roadside ditch 8950, and appeared to be contemporary with Phase 5 roadside gullies 10040 and 10240. It is possible that the posts carried the ridge pole of a structure whose other components did not survive (see below).

South-west of the post-row was a shallow hollow filled by deposit 9333, the south-western limit of which being defined by SW2/SW3 boundary gullies 9570 and 9580; the deposit extended over a very well-defined rectangular area of approximately 32 sq. m. It produced a reasonably large pottery assemblage (over 4 kg - see Chapter 6, Assemblage 34) indicating a date which places it in Phase 5, an iron nail and a fragment of glass from a blue-green tubular rimmed bowl (SF1512; see Cool, Chapter 5, Cat. no. 38; Fig. 5.4). The dark grey silt clay of 9333 probably formed through gleying as the deposit had organic inclusions and was most likely seasonally water-logged. Such a scenario coincides well with the inter-pretation that this deposit represents animal penning. The shallow depth of the soil, on average 0.08 m, its irregular undulations throughout, and its reasonably well-defined area all suggest a trample deposit. If so, the shallow hollow thus created would have held surface water throughout much of the winter, while also having a concentration of organic inclusions in the form of manure, hay and bedding.

A sub-circular waterhole 10125 was located north-west of the gleyed area (Fig. 3.32, section 1386). This feature had a diameter of 3.2 m, was hand excavated to a depth of 1.94 m and augured to a depth of 4.14 m below ground level without encountering natural geology. The two lowest recorded auger deposits consisted of blue-grey silt clays with occasional in-clusions of charcoal and wood fragments, overlain by a blue-orange silt clay 0.60 m deep. The latter was sealed by two deposits of blue-grey silt clay, which had bands of, dark green clay throughout, above which was a mixed blue-orange silt clay. The hand-excavated deposits above this comprised a grey-yellow clay (10207) that was deposited around the internal circumference of the waterhole to create a vertical shaft. This was then sealed and consolidated by a layer of light grey clay (10206), which appears to have formed the lining of the waterhole. The shaft defined by 10206 was filled with a deposit of grey-blue silt clay (10164) 0.96 m deep, overlying which were three grey silt clay deposits (10126-101280, all producing pottery dated AD 130-200.

Plot SW3 (Figs 3.33-3.35)

Plot SW3 was *c* 19 m wide and of uncertain length. It was divided longitudinally into two strips respec-tively *c.* 9 m and *c.* 10 m wide. These are considered to represent two halves of the same plot rather than two separate, unusually narrow plots. A structure was placed, or partly placed, in each half (Figs 3.29 and 3.33-3.35).

The north-east boundary of plot SW3 was defined by successive Phase 4 gullies, 9570 and 9580. Gully 9570 was heavily truncated by the later 9580 and only seen in plan towards the south-east, where it neared the line of the road, and towards the far north-west (Fig. 3.33, section 1143, cut 9053). Its fills produced a small group of pottery (see Chapter 6, Assemblage 20C). By analogy with the sequence of the two stages

of gully definition within plots SW1 and SW2, 9570 would most likely have run to the north-east corner of the plot and turned south-westwards to follow the line of the road, most probably as ditch 10410 which extended for 30 m across the frontage of plot SW3, before ending in a rounded terminal in front of plot SW4. The south-east edge of 10410 was cut along its entire length by ditch 10050, although what did re-main suggested a feature 0.75 m wide at the north-east end becoming gradually wider, up to 0.95 m, at its south-western end. The depth of ditch 10410 re-mained consistent at 0.3 m, as did the round based and broad U-shaped profile (Fig. 3.33, section 1355, cut 9964; section 1432, cut 10289).

The second stage plot SW2/SW3 boundary gully, 9580, terminated at the north-east corner of plot SW3 to respect the NE-SW line of ditch 10050. The latter formed the south-east boundary of plots SW2, SW3 and part of SW4 at this stage in the Phase 4 develop-ment of the site. Gully 9580 (Fig. 3.33, section 1143, cut 9547; section 1018) had a U-shaped profile and was filled with a single grey silt clay which produced an illegible early Roman coin (SF1494; see Guest, Chapter 5, Table 5.5) and a small group of pottery (see Chapter 6, Assemblage 22C).

A localised later development of the plot SW3 frontage was represented by a short length of gully 10280 (Fig. 3.35; see Fig. 3.33, section 1355, cut 9963), probably analogous with 10240 at the front of plot SW2 (Fig. 3.35). A gap of *c* 4 m between these two fea-tures at the north-east corner of plot SW3 may have defined a late (Phase 5) entrance into the plot. Post-holes 10325 and 9834 (Fig. 3.35), set back from the terminals of 10240 and 10280 respectively, may have carried gateposts.

The south-west side of plot SW3 (the SW3/SW4 boundary) was defined initially by ditch 10180/8510, extending some 49 m from the edge of Area B to the roadside ditches. At that point it may have termi-nated to respect the line of ditch 10050 (see above), but the relationship was largely removed by a large post-medieval ditch (9130) and this interpretation is speculative. An initial impression was that ditch 8510 terminated just south-east of the line of 10050 and was therefore later than it. This, however, would have left the south-west side of plot SW3 undefined in the first part of Phase 4 and it is likely that the south-east end of 8510 was a recut which had completely removed an earlier phase of boundary on this alignment. This recut, which probably included cuts 8796 and 8893, had an estimated length of 15 m. If this interpreta-tion is correct the position of an original south-east terminal for ditch 8510, and thus its relationship to the roadside ditch sequence, is unknown.

As initially defined, ditch 8510 was L-shaped in plan, extending from the roadside and then turning a right angle to the north-east at the point of junc-tion with ditch 10180, which continued the line of the south-eastern length of 8510 to form the north-western part of the plot SW3/SW4 boundary. No relation-ship could be identified between 8510 and 10180 at the point of junction and they are therefore assumed

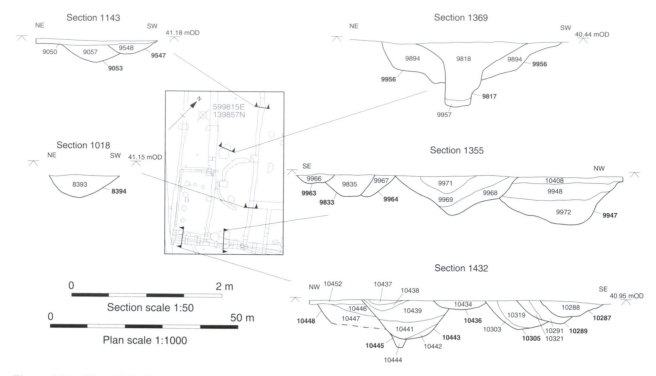

Figure 3.33 Plot SW3: Sections of gullies 9570, 9580, 10410 and 9580: Gully 9570: section 1143 (cut 9053); gully 9580: section 1143 (cut 9547); gully 10410: section 1355 (cut 9964), section 1432 (cut 10289); gully 9580: section 1018.

to have been contemporary. The north-easterly arm of 8510 extended for 8 m to a junction with ditch 10230/10270, which formed the longitudinal subdivision of the plot. Ditch 8510 must have been the later of these features.

Ditch 10180/8510 had an average width of 0.81 m and a depth of 0.22 m with moderately sloping sides and a rounded base (Fig. 3.35, section 1074, cut 8694; section 1105, cut 8796 (the latter representing the 'recut' version on the interpretation offered here)). Throughout its length it was filled with a grey-brown silt clay, except in one section midway along its length, which had a more varied sequence of, fills (Fig. 3.35, section 1269, cut 9593). These fills consisted of three silt clays, of which the secondary and uppermost produced a large amount of charred remains (approximately 80%) and fired clay, possibly derived from activity within structure D some 15 m to the south-east.

Ditch 10180/8510 produced nine small finds comprising four fragments of glass (three sherds (SF1453, SF1454 and SF1456) from a late 2nd- to 3rd-century spouted jug (see Cool, Chapter 5, Cat. no. 51; Fig. 5.5) and the fourth sherd (SF1487) a blue green body fragment), two pieces from a copper alloy steelyard (SF1451, SF1452; see Cool, Chapter 5, Cat. no. 80; Fig. 5.6), a biconical lead weight (SF1321; see Cool, Chapter 5, Cat. no. 83) and two iron nails.

Plot SW3 was divided longitudinally by ditch 10230/10270. This had steep sides and a rounded base with an average width and depth of 0.85 m and 0.5 m respectively (Fig. 3.35, section 1226, cut 9401; section 1070, cut 8712). The feature extended for the entire length

of the plot as revealed in Area B, terminating at the roadside adjacent to ditch 10050, with which it may have been broadly contemporary, though an earlier date is perhaps more likely. The fills of 10230/10270 were a primary of grey-yellow silt clay, and an upper fill of dark grey clay silt, which contained occasional charred remains and fired clay.

Plot SW3 contained evidence of two structures, Structure E and Structure D. The former was only partly contained within the plot, and presumably predated its establishment, while the latter was well-defined by surrounding gullies.

Structure E (?Phase 4) (Fig. 3.34)

Structure E was represented by drainage gully groups 10250/10260, and lay on the north-east side of the plot, set back *c* 8 m from the contemporary roadside gully. The gullies defined approximately half of what may originally have been a circular structure with an approximate diameter of 12 m, in which case it must have predated the establishment of the south-west plots (see below). The profile of both gullies varied from shallow to steep sided; 10260 had moderate sloping sides and an irregular base (Fig. 3.34, sections 1153 and 1154), while 10250 had consistently irregular sides and base (Fig. 3.34, section 1151, cut 8895; and section 1152). A primary deposit of grey-brown clay was observed within both features, overlain by a dark grey silt clay containing occasional pieces of wood charcoal. The late 2nd-century pottery assemblage from these gullies (see Chapter 6, Assemblage 28)

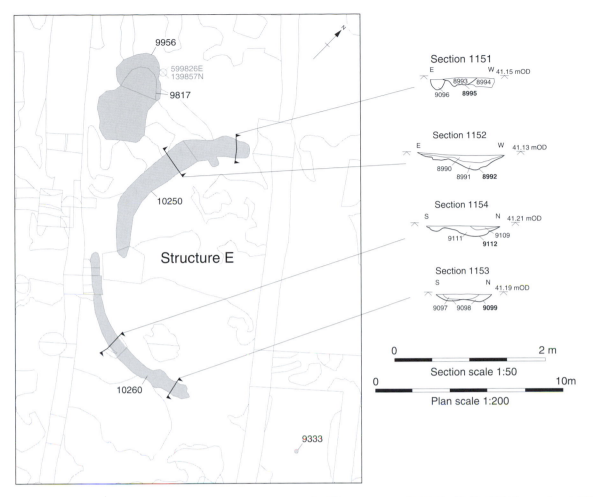

Figure 3.34   Plot SW3: Plan of Structure E and sections of gullies 10250 and 10260: Gully 10250: section 1151 (cut 8895), section 1152; gully 10260: section 1153, section 1154.

corresponded with the pottery retrieved from the later of two adjacent intercutting pits. An earlier feature, pit 9956, 2 m to the north-west was roughly circular, with a maximum diameter of 2.46 m and a depth of 0.52 m (Fig. 3.33, section 1369). Its sides were generally steep and the base was slightly irregular, but predominantly flat. The only fill was a yellow-grey clay which may have been deliberately deposited, but contained no dating material. Pit 9956 was cut by pit 9817 which was 1.5 m in diameter and 0.88 m deep. This had near vertical sides with splayed upper edges and was filled with a grey-yellow silt clay, sealed by a dark reddish-grey silt clay (9818) containing much charcoal and a large pottery assemblage.

Structure D (Phase 4-5) (Fig. 3.35)

Structure D (Fig. 3.35) was located between the south-west boundary of plot SW3 (ditch 10180/8510) and the longitudinal plot subdivision (ditch 10230/10270). The latter was in existence before structure D was constructed, as the postholes of the north-east side of the building cut into the fills of 10230/10270. The L-shaped plan of 8510, however, is likely to have

been cut either to respect the position of an existing structure or to accommodate one which was to be constructed soon after.

A second stage of definition around structure D was marked by features post-dating ditch 8510. A gully (10170) was cut along the inner edge of ditch 8510 and followed its L-shaped plan. The south-east terminus of the gully fell a little short of the road-side ditches and of the south-east corner of Building D. Its north-east arm terminated at the junction with earlier ditch 10270, where it met a small, steep-sided pit, 9199, 0.54 m in diameter and 0.47 m deep. The gully was typically 0.5 m wide m and had moderate to steep sloping sides and a flat base. It increased in depth from 0.2 m to 0.34 m from the south-east to the north-east. It was filled with a consistent dark grey-brown silt clay along its length (Fig. 3.35, section 1105, cut 8795; section 1074, cut 8696), with localised concentrations of charred remains and fired clay. The fill of pit 9199 was a similar dark grey clay.

The line of feature 10270 adjacent to structure D was not redefined, but north-west of the building the line of the longitudinal plot division was renewed by ditch 10190 which cut the top of 10230 for a distance of at least 31 m (to the edge of Area B) and ended in a rounded south-east terminal about 1 m from pit 9199. The profile of this ditch, with moderately sloping sides and a rounded base at the north-west, became more steep-sided as it extended to the south-east. The sequence of fills also varied with grey-brown clay silts observed at the north-west and south-east extremities, but a more complex series of deposits noted near the middle of the feature (Fig. 3.35, section 1226, cut 9402). These consisted of three silt clay

deposits overlain by two grey upper silting fills. The secondary deposit within this ditch produced a *sestertius* of 161-180 (SF1515).

Structure D itself was represented by eleven post-holes out of a presumed original total of fourteen (Fig. 3.35). Only two postholes were found on the north-east side of the building, both cut into the fill of ditch 10270. The three fronting the road cut into the fills of Phase 3 continuous roadside ditch 10070. On average the postholes were 0.96 m in diameter and 0.37 m in

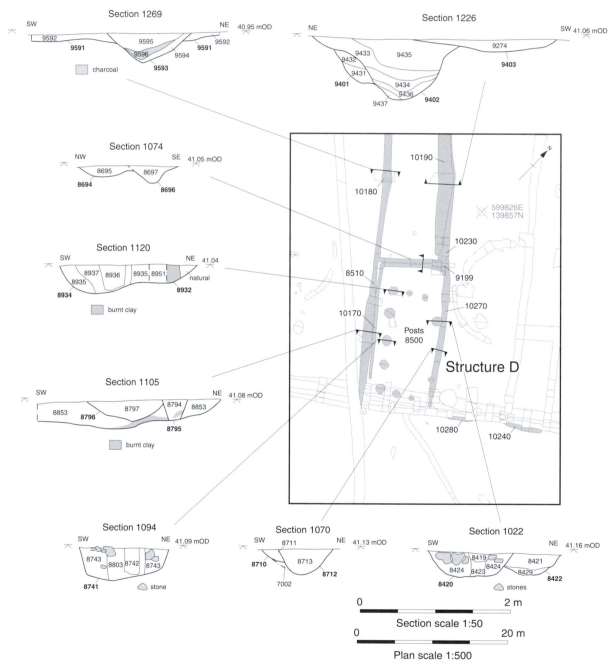

Figure 3.35   Plot SW3: Plan of Structure D and sections of Drainage gully 10180/8510, and gullies 10170, 10190 and 10230/10270: Drainage gully 10180/8510: section 1074 (cut 8694), section 1105 (cut 8796), section 1269 (cut 9593); gully 10170: section 1105 (cut 8795), section 1074 (cut 8696); gully 10190: section 1226 (cut 9402); gully 10230/10270: section 1226 (cut 9401), section 1070 (cut 8712).

depth, near vertically-sided and flat-bottomed. They all had separate packing and post pipe deposits. The former consisted of a yellow-brown silt clay with large Ragstone packing stones measuring on average 0.2 by 0.14 by 0.14 m and occasional flint measuring 0.1 x 0.05 m, while the post pipe fills were dark grey silt clay with occasional charcoal flecking. The post pipes measured between 0.4 and 0.5 m in diameter. Two of the postholes fronting the road produced an iron nail and a blue-green glass bottle fragment datable to the late 1st to early 3rd century (SF1493; see Cool, Chapter 5, Cat. no. 56; Fig. 5.5). Together the post-pits contained 111 sherds of pottery collectively indicating a later 2nd-century date for the structure (see Chapter 6, Assemblage 26). As mentioned above, three of the projected postholes in the north-east side of the building, including the two corner posts, were not located. The reason for this is not clear, but is unlikely to have been because of plough truncation since the other postholes were all fairly uniformly substantial.

There was very little indication of internal features within the building. A small feature (8932) projecting from the south-west corner post-pit (8934) represents the cut for an oven excavated by KARU in evaluation Trench 4 (Fig. 3.35, section 1120). Since this feature was cut by the post-pit, it must therefore have pre-dated the use of the building. A further shallow pit containing two 'burnt zones' was also examined by KARU immediately east of post-pit 8741, but no trace of this was identified in 1999. From its position this feature, which was 0.80 m wide and projected at least *c* 1.30 m into the building from the wall line, could have been contemporary with the use of the building, but its function is uncertain Features associated with the structure - principally the surrounding gullies - produced pottery indicative of activity up to *c* AD 250 (see Chapter 6, Assemblage 27).

Plot SW4 *(Fig. 3.36)*

This was the widest of the south-west group of plots, measuring 22 m across, possibly as a consequence of the existence of structure C within it (Fig. 3.29). Its north-east boundary was defined by ditch 10180/8510 as described above, and the plot was bounded to the south-west by gully 9370 (see plot SW5). (For the boundary ditches alongside the road and the alignment of seven postholes (group 9470) just south-east of the ditches, see Plot SW5 below.)

Structure C *(Phase 4)*

Approximately 16 m south-west of possible circular structure E (in plot SW3) was structure C, represented by gully group 9280. This consisted of four distinct segments of curvilinear drainage gully with an internal diameter of 13.30 m. The truncated gullies had an average width of 0.30 m and an average depth of only 0.06 m (Fig. 3.36, sections 1189, 1187, 1194, 1192). They were all filled with a single deposit of grey-brown silt clay which produced amongst

other finds a fragmentary coin of Hadrian (SF1388, see Guest, Chapter 5, Table 5.5) and a group of pottery dated roughly to the mid 2nd century AD (see Chapter 6, Assemblage 24).

Although in origin this structure may have pre-dated the establishment of organised property divisions in Phase 4, its central position within the area defined by gullies 10180/8510 and 9370 cannot merely be coincidence. It is clear that structure C was still in existence at the time of the layout of plot SW4, the boundaries of which were positioned to respect its location.

Internal features include postholes 9295 and 9323. The former was located just inside the south-east side of the structure and was 0.4 m in diameter and 0.08 m deep, with vertical sides and a rounded base. It was filled with a single deposit of dark grey silt clay and at the very base were the remains of a vessel dated AD 43-200, lying on its side (Fig. 3.36, section 1200). Within the central area of structure C was isolated posthole 9323 possibly associated with hearth base 9324 (Fig. 3.36, section 1213). This posthole had vertical sides and a rounded base and was filled by a primary yellow-brown silt clay, overlain by a dark grey clay silt containing large amounts of charcoal and lumps of burnt clay. A quern fragment within this deposit may possibly have been used as post packing. Feature 9324, tentatively recorded as a hearth base, was 0.45 m in diameter and only 0.03 m deep. All that remained therefore was a shallow depression filled with a layer of charcoal rich clay silt. This overlay the natural clay base which was fire reddened. A thin layer of grey silt extending from the south-east edge of 9324 also had patches of *in situ* scorching, but no concentrations of wood charcoal.

Pit 9315 and later pit 9317 were sub-circular and located towards the western side of structure C (Fig. 3.36, section 1208). The former was 0.9 m in diameter and 0.2 m deep and the latter 0.9 m in diameter and 0.1 m depth. Both had shallow sides and a rounded base and were filled with a grey brown silt clay. Pit 9304 to the east was 0.55 m in diameter and 0.07 m deep (Fig. 3.36, section 1204). This was filled with a dark grey silt clay, which like the other pits produced nothing to determine the function of these features. A 3.5 m long stretch of gully (group 9310) also lay in the south-east part of the structure. This had regular sides sloping at 45° and a flat base and was on average 0.65 m wide and 0.11 m deep with well-defined termini at each end (Fig. 3.36, section 1202, cut 9300; section 1203, cut 9302). This was the only internal structural feature demonstrably contemporary with the drainage gullies defining structure C.

Grave 8160

Just inside the north-west perimeter of structure C was grave 8160 (Fig. 3.36, sections 1448 and 1449), which was rectangular, aligned NE-SW, and measured 1.94 m long, 0.76 m wide and 0.24 m deep. No skeletal remains survived due to the acidic nature of the soil, but a 0.02 m deep coffin stain (8548) of dark

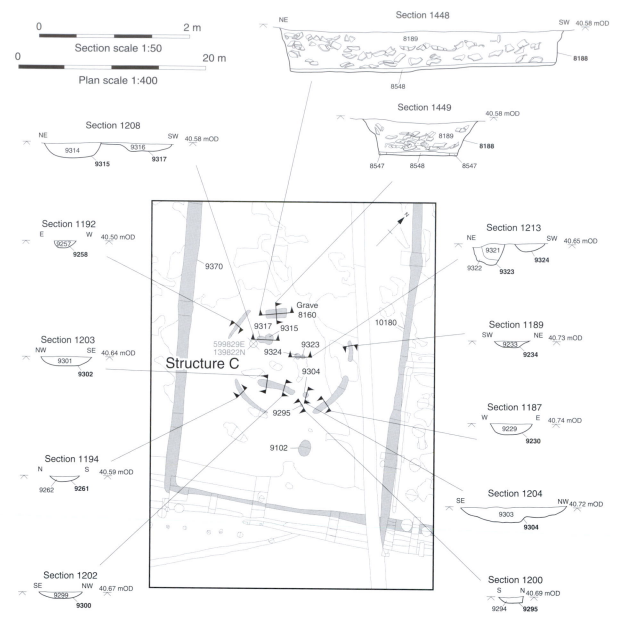

Figure 3.36   Plot SW4: Plan of Structure C and sections of gullies 9280, 9310, and Grave 8160: Gully 9280: sections 1192, 1194, 1189, 1187; gully 9310: sections 1202, 1203; Grave 8160: sections 1448 and 1449.

grey clay, was visible extending around the internal edge of the grave cut at its base. Two nails and a fragment of iron (SF1440-1442) along the south-west edge of the grave cut also suggested the existence of a wooden coffin. Around 8548 was a fairly clean light grey silt clay (8547). Above this the uppermost 0.20 m of the grave was backfilled with a very similar clay (8189), distinguished by containing a very large quantity of pottery fragments (see Chapter 6, Assemblage 25). Many of the pottery vessels appeared to have been deliberately broken before being placed into the grave. The only exception is a small, but complete crucible. The date of deposition of the ceramic assemblage from the grave (c AD 170) presumably indicates the end of use of Structure C.

Other features

Features outside structure C consisted largely of irregularly-shaped root holes, with oval pit 9102 the only exception (Fig. 3.36). This measured 1.7 m x 1.4 m and 0.35 m deep, and had steeply sloping sides and an uneven base. The primary fill was a grey-yellow silt clay which had two pieces of stone measuring 0.1 m by 0.15 m pressed through it and into the sides of the pit. Overlying this was a dumped deposit of charcoal-rich clay silt with occasional lumps of burnt clay. The original function of the pit is unclear, although it was eventually used to deposit occupation debris. The pit may have been associated with Structure C, although the dumped backfill produced pottery dated to AD 200-270, suggesting that the feature post-dated the abandonment of the structure.

Plot SW5 (Fig. 3.37)

The plot SW4/SW5 boundary was formed by gully 9370 (Figs 3.29 and 3.37). This extended some 43 m from the north-western edge of Area B to the roadside ditch alignment. It had an average width and depth of 1.4 m and 0.4 m respectively and moderately sloping sides and a slightly rounded base (Fig. 3.37, sections 1217 and 1176). Throughout its length the gully was filled with a yellow-brown silt clay; in places a grey-brown clay silt sealed the latter. These fills produced a group of generally very broken pottery (see Chapter 6, Assemblage 22D). At its south-eastern end 9370 cut earlier roadside ditches 8950 (Phase 2) and 10070 (Phase 3), eventually ending in a well-defined terminal at the junction with the contemporaneous Phase 4 ditch 10420 (Fig. 3.37, section 1220). Just south-east of this junction was a 16 m length of shallow U-shaped drainage gully, group 10430, which cut the top of 10420 along its length and was filled with grey silt clays (Fig. 3.37, section 1428, cut 10257). This stretch of gully was contemporary in date (Phase 5) with other short gully segments to the north-east, which may suggest that the north-west roadside boundary was not defined by a substantial and continuous ditch during the later phases of occupation. Alternatively, since 10430 did not have well-defined termini and it may have merely been cut into 10420 to facilitate drainage from the road.

Immediately south-east of gully 10430 and parallel to it was a row of seven postholes, group 9470, which extended for 12 m, essentially fronting plot SW4 (Fig. 3.29). Of the four excavated all had near vertical sides and a flat base, while three had distinct post pipes, with diameters between 0.13 and 0.2 m, while overall the postholes had an average diameter and depth of 0.5 m and 0.28 m respectively. The postholes contained yellow-brown silt clay packing fill, with occasional stone fragments typically 0.15 by 0.08 by 0.10 m and the pipes were filled with a dark grey silt clay (Fig. 3.38). The function of the postholes is uncertain. They were not obviously part of a structure and they may simply have formed a short fenceline, but in this case their associations are not clear. They are assigned tentatively to Phase 5. Further small pits or postholes clustered at the road margin in line with the plot SW4/SW5 boundary.

Internal features in plot SW5 consisted of a few discrete pits and the remains of a cremation grave. Pit 10249 (Fig. 3.37, section 1426) measured 1.9 m by 3 m and was only 0.15 m deep. It had a very uneven base and sides and may have been the remains of a tree-hole. Nevertheless its grey silting fill produced pottery datable to Phase 3. Further north-west were Phase 4 features 10337 and 10335. The upper part of cremation grave 10337 had been removed by 10335, and all that remained was a circular pit with steep near vertical sides only 0.06 m deep. The dark brown silt clay fill of 10337 contained *c* 30% charcoal fragments and 268 g of cremated bone from an unsexed adult. Feature 10335, which cut across the top of the

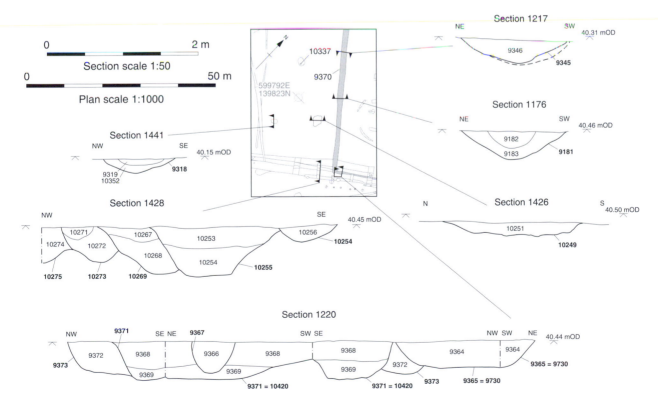

Figure 3.37   Plot SW5: Plan and sections of gullies 9370 and 10430; and location of truncated cremation pit 10337: Gully 9370: sections 1217, 1176, 1220 (cut 9365); gully 10430: section 1428 (cut 10257).

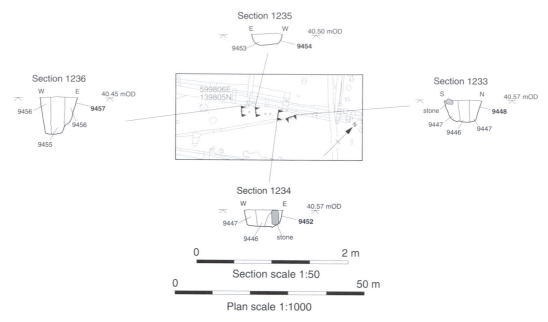

Section 1235

Section 1236

Section 1233

Section 1234

Section scale 1:50

Plan scale 1:1000

Figure 3.38   Plot SW4/SW5: Plan and sections of posthole group 9470.

grave, was 2 m in diameter and 0.12 m deep. It was filled with a grey silt clay, which contained 2 g of cremated bone. Phase 5 pit 9318, which lay south-west of pit 10249, was sub-circular, and measured 1 m by 1.5 m and was 0.18 m deep with moderately sloping sides and was filled by two deposits of grey silt clay (Fig. 3.37, section 1441).

Plot SW6 *(Figs 3.29 and 3.39)*

Plot SW6 was bounded to the north-east by gully 9210 and perhaps by its predecessor 8930, but did not have a clearly defined south-western boundary within the excavation area. Gully 8930 was laid out at right-angles to the roadside ditches, parallel to the north-east boundary of plot SW5 and 20 m from it. It was traced over a distance of some 33 m from the north-west edge of Area B and terminated c 1.5 m short of the Phase 2 roadside ditch 8950. The gully was generally c 0.4 m wide and 0.15 m deep (Fig.3.40, sections 1186 and 1092). However, the pottery derived from its fills suggested a Phase 2 or early Phase 3 date, thus predating the establishment of the south-west plots and probably associated with the adjacent Structures A and B (see below).

Gully 9210 seems to have formed the Phase 4 boundary between plots SW5 and SW6. Curiously, this was not perpendicular to the main road alignment, but instead followed a WNW-ESE course, some 20 m from and parallel to a relict length of the prehistoric field system (feature 9480) lying to the south. Gully 9210 cut across the fills of 8930 and the Phase 2 and 3 roadside ditches 8950 and 10070 and ran into the top of roadside ditch 10420. Its average width and depth were 0.9 m and 0.35 m and it was filled consistently with a primary brown-yellow silt clay sealed by a grey silting deposit (Fig. 3.39, section

1170, cut 9143; and section 1093, cut 8856), except at the junction with the roadside ditch, where the gully (Fig. 3.39, section 1443, cut 10364) had only a single silting fill, which extended across the top of ditch 10420 (Fig. 3.39, section 1443, cut 10362).

The prehistoric ditch alignment 9480 must have survived as a landscape feature in some way. A deposit (context 9543) overlying its fills produced a small pottery assemblage probably of pre-Flavian date (see Chapter 6, Assemblage 2). This feature may have served to define the south-west side of a 'plot' in Phase 2 and perhaps into Phase 3, corresponding to gully 8930 to the north, but with no indication that it provided any definition of the south-west side of plot SW6 at any later date.

Features within the area of SW6 consisted of two probable Phase 2 structures and a Phase 5 pit; the structures predated the organisation of the area north-west of the road into regular plots. Even though there was no stratigraphic relationship between the two structures, and the component features of Structure B produced no useful dating material, their proximity suggests that they were closely contemporaneous.

Structure A (Phase 2) (Fig. 3.40)

Structure A was defined by a penannular gully (group 8790) with an internal diameter of 9.5 m and an average width and depth of 0.60 m and 0.10 m respectively. The widely-spaced termini of this feature, facing north-east, probably did not reflect its original layout as their profiles, becoming gradually shallower with ill-defined ends, suggest plough truncation rather than a structural characteristic. The gully was filled with a single brown-grey silt clay containing moderate amounts of wood charcoal and occasional sub-rounded pieces of flint and stone. This deposit

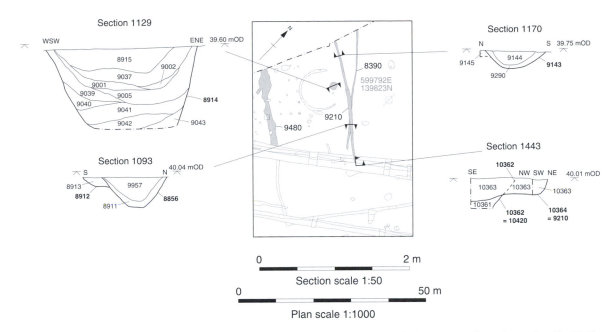

Figure 3.39   Plot SW6: Plan of ditches and gullies 9480, 9210 and 8390, and pit 8914, and sections of gully 9210, and pit 8914: Gully 9210: section 1170 (cut 9143), section 1093 (cut 8856), section 1443 (cut 10364); pit 8914: section 1129.

also produced a (probably intrusive) fragment from a prismatic bottle of blue-green glass (SF1462) broadly dated late 1st-early 3rd century. Otherwise the fills of this feature produced 495 sherds (4236 g) of pottery mostly of pre-Flavian character, suggesting that the fill of the gully was contemporary with deposit 9543 (above) overlying the fills of prehistoric ditch 9480 (see Chapter 6, Assemblage 3). There were no internal surfaces or features (but see pit 8914 below).

Structure B (Phase 2) (Fig. 3.40)

Structure B consisted of a rectilinear setting of seven postholes (Group 10480). This group was aligned broadly north-west to south-east and probably defined the whole of the SE and NE sides and part of the SW side of a small building located immediately south-west of the penannular structure A. The structure was *c* 5 m wide and perhaps 10 m long. The postholes were on average 0.50 m in diameter and 0.10-0.20 m deep and they were all filled with a dark grey-brown silt clay. As with structure A there were no internal surfaces or features.

Pit 8914

Pit 8914 was located south-west of gully 9210 and would have lain within the north-east part of structure A if it is assumed that gully 8790 was originally circular in plan. The pit was, however, dated to Phase 5. It was 2.0 m diameter and was excavated to a depth of 1.10 m without reaching the natural clay (Fig. 3.39, section 1129). It was filled by a series of silt clay deposits, including a number of sterile clays which derived from the erosion of the natural edges. Sealing these was an upper silting deposit which included a

purpose-made fired clay counter (SF1486; see Cool, Chapter 5, Cat. no. 79) among other ceramic finds. The latter were mostly not closely dated, but two small sherds pottery were of 3rd-century date. On this basis the feature was somewhat tentatively assigned to Phase 5.

North-East Enclosure Area

Ditch sequences (Figs 3.41-3.43)

At the north-east edge of Area B were the ditches of what appeared to be a double ditched enclosure (Fig. 3.41). The ditches ran parallel to the edge of Area B. At their north-west end the majority of these ditches turned north-eastwards and, to judge from the results of the gradiometer survey, they extended along the line of the Canterbury road. The excavations also showed that the ditches turned north-eastwards at their south-eastern extents. Only the south-western side of the enclosure lay within the excavation area, and therefore the function of the ditches was not fully established. The enclosure appears to have been established in Phase 3 and its boundaries were redefined several times in Phase 4 before falling out of use in Phase 5.

Cremation grave (Phase 2)

The primary feature in the area was an apparently isolated late Iron Age or early Roman unurned cremation burial within a sub-rectangular shallow pit (1261) (Fig. 3.41), measuring 0.46 m by 0.2 m by 0.12 m deep. At the north-east end of the pit was an ancillary vessel (1262), which can be dated late Iron Age to *c* AD 50. This was found in an upright position, though it had been truncated, probably by post-Roman ploughing. The remainder of the pit was filled with a single deposit of mid-grey clay silt, 1263, which contained the remains of the cremated bone (see Chapter 8).

Ditches 1721 and 1750 (Phase 3) (Figs 3.41-3.42)

The earliest ditches in the enclosure sequence were 1721 and 1750, both dated to Phase 3. Ditch 1721 was only observed on the north-east side of later ditch 1765 (Fig. 3.42, section 132, cut 519) and in the excavated sections underlying structure R (Fig. 3.42, section 347, cut 1671), consequently its extent to the north-west is quite unknown. Owing to the degree of truncation by later ditches, only a small part of the profile survived in each excavated section. This had a consistently broad, flat base and increased gradually in width and depth towards the south-east, the depth ranging from 0.3 m at the north-west to 0.8 m at the south-east. The most complete profile had a broad flat

base with a sharp change to sides sloping at 40°. These splayed dramatically at an average depth of 0.4 m, to sides sloping at 10°, possibly suggesting a surface width in excess of 3 m. Generally the ditch was filled with a single deposit of grey-brown clay silt which produced pottery and an illegible early Roman coin (SF252; see Guest, Chapter 5, Table 5.5). In the vicinity of structure R, however, the ditch contained a sterile brown-yellow silt clay, which appeared to be redeposited natural. This perhaps derived from the excavation of the next phase of ditch, and may have been deliberately deposited to level out an area in anticipation of the construction of structure R.

Ditch 1750 was also heavily truncated along its length by a later (Phase 4-5) ditch (1740), and therefore its original surface width was never determined. The ditch had a splayed V-shaped profile with an average depth of 0.4 m, filled with a single deposit of mid brown clay silt (Fig. 3.42, section 229, cut 1078; section 57, cut 341). Its extent to the south-east and

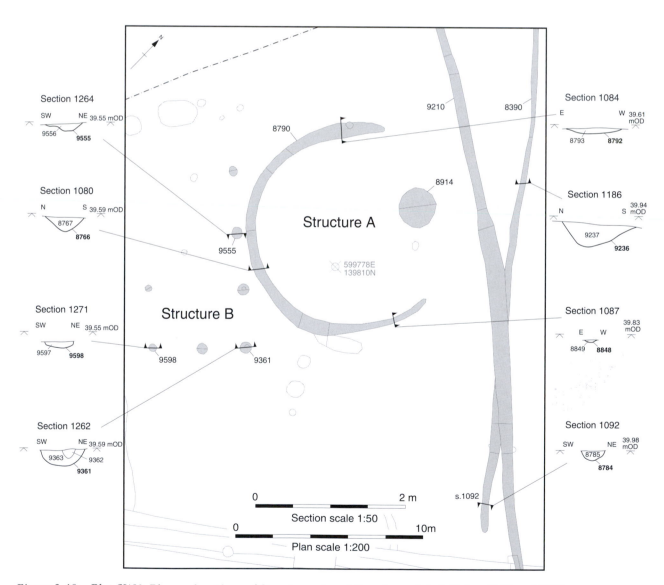

Figure 3.40   Plot SW6: Plan and sections of Structures A and B and associated ditches 8390 and 9210.

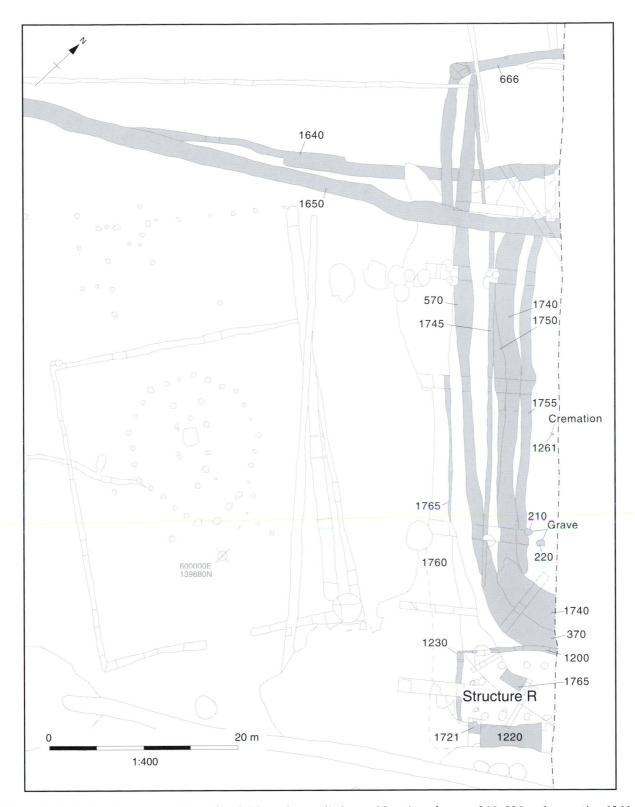

Figure 3.41   NE enclosure area: Plan of multiple enclosure ditches and location of graves 210, 220 and cremation 1261.

north-west is not known owing to truncation by later features, but it is possible that 1750 continued beneath 1740 and turned to the north-east. Close to the point where this change of alignment may have occurred a shallow hollow some 3 m wide (1107) lay immediately south-west of the putative line of 1750. This feature was also assigned to Phase 3.

A short length of gully (690), lying at the south-east margin of the Canterbury road immediately adjacent to the north-east edge of Area B, was tentatively

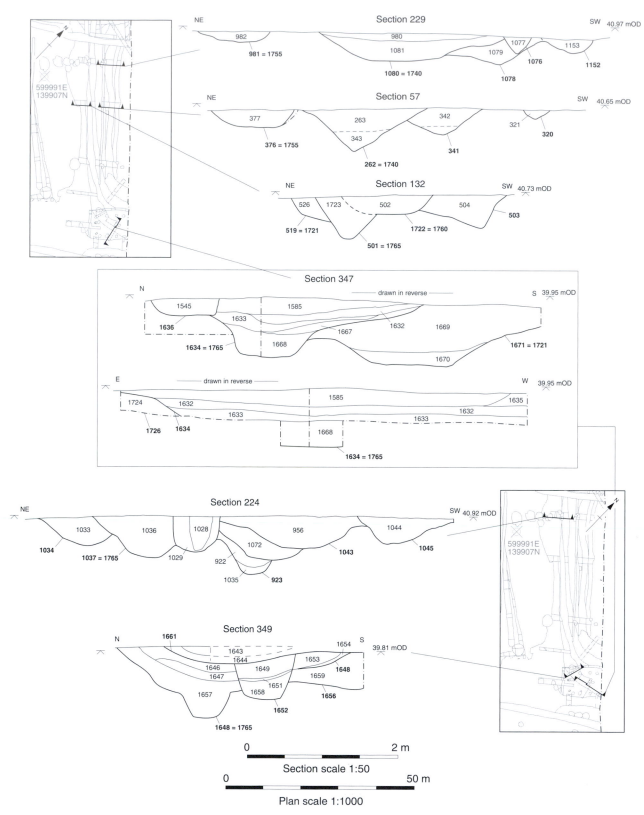

Figure 3.42   NE enclosure area: Sections through multiple enclosure ditches: Sections of ditch 1721: section 132 (cut 519), section 347 (cut 1671); ditch 1750: section 229 (cut 1078); section 57 (cut 341); ditch 1740: section 229 (cut 1080), section 57 (cut 262); ditch 1760: section 132 (cut 1722); ditch 1755: section 229 (cut 981), section 57 (cut 376); ditch 1765: section 132 (cut 501), section 347 (cut 1634), section 224 (cut 1037), section 349 (cut 1648).

assigned to Phase 3 and may possibly have been related.

Ditch 1765 (Phase 4) (Figs 3.41-3.42)

Ditch 1765 represented a re-cut of ditch 1721. It was cut along its length by a later Phase 4 ditch 1760. Where a complete or partly truncated profile survived, the ditch was 3.2 m wide and 0.8-0.9 m deep. It had a well-defined flat base with steep sloping edges (Fig. 3.42, section 224, cut 1073; section 349, cut 1648; section 132, cut 501). The majority of the fills throughout the length of the ditch consisted of orange-grey and brown-grey clay silts, but a section excavated across the ditch beneath structure R (Fig. 3.42, section 347, cut 1634) showed that the feature had been purposely backfilled to level out this area. The silt clays contained occasional charcoal flecking and small sub-angular flints. They produced a late 1st- to early 3rd-century glass bottle handle fragment (SF274; see Cool, Chapter 5, Cat. no. 60), and ceramic evidence indicating that the ditch was dug about the middle of the 2nd century, and back-filled c AD 200 (see Chapter 6, Assemblage 23). The upper part of 1765 in the vicinity of structure R - used for ironworking - was filled with a clay silt containing dense hammerscale debris to a depth of 0.2 m, presumably contemporary with the use of the structure. This implies that a shallow hollow must still have existed over parts of 1765, while the next phase of ditch, 1760, was open. The presence of furnace debris within the lower fills of 1760 suggests that slag and other furnace debris were deposited to the south-west of the building, whilst waste from the secondary iron processing stage was deposited within the interior of the structure, and therefore into the top of 1765. Ditch 666 was probably an extension of ditch 1765 to the north-west, forming the west corner of the probable enclosure. This corner was relatively square in plan, contrasting with the more rounded corner to the south.

Ditches 570 and 1755 (Phase 4) (Figs 3.41-3.43)

Ditch 570 was paired with 1755 to form the south-west side of a double ditched enclosure also in Phase 4. Both features were truncated by ditch 1740, and were on average 5 m apart, which appears to have been the spacing employed quite consistently for all of the paired ditches in this part of the site. Ditch 570 had a broad splayed U-shaped profile with a depth of 0.3-0.35 m and an average width of 1 m, widening to 2.4 m as it turned at its south-eastern end (Fig. 3.43, section 295, cut 1371). Throughout the length of the ditch it was filled with a single dark brown silting deposit, containing sub-rounded stone and small sub-angular flints (Fig. 3.43, section 257, cut 1205; section 131; section 185, cut 775).

Ditch 1755 had a shallow bowl-shaped profile with a slightly rounded base. It was between 1 m and 1.2 m wide and gradually increased in depth from 0.15 m at the north-west to 0.3 m at the south-east. The ditch had a possible south-east terminal, but this was not well-defined due to the extent of later truncation. The north-western limit of the ditch was also difficult to locate presumably because it was totally truncated by ditch 1740. The full length of the ditch was filled with a single dark brown silting deposit (Figs 3.42, section 229, cut 981; section 57, cut 376; 3.43, section 185, cut 784).

The relationship between these features and ditch 1765/666 was not clearly demonstrated, but as ditch 570 appeared to terminate against the line of ditch 666 at the side of the Canterbury road it is assumed that 570 and its fellow (1755) were slightly later than 1765/666 (Fig. 3.41).

Ditches 1740 and 1760 (Phase 4-5) (Figs 3.41-3.43)

A further pair of enclosure ditches also seems to have originated in Phase 4. Ditch 1740 emerged from the north-eastern edge of Area B and extended south-eastwards before returning to the north-east again beyond the limit of excavation. This feature had a marginal relationship with both ditches 570 and 1755, but appears perhaps to have cut both. It was most likely paired with the Phase 4-5 ditch 1760, which lay approximately 5 m further to the south-west and extended along the south-west edge of structure R before turning to the north-east as ditch 1220. Ditch 1760 certainly cut ditch 1765.

The profile of 1740 was relatively consistent throughout its length, with straight sides sloping at 45° and a flat base. The width varied from 2-2.5 m and the depth from 0.5-0.6 m (Fig. 3.42, section 229, cut 1080; section 57, cut 262; Fig. 3.43, section 185, cut 782; section 295, cut 1354). There were generally two or three clay silt deposits within the ditch. The primary fill, a mid grey clay silt, produced a strip of lead alloy (SF192; see Cool, Chapter 5, Cat. no. 128) and a light green glass indented beaker body fragment (SF193; see Cool, Chapter 5, Cat. no. 42). A secondary deposit of reddish brown clay silt with occasional charcoal flecking and a high density of manganese overlay this. This deposit yielded a bronze nail with a leaded terminal (SF158), a fragmentary coin of Trajan (SF152; see Guest, Chapter 5, Table 5.5), two fragments of glass (SF112 and SF191) and two iron nails, as well as pottery (see Chapter 6, Assemblage 21, including residual material from the primary fills of 1740). At the south-east end of the ditch, as it turned along the north-west side of structure R, a mottled grey-brown silt, 1352 (Fig. 3.43, section 295, cut 1354), which contained a high proportion of charred material, was spread across the top of the ditch, partially sealing and obscuring the fills of earlier ditch 570. Similarly, at the north-west end of the ditch, a dark grey silt (805) containing a large amount of furnace debris, and a coin dated AD 161-175 (SF176; see Guest, Chapter 5, Table 5.5), extended across the top of 1740 and obscured its southern edge. Despite this it is very likely that the west corner of this phase of inner enclosure ditch was marked by features 1714 and 1716. The relationship between these was not examined, but 1716 was more closely comparable in

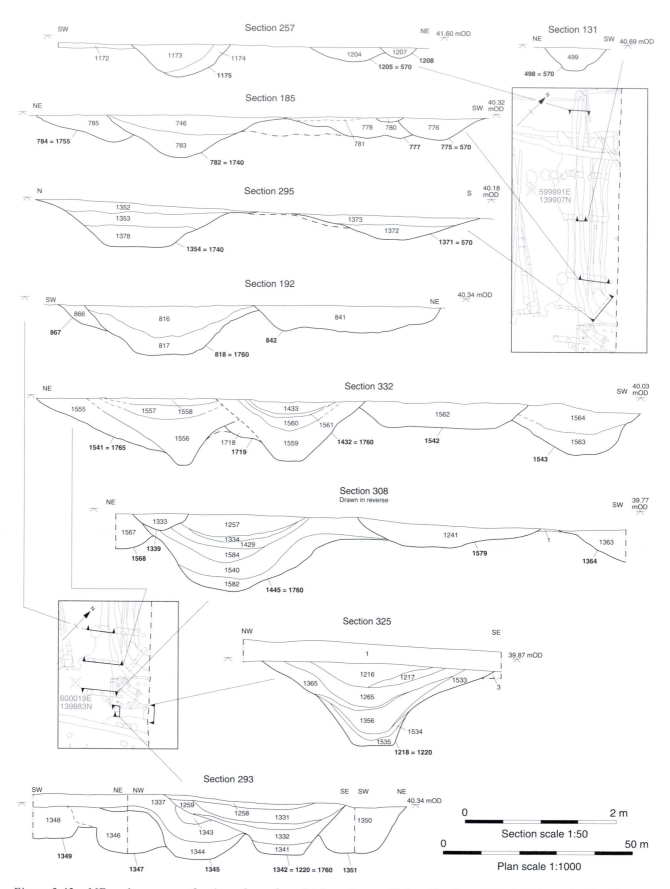

Figure 3.43   NE enclosure area: Sections through multiple enclosure ditches: Sections of ditch 570: section 257 (cut 1205), section 131 (cut 498), section 185 (cut 775), section 295 (cut 1371); ditch 1740: section 185 (cut 782), section 295 (cut 1354); ditch 1760: section 192 (cut 818), section 332 (cut 1432), section 308 (cut 1445); ditch 1760/1220: section 293 (cut 1342); ditch 1220: section 325 (cut 1218); gully 1230: section 308 (cut 1339).

dimensions to 1740 and was presumably its continuation. The corner here was again markedly squared, in contrast with the more rounded southern corner.

Phase 4-5 ditch 1760 ran from NW-SE and then turned to the north-east as ditch 1220 to bound the south-east side of structure R. The profile of the ditch showed a distinct progression in its course south-eastwards. At the north-west end it was 2-2.5 m wide and only 0.2 m deep, though with moderately sloping sides and a well-defined flat base (Fig. 3.42, section 132, cut 1722; Fig. 3.43, section 192, cut 818). The minimal depth of the feature at this point, suggesting heavy truncation, may explain why it was not traced as far as the west corner of the enclosure - where only the earlier ditches 666 and 570 were seen. The ditch became deeper as it approached the vicinity of structure R, with the upper deposits containing higher amounts of charcoal and iron slag (Fig. 3.43, section 332, cut 1432). At the point where it formed the south-west boundary of structure R, it was 3 m wide and 1 m deep, with splayed upper edges becoming steeper with a sharp change of angle to a flat base (Fig. 3.43, section 308, cut 1445). The ditch within this area appeared to have been cut into an area of existing pits which explained why its south-western edge was wide and shallow. This part of 1760 was also backfilled with furnace debris to the extent that ditch 1230 was cut into the top to facilitate drainage, as obviously the debris was effectively damming 1760 at this point. The rest of the ditch was generally filled with a primary grey-brown silt clay, overlain by a series of dark grey clay silts, which contained moderate to high amounts of furnace debris in the vicinity of structure R. The uppermost deposit produced a fragment of lava quern (SF243; see Roe, Chapter 5, Cat. no. 14).

Ditch 1220 was the SW-NE aligned continuation of ditch 1760. It extended north-eastwards beyond the limit of excavation, although the geophysical survey suggests that it did not run much further. The ditch had the same profile as 1760, with a depth between 0.7 m and 1.1 m and a surface width between 2.5 m and 3 m. The deposits within the ditch were all silt clays containing large quantities of fired clay and iron slag (Fig. 3.43 section 293, cut 1342; section 325).

Metalworking installations

Structure R (Figs 3.44-3.45 and Plate 3.5)

Structure R at the south-east corner of the ditched enclosure (above) was a structure with at least six posts bounded to the north-west by gully 1200, to the south-west by gully 1230 and to the south-east by ditch 1220. As excavated, the post structure measured 5.5 m x at least 6 m internally, though it will have been longer as its north-eastern limit lay beyond the area of investigation. (See Paynter, Chapter 7 for a more detailed description of the building in relation to its metalworking function.)

Gully 1200 extended NE-SW for 10.5 m and terminated to the south-west at the junction with gully 1230. It was on average 0.6 m wide and 0.25 m deep, with a rounded profile, and was filled by two silt clays, both rich in wood charcoal (oak) and iron slag (Fig. 3.44, sections 262 and 266). Cutting into the top of gully 1200 was pit 1233. This was oval measuring 1 m across and 0.3 m deep, with sloping sides and a flat base. The pit was filled with a primary dark grey clay silt which contained a high proportion of charcoal, overlain by a dark grey clay silt which contained less charcoal, but large amounts of iron slag and ceramic building material (Fig. 3.44, section 269).

Gully 1230 succeeded ditch 1760 as the south-western boundary of structure R. It extended for 7.5 m, but lacked clearly defined termini or stratigraphic relationships with the ditches at either end. It had a maximum width of 1.0 m, and a depth of 0.2 m, with a rounded shallow profile, and was filled with grey silting deposits along its length (Fig. 3.43, section 308, cut 1339). The apparent absence of clear terminals at either end is most likely because the gully was cut through the furnace debris which had been dumped into that area of ditch 1760. The remainder of 1760, away from the immediate vicinity of structure R, was not backfilled to this extent and was still functioning, draining water from the north-west towards structure R. Gully 1230 may therefore have been cut into otherwise open ditches 1760 and 1220 to facilitate continued drainage.

The postholes of structure R formed two NE-SW aligned rows, 5.5 m apart, with the centres of the postholes 2-2.5 m distant from each other. Their profiles were generally steep-sided, tapering to a pointed base, but in two instances the base was flat. The postholes ranged from 0.7-0.85 m in diameter and 0.35-0.7 m in depth, with the majority filled with a single deposit of dark grey clay silt, containing notable amounts of wood charcoal, iron slag and fired clay. One of the postholes had a post-pipe 0.32 m in diameter which consisted of a dark brown clay silt with infrequent charcoal and small pieces of iron slag, surrounded by a yellow-brown silt clay packing fill. In no other case was there evidence for the post rotting *in situ*; the posts were presumably removed and the remaining voids rapidly in-filled (Fig. 3.44, sections 311-313, 349, 329, 326, 323, 338).

A number of internal features were noted in the central and north-east parts of structure R. At the north-east end adjacent to the site baulk was a group of possible smithing hearths 1526, 1530 and 1531 (Fig. 3.45, section 331). Hearth 1526 was rectangular in shape with steeply sloping sides and a flat base, measuring 0.7 m by 0.44 m by 0.18 m. It was filled with a dark grey clay silt, rich in charcoal and occasional iron slag lumps. Feature 1531 also had steep sides, and a flat base. It measured 1.2 m x 0.4 m x 0.2 m and was filled with four dark grey silt clay deposits, all rich in charred remains. Hearth 1530 was earlier than 1531 and 1526 and only its south-eastern edge survived. It was filled with a single deposit of dark grey clay silt which was also rich in charcoal. All these features extended beyond the edge of excavation so their full extent is not known.

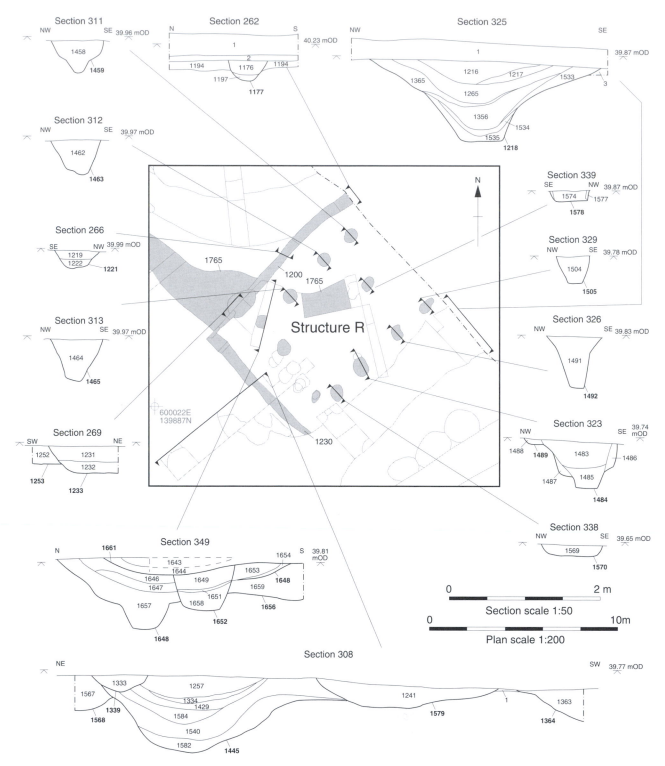

Figure 3.44   Plan of Structure R with sections of ditch 1220, and gully 1230: Ditch 1220: section 325 (cut 1218); section 262 (cut 1177), section 266 (cut 1221); gully 1230: section 308 (cut 1339); pit 1661: section 349.

An occupation spread (1585) was uncovered in the central part of the structure, surviving partly within a slight depression caused by an underlying earlier ditch. It comprised a charcoal-rich clay silt, which contained a very high proportion of hammerscale (Fig. 3.42, section 347). The deposit measured 5.8 m by 3.5 m and its relatively straight south-westerly edge in line with postholes 1465 and 1484 indicates the position of the end of the building. The distribution of hammerscale was established by sampling on a 0.5 m grid. A probable smithing hearth 1578, measuring 0.7 m by 0.5 m, was observed within 1585

Plate 3.5   View of Structure R before excavation.

(Fig. 3.44, section 339). Close by was a sub-rectangular it 1636, which measured 0.9 m by 0.9 m by 0.25 m deep. It had steep sides and a flat base and was cut into the top of earlier ditch 1765 (Fig. 3.42, section 347, cut 1634). The pit contained a near complete storage jar, 1546, which was found in an upright position and was filled with a dark brown clay silt with fragments of charcoal and slag throughout.

A shallow pit (1661), which not only cut the fill of ditch 1765 but also 1652 one of the posts from structure R, was for that reason assigned to Phase 6. The feature was 1.7 m by 1.3 m by 0.23 m deep with sloping sides and a slightly rounded base. It was filled by a dark grey charcoal rich clay silt, and sealed by a brown clay silt containing charcoal, slag and fired clay (Fig. 3.44, section 349). This was the only feature dated to Phase 6 in this area of the site. Together the component features of the structure - the surrounding gullies, the postholes and pit 1636 - produced a small quantity of pottery of 3rd-century date (see Chapter 6, Assemblage 36).

A NW-SE row of four groups of hearths/furnaces aligned on the long axis of the building was located south-west of the post structure, but inside gully 1230 (Fig. 3.45; Plate 3.6). From the north-west these consisted of intercutting furnaces 1455, 1451 and 1449 (Fig. 3.45, section 310), 1443 and 1438 (Fig. 3.45, section 309), 1428 and 1425 (Fig. 3.45, section 306), and single hearth 1383 (Fig. 3.45, section 298).

Furnace 1455 was sub-rectangular, measuring 0.6 m by 0.5 m by 0.15 m. The sides were steep at 70° and the base flat. A primary deposit of scorched natural clay was overlain by a fired clay lining. This in turn was sealed by a dark brown silt clay containing charcoal and slag. The feature was cut on its north-east edge by 1451, which was 0.55 m in diameter, 0.1 m deep and was filled with a dark red clay silt possibly representing *in situ* burning. This was cut in turn on its north-east edge by furnace 1449. This was sub-rectangular measuring 0.8 m by 0.6 m by 0.11 m deep, with steep sides and a flat base. It was filled with a single deposit of charcoal-rich clay silt (Fig. 3.45, section 310).

Furnace 1443 was sub-rectangular, measuring 0.7 m by 0.5 m by 0.24 m deep, with near vertical sides and a flat base. Its base was fire reddened, indicating *in situ* burning, and was overlain by a grey clay silt. This was covered by a layer of fired clay which extended up the sides of the feature, and in turn sealed by a grey clay silt containing charcoal and lumps of fired clay. This was cut by furnace 1438 which was oval shaped and measured 0.9 m by 0.8 m by 0.25 m deep. The sides dropped steeply at 70° to a flat base, and it was filled with a single deposit of black clay silt containing 20% wood charcoal and iron slag (Fig. 3.45, section 309).

Furnace 1425 was oval shaped and measured 0.6 m x 0.4 m x 0.15 m deep, with steep sides and a flat base.

A fire reddened clay lining the base was overlain by a yellow-brown silt clay containing occasional charcoal flecks and slag. This was cut by 1428 which was circular with a diameter of 0.65 m and a depth of 0.18 m. The sides fell steeply to a rounded base. The primary deposit was a dark red silt clay probably representing *in situ* burning, overlain by a grey-brown silt clay which contained a low density of wood charcoal (Fig. 3.45, section 306).

Hearth 1383 measured 0.6 m x 0.4 m x 0.05 m deep, with sides sloping at 60° and a concave base. The natural clay edges were fire reddened, and the remainder of the feature was filled with a dark grey clay silt with occasional charcoal and slag (Fig. 3.45, section 298).

The debris from all of the above features appears to have been dumped directly to the south west, lo-cally filling part of ditch 1760. Debris was dumped in surrounding ditches 1220 and 1200 in lesser concentrations.

Other features to the south-east

Circular features to the south-west and south-east of structure R were interpreted as clay extraction pits for the construction of the furnaces of the metalworking area (Fig. 3.17). A number of pits, immediately south-west of boundary ditch 1760, were between 0.6 and 2.4 m diameter and on average 0.6 m in depth, with moderate to steep sides and flat bases. All were filled with a single deposit of orange-grey silt clay with a large amount of manganese throughout. Further north-west was another series of pits along the edge of ditch 1760 which were similar in profile and

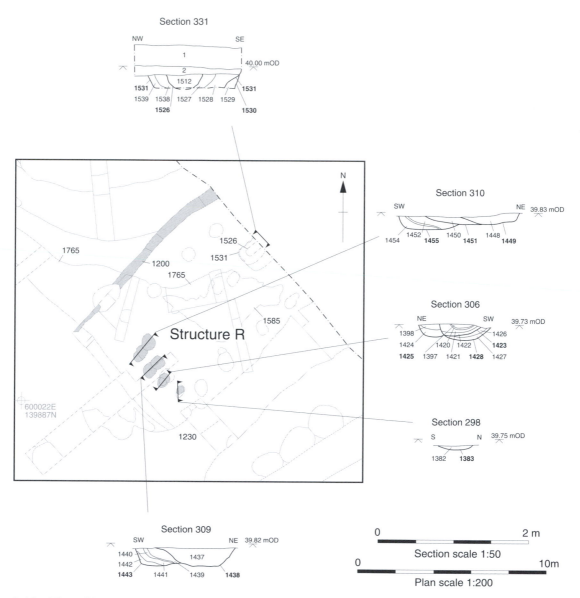

Figure 3.45 Plan of Structure R with sections of internal features including furnaces and hearths: Furnaces 1455, 1451, 1449: section 310; Furnaces 1443, 1438: section 309; Furnaces 1425, 1428: section 306; Furnace 1383: section 298; Hearths 1526, 1531 and 1530: section 331.

Plate 3.6   Furnaces after excavation.

dimension to the above mentioned pits. These pits were also inter-cutting and filled with a single sterile silt clay deposit.

A series of oval pits in the extreme east corner of the excavation area, with surface diameters ranging from 0.8-1.5 m, were not excavated. Their fills resembled those of the excavated pits, consisting of an orange-grey silt clay with no visible inclusions other than large amounts of manganese.

Cremation burials (Fig. 3.41)

Three cremation burials were located north east of the ditch sequences within the north-east enclosure area. Grave 1261 was the most north-westerly of the three, while groups 210 and 220 were situated approximately 12 m north-west of structure R. Grave 1261, dated to the late Iron Age up to AD 50 has been described above. The three burials are itemised in full in Chapter 8; the evidence is only summarised here.

Cremation burial 210 (Figs 3.41 and 8.21), dated AD 170-200, was in a sub-oval grave which cut the north-east edge of enclosure ditch 1755. The pit was near vertical sided with a slightly uneven base. Some 386 g of cremated bone from an adult female lay partly within a truncated cremation urn (205) and partly distributed across the fill of the grave and over some of the ancillary vessels, presumably, but not certainly, as a result of post-Roman disturbance.

The cremation urn was accompanied by six further pottery vessels set out in a way that suggested that they had been placed in a wooden box. The ancillary vessels consisted of samian ware forms 33 and 31 and four coarse ware vessels - two beakers and two bowls. The majority of the vessels had suffered from post-Roman ploughing. None ceramic finds - copper alloy needle (SF32; see Cool, Chapter 5, Cat. no. 34; Fig. 5.4) and a group of 27 hobnails (see Scott, Chapter 5, Table 5.22) - were found at the base of the pit.

Cremation grave 220 (Figs 3.41 and 8.22; Plate 3.7), contained pottery dated AD 200-250, but was probably closely comparable in date to burial 210. The pit was rectangular in shape with near vertical sides and a flat base. Some 1364 g of cremated bone from a young adult female were placed in a cremation urn accompanied by a further nine pottery vessels, seven of them samian (two form 33 cups and five form 31 bowls), the other vessels being an Upchurch beaker and a BB2 platter. The rectangular grave cut and the very formal rectangular layout of the grave group again suggested that this was a box burial. This was further substantiated by the recovery of three iron nails (SF29-31) along the north-west edge of the pit. A box roughly 0.60 m square would have accommodated the finds as they were recovered. All the pottery vessels were found in an upright position, with only the cremation urn 218 showing significant plough damage. A shallow samian bowl (221) to the south of the cremation urn was placed on top of 74 hobnails (SF34), indicating that as in burial 210 a pair of shoes had been placed in the bottom of the grave, in this case towards the eastern corner (see Chapter 8).

Shrine Area (Figs 3.10, 3.41, 3.46-3.49)

To the south-west of the north-east enclosure lay an open area containing a polygonal shrine within a rectangular enclosure. The area was defined on its north-east side by the successive ditches of the North-east enclosure. On its north-west it was defined by the main road through the settlement, although there was no identifiable linear feature other than the road on this side of the area until relatively late in the roadside sequence when gully 43/595 was cut. The open area was defined on its south-west side by the evolving sequence of linear features defining the southern settlement area (see below) and linked to the sequence of ditches alongside the main Canterbury road. The south-east limit of the open area appears not to be defined, and the geophysical survey showed no indication of a boundary beyond the edge of Area B in this direction.

The open area was irregular in shape and was gradually eroded by the encroachment of boundaries on the southern side, but even at a late stage in this process it occupied a frontage of *c* 100 m on the south-east side of the Canterbury road, while the width of the area south-east of the shrine enclosure, between the south trackway and structure R, was c 70 m.

The main features within the open area were the shrine and its rectangular enclosure already noted and large waterhole 9179, but there was also a group of pits and possible postholes.

Pits (Fig. 3.17 and 3.41)

The pits and possible postholes were located immediately to the south-west of the ditched enclosure (see above) and formed an approximately linear arrangement extending SW from the enclosure ditches. These features exhibited some signs of intercutting and so were not all contemporary, but the relatively regular nature of their alignment suggested that they were broadly contemporaneous. The pottery evidence, albeit limited, and the stratigraphic relationships with ditch group 570, suggest a Phase 5 date.

Rectilinear shrine enclosure (Fig. 3.46, Plates 3.8-3.9)

The rectilinear enclosure was defined by a slight ditch (group 70) and assigned to Phase 3. It was located towards the northern side of the open area (Plate 3.8).

Plate 3.7   Cremation group 220.

Ditch group 70 enclosed an area 27 m NNE-SSW by 31 m maximum WNW-ESE, forming an almost exact rectangle, with an entrance 4.8 m wide facing southeast (Fig. 3.46; Plate 3.9). The average dimensions of the ditch were 0.65 m wide and 0.25 m deep, although at the eastern corner it broadened to 1.2 m wide and

0.5 m deep (Fig. 3.46, sections 112 and 116). The profile varied slightly along its length from moderately sloping sides and rounded base to V-shaped with a flat base. The ditch was filled with a characteristic dark grey homogeneous silt containing sub-angular flint and small sub-rounded stone. A *denarius* of AD

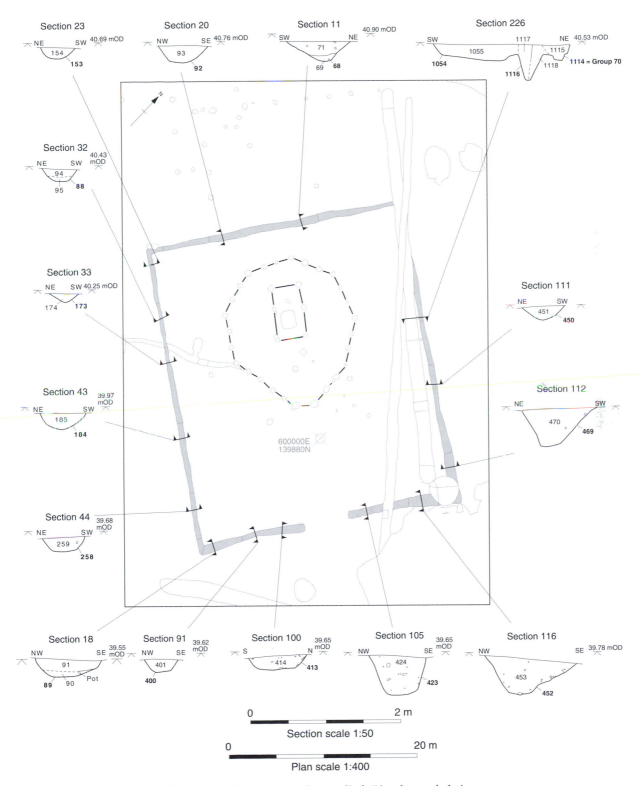

Figure 3.46   Shrine: Plan with sections of primary enclosure ditch 70 polygonal shrine.

Plate 3.8   *Shrine enclosure ditch during excavation and view of site beyond.*

Plate 3.9   *View of shrine enclosure from south-east.*

91 (SF21, see Guest, Chapter 5, Table 5.5) retrieved from the fill (context 185, Fig. 3.46, section 43) at the south-west side of the enclosure. At two points along the north-west (Fig. 3.46, section 11) and south-west sides (Fig. 3.46, section 32) this layer was overlain by another deposit of dark grey silt. A notable amount of wood charcoal with fragments averaging 0.03 m x 0.03 m was noted within the base of the ditch along the north-west side, and excavated sections either side revealed a number of stakeholes and postholes. A series of five stakeholes was seen cutting through the primary fill and into the base of the ditch 17 m from the west corner. All the stakeholes were circular, having an average diameter of 0.10 m and a depth of 0.12 m, with almost vertical sides tapering to a rounded point. The two postholes located on the outer edge of the west corner had steep sides and flat bases and both were roughly 0.6 m in diameter and 0.3 m deep. All of these features were filled with the upper dark grey silting fill suggesting that they were broadly contemporary with the enclosure ditch fills. The latter produced a small group of pottery, none of which need be later than the end of the 1st century AD (see Chapter 6, Assemblage 12).

Ditch 970 and posthole group 1070 *(Fig. 3.47)*

A second phase of boundary, in the form of Phase 4 ditch 970, was created on the north-east side of the shrine enclosure (Fig. 3.47). This ditch terminated at its south-east end by pit 529 located at the original east corner of the primary Phase 3 enclosure. It extended to a terminal 13 m north-west of the north corner of the Phase 3 enclosure ditch. From this point a posthole alignment, group 1070, extended south-westwards at a right angle to ditch 970 for a distance of at least 20 m, perhaps supporting a fence which separated the temple area from the road to the north-west.

Ditch 970 had an average width and depth of 1.4 m and 0.2 m and had shallow sloping sides and a flat base. It was filled with a single deposit of light grey silt which contained occasional sub-angular flints. Pit 529 (Fig. 3.47, sections 167-68) was 2.2 m in diameter and 0.95 m deep with moderately sloping sides and a flat base. The primary and secondary fills comprised grey clays suggesting that the pit was open for some time and probably held water. Both deposits contained amounts of furnace debris and the lower fill produced three iron nails (SF117-119). Overlying these were two grey-brown silt clays containing large amounts of iron slag and fired clay and including two further iron nails (SF93, SF96) and a paddle-shaped iron object of uncertain function (SF92, see Scott, Chapter 5, Cat. no.7). The latest deposits in this sequence consisted of a dark brown silt with frequent small sub-rounded stone, overlain by a dark grey silt, which had accumulated in a shallow void within the centre of the pit. Group 1070 consisted of ten postholes which were on average 0.41 m in diameter and 0.15 m deep. Their profiles varied from shallow to moderate steep sided with a flat base, and they were

all filled with a homogeneous grey silt (Fig. 3.47, sections 260, 243 and 250).

Shrine structure *(Fig. 3.48, Plate 3.10)*

The evidence for the shrine consists entirely of settings for vertical posts, forming an outer wall line and internal features or structures.

Walls of the shrine

The shrine was a nine-sided structure set on the central NW-SE axis of the surrounding enclosure (Fig. 3.48). The perimeter of the structure was defined by 28 postholes, including two posts forming a south-east facing entrance (Plate 3.10). Each side of the structure (numbered 1 to 9 commencing from the right of the entrance as seen from the outside, with the entrance itself being side 9) was made up of four posts, including the end posts, which are shared with adjacent sides, except for that on the south-west side of the presumed entrance (side 8), which had six, and the narrow entrance itself. The lengths of the sides were quite consistent, being approximately 5.3 m, 5.1 m, 5.2 m, 5.8 m, 5.8 m, 5.2m, 5.2 m and 7.8 m. The south-east facing entrance posts were c 1.9 m apart. The extra length of the two sides (4 and 5) furthest from the entrance may have been deliberate, and overall the structure seems to have been carefully planned, though the extra length of side 8 is puzzling. It may be noted, however, that the length of this side is exactly one and a half times that of the typical side length of 5.2 m, so although it is anomalous the length may still have been of particular significance rather than resulting from an error in layout of the structure.

Posthole 192 on the south-west side of the entrance was sub-rectangular, measuring 1.2 m by 1.0 m by 0.5 m deep. The north-east entrance posthole (337) was oval and measured 0.9 m by 0.8 m by 0.46 m deep. Both had steep, near vertical sides and a flat base, filled with brown clay packing surrounding post pipes c 0.2-0.3 m across. These had dark grey silt clay within the base, incorporating the remains of the rotted post, overlain by mid brown silt which had accumulated within the post void. The average dimensions of the remaining posts were 0.49 m diameter and 0.16 m depth, with the corner posts in some cases being slightly wider, between 0.38 m and 0.6 m, but not notably deeper than the others. The post at the corner of sides 1 and 2 was the only one to show the remains of a post pipe; all the others were filled with a consistent single mid brown silt. The majority of the postholes had steep sides and a flat base, but occasionally this changed to a more V-shaped profile with a tapered base.

Features within the shrine

There were 11 internal postholes plus a central post setting and a possible small pit (Fig. 3.49). Six postholes (146, 566, 148, 141, 631 and 571, of which the two last were probably replaced by 633 and 568 respectively)

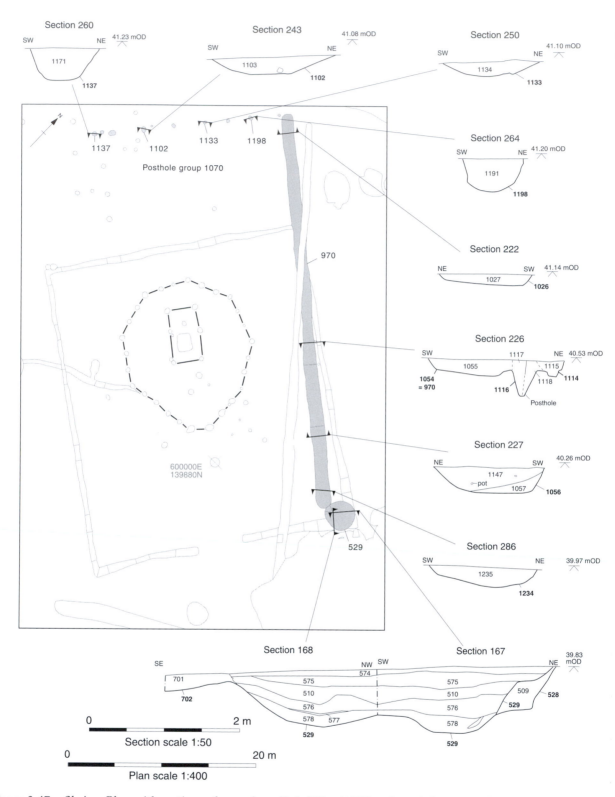

Figure 3.47   Shrine: Plan with sections of secondary ditch 970, pit 529 and posthole group 1070.

may have formed a rectangle measuring 5.5 m by 3 m which enclosed the central feature (415), with another posthole (131) 1 m north-west of 415. All these posts were filled with a single deposit of mid brown silt. The first six postholes generally had steep sides with a sharp break to a flat base, with average di-

mensions of 0.51 m diameter and 0.21 m depth. Finds from them included an iron nail (SF114) and a fragment of blue-green glass (SF9). The two re-cuts had similar profiles and were 0.28 m in diameter and 0.16 m deep (633) and 0.5 m in diameter and 0.2 m deep (568).

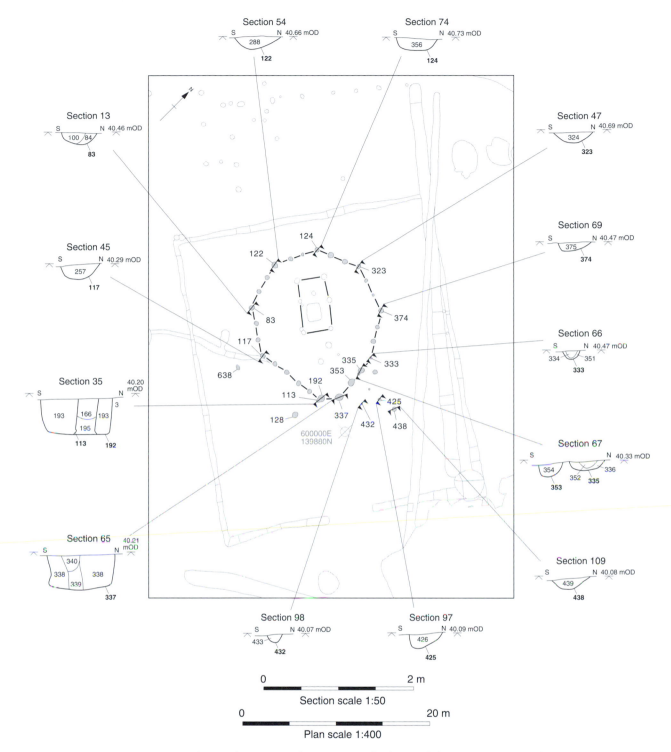

Figure 3.48   Shrine structure: Plan with sections of outer posts of polygonal shrine and external features.

The remaining internal postholes (204 and 443) were located east of the rectangular arrangement of postholes. Both were circular with depths of 0.1 m and 0.15 m and were filled with a single deposit of mid brown silt. Neither post seemed to form an obvious part of the post structure. North-west of these postholes was a possible pit 421. This had a rounded base and sides and was 0.69 m in diameter and 0.23 m deep. A single deposit of dark grey silt containing small sub-rounded stones filled the whole of the pit, which was positioned near the 'front' of the rectangular arrangement of postholes.

The central feature was a rectangular pit (415), measuring 1.97 m by 1.47 m by 0.85 m deep (Fig. 3.49, sections 103-104). The sides were all nearly vertical apart from the north-west edge which sloped at 70°;

the base was flat. The primary deposit (461) was a sub-rectangular patch of compact dark grey silt clay, roughly 0.6 by 0.6 m, which produced three iron objects (SF81-83; see Scott, Chapter 5, Table 5.27) and a 1st- to 2nd-century coin (SF80; see Guest, Chapter 5, Table 5.5). The deposit is thought to represent *in situ* decay of a post or other wooden feature, rather than silting after the removal of such an item. A dark yellow silt clay (416), surrounding the primary deposit, contained occasional sub-angular flint and represented the packing around the central post. This produced a single iron nail (SF84) and two 1st-2nd century coins, one illegible (SF91) and one of Hadrian (SF95) (see Guest, Chapter 5, Table 5.5), the latter discovered at the very base of the deposit. Fill 416 also produced a charred fragment of *Pinus pinea* (stone pine) nut shell (see Pelling, Chapter 9). The latest deposit, 417, was a dark grey-brown clay silt which contained small sub-rounded stone and occasional sub-angular flint. This produced five iron nails (SF75-78 and SF90), a possible iron hinge strap (SF88; see Scott, Chapter 5, Cat. no. 13), another 1st-2nd century coin (SF89; see Guest, Chapter 5, Table 5.5) and a 4th century glass fragment (SF281; see Cool, Chapter 5, Cat. no. 53; Fig. 5.5). This upper deposit represented the backfill of the void formed by the removal of the central post, an event dated after *c* AD 350 by associated pottery (see Chapter 6, Assemblage 41), making 417 the

only context in Area B certainly attributed Phase 7 of Period 2.

Other features within the rectilinear enclosure

A number of postholes lay within the rectilinear enclosure, but outside the polygonal structure. Five of them formed a small group situated north-east of the entrance to the shrine. These ranged from 0.16-0.48 m in diameter and from 0.1-0.25 m in depth and each was filled with a single deposit of dark grey silt. They were notably smaller than the postholes associated with the temple structure and did not form any discernible structure of their own. Another two features to the south of the polygonal structure appeared to be shallow pits rather than isolated postholes as their profiles had very shallow sloping sides unlike the near vertical sides of the postholes. Pit 128, located south of the entrance, was sub-circular with a shallow bowl-shaped profile 0.55 m in diameter and 0.08 m deep, filled by a single deposit of dark grey silt. Pit 638, outside the south-western side of the shrine, was 0.6 m in diameter and 0.1 m deep. This was oval in shape with shallow sides and a flat base, filled with a charcoal rich clay silt, and overlain by a mid brown clay silt which contained a significant amount of charcoal.

The date of these features is uncertain in many cases, owing to a paucity of dating material. Many

Plate 3.10   *View of shrine structure from east.*

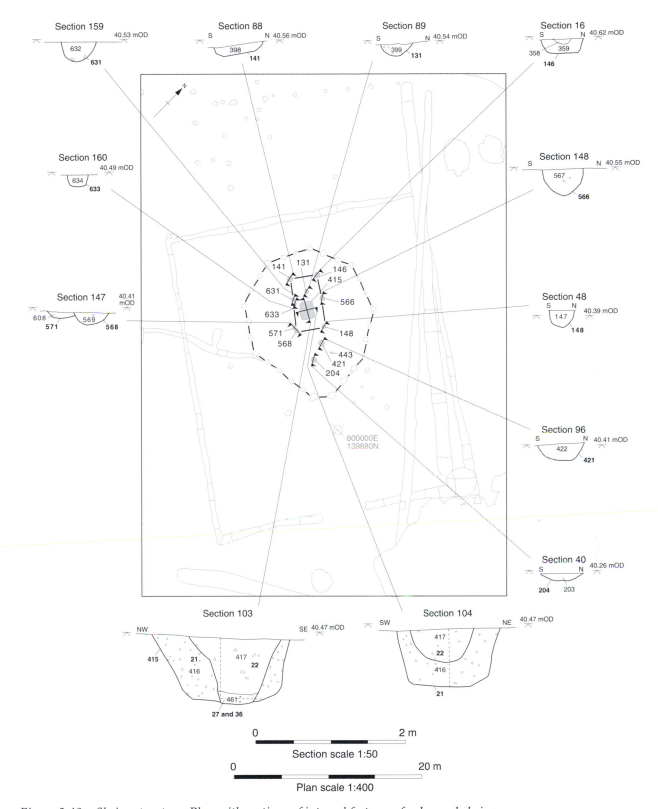

Figure 3.49   Shrine structure: Plan with sections of internal features of polygonal shrine.

individual features were not dated except by association with the shrine complex. The inception of the shrine is assigned to Phase 3 and the remodelling of the north-eastern enclosure boundary to Phase 4. It is assumed that the rest of the (Phase 3) enclosure group

70 fell out of use at this time. The date range of the internal posthole structures is much less certain. The only fixed point is provided by the removal of the central post, an event assigned (uniquely) to Phase 7. It is possible, but unlikely given the total absence of

evidence, that the remainder of the shrine remained in use as late as this. For present purposes it has been assumed that the bulk of the structure did not outlast the majority of adjacent settlement components and the relevant features have been assigned to Phases 3-5 (see below).

Waterhole 9179 *(Fig. 3.50; Plates 3.11-3.13; Table 3.3)*

Waterhole 9179 lay approximately 25 m south-west of the shrine structure and comprised a vertical sided circular shaft, with an approximate diameter of 8 m in the upper parts and a depth of *c* 3.80 m. At the surface it broadened out to a shallow irregular ovoid shaped depression, which measured 17.50 m x 13 m with a depth of 0.30 m. Due to its size, this feature was largely excavated by machine, and deposits below its base, which were not readily distinguished from the lower fills, were investigated using an auger to a depth of 6.30 m at 33.52 m above OD (Plates 3.11 and 3.12).

The lowest fills encountered with the auger above the Wealden Clay - layers 10159, 10158, 10119, 10118 - were all very clean and characteristically showed no evidence of organic remains Table 3.3).

Layer 9421, above 10118, and the layers up and including to layer 9413 were machine excavated. (Finds from machine-excavated contexts (9421 to 9413) were grouped together as finds reference number 9422.) Above layer 9421 were successively layers 9420, 9419 and 9418. None of these layers produced dateable finds. Layer 9417 was the lowest deposit in the sequence to produce finds. These comprise pottery dated to AD 100-150, and a timber plank (10079) 3.80 m long, 0.07 m wide and 0.03 m thick, lying horizontally and aligned NE-SW.

Overlying 9417 was 9416, a deposit consisting of a series of thin clay lenses of varying blue, grey and yellow colours. Layer 9415 was next layer in the sequence. Above 9415 was layer 9414, which produced two further timber planks, 9991 and 9992, both horizontal. The former was 1.60 m long, 0.23 m wide and 0.10 m thick and lay NW-SE in the base of deposit 9414, overlying 9992 at its north-east end. The latter was 0.90 m long, 0.43 m wide and 0.03 m thick and lay NNW-SSE. These timbers were not *in situ*, but possibly represented part of a collapsed structure - a lining? - associated with the waterhole.

Above 9414 was a dark grey clay deposit 9413, which produced pottery dated to AD 150-200+ as well as further timber planks (9958 and 9959), which again were lying horizontally (Plate 3.13). Timber 9958 was 1.30 m long, 0.27 m width and 0.05 m thick and lay ENE-WSW, while 9959 was 1.30 m long, 0.13 m wide and 0.06 m thick and aligned north-south. One end of this timber appeared to have been fashioned into a point. Again these timbers were not *in situ*, but are likely to have been structural in some way.

As noted above, context 9422 was the combined finds reference for the machine excavated deposits. Included amongst the finds with context number was a large piece of unworked oak found in an upright position against the south-west edge of the feature. It is possible that it had been placed deliberately within the waterhole, but it may simply have derived naturally from a tree in the immediate vicinity. The timber formed part of the trunk of a small, slow grown mature oak (c 0.3 m diameter with a mean of 313 rings), but unfortunately the dendrochronological sequence could not be matched (D Miles pers. comm., report in archive) and perhaps would not have been useful

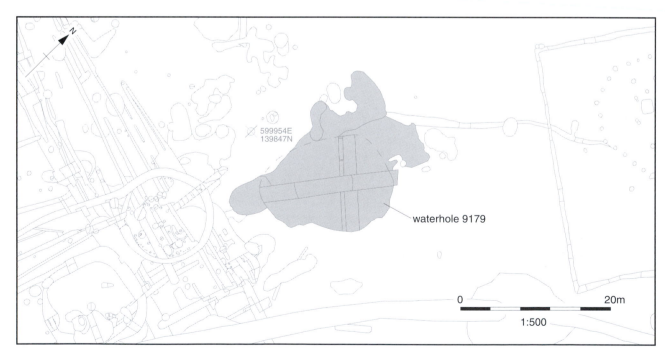

Figure 3.50   Plan of waterhole 9179.

Plate 3.11   Upper portion of waterhole 9179.

Plate 3.12   Waterhole 9179 after machine excavation.

Table 3.3   Waterhole 9179: Summary of contexts, finds and dating evidence, from the earliest (10159) to the latest fill (7128)

Context	Description	Depth	Method	Finds
10159	light grey clay	0.15 m	auger	
10158	tenacious dark grey clay with white flecking	0.45 m	auger	
10119	pale grey silt clay	0.25 m	auger	
10118	dark grey clay	0.35 m	auger	
9421	compact dark grey clay	0.18 m	machine dug	
9420	blue clay with orange flecking	0.20 m	machine dug	
9419	dark blue clay with white flecks	0.15 m	machine dug	
9418	blue yellow clay	0.65 m	machine dug	
9417	blue yellow clay	0.58 m	machine dug	pottery 100-150; wood plank (10079)
9416	series of clay lenses or blue, grey and yellow	0.35 m	machine dug	
9415	dark brown clay silt	0.15 m	machine dug	
9414	dark blue clay		machine dug	2 x wood planks (9991-9992)
9413	dark grey clay	0.26 m	machine dug	pottery AD 150-200+; wood planks (9958-9959)
9422	finds from contexts 9421 to 9413		machine dug	unworked oak; quernstone fragment (SF1518)
9188	blue grey clay	0.20 m	hand	
9187	light grey silt clay occasional sub rounded stones	0.26 m	hand	
9185	light grey silt clay	0.40 m	hand	
7258	compact orange brown clay	0.10 m	hand	glass bottle sherd (SF976)
9186	light grey clay	0.30 m	hand	
7129	grey blue clay silt	0.40 m	hand	pottery AD 150-200; wood fragments
9184	light grey clay silt		hand	
7128	compact grey clay silt with ironpanning		hand	2 x coins 'early Roman' (SF931-932); quern fragment; cu alloy bead (SF939)

Waterhole 9179 produced Pottery Assemblage 37, mid to late 2nd century

Plate 3.13   Timbers 9958 and 9959 from waterhole 9179.

(9186). Above this was layer 7129, which produced pottery dated AD 150-200 as well as a number of wood fragments. Layer 9184 comprised a light grey silt clay, which had accumulated within the centre of the waterhole. The uppermost deposit, silting layer 7128, filled the wide (*c* 17.50 m x 13 m), shallow, hollow overlying the main waterhole fill sequence. It consisted of a compact grey clay silt with a high quantity of iron panning. Two coins, a quern fragment and a rare copper alloy bead (SF939) were recovered in the course of a metal-detector examination of the upper part of this deposit. The coins, SF931 and SF932, were both heavily corroded and only dated broadly to the early Roman period. The finds reference contexts assigned to these objects (7088, 7087 and 7081 respectively) all form part of fill 7128.

The total quantity of pottery recovered from the waterhole was very small, but indicated a late 2nd- to early 3rd-century *terminus post quem* for the upper fills of the feature (see Chapter 6, Assemblage 37).

Southern Settlement Area

To the south side of the open area containing the Shrine and waterhole 9179, was a series of plots and enclosures, the northern margins of which were generally defined by ditches and gullies originally linked in some way to the south-east roadside ditch/gully sequence. These plots and enclosures were for the most part less well-defined than those on the north side of the Canterbury road, although for the most part they were approximately rectilinear and contained a variety of structures and other features. For ease of reference the plots/enclosures have been allocated numbers in a 'south-central' series (SC1-SC6 from west to east) in the same way as the roadside plots, but because the definition of individual units was not always so clear these labels have more value in some phases than in others. The general developmental sequence in this part of the site saw a northward movement of the northern boundary of the area and, to a lesser extent, a west to east sequence of establishment of enclosures. The north-south trackway which entered the shrine open area seems to have been a component of this arrangement from an early stage, however.

It should be noted that a particularly high concentration of discrete features, particularly small pits and/or postholes, was encountered in this part of the site. It was not possible to examine all of these, and many that were excavated were not well-dated. It is likely that rather more posthole structures than those described below originally existed here.

Plot SC1 (Figs 3.4, 3.10, 3.14, 3.17 and 3.51)

Phase 2 (Fig. 3.4)

The earliest stage of development in this area was marked by the curvilinear ditch 8620 which was a continuation of the primary south-east roadside ditch. This feature curved first to the south-east and then doubled back to the south-west, eventually fading out about 150 m south of the contemporary edge of the shrine area. The definition of its south-west end was unclear, however, and the ditch may originally have extended further in that direction. Although ditch 8620 partly enclosed the position of a circular structure (Structure K) this was dated to the following Phase 3 (plot SC1). No features assigned to Phase 2 were identified within the area 'enclosed' by the ditch.

Phase 3 (Fig. 3.10)

The curvilinear Phase 2 ditch 8620 and the associated primary south-east roadside ditch were superseded by roadside ditch 8670 which turned at an angle of *c* 60° to form part of the southern boundary of the shrine area in this phase. The ditch effectively provided a more rectilinear arrangement of the 'front' of plot SC1, with a gap probably at least 2 m wide some 14 m from the north-west corner perhaps forming an entrance. A rear boundary or boundaries of the plot may have been formed by parallel ditches 9090 and 9100. These were aligned roughly NW-SE and extended for *c* 40 m from the vicinity of (but without having a direct relationship with) the south-east roadside ditch. At their south-east ends they terminated short of Phase 2 ditch 8620, with the implication that they may have respected the surviving alignment of this feature. Ditches 9090 and 9100 were up to 1.05 m wide and 0.52 m deep (Fig. 3.51, section 879, cut 9100). Their profiles varied throughout their length from rounded to straight-sided with a flat base, but the fills were a consistent grey clay silt which produced a fragment of lava quern (SF1340) from ditch 9100. The ditches were also consistently parallel, on average 5 m apart, and may have formed some sort of trackway access to the rear of the south-centre block of plots.

Structure K, part of plot SC1 (Phase 3), was represented by the remnants of a curvilinear drainage gully (9990) extending for approximately 9.5 m (Fig. 3.51). The gully was on average 0.60 m wide and 0.20 m deep, with a projected diameter of *c* 15 m if originally circular or penannular. The profile of the gully was steep sided and flat based, and throughout its length was filled with a single grey silting deposit containing early-mid 2nd century pottery (see Chapter 6, Assemblage 14). The only feature remaining which was possibly associated with a structure was posthole 7511 situated just east of and inside the identified south end of the gully. This was circular with steep sides and a flat base, measured 0.72 m diameter and 0.24 m deep and was filled with a brown grey silt clay containing charcoal flecking.

A group of three pits lay just west of the south end of the gully. These were not excavated, but surface finds suggested that they were probably contemporary with structure K. Four postholes immediately west of these features may have formed part of a structure or a fence some 7.5 m long. These features were undated, however, and their relationship to structure K is unknown.

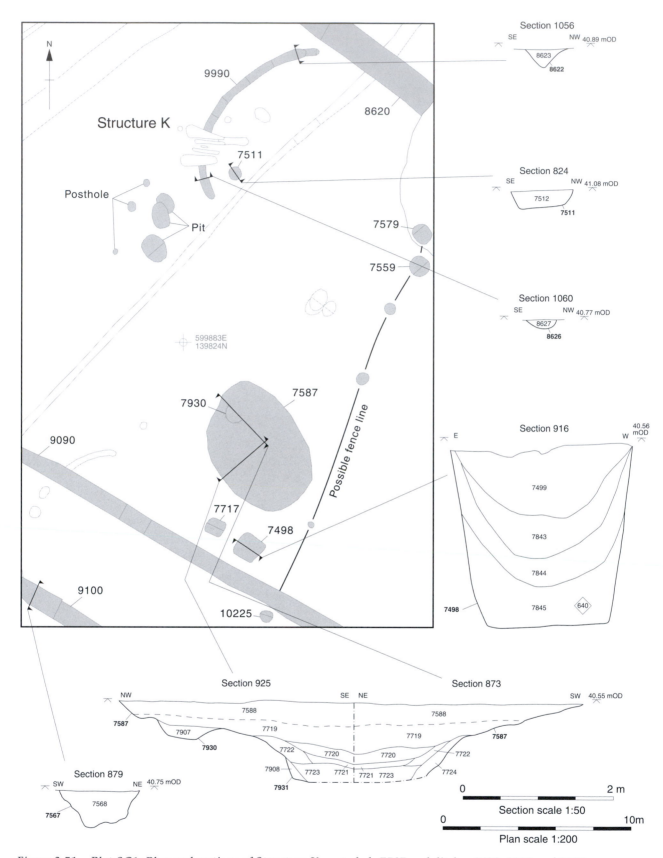

Figure 3.51   Plot SC1: Plan and sections of Structure K, waterhole 7587 and ditches 8620, 9090 and 9100.

Waterhole 7587 was south of structure K; it was *c* 6.5 m x 4.5 m in plan and excavated to a depth of 1.1 m (Fig. 3.51, sections 873/925). The two lowest excavated deposits comprised orange-grey silt clays, both encountered at the level of the current water table. The earlier fill represented erosion and slippage of the edges while the latter appeared to have accumulated slowly within the centre of the feature. Overlying these was a compact orange silt, and an orange-grey silt clay, which contained a small amount of charred, remains. Sealing these lower deposits were three distinct grey clay silt layers, which all contained notable amounts of charred remains, fragments of ceramic building material and (unusually) some animal bone. The uppermost silt extended across the top of the waterhole and produced a yellow-green glass fragment from the base of a jar or jug (SF1317; see Cool, Chapter 5, Cat. no. 50).

At the time this waterhole was dug, two small pits appear to have been deliberately cut into its edge, both on the north-west side. The first (7930) was cut into the top of the feature, while the other (7931) was located at the lowest excavated point. Both were sealed by the fills within the waterhole. Pit 7930 had a diameter of 0.5 m and a depth of 0.25 m and was filled with a single dump deposit consisting largely of broken pottery sherds in a matrix of orange-brown silt clay. Pit 7931, dug into the steeply-sloping side of the waterhole, was 0.35 m across and 0.3 m deep and was filled with orange-grey silt clay. This deposit (7908) held the remains of a near complete vessel, which may have represented a deliberate deposit. The waterhole and associated pits collectively produced a small early 2nd century pottery assemblage, though the pot in 7908 probably did not date much before the middle of the 2nd century (the end of Phase 3) at the earliest.

Phase 4 (Fig. 3.14)

The southern edge of the shrine area was defined in Phase 4 by a complex sequence of gullies, generally on a line advanced at least 5 m north of that in use in Phase 3. At the south-west corner of the shrine area the Canterbury road south-east ditch 8680 turned to the east, terminating after 28 m at the north-west corner of plot SC2.

There was no significant indication of activity in plot SC1 in this phase. Two square pits were located at the southern edge of Phase 3 waterhole 7587. Pit 7498 was 1.2 m across and excavated to the depth of the water table, at 1.2 m (Fig. 3.51, section 916). The lowest fill examined was a grey-brown silt clay containing small amounts of charred remains. This was overlain by a clean yellow silt clay, which appears to have eroded from the edge of the pit. Sealing these deposits were two fills of light grey clay silt which gradually accumulated into the top of the feature. An adjacent pit, 7717, 1.05 m across and 0.3 m deep, with vertical sides and a flat base, was filled with a single deposit of grey-brown clay silt which

produced four iron nails (SF1341-4), but no closely dateable pottery. A Phase 3 or later date is possible for this feature.

Phase 5 (Fig. 3.17)

Despite widespread redefinition of boundaries in this part of the site in this phase the main evidence of activity was confined to an apparently new enclosure (plot SE1) to the south-west of SC1 and to plots SC4 and SC5. In particular there were very few features of this phase in plots SC1-SC3.

A number of small pits and postholes, north-east of plot SE1 - both within the area of Plot SC1 and south of the Phase 3 gullies which originally defined it – mat be tentatively assigned to this phase. These averaged 0.2 m in diameter and 0.2 m deep with steep sides and flat bases and were are all filled with yellow-brown silt.

More certainly of this phase was a roughly NNE-SSW aligned row of six irregularly spaced postholes extending over some 28.5 m from 10225 at the south to 7579 at the north (Fig. 3.51). These, if truly associated with each other, may have formed a fenceline. The excavated examples were steep sided and flat based, on average 0.4 m in diameter and 0.2 m deep. They were filled with a single deposit of light grey clay silt and all produced Phase 5 pottery.

Plot SC2

Phase 2 (Figs 3.4, 3.52)

In Phase 2 SC2 was defined on its west side by ditch 8620 and on the east side by ditch 9270. Ditch 9270 together with ditch 9108 formed an enclosure defined to the west in part by 8620 and probably utilising ditch 9360 (which extended south-east from 8620 for at least 25 m) to form the northern boundary. In this form plot SC2 had overall dimensions of *c* 15 m by 35 m. Both 9270 and 9108 had moderately-sloping sides and a rounded base with an average width of 1.10 m and depth of 0.26 m. Both were filled with a single deposit of light grey silt. At the south-east corner of the enclosure, the probable junction of these ditches and cutting both of them, was a relatively shallow waterhole, group 10460, measuring 5 m by 6 m across, and excavated in quadrants to a depth of 1.10 m (Fig. 3.52, section 926). The eastern quadrant was filled with a series of grey-yellow silt clays which appear to have derived from the erosion of the feature's edge. The western quadrant, which was located within the enclosure, had higher concentrations of charred remains and more instances of dumped deposits, most likely indicating activity within the enclosed area. The lower excavated deposits comprised dark grey silt clays with sporadic concentrations of charred remains. These were overlain by three distinct layers of grey-orange silt clay which again showed high densities of charred remains. A dumped layer of silt clay containing ceramic building material

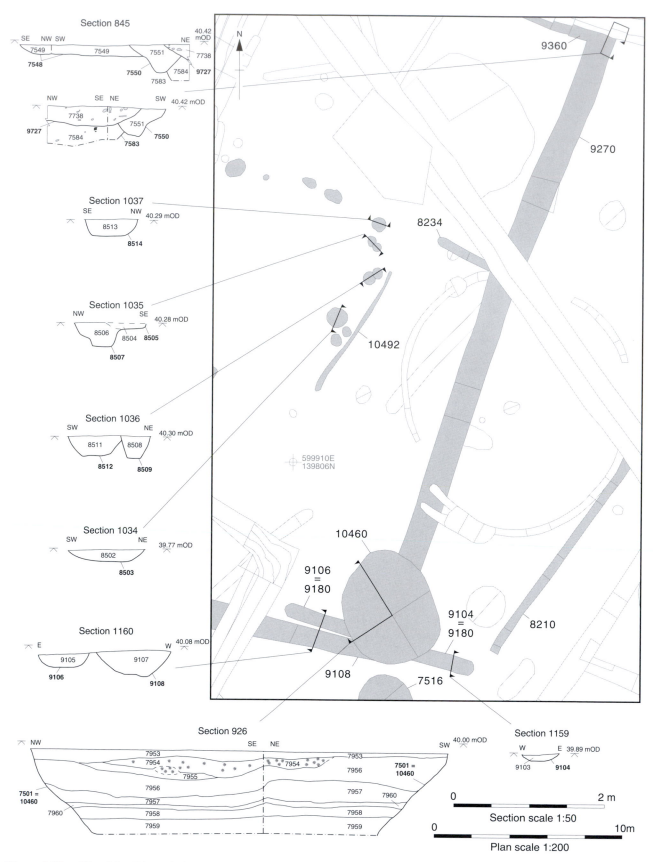

Section 845

Section 1037

Section 1035

Section 1036

Section 1034

Section 1160

Section 926

Section 1159

9360
9270
8234
10492
10460
9106 = 9180
9104 = 9180
8210
9108
7516
599910E
139806N

0   2 m
Section scale 1:50

0   10m
Plan scale 1:200

Figure 3.52   Plot SC2: Plan of Phase 2 and possible Phase 2 features, including enclosure ditch 9270 and waterhole 10460, with sections.

fragments overlay this, and extended 1.80 m from the north-west edge of the feature. This was overlain by another dumped deposit tipped from the north-west, that is, within the area defined by the enclosure. This consisted largely of charred plant remains in a very dark grey silt clay matrix. The uppermost deposit which extended across the top of the entire feature was a grey silt clay which contained relatively little charred material, but produced a group of pottery which may have been deposited no later than *c* AD 50-60 (see Chapter 6, Assemblage 7).

A four-post structure (S) was located in the south-west corner of plot SC2 (Fig. 3.4). This had dimensions of 2 m by 2.50 m and was interpreted as a grain store. No other features related to this phase appeared to survive within the enclosed area, although a group of postholes and slots north of structure S might have originated in this phase (see Phase 3 below).

Phase 3 (Figs 3.10, 3.53)

Plots SC2 and SC3 seem to have been combined in Phase 3 as the initial east boundary of plot SC2 – ditch 9270 - was overlain by a probable circular structure (L). The structure lay within the area defined to the north by gully 9730, an easterly extension of the line of 8670 in front of plot SC1, and on the east by ditch 7840 (see also south-east roadside ditches above). The south-western return of ditch 7840 extended for 128 m.

Phase 2 features probably continued to provide definition of the west and part of the south side of the plot, although gullies 9180 and 8210, located towards the south-east corner, south and east of structure L (see below), were new to this phase (Fig. 3.52). The features were 10 m and 12 m long and 0.75 m and 0.45 m wide respectively. Both had steep sides and a flat base, with an average depth of 0.12 m. The former feature, clearly dated to Phase 3 by pottery and on the basis of spatial evidence, should have cut the fills of waterhole 10460, equally clearly dated to Phase 2, although this relationship was not evident either in plan or in section. It is perhaps possible that the waterhole was of later date, but that its fills contained only redeposited Phase 2 material. Just south of 10460 outside the southern boundary of the plot was a large contemporary pit (7516) 2.60 m in diameter and 1.50 m deep. This was filled with a primary deposit of blue-grey clay sealed by a grey-brown clay silt. Overlying this was a substantial grey silting deposit containing occasional fragments of wood charcoal and finds including a blue-green ribbed glass fragment (SF1268; see Cool, Chapter 5, Cat. no. 73) and SF1288 (a fragment of lead).

Structure L (group 8270) was defined by three main segments of curvilinear gully enclosing a slightly oval area some 12-13 m across (Fig. 3.53). The gullies on the south and west sides were both cut by a modern feature. Elsewhere definition was imperfect, but the length of gully on the south-east side had a well-defined terminal at its western end, coincident with the line of the Phase 2 ditch 9270. At this point there was a short length of subsidiary gully just outside the line of the main feature, perhaps emphasising the importance of drainage here. The gullies were on average 0.3 m wide and 0.1 m deep, but in places the depth was reduced to 0.03 m due to truncation. All three gully segments were filled with grey clay silt and produced 1st-2nd century pottery (see Chapter 6, Assemblage 16).

A posthole (8236) in the centre of the circle defined by the gullies may have been a component of the structure. This was 0.65 m in diameter and 0.19 m deep. The post appears to have been removed and the void filled with a deliberate deposit of fired clay, charred remains and pottery fragments (see Chapter 6, Assemblage 15), in a clay silt matrix. No other potential structural components were identified.

Pit 7733 was located just south of structure L (Fig. 3.53). This was 2.2 m across and steep sided, but the base was not recorded as excavation ceased at a depth of 1.2 m. Orange-grey silt clays within the base of the pit, most likely deriving from the erosion of the edges, were overlain by two grey silting deposits. All the deposits were reasonably clean with no obvious domestic debris; only one of the upper silting deposits produced pottery datable to AD 70-150. Other features in the area were not well-dated and their phasing is somewhat speculative. They included a group of four small pits located to the north of structure L which may possibly have been associated with it. Only one of these, pit 7473, was excavated, and was 1.45 m in diameter and 0.54 m deep (Fig. 3.53, section 850). It was filled with three very similar deposits of grey-brown silt clay containing occasional small sub-rounded stone.

An unexcavated gully (10492), *c* 7.5 m long and varying in width from 0.12-0.25 m, filled with grey clay silt was located west of structure L and parallel with gully 8210. At right-angles to this feature was a further, more substantial gully (8234). This was only 3 m long, but was truncated at its east end by a modern field boundary, also removing the relationship between 8234 and both the Phase 2 ditch 9270 and structure L, although it is possible that the latter of these was quite closely contemporary with 8234. The gully, steep sided with a rounded base, had a width of 0.5 m and a depth of 0.2 m.

These features may have been associated with a roughly rectilinear arrangement of postholes immediately to the west (Fig. 3.52). These formed a north-south line some 8 m long before turning to the west for a further 9 m. The excavated postholes had steep sides and flat bases and ranged in diameter from 0.45 m to 1 m, with an average depth of 0.26 m. All the postholes were filled with a light grey clay silt, containing small sub-rounded stone and occasional pieces of wood charcoal. The postholes were not closely dated and it is possible that they related to the Phase 2 layout of the plot, but the limited amount of pottery recovered from their fills was consistent with Phase 3. Forming only two sides of a structure, they are perhaps more likely to have represented part of a small enclosure than a building.

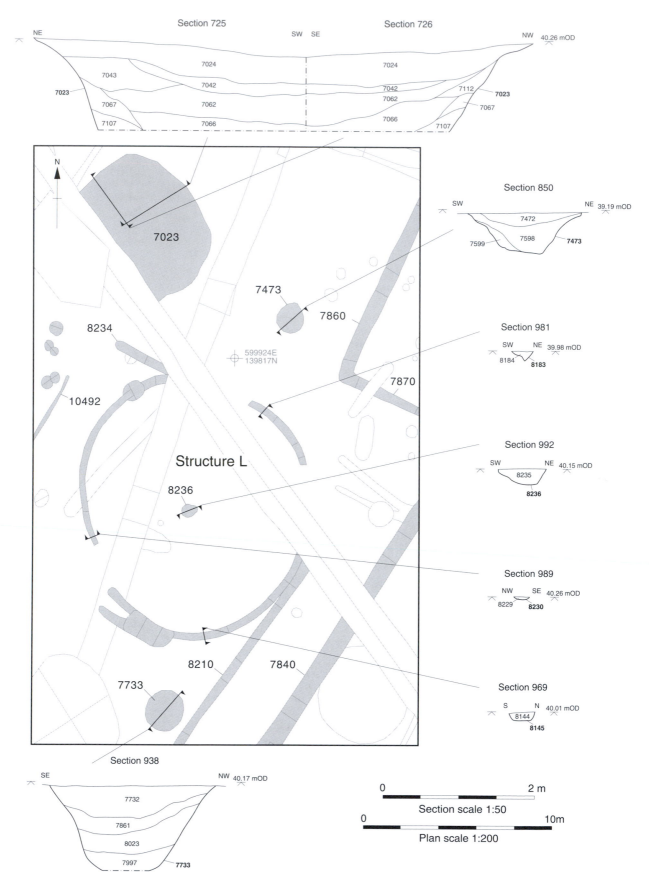

Figure 3.53   Plot SC2: Plan of Phase 3 and possible Phase 3 features, including Structure L, and waterhole 7023, pits 7473 and 7733, and associated gullies, with sections.

Phase 4 (Fig. 3.14)

The expanded single plot SC2/SC3 was maintained in this phase. The terminus of ditch 8680, extending from the south-east roadside margin, was exactly in line with the redefined plot SC1/SC2 boundary. There was a possible entrance some 2 m wide before the alignment resumed as feature 9500. This continued to extend eastwards in the form of gully segments 7780 and 10479.

A number of other gullies lay either side of 9500 and followed the same E-W alignment in this phase. Gullies 9740, 7800 and 7750/60 either complemented the main boundary, or represented a form of intermediary boundary located between the main boundary alignment and its predecessor (Fig. 3.14). Gully 9740 was 16 m long and cut into the top of Phase 3 ditch 7850. Gully 7800 was some 36 m long and extended to the east across the front of both plot SC2/SC3 and plot SC4. Gully 7800 was succeeded by a series of broadly contemporary ditch segments which eventually extended to the western boundary of the north-south trackway. From west to east these consisted of 9490, 7790 and 8140 (Fig. 3.14).

The latest gullies in this Phase 4 sequence were 7750 and 7760, cut on the same alignment, 7760 being the later of the two. Like 7800 these gullies extended part way across the northern side of plot SC4 and they were cut by Phase 5 penannular structure P (group 7500). Here their easterly extent was occasionally obscured by spreads of occupation debris. However, 7750 is likely to have corresponded to 7770 which ran eastward from structure P across the north side of plot SC5 and up to the junction with N-S ditch 8020. All gullies were filled with a same similar deposit of light grey clay silt which had occasional inclusions of iron slag, fired clay and charred remains.

The west side of plot SC2 was refashioned in this phase, possibly for the first time, although the offset alignments of Phase 3 ditches north of plots SC1 and SC2 suggest the existence of a predecessor of the Phase 4 boundary, presumably completely removed by later features. The Phase 4 boundary itself (8980/9350) was extensively truncated by successive phases of gully. The northern end of the new boundary (9350) was discernibly the earliest in a sequence of three gullies (Fig. 3.16, section 860, cut 7871) and clearly terminated to respect the eastern terminal of roadside ditch 8680 (Fig. 3.14). The continuation of this boundary to the south (8980) followed a zig-zag plan (Fig. 3.14) as far as a point 10 m south of the Phase 2 ditch 9060 where it terminated with no apparent reason.

The east side of plot SC2/SC3 was less clearly defined in this phase. Its principal component may have been a shallow NNE-SSW aligned gully (7369). This was 28 m long with its northern terminal some 17 m short of the broadly contemporary east-west gully 7800 (the southern end of the feature may have lain beyond the edge of the excavated area). Only 2 m further east a parallel gully (7670) was associated with structure O in plot SC4 (see below).

A circular waterhole 7023, south-east of the Phase 4 boundary gully 9350 and partly truncated by a modern ditch, had a maximum diameter of 7.5 m (Fig. 3.53). It was excavated to a depth of 1.2 m. The two lowest deposits excavated consisted of yellow-brown clay silt which had accumulated on the north-western edge of the feature. These were overlain by a substantial layer of grey silt clay which contained fragments of sandstone and a blue-green glass handle. A sterile orange-grey clay silt above this lay on the north-west slope of the waterhole. This was sealed by two grey clay silt deposits, both containing sub-angular natural flint nodules and occasional charcoal. A layer of dark grey clay silt, with fine lenses of grey clay throughout, overlay these deposits. This contained discrete patches of charred remains and occasional fired clay, as well as producing five iron nails and a fragment of blue-green glass. The uppermost fill of the waterhole was a grey silt clay with orange oxidisation mottling. Sub-angular flint nodules and small rounded stone was present throughout this layer which produced four iron nails and a short length of copper alloy wire (SF907).

Some 9 m east of the waterhole was an L-shaped length of gully 23 m long (groups 7860 and 7870) which enclosed most of the north-east corner of plot SC2/SC3, an area which included a cluster of postholes (Fig. 3.14). The north-west end of this feature lay adjacent to the east terminal of east-west gully 9740. The gully was on average 0.48 m wide and 0.17 m deep, with moderate sides and a rounded base. The NNE-SSW arm of the gully was filled almost entirely with wood charcoal (the largest pieces measuring 0.04 by 0.03 m) and notable amounts of iron slag in a black clay silt matrix. A dumped deposit of yellow to light grey ash was found at the part of the gully where it turned 90° eastwards at its southern end; the fill was covered by the black clay silt noted above. A dark grey clay silt overlying this and restricted to this point, contained occasional iron slag pieces, frequent charcoal and two iron nails (SF943, SF944). As the feature extended ESE the sequence of dumped deposits ceased and the remainder of the gully was filled with a single light grey clay silt with occasional sub-rounded stones.

The postholes enclosed by the gully were all near vertical sided with flat bases, and had average dimensions of 0.44 m diameter and 0.26 m depth. The largest posthole in this group, 8777, was the only one which appears to have been later in date than the rest, as it contained 15 fragments of pottery dated to AD 200+, while the small assemblages from the other features were consistent with a Phase 4 date.

Phase 5 (Fig. 3.17)

Plots SC2 and SC3 seem to have remained as a single unit in this phase. The boundary between plot SC1 and plot SC2/SC3 was defined by gully 8770 which followed the dogleg alignment of its Phase 4 predecessor before eventually linking to the alignment of the Phase 3 gully 7840 some 90 m south of the contemporary boundary of the shrine area (Fig. 3.17).

There was no indication of activity within the northern part of plots SC2 and SC3. However, another cluster of pits was uncovered south-west of the rear of these plots as originally defined and adjacent to gully 8770. The largest of these, 7502, had a diameter of 2.2 m and a depth of 0.26 m, with shallow sloping sides and a rounded base. It had a primary fill of dark grey silt clay with frequent charcoal fragments, overlain by an orange-grey clay silt containing a little charcoal. A smaller pit, 7507, lying 2 m to the west, was 0.98 m in diameter and 0.27 m deep, with moderately sloping sides and a rounded base. The primary fill was a redeposited yellow clay containing frequent fired clay fragments and occasional charcoal flecks. Overlying this was a dark grey clay silt with smaller amounts of charcoal and fired clay, sealed by a light grey clay silting deposit. The other pits in this area were typically shallow with an average diameter of 1.0 m and depth of 0.16 m; all were filled with a single deposit of light grey clay silt.

Plot SC3

Phase 2 (Fig. 3.4)

This plot was bounded by gully 9270 to the west and presumably by Phase 2 ditch 9360 to the north, although this could not be traced all the way to the putative north-east corner of the plot because it was cut away by Phase 3 ditch 7850 at its east end (Figs 3.4 and 3.10). The eastern side of the plot was defined by a NNE-SSW aligned Phase 2 gully 7820, giving an approximate plot width of 21-22 m. At the north end this feature appeared to have a shallow terminus immediately south of Phase 5 structure P and associated occupation spread 7439, while to the south it extended beyond the edge of the excavated area. Gully 7820 had steep sides sloping at 70° to a flat base and on average was 0.7 m wide and 0.21 m deep. Its fills were a primary brown silt clay sealed by a light grey clay silt and contained 1st century pottery except for a single upper fill (7078) which contained a group of pottery of Phase 4 date. This material was either intrusive or, perhaps more likely, related to a very localised recut of the feature.

No internal features in plot SC2 were certainly attributable to this phase. There was a large possible waterhole in the southern part of the plot. This feature was not excavated or dated by finds, but it may have been of Phase 2 date on the basis of a marginal relationship with a Phase 3 gully. No Phase 2 features were identified in the area east of plot SC3.

Phase 3 (Fig. 3.10)

Plot SC3 was at least partly incorporated with plot SC2 in this phase. The plot was bisected approximately by a ditch (7840) interpreted as a boundary between the augmented plot SC2 to the west and a new plot (SC4) to the east. The latter also incorporated part of the space previously (and again subsequently) assigned to plot SC3.

Phases 4 and 5

See plot SC2 above.

Plot SC4 *(Fig. 3.54)*

Phase 3 (Fig. 3.10)

There was no definable plan element in this part of the south settlement area before Phase 3. The establishment of ditch group 7840 at that time had the effect of bisecting plot SC3 at a slightly odd angle (see plot SC2 above). The area east of this alignment was defined as plot SC3/SC4 in this phase (Figs 3.10 and 3.54). The approximate line of the original eastern boundary of plot SC3 may have been maintained, however, by two north-south gullies (7369, and 7774 = group 10380) though the phasing of these features is not absolutely certain. A number of other gullies uncovered between 7840 and 10380, despite their sparse dating evidence, were assigned to phase 3 on the basis of their layout. These included 10400, a narrow (typically 0.25-0.30 m wide) slot running roughly parallel to 7840 some 5 m east of it, which turned a sharply-defined right-angle to the east at its southern end. Neither the eastern nor the northern end of 10400 was confidently located and its interpretation is uncertain. Close to the corner of the gully the gap between 7840 and 10400 was closed by a broader gully 8280. This was undated, and could perhaps have been of Phase 4 date. Just north-east of this gully was a large discrete feature *c* 4.75 m across. This was not excavated, but its size suggests that it could have been a waterhole. It had a marginal relationship with ditch 7840, which may have been the later of the two. On the basis of its position, however, the feature was perhaps broadly contemporary with the surrounding linear features. A Phase 2 or 3 date is likely.

Further east another N-S aligned feature, ditch 7740, lay a little to the west of the line later more clearly defined as the boundary between plots SC4 and SC5. Ditch 7740 had a minimum length of 29 m and was truncated at its south end by a post-medieval feature. At its northern end it extended almost 8 m beyond the line of the slightly earlier Phase 3 E-W ditch which notionally marked the northern boundary of the plots in this phase. The average width and depth of 7740 were 1 m and 0.3 m respectively, and it had a consistent profile with moderate sides and a flat base. The ditch was mostly filled with a single deposit of light grey silt clay, which contained occasional charcoal flecks, but at the north end the deposit sequence changed. Here it consisted of primary and secondary fills of light grey silt clay, overlain by a yellow-grey silt clay containing a large amount of charcoal and patches of burnt clay. This may have been intrusive material associated with the later structure O which directly overlay 7740.

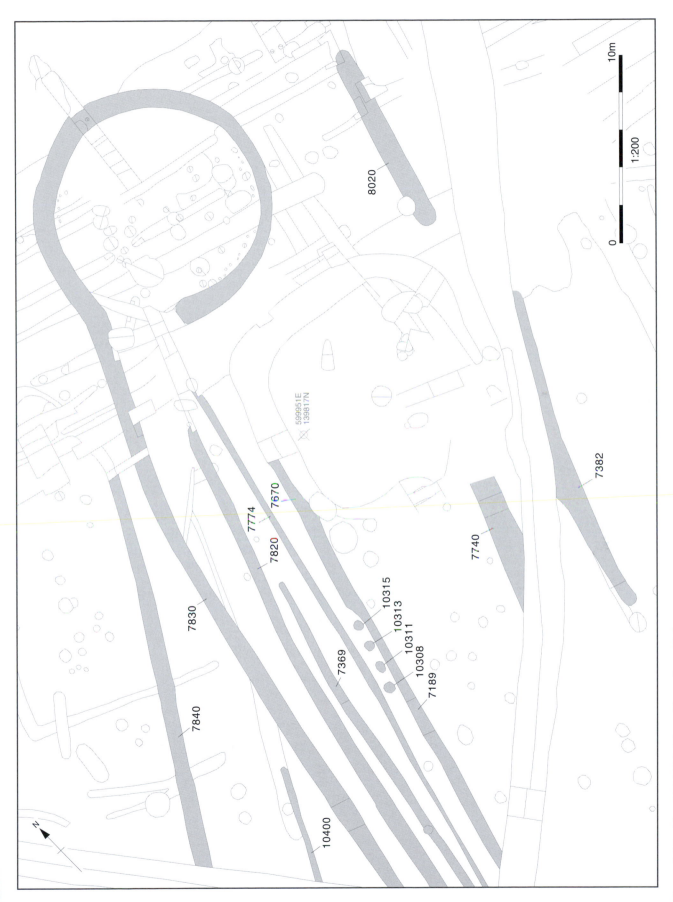

Figure 3.54   Plot SC3/SC4: Plan of boundary ditches.

Phase 4 (Figs 3.14, 3.54-3.55)

As defined in this phase plot SC4 was perhaps up to 20 m wide and distinguished principally by the presence of structure O in its north-west corner (Fig. 3.14). The main boundary between plot SC4 and plot SC3 was 7670 which extended southwards from the edge of the ditch surrounding structure O. Gully 7670 was 0.71 m wide and 0.23 m deep and had the same profile as the smaller gully, 7369, just to the west (see above). It was filled with a mid grey clay silt which contained occasional charcoal fragments (10%) and two iron nails (SF987, SF1000). Four unexcavated postholes, bordering the western edge of 7670, were set about 1 m apart from centre to centre. These each measured *c* 0.5 m in diameter and filled with light grey clay silt.

The north side of the plot was marked by a series of gullies, most of which were continuous with features bounding plot SC2/SC3 (see above). A number of these gullies appeared to have an eastern terminus in line with the east side of the ditch defining structure O, and it is possible that the east side of the plot in this phase was in line with these termini, on an alignment followed by Phase 5 gullies 8020 and 7382. Alternatively, a division between plots SC4 and SC5 was marked by ditch 10495 some 8 m further east (see below).

Structure O was defined by a gully (group 7660) roughly square in plan with an opening to the east and internal dimensions of 10 m by 10 m (Fig. 3.55). The termini were rounded and well-defined, forming an entrance *c* 1.5 m wide. The average surviving width and depth of the gully were 1.0 m and 0.18 m respectively and it had a consistently sloping-sided and flat-bottomed profile. The gully was filled with a single deposit of light grey clay silt containing infrequent amounts of wood charcoal and pottery dated to the late 2nd century AD (see Chapter 6, Assemblage 31). At a point along the southern edge of the structure three phases of gully were observed in section; however, in other areas of excavation the latest phase of gully had truncated the previous two completely. The profile of the gully surrounding structure O suggests that it was for drainage rather than structural purposes.

Internal features included a number of pits, postholes and a hearth. Very few of these, however, were clearly recognisable as structural features which may have shed light on the form of the building. The only possible exception was a shallow pit (7687), which lay in the centre of the structure and could perhaps have carried a central post. This was 1.0 m in diameter and 0.05 m deep with steep sides and a flat base, and was filled with a brown silt clay which contained small lumps of fired clay and fragments of iron slag. Pit 7716 was sub-rectangular, measured 1.25 m by 0.45 m by 0.10 m deep, and had steep sides to a rounded base. It was filled with a light grey clay silt. A further pit (7611) was located at the eastern internal edge of the structure. This measured 2.0 m by 1.2 m by 0.76 m deep and was again steep-sided with a flat base. It

had a primary fill of red-brown clay silt with occasional charcoal flecking, sealed by dark grey clay silt. Posthole 7699 was near vertical sided and flat based, filled with a dark grey clay silt containing a large amount of wood charcoal. It may have been associated with a hearth (7697) which lay directly to the east. Measuring 1.10 m by 0.7 m by 0.23 m this was sub-rectangular with steep sides and a flat base. The primary deposit was a lining of fire-reddened, re-deposited, natural clay. A charcoal-rich, dark grey clay silt overlay this. A discrete patch of fire reddened clay above this represented a second episode of firing; this was in turn sealed by another deposit of charcoal-rich clay silt. Patches of fired clay around the hearth may have represented the remains of similar features, or merely have derived from 7697. The hearth and the posthole cut through 7666, a light grey silt clay on average 0.1 m thick, which contained a large amount of pottery fragments and a curved bronze rod or ring fragment (SF1333; see Cool, Chapter 5, Cat. no. 115). This deposit represented a gradual accumulation of silt within the interior of the structure.

A small pit (7582) at the entrance of structure O contained the remnants of a near complete pot. The pot was in an upright position and fitted snugly into the pit which had a diameter of 0.6 m and a depth of 0.3 m. The southern edge of the pot had collapsed, the broken pieces being found within the silt clay deposit which filled it; additionally, there was some plough damage to the surviving upper part of the vessel. A larger pit (7213) was located to the rear of the building in the angle between gully 7660 and plot SC3/SC4 boundary gully 7670. Measuring 1.5 m in diameter and 0.32 m deep, 7213 had steep sides and a rounded base and was filled with a single deposit of light grey silt with occasional small angular flint nodules. The fill contained no material diagnostic of a particular function. It may perhaps have been used for storage. An adjacent (unexcavated) pit cut the fills of gully 7660 and may perhaps have been of Phase 5 rather than Phase 4 date.

Phase 5 (Fig. 3.17)

The plot SC3/SC4 boundary was formed by a N-S gully 7830 contemporary with penannular structure P. Gully 7830 extended *c* 47 m southwards from the gully surrounding that structure to the edge of Area B and was typically 0.8 m wide and 0.25 m deep. The sides of the gully sloped at 70° to a flat base, and it was consistently filled with a single light grey clay silt, which contained occasional small rounded stone and a blue-green glass bottle fragment (SF996).

Structure P (Group 7500) was defined by a penannular gully which enclosed an area with an internal diameter of 11 m (Fig. 3.55). The gully terminated to provide an entrance to the south-west 4.5 m wide. Generally the gully had sides sloping at 70° to a flat base, although at two points along its length the base was slightly rounded, and the overall average width was 0.9 m and depth 0.28 m. A primary light grey clay silt was noted along the length of the gully, although

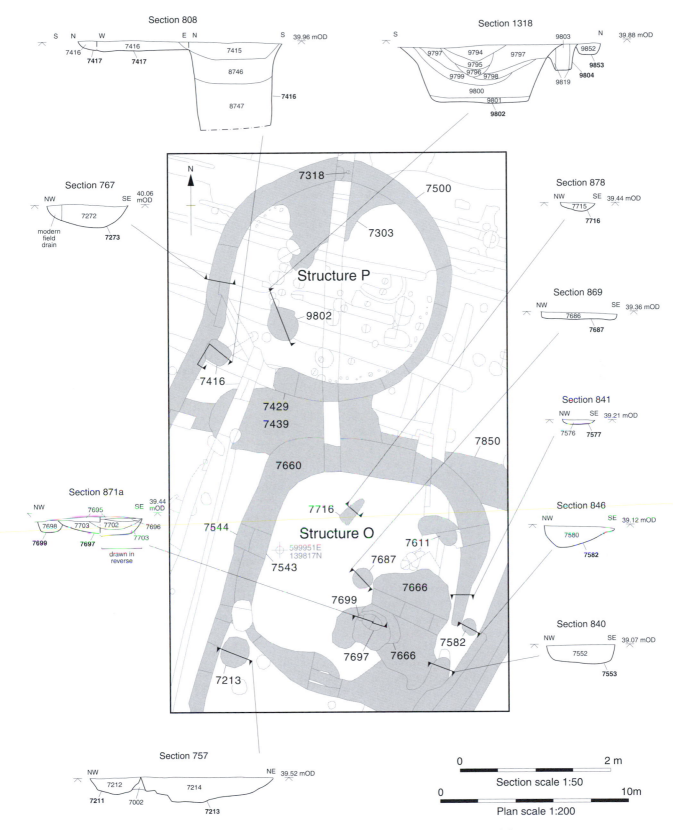

Figure 3.55   Plot SC4: Plan of Structures O and P with plans and sections of associated features.

at both termini this deposit was much darker and contained more charcoal; along the eastern arc of the gully a dump of fired clay was deposited within the base. This deposit produced a neck fragment from a blue-green glass bottle (SF1104; see Cool, Chapter 5, Cat. no. 63) and two bronze coins, one of Augustus dated 28-25 BC (SF1224) and the other illegible, but early Roman (SF1225) (see Guest, Chapter 5, Table 5.5). Also within this part of the gully was a secondary deposit of dark grey clay silt which extended for approximately 10 m. This contained a large amount of dumped material including fired clay and charcoal fragments, a reeded bottle handle of blue-green glass (SF1006; see Cool, Chapter 5, Cat. no. 58; Fig. 5.5), and a cluster of five nails (SF1067-69, SF1073-4), all located above posthole 7318 which was cut into the base of the gully. At the southern terminal the light grey clay silts of two earlier gullies were noted, extending to the west and north west. These most likely represented earlier stages of entrance to the structure. Collectively the gullies produced a substantial group of pottery generally of early 3rd century date (see Chapter 6, Assemblage 35).

A series of 22 stakeholes was ranged around the northern and southern arcs inside the penannular gully. These ranged between 0.1 m and 0.13 m deep with an average diameter of 0.2 m, and presumably formed part of the wall line for an internal structure. A series of soil spreads was uncovered within the lines indicated by the stakeholes. Spread 7303, situated within the northern edge of the structure, had a consistent depth of 0.07 m and consisted of a dark grey clay silt which contained occasional slag fragments and wood charcoal. Soil spread 7439 consisted of a dark grey clay silt with occasional charcoal flecks throughout, and was located at the southern edge of the structure. Covering an area c 9 m by 3.4 m, and with a depth of 0.06 m, this appeared to have survived plough truncation by settling into the slight depression created by earlier ditch 7850. There were 25 postholes or small pits within the centre of the structure. All of these features had steep, near vertical, sides and flat or rounded bases. Their diameters ranged from 0.20-0.45 m and the depths from 0.10-0.26 m and they were all filled with a light grey clay silt, mottled with red silt patches. The majority produced pottery, but very little else was recovered other than occasional iron slag fragments and small amounts of charcoal.

A large pit (9802) was located just inside the entrance to the structure, and another waterhole 7416 was positioned outside the entrance west of the south-west terminal of the penannular gully. Pit 9802 was square in plan with vertical sides 1.7 m long and 0.78 m deep. The two lowest fills were natural silts, overlain by a dump deposit of yellow clay containing a large amount of fired clay and much charcoal. Overlying this were two grey silting deposits, sealed by a dark grey silt clay, which contained a large amount of, charred remains. A yellow redeposited clay above this contained occasional pieces of fired clay and the uppermost fill was a grey silt with infrequent charcoal

flecks. Pit 7416 was also square in plan, 1.3 m across, with vertical sides at least 1.2 m deep. The lowest fill was a blue-grey clay containing occasional iron slag fragments, overlain by a red-grey clay with patches of light grey clay throughout. These were sealed by an upper deposit of dark grey clay silt containing a large amount of fired clay and wood charcoal.

Plot SC5

Phase 3 (Figs 3.10, 3.56)

Plot SC5 was defined to the west by ditch 7740 and to the north by ditch 7850. Ditch 7850 turned southwards at the north-east corner of the plot apparently to form the west side of the north-south trackway. The existence of a ditch on the west side of the trackway in this phase cannot be demonstrated conclusively since the direct evidence for its presence would have been removed by later ditches on the same line, but seems to be required by the spacing and layout of all the features in this part of the site. This gave an approximate maximum width of 26 m for the plot (Fig. 3.10). Its length is uncertain, however, because there was no clear evidence for a southern boundary in this phase. Short, isolated lengths of undated gully lying some 45-50 m from the line of 7850 may have indicated the position of such a boundary, but this is uncertain. There were indications, however, of a northerly extension to the plot, suggested by a gully (8140) lying parallel to 7850 and some 5 m north of it. This may have been associated with the northward extension of ditch 7740 beyond the line of 7850, but the two features did not meet.

The plot contained a large number of poorly-dated discrete features, few of which could be assigned with confidence to this phase. They were so assigned principally on the basis of their spatial arrangement in relation to features such as ditch 7740. An approximate southerly projection of the line of 7740, beyond its presumed terminus beneath the modern ditch, was marked by a linear arrangement of small pits or (less likely) large postholes extending north-south for some 7 m, before turning to the east for a further 6 m. These were unexcavated, but were mostly from 0.7 m to 1 m across, with an occasional smaller example. All had an upper fill of light grey silt. Additional possibly related features lay a little further to the east, where they were interspersed with postholes assigned to a probable six post structure (Structure M), on a similar alignment. It is possible that these features related to a structure rather than simply forming linear groups of discrete pits. This possibility is discussed further below.

Structure M (Fig. 3.56) was square and measured 3 m by 3 m, with the individual postholes ranging from 0.25 m to (exceptionally) c 0.75 m in diameter. It had suffered heavy truncation from ploughing. A line of four further postholes extended northwards from the north-east corner of the structure while a group of undated pits to the north may also have been associated with it.

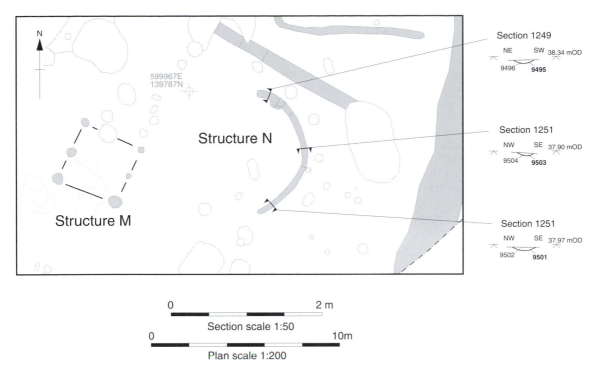

Figure 3.56   Plot SC5: Plan and sections of Structures M and N.

A short length of curvilinear gully (group 9970), equidistant between Structure M and the north-south trackway to the east, had an average width of 0.30 m and was only *c* 0.05 m deep (Figure 3.56). Neither terminal was well-defined, however, and it is likely that the gully was originally more extensive. It may have surrounded the eastern side of a circular structure (N), which would have had a diameter of approximately 7 m. Dating material from the gully was scarce, but was consistent with a Phase 3 date.

Phase 4 (Figs 3.14, 3.57)

The north side of a small rectilinear enclosure was formed by ditch 9960 (Figs 3.14 and 3.57). Its west side (ditch 10495), which lay 8 m east of structure O, was traced for 13 m and, although the north-west corner was obscured, it is almost certain that this feature was linked with an E-W ditch alignment recutting the Phase 3 boundary 7850 and extending eastwards to the west side of the N-S trackway, where it turned again to the south. Here it followed the alignment of the trackway for 20 m before either being lost to a later ditch (ditch group 10450, which defined the full length of the west side of the trackway was thought to span both Phases 4 and 5) through truncation or (perhaps more likely on the basis of the plan) terminating. The resulting enclosure, lacked a south side, but had approximate maximum dimensions of 20 m (N-S) by 13 m (E-W). On average, ditch 9960 was 1.0 m wide and 0.4 m deep, filled with a primary yellow-grey silt clay, overlain by two mid grey silt clay deposits with occasional fragments of charcoal and small pieces of fired clay. The profile varied little and

generally had sides sloping at 45-60° to a slightly rounded base. Ditch 10495 was similar, but wider, being up to 1.5 m across.

At the south-east corner of this enclosure a further, smaller rectilinear enclosure was defined by narrow (unexcavated) gullies surrounding an area roughly 10 m by 9 m apparently facing the west side of the N-S trackway. It is possible that these gullies, together with a row of four possible postholes towards the eastern side, defined a structure, but their combined character was reminiscent of features lying just north of the Phase 2 structure S in Plot SC2, which is interpreted as an enclosure. This interpretation is tentatively favoured here. The north-west corner of the enclosure feature was obscured by an irregular soil spread 7204 measuring approximately 11 m by 5 m, which survived within a slight hollow. This comprised a primary reddish-brown silt clay with charred remains and fragments of ceramic building material, overlain by a dark grey clay silt containing moderate amounts of wood charcoal. Pottery from the upper fill (7125) was of Phase 4 or possibly Phase 5 date.

A series of postholes and two short segments of gully within the north-east corner of the area defined by enclosure 9960 possibly represented the remains of a circular or sub-rectangular structure, labelled T (Fig. 3.57). The majority of the features were very ephemeral with diffuse edges, which makes this interpretation rather speculative. A rectangular arrangement of four postholes could have formed an entrance which would have faced south. The rest of the structure may have been formed by a roughly L-shaped arrangement of postholes which survived around the south eastern edge of the building. A western side to this structure may have been marked by a 4 m length of possible drainage gully, and another gully segment only 1.4 m in length was seen at the eastern external edge of the putative entrance. No dating evidence was retrieved from this possible structure, but its position within the enclosure indicates that it was probably of Phase 4 date.

Phase 5 (Fig. 3.17)

Structure P was the only feature at the northern, or front, end of plot SC4 in this phase. Plot SC5, in contrast, was more closely defined. Its northern boundary was formed by ditch 8070 which ran roughly east-west for 21 m before turning to the south as ditch

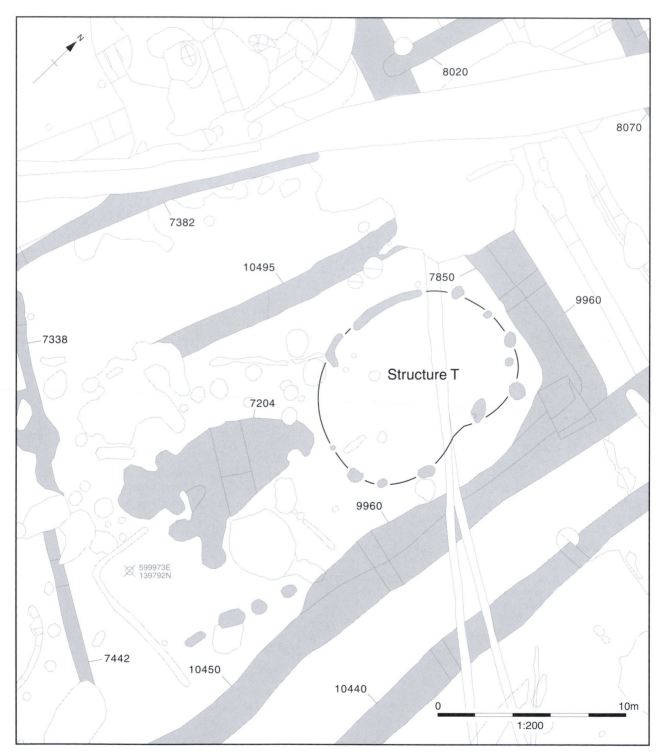

Figure 3.57   Plot SC5: Plan of Structure T with associated enclosure ditches 7850, 9960, and 10495, and trackway ditches 10450 and 10440.

10450, which formed the western ditch of the north-south trackway. The profile of ditch 8070 remained consistent along its length of the feature, with sides sloping at 70° to a flat base. The fills were generally a light grey silt clay, overlain by a grey silt clay mottled with patches of red silt. However, at the point where the ditch turned to the south, the corner segment was filled with a different sequence of deposits. This comprised two orange-grey silt clays, derived from the erosion of the ditch edges, sealed by a red-brown clay silt containing fragments of fired clay and ceramic building material. Overlying this were two light brown clay silts containing occasional slag fragments and small sub-angular stone. Ditch 10450, the southerly continuation of ditch 8070, had an average width of 1.10 m and depth of 0.52 m, with sides sloping at 60° to a flat base. The primary fill was consistently a blue-grey silt clay, overlain by a grey silt clay with infrequent charcoal flecks, slag and fired clay fragments.

Four segments of gully – 7442, 7338, 7382 and 8020 - combined with the trackway ditch to form an approximately rectangular enclosure with maximum dimensions of *c* 23 m by 39 m (Fig. 3.17). The western boundary of plot SC5 was formed by gully 8020, which began 1.5 m south of the western terminal of ditch 8070 and was 10 m long with clearly defined rounded termini. Its average width was 1.0 m and the depth 0.3 m. Some 5 m from the southern terminal of 8020 the line of the boundary was continued by ditch 7382. This was 18 m long, up to 1 m wide, and ended in a rounded terminal 0.7 m wide and 0.1 m deep with shallow sides and an undulating irregular base. Gullies 7338 and 7442, were most likely part of the same feature, and extended south-eastwards from the end of 7382 to form the rear (south-west) boundary of the plot. Both had shallow sloping sides and an irregular to flat base with an average width of 0.75 m and depth of 0.15 m. All these gully segments were filled with a single deposit of dark grey silt clay containing infrequent charred remains.

A series of pits was uncovered within plot SC5, though not all were closely dated. The small sample excavated was filled with a single deposit of grey silt clay containing occasional charcoal and fragments of animal bone. They were mostly shallow, with sides sloping gently to a flat base, and on average were 0.8 m in diameter and 0.15 m deep, although the larger unexcavated pits had a maximum diameter of 2 m.

Trackway ditch 10450 was paralleled to the east by ditch 10440 (Figs 3.17 and 3.57). These features and their predecessors combined to form a trackway generally 3.5m to 4 m wide between plots SC1-SC5 to the west and plot SC6 to the east. The trackway gave access to the open area and shrine complex from the south. Both ditches extended beyond the excavated area, but within the confines of Area B they extended for approximately 95 m. The southernmost observations of these features were made in trenches excavated in 1998, where the southward continuation of ditch group 10440 was defined as group 1000.

Ditch 10450 was typically *c* 1.10 m wide, while 10440/1000 was from 1.80 m to 2.35 m wide and 0.55-0.85 m deep. It had a slightly different profile from 10450, with sides sloping at 60° to a more pointed V-shaped base. A primary light grey-brown silt clay was found throughout the length of the ditch, and was overlain by a dark grey clay silt which contained occasional fragments of slag and ceramic building material and the base of a blue-green glass vessel (SF1026; see Cool, Chapter 5, Cat. no. 65; Fig. 5.5). At its northern end, at the margin of the shrine area, 10440 returned to the east for at least 30 m.

The uppermost fills of both 10450 and 10440 were assigned to Phase 5 on the basis of pottery evidence. As already indicated, however, it is likely that ditch 10450 was cut in Phase 4, and may very well have had a predecessor in Phase 3. The same may be presumed for ditch 10440. At the very least, a Phase 4 ditch on this alignment is required by the presence of plot SC6 (see below) and appears to have been represented by ditch 1000. Whether the east side of the trackway was defined by a ditch in Phase 3 is less certain, but is quite likely in view of the suggested or possible phasing of features such as 1030 and 1020 in and adjacent to the area of plot SC6 (see below).

Plot SC6 - south-eastern settlement area (Fig. 3.58)

This plot was located to the east of the north-south side road and defined on its west and north sides by ditch 10440/1000. Ditch 1040, assigned to Phase 4, was located east of 10440/1000 on a NNE-SSW alignment (Figs 3.14 and 3.58) and was seen in two extensions of Area B, which showed that it had a minimum length of 57 m. Although its northerly limit is not known; it is likely that it terminated at a junction with the eastern return of 10440, but this is not certain. Characteristically, 1040 had moderately sloping sides and a flat base with a width of 0.7 m and a depth of 0.34 m. It was filled with a light grey silt clay, overlain by a mid grey clay silt with infrequent charcoal flecks (Fig. 58, section 236, and section 274, cut 1281).

Ditch 1040 is interpreted here as defining the south-eastern side of a somewhat hypothetical plot SC6 in the south-east angle of ditch 10440. In general 1040 appears to have been the last substantial boundary extending south-eastwards down the slope towards the Whitewater Dyke. A number of gullies perpendicular to it, including 1280 and 1290, terminated to respect its line and only one earlier gully (1030) - possibly Phase 3 - extended south-east of it and continued beyond the limit of excavation (Fig. 3.10). It is noteworthy that while the east-west arm of ditch 10440 extended beyond the edge of the excavated area its recorded length is almost exactly that seen on the gradiometer survey, which shows the feature apparently coming to a clear stop. It therefore seems likely that the north-east corner of plot SC6, possibly formed by the junction of 10440 and 1040, and falling just outside the excavated area, marked the limit of significant activity at the south-east margin of the settlement.

Features 1280 and 1290 were two parallel segments of shallow ditch, neither extending as far west as trackway ditch 10440/1000. The former had moderate

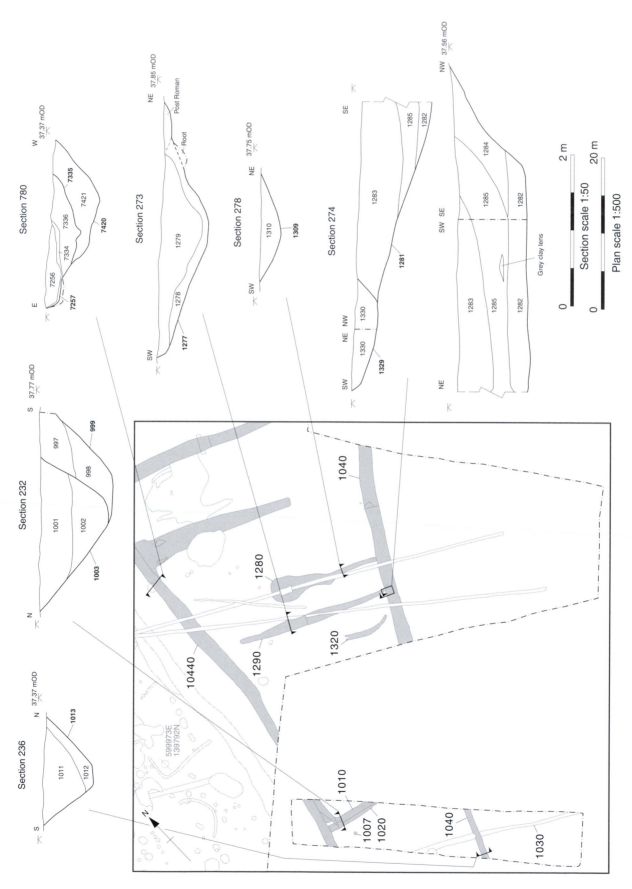

Figure 3.58   Plot SC6: Plan showing trackway ditch 10440/1000, enclosure ditches 1040 and 1020, and gullies 1030, 1290, 1280 and 1320, with cremation grave 1007, with selected ditch and gully sections.

sloping sides and a rounded base with a width and depth of 1 m and 0.2 m (Fig. 3.58, section 278). This was filled with a single deposit of dark brown clay silt which produced two blue-green glass fragments, one a ribbed body sherd (SF202; see Cool, Chapter 5, Cat. no. 72) and the other a sherd from a tubular rimmed bowl (SF203; see Cool, Chapter 5, Cat. no. 37; Fig. 5.4), dated to the mid 1st to mid 2nd century. Ditch 1290 also had moderate sloping sides, but a flat base, with an average width and depth of 1.4 m and 0.32 m respectively (Fig. 3.58, section 273). Both ends narrowed to ill-defined termini. A dark grey clay silt with occasional charcoal flecking overlay a primary grey-brown silting fill. South of these ditches was a curvilinear segment of gully (1830) which terminated before reaching a junction with ditch 1040. This was heavily truncated by post-Roman plough damage and had a maximum width of 0.7 m and an average surviving depth of 0.07 m, being only 0.03 m deep at either end. Gully 1830 had the same profile as ditch 1290 and was filled with a single deposit of light grey clay silt.

Approximately 20 m south of this group of features two further gullies extended from the trackway ditch 10440/1000 eastwards beyond the edge of the excavation. Gully 1020 was the earlier of the two with a width and depth of 1 m and 0.4 m, moderate sloping sides and a flat base (Fig. 3.58, section 232, cut 999). This extended from ditch 10440/1000 for at least 7 m. Gullies 1020 and 1000 were probably broadly contemporary, but the fill of feature 1020 was truncated by part of ditch 1000. Since 1020 did not extent beyond the line of ditch 1000 it may originally have related to an earlier feature on the same alignment as 1000. A later feature, gully 1010, ran parallel with ditch 10440 for 5 m before turning to the east and cutting into the top of gully 1020 for a further 5 m. This later gully had similar dimensions and profile as its predecessor and both were filled with orange-grey silt clay overlain by brown-grey clay silt (Fig. 3.58, section 232, cut 1003). In combination with the trackway ditches 10440/1000, gullies 1020 and 1010 probably defined the south-west corner of plot SC6.

A single adult cremation burial in grave 1007 was uncovered a few metres south of gully 1020. The grave had a diameter of 0.36 m, a depth of 0.15 m, and contained a single vessel (1004), a storage jar holding 1225 g of cremated bone. The vessel was in poor condition due to plough damage, and was lifted along with the remains to be excavated off site. It was dated *c* AD 43-100, placing the burial in Phase 2 or 3 (see Chapter 8).

Gully 1030, approximately 8 m to the south, presumably also originated at a junction with ditch 10440, although the evidence for this lay outside the excavated area. If it did join 10440, then it would have extended for at least 32 m south-eastwards from the line of 10440. This feature had the same moderate sided profile and flat base as seen in the other gullies in this part of the site, and was 0.7 m wide and 0.2 m deep. It was filled with a light brown-orange clay silt, which became slightly more clayey in composition as it extended down slope to the south-east.

Apart from the isolated cremation burial, there were no features associated with the gullies to indicate the type of activity in the area. This part of Area B was well away from the more intensive areas of settlement, and may possibly have been prone to seasonal flooding from the Whitewater Dyke located to the south-east. A probable alluvial deposit on average not more than 0.15 m deep was noted beneath the subsoil during the machine excavation of these areas. This was not dated, however, so it is not known if it was contemporary with the settlement.

Southern Peripheral Area

Plot SE1 (Fig. 3.59)

This plot lay south-east of the Canterbury road and south of plot SC1 and was defined by three parallel NW-SE aligned gullies (9150, 9160 and 9170), which were angled slightly of the perpendicular in relation to the Canterbury road it. They may have formed field boundaries, but in view of their spacing and their location opposite the south-west block of plots, it is perhaps more probable that they enclosed a single property unit (SE1). The rear (south-east side) of this plot appears to have been defined by the residual line of the Phase 2 ditch 9060, giving a maximum plot depth of *c* 65 m, while at the north-western street frontage none of the gullies extended as far as the roadside gullies, though this area was quite heavily disturbed by post-medieval ditches which could have completely removed portions of some of the gullies.

The most south-westerly gully was 9170, which had an average width of 0.97 m and depth of 0.28 m. A slighter gully, 9160, was only *c* 1 m north-east of 9170. This had steep sides and a slightly rounded base with an average width of 0.44 m and depth of 0.13 m. It was filled with a single deposit of grey-orange silt with high densities of manganese. This gully became gradually shallower to the south-east, rather than ending in a formal terminal. In its north-western part it was cut by a number of pits and other features (see below), while close to its north-western terminal it appeared to cut the north-east edge of a 4.8 m length of a rather broader gully (9165). Some 20 m north-east of 9170 was 9150, which was on average 1.14 m wide and 0.27 m deep. A localised recut 11 m long at the north-west end of the feature (9190) was up to 2 m wide and 0.37 m deep. Both 9150 and 9170 were steep-sided with a flat base and, like 9160, became gradually shallower to the south-east. Both had a similar single grey clay silt fill.

A group of small unexcavated pits projected the alignment of 9160 at its north-western end and a further cluster of undated pits (9138, 9134, 9131, 10493 and 10494) cut into the top of 9160 and partly into 9170 some 25 m from the road edge. Further south-east an isolated pit (8214) lay immediately north-east of 9160. This was oval in shape, *c* 1.56 m by 1.2 m and excavated to a depth of 1.2 m without reaching the natural clay. The lowest deposit excavated was an orange-brown silt clay with lenses of light grey clay throughout. This

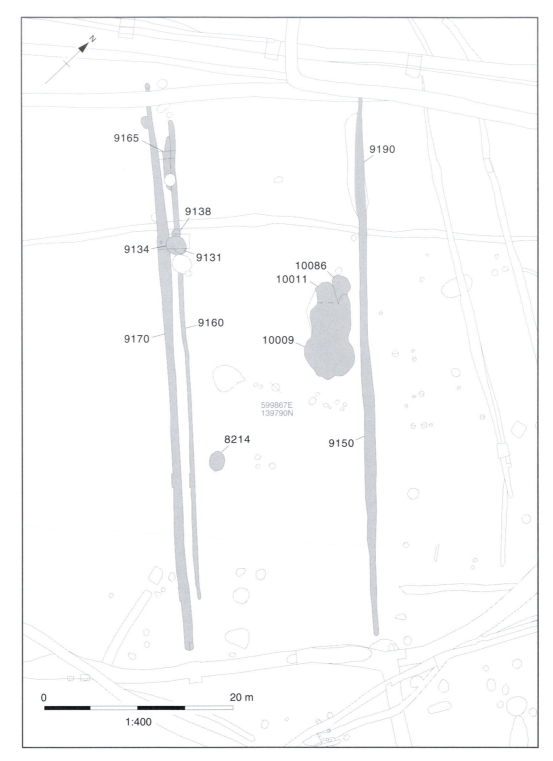

Figure 3.59   Plot SE1: Plan showing ditches 9150, 9160 and 9170 and associated features.

was overlain by a grey-orange clay silt containing occasional fragments of burnt stone and charcoal and the uppermost fill was a grey-orange clay silt with a high density of manganese and frequent small rounded stone.

A group of slightly irregular intercutting pits covering an area approximately 10 m by 4 m was located towards the north-east side of the plot. The pits

excavated at the north-west end of this group (10009, 10011 and 10086) all had moderate sloping sides with a rounded base, and were on average 0.41 m deep, ranging from *c* 1.2 m to *c* 3 m across. Their primary fills were consistent yellow-brown silt clays, sealed by series of grey-brown silt clays. The uppermost deposit in all cases contained frequent amounts of charred remains.

The chronology of the features of plot SE1 is a little uncertain. The primary boundaries of the plot were probably formed by 9150 and 9160, both of which could, on the basis of the limited pottery recovered from their fills, have been as early as Phase 3 in date. It seems unlikely that 9170 and 9150 were contemporary use. The only complicating factor is that the upper fill of the small gully 9165, apparently cut by 9160, was clearly of Phase 5 date. Material in this fill could have been intrusive, but it may be that the relationship between 9160 and 9165 was incorrectly observed, a suggestion supported by the fact that the corresponding feature (9190) relating to ditch 9150 to the north was the later of the two and was also of Phase 5 date. The plot could have originated either in Phase 3 or Phase 4, though the fact that the ditches seem to have respected the major Phase 2 alignment at their south-east ends argues for an earlier rather than a later date. Ditch 9170 could have replaced 9160 either in Phase 4 or Phase 5. The pits which cut 9160 and impinged marginally on 9170 were, like most of the ditches, poorly dated. Unequivocal Phase 5 material came from a single upper fill (9168) of ditch 9170, from the two localised ?recuts 9165 and 9190, from the upper fill of isolated pit 8214, and from 10011, one of the group of irregularly-shaped pits adjacent to ditch 9150.

Possible mortuary enclosure *(Fig. 3.60)*

A small square ditched enclosure (group 8730) was uncovered in the south-western part of Area B, approximately 26 m south-east of the road (Figs 3.10 and 3.60). This consisted of a single ditch defining an area with an internal width of 10 m and a north-west facing entrance 1.4 m wide. The average width and depth of the ditch, which had steeply sloping sides and a flat base, were 0.93 m and 0.3 m. It had a single fill of light yellow-brown clay silt which produced a small quantity of undiagnostic 1st-2nd century pottery. The only remaining internal feature was a posthole located centrally in the enclosure. This measured 0.5 m by 0.4 m and 0.07 m deep and had vertical sides and a flat base. It was filled with a single deposit of mid brown silt clay containing occasional charcoal flecks. A rather larger, very amorphous feature cut by the posthole was probably a tree throw hollow. The date of this feature remains unclear. It was tentatively assigned to Phase 3.

Other features *(Fig. 3.61)*

Cremation graves

Two isolated cremation burials, 9860 and 9940, 4.5 m apart lay at the extreme south-eastern margin of Area B, immediately south-east of NE-SW aligned ditch 7840. The grave of 9940 was roughly circular with steep sides and a rounded base measuring 0.6 m in diameter and 0.32 m deep. An upright cremation urn within the pit was filled with a light grey silt clay, which contained the cremated bone. Above this deposit was an inverted samian bowl, which appeared to have been placed deliberately to act as a form of lid for the burial. Cremation grave 9860 was sub-rectangular and measured 0.6 m by 0.7 m, but only survived to a depth of 0.03 m (Plate 3.14). Within the pit were the remains of a flagon lying on its side, and the heavily broken up remains of a jar. The majority of the cremated bone was within

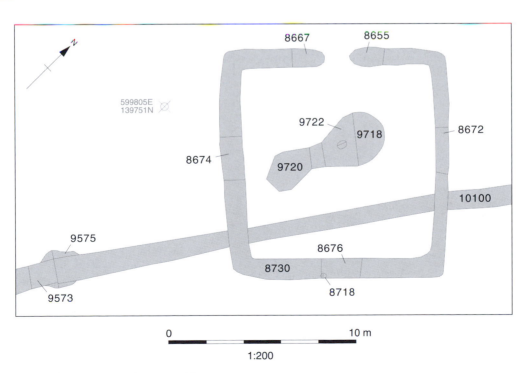

Figure 3.60   Plan of mortuary enclosure 8730.

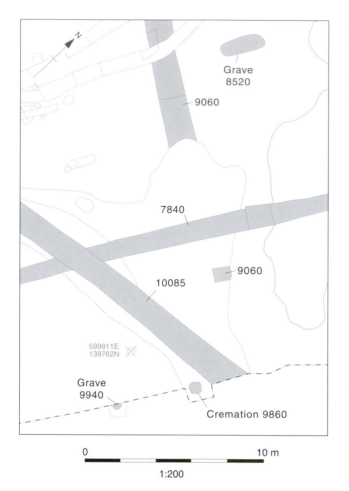

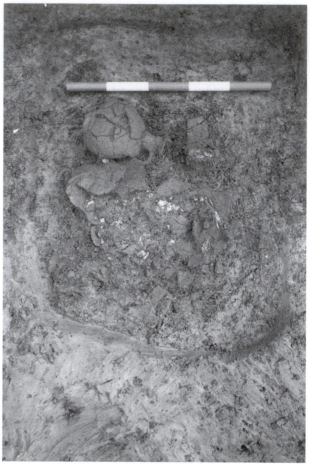

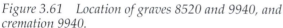

0   10 m

1:200

Figure 3.61   Location of graves 8520 and 9940, and cremation 9940.

Plate 3.14   Cremation group 9860.

a shallow bowl-shaped depression in the centre of the cremation cut and does not seem to have been placed within the jar. It may originally have been held in a bag or some other organic container. Both cremation pits were back-filled with redeposited natural silt clay (see Chapter 8).

Inhumation grave

A single inhumation grave 8520, aligned roughly NE-SW, was situated approximately 19 m north-west of the cremations mentioned above. The grave was sub-rectangular in shape, with a maximum width of 0.75 m, tapering to 0.43 m at either end, and a length of 2.46 m. The edges of the grave were irregular and near vertical; the base had maximum surviving depth of 0.14 m. The bone preservation was very poor due to the acidic nature of the soil, and only incomplete parts of the right and left tibia and the right femur survived. The grave contained three ancillary vessels. A samian bowl and a heavily broken up flagon were set in an upright position on the base of the grave in the vicinity of the right foot. At the north-east end of the grave, close to where the head would have been, were the remains of a small grey ware flask. This lay

on its side with only half of the base surviving. Also at the north-east edge of the grave was a single iron nail (SF1406), the only surviving evidence for a coffin (see Chapter 8).

Area C (Figs 3.62-3.63)

Cemetery

A small cemetery was located to the north-west of Area A beyond the main settlement boundary. Eleven cremations and eight possible inhumations were examined within a well-defined enclosure.

Ditches

The south-east boundary of the cemetery (and of the whole of Area C) was marked by a substantial NE-SW ditch alignment (5174). This divided the cemetery from the adjacent settlement in all phases; indeed, its alignment is perpetuated by a modern hedge and tree line up to the present day. Only some of the later phases of ditch 5174, however, were observed within the limits of Area C.

A NW-SE aligned ditch (5270) was stratigraphically the earliest linear feature within the cemetery

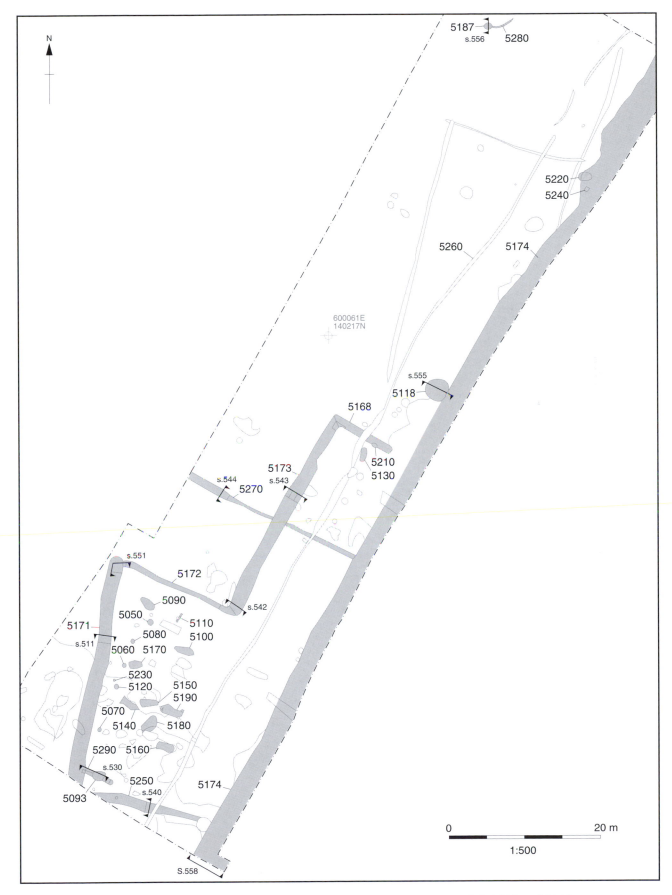

Figure 3.62   Area C: Plan of cemetery enclosed within ditches 5250, 5174, 5171, 5172, 5173 and 5168.

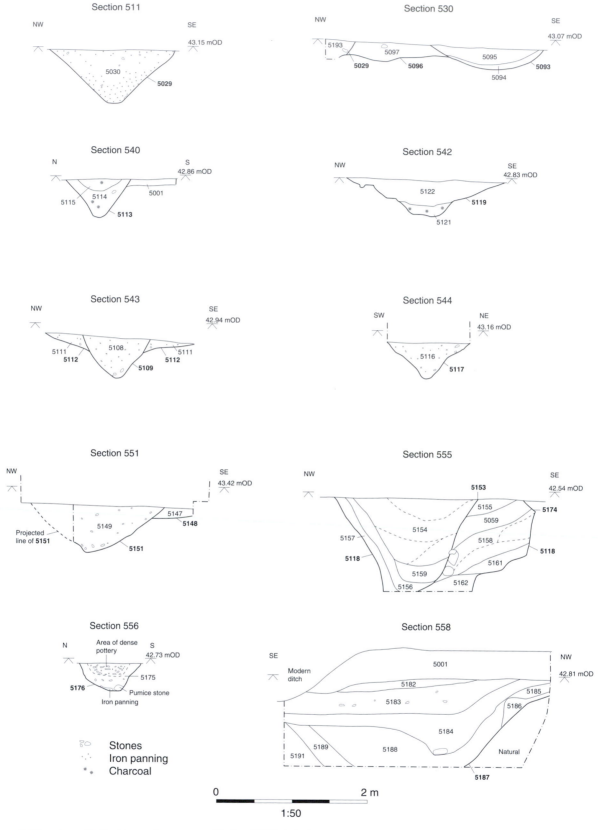

Figure 3.63   Area C: Sections of cemetery ditches 5250, 5171, 5172, 5173, 5174, ditch 5270, gully 5290, waterhole 5118, and pit 5176: Ditch 5250: section 540 (cut 5113); ditch 5171: section 511 (cut 5029), section 551 (cut 5151); ditch 5172: section 551 (cut 5148); ditch 5173: section 542 (cut 5119), section 543 (cut 5109); ditch 5174: section 558 (cut 5187), ditch 5270: section 544 (cut 5117), gully 5290: section 530 (cut 5096), waterhole 5118: section 555; and pit 5176: section 556.

area. Ditch 5270 was 1.10 m wide and 0.45 m deep and had a splayed V-shaped profile (Fig. 3.63, section 544). The light grey silt clay fill may have represented a single episode of backfilling, rather than a gradual silting event. Ditch 5270 may have represented an early form of boundary for the north-east side of the cemetery, before it was succeeded by a more elaborate cemetery enclosure consisting of ditches 5171, 5172, 5173 and 5168.

The NE-SW ditch 5174 was most likely, judging by the evidence of the gradiometer survey, a continuation of ditch 840 recorded in Area B. This feature paralleled the alignment of the Canterbury road, but lay to the rear of the settlement plots north-west of the road, separating the cemetery from the main settlement area. It is likely that this alignment was in place from a very early stage in the life of the settlement and would have been in existence before the ditches associated with the cemetery boundary (5171, 5172, 5173, 5168) were established. Ditch 5174 had an average width of 4.0 m and a depth of 1.50 m, with steeply sloping sides and a flat base (Fig. 3.63, section 558). A yellow-brown silt clay on both sides of the ditch represented the erosion and slippage of the original edges. This was overlain by a yellow-brown silt clay, which contained moderate amounts of charcoal, tipping into the ditch from the south-east edge. Above these fills were two grey silt clay deposits, both containing large amounts of charcoal. The latter of these deposits was of substantial depth (0.55 m) and represented a single episode of infill. This was interpreted as a possible flood deposit, or the fill at least suggested that the ditch had contained standing water for a time. These deposits were sealed by a dark grey silt, which represented a more gradual accumulation in the ditch.

Ditches 5250, 5171, 5172, 5173 and 5168 comprised a rectilinear series of boundaries which formed a more elaborate enclosure for the cemetery area. Features 5172, 5173 and 5168 formed one continuous ditch which eventually terminated to respect the alignment of boundary ditch 5174 at the north-east corner of the cemetery enclosure. This ditch ranged considerably in width from 0.60 m to 2.20 m and in depth from 0.12 m to 0.50 m. Its shallow U-shaped profile at its western limit changed as it extended eastwards to a ditch to a profile with shallow sloping sides, which stepped down steeply to a flat base. A blue-grey primary silt clay fill was recorded along its length, overlain by grey-brown silting deposit which contained occasional pieces of hearth bottom slag. The ditch produced pottery mostly dated *c* AD 43-100, although an upper silting deposit (5122; Fig. 3.63, section 542) within the NE-SW stretch of the ditch produced (in a larger assemblage) a few small sherds dated after AD 200 which were probably intrusive. It was within this area of the ditch that a re-cut (5109) was recorded, running on the same axis for approximately 22 m (Fig. 3.63, section 543). This was 0.9 m wide and 0.5 m deep and had steep sides and a rounded base filled with a pale grey clay silting deposit which contained a bronze Colchester

derivative brooch (SF501) dated mid-late 1st- to early 2nd-century (see Cool, Chapter 5, Cat. no.10).

Ditch 5171 was aligned roughly NNE-SSW and formed the western boundary of the cemetery area. This feature was up to 1.67 m wide and 0.72 m deep and had sides sloping at 45° to a flat base (Fig. 3.63, section 511). It was filled by a blue-grey silt clay mottled with flecks of orange silt, which produced an illegible 1st-2nd century coin (SF505; see Guest, Chapter 5, Table 5.5). A short stretch of gully, group 5290, extended 4 m to the south-east from the line of ditch 5171 (Fig. 3.63, section 530). This had a shallow U-shaped profile and measured on average 0.8 m wide and 0.2 m deep, although to the south-east it ended in an ill-defined terminal only 0.08 m deep. The gully was filled with brown-grey clay. A sub-circular pit (5093), 1.5 m in diameter and 0.3 m deep, was cut into the top of gully 5290. It had a primary fill of grey-orange silt clay overlain by a dark brown clay silting fill containing infrequent charcoal flecks.

Ditch 5250, aligned roughly WNW-ESE, probably formed the south-western boundary of the cemetery area. To the south-east it ran into pit 5196 before the junction with main boundary 5174. To the north-west it extended beyond the area of excavation, but it is likely to have returned to the north as ditch 5171. Ditch 5250 was typically 0.9 m wide and 0.5 m deep, with sides sloping at 45° to a slightly rounded base, and it was filled with grey-brown silt clay overlain by a dark grey silting deposit (Fig. 3.63, section 540).

Graves

Nineteen graves, ten cremation and nine possible inhumation graves, were excavated within Area C. Most of the burials were in discrete features, as a result of which the dating of some of them was problematic. It is emphasised that no unburnt human bone survived and the identification of inhumation burials was based on feature morphology, in some cases aided by the inclusions of pottery vessels which might have been placed in the features intact and therefore suggest grave goods. The graves and their contents are itemised in full in Chapter 8; this evidence is only summarised here in approximate chronological sequence (Table 3.4)

Two inhumation graves, 5130 and 5190, some 42 m apart, were tentatively assigned to Phase 2 on the basis of associated finds. Two further inhumations adjacent to 5190 - 5160 parallel to it to the south and 5180 roughly at a right angle between 5190 and 5160 - could also have been as early as Phase 2 in date, but the pottery redeposited in the grave fills could not be more closely dated than Phases 2-4. Three cremation burials, 5110, 5120 and 5230, might also have been as early as Phase 2 in date, but could only be assigned wide date ranges. The last two of these formed part of a row of cremations some 18 m long (from south to north 5070, 5230, 5120, 5060, 5080, 5050 and 5090) which extended roughly SSW-NNE inside the line of ditch 5171, but not quite parallel to it (see below).

Table 3.4   Area C cemetery: Summary of burials

Phase	Type	Grave group no	Cut	Alignment	Maximum dimensions (m)	Main fill	Grave goods
2	Inhum	5130	5047	E-W	1.80 x 0.90 x 0.12	5046	Drinking vessel
2	Inhum	5190	5085	NW-SE	3.00 x 1.00 x 0.20	5084	
2-3	Crem	5110	5026		0.35 dia x 0.15	5033	Urn
2-4	Inhum	5160	5072	NW-SE	2.30 x 1.10 x 0.19	5071	
2-4	Inhum	5180	5099	c N-S	2.10 x 1.10 x 0.12	5098	
2-5	Crem	5120	5043		0.60 dia x 0.15	5040	Urn
2-5	Crem	5230	5146		0.33 dia x 0.07	5143	Urn
3	Crem	5220	5131		1.70 x 1.10 x 0.20	5132	?Wooden box, urn, 3 other vessels, animal bone, hobnails
3	Crem	5240	5166		0.54 x 0.51x 0.07	5163	Possible box?? Urn
3	Inhum	5170	5023	E-W	1.90 x 1.00 x 0.10	5022	
3-5	Inhum	5100	5032	E-W	2.80 x 1.00 x 0.15	5031	
4-5	Crem	5080	5021		0.60 dia x 0.15	5017	Urn and flagon
5	Crem	5050	5010		0.65 x 0.40 x 0.15	5011	Urn and intaglio
5	Crem	5070	5061		0.70 x 0.60 x 0.15	5062	Urn and drinking vessel
5	Crem	5210	5128		0.94 x 0.52 x 0.05	5127	Drinking vessel
5	?Inhum (infant)	5060	5016		0.50 dia x 0.12	5012	2 vessels
5	Inhum	5150	5054	E-W	2.50 x 1.10 x 0.18	5053	
6	Crem	5090	5028		c 1.00 x 0.70 x 0.25	5024	Urn, 3 other vessels, animal bone, jet beads and cu bracelet
6	Inhum	5140	5052	NW-SE	3.00 x 1.20 x 0.20.	5051	

Two cremation graves (5220 and 5240) and a single inhumation grave (5170) were assigned to Phase 3. The first of these was certainly contained within a wooden box, and 5240 was possibly treated similarly, although this suggestion is only based on the square shape of the grave. These two graves lay well to the north of the rest of the cemetery immediately north-west of ditch 5174, while inhumation grave 5170 lay close to the line of predominantly Phase 5 cremation burials. A further inhumation, 5100, a little to the east of 5170, was on a similar WNW-ESE alignment to the ?Phase 2 inhumation grave 5160 and 5190 further south. It could only be dated within a wide Phase 3-5 bracket and may therefore have been roughly contemporary with 5170 or rather later.

The row of cremation graves (5070 to 5090) included the majority of those assigned certainly or probably to Phase 5. The spacing of these features varied from c 1.5 m to 3.5 m. The character of burial 5060 was uncertain since no cremation urn or cremated bone was recovered. It is possible that this feature contained an infant inhumation rather than a cremation. The most northerly burial of this row, 5090, was assigned to Phase 6, although a late 3rd century (Phase 5) date is just possible. This cremation group lay in a cut approximately 1.0 m by 0.70 m and 0.25 m deep at the south-east edge of what initially resembled a sub-rectangular inhumation cut. It contained a complete beaker (5003), a fragmented flagon (5027) and a complete cremation urn (5026) at the south-east edge of the pit (Plate 3.15). This latter was lifted and excavated in the laboratory at OA. During excavation a ceramic lid was discovered within the jar, beneath which was a bracelet of copper alloy and a configuration of jet and lignite beads forming a necklace and an armlet (Figs 5.8, 8.6). The necklace was found to consist entirely of jet, while the armlet was a mixture of jet and lignite (see Allason-Jones, Chapter 5; see also Cool, Chapter 5). Below the jet and lignite jewellery, which was unburnt, were the cremated remains of a young adult male (See Chapter 8 below).

A further Phase 5 cremation group, 5210, was located over 30 m north-east of the nearest contemporaneous cremation burial in a sub-rectangular grave cut into the edge of the north-eastern arm of ditch 5171 that defined the cemetery area. This was the only certain burial with such a relationship; an unexcavated feature (5194) which cut 5171 towards the south-west edge of Area C was thought to be a pit rather than a grave.

Late inhumation burials were 5150, aligned E-W and assigned to Phase 5, and the immediately adjacent 5140, aligned roughly NW-SE, assigned to Phase 6 on the basis of a small number of sherds in the backfill of the feature. The former grave cut an earlier gully (5069) and pit (5067).

Other features

A waterhole (5118) with a re-cut (5153) was situated north-east of the cemetery area and was truncated slightly by the north-west edge of ditch 5174. Feature 5118 was roughly circular with a diameter of 3.5 m (Plate 3.16). The sides were near vertical, but the base was not recorded as the feature could only be excavated to a depth of 1.5 m (Fig. 3.63, section 5550. The lowest deposits at the south-east and north-west edges of the waterhole consisted of silt clays deriving from the erosion of the natural edges. Overlying these lower deposits was a substantial layer of light grey silt clay containing charcoal flecks and fragments of stone. This layer (5158), approximately half way down the excavated section of the waterhole, appears to have been waterlogged at one time, as a

Plate 3.15   Grave group 5090 showing grave goods in situ.

Plate 3.16   Well 5118.

high concentration of compacted organic debris was very visible. At the point of recording, however, oxidised flecking was observed throughout the deposit. The penultimate deposit consisted of a dense layer of redeposited natural clay, which contained few inclusions, but did produce a light yellow-brown glass fragment of 1st- to 2nd-century date (SF502). This deposit may possibly consist of upcast derived from the excavation of ditch 5174, or from the re-definition of the edges of the ditch. The uppermost deposit within waterhole 5118 was a light grey silt with occasional flecks of charcoal.

Re-cut 5153 was oval in shape and cut into the north-west edge of waterhole 5118. It measured 2.5 m by 2 m and 1.5 m deep, with near vertical sides and a rounded base. The primary fill within the base of 5153 was a 0.4 m thick dark grey clay silt, which contained a large amount of organic debris and occasional charcoal flecks. This was overlain by a substantial layer (1 m thick) of yellow-brown silt clay, which resembled redeposited natural, perhaps indicating deliberate backfill of the disused waterhole.

A further pit (5176) lay in the northern part of Area C and was probably related to gully segment 5280, which ran from its eastern edge. The pit was 0.60 m in diameter and 0.40 m deep, with steep sloping sides and a flat base. The original function of the pit is uncertain, but it was backfilled with a single deposit of redeposited natural clay which contained fragments of ceramic building material and fragments of at least four flagons probably of late 1st-century date (see Chapter 6 below, Assemblage 1). Gully 5280 was curvilinear, approximately 3 m long and on average 0.3 m wide and 0.1 m deep, with a wide U-shaped profile (Fig. 3.63, section 556). It was backfilled with the same material seen in pit 5176, and included fragments from a further flagon related to those from the pit.

A narrow gully (5260) was generally aligned parallel to the main Roman boundary 5174 some 6-8 m distant from it and extended across the length of Area C. This feature, on average 0.6 m wide and 0.2 m deep, was filled with a mottled grey-brown silt clay which contained many abraded fragments of Roman pottery. The nature of these finds and the fact that it cut all features along its course through the site, suggested that the gully was of post-Roman, and most likely post-medieval, date. Its alignment was followed by that of two field drains which ran the length of Area C.

Chapter 4:   Periods 3-4 - Medieval and Post-Medieval Activity

PERIOD 3: MEDIEVAL FEATURES

Medieval activity was concentrated entirely at the southern margin of Area B (Fig. 4.1). Sampling of features in this part of the site was at a low level and there may originally have been more features of medieval date than are identified here. In addition, while the dated activity seems to have concentrated in the 13th century the presence of spatially related features apparently of post-medieval date may indicate more extended low level activity in the late medieval period.

A ditch *c* 0.9-1.0 m wide (group 10350) extended approximately northwards from the southern margin of Area B. Its course was partly obscured by later features but it probably ran up or very close to a possible waterhole or small pond (10078). This feature, up to *c* 7 m by 5 m, lay just south-east of the Phase 2 ditch 9060 and contained a fill (10077) which produced 13th century pottery (see Chapter 6 below, Assemblage 42).

In the vicinity of feature 10078 were two pits of medieval date. To the north-east pit 9987 was oval in shape with steep sides and a narrow rounded base and was 2.65 m in diameter and 0.85 m deep. The primary fill was a substantial dumped deposit of grey silt clay which contained a large amount of domestic debris including charred remains and pottery fragments (see Chapter 6 below, Assemblage 43) and an iron bucket handle (SF1534), overlain by a grey silting deposit. To the south, pit 10131 had moderately sloping sides a rounded base and measured 2 m in diameter and 0.4 m deep. This similarly was filled with a substantial dumped deposit containing a large amount of wood charcoal and fragments of burnt clay, overlain by another grey silting deposit.

The remains of an oven 9978, located immediately south-west of feature 10078, consisted of a subcircular pit with gradually sloping sides and a flat base. A series of sixteen stakeholes within the bottom of the half-sectioned pit survived to an average depth of 0.07 m below the base of the pit. The primary fill within the remains of the oven was a lining of redeposited natural clay which showed evidence of *in situ* scorching. This was overlain by a charcoal-rich silt-clay, in turn sealed by a mid grey silting deposit with infrequent charcoal flecking and small subrounded stone. There was no direct dating evidence from this feature. A medieval date is assumed but not proved.

Two approximately parallel lengths of gully, groups 10310 and 10300, were recorded east of these features. The latter, some 0.7-0.8 m across was approximately 18.5 m long, with a roughly-defined terminal at each end. Gully 10310 was narrower (0.4-0.5 m

wide) and both ends were obscured but it is unlikely to have been much longer than 10300. Both features produced small groups of medieval sherds in a similar fabric to that of assemblages 42 and 43. A third gully, to the east of 10300 and similarly aligned, was not dated. It has been assigned to the post-medieval period, but an earlier date is possible.

PERIOD 4: POST-MEDIEVAL FEATURES

A number of post-medieval field boundaries were present in Areas B and C. These are not treated in any detail here. The most significant of these alignments were parallel ditches 10000 and 9000 running NE-SW through Area B, the former keeping roughly to the alignment of the Weald to Canterbury road. A series of ditches and some slighter features ran approximately perpendicular to these boundaries. These included an existing hedge-line which extended NW-SE through Area B, but further boundaries were present which had not survived into recent times. Overall the boundaries indicate the existence of a pattern of fields of more than one phase. This consisted originally of rather smaller fields than survived just prior to the excavation, and was for the most part similar to the pattern seen on the Tithe Map of 1839. This pattern of smaller fields is therefore of early 19th century or earlier date.

At the southern margin of Area B the layout of probable post-medieval boundaries departed from the fairly regular rectilinear pattern seen elsewhere in the area and was apparently related in part to earlier alignments. Two parallel ditches (groups 10290 and 10320) running SSE from the line of ditch group 10085 were aligned similarly to medieval gullies 10300 and 10310, while just west of these features, ditch 10340 connected further post-medieval boundaries with feature 10078. The latter, perhaps a waterhole or pond in Period 3, may have continued to serve a similar function in Period 4. To the south of this feature ditch 10360 extended north-eastwards from the edge of excavation for 12 m, before turning through a right angle and running some 9 m to a south-east terminal. The upper fill of this feature was associated with a scatter of post-medieval ceramic building material and a single sherd of pottery possibly of 16th century date. The Kingsnorth Tithe Map of 1839 shows a small building very close to this location.

The base of an isolated wooden post (10515) was encountered towards the south-western end of Area B. This was unremarkable, except that its position correlated closely with that of a feature shown on 19th-century editions of the 25 inch Ordnance Survey map

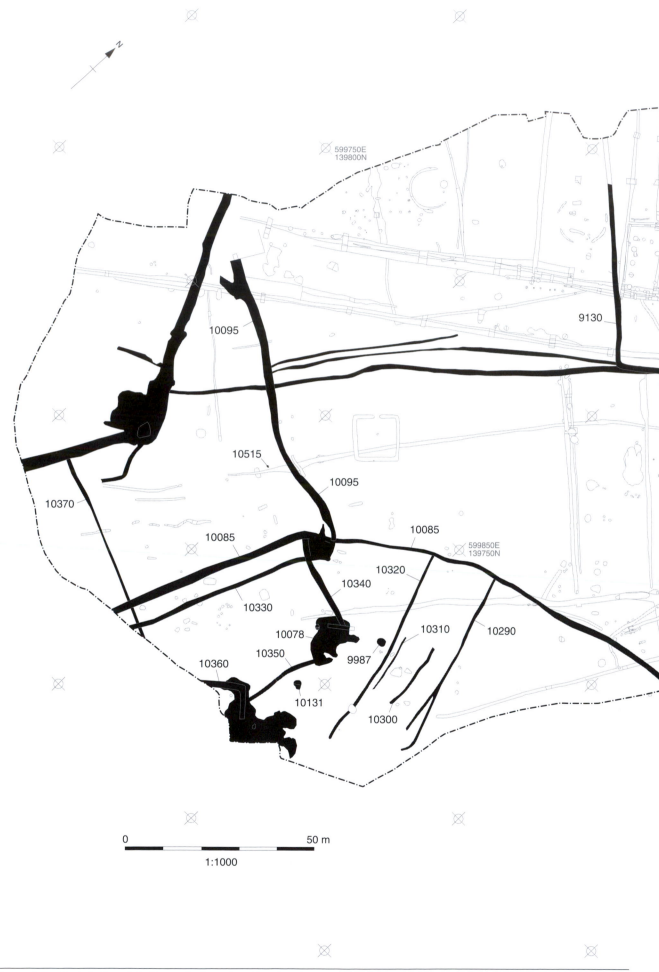

10095

599750E
139800N

9130

10515

10095

10370

10085

10085

599850E
139750N

10320

10330

10340

10290

10078

10310

9987

10350

10360

10300

10131

0   50 m

1:1000

Figure 4.1   Periods 3 and 4, General plan of medieval and post-medieval features.

599800E
139900N

10105

9140

9020

1730

1048

8600

7546

8860

599950E
139900N

7863

883

1650

963

8600

1645

1745

9000

1655

1660

600050E
139900N

600050E
139800N

as marking the south-westerly limit of a projection of the parish boundary of Ashford into land otherwise assigned to Kingsnorth parish. The post, situated in the middle of a field, was presumably intended specifically to mark the boundary.

Other post-medieval features included frequent ceramic field drains and a number of modern disturbances, of which the most substantial was a large pipe trench and manhole cut in recent times at the south-west end of Area B.

Chapter 5:   Coins and Non-Ceramic Finds

COINS
by Peter Guest

Introduction

The excavations at Westhawk Farm produced 237 coins in total, the overwhelming majority of which being Roman bronze denominations struck between the 1st and early 3rd centuries AD. A further 89 coins, including the single Iron Age coin from the site, were recovered during a metal-detector survey undertaken prior to excavation. The site also produced ten post-Roman coins (nine from the excavations and one from the metal-detector survey). The full list of excavated coins from Westhawk Farm is contained in Table 5.5, while the coins recovered by metal detector are listed in Table 5.6. Summaries of these two groups of coins are presented in Tables 5.1 and 5.2 respectively. Generally the coins from Westhawk Farm were rather worn, although in most cases the soil conditions had caused considerable corrosion and decay.

Coins

The Iron Age coin is a gold quarter-stater, struck at the beginning of the 1st century AD in the name of Eppilus, with the inscription COM.F on the obverse and a horse and flower below IPPI on the reverse (metal detector find SF150; Plate 5.1). Analysis at Cardiff University indicated that the metal from which this coin was struck was a heavily debased gold-silver alloy.

Of the 227 excavated Roman coins, 126 could be identified to individual emperors' reigns. The summary tables clearly show that most of these coins were produced during the 1st, 2nd and early 3rd centuries, with a particular concentration of coins from the 2nd century. Most of these coins are bronze denominations (*sestertii*, *dupondii* and *asses*), although the assemblage also included a number of smaller *semisses*. Only ten silver *denarii* were recovered, although this preponderance of bronze coinage is typical of site-finds from Romano-British settlements. The remaining 101 coins could only be described in more vague terms - 'early Roman', that is from the 1st to early-mid 3rd centuries.

The earliest Roman coin is a very worn *denarius* of the later 2nd century BC, showing the head of Roma on the obverse and a *quadriga* on the reverse (SF1141). The three coins of Augustus include a *dupondius* from Pergamum, struck between 28 and 15 BC (SF1224), and an *as* from Nimes (SF983).

The main concentration of coins from Westhawk Farm, however, extends from the Flavian period until the reign of Commodus at the end of the 2nd century (representing 83% of identifiable coins). At first the smaller *dupondii* and *asses* were almost as common as the larger *sestertius*, but by the end of the 2nd century this latter denomination was by far the most common. The Severan period (AD 193-235) is represented by seven coins, including a *denarius* of Caracalla as Caesar from Laodicea (SF1271) and a most unusual Roman provincial bronze denomination struck by the city of Cius in Bythinia for Elagabalus, showing two rearing goats and a large amphora on the reverse (SF167; Plate 5.2). Although bronze coins from the eastern provinces of the Roman Empire do turn up in Britain, they do so in very small numbers (Walker 1988). The Westhawk coin's size and weight suggest that it could have circulated at the equivalent value of a western *as*.

Only ten coins from the Westhawk Farm excavations post-date AD 235, a most unusual situation for a Romano-British settlement. These included three *asses* of Gordian III and Philip I, six radiates of the middle and later 3rd century (of which three were barbarous copies), and a single 4th-century coin struck in AD 316. The metal-detector survey produced a further six 4th-century coins, suggesting that some form of occupation might have continued to the east of the excavated area in the 4th century, although certainly not at the same intensity as in the early Roman period. The absence of usually common bronze coins from the second half of the 4th century, such as the *Fel Temp Reparatio* or Valentinianic issues, suggests that the settlement at Westhawk Farm was abandoned by AD 350 at the latest (and probably some years earlier).

Coins as site-finds

The Westhawk Farm coins are perhaps most intriguing and informative as an assemblage. Table 5.1 shows quite clearly that these coins, as a group, are dominated by the large bronze denominations of the early Roman period. Our understanding of site-finds indicates that this situation is unusual for Roman Britain, where most settlements produce significantly greater quantities of 3rd-century radiates and small 4th-century bronzes than these early-Roman coins.

Fortunately a methodology has been developed in the past few years that allows us to compare quantitatively coins from any sites against the background of coin-supply to Britain, and thereby see when and how they deviate from the notionally average Romano-British site (Reece 1995a). The calculations required for this approach are presented on Table 5.3. First, the coins must be converted into 'coins per thousand' values and then added cumulatively. Then these figures

Table 5.1   Coins: Summary list of coins from excavated contexts (for detailed list see Table 5.5).

Up to AD 296	Den	Ant	Ses	Dup/as	Dup	As	Sem	others	Total
Republic	1								1
Augustus					1	1	1		3
Nero			1						1
Vespasian	1		2			1			4
Domitian	1		1	1		1			4
Nerva	2								2
Trajan			5		3	2		1 (AE frag)	11
Hadrian			*6*	*1*	*2*	*3*			*12*
Sabina			*1*						*1*
Hadrian, total			7	1	2	3			13
Antoninus Pius	*1*		*6*	*1*		*5*		*1 (AE copy)*	*14*
Faustina I	*1*		*6*	*1*					*8*
Marcus Caesar			*2*	*1*					*3*
Faustina II			*1*	*1*					*2*
Antoninus, total	2		15	4		5		1	27
Marcus Aurelius			*18*						*18*
Lucius Verus			*1*						*1*
Faustina II			*7*			*1*			*8*
Lucilla			*5*						*5*
Marcus, total			31			1			32
Commodus			8					1 (plated)	9
Caracalla Caesar	*2*								*2*
Julia Domna			*1*						*1*
Plautilla	*1*								*1*
uncertain empress			*1*						*1*
Severus, total	3		2						5
Elagabalus								1	1
Alex Severus			1						1
Gordian III						1			1
Philp I		*1*				*1*			*2*
Otacilia Severa						*1*			*1*
Philip I, total		1				2			3
Gallienus		1							1
Claudius II		1							1
as Tetricus I		*1*							*1*
as uncertain emp		*2*							*2*
Barb radiates, total		3							3

Uncertain coins up to AwD 296	Den	Dup/as	Semis	AE1	AE2	Copies	Total
Flavian					1	1	2
Antonine empress		4					4
'early Roman'	1		1	48	48		98

Fourth century bronze coin	Trier
313-318	1

Post-Roman Coins	Groat	Penny	Halfpenny	Farthing	Jeton	Total
Edward III	1					1
George III			2			2
George IV			1			1
Victoria		1	1			2
George VI			1			1
12th-13thC				1 cut		1
17thC					1	1

Table 5.2   Coins: Summary list of coins recovered by pre-excavation metal-detector survey (for detailed list see Table 5.6).

Iron Age coin

	AU ¼ stater
Eppilus	1

Up to AD 296	Den	Ant	Ses	Dup/as	Dup	As	Total
Republic	1						1
Claudius	1						1
Vespasian						1	1
Trajan	1		1	1			3
Hadrian	1		1				2
Faustina I	*1*						*1*
Antoninus, total	1						1
Marcus Aurelius			2				*2*
Lucius Verus			1				*1*
Marcus, total			3				3
Gallienus		1					1
Postumus		1					1
as Tetricus I		1					*1*
as uncertain emp		1					*1*
Barb radiates, total		2					2

Uncertain coins up to AD 296	Den	Sestertius	Dp/as	AE1	AE2	Copies	Total
Antonine emperor				3	3		6
Faustina II	2	1	1				4
'early Roman'	3			21	26		50

Fourth-century bronze coins

	uncertain mint
313-18	1
324-30	2
335-41	2
350-53	1

Uncertain Roman bronze coins

	AE3
late 3rd-4thC	2
Roman	3

Post-Roman Coin

	Jeton
17thC	1

Plate 5.1   Late Iron Age gold quarter-stater of Eppillus, showing (a) obverse and (b) reverse.

Plate 5.2   Bronze as of Elagabalus, showing (a) obverse and (b) reverse.

Table 5.3   Coins: Chronological distribution of excavated Roman coins from Westhawk Farm by Issue Period.

Issue Period	Date	No. of coins	Coins per 1000	Cumulative values	AWF minus Brit
I	up to AD 41	4	31.7	31.7	25.2
II	41-54			31.7	13.5
III	54-68	1	7.9	39.7	15.6
IV	69-96	10	79.4	119.0	64.0
V	96-117	13	103.2	222.2	147.4
VI	117-138	13	103.2	325.4	234.8
VII	138-161	27	214.3	539.7	430.4
VIII	161-180	32	254.0	793.7	672.9
IX	180-192	9	71.4	865.1	739.6
X	193-222	5	39.7	904.8	764.1
XI	222-235	2	15.9	920.6	772.6
XII	235-260	4	31.7	952.4	796.4
XIII	260-275	2	15.9	968.3	668.0
XIV	275-296	3	23.8	992.1	570.5
XV	296-318	1	7.9	1000	560.9
XVI	318-330		0	1000	516.8
XVII	330-348		0	1000	271.3
XVIII	348-364		0	1000	173.0
IXX	364-378		0	1000	55.0
XX	378-388		0	1000	50.2
XXI	388-402		0	1000	0
		126	1000		

are deducted from the Romano-British mean (an average of the coins from 140 sites) to produce a sequence of numbers that shows, generally speaking, when and to what extent the Westhawk Farm coins deviate from this mean.

Figure 5.1 plots the same data as a graph (the x-axis representing the Romano-British background) and the strong bias of coins from the Flavian to Severan periods is obvious, as is the sharp decline from the middle of the 3rd century onwards. That the Westhawk Farm coins are always above the x-axis is due to the fact that the site produced significantly more early coins (and significantly fewer later 3rd- and 4th-century coins), than is normal for a settlement in Roman Britain.

The great advantage of this methodology is that it allows sites to be compared with each other, so that groups of similar site-find assemblages can be identified. Figure 5.2 shows the sites with which Westhawk Farm's pattern of coin loss is most similar. These include two groups of coins from London, the forts at Brecon and Ribchester, the early *Classis Britannica* forts at Dover, the large early villa at Fishbourne, and the watery deposits at Bath and Coventina's Well. All of these assemblages produce the same peak of

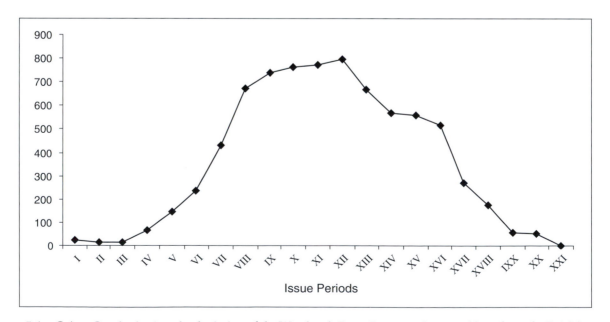

Figure 5.1   Coins: Graph plotting the deviation of the Westhawk Farm Roman coin assemblage from the British mean. Based on figures in Table 5.3.

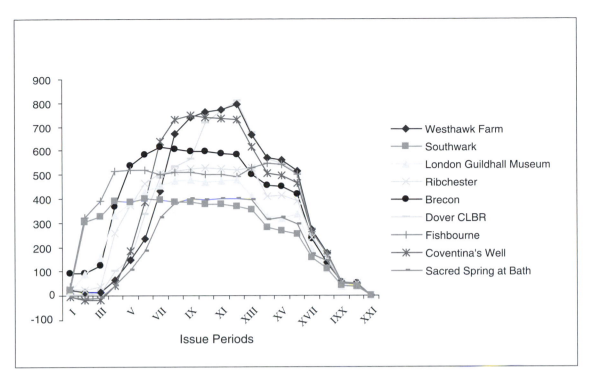

Figure 5.2   Coins: Graph plotting the deviation of the Westhawk Farm coin assemblage from the British mean, together with plots for selected sites showing a similar pattern.

early coins and a relatively weak pattern of coin loss from the beginning of the 3rd century onwards. Having identified that a particular group of sites shares similar coin loss profiles, the next stage is to understand why this might have occurred. It has long been thought that Roman coins initially arrived in Britain in order to pay the army (among other groups, perhaps), and the preponderance of early Roman coins at military sites certainly seems to bear this out. Other than the three forts shown on Figure 5.2, the palace at Fishbourne was preceded by a phase of occupation that might have been a military supply base; a military presence has been postulated at Southwark, and Coventina's Well is just outside the fort at Carrawburgh on Hadrian's Wall. Of course, the precise nature of the settlement at Westhawk Farm cannot be identified from the coins alone, but a strong military influence seems certain.

Coins and the context of deposition

It is interesting that the coins from Westhawk Farm are most similar to two assemblages from sites of religious significance. Excavations at Bath recovered over 12,500 coins from the sacred spring itself, while the well to Coventina at Carrawburgh produced perhaps 16,000 coins in total, as well as stone altars and stele, numerous items of jewellery, an incense-burner, bronze masks, mounts and fittings, and ceramic and glass vessels. There can be little doubt that these large groups of coins represent votive offerings to the deities worshipped at these places, a common practice at places dedicated to water-deities in Brit-

ain and the north-western provinces of the Roman empire (Allason-Jones and McKay 1985, 6-11).

The Westhawk Farm coins, however, are more closely similar to the assemblages from Coventina's Well and Bath than their profiles suggest. Approximately half of the recorded coins from Westhawk Farm were recovered in stratified deposits (the remaining coins are described as unstratified or from topsoil deposits). Generally, one, two, or sometimes three coins came from individual contexts, although four deposits stand out as exceptional due to the fact that they produced significantly more coins than most other contexts, as Table 5.4 shows.

Contexts 303, 677, 723 and 739 as a group account for 57 coins. In fact, it is better to treat them as a single group (or inter-related groups perhaps), as each of these four contexts represents deposits that filled

Table 5.4   Coins: Summary of coin numbers from stratified contexts producing two or more coins.

Context	No. of coins	Context	No. of coins
255 *	2	7644	2
379 *	2	8014	2
427 *	2	302 *	3
675 *	2	416	3
676 *	2	739 *	6
7081	2	303 *	9
7237	2	677 *	21
7428	2	723 *	21

* Contexts marked with an asterisk are fills of Waterhole 796.

Table 5.5 Coins: Detailed list of coins from excavated contexts.

Roman Coins

SF no.	Context	Denomination	Wt (g)	Date	Obverse	Reverse	Mint	Reference	Comment
1141	7000	Denarius	3.8	late 2ndC BC	Head of Roma	Quadriga	Rome		very worn
1224	7428	Dup	5.7	28-15 BC	AUGUSTUS	CA in laurel-wreath & rostra	Pergamum	RIC: 497/9	
983	7185	As	4.9	20-10 BC	AUGUSTUS & AGRIPPA	COL-NIM & crocodile	Nimes	RIC: 156	
165	677	Semis	4.2	early 1st C	AUGUSTUS?	illegible			Left facing bare-headed bust
1170	7004	Semis	15.3	early 1st C	illegible	illegible			'Julio-Claudian' bust
1024	7238	AE1	18.5	54-68	NERO	illegible			
222	723	Sestertius	9.5	69-79	VESPASIAN	illegible			
1143	7004	Denarius	7.8	69-79	VESPASIAN	illegible			
1161	7004	Sestertius	–	69-79	VESPASIAN	illegilble			Very corroded
1382	7836	As	4.0	69-79	VESPASIAN	illegible			
1180	7004	AE frag	2.0	69-96	illegible	illegible			'Flavian' bust
1413	8209	AE2 copy	7.8	69-96	illegible	illegible			'Flavian' bust
128	676	AE2	8.0	81-96	DOMITIAN	illegible			Damaged
1183	7004	AE1		81-96	DOMITIAN	illegible			Damaged
1394	7906	As?		81-96	DOMITIAN	illegible			Left facing 'Flavian' bust
21	185	Denarius		91	DOMITIAN	IMP XXI COS XV CENS PP	Rome	RIC: 156	
1237	7004	Denarius		96-97	NERVA	CONCORDIA EXERCITVVM	Rome		
1308	644	Denarius		97	NERVA	COS III PATER PATRIAE	Rome	RIC: 24	
140	677	Dupondius	5.9	98-117	TRAJAN	illegible			
152	746	AE frag	–	98-117	TRAJAN	illegible			
272	1674	Sestertius		98-117	TRAJAN	illegible			Damaged
1203	7003	Sestertius	16.0	98-117	TRAJAN	illegible			
1160	7004	Dupondius	6.2	98-117	TRAJAN	illegible			
1244	7004	Dupondius	–	98-117	TRAJAN	illegible			Damaged
1305	7004	As	4.4	98-117	TRAJAN	illegible			
1346	7734	Sestertius	–	98-117	TRAJAN	illegible			Damaged
1381	7835	Sestertius	22.5	98-117	TRAJAN	illegible			
1546	10351	As	5.8	98-117	TRAJAN	illegible			
1366	7769	Sestertius	13.8	103-11	TRAJAN	SPQR OPTIMO PRINCIPI - SC (Concordia)	Rome	RIC: 496	Damaged
10	126	Dupondius	1.5	117-38	HADRIAN	illegible			Cut to 20mm diam. module
95	416	As	9.9	117-38	HADRIAN	illegible			
239	723	As	6.5	117-38	HADRIAN	illegible			
1162	7004	Sestertius	7.1	117-38	HADRIAN	illegible			Cut to 24mm diam. module
1166	7004	Sestertius	14.3	117-38	HADRIAN	illegible			
1169	7004	Sestertius	11.1	117-38	HADRIAN	illegible			Cut to 21mm diam. module
1174	7004	As	2.7	117-38	HADRIAN	PONT MAX TR POT COS III - SC. PIE AVG	Rome	RIC: 579	
1233	7004	Sestertius	3.2	117-38	HADRIAN	illegible			Damaged
1371	7004	Sestertius	15.2	117-38	HADRIAN	illegible			
1067	7294	Sestertius	19.5	117-38	HADRIAN	illegible			
1388	7837	AE frag	3.4	117-38	HADRIAN	illegible			
1168	7004	Dupondius	7.2	119-21	HADRIAN	VIRTVTI AVGVSTI - SC	Rome	RIC: 605	
62	303	Sestertius	21.0	119-38	SABINA	illegible			

No.	Cat.	Denomination	Wt	Date	Person	Reverse legend	Note	RIC	Comment
141	677	Sestertius	17.5	139	ANTONINUS PIUS	Libertas [Publica Cos II] - SC	RIC: 538		
24	255	AE1 frag	9.6	138-61	ANTONINUS PIUS	Libertas left			
41	266	As	9.4	138-61	ANTONINUS PIUS	illegible			
54	302	As	12.5	138-61	ANTONINUS PIUS	illegible			
146	677	As	12.4	138-61	ANTONINUS PIUS	illegible			
225	723	Sestertius	20.2	138-61	ANTONINUS PIUS	illegible			
151	739	Sestertius	14.8	138-61	ANTONINUS PIUS	illegible			damaged
1154	7004	Sestertius	-	138-61	FAUSTINA II	illegible			
1282	7004	As	8.4	138-61	ANTONINUS PIUS	illegible			
1338	7004	AE1	16.2	138-61	ANTONINUS PIUS	illegible			
1360	7004	AE2 frag	3.8	138-61	ANTONINUS PIUS?	illegible			
228	723	AE copy	7.7	1st-2nd C	as Antonius Pius?	illegible	copy		Right facing bust - big nose
240	724	Dupondius/as	6.0	138-80	uncertain empress	illegible			
233	723	Dupondius/as	5.6	141-61	DIVA FAUSTINA I	AETERNITAS - SC			
234	723	Sestertius	17.9	141-61	DIVA FAUSTINA I	AETERNITAS - SC			
267	723	Sestertius	25.9	141-61	DIVA FAUSTINA I	AVGVSTA (Vesta) - SC		RIC: 1126	
219	739	Sestertius	22.8	141-61	DIVA FAUSTINA I	AVGVSTA - SC			
266	739	Sestertius	14.1	141-61	DIVA FAUSTINA I	illegible			
1142	7004	Denarius	-	141-61	DIVA FAUSTINA I	AETERNITAS (Aeternitas)	Rome	RIC: 347	
1165	7004	Sestertius	23.3	141-61	DIVA FAUSTINA I	illegible			damaged
937	7086	Sestertius	20.6	141-61	DIVA FAUSTINA I	illegible			
65	303	Sestertius		145-61	MARCUS AURELIUS	illegible			
					Caesar				
1230	7004	Dupondius/as	7.0	145-61	FAUSTINA II (Pius)	VENVS - SC		RIC: 1387	
224	739	Sestertius	24.1	145-75	FAUSTINA II?	illegible			
264	739	Sestertius	20.6	145-75	FAUSTINA II	illegible			
1409	8043	Dupondius/as	4.1	145-75	FAUSTINA II	PRIMI/DECEN/NALES/COS III - SC		RIC: 846	
145	677	Sestertius	13.6	147-48	MARCUS AURELIUS				
221	723	Sestertius	22.8	151-53	ANTONINUS PIUS	SALVS AVG COS III - SC	Rome	RIC: 221	
1144	7004	Denarius		152-53	ANTONINUS PIUS	COS IIII (Annona)		RIC: 934	
1077	7279	As	7.3	154-55	ANTONINUS PIUS	BRITANNIA		RIC: 1350	
168	677	AE2 copy?	2.4	158-59	MARCUS AURELIUS	TR POT XIII [COS II] - SC			
					Caesar				
61	303	Sestertius	19.5	161-69	LUCILLA	[Pietas] - SC		RIC: 1756	
64	303	Sestertius	25.8	161-69	LUCILLA	VENVS - SC		RIC: 1763	
276	379	Sestertius	27.3	161-69	LUCILLA	HILARITAS - SC		RIC: 1740	
162	677	Sestertius	22.7	161-69	LUCILLA	VENVS - SC		RIC: 1763	
1158	7004	Sestertius	20.3	161-69	LUCILLA	VENVS - SC			
22	2	Sestertius	-	161-75	FAUSTINA II	[Laetitia] - SC			damaged
227	723	Sestertius	21.3	161-75	FAUSTINA II	[Laetitia] - SC		RIC: 1654	
269	723	As	10.0	161-75	FAUSTINA II	[Iuno] - SC		RIC: 1647	
176	805	Sestertius	-	161-75	FAUSTINA II	[Iuno] - SC		RIC: 1645	damaged
1188	7001	Sest copy	-	161-75	as Faustina II	as Salus std l.			damaged
1306	7004	Sestertius	11.9	161-75	FAUSTINA II	[Laetitia] - SC			
1435	7004	Sestertius	19.1	161-75	FAUSTINA II	[Venus Felix] - SC		RIC: 1686	
929	7076	Sestertius	21.9	161-75	FAUSTINA II	[Venus Felix] - SC		RIC: 1686	

(Continued on next page)

Table 5.5 (continued)

SF no.	Context	Denomination	Wt (g)	Date	Obverse	Reverse	Mint	Reference	Comment
60	303	Sestertius	14.5	161-80	MARCUS AURELIUS	Fig stdg l. with cornucopiae			
217	427	Sestertius	24.2	161-80	MARCUS AURELIUS	illegible			
144	677	Sestertius	16.0	161-80	MARCUS AURELIUS	Salus? seated l feeding snake around altar			
230	723	Sestertius	14.6	161-80	MARCUS AURELIUS	Fig stdg r. holding spear			fragment
1404	8014	Sestertius	-	161-80	MARCUS AURELIUS	illegible			
1515	9436	Sestertius copy?	6.9	161-80	MARCUS AURELIUS	illegible			
265	739	Sestertius	22.7	166-75	MARCUS AURELIUS	Roma seated with Victory, spear & shield			
271	1673	Sestertius	-	166	LUCIUS VERUS	[Trp Pot VI Imp IIII Cos II] - SC		RIC: 1457	fragment
135	677	Sestertius	19.9	168-69	LUCIUS VERUS	Aequitas seated l.			
226	723	Sestertius	17.6	168-71	MARCUS AURELIUS	Salus with sceptre feeding snake around altar			
985	7187	Sestertius	16.6	168-71	MARCUS AURELIUS	Salus with sceptre feeding snake around altar			
220	723	Sestertius	23.7	169-70	MARCUS AURELIUS	[Saluti Aug Cos III] - SC		RIC: 979	
275	379	Sestertius	20.2	170-71	MARCUS AURELIUS	IMP VI COS III (Victory setting shield on tree) - SC		RIC: 1001	
268	723	Sestertius	23.5	170-71	MARCUS AURELIUS	VOTA SUSCEPTA DECENN II COS III - SC		RIC: 1017	
129	676	Sestertius	20.3	171-72	MARCUS AURELIUS	[Imp VI Cos III] (Roma with shield) - SC		RIC: 1033	
139	677	Sestertius	18.9	171-72	MARCUS AURELIUS	IMP VI COS [III] (Roma with shield) - SC		RIC: 1033	
236	723	Sestertius	17.7	172-73	MARCUS AURELIUS	VICT/GERMA/IMP VI/COS III/SC		RIC: 1090	
1348	7004	Sestertius	12.6	176-77	MARCUS AURELIUS	Trophy with 2 seated captives at base			
1146	7004	Sestertius	13.8	177-78	MARCUS AURELIUS	[Imp VIIII Cos III PP] (Aequitas) - SC		RIC: 1230	
1310	7580	Sestertius	12.0	180	COMMODUS	IOVI VICTOR [Imp III Cos II PP] (Victory) - SC		RIC: 291	
137	677	Sestertius	12.8	183	COMMODUS	TRP VIII IMP VI COS PP (Victory) - SC		RIC: 374	
218	427	Sestertius	12.3	186	COMMODUS	FID EXERCIT		RIC: 468	
68	303	Sestertius	19.6	180-92	COMMODUS	Hercules stdg front			
229	723	Sestertius	18.3	180-92	COMMODUS	Fig. stdg with cornucopiae			
232	723	Sestertius	21.6	180-92	COMMODUS	illegible			
1175	7004	Sestertius	11.8	180-92	COMMODUS	illegible			
1022	7237	Sestertius	14.3	180-92	COMMODUS	illegible			
132	677	Plated denarius		192	-	[...] COS VII PP (Pietas std l.)	copy		single sheet of silver foil around remnants of CuA core. Probably copying denarius of Commodus
1150	7004	Sestertius	15.7	193-217	JULIA DOMNA	illegible			
1286	7646	Denarius		196-211	CARACALLA	illegible			fragment

No.	Cat.	Denomination	Wt./diam.	Date	Ruler	Reverse	Mint	Reference	Notes
1271	7004	Denarius		198	CARACALLA	SPES PVBLICA	Laodicea	RIC: 338b	
1359	7004	Denarius		202-05	PLAUTILLA	VENVS VICTRIX	Rome	RIC: 369	
167	677	Ae, diameter 22 mm	5.2	218-22	Elagabalus (M AVR ANTO-NINVS AVG)	[KIANON] 2 goats and large amphora	Cius, Bythinia	BMC: 40	damaged
23	255	Sestertius	-	222-35	SEVERUS ALEXANDER	illegible			
1010	7004	AE2	3.5	222-38	Severan empress	illegible			
238	723	As	4.8	238-44	GORDIAN III	illegible			
124	675	As	-	244-49	PHILIP I	VICTORIA AVG - SC		RIC: 191var	damaged
223	723	As	3.1	244-49	OTACILIA SEVERA	illegible			
163	677	Radiate	4.7	247-49	PHILIP I	FIDES EXERCITVS		RIC: 62	
1281	7644	Denarius	8.4	1st-early 3rdC	illegible	illegible			
35	2	AE2	14.7	1st-mid 3rdC	illegible	illegible			
49	302	AE1	4.9	1st-mid 3rdC	illegible	illegible			
58	302	AE1	14.8	1st-mid 3rdC	illegible	illegible			
56	303	AE2	18.4	1st-mid 3rdC	illegible	illegible			
57	303	AE1	4.6	1st-mid 3rdC	illegible	illegible			
63	303	AE1	7.1	1st-mid 3rdC	illegible	illegible			
80	416	AE1	5.1	1st-mid 3rdC	illegible	illegible			
91	416	AE1	4.2	1st-mid 3rdC	illegible	illegible			
89	417	AE1	21.8	1st-mid 3rdC	illegible	illegible			
121	675	AE1	14.6	1st-mid 3rdC	illegible	illegible			
131	677	AE1	9.3	1st-mid 3rdC	illegible	illegible			
133	677	AE1	0.1	1st-mid 3rdC	illegible	illegible			
134	677	AE1	15.8	1st-mid 3rdC	illegible	illegible			
142	677	AE3	4.8	1st-mid 3rdC	illegible	illegible			
231	723	AE1	2.9	1st-mid 3rdC	illegible	illegible			
235	723	AE2	7.1	1st-mid 3rdC	illegible	illegible			
174	819	AE2	9.7	1st-mid 3rdC	illegible	illegible			
175	841	AE1	5.5	1st-mid 3rdC	illegible	illegible			
194	1089	AE1	3.8	1st-mid 3rdC	illegible	illegible			
258	1380	AE1	3.7	1st-mid 3rdC	illegible	illegible			
252	1567	AE2	3.7	1st-mid 3rdC	illegible	illegible			
505	5030	AE2	12.7	1st-mid 3rdC	illegible	illegible			
1148	7000	AE2	1.6	1st-mid 3rdC	illegible	illegible			
1179	7000	AE1	17.4	1st-mid 3rdC	illegible	illegible			
1204	7003	AE2	9.7	1st-mid 3rdC	illegible	illegible			
1014	7004	AE1	11.1	1st-mid 3rdC	illegible	illegible			
1145	7004	AE1	10.4	1st-mid 3rdC	illegible	illegible			
1149	7004	AE1	3.8	1st-mid 3rdC	illegible	illegible			
1152	7004	AE1	2.9	1st-mid 3rdC	illegible	illegible			
1153	7004	AE2	4.3	1st-mid 3rdC	illegible	illegible			
1155	7004	AE2	3.0	1st-mid 3rdC	illegible	illegible			
1156	7004	AE2	2.8	1st-mid 3rdC	illegible	illegible			
1157	7004	AE2		1st-mid 3rdC	illegible	illegible			
1159	7004	AE2		1st-mid 3rdC	illegible	illegible			

(Continued on next page)

Table 5.5 (continued)

SF no.	Context	Denomination	Wt (g)	Date	Obverse	Reverse	Mint	Reference	Comment
1163	7004	AE1	11.1	1st-mid 3rdC	illegible	illegible			
1171	7004	AE1	3.9	1st-mid 3rdC	illegible	illegible			
1172	7004	AE2	2.7	1st-mid 3rdC	illegible	illegible			
1176	7004	AE2	1.7	1st-mid 3rdC	illegible	illegible			
1178	7004	AE2	2.3	1st-mid 3rdC	illegible	illegible			
1195	7004	AE2	3.4	1st-mid 3rdC	illegible	illegible			
1200	7004	AE1	7.6	1st-mid 3rdC	illegible	illegible			
1201	7004	AE1	11.3	1st-mid 3rdC	illegible	illegible			
1213	7004	AE1	10.6	1st-mid 3rdC	illegible	illegible			
1218	7004	AE2	1.8	1st-mid 3rdC	illegible	illegible			
1231	7004	AE1	4.9	1st-mid 3rdC	illegible	illegible			
1232	7004	AE1	3.4	1st-mid 3rdC	illegible	illegible			
1234	7004	AE2	1.5	1st-mid 3rdC	illegible	illegible			
1235	7004	AE1	3.6	1st-mid 3rdC	illegible	illegible			
1236	7004	AE2	1.1	1st-mid 3rdC	illegible	illegible			
1238	7004	AE1	4.0	1st-mid 3rdC	illegible	illegible			
1240	7004	AE2	3.9	1st-mid 3rdC	illegible	illegible			
1241	7004	AE2	3.9	1st-mid 3rdC	illegible	illegible			
1245	7004	AE1	6.3	1st-mid 3rdC	illegible	illegible			
1248	7004	AE1	4.5	1st-mid 3rdC	illegible	illegible			
1257	7004	AE1	8.2	1st-mid 3rdC	illegible	illegible			
1270	7004	AE1	9.7	1st-mid 3rdC	illegible	illegible			
1277	7004	AE2	2.1	1st-mid 3rdC	illegible	illegible			
1307	7004	AE2	1.9	1st-mid 3rdC	illegible	illegible			
1312	7004	AE2	4.5	1st-mid 3rdC	illegible	illegible			
1347	7004	AE2	3.6	1st-mid 3rdC	illegible	illegible			
1349	7004	AE2	3.8	1st-mid 3rdC	illegible	illegible			
1362	7004	AE2	0.7	1st-mid 3rdC	illegible	illegible			
1363	7004	AE1	11.3	1st-mid 3rdC	illegible	illegible			
1370	7004	AE1	4.2	1st-mid 3rdC	illegible	illegible			
1373	7004	AE1	8.8	1st-mid 3rdC	illegible	illegible			
1385	7004	AE1	3.3	1st-mid 3rdC	illegible	illegible			
1414	7004	AE2	4.4	1st-mid 3rdC	illegible	illegible			
900	7005	AE2	2.4	1st-mid 3rdC	illegible	illegible			
903	7005	AE2	2.5	1st-mid 3rdC	illegible	illegible			
904	7008	AE1	5.3	1st-mid 3rdC	illegible	illegible			
906	7022	AE2	2.3	1st-mid 3rdC	illegible	illegible			
927	7074	AE2	3.3	1st-mid 3rdC	illegible	illegible			
928	7075	AE2	3.0	1st-mid 3rdC	illegible	illegible			
931	7081	AE1	6.8	1st-mid 3rdC	illegible	illegible			
932	7081	AE2	3.9	1st-mid 3rdC	illegible	illegible			
936	7085	AE1	4.6	1st-mid 3rdC	illegible	illegible			

957	7120	AE2	2.2	1st-mid 3rdC	illegible	illegible		
986	7188	AE2	2.7	1st-mid 3rdC	illegible	illegible		
999	7210	AE1	7.4	1st-mid 3rdC	illegible	illegible		
1021	7237	AE1	5.2	1st-mid 3rdC	illegible	illegible		
1208	7426	AE2	4.2	1st-mid 3rdC	illegible	illegible		
1225	7428	AE2	3.5	1st-mid 3rdC	illegible	illegible		
1272	7637	AE1	15.3	1st-mid 3rdC	illegible	illegible		
1400	7639	AE2	4.2	1st-mid 3rdC	illegible	illegible		
1275	7640	AE1	8.5	1st-mid 3rdC	illegible	illegible		
1280	7643	AE2	3.8	1st-mid 3rdC	illegible	illegible		context no. unclear
1364	7789	AE2	2.2	1st-mid 3rdC	illegible	illegible		
1369	7793	AE1	4.0	1st-mid 3rdC	illegible	illegible		
1376	7828	AE2	4.0	1st-mid 3rdC	illegible	illegible		
1377	7829	AE2	2.3	1st-mid 3rdC	illegible	illegible		
1379	7833	AE1	4.1	1st-mid 3rdC	illegible	illegible		
1405	8014	AE2	2.9	1st-mid 3rdC	illegible	illegible		
1494	8393	AE1	3.3	1st-mid 3rdC	illegible	illegible		
1509	9155	AE2	2.5	1st-mid 3rdC	illegible	illegible		
1304	u/s	AE1	6.5	1st-mid 3rdC	illegible	illegible		
59	344	Radiate		260-68	GALLIENUS	illegible		
51	298	Radiate		268-70	CLAUDIUS II	MARS VLTOR		
138	677	Barb radiate		270-90	illegible	illegible		
164	677	Barb radiate		270-90	as Tetricus I	as Pax		
1438	7004	Barb radiate		270-90	illegible	illegible		
166	677	AE3		316	LICINIUS	GENIO POP ROM	RIC: Tr120 T/F/ATR	

Post-Roman Coins

1276	7641	Cut farthing		12th-13thC	illegible			
956	7003	Groat		1351-61	EDWARD III			pre-Treaty coinage
1147	7004	Rose farthing		17thC				
36	2	Token		18thC?	illegible			
1173	7003	Halfpenny		1806	GEORGE III			
1408	7004	Halfpenny		1760-1820	GEORGE III			
1008	7004	Halfpenny		1826	GEORGE IV			
1151	7004	Halfpenny		1861	VICTORIA			
1167	7004	Penny		1861	VICTORIA			
1351	7004	Halfpenny		1939	GEORGE VI			

Table 5.6   Coins: Detailed list of coins from pre-excavation metal-detector survey.

SF no	Denomination	wt (g)	Date	Obverse	Reverse	Mint	Reference	Comment
Iron Age Coins								
150	quarter-stater	1.2	early 1stC AD	COM.F, pellet border	Horse with mane r., above IPPI, below flower		VA437	
Roman Coins								
275	Denarius		early 1stC BC	Head of Apollo	Quadriga			worn
213	Denarius		1stC BC-1stC AD	illegible	illegible			
85	Denarius		46-47	CLAUDIUS	DE BRITANN			
180	As	9.4	69-79	VESPASIAN	illegible			
137	Sestertius	20.5	98-117	TRAJAN	illegible			
144	Dupondius/as	4.6	98-117	TRAJAN	illegible			
229	Denarius		98-117	TRAJAN	illegible			
104	Sestertius	16.6	117-25	HADRIAN	illegible			
329	Denarius		125-28	HADRIAN	COS III (Abundantia)	Rome	RIC: 169	
67	AE1	17.2	138-92	Antonine emperor	illegible			
145	AE1	12.2	138-92	Antonine emperor	illegible			
161	AE2	3.7	138-92	Antonine emperor	illegible			
201	AE2	-	138-92	Antonine emperor	illegible			damaged
241	AE2	6.2	138-92	Antonine emperor	illegible			
309	AE1	15.9	138-92	Antonine emperor	illegible			
265	Denarius		141-61	DIVA FAUSTINA I	illegible			
158	Denarius		145-75	FAUSTINA II	illegible			
251	Denarius		145-75	FAUSTINA II	illegible			
296	Sestertius	12.8	145-75	FAUSTINA II	illegible			
340	Dupondius/as	9.8	145-75	FAUSTINA II	illegible			
91	Sestertius	20.5	161-80	MARCUS AURELIUS	illegible			
103	Sestertius	12.3	161-80	MARCUS AURELIUS	illegible			
181	Denarius		163-64	LUCIUS VERUS	TRP IIII IMP II COS II (Mars)	Rome	RIC: 515	
3	AE2	-	1st-early 3rdC	illegible	illegible			damaged
14	AE2	6.8	1st-early 3rdC	illegible	illegible			
22	AE2	9.2	1st-early 3rdC	illegible	illegible			
30	AE1	12.5	1st-early 3rdC	illegible	illegible			
61	AE2	5.6	1st-early 3rdC	illegible	illegible			
62	AE1	17.2	1st-early 3rdC	illegible	illegible			
72	AE1	13.1	1st-early 3rdC	illegible	illegible			
76	AE2	7.7	1st-early 3rdC	illegible	illegible			
80	AE2	5.6	1st-early 3rdC	illegible	illegible			
93	AE2	8.8	1st-early 3rdC	illegible	illegible			
96	AE2	3.9	1st-early 3rdC	illegible	illegible			
105	AE2	6.7	1st-early 3rdC	illegible	illegible			
115	AE2	7	1st-early 3rdC	illegible	illegible			
121	AE1	15.9	1st-early 3rdC	illegible	illegible			
122	AE1	15.1	1st-early 3rdC	illegible	illegible			
127	AE2	4.3	1st-early 3rdC	illegible	illegible			
128	AE2	6.7	1st-early 3rdC	illegible	illegible			
130	AE1	-	1st-early 3rdC	illegible	illegible			damaged
133	AE1	5.4	1st-early 3rdC	illegible	illegible			
148	AE2	5.7	1st-early 3rdC	illegible	illegible			
149	AE1	9.5	1st-early 3rdC	illegible	illegible			
154	AE1	5.9	1st-early 3rdC	illegible	illegible			
185	AE2	5.7	1st-early 3rdC	illegible	illegible			
195	AE2	5.1	1st-early 3rdC	illegible	illegible			
196	AE1	12.6	1st-early 3rdC	illegible	illegible			
200	AE1	13.5	1st-early 3rdC	illegible	illegible			
211	Denarius		1st-early 3rdC	illegible	illegible			
214	AE1	8.1	1st-early 3rdC	illegible	illegible			
218	AE2	4.7	1st-early 3rdC	illegible	illegible			
220	AE2	7.3	1st-early 3rdC	illegible	illegible			
224	AE1	11	1st-early 3rdC	illegible	illegible			
227	AE2	4.9	1st-early 3rdC	illegible	illegible			
228	AE1	11.6	1st-early 3rdC	illegible	illegible			
235	AE2	4.3	1st-early 3rdC	illegible	illegible			
237	AE1	12.1	1st-early 3rdC	illegible	illegible			

Table 5.6 (continued)

SF no	Denomination	wt (g)	Date	Obverse	Reverse	Mint	Reference	Comment
237A	AE2	6.9	1st-early 3rdC	illegible	illegible			
238	AE1	9.3	1st-early 3rdC	illegible	illegible			
250	AE2	7.2	1st-early 3rdC	illegible	illegible			
274	AE1	5.9	1st-early 3rdC	illegible	illegible			
277	AE2	6.9	1st-early 3rdC	illegible	illegible			
294	AE1	10	1st-early 3rdC	illegible	illegible			
299	AE2	3.9	1st-early 3rdC	illegible	illegible			
301	AE1	8.2	1st-early 3rdC	illegible	illegible			
308	AE1	8.8	1st-early 3rdC	illegible	illegible			
312	AE2	3.9	1st-early 3rdC	illegible	illegible			
317	AE3	5.5	1st-early 3rdC	illegible	illegible			
318	Denarius		1st-early 3rdC	illegible	illegible			
319	AE2	5.7	1st-early 3rdC	illegible	illegible			
330	AE1	-	1st-early 3rdC	illegible	illegible			damaged
66	Radiate		260-68	GALLIENVS	GERMANICVS MAX V	Lyons	RIC: 18	
87	Radiate		260-68	POSTUMUS	PAX			
68	Barb radiate		270-90	illegible	illegible			
136	Barb radiate		270-90	as Tetricus I	as Victoria?			
332	AE3		313-18	Constantine I	SOLI INVICTO COMITI	T/F/[.....]		
69	AE3		324-30	House of Constantine	Camp gate	-		
324	AE3		324-30	House of Constantine	PROVIDENTIAE CAESS	-		
78	AE3		335-41	House of Constantine	GLORIA EXERCITVS (1 std)	-		
94	AE3		335-41	House of Constantine	GLORIA EXERCITVS (1 std)	-		
54	AE3		350-53	illegible	Emperor stdg facing holding standard	-		
273	AE3		late 3rd-4thC	illegible	illegible			
336	AE3		late 3rd-4thC	illegible	illegible			
239	AE3	-	Roman	illegible	illegible			
244	AE3	-	Roman	illegible	illegible			
262	AE3	-	Roman	illegible	illegible			
Later Coins								
117	Token?		17thC?	illegible	illegible			

Table 5.7   Objects and vessels of non-ferrous metal, fired clay and glass: Summary quantification (fragment count) by Phase and material.

Phase	Copper alloy	Lead alloy	Modern alloys	All non-ferrous metal finds	Fired Clay	Frit	Glass	All non-metallic finds	Total
2	1	-	-	1	-	1	2	3	4
3	10	-	-	10	1	-	39	40	50
4	16	3	-	19	1	2	73	76	95
5	11	5	-	16	-	-	45	45	61
6	1	2	-	3	-	-	9	9	12
Unphased	57	57	4	118	-	-	10	10	128
Total	96	67	4	167	2	3	178	183	350

Table 5.8   Objects and vessels of non-ferrous metal, fired clay and glass: Percentages of small finds and vessel fragments by material in the phased and unphased contexts. (Quantification by fragment count, see Table 5.7).

Phase	Copper alloy	Lead alloy	Modern alloys	All non-ferrous metals finds	Fired Clay	Frit	Glass	All non-metallic finds
Phased	41%	15%	0%	29.4%	100%	100%	94%	94.5%
Unphased	59%	85%	100%	70.6%	0%	0%	6%	5.5%

waterhole 796 in plot NW2, close to structure J (see Chapter 3 above). Including the smaller numbers of coins from other component contexts the upper fills of this feature produced a total of 73 coins, or just over half of all the stratified coins from the excavations. This is remarkably close to the patterns observed at the Sacred Spring at Bath and Coventina's Well. In both cases large numbers of coins, among other things, were recovered from watery contexts where, it is generally agreed, they were deposited singly or in groups as offerings to the deities that could be approached, it was thought, via these sources of ground water.

Yet, the excavated stratigraphy at Westhawk Farm indicates that those coins recovered from waterhole 796, despite appearances, should not be interpreted as *in situ* votive deposits. Instead the excavators argue that this feature's upper fills comprised a series of cleaning deposits, collected from elsewhere in the settlement, and thrown into the waterhole sometime in the early 4th century. Although only five of the 57 coins from the waterhole were struck after AD 200, these included two barbarous radiates from the late 3rd century (SF138 and SF164), and a reduced *follis* of 316 struck in the name of Licinius I (SF166). Nevertheless, the proximity of plot NW2 to the temple enclosure to the south-east, might suggest that the coins from waterhole 796 did indeed originate from a votive context before being cleaned up and finally disposed of in a shallow pond across the road.

OBJECTS AND VESSELS OF NON-FERROUS METAL, FIRED CLAY AND GLASS
by H E M Cool

Introduction

The archaeological investigations at Westhawk Farm produced a total of 350 fragments of non-ferrous metal, fired clay and glass small finds and vessels as summarised in Table 5.7. (In addition, fragments of copper alloy wire were also found stringing together the elements of the jet bracelet - Allason-Jones below). In Table 5.7, for ease of comprehension, the material from contexts assigned to more than one phase (2-3, 2-4 etc) has been placed in the later or latest phase.

The high figure for the unphased material reflects the extensive metal detecting that was undertaken as most finds thus recovered came from plough or sub-soil contexts. The effect of this metal detecting programme can easily be seen from Table 5.8 where the assemblage is summarised according to material and whether it came from phased or unphased contexts. Approximately 70% of the non-ferrous metal came from unphased contexts, whereas the corresponding figure for the other types of material is a little over 5%.

Of the unphased material, virtually all of the glass could be assigned to the Roman period on typological grounds. For the non-ferrous metal, 31 items (26.3%

of the unphased metalwork) were typologically Roman. The other dateable items in the unphased metalwork point to casual use of the land from the late medieval period onwards. There is, for example, a much damaged seal (SF1439) depicting a bird centrally which belongs to Rigold's banal type and which may be dated to the 14th century. There was also a button and several buckles of the late medieval to early post medieval period, as well as musket balls, bullet casings, buttons and buckles of the post medieval to modern periods. In total 60 items (50.8% of the unphased metalwork) could be assigned to the late medieval or later period. The remaining metalwork is not chronologically diagnostic.

This report considers all the material that can be regarded as having been used by the Romano-British inhabitants of the settlement, both from the unphased and phased contexts. It is probable that some of the undiagnostic metalwork in the unphased contexts is also of Roman date but as it would not contribute anything to our understanding of the site; it is not considered further here.

One important factor that must be kept in mind when considering the small finds from Westhawk Farm is that the soil conditions have had a deleterious effect on them, and this has undoubtedly biased the assemblage. The underlying geology is capped by moderately acidic soil (see Chapter 1 above). This has resulted in most of the non-ferrous metalwork being in very poor condition. As Fell has noted (conservation report in project archive), there appears to have been decuprification of the surfaces of the copper alloy, and on many items the surface is poorly preserved. The disappearance of the surface has often removed features which would have allowed more precise identification of the items. The total lack of worked bone is also probably a result of the soil conditions rather than reflecting a true absence. Worked bone often served the role in antiquity that plastic serves in the modern world, and its lack severely biases the assemblage from the site.

The first part of the report presents the individual items found, placing them in their chronological and typological context, and is structured according to the functional categories developed by Crummy (1983). The assemblage as a whole is then considered from the point of view of chronology and what it can tell us of the character of the population, their status and their links with the wider world. Finally the combination of metal detecting and excavation at the same site allows a comparison to be made between the types of metal finds that the two methodologies recover.

Finds by function

The Roman finds are summarised by functional category in Table 5.9. Personal ornaments are well represented. The high total for the household category is due to the quantity of vessel glass found. An unusual feature of this assemblage is the quantity of weigh-

Table 5.9   Objects and vessels of non-ferrous metal, fired clay and glass: Summary quantification (fragment count) by functional category and material.

Function	Copper alloy	Lead alloy	Fired Clay	Frit	Glass	Total
Personal	18	-	-	3	5	26
Toilet	5	-	-	-	1	6
Textile	2	-	-	-	-	2
Household	3	1	-	-	165	169
Recreation	-	-	1	-	-	1
Weighing	2	10	-	-	-	12
Buildings	-	-	-	-	2	2
Fasteners	9	-	-	-	-	9
Religion	-	-	1	-	-	1
Craft and Industry	2	-	-	-	2	4
Miscellaneous	13	12	-	-	-	25
Total	54	23	2	3	175	257

ing equipment recovered, and this will be further discussed in the next part of the report.

Personal ornaments and jewellery

Personal ornaments are dominated by brooches with 15 examples. A remarkable feature about this group is its typological homogeneity. With the exception of the knee brooch no. 15, all of the brooches that can be assigned to a type (nos 1-13) are Colchester Derivatives. They all have semi-cylindrical spring covers with a double perforated lug behind the head. This holds the chord of the spring in the upper perforation and the bar which holds the spring in the lower one. They also have D-sectioned bows and, where preserved, perforated catch-plates. These features mean that they belong to what Hull variously designated his Colchester BB type (Hull 1968, 79) or Type 93 (Crummy 1983, 12). Hull noted that these were very common in Kent, and proposed a Flavian date (Hull 1959, 48-9, nos 4, 6-9). In Kent examples found in later 1st-century contexts include those from Springhead (op. cit.), Eastwood Farm, Fawkham (Hull 1964, 70, nos 4-6, fig. 3) and Lullingstone (Meates 1987, 65, no. 60, fig. 24). The contextual information from Westhawk Farm is not particularly useful for dating the type. The three brooches (nos 2, 4, and 8) broadly contemporary with the *floruit* of the type derived from contexts that could not be closely dated within Phases 2-3.

The various types of the Colchester Derivative brooch were the commonest type in use during the second half of the 1st century in the south-east of England, and it is becoming increasingly clear that the variants had regional significance. The type where the spring is held by a rearward facing hook is found in large numbers in the Norfolk/Suffolk areas and is relatively frequent in Essex. Mackreth suggests that this should be seen as the type specific to the Iceni with its disappearance after *c* AD 65 being attributable to the suppression of the tribe after the Boudican rising (Mackreth 1996, 300). The form with a spring fixing mechanism similar to the ones found at Westhawk Farm, but with a bow with cavetto mouldings down the front frequently combined with rocker arm ornament (Colchester B or Hull Type 92 - Crummy 1983, 12) appears to be the form worn by the Trinovantes and Catuvellauni in the mid 1st century. Mackreth has designated this the Harlow type and has drawn attention to the regional distribution; he notes that many of the well-dated examples are from contexts that predate AD 75/80 (Mackreth 1995, 959-61, nos 10-18). The popularity of the type found at Westhawk Farm perhaps points to it being the equivalent brooch for the Cantiaci.

It is clear that even if this were the preferred type south of the Thames, it did not dominate at all sites in Kent to the extent that the Catuvellaunian/Trinovantes type did to the north. Harlow brooches are frequently encountered in assemblages from sites in Kent. At the Marlowe excavations at Canterbury (Mackreth 1995, 959-61, nos 10-18) and at Richborough (Hull 1968, 80), for example, they are in the majority. The domination of the Westhawk assemblage by the Colchester BB is thus remarkable. One explanation may be chronological. If the Harlow type was indeed passing from fashion in the 80s, the Colchester BB perhaps continued in use for longer and perhaps at Westhawk the fashion of wearing (and losing) brooches was a late 1st century one. This does not seem a very satisfactory explanation given the popularity of brooch wearing in the south-east throughout the 1st century, and the undoubted occupation on the site prior to the later 1st century. Alternately, if this variant was indeed the preferred variant of the Cantiaci, then perhaps it is hinting that at Westhawk Farm we have a native population whose dress habits were relatively untouched by foreign influences - be those influences continental or foreign in the sense that they came from another British tribe. Both Richborough and Canterbury could be expected to have been far more cosmopolitan than Westhawk Farm. It is noticeable that at the Keston villa, a site that may be more comparable to Westhawk Farm, it is again the Colchester BB that is present (Philp *et al.* 1991, 171-3, nos 96-8, 101), with only one possible Harlow type (Philp *et al.* 1999, 92, no. 975, fig. 40).

The brooches come in two clear size ranges: large examples frequently with elaborate decoration (nos 1-7 and probably the fragmentary no. 13) and smaller, plainer ones (nos 8-11). In considering the examples from Springhead, Hull hypothesised that the larger ones might be the earlier (Hull 1959, 48, no. 4), but both variants often seem to be found contemporaneously. An alternative explanation may be that the smaller plain examples were used to fasten inner garments, and the larger ones for garments made of thicker fabric, possibly outer garments where the decoration on the brooches would be better displayed and appreciated.

Brooch wearing only really died out amongst the bulk of the civilian native population of Britain in the mid to late 2nd century. Colchester Derivatives are normally considered to be a 1st-century form. Unless we assume that the population at Westhawk Farm gave up wearing brooches early in the 2nd century, which again seems unlikely, then one must assume that here the Colchester BB form had a long life, well into the 2nd century. This may be hinted at by the contexts in which they were found. As already noted only three were from contexts of Phases 2-3. One (no. 1) was found in a Phase 4 pit fill and a poorly preserved fragmentary one (no. 11) from a similar context belonging to Phase 3-4. Though the latter may be residual, this seems unlikely in the case of no. 1 which, given the generally poor condition of the Westhawk Farm metalwork, is in very good condition. Such longevity is also suggested elsewhere. A large example of the type in good condition was found at Keston in the clay lining of a pond dug in the mid 2nd century (Philp *et al.* 1991, 171, no. 96, fig. 52).

The other identifiable brooch from Westhawk Farm (no. 15) is a knee brooch of Snape Type 5.1A (Snape 1993, table 3 and fig. 3) dateable to the later 2nd to earlier 3rd centuries. As already noted the habit of wearing brooches amongst the civilian population declined in the mid 2nd century, and it is noticeable that sites with large assemblages of knee brooches tend to be northern military ones (see, for example, Snape 1993, 122, Appendix IIb; Mackreth 2002). This suggests that in Britain the people who were wearing them may well have been soldiers, or officials of some other kind, who adopted a different style of dress from the majority of the civilian population. Elsewhere in Kent, knee brooches tend to be found on sites where an official presence could be expected, though they are never common. Amongst the very large assemblage of brooches published from Richborough only three fall into this category (Hull 1968, 92, no. 84, plate xxxiii; Henderson 1949, 118, nos 51 and 52, plate xxix, (of which the last is of the same variant as our no. 15)). A small number has also been recovered from Canterbury (Mackreth 1995, 979, nos 111-2, fig. 409), but it is noticeable that they appear to be absent on extensively excavated sites with later 2nd-century occupation such as at Lullingstone and Springhead, where the likelihood of military or official involvement is less. The presence of a knee brooch at Westhawk Farm is thus of some interest, perhaps hinting at official interest in the site during the later 2nd to 3rd centuries.

One of the ways in which changing fashion amongst the female population can be most easily traced is via hairpins which were needed when the Romanised hairstyles were adopted. That they were adopted in some quantity at other sites in Kent is clear from the development of local north Kent variants in copper alloy (Cool 1991, 175). The only metal hairpin from this site (no. 16) is from a Phase 5 context and is of a type that, while most likely to have been commonest during the 2nd century, could have been contemporary with its date of deposition (Cool 1991, 170, group 24). By far the majority of hairpins, however, were made in bone, and so the non-survival of bone artefacts at the site is a particular loss. Had bone survived, by comparing the brooch evidence with that of hairpins, it would have been possible to test the suggestion made above that the population at Westhawk Farm may have been relatively uninterested in adopting new styles of dress and ornamentation in the 1st to 2nd centuries.

Where the date of various other undoubted items of female jewellery can be established either by the context in which they were found or by typological parallels, they all appear most likely to be of late 2nd-century date or later. This again makes it difficult to place the brooch evidence in context. The earring no. 17 is of a long-lived type (Allason-Jones 1989a, 2, type 1), but was found in a Phase 5 context. The three small glass beads (nos 18-20) are all forms that are commonest in the late Roman period, though the contexts of two of them (nos 18-19) suggest they might be evidence for the wearing of necklaces in the 2nd to 3rd centuries. Blue segmented beads such as no. 18 have occasionally been found in early 2nd-century contexts (see Brewer 1986a, 148; fig. 48, no. 11), but by far the majority come from later 3rd- to 4th-century ones (Guido 1978, 92). It is possible that this example, which came from a Phase 3-4 pit fill, might be an early example. Translucent blue/green spherical beads such as no. 19 are not particularly common and few have come from well-dated contexts, so the discovery of this one in a Phase 5 dump is a valuable addition to the corpus. The small polychrome bead (no. 20) from the Phase 6 silting of the waterhole is of type that first appears in Britain in the later 2nd to early 3rd century (Brewer 1986a, 151; fig. 48, no. 73; Wedlake 1982, 154, no. 5), though again is most frequently encountered in late Roman contexts as here. This example very clearly shows the intricate way in which the beads were made.

One ornament type that is strikingly absent from the assemblage is the bracelet. On most Romano-British sites occupied during the 4th century, fragments of copper alloy bracelets are normally found (Swift 2000, 119-20), probably reflecting the female fashion for wearing several to a wrist at that time. Here the only copper alloy bracelet (no. 21) is from the cremation burial of a male. No fragments have been recognised within the site assemblage. No. 21 now appears to be a massive plain penannular bracelet. Unfortunately the terminals are missing and the whole surface badly damaged by corrosion, so the possibility that it originally had joining terminals and some decoration cannot be entirely ruled out. What can be said is that it would have been amongst the less common bracelet types in use in the 4th century, as most women wore several light bangles together, rather than a more massive single bracelet as here.

Finger-rings are also absent but their presence is indicated by one intaglio (no. 22) and probably by the glass setting no. 23. No. 22 is a very small example of the type of moulded glass intaglio of 'an extremely barbarous sort', which is a common 3rd-century Romano-British type thought possibly to be based on radiate coinage and to represent the spread of signet wearing to the rural peasantry (Henig 1974, 164-65). Most commonly these have a recognisable human figure, which Henig suggests may have been intended to be Virtus, Sol or Pax. Interpreting the design on no. 22 is complicated by its very small size, but it may have been intended to be Henig's figure type 4 (ibid., key to fig. 3). The intaglio was found in the fill of the cremation urn and may well have been a pyre good. It shows no obvious evidence of having been affected by heat, but this may simply indicate that the pyre did not reach a temperature high enough to affect the glass. To melt Roman glass requires a temperature in excess of 1100°C (Henderson 2000, 39, fig 3.24).

The small blue glass hemisphere (no. 23) is of a size that would have been appropriate for a finger-ring with constricted shoulders and a deep box-bezel, such as those found at Silchester in a bank with material dated to AD 190-210 (Cotton 1947, fig. 9.5) and at Verulamium in a destruction deposit containing late 3rd-century material (Cotton and Wheeler 1953, fig. 1.10). Such rings appear to have been in use in the late 2nd to 3rd century, mainly in the south-west and south central parts of England (Cool forthcoming), but occasional examples have been found in the east such as an example from the Marlowe Car Park, Canterbury (Henig 1995, 1001, no. 199, fig. 419).

Finally in this section the presence of three melon beads (nos 24-26) may be noted. These are a common find on 1st- to mid 2nd-century sites (Cool and Philo 1998, 181), especially military ones. There are some doubts as to whether these were ornaments for people. Many years ago, Fox (1940, 132) suggested these were harness ornaments, a supposition borne out by excavation of a horse wearing a copper alloy neck ring threaded with both frit and blue glass melon beads at Krefeld-Gellep (Pirling 1997, 58-9). Though they are a very typical Roman artefact, the presence of these beads at Westhawk Farm in an early Phase 2 context (no. 25) cannot, therefore, be taken as an indication of the early adoption of Roman fashions by humans. No. 24 is of interest because of the very heavy wear it shows at either end, as if tightly strung against other beads of a similar size.

Toilet and medical equipment

The site has produced an interesting range of finds that can be assigned to this category. Nos 27 and 28 are both fragments of rectangular mirrors of Lloyd-Morgan Group A (1981). No. 27 came from the Phase 4 fill of the roadside ditch and no. 28 was unstratified in the subsoil. They may have come from the same mirror but it should be noted that no. 27 is bevelled in from the reflecting edge while that of no. 28 is bevelled out, possibly suggesting that the two fragments came from different mirrors. Rectangular mirrors are a common 1st-century form which is not believed to have been made after that date, though of course they could have continued in use well into the 2nd century. A third mirror is represented by an internal fragment (no. 29). Unlike the rectangular mirrors which can be polished to a reflecting surfaces because they are made of a high tin bronze, this one

has been deliberately tinned to produce the reflecting surface; on the other side there is a raised ring. The fragment is in very poor condition but the ring may be turned. This seems most likely to have come from a hand mirror, perhaps from Lloyd-Morgan group G (1981), another 1st-century form. Although now represented only by a very fragile fragment, originally this mirror would have been a much more luxurious item than the mirrors represented by nos 27-8, which are almost the equivalent of handbag mirrors kept in a wooden frame (see, for example, Lloyd-Morgan 1983). By contrast, no. 29 is likely to belong to the same family as the silver mirrors in the Boscoreale treasure (Baratte 1986, 45-7), consisting of a large reflecting disc held on a projecting handle.

Mirrors are not often found in such quantities outside urban and military sites. Glass stirring rods such as no. 30 are also commonest on military and urban sites during the 1st and to a lesser extent the 2nd centuries (Manning *et al.* 1995, 306). No. 30 came from a Phase 5 context suggesting it was probably residual. When complete the rod might either have had another disc terminal like the extant one or perhaps a bird such as on the yellow example from the cemetery at the Artillery Barracks at Canterbury (Brent 1879, 39, plate 6, no. 1).

Another unusual find at a site like Westhawk Farm is no. 31. This appears to be the terminal and upper part of the arms of a set of forceps, see for example those of Coudé type found near Littleborough, Notts (Jackson and Leahy 1990). Here because most of the arms and jaws are missing the precise type is unknown. No. 31 may have been a medical instrument used by a doctor (Jackson 1986, 137), but smooth-jawed forceps could also be used in depilation and this may have been the purpose of the examples found at bathhouses such as those at Caerleon (Brewer 1986b, 189, no. 188) and Castleford (Cool and Philo 1998, 139, no. 138). When this item would have been in use during the Roman period is unknown as they are not closely dateable and the fragment was found in an unstratified context. A similar problem besets the tweezers (no. 32).

This assemblage of toilet equipment is curiously unbalanced consisting as it does of unusual and less commonly encountered types, with the normally ubiquitous chatelaine implements and long-handled implements such as *ligulae* only being represented by the tweezers.

Textile equipment

Two lengths of copper alloy wire may have come from needles. On no. 33 the head is missing but the upper end is thinning in the normal way. No. 34 is broken at both ends but retains the grooves often seen below the eyes of copper alloy needles (Crummy 1983, 67, type 3), though the extant length would be long for such an artefact. These needles may have been used in textile work though it should be noted that there is some evidence that metal needles were preferred for leatherwork (Cool 2002, 35) and they may have been used for this purpose. Again the absence of bone probably means the category is under represented in the assemblage, as many needles were made of that material.

Household equipment

This category is dominated by fragments from glass vessels but there is also at least one metal vessel and part of a candlestick.

Glass vessels

In total 168 fragments of vessel glass were found during the excavations and these are summarised by phase and colour in Table 5.10. Though glass was found stratified in contexts of Phases 2 to 6, both the colours and the types represented suggest that glass vessels were primarily in use during Phases 3 and 4, that is, the later 1st and 2nd centuries. There is very little material that could be attributed to the 3rd century with any certainty and only one fragment (no. 53) made of the typical bubbly light green glass of the 4th century, and this seems to have been intrusive in the context in which it was found.

The earliest vessel on the site is represented by nos. 35 and 36 which could come from a single blue/green pillar moulded bowl. These were in use from the conquest until the late 1st century (Price and Cottam 1998, 44), and this example may have arrived on site in the middle of the century as no. 36 was found in a Phase 2 context. Large bowls are also represented by fragments from the tubular-rimmed form (nos 37-40). As these were a common mid 1st- to mid-century type (ibid., 78), no. 39 found in a Phase 5 context is almost certainly residual.

Drinking vessels are rare in the assemblage. Fragments from two indented beakers (nos 41-2) were recovered from Phase 4 ditch and gully fills, but again they are likely to be residual as the form is commonest in the later 1st century, going out of use early in the 2nd century (Price and Cottam 1998, 85).

A similar date is appropriate for the collared jar no. 43 (ibid., 137) and globular jugs nos 45 and 46 (ibid.,

150). The lower body and base fragments (nos 48-50) are also likely to have come from vessels of this sort. The handle fragment no. 47 could either come from a globular jug or the conical form (ibid., 155) which continued in use into the third quarter of the 2nd century. All of this range of vessels, as well as the tubular rimmed bowls, were often decorated with ribs and it is highly probable that the ribbed body fragments nos 69-74 could have come from vessels of the same range.

Another jug form is represented by no. 51, one fragment of which was found in a context dated to Phases 4-5. This is a funnel-mouthed jug with a folded-in rim and pinched-in spout, the neck is short and the body possibly globular or ovoid. These features would suggest it was in use during the later 1st or first half of the 2nd century (Cool and Price 1995, 131). The spouted jugs of that date normally have a trefoil outline to the rim, see for example those found in contexts of the second half of the 1st century at Leadenhall Court London (Shepherd 1996, 110, nos 144-51, fig. 65). Though the spout of no. 51 is missing there are distinct suggestions that as well as being pinched in, it might have been pulled up at the tip. This was generally a 2nd-century fashion (Cool and Price 1995, 133) and so a 2nd century date may be favoured for no. 51. Such a date would fit with its context and also with the substantial amount recovered which does not hint that the fragments were residual. Another 1st- or 2nd-century jug is represented by the handle fragment no. 52. A variety of small jugs of that date had such pinched attachments, but it is not possible to identify the precise form from the fragment.

As is normally the case in 1st- to 2nd-century assemblages, blue/green bottles are very common (nos 55-64). Where it is possible to identify the shape, the fragments come from the square variant (see Price and Cottam 1998, 194). These became common during the later 1st century, were in use throughout the 2nd century and seem to have finally disappeared during the early to mid 3rd century (see Cool 2004).

The final vessel forms of the 1st or 2nd century are a jar with a fire rounded rim (no. 44 - see Cool and Price 1995, 113) and some form of globular flask (no.

Table 5.10   Roman vessel glass: Summary quantification (fragment count) by Phase and glass colour.

Phase	Blue Green	Bottle	Deep Blue	Light Green	Yellow Brown	Yellow Green	Colourless	4th century	Total
2	1	1	-	-	-	-	-	-	2
2-3	2	-	-	-	-	4	-	-	6
2-4	3	-	-	-	-	-	-	-	3
3	19	5	-	2	5	1	-	1	33
3-4	6	-	1	-	1	-	-	-	8
3-5	3	-	-	-	-	-	-	-	3
4	31	8	-	3	-	11	5	-	58
4-5	3	1	-	-	1	-	-	-	5
5	13	18	-	-	-	-	1	-	32
6	1	4	-	-	-	-	3	-	8
U/S	8	2	-	-	-	-	-	-	10
Total	90	39	1	5	7	16	9	1	168

54) from a Phase 3 context, but as this is only represented by a lower body and base fragment, the precise form cannot be suggested.

A very noticeable absence from this assemblage is the colourless cylindrical cup with double base ring (Price and Cottam 1998, 99). This generally occurs in such large numbers on later 2nd- to mid 3rd-century sites, that it can almost be taken as a type fossil for that period. Its absence at Westhawk Farm strongly suggests that glass vessels were not much in use after the mid 2nd century in the part of the site excavated.

The latest piece of glass recognised in the assemblage is no. 53. This is made in the typical bubbly glass of the 4th century, and the base form strongly suggests it came from a jug on a high foot, a common 4th-century form (Cool and Price 1995, 136, no. 1160).

The 1st- to 2nd-century glass assemblage can be summarised according to broad vessel type. As can be seen from Table 5.11, the assemblage is dominated by bowls and bottles, with other vessel types playing a much smaller role. In a survey of vessel glass use in Roman Britain, it was obvious that there was a marked difference in the consumption patterns of urban and military sites in the later 1st to mid 2nd century. It was suggested that the consumption patterns of rural sites at the time were far more akin to military ones than those on urban sites, but the small size of rural assemblages and the fact they were frequently poorly published made it difficult to be certain of this (Cool and Baxter 1999, 84-5). The bowl and bottle pattern seen at Westhawk Farm is typical of the proposed rural pattern, and provides more evidence that on such sites large bowls of both glass and samian pottery were playing a special role in society.

Other items

In the light of this proposed special role for large bowls in rural society, it is interesting to note that the one metal vessel that can be recognised with certainty at Westhawk Farm would also have fallen into this category. The escutcheon no. 75 was clearly designed to be mounted on the side of a vessel so that the open loop would have been closed by the side wall. This style of escutcheon was favoured on shallower bowls (see, for example, den Boesterd 1956, 55-6, nos 189, 193, plate viii) where the escutcheons held small rings. This escutcheon is a substantial cast piece, obviously designed to fit onto a vessel of large diameter (perhaps *c* 210-220 mm), but whether it would have been in use during the 1st to 2nd centuries cannot be suggested with certainty. It was found in the sub-

soil and cannot therefore be dated by its context, and no precisely similar parallel has been traced which would allow it to be dated on typological grounds. It does have a broad generic similarity with some escutcheons designed to project above the rim edge of deeper buckets. The foliate edging and heavy casting, for example, is also seen on two escutcheons of that sort with female masks found at Carlisle (Padley 1991, 113 no 68) and Castel Collen (Britnell *et al.* 1999, 53, no. 9, fig. 6); unfortunately neither of these came from a usefully dated context.

The presence of two other copper alloy vessels can be suggested more tentatively. The features seen on no. 76 are consistent with it being from the base of a turned vessel, but the fragment is so corroded that no original surface survives and the identification cannot be made with certainty. The small mount no. 77 may have come from the lid of a trefoil mouthed jug. The knobs on these often took a zoomorphic form, frequently of a small bird. These could be cast in one with the lid (see, for example, Goodburn 1984, 51, no. 175, fig. 19), but frequently must have been made separately and inserted, as in the case of an example from Usk (Manning *et al.* 1995, 194, no. 2, fig. 51).

Finally in this category, the lead strip (no. 78) from waterhole 796 may be one leg of a three-legged candlestick. Fragments of such items have been recovered from time to time in urban sites in the Essex/Suffolk region in contexts suggesting a later 2nd- to 3rd-century date (Crummy 1983, 168, no. 4709; Major and Eddy 1986), but it was not until the discovery of a virtually complete example still bent in shape from Culver St., Colchester (N Crummy 1992, 163, no. 608) that it was realised what the object was. The dimensions of no. 78 match those of the legs of the other examples quite closely and the pelleted decoration is frequently encountered on them as well. While the identification cannot be made with total certainty, it does seem very likely. The date of the context it came from would also be appropriate. It may be noted that the type was not exclusively a south-eastern one as an example is known from Piercebridge, Co. Durham (Scott 1977, 50, no. 3, fig. 2), though the moulded decoration on the latter seems to differ from the patterns seen on the south-eastern ones.

Recreation

The only item in this category is a purpose-made fired clay counter (no. 79) from a Phase 3 pit fill. Purpose-made counters like this are unusual finds. In the late 1st to mid 2nd centuries plano-convex glass counters were very common, declining in numbers towards the end of the period as bone counters come to dominate

Table 5.11   Roman vessel glass: Summary of the 1st- to 2nd-century assemblage by functional type. Quantification by estimated vessel equivalents (EVE).

	Cup/beaker	Bowl	Jar	Flask	Jug	Bottle
EVE	60	200	92	40	126	238
%age	7.9%	26.5%	12.1%	5.3%	16.7%	31.5%

(Cool *et al.* 1995, 1555). In the soil conditions at Westhawk Farm, bone counters are not to be expected, but the absence of glass ones is noteworthy. As there is no other evidence of board games at the site, it is possible that no. 79 was not intended to be used as a counter, but could instead have functioned as something like a stopper to a vessel.

Weighing equipment

As already noted, a remarkable feature of this assemblage is the number of items associated with weighing that have been recovered. These include a steelyard (no. 80), nine steelyard weights (nos 81-89) and at least one weight for an equal-armed balance (no. 90).

The virtually complete steelyard arm, found in a ditch fill of Phase 4-5, retains sufficient of the scale markings to show that it was intended to weigh items up to 45 Roman pounds or *librae* (*c* 14.74 kg). (For an explanation of how steelyards work see Crummy 1983, 99.) The scale along one arm runs up to 9 *librae*. The space between each *libra* marking is divided up into 12 portions by 11 dots. These indicate the ounce (*uncia*) markings. When the scale was turned over and suspended from the second fulcrum, it could be used to measure weights between 10 and 45 *librae* with the grooves along the edge denoting the individual pounds. Corrosion has removed some of the markings but it seems likely that on the 1 to 9 side the full numerals were not scratched along the side but instead the sequence I, II, III, IIII, V, I, II, III, IIII was used. This was presumably because the scale along the edge did not have precise marks where the pound divisions were, such as on the steelyard from a Boudican context at Colchester (Crummy 1983, 99, no. 2508), but only slight gaps in the dot sequence. The repeated use of I, II, III, IIII rather than VI, VII, VIII, VIIII would have made it easier to position the weight accurately as the gaps would have been more narrowly pinpointed. Only the suspension loop of the weight remains and this is very heavily corroded with the surface removed at the point where it would have rested on the arm. It appears, however, to have been rectangular-sectioned and may have narrowed slightly at the point of contact allowing it to have been placed with some precision.

Not all steelyards have the scale marked as clearly as on the Westhawk example. The Colchester example did not have clearly marked scales, and nor did those from Whitton, South Glamorgan (Webster 1981, 182, no. 48, fig. 72) and Gestingthorpe, Essex (Draper 1985, 41, no. 136, fig. 17). Three steelyards from London, however, have clearly marked scales and some other similarities with the Westhawk arm. A fragmentary steelyard from Austin Friars (Wheeler 1930, 87, fig. 23) has the lower scale divided by dots into *unciae* and the larger by grooves into *librae*. The markings for the greater scale on this also seem to suppress the 'X's for measurements such as XV, as in the case of no. 80. Though the terminal end of this arm is missing, the fact that on steelyards the greater scale starts where the lesser scale finishes indicates that it would have weighed objects up to 5 or 6 *librae* on the lesser scale and up to perhaps 30 *librae* on the greater scale. A complete steelyard with suspension loops and weights was found in the Walbrook (Brailsford 1958, 78, no. 11, fig. 40). The lesser scale on this measures up to 8 *librae* and the drawing would appear to indicate that the *unciae* marks were dots. The other scale is unfortunately neither illustrated nor described, so it is not possible to see if the 'X's are suppressed. It does however have an identical spur at the fulcrum end above the terminal suspension loop to that seen on the Westhawk arm. There are hints that something similar may have been present on the Austin Friars steelyard but the drawing is not sufficiently detailed to be sure of this. A second steelyard from the Walbrook (Merrifield 1965, 186, plate 128) has a lesser scale running up to 6 in Roman numerals, but no details of the greater scale or the gradations along the edges are illustrated or described. It shares with the other Walbrook steelyard and the Westhawk example the shallow conical terminal. This is not an invariable terminal type for steelyards. The example from Colchester had a crossbar and that from Gestingthorpe had a perforated disc terminal. The same combination of numbering, conical terminal and possible spur on the fulcrum is also seen on a steelyard found at Benwell (Petch 1927, 189, no. 18, fig. 13).

There are, therefore, slight hints here that these steelyards may have come from the same source. A short steelyard found in a late Neronian to Flavian context at Canterbury has a similar terminal and what would appear to be the greater scale clearly marked with numerals and grooves to denote the individual *librae* (Frere 1970, 112, no. 6, fig. 13), but the quality of the description and illustration is too poor to be certain whether or not it could have been another product of the same workshop. If the workshop was a common source then the presence of two complete examples from the Walbrook might suggest it was active between the mid 1st and mid 2nd century. The Walbrook has produced large quantities of artefacts in pristine condition and though there is some dispute about the precise nature of the deposition (Shepherd 1998, 218), the date advanced for it by Merrifield (1962) is not in dispute. No. 80 was found in a deposit dated to Phase 4 to 5 (*c* AD 150-250) but it was clearly old when discarded, as one of the suspension loops is broken and the other shows distinct signs of wear through long use.

The production of steelyards would have been a specialist arm of the bronzesmith's trade. Much ancient commerce and accounting was conducted using measures of weight or volume as a glance at the price edict of Diocletian (Graser 1940) or the Vindolanda tablets (see, for example, Bowman and Thomas 1994, nos 180, 182, 190 and 192) will show. It would have been important that such measures were reliable and trustworthy within the bounds that was possible across the empire (for discussion see *RIB* II.2, 1-5), and there are some grounds for thinking that attempts were made to standardise weighing equipment. A steelyard from Pompeii, for example, has an inscription indicating that it was calibrated according to the 'Articuleiana' standard as laid down in the year AD 47 at Rome (Ward-Perkins and Claridge 1976, no. 248). A weight of 1 *libra* from Alchester, Oxon. (*RIB* II.2, no 2412.99) had the inscription CAES-AUG around the sides suggesting it might have been an official standard, although it would have been approximately 2% underweight. A workshop producing weighing equipment might be expected in London as, whatever its precise status, the city was undoubtedly a place where much official provincial business was transacted, and also a place where the calibration of weighing instruments could be conducted. Whether the apparent concentration of steelyards of this type in the London/Kent area is a true reflection of their distribution is, however, open to question. As will already be clear, the publication of steelyards is frequently inadequate, which makes it difficult to characterise them correctly. The possibility that one has been identified at Benwell suggests that the distribution may have been much wider.

Of the steelyard weights there is one small example in copper alloy in the form of an acorn (no. 81). As Webster (1992, 157, no. 366) has noted, there has been some discussion as to whether these small acorns were intended as steelyard weights, but given the plethora of other weights in the assemblage, this seems an appropriate identification here. The other steelyard weights are all made of lead with iron wires running through the centre to provide the attachment loops. Nos. 82-87 are all of the classic biconical form, frequently used in the Roman period. It is, for example, the type of weight used on the steelyards from the Walbrook discussed above. No. 88 is less common as it has a cylindrical middle section, and no. 89 is now hemispherical over its lower parts.

The weight for the equal-armed balance (no. 90) now weighs 12 g and, given the damage it has sustained may well have been a half *uncia* weight (13.6 g). Its cylindrical shape is one of the commoner Roman forms (*RIB* II.2, 5, fig. 1a), but the surface damage makes it impossible to see if it retained any marking to indicate its calibration. No. 91 might be another weight of the same type but it is now so damaged that the identification cannot be a secure one.

Of all these weights, only no. 82 comes from a stratified and phased context which is broadly contemporary with the steelyard beam context. Given their typology, however, there seems little doubt of their Roman date, and they must strongly suggest that the inhabitants of Westhawk Farm were regularly called upon to weigh things. The range of sizes would also suggest that a variety of commodities were involved.

Structural finds

Fragments of cast window glass were found in a Phase 4 context (no. 92) and one of Phase 5 (no. 93). This is the typical Roman window glass of the 1st to 3rd centuries and indicates that at least one of the buildings in the settlement had glazed windows. The fragments may hint of the presence of a bathhouse as suggested by the tile evidence (see Harrison, Chapter 6 below), as glazed windows were an important feature of bathhouse architecture allowing illumination while at the same time keeping heat in.

Fasteners and fittings

The commonest item in this category is the bell-shaped stud (Allason-Jones 1985). Three examples were found (nos 94-6), all of which have integral shanks cast in one with the head. No. 96 is likely to have belonged to Allason-Jones' Type 2 which has a perforation through its lower extremity. Nos. 94-5 may have belonged to this type but the short lengths of shank that remain are more reminiscent of the type defined by Webster (1992, 136) where the shank is short and tapering. The various types of bell-shaped studs were in use throughout the Roman period and had a variety of purposes, but those with integral shanks seem most likely to have been parts of the fittings of large chests or boxes with the examples with perforated terminals forming part of the lock mechanism. Nos 94-6 are therefore likely to reflect the presence of such chests among the furnishings of the houses at Westhawk Farm. No. 97 may be part of another box fitting, as it could be part of a lock. The sheet copper alloy clearly contains some form of mechanism, but the interior is now too corroded to ascertain, even with the aid of X-radiographs, what it might have been.

Some of the small fittings (nos 98-100) could also have been used decorate items of furniture. The small horse head mount (no. 98) was found unstratified but is typical of the small end mounted terminals that could be either for furniture or the ends of handles. Of the other items in this category only the mount no. 102 calls for special comment. This is very corroded, but seems very likely to have been in the form of a dolphin and to have been very similar to examples from Caerleon (Wheeler and Wheeler 1928, 168, no. 42, fig. 15) and Birdoswald (Wilmott *et al.* forthcoming). Those were in better condition and were so similar that it seemed possible they could have come from the same mould. This example seems to be swimming in the opposite direction suggesting that they were mounted as pairs. Neither the Caerleon nor the Birdoswald examples came from usefully dated contexts, and so the discovery of this example in the Phase 2 primary silt of the roadway is a useful addition to the corpus.

Religious items

The only object in this category is a fragment of a Central Gaulish pipe clay Venus figurine (no. 103) of the type where the semi-draped goddess raises her right hand to her hair at the side of her neck. This is the commonest figurine type found in Britain. When Jenkins first studied them, he could point to a hundred examples (Jenkins 1958). In a more recent study that number had almost doubled (van Boeckel 1993, 247), and the figure has continued to rise in the decade or more since. They were in use primarily in the 2nd century, and the Phase 4 context of no. 103 shows it was broken and lost within that period. In the southeast, these and other pipe clay figurines are common finds on a wide range of site types (ibid., fig. 110), and presumably all parts of the population found a use for them.

Evidence of craft and industry

There is a small amount of evidence to indicate that non-ferrous metalworking took place at the site from time to time. No. 104 is an off-cut from working copper alloy sheet found in the Phase 2-3 fill of a boundary ditch. Although found in the subsoil, the fragment of casting waste no. 104 presumably also relates to Romano-British activity. The small blue glass hemisphere no. 106 has a superficial resemblance to a bead, but the lack of a perforation and its highly vesicular nature would indicate that it is more like to be a by-product of high temperature activity. This need not have been concerned with working glass, as such a small vesicular fragment might have arisen as part of the processes that produce fuel ash slags.

Most tools would not have been made of the materials under consideration here, but no. 107 is a fragment of a blue/green bottle that has been flaked like a piece of flint to provide a sharp edge to be used in some cutting activity. This sort of re-use is frequently observed on Roman sites where bottle glass may have been a more easily accessible raw material for knapping than flint.

Miscellaneous

The remaining catalogued items cannot be assigned to a particular functional category, either because they may have had many functions, or because their function is unknown or because they are too fragmentary to identify. In the first category there is the bell, no. 108. Though from an unphased context it is typical of the small bells in use during the Roman period (see for example Manning *et al.* 1995, 55, fig. 20). Apart from the more utilitarian functions, such as animal bells, they also served to ward off evil spirits. In the second category lie the lead whorls, nos 109-13. These all derive from the sub- or plough-soil and there is no certainty that they are Roman as whorls of this sort are rarely encountered in Roman contexts. Roman lead spindle whorls tend to be flat (see Mould 1998, 121, nos 1-5, fig. 43), and the Westhawk Farm whorls in any case have perforations that would be too wide for the narrow spindle of the Roman era. Given the number of steelyard weights at the site, one possibility might be that they were removable counter weights, added where necessary to the chains from which the item to be weighed was suspended.

The Finds as an assemblage

It is clear that the finds reflect the life of the occupants at Westhawk Farm in the later 1st and 2nd centuries. There is a distinct scarcity of material that would have been in use in the middle of the 1st century and have gone out of use by the end of it. Only the pillar moulded glass bowl fragments (nos 35-6) fall into this category. The bulk of the dateable finds have a *floruit* of the second half of the 1st century running into the 2nd century. Material that would have been in use within the mid 1st- to mid 2nd-century period includes all of the Colchester Derivative brooches, the melon beads, the mirrors, the stirring rod and most of the vessel glass. It was suggested above that the steelyard might be the product of a workshop that operated in the period between the mid 1st and mid 2nd centuries. If this is correct then the steelyard would also fall into this category.

Material with a 2nd-century date consists of the pipe clay figurine and hairpin. Later 2nd- to 3rd-century items include the knee brooch and the lead candlestick, and possibly the glass beads. The 3rd century is represented by the glass intaglio and possibly the ring setting (no. 23) and the 4th century by a single fragment of vessel glass and presumably the bracelet no. 21. This date range is reflected, in part, by the stratified contexts in which the items were found. As can be seen from Table 5.7, two-thirds of the stratified items had been deposited by the end of Phase 4 at the latest. It is also noticeable that two of the very small number of late items (the intaglio and the bracelet) come from burials rather than settlement contexts.

What do the finds tell us of the people who lived here in the later 1st and 2nd centuries? There are hints from the brooches that they were conservative in their dress, not rapidly adopting new fashions. Their glass and metal vessels fall into the rural pattern of consumption, hinting that dining here would have been a somewhat different experience to dining in the developing local towns. There is also, however, a relatively substantial amount of items that suggest an interest in acquiring Romanised material culture, and the resources to acquire it, so it may well be that the conservatism applied to particular facets of life, not to all of it.

It is also probable that the acquisition of Romanised material culture increased with time. This is hinted at by the increasing range of functional categories present in the stratified material. Table 5.12 summarises this. The possible counter (no. 79) from a Phase 3 context has been excluded on the grounds that the identification of function is not secure, and the vessel glass has been excluded from household category. As can be seen from the table, the later part of the occupation shows a noticeable expansion of functional types present, as though the trappings of a Romanised life were being more enthusiastically embraced.

This development may have been a natural development of the indigenous population, but it is worth

Table 5.12   Objects and vessels of non-ferrous metal, fired clay and glass: Presence of different functional categories amongst the phased finds.

	Phase 2	Phase 3	Phase 4	Phase 5
Personal	Present	Present	Present	Present
Toilet	-	-	Present	Present
Textile	-	Present	Present	-
Household	-	Present	-	Present
Weighing	-	-	-	Present
Buildings	-	-	Present	Present
Fasteners	Present	-	Present	Present
Religion	-	-	Present	-
Industry	-	Present	Present	Present
Number of categories	2	4	7	7

considering whether it might reflect some changing function within the settlement. As already noted the knee brooch may hint at the presence of an official. The presence of the small glass beads no. 18, from a Phase 3-4 context, and no. 19, from a Phase 5 context, is also of interest. Glass bead necklaces do not appear to have become fashionable for the majority of the population until the later 3rd and 4th centuries. If the contexts of these are to be believed, the women of the Westhawk Farm settlement were very early adopters of the fashion, which stands in marked contrast to the earlier conservatism with regard to fashions in brooches.

As already noted, the number of items associated with weighing at this site is unusual as normally such items form a small part of any assemblage. How unusual the Westhawk Farm assemblage is can be seen from Table 5.13. In this the number of weights, steelyards and balances has been compared to the number of brooches from a range of ex-

cavations of sites which include 1st and 2nd century occupation and have produced large finds assemblages. Brooches have been chosen as a standard against which to compare the weighing equipment as they are a common find and, given their privileged status within Romano-British finds research, can be relied on to be fully published. The weighing equipment is shown as a percentage of the brooch total. This is admittedly a crude measure, but serves to put the Westhawk Farm figures into perspective. The *vicus* at Caersws stands out and here a conservative interpretation of the lead weights has been taken, including only those with the standard dot markings indicating their weight. Generally, however, weighing equipment totals are 10% or less of brooch totals at most sites no matter what their status. Even if only the stratified and phased material from Westhawk Farm was considered (9 brooches, 1 steelyard and 1 weight), the weighing equipment percentage (22%) would still be only second to Caersws.

Such a plethora of weighing equipment in the finds assemblage would suggest a greater than normal interest in measuring commodities. At Caersws the weights were associated with an area of the *vicus* that could be plausibly interpreted as a commercial site. The weights there, however, were all for an equal-armed balance requiring a range of weights to be useful. At Westhawk Farm, by contrast, the weights are for steelyards which only need one weight, and the number of such weights found must indicate that a large number of steelyards were in use. This may have been for straightforward commercial transactions as is likely in the *vicus* at Caersws, but the timing of this activity may be significant. Only the steelyard (no. 80) and one of the steelyard weights (no. 82) were from phased contexts, and assigned to Phases 4-5 when the increased range of functional

Table 5.13   Objects and vessels of non-ferrous metal, fired clay and glass: Comparison of numbers of brooches and items of weighing equipment from selected sites, with the number of items of weighing equipment expressed as a percentage of the number of brooches from each site.

Site	Site type	Source	Brooch	Weights etc	%
Westhawk Farm	Rural settlement	this report	15	11	73%
Stonea	Rural settlement	Jackson and Potter 1996	108	6	6%
Wilcote	Rural settlement	Hands 1993; 1998	47	1	2%
Dragonby	Rural settlement	May 1996	157	1	>1%
Cirencester	Town	Viner 1998	133	18	14%
Verulamium	Town	Waugh and Goodburn 1972; Goodburn 1984	80	10	10%
Wroxeter	Town	Barker et al 1997	181	16	9%
Colchester	Town	Crummy 1983, 1992a & b	161	10	6%
Canterbury	Town	Blockley *et al* 1995	139	1	>1%
Leicester	Town	Cooper 1999	29	0	0%
Caersws	vicus	Britnell 1989.	15	11	73%
Castleford	Fort and *vicus*	Cool and Philo 1995	150	12	8%
Caerleon	*Vicus*	Evans 2000	50	4	8%
Richborough	Fort and civil settlement	Bushe Fox 1926, 1928, 1932, 1949; Cunliffe 1968.	210	13	6%
Gorhambury	Villa	Neal et al 1990	47	10	21%
Gadebridge Park	Villa	Neal 1974	31	2	7%
Frocester Court	Villa	Price 2000	75	4	5%

types is noticeable at the site. This is also the period when the state was moving towards supplying the troops with their rations directly, without deducting the cost from their pay, and acquiring those rations, at least in part, by direct requisitions. Precisely when this system (the *annona militaris*) was introduced, if it was indeed a single decision, is unknown. A recent consideration, however, suggests a date at the end of the 2nd century to the early 3rd century might be appropriate (Roth 1999, 241). How it was administered in practice is equally unclear (Millett 1990, 149). One might speculate, however, that if direct requisitions were starting to occur towards the end of the 2nd century, 'rural' sites such as the settlement at Westhawk Farm on the junction of two important roads might have had a role to play as collection points.

If there were to have been some form of change of role, with or without official involvement, for the settlement, it might also explain some of the conflicting strands of evidence in the finds assemblage. As noted in the previous section, the composition of some categories of finds, such as the toilet equipment, is more typical of an urban or military site than a rural one of the type demonstrated by the brooch and vessel glass assemblages. The later burials on the site with small finds also hint at a slightly more cosmopolitan society.

It is difficult to assess the status of the individual whose remains were found in cremation urn 5009 (cremation group 5050) together with the intaglio no. 22. As already noted (see above) this is an intaglio type that is thought to be associated with the spread of signet ring use to the rural peasantry. Its presence as a probable pyre good, however, is most unusual. Philpott (1991, 163) knew of only two intaglios from cremation burials in Britain. To these a third may be added from a mid 2nd-century burial at West Tenter Street in the East Cemetery at London (Whytehead 1986, 94, fig. 41; Barber and Bowsher 2000, fig. 85) and a fourth from a mid 3rd-century burial at Brougham (Cool 2004, 382). But the total is still tiny and in two of the cases where it is known the deceased is likely to have been a soldier.

The person buried with the jet necklace and bracelets of jet/lignite (see Allason-Jones, below) and copper alloy (no. 21) in cremation urn 5026 (cremation group 5090), however, may have been a most exotic individual. He was an adult male which makes the association with a necklace and bracelets most unusual, as these are normally ornament types associated with females. Precisely the same combination of ornaments, however, was worn by a young adult male buried in an inhumation grave at Catterick, where the copper alloy 'bracelet' was being worn as an anklet (Cool 2002). Beads from a similar jet bead bracelet were found with the cremated remains of an adult male in a 3rd-century burial at Brougham (Cool 2004, 391). In the East cemetery at London a male of 19-25 years was found wearing a copper alloy bracelet in a late 3rd- to 4th-century inhumation and was accompanied by an unworn jet necklace with Medusa pendant and a separate jet pendant in the form of

a palmette (Barber and Bowsher 2000, 226-7, burial 709). The sex of the individuals cremated with a similar bead bracelet at Ospringe (Whiting 1926, 146, group lxii; Whiting *et al.* 1931, plate lvii, fig. 2), and inhumed with them at Verulamium (Wheeler and Wheeler 1936, 210, no. 48, fig. 45) and York (*Eburacum*, 94, burial IV k (vi); Allason-Jones 1996, 28, no. 28) is unknown.

There can be no doubt that if the young man at Catterick had worn the ornaments in life, as he did in death, then he would have been regarded as a transvestite, and it was suggested he may have been one of the castrated priests of Cybele, as the ornaments are of the types they are regarded as having worn. There were also sufficient unusual features surrounding the deposition of the individual at Brougham with the jet bracelet, to suggest that he may too have been regarded as 'other' in some way. The man in the East London cemetery too may have been 'different' as his grave was one of two isolated burials at what the excavators describe as on 'an odd alignment' (Barber and Bowsher 2000, 45). The individual buried at Westhawk Farm with these ornaments may also have been in some way unusual, perhaps because he was a priest or had adopted a different gender role to his biological sex. This might also explain the choice of a less common copper alloy bracelet form for inclusion in the grave.

Comparison of the stratified and non-stratified non-ferrous metal small finds

Previous work with metal detected assemblages has suggested that not all categories and shapes of Roman finds are as likely to be found by metal detecting as by excavation (Britnell *et al.* 1999, 47). This supposition has been strengthened by an examination of the Roman small finds in the Portable Antiquities Database (Cool 2001) which suggested that long thin items such as most types of toilet implements and hair pins were seriously underrepresented in metal detected assemblages. Other types that were underrepresented were penannular brooches and bracelets which could, of course, be regarded as long thin items bent into a circle. The extensive metal detecting undertaken at Westhawk Farm allows a comparison of the stratified and unstratified material from the topsoil to see if the latter is a good reflection of the former.

In order to investigate this the recognisable Roman non-ferrous finds have been characterised in two ways: in the first they were weighed, and in the second they were assigned to one of five broad shape categories. The current state of the items has been taken into account, thus bow brooches in a good condition are assigned to the solid three dimensional categories, whereas those that are damaged and have lost their wings and springs are better described as being long and thin.

The weight is summarised in Table 5.14. The top two rows show the complete data set. In both cases this is distorted by the recovery of a small number of

Table 5.14   Roman non-ferrous metalwork: Summary of the numbers of pieces, and comparison of the ranges of weights, and mean weights of objects recovered by excavation and by metal detecting.

	Number	Range	Mean
Excavated	27	1 - 183g	14.6g
Metal-detected	26	1 - 581g	56.7g
Excavated less than 100g	26	1 - 62g	8.1g
Metal-detected less than 100g	23	1 - 95g	22.9g

heavy items, so the third and fourth rows summarise those items of 100 g or less. As can be seen the metal-detected items are regularly heavier and by implication larger than the excavated pieces.

Table 5.15 summarises the shape of the items and as may be seen the bulk of the metal-detected items may be characterised as being three-dimensional, whereas a wider range of shapes is found in the excavated assemblage. Flat and narrow items appear much more likely to be recovered through excavation than through metal-detecting. The difference in size is not surprising as large items are more likely to survive in the plough soil than small ones, but the increasing evidence that metal detecting may be better at recovering items of particular shapes is of some importance as it has implications for how best to make use of the increasingly large amounts of data available from metal-detecting, both within archaeological work and from such initiatives as the Portable Antiquities Scheme (cf. DCMS 2000). If certain cat-

egories of finds are always going to be rare within such material, then clearly it would be sensible to devise any research schemes that are going to make use of metal detected data with this in mind.

Catalogue

Personal ornaments and jewellery

Brooches (Fig. 5.3: 3-9, 15)

1   (*not illustrated*) **Colchester derivative brooch.** Copper alloy. Semi-circular spring cover, ends broken, front of cover decorated by alternating pairs of narrow ribs with wide curved ribs. Double perforated lug behind cover, outer edge of this cast into series of scalloped ribs which continue over top of bow to form crest in the form of a skeuomorphic forward facing hook. Fragmentary spring of at least 12 turns with chord held in upper perforation of lug and bar retaining spring in lower perforation. D-sectioned bow with side flanges and three narrow ribs running down centre; rocker arm ornament down flanges and down outer edge of central triple rib group. Foot and catchplate missing. Extant L: 44 mm. Context 7377, SF1101, Phase 4.

2   (*not illustrated*) **Colchester derivative brooch.** Copper alloy. Wide semi-cylindrical spring cover, ends broken; front of cover decorated by alternating pairs of narrow ribs with wide curved ribs. Double perforated lug behind, top broken; small fragment of chord retained in

Table 5.15   Roman non-ferrous metalwork: Comparison of numbers of stratified and unstratified finds characterised by shape and size.

Shape	Type	Stratified		U/S	
Solid three dimensional	Bow brooch	9		3	
	Steelyard weight	1		8	
	Cylindrical weight	1		1	
	Bell-shaped stud	1		2	
	Vessel	-		2	
	Fitting	1		2	
	Lead whorl	-		4	
	Subtotal		13		22
Three dimensional	Lock casing	1		-	
	Bell	-		1	
	Forceps	-		1	
	Subtotal		1		2
Solid flat	Mirror	2		1	
	Steelyard beam	1		-	
	Dolphin mount	1		-	
	Vessel	1		-	
	Lead disc	1		-	
	Subtotal		6		1
Long thin	Brootch	2		1	
	Tweezer	1		-	
	Needle	2		-	
	Candlestick	1		-	
	Subtotal		6		1
Ring	Earring	1		-	
	Subtotal		1		0
Total		27		26	

broken upper perforation, bar holding spring through lower perforation; spring of at least 12 turns, parts missing; front of spring cover has pairs of narrow ribs alternating with wide plain zones. D-sectioned bow with side flanges and central rib joining perforated lug as a crest, pair of grooves marking the junction. Foot missing, majority of perforated catchplate missing. In two joining corroded fragments, twisted out of shape. Context 50, SF5, Phase 2-3.

3 **Colchester derivative brooch**. Copper alloy. Semicircular spring cover, ends broken; front decorated by narrow vertical ribs. Double perforated lug behind; spring of at least 12 turns, chord held in upper perforation of lug, spring held by ?iron central bar that would have passed through lower perforation. D-section bow with upper face divided into 5 ribs; upper part of perforated lug forms small projection, below on central rib two diagonal grooves separated by horizontal grooves, traces of similar cross motif on right-hand rib. Bow tapering to missing foot, part of catch plate with triangular perforation extant. Extant L: 57 mm, extant W of wings: 42 mm. Context 7004 (subsoil), SF1127, unphased.

4 **Colchester derivative brooch**. Copper alloy. Semi-circular plain spring cover, both ends broken, with double perforated lug behind retaining part of chord of spring in upper perforation and bar holding mostly missing spring in lower. D-sectioned bow with central rib separated from top of perforated lug by notch; bow tapering to missing foot; most of catch plate also missing but retains upper part of perforation. Surfaces poorly preserved but isolated traces of rocker arm ornament suggest originally a band running down either side of central rib. Extant L: 49 mm, extant W of wings: 25 mm. Context 892, SF183, Phase 2-3.

5 **Colchester derivative brooch**. Copper alloy. Upper part of brooch only. Part of semi-circular plain spring cover with double perforated lug retaining part of chord in upper perforation and central bar for spring in lower perforation; small fragment of spring retained by lug. D-sectioned bow with central rib becoming crest at top of perforated lug, with slight notch marking junction. Extant W: 17 mm. Context 7412, SF1202, Phase 4-5.

6 **Colchester derivative brooch**. Copper alloy. Stumps of semi-cylindrical spring case preserved either side of broken head; stumps of double perforated lug behind. D-sectioned bow with 3 gently rounded vertical ribs and side flanges; central rib probably divided from perforated lug by notch. Foot missing and catch plate mostly broken away. Extant L: 51 mm. Context 7186, SF984, unphased.

7 **Colchester derivative brooch**. Copper alloy. Semi-cylindrical spring cover with ends missing; front divided into three zones either side of the bow, two outer zones diagonally grooved, central plain with convex-surface. Spring mostly missing but chord held in upper perforation of double perforated lug at rear of head, lower perforation retains part of iron bar holding spring. Bow has stepped D-section; central rib continues over the head to merge with perforated lug and is decorated with groups of diagonal lines arranged in vertical chevron pattern; plain convex-curved ribs on either side; low flange on either side horizontally grooved to give close-milled effect. Foot broken, triangular catch plate has broken edge, and triangular perforation obscured by corrosion. Context 7004 (subsoil), SF1128, unphased.

8 **Colchester derivative brooch**. Copper alloy. Semi-cylindrical plain spring cover, one end chipped; double perforated lug behind retaining chord of spring in upper perforation and iron bar holding spring in lower perforation, only one turn of spring extant. Much of surface of bow now missing but over head a pronounced central rib forming crest with top of lug, with two transverse grooves marking junction; some evidence that this rib continued down centre of bow. Catchplate and lower part of bow missing. W of spring cover: 17 mm, extant L: 23 mm. Context 28, SF2, Phase 2-3.

9 **Colchester derivative brooch**. Copper alloy. Heavily corroded and virtually no original surface remaining. Semi-cylindrical spring cover, with stumps of double perforated lug behind. One detached coil of spring extant. D-sectioned bow forming slight crest over head where joined with perforated lug. Foot and catchplate missing. Bow now bent up over head. Depth of spring cover 4.5 mm, extant L: as bent: 20 mm. Context 7089, SF940, unphased.

10 (*not illustrated*) **Colchester derivative brooch**. Copper alloy. Small fragment of semi-cylindrical spring cover either side of head, double perforated lug behind head with curved mouldings over upper part. D-sectioned bow with central rib. Foot and catchplate missing. The whole very corroded and surface poorly preserved but the central rib may have had band of rocker arm ornament down front. Extant L: 42 mm. Context 5007, SF501, Phase 5.

11 (*not illustrated*) **Colchester derivative brooch**. Copper alloy; the whole much corroded and no original surfaces remaining. Semi-cylindrical spring cover, ends broken, with double perforated lug behind. D-sectioned bow forming slight crest over head where joins with perforated lug. Foot and catchplate missing. Depth of spring cover 5 mm, extant L: 22 mm. Context 7808, SF1374, phase 3-4.

12 (*not illustrated*) **Colchester derivative brooch**. Copper alloy; two fragments from head. Very heavily corroded and details obscured. Remains of lower part of spring cover preserved below head. Spring of *c* 10 turns with chord held in forward facing hook or pierced lug. Upper part of D-sectioned, apparently plain bow. Extant L:

18 mm, W of spring: *c* 19 mm. Context 565, SF106, Phase 3-4.

13 (*not illustrated*) **Colchester derivative brooch**. Copper alloy. Two very corroded fragments consisting of head and one side of spring cover and detached spring fragment. Semi-cylindrical spring cover, stumps of double perforated lug behind; front of spring cover has traces of paired narrow ribs. Traces of grooves on each side of head. Detached fragment consists of spring of at least 6 turns with central bar. Extant W of spring cover: 19 mm. Context 869, SF181, Phase 3-4.

14 (*not illustrated*) **Brooch**. Copper alloy. Shallow D-sectioned bow, probably originally with narrow flanges on either side, now mostly missing. Triangular catch plate. Much corroded and much of original surface missing. Extant L: 33 mm. Context 7004, SF1129, subsoil.

15 **Knee brooch**. Copper alloy. Cylindrical spring cover with central iron bar for spring held in pierced ends, spring of *c* 6 turns with chord running below missing pin. Angular bow with stepped junction with spring cover, bow expanding slightly to flat-based foot, broken rod catch-plate. Heavily corroded and much of the surface now missing. L: 35 mm, W of spring cover: 22 mm. Context 7642, SF1279, unphased.

Other personal ornaments (Fig. 5.3: 16; Fig. 5.4: 17-24)

16 **Hairpin**. Copper alloy. Circular-sectioned tapering rod with shallow conical terminal, other end broken. Bent out of shape. Maximum section: 3.5 mm, Extant L: 63 mm. Context 7298, SF1072, Phase 5.

17 **Earring**. Copper alloy. Penannular D-sectioned wire ring tapering to pointed ends. In two fragments, the whole much corroded and no original surfaces extant. D: *c* 20 x 13 mm. Context 7279, SF1028, Phase 5.

18 **Bead**. Deep blue opaque glass. Segmented, parts of two segments remaining. Extant L: 6 mm, D: 4.5 mm. perforation D: 2 mm. Context 872, SF284, Phase 3-4.

19 **Bead**. Blue/green glass. Spherical with traces of winding visible at perforation. L: 8mm, section: 7.5 mm, perforation D: 2 mm. Context 687, SF277, Phase 5.

20 **Bead**. Opaque blue glass with opaque white and red chevron. Made from cane layered blue, white, red, white red, bead formed of two slices of cane shaped round former; junction clearly marked. Cubic. L: 4.5 mm, section: 3 mm, perforation D: 1.5 mm. Context 379, Sample 16, Phase 6.

21 **Bracelet**. Copper alloy. Oval section tapering to either end; terminals now broken. Casting flange runs around one side. The whole surface much eroded. D: 66 x 51 mm, maximum section: 5 x 4 mm. Context 5025, SF563, Phase 6.

22 **Intaglio**. Very pale translucent green-tinged co-lourless glass with streak of opaque turquoise. Oval with bevelled edges. Moulded design - in impression an H -shape with small dots between arms. L: 6.5 mm, W: 6 mm, Th: 3.5 mm. Context 5008, SF508, Phase 4-5.

23 **Jewellery setting**. Deep blue translucent glass; hemispherical. D: 7 mm, Th: 4.5 mm. Context 865, SF278, Phase 3-4.

24 **Melon bead**. Frit retaining turquoise glaze. Complete with heavily worn edges to the perforation. L: 15 mm, D: 23 mm, perforation D: 12.5 mm. Context 161, SF14, Phase 3-4.

25 (*not illustrated*) **Melon bead**. Frit retaining turquoise glaze. Half extant in two joining fragments. L: 12 mm, D: 15 mm, perforation D: 7 mm. Context 7478, SF1251, Phase 2.

26 (*not illustrated*) **Melon bead**. Frit. Approximately one quarter extant. L: 11 mm. Context 10303, SF1543, Phase 4.

Toilet and medical equipment (Fig. 5.4: 27-32)

27 **Mirror**. High tin bronze (XRF analysis). Parts of two bevelled edges extant, other sides broken. Slightly convex reflecting surface much obscured by corrosion blisters. Dimensions: 63 x 38 mm. Context 7491, SF1249, Phase 4.

28 **Mirror**. Copper alloy. One straight bevelled edge; other edges broken. Back unfinished. Dimensions: 23 x 23 mm, Th: 1mm. Context 7004 (subsoil), SF1013, unphased.

29 **Mirror**. Copper alloy. Slightly convex reflecting surface retaining white metal coating; circular ring or frame in back with groove around outer edge. XRF indicated tin or tin/lead coating on bronze with the lead possibly being present in the base alloy. Dimensions: 33 x 11 mm, outer D: of ring *c* 50 mm, Th: 1.5 mm. Context 871, SF182, Phase 3-4.

30 **Stirring rod**. Blue/green glass. Cylindrical rod with four pronounced ribs on side with right-hand twist; one end broken, other has flattened disc terminal with curving lines from twist on underside. Extant L: 35 mm, D of terminal: 17 mm, section of rod: 9mm. Context 9088, SF1499, Phase 5.

31 **Forceps**. Copper alloy. Circular-sectioned pear-shaped terminal with chipped point; square-sectioned unit with 3 ribs; upper parts of two arms. Section (maximum): 7 x 7 mm, extant L: 31 mm. Context 7787, SF1367, unphased.

32 **Tweezers**. Copper alloy. Rectangular-sectioned bar bent in half to form tweezers, jaws missing on each arm. Outer face of arms have groove parallel to each edge. Extant L: 46 mm. Context 7293, SF1066, unphased.

Textile equipment (Fig. 5.4: 34)

33 (*not illustrated*) **Needle**. ?Copper alloy. Circular-sectioned shaft tapering to point, flattening to-

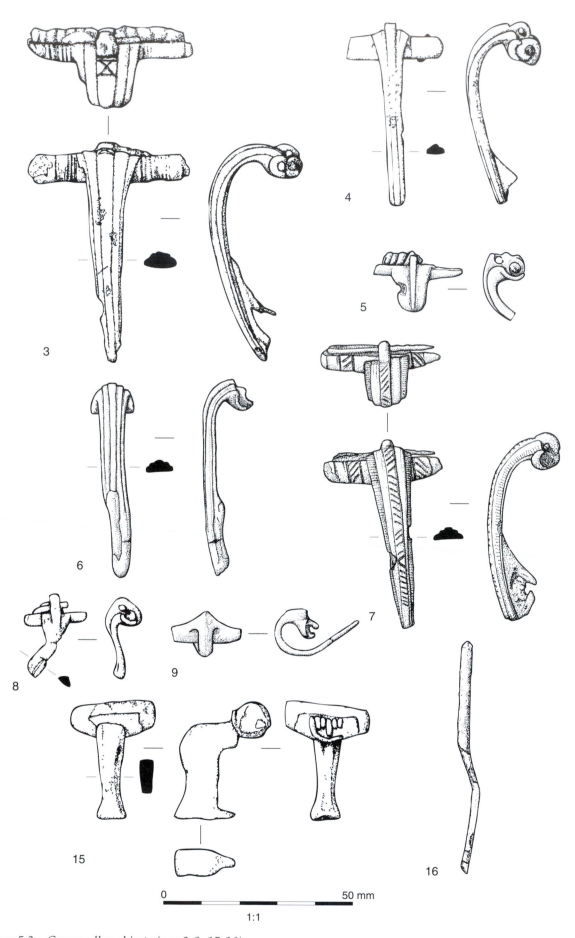

Figure 5.3   Copper alloy objects (nos 3-9, 15-16).

wards broken head. Section: 2 mm, extant L: 45 mm. Context 8239, SF1430, Phase 2-3.

34 **Needle**. Copper alloy. Circular-sectioned; broken into three fragments; one end broken, other flattens with groove below missing eye. Section D: 2.5 mm, extant L: 140 mm. Context 233, SF32, Phase 4.

Household equipment

Glass vessels (Fig. 5.4: 37-38; Fig. 5.5: 40, 44, 51-53, 55-56, 58-59, 65)

35 (*not illustrated*) **Pillar-moulded bowl**. Blue/green glass; wheel polished internally, fire polished externally. Two body fragments, one from side and one from base. Dimensions (largest): 27 x 25 mm. EVE 0.40. Context 5098, SF504, Phase 2-4.

36 (*not illustrated*) **Pillar-moulded bowl**. Blue/green glass, wheel-polished internally, fire-polished externally. Lower body fragment retaining parts of four ribs, abraded band internally. Dimension 28 x 24 mm. EVE 0.20. Context 5084, SF503, Phase 2.

37 **Tubular-rimmed bowl**. Blue/green glass. Rim fragment, outbent rim, edge bent down and in; straight side. Rim D: *c* 130 mm, wall Th: 2 mm, present Ht: 15 mm. EVE 0.40. Context 1272, SF203, Phase 3.

38 **Tubular-rimmed bowl**. Blue/green glass. Rim fragment, rim bent out and down, rim slightly incurved; body curving in. Rim D: 160 mm, present Ht: 12 mm, wall Th: 1 mm. EVE 0.20. Context 9333, SF1512, Phase 4-5.

39 (*not illustrated*) **Tubular-rimmed bowl**. Blue/green glass. Rim fragment, edge bent out and down with tube at upper point. Extant Ht: 14 mm. EVE 0.20. Context 7244, SF1550, Phase 5.

40 **Tubular-rimmed bowl?** Blue/green glass with many bubbles. Complete base fragment, wide lower body broken at junction with side; applied true base ring of oval outline with post technique scars. Base D: 65 x 58 mm, wall Th: 2 mm, present Ht: 15 mm. EVE 0.60. Context 551, SF103, Phase 3.

41 (*not illustrated*) **Indented beaker**. Blue/green glass. Seven body fragments, four joining; vertical side retaining part of two indentations. Extant Ht: 65 mm, wall Th: 1 mm. EVE 0.20. Context 7154, SF966, Phase 4.

42 (*not illustrated*) **Indented beaker**. Light green glass, many bubbles. Two body fragments with parts of indentations, including base of indentation. Dimensions (largest): 37 x 28 mm, wall Th: 1 mm. EVE 0.20. Context 1081, SF193, Phase 4.

43 (*not illustrated*) **Collared jar**. Yellow/green glass. 14 body fragments, many joining; broken at junction with rim, wide upper body with rounded carination to lower body, vertical tooled ribs on lower body. Maximum body D: 120-130 mm, wall Th: 1.5-2.5 mm, present Ht: *c* 70 mm. EVE 0.52. Context 7528, SF1283, Phase 4.

44 **Jar**. Blue/green glass. Rim fragment; asymmetric out-bent rim, edge fire-rounded. Rim D: 65mm, wall Th: 1mm, present Ht: 13 mm. EVE 0.40. Context 64, SF6, Phase 2-4.

45 (*not illustrated*) **Globular jug**. Light yellow/brown glass. Four neck and shoulder fragments, 3 joining. Cylindrical neck with slight tooling marks at base, curving out to wide shoulder. Neck D: *c* 20 mm, wall Th: 1.5 mm, present Ht: 34 mm. EVE 0.28. Context 159, SF13, Phase 3.

46 (*not illustrated*) **Globular jug**. Blue/green glass. Shoulder fragment broken at junction with tooled base of neck; vertical tooled ribs. Dimensions: 41 x 30 mm, wall Th: 2mm. EVE 0.14. Context 742, SF157, Phase 2-3.

47 (*not illustrated*) **Jug**. Light green glass. Handle fragment ribbon with central rib. Section excluding rib: 28 x 5 mm. EVE 0.14. Context 171, SF27, Phase 3.

48 (*not illustrated*) **Jar or jug**. Yellow/green glass. Two joining lower body and open pushed-in base fragments. Base D: 70 mm, wall Th: 1.5 mm, present Ht: 21 mm. EVE 0.28. Context 7157, SF967 and SF968, Phase 4.

49 (*not illustrated*) **Jug or jar**. Blue/green glass. Lower body and base fragment; side sloping in to open pushed-in base ring, horizontal scratch marks on side above base ring. Base D: 75 mm, wall Th: 2 mm, present Ht: 18 mm. EVE 0.14. Context 8546, SF1551, Phase 3-4.

50 (*not illustrated*) **Jug or jar**. Pale green glass. Lower body fragment, convex-curved retaining small part of open pushed-in base ring. Dimensions: 37 x 24 mm, wall Th: 1.5 mm. EVE 0.14. Context 7588, SF1317, Phase 4.

51 **Spouted jug**. Blue/green glass; many bubbles; some large. Three joining rim, neck and handle fragments. Slightly funnel-shaped mouth, rim edge bent in and down, rim pinched in to form lobate outline, spout missing and possibly slightly pulled up; short neck curving out to shoulder. 'D'-sectioned rod handle with simple lower attachment, handle attached to back of rim, trailed up and down and re-attached to top of rim with small return trail. Handle between two upper attachments pinched together, flattened and bent back to form a thumb rest, the upper part of this thumb rest shows tapering points of pincers used in flattening and bending process. W of rim: 56 mm, handle section: 9 x 5 mm, present Ht: 62 mm. Context 8797, SF1453-1454 and SF1456, Phase 4-5.

52 **Jug**. Blue/green glass with streaky green impurities and many bubbles. Handle fragment, rod handle with single pinched projection at lower handle attachment which retains small fragment of convex-curved shoulder. Handle section: 9 x 7 mm. EVE 0.14. Context 530, SF100, Phase 3-4.

53 **Jug**. Light green bubbly glass. High pushed-in base ring, side and base missing. Base D: *c* 65 mm. EVE 0.14. Context 417, SF281, Phase 7.

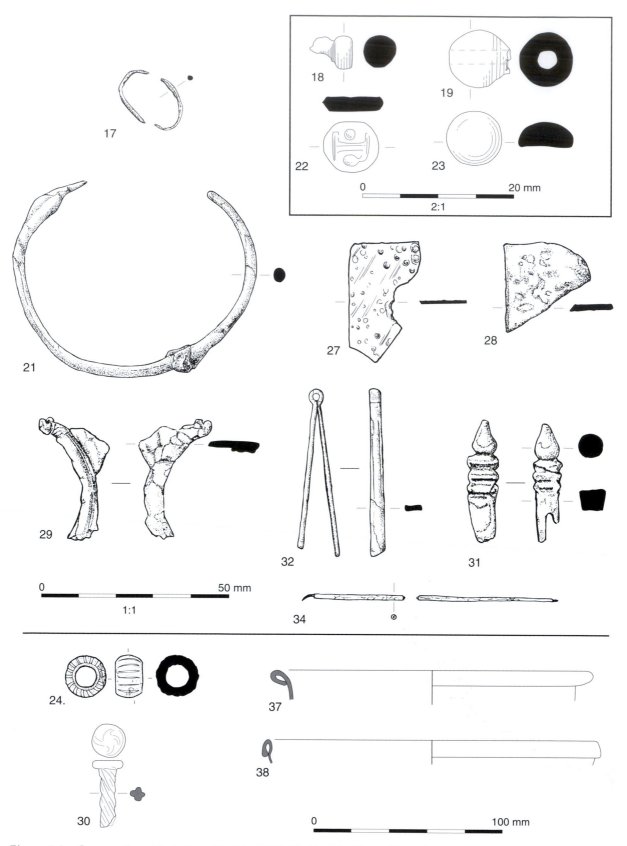

Figure 5.4   Copper alloy objects (nos 17, 21, 27-29, 31-32, 34); Glass objects (nos 18-19, 22-24, 30, 37-38).

54 (*not illustrated*) **Flask?** Blue/green glass; many bubbles, streaky green impurities. Base fragment; side curving into concave base. Base D: c 50 mm, wall Th: 1 mm, present Ht: 13 mm. EVE 0.40. Context 177, SF19, Phase 3.

55 **Prismatic bottle**. Blue/green glass; many bubbles, some large. Four joining rim, neck, handle and shoulder fragments; rim bent out, up, in and flattened; cylindrical neck; flat shoulder; angular ribbon handle with simple lower attachment, upper attachment on neck with return trail between handle and rim edge. Rim D: c 45mm; handle section: 21 x 2.5 mm, present Ht: 41 mm. EVE 0.56. Context 8857, SF1457, Phase 4.

56 **Bottle**. Blue/green glass; streaky green impurities. Rim and neck fragment, rim folded out, up, in and flattened; narrow cylindrical neck with tooling marks at base; bending out to shoulder. Fragment of folded upper handle attachment on neck below rim. Rim D: 30 mm, shoulder Th: 2.5 mm, present Ht: 44 mm. EVE 0.42. Context 9059, SF1493, Phase 4.

57 (*not illustrated*) **Bottle**. Blue/green glass. Rim and neck fragment, rim bent out, up, in and flattened; vertical neck. Rim D: 40 mm. EVE 0.28. Context 7029, SF922, unphased.

58 **Bottle**. Blue/green glass. Three joining handle fragments; angular reeded handle with simple lower handle attachment retaining part of shoulder. Handle section 28 x 4 mm, Ht of handle: 37 mm. EVE 0.28. Also one body fragment possibly from this vessel. Context 7225, SF1006, Phase 5.

59 **Prismatic bottle**. Blue/green glass. Handle fragment; angular with pronounced side ribs, simple lower attachment retaining part of shoulder. Handle section: 38 x 5 mm. EVE 0.28. Context 7066, SF941, Phase 4.

60 (*not illustrated*) **Bottle**. Blue/green glass. Handle fragment. EVE 0.14. Context 1633, SF274, Phase 4-5.

61 (*not illustrated*) **Bottle or jug**. Blue/green glass. Handle, fragment from folded upper attachment. Dimensions: 18 x 15 mm. Context 675, SF150, Phase 6.

62 (*not illustrated*) **Bottle**. Blue/green glass. Neck fragment. Context 677, SF136, Phase 5.

63 (*not illustrated*) **Bottle**. Blue/green glass. Shoulder fragment broken at tooled junction with cylindrical neck. Neck D: c 50 mm. EVE 0.14. Context 7347, SF1104, Phase 5.

64 (*not illustrated*) **Prismatic bottle**. Blue/green glass. Base fragment. Base design - at least two concentric circular mouldings. Dimensions: 17 x 17 mm. EVE 0.14. Context 675, SF122, Phase 6.

65 **Base fragment**. Blue/green glass. Base fragment; high pushed-in base ring, concave base. Base D: 70 mm, present Ht: 13 mm. Context 7255, SF1026, Phase 5.

66 (*not illustrated*) **Base fragment**. Blue/green glass; many bubbles. Two joining base fragments; wide lower body fragment broken at junction with side; solid, possibly trailed base ring, base missing. Base D: 40 mm, wall Th: 2 mm, present Ht: 11 mm. Context 7279, SF1096, Phase 5.

67 (*not illustrated*) **Base fragment**. Blue/green glass. Side sloping into concave base with pontil scar, edge of base heavily worn. Base D: c 80 mm, wall Th: 2.5 mm. Context 7562, SF1295, Phase 4.

68 (*not illustrated*) **Base fragment**. Colourless glass. Solid pushed-in base ring, part of base, side grazed. Base D: c 80 mm. Context 758, SF196, Phase 6.

69 (*not illustrated*) **Body fragment**. Yellow/green glass. Convex-curved with part of one rib. Dimensions: 25 x 15 mm, wall Th: 1 mm. Context 868, SF180, Phase 2-3.

70 (*not illustrated*) **Body fragment**. Light green glass. Convex-curved with optic blown rib. Dimensions: 15 x 12.5 mm, wall Th: 1.5 mm. Context 7813, SF1375, Phase 3.

71 (*not illustrated*) **Body fragment**. Blue/green glass. Convex-curved with vertical tooled ribs. Dimensions: 34 x 24 mm, wall Th: 2.5 mm. Context 868, SF179, Phase 2-3.

72 (*not illustrated*) **Body fragment**. Blue/green glass. Parts of two optic blown ribs. Dimensions: 27 x 23 mm, wall Th: 2 mm. Context 1272, SF202, Phase 3.

73 (*not illustrated*) **Body fragment**. Blue/green glass. Convex-curved, retaining parts of two vertical ribs. Dimensions: 21 x 16 mm, wall Th: 1.5 mm. Context 7514, SF1268, Phase 3.

74 (*not illustrated*) **Body fragment**. Blue/green glass. Convex-curved with parts of three vertical optic blown ribs. Dimensions: 29 x 16 mm. 7 Context 045, SF923, Phase 3-4.

Other items (Fig. 5.5: 75-78)

75 **Escutcheon**. Copper alloy. Triangular leaf-shaped plate with unfinished back; rectangular-sectioned loop at right angles to plate, tapering to rounded point. Dimensions of plate: 39 x 33 mm. Context 7004 (subsoil), SF1434, unphased.

76 **Vessel?** Copper alloy. Very heavily corroded with no original surface remaining. Flat plate with low angular projecting ring - possibly turned base ring. Dimensions: 25 x 12 mm, D: of ring c 35-40 mm. Context 172, SF17, Phase 2-3.

77 **Mount**. Copper alloy. Flat-bottomed oval casting with 'neck' at one end. Short-circular-sectioned shank centrally below with convex end. L: 16.5 mm, section: 10 x 6 mm. Context 7639, SF1274, unphased.

78 **Candlestick?** Lead alloy. Rectangular strip, one end cut across, other broken at point where it may have widened out, central row of pellets. L: 52 mm, section (excluding pellets): 8 x 3 mm. Context 707, SF161, Phase 6.

Recreation

79 (*not illustrated*) **Counter**. Fired clay, oxidised. Circular disc with concave faces. D: 27 mm, Th: 9 mm. Context 8915, SF1486, Phase 3.

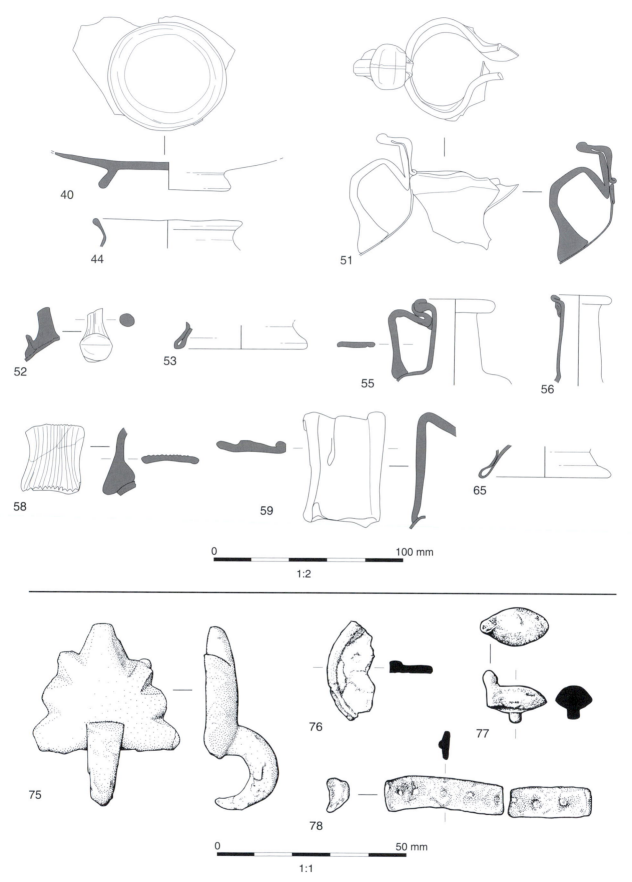

Figure 5.5   Glass objects (nos 40, 44, 51-53, 55-56, 58-59, 65); Copper alloy objects (nos 75-77); Lead alloy object (no. 78).

Weighing equipment (Fig. 5.6: 80, 84, 86-88, 90)

80 **Steelyard**. Copper alloy. Pointed oval-sectioned arm tapering to conical terminal, fulcrum end rectangular-sectioned with three suspension loops, one broken; small double pointed spur on edge close to end suspension loop. Corroded and original surface frequently missing on sides. Two scales marked by divisions along edges and numerals scratched on side. The corrosion means that in some cases numerals are represented by 'ghosts' below the missing surface. Scale corresponding to suspension from outer (broken) loop marked by groups of 11 dots on edge, generally with small gaps between them. The dots have been removed by corrosion between fulcrum and first division, are intermittently present between first and second division and are thereafter clearly marked. On side corresponding to gaps, I and II are represented by ghosts; III present, IIII represented by one stroke and 3 ghosts, upper ends of V present; VI represented by tip of one stroke; VII by upper ends of II, VIII by upper ends of III; and VIIII by III prior to deep corrosion. In the case of VI, VII, VIII and VIIII there are no ghosts or tips of strokes to suggest that the 'V's were ever present. The suggested sequence is therefore I, II, III, IIII, V, I, II, III, IIII with the 'V's being assumed in the latter case. Scale represented by suspension from inner loop marked by short grooves across edge with corrosion removing most of those between fulcrum and the 2nd division, thereafter most remain. First division marked by upper part of X, then V, XX, V, XXX, V, XXXX mark includes three ghosts, possible ghost of final V at end by terminal. There are 5 edge grooves between each numeral. Wire suspension loop probably for weight found with arm, now much corroded. Rectangular sectioned wire bent to form loop and free end wrapped around shank at least 5 times to secure it. Arm: L: 206 mm, section by fulcrum: 16 x 4 mm, suspension loop: 34 mm. Context 8796, SF1451 and SF1452, Phase 4-5.

81 **Steelyard weight**. Copper alloy. In shape of acorn, broken across base of loop terminal. Maximum D: 11.5 x 10 mm, L: 21 mm, Wt: 7 g. Context 7004 (subsoil), SF1132, unphased.

82 (*not illustrated*) **Steelyard weight**. Lead. Biconical with iron wire through centre, one end has stump of two wires from a loop, other has central stump of wire with a second wound around it. L: 49 mm, D: 37.5 x 36 mm, Wt: 183 g. Context 7412, SF1207, Phase 4-5.

83 (*not illustrated*) **Steelyard weight**. Lead. Biconical with iron corrosion at one end and possible trace of wire at end. L: 70 mm, D: 54 mm, weight 581 g. Context 7627, SF1321, unphased.

84 **Steelyard weight**. Lead. Biconical with stump of iron loop at one end and traces of iron wire at other. L: 39 mm, D: 30 mm, Wt: 105 g. Context 7004 (subsoil), SF1326, unphased.

85 (*not illustrated*) **Steelyard weight**. Lead. Biconical with stump of iron suspension loop at one end. L: 32 mm, D: 37.5 x 31 mm, Wt: 95 g. Context 7004 (subsoil), SF1115, unphased.

86 **Steelyard weight**. Lead. Assymetrical biconical, iron visible at either end. L: 21 mm, D: 23 x 21 mm, Wt: 32 g. Context 7077, SF930, unphased.

87 **Steelyard weight**. Lead. Biconical with traces of iron wire at either end. L: 27 mm, D: 20 mm, Wt: 30 g. Context 7004 (subsoil), SF1116, unphased.

88 **Steelyard weight**. Lead. Biconical with cylindrical central part. Traces of iron wire at apex. L: 39 mm, D: 39 mm, Wt: 260 g. Context 7238, SF1496, unphased.

89 (*not illustrated*) **Steelyard weight**. Lead. Rounded biconical with conical upper part and rounded lower part. Broken stump of iron loop in apex. Damaged on one side. L: 31mm, D: 25 mm, Wt: 69 g. Context 7004 (subsoil), SF1258, unphased.

90 **Weight**. Lead. Cylindrical disc, damaged on one edge and much of original surface missing. D: 18 mm, Th: 5.5 mm, Wt: 12 g. Context 7426, SF1209, unphased.

91 (*not illustrated*) **Weight?** Lead. Disc with damaged edges. D: 27 mm, Th: 6.5 mm, Wt: 23 g. Context 7004 (subsoil), SF1122, unphased.

Structural finds

92 (*not illustrated*) **Window**. Blue/green glass. Cast, matt/glossy. Area 31 cm². Context 922, SF188, Phase 4.

93 (*not illustrated*) **Window**. Blue/green glass. Cast matt/glossy. Area 1 cm². Context 7240, SF959, Phase 5.

Fasteners and fittings (Fig. 5.6: 95-96; Fig. 5.7: 97-100)

94 (*not illustrated*) **Bell-shaped stud**. Copper alloy. Moulding around outer edge of base of central cone; circular-sectioned broken shank. D: 23 mm, extant L: 21 mm. Context 7237, SF1023, Phase 5.

95 **Bell-shaped stud**. Copper alloy. Upper margin chipped but retains internal groove; circular rib around central cone; broken circular-sectioned shank. D: 20 mm, extant L: 19 mm. Context 7004 (subsoil), SF1206, unphased.

96 **Bell-shaped stud**. Copper alloy. Circular head chipped on one side; turning grooves internally and forming effect of rib around base of conical centre; rectangular-sectioned integral shank, broken at end. Head D: 36 mm, shank section: 10 x 7 mm, extant L: 39 mm. Context 7004 (subsoil), SF1139, unphased.

97 **Lock casing?** Copper alloy. Rectangular sheet retaining one rounded corner and parts of two parallel edges, other edges broken. Second sheet, rivetted to back, bent to form a square casing, parts of four round-headed rivets remaining. Much corroded remains of ?mechanism internally, possibly of iron as corrosion products are blue suggesting vivianite. W: 40 mm, extant L: 48 mm. Context 7279, SF1063, Phase 5.

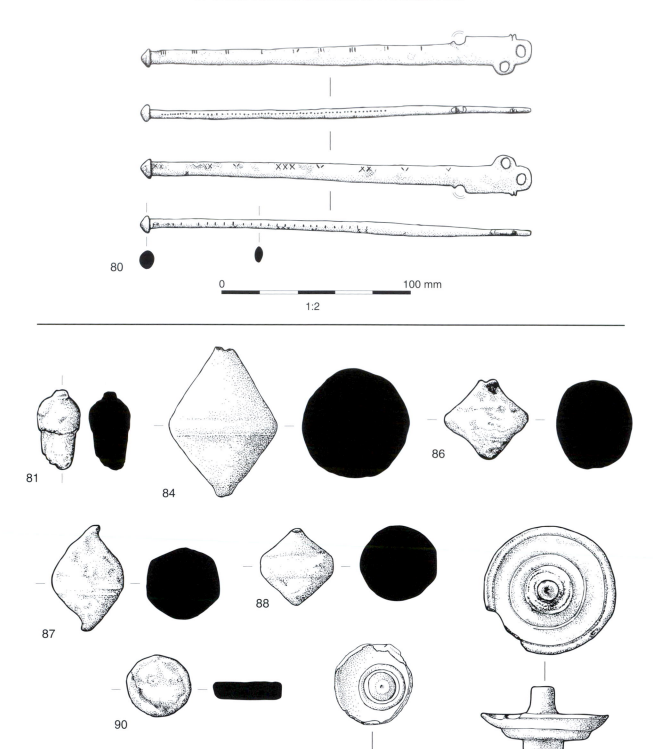

Figure 5.6   Copper alloy objects (nos 80-81, 95-96); Lead objects (nos 84, 86-88, 90).

98 **Fitting**. Copper alloy. Cast horse head with elongated muzzle and prominent ears, traces of eyes, mouth and nostrils; broken shank. section: 8 x 6 mm, extant L: 19 mm. Context 7628, SF1322, unphased.

99 **Fitting**. Copper alloy. Discoid with large central perforation now filled with iron corrosion products. L: 9 mm, D: 16mm, perforation D: 7 mm. Context 7088, SF939, unphased.

100 **Nail**. Possibly leaded copper alloy. Spherical knob terminal with broken circular-sectioned shank. D: 13.5 mm. Context 806, SF158, Phase 4.

101 (*not illustrated*) **Rivet and washer**. Copper alloy. Oval slightly domed head with chipped edges; circular shank; flat integral washer with chipped edges. L: 7.5 mm, head D: 11 x 9 mm. Context 10293, SF1541, Phase 4.

102 (*not illustrated*) **Dolphin mount**. Copper alloy. Hollow-backed, curved, one end broken across perforation within forked tail, centrally on upper edge the remains of the fins; head divided from attachment area by vertical rib, small iron rivet beyond rib and edge beyond broken. All of the original surface lost. Extant L: 42 mm. Context 7536, SF1300, Phase 2.

Religious items

103 (*not illustrated*) **Venus figurine**. Pipe clay. Back of head and neck, fragment has divided from front of head at mould seam. Hair including bun at base of neck clearly moulded with ringlet on each shoulder and tip of right hand touching one ringlet. W of head: 26 mm, extant L: 35 mm. Context 7573, SF1303, Phase 4.

Craft and industry

104 (*not illustrated*) **Offcut**. Copper alloy. Narrow twisted strip with many fragmented crumbs. L: 39 mm. Context 61, SF7, Phase 2-3.

105 (*not illustrated*) **Casting waste**. Copper alloy. Fragment. Context 7004 (subsoil), SF1393, unphased.

106 (*not illustrated*) **Fragment**. Melted opaque dark blue glass, vesicular. D: *c* 5.5 mm, Th: 3.5 mm. Context 1529, SF279, Phase 5.

107 (*not illustrated*) **Scraper**, Blue/green glass. Flat prismatic bottle body fragment showing flaking and deliberate retouch along one side. Dimensions: 46 x 31 mm, wall Th: 7 mm. Context 7258, SF976, Phase 4.

Miscellaneous (Fig. 5.7: 108-112, 126)

108 **Bell**. Copper alloy. Upper part of conical body with complete but much corroded upper suspension loop and internal rectangular-sectioned suspension loop for missing clapper. Body of bell has external white metal coating, possibly a high tin bronze with surface enhancement. Present Ht: *c* 47 mm. Context 7638, SF1273, unphased.

109 **Whorl**. Lead. Tall plano-convex. L: 16 mm, D: 20 x 17.5mm, perforation D: 10 mm, weight 31 g. Context 7004 (subsoil), SF1415, unphased.

110 **Whorl**. Lead. Plano-convex. L: 9 mm, D: 23 mm, perforation D: 8 mm, weight 29 g. Context 7003 (ploughsoil), SF1215, unphased.

111 **Whorl**. Lead. Plano-convex. L: 7 mm, D: 18 mm, perforation D: 9 mm, weight 10 g. Context 7004 (subsoil), SF1416, unphased.

112 **Whorl**. Lead. Cylindrical. L: 15.5 mm, D: 23 mm, perforation D: 10 mm, weight 38 g. Context 7003 (ploughsoil), SF1120, unphased.

113 (*not illustrated*) **Weight**. Lead. Lentoid-sectioned slightly bent disc, with oval perforation. D: 23 x 21 mm, Th: 4 mm, perforation D: 8 x 5.5 mm, weight 9 g. Context 7579, SF1309, Phase 6.

114 (*not illustrated*) **Strap fitting?** Copper alloy. End of rectangular folded sheet with possible traces of minerally preserved organic material internally. Dimensions: 14 x 10 mm, Th: 0.5 mm. Context 8239, SF1428, Phase 2-3.

115 (*not illustrated*) **Ring?** Copper alloy. Approximately circular-sectioned slightly curved rod, possibly from a large ring; both ends broken; much corroded. Section: 4 mm, L: *c* 35 mm. Context 7666, SF1333, Phase 4.

116 (*not illustrated*) **Rod**. Copper alloy. Circular-sectioned, tapering; both ends broken. Section (maximum): 3 mm, extant L: 34 mm. Context 9481, SF1519, Phase 4.

117 (*not illustrated*) **Rod**, Copper alloy. Circular-sectioned, both ends broken. White metal coating on surface. D: 2.5 mm, extant L: 41 mm. Context 7529, SF1284, Phase 4.

118 (*not illustrated*) **Rod**. Copper alloy. Tapering circular-sectioned rod; both ends broken. L: 59 mm, section: 2.5 mm. Context 686, SF130, Phase 4.

119 (*not illustrated*) **Shank?** Copper alloy. Circular-sectioned rod tapering to point, other end broken. Section: 3 mm, extant L: 75 mm. Context 9031, SF1490, Phase 4.

120 (*not illustrated*) **Sheet**. Copper alloy. Sheet folded into bar. Dimensions: 59 x 14 x 10 mm. Context 8855, SF1469, Phase 5.

121 (*not illustrated*) **Terminal**. Copper alloy. Hemispherical rounded terminal at end of angular plate. Plate now fragmented. D of knob: 6 mm, Th of plate: 2 mm. Context 8475, SF1433, Phase 3.

122 (*not illustrated*) **Wire**. Copper alloy. Both ends broken. L: 5 mm. Context 8425, SF1432, Phase 2-3.

123 (*not illustrated*) **Wire**. Copper alloy. Both ends broken; no original surfaces now extant. L: 70 mm. Context 7024, SF907, Phase 4.

124 (*not illustrated*) **Fragment**. Copper alloy. Approximately D-sectioned cast. Section: 11 x 8 mm, extant L: 17 mm. Context 7395, SF1219, Phase 3.

125 (*not illustrated*) **Fragment**. Copper alloy. Cast fragment, all edges broken. Dimensions: 13 x 13 x 4 mm. Context 1258, SF214, Phase 5.

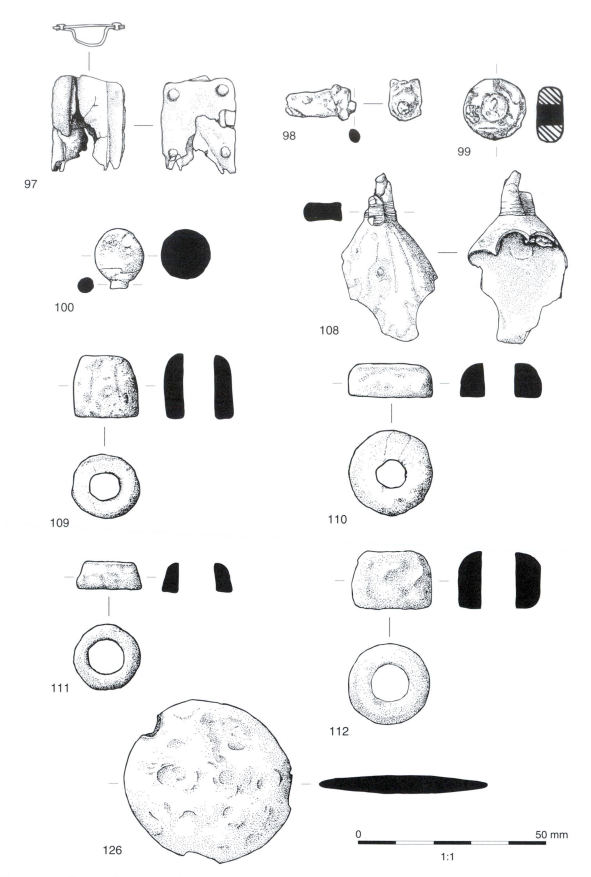

Figure 5.7   Copper alloy objects (nos 97-98, 100, 108); Copper alloy and iron object (no. 99); Lead objects (nos 109-112, 126).

126 **Disc**. Lead. D: 46 mm, Th: 5 mm, weight 44 g. Context 7127, SF981, Phase 4.

127 (*not illustrated*) **Sheet**. Lead. Fragmented strip retaining parts of two perforations. W: 29 mm, Wt: 15 g. Context 7244, SF998, Phase 5.

128 (*not illustrated*) **Strip**, Lead. Bent. L: 31 mm, W: 5 mm, Wt: 2 g. Context 1081, SF192, Phase 4.

129 (*not illustrated*) **Fragment**, Lead. Wt: 7 g. Context 8218, SF1420, Phase 4.

130 (*not illustrated*) **Run-off**. Lead. Wt: 7 g. Context 7237, SF1019, Phase 5.

131 (*not illustrated*) **Run-off**. Lead. Wt: 2 g. Context 720, SF172, Phase 6.

132 (*not illustrated*) **Run-off**. Lead. Wt: 18 g. Context 7237, SF1016, Phase 5.

133 (*not illustrated*) **Run-off**. Lead. Wt: 16 g. Context 723, SF270, Phase 6.

JET AND LIGNITE OBJECTS FROM GRAVE 5090
by Lindsay Allason-Jones

Catalogue (*Figs 5.8-5.9, 8.5*)

1 **Cylinder necklace beads**, jet. There are 183 examples. Two beads were long and decorated with panels of grooves (Fig. 5.8: 1-2). The majority of the cylinder beads (Fig. 5.8: 3-5) were short but made from long tubes with scored encircling line decoration. Each bead has been snapped off at a scored line usually leaving one line as a central decoration on each individual bead; eight beads are decorated with two lines and one bead has three, suggesting that the bead-maker was not always careful to make the beads a uniform length. Occasionally a rough spelk of jet has been left as a result of the initial snapping; the fact that these are still visible and sharp suggests that the necklace had not been worn extensively by its owner before deposition. Long cylinder beads: L: 28 mm, D: 4 mm - 5 mm; short cylinder beads: L: 2.5 mm – 7 mm, D: 4 mm. Context 5025, SF504, SF512-19, SF521-39, SF541-49, SF586, SF589-610, SF643-53, SF659-738

The short cylinder bead is the commonest form of jet bead found in Roman Britain and Germany: see Allason-Jones 1996. The type seems first appear in the late 2nd century AD and continues in use into the 4th century.

2 **Armlet**. Made from three large, **oval, ridge-backed beads** (Fig. 5.8: 6-8), on which traces of gold leaf were found, and 25 **flat elliptical beads** (Fig. 5.8: 9-31) with one edge more markedly curved than the other and decorated with a deeply cut motif. Twenty-two of the latter divide into the main two types of armlet beads to be found in Britain: Fifteen examples have a central Z-motif flanked by ovals, while seven simply have ovals. Of the remaining two, one has a central, waisted oval motif flanked by zigzags while the other is notched along one edge. Both the ridge-backed beads and the elliptical beads are pierced laterally by two circular holes. Ridge-backed beads: 36 x 27 mm, 22 x 28 mm, 22 x 24 mm; elliptical beads: 16 x 9 mm – 29 x 13 mm. Context 5025, elliptical beads: SF511, SF520, SF565-575, SF577-584, SF654, SF656-658; ridge-backed beads: SF564, SF576, SF655.

Parallels to the oval-decorated elliptical beads can be found at York (Allason-Jones 1996, no. 28) and Colchester (Crummy 1983, fig. 37, no. 1498), as well as in the Rhineland (Hagen 1937, Taf. 25, Abb. 2, C38). The type with a central Z-motif flanked by ovals is more common in Britain (Allason-Jones and Miket 1984, no. 7.28) although it does occur occasionally in France (Deyber 1989) and at Aquincum in Hungary where examples are also known in lignite (Aquincum Museum unpubl.). The larger ridge-backed beads, however, are almost exclusively confined to the Rhineland being particularly prominent in the cemeteries of Cologne (Hagen 1937, Taf. 25, Abb. 2, C45; Taf. 27, Abb. 1, C27), although a few examples are known from British contexts, for example Silchester (Lawson 1975, fig. 1.4) and London (unpublished, MSL87.1914.SF642-7).

The beads when found still had fragments of copper alloy wire *in situ* making it clear that a complete, strung armlet was deposited as part of the funerary rite, rather than a handful of loose beads (see Fig. 5.8: 25). However, both the mixture of bead types and the arrangement of the beads makes it equally clear that the armlet had been made from beads recycled from at least five other armlets. Armlet beads were designed to be graded in size with the largest in the centre, tapering to the smallest at each terminal; this made the armlet more comfortable for the wearer and made it fit the wrist more snugly. The decorative motifs on the curved outer faces of each bead were also carefully carved so that when the beads were in the right order the design flowed. On this armlet one of the ridge-backed beads was set at each terminal with the third dividing the elliptical beads into two sets. Only the most cursory attempt has been made to grade the beads so that the largest are in the middle of each set and the two main types of decorative motifs have been mixed.

Analysis

Analysis of ten samples taken from the beads (see Table 5.16) was carried out by Dr J M Jones, Fossil Fuels and Environmental Geochemistry (Postgraduate) Institute, University of Newcastle-upon-Tyne, using reflected light microscopy (Allason-Jones and Jones 2001). This revealed that the necklace beads were all likely to be of jet while the armlet beads were a mixture of lignite and jet beads.

The jet fits in well with that found from Yorkshire, although it should not be presumed that it could only have been found in Yorkshire. Pirite specks present in the sample from ridged bead 655 may suggest a Rhineland source. The lignite, on the other hand, appears

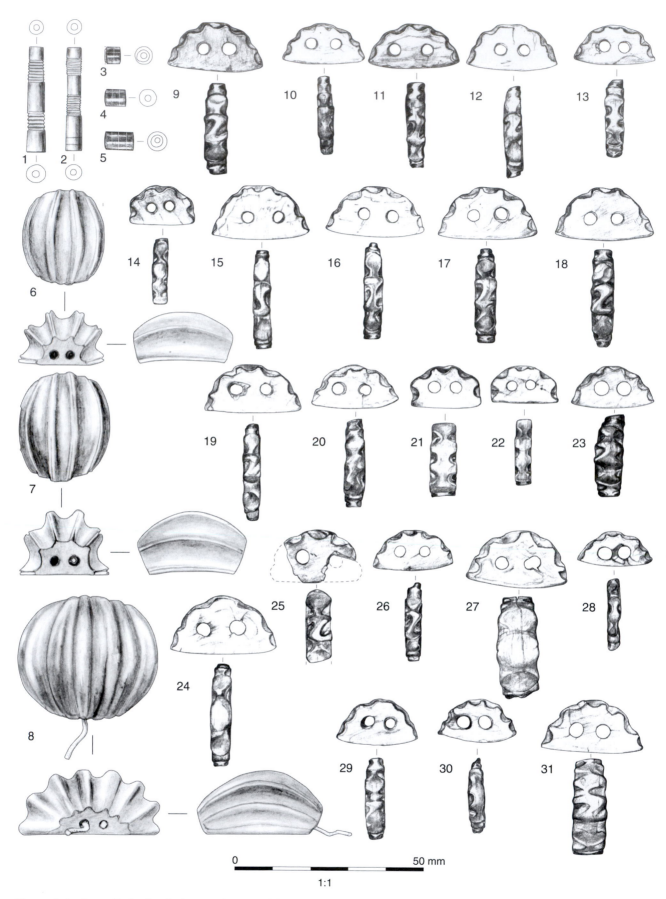

Figure 5.8   Jet cylinder beads (nos 1-5); Jet and lignite ridged-back beads (nos 6-8) and flat elliptical beads for an armlet (9-31) from Burial 5090.

Figure 5.9   Reconstruction of jet and lignite armlet from burial 5090.

0   50 mm

1:1

to have come from a local source. Local sources of lignite with their reflectance measurements is summarised in Table 5.17.

It is unlikely that the lignite source could be pinned down to one particular bed in a foolproof way but it seems likely that whoever carved this group of beads had not travelled far for the raw material. This is the first time that lignite has been found worked as jewellery in a Romano-British context. Because the armlet appears to have been made from beads recycled from five armlets it is not possible to suggest that all the beads are of British manufacture; the use of the ridge-backed beads, indeed, may suggest some influence from the Rhineland.

The fact that traces of gold were found on one of the ridge-backed beads is of great importance as this is the first time gold has been found on a piece of Romano-British black jewellery (Allason-Jones 1999). Gold has been found on jewellery from Roman Germany as wire, twisted around cable armlets (eg Cologne - la Baume 1971), and applied in the form of gold leaf on octagonal armlets (Allason-Jones 1996, fig. 12), but not previously on armlet beads. Because only minute traces of gold were found it is not clear if the beads were completely gilded or if the gilding was confined to the valleys of the decoration or applied as spots.

Although the wearing of jet and jet-like jewellery started in the late 2nd century in Britain it became particularly fashionable in the late 3rd to 4th centuries. Each of the Ashford objects could have derived from almost any period within the late 2nd to 4th century timescale but, as an assemblage, is more likely to be early 4th century in date.

IRONWORK
by Ian Scott

Introduction

Composition of the assemblage

The ironwork assemblage comprises 676 fragments. The range of material represented is limited (Tables 5.18 and 5.19). Only 31 pieces (4.6% of the total assemblage by count) are identifiable objects (see Table 5.20). The

Table 5.16   Jet and lignite from Grave 5090: Summary of results of reflected light microscopy analysis of samples from beads. (10 samples selected).

SF number	Type	Reflectance	Material
582A	Elliptical bead	0.27% R.O	Lignite
570	Elliptical bead	0.34% R.O	Lignite
654	Elliptical bead	0.3% R.O	Lignite
581	Elliptical bead	0.28% R.O	Lignite
582B	Bead frags.	0.27% R.O	Lignite
569	Elliptical bead	0.26% R.O	Lignite
576	Ridged bead	0.18% R.O	Jet
655	Ridged bead	0.19% R.O	Jet
641	Cylinder bead	0.18% R.O	Jet
642	Cylinder bead	0.18% R.O	Jet

Table 5.17   Jet and lignite from Grave 5090: Comparison of reflectance measurements for local sources of lignite.

Source	Reflectance
Lignite Wealden	0.25% R.O
Lignite Weald Clay	0.32% R.O
Lignite Lulworth	0.34% R.O
Shale Ashdown beds	0.37% R.O
Lignite Hastings	0.38% R.O
Shale Hastings beds	0.4% R.O

largest categories of object are nails, which comprise 49.9% of the assemblage by number (337 nails or nail fragments, see Table 5.21) and hobnails, which form 24.1% of the assemblage (163 hobnails or hobnail strips, see Table 5.22). The remainder of the assemblage comprises 83 miscellaneous pieces of strip, rod, sheet, etc (see Table 5.23) and 30 pieces of uncertain identification (see Table 5.24), which together form 16.7% of the assemblage. The latter comprise fragments of objects that cannot be identified to a specific object or function. Finally there are 32 small unidentifiable scraps (see Table 5.25). A number of pieces of slag (40 pieces) and cinder and possible hammerscale (115 pieces), which were bagged with the artefacts, have been omitted from consideration in this report.

The material was largely recovered by hand, although some finds, mainly hobnails and small fragments, were recovered from sieving. The assemblage is comparatively small when its composition and the extent of the excavations are taken into account. In particular the number of identifiable objects, excluding nails and hobnails, is very small.

Methodology

Because of the limited number of objects which can be identified to function, the emphasis in this report is on the assemblage as a whole rather than on individual objects. The ironwork from the site was classified to function in broad terms during the recording process. The system employed is based on the Colchester system (Crummy 1983, 4-6), but with the addition of classifications for material which cannot be identified as specific objects, or identified to a particular function or process. Fragments of strip, sheet, rod and wire are classed as 'miscellaneous'; other fragments which may have formed parts of larger objects, but which now cannot be identified, are classed as being of 'uncertain identification'. The material which could not be classified to function, mainly small fragments, is classed as 'unidentifiable'. These classifications are used in this report and in the archive database.

Report structure

The ironwork assemblage is considered from two points of view: the assemblage as a whole and the individual phase assemblages. The comparison of different types of material across the phases is briefly considered, but given the small size of the assemblage,

Table 5.18   Ironwork: Summary quantification (fragment count) by functional category and Phase, showing percentage of each functional category in each Phase.

Phase	Objects (excl hobnails)		Hobnails and hobnail strips		Nails		Misc		Uncertain ID		Unidentifiable		All classes	
	No.	%	No.	%	No.	%	No.	%	No.	%	No.	%	No.	%
2	-	-	-	-	6	1.8%	1	1.2%	-	-	11	34.4%	18	2.7%
3	5	16.1%	45	27.6%	40	11.9%	10	12%	4	13.3%	-	-	104	15.4%
4	5	16.1%	32	19.6%	92	27.3%	29	34.9%	10	33.3%	10	31.3%	178	26.3%
5	5	16.1%	80	49.1%	112	33.2%	24	28.9%	7	23.3%	9	28.1%	237	35.1%
6	3	9.7%	6	3.6%	26	7.7%	2	2.4%	1	3.3%	-	-	38	5.6%
Uncertain	3 }	41.9%	-	-	28 }	18.1%	10 }	20.5%	5 }	26.7%	2 }	6.3%	48 }	14.9%
Unphased	10 }		-		33 }		7 }		3 }		0 }		53 }	
Total	31	99.9%	163	99.9%	337	100%	83	99.9%	30	99.9%	32	100.1%	676	100%

Table 5.19   Ironwork: Summary quantification (fragment count) by functional category and Phase, showing each functional category as a percentage of each per Phase assemblage.

Phase	Objects No /% age	Hobnails No / % age	Nails No / % age	Miscellaneous No / % age	Uncertain ID No / % age	Unidentifiable No / % age	All classes No
2	-	-	6	1	-	11	18
	-	-	33.3%	5.6%	-	61.1%	= 100%
3	5	45	40	10	4	-	104
	4.8%	43.3%	38.5%	9.6%	3.8%	-	= 100 %
4	5	32	92	29	10	10	178
	2.8%	18%	51.7%	16.3%	5.6%)	5.6%	= 100%
5	5	80	112	24	7	9	237
	2.1%	33.8%	47.3%	10.1%	3%	3.8%	= 100.1%
6	3	6	26	2	1	-	38
	7.9%	15.8%	68.4%	5.3%	2.6%	-	= 100%
Uncertain	3	-	28	10	5	2	48
Unphased	10	-	33	7	3	-	53
Total	31	163	337	83	30	32	676
	4.6%	24.1%	49.9%	12.3%	4.4%	4.7%	= 100%

this has not proved to give any interesting information. The contents of the assemblage are summarised in the tables and only the identifiable objects are catalogued in detail. Most of the latter are also illustrated (Figs 5.10-5.12). Although percentages are given in the various summary tables, these are provided only to give an indication of the composition of the phase assemblages and of the various categories of finds. The assemblage is small and on this account any statistics are unreliable except in the broadest terms.

Assemblage as a whole

Range of finds present

The range of identified objects is typical of any Roman site; structural pieces, some horse/cart gear, a few personal items, etc. are largely unphased (Table 5.20). What is atypical is the small proportion of the assemblage that can be identified to function. The paucity of finds perhaps reflects the comparatively early abandonment of the site. It is only an impression based on observation of a number of finds assemblages as yet without statistical evidence to support it, but it does seem that the metal finds from earlier phases of Roman sites tend to be less prolific than those from later

phases. Where a site has a long occupation history this can be attributed to the gathering up and recycling of earlier material by later occupants. However, the Westhawk Farm site was not occupied throughout the Roman period – as witnessed by the coin list – and it is arguable that the absence of substantial numbers of metal objects reflects a genuine absence and careful husbanding of valuable re-usable resources. The impact of any post-depositional erosion of deposits needs to be considered as well. It is worth noting that it is not simply the ironwork assemblage which is limited. Other metal finds assemblages are also limited.

Amongst the identifiable objects, there is little that would be out of place on any Romano-British site, civil or military. Only the iron billet (catalogue no. 2), smith's wedge (no. 1) and possibly the small dense iron block (no. 3) can be directly connected with one of the main economic functions of the site. What is generally recovered from archaeological contexts on Romano-British sites comprises small broken fragments, which have been lost, and more rarely structural fragments *in situ* and deliberate deposits of material such as grave furniture. Substantial objects and largely complete pieces are generally only found in demolition, rubbish, or ritual deposits, where they

Table 5.20   Ironwork: Summary of identified objects by Phase, Structure, and group/feature.

Phase	Structure	Group	Context	SF No	No	L (mm)	Cat No	Description and Comments
3	Structure I	1790	542	104	1	85	24	Split spike loop.
	Structure Q	80	417	88	1	101	13	Possible hinge strap
	Waterhole	7239	9155	1508	1	115	11	L-shaped lift, or slide, key.
	Waterhole	7239	9155	1507	1	42	26	?L-shaped staple fragment
	-	8530	7950	1397	1	c 93	21	looped pin or spike
3			**Sub-total**		**5**			
4	Waterhole	796	1547	248	1	217;124	15	Bucket handle
	Waterhole	796	1547	253	1	93	16	bucket handle mount
		1260	510	92	1	124	7	Chisel-, or paddle-, shaped object
	-	8160	8189	1447	1	62	5	possible awl,
	-	9210	8857	1461	1	52	22	loop headed spike fragment
4			**Sub-total**		**5**			
5	Waterhole	796	367	73	1	205	19	Large collar of thin rectangular section.
	Waterhole	796	1359	259	1	103	25	T-shaped staple, incomplete.
	-	-	7235	1018	1	150	8	linch pin, with spatulate head
	-	-	7237	1504	1	44	4	carpenter's ?chisel, blade fragment. Firmer chisel
	-	-	8855	1467	1	50	18	chain links or looped junction
5			**Sub-total**		**5**			
6	Waterhole	796	255	28	1	81	20	Hook formed from rectangular strip
	Waterhole	796	723	147	1	60	9	Bell fragment
	Waterhole	796	739	263	1	57	23	L-shaped binding with tear-shaped plate.
6			**Sub-total**		**3**			
8?		8600	7054	925	1	93	17	knife fragment, uncertain form
	-	9000	7082	933	1	142	6	spade shoe, fragment
	-	-	9989	1534	1	135	-	handle with rolled over loop at one end
8?			**Sub-total**		**3**			
Unphased	-	-	7000	1123	1	43	-	rectangular buckle frame, almost complete, with probable sheet metal roller.
	-	-	7003	1126	1	88	-	scissors handle.
	-	-	7003	1124	1	44	-	rectangular buckle frame, almost complete. Probably had a sheet metal roller.
	-	-	7004	1090	1	110	-	horseshoe, complete.
	-	-	7004	1256	1	77	1	smith's wedge.
	-	-	7009	905	1	320	2	Large pointed billet
	-	-	7083	934	1	65	10	L-shaped slide key, small.
	-	-	7626	1320	1	66	14	L-shaped ?hinge staple
	-	-	8014	1403	1	70	3	block of iron
	-	-	8015	1446	1	100	12	Possible hinge strap
Unphased			**Sub-total**		**10**			
			Total		31			

have been placed deliberately. Examples of such deposits are well known: the pit deposits from the Flavian fort at Newstead (Curle 1911), the 3rd century abandonment deposits from Künzing on the Danube (Hermann 1969), deliberate deposition in wells at Baldock, Herts (Stead and Rigby 1986, 147-9) and at Dalton Parlours, North Yorks (Wrathmell and Nicholson 1990, 195-272). Perhaps most famous is the deposit of almost 10 tons of both used and unused nails found together with nine wheel-tyres in a single pit in the *fabrica* at Inchtuthil (Angus *et al.* 1962; Pitts and St Joseph 1985, 109-13, 289 and plates xix and xx).

It can be argued that all these deposits are more than purely demolition deposits. Hingley has recently argued that such deposits were made for ritual as well as practical reasons (Hingley 2006 *passim*). Of course ritual activities and practical or pragmatic behaviour are not mutually exclusive. Indeed it can be argued that Roman religion was supremely pragmatic, and that much of the associated ritual behaviour was intended to ensure the success of both public and personal endeavours through the performance of sacrifices or the making of vows. Everything from success in warfare and diplomacy, to more personal concerns - safe return from voyages, success in business ventures and fertility of crops - were all perceived as being subject to the whim of the gods.

The number of nails recovered from the Westhawk Farm site (Table 5.21), is too small to be significant in terms of distribution or site use, with the possible exception of a few cases which are considered in discussion of the phase assemblages below. Again, consideration should also be given to the possibility that the deposition of such seemingly humble objects as nails might have had ritual significance (see for example the discussion by Dungworth 1998). There are no substantial deposits of nails indicative of demolition deposits, or caches of stored nails. The quantities of nails required for structural work would have been enormous, and more readily quantifiable by

Table 5.21   Ironwork: Quantification (fragment count) of nails and nail fragments by Phase, Structure and group/context comparing finds from Structures and stratigraphic groups or features to finds from contexts not assigned to a stratigraphic group or feature.

Phase	Structure	Group/Feature	No.	
2	-	8620	6	= 6
	-	No group	0	= 0
2		**Sub-total**		**= 6**
2 to 3		40	1	
		8730	1	= 2
2 to 3		No group	0	= 0
2 to 3		**Sub-total**		**= 2**
2 to 4		Groups	0	= 0
		No group	2	= 2
2 to 4		**Sub-total**		**= 2**
2 to 5		5120	1	= 1
		No group	0	= 0
2 to 5		**Sub-total**		**= 1**
3	Structure Q	80	16	
	Structure I	200	1	
	-	5220	8	
	-	8520	1	
	-	8790	1	
	-	9990	1	= 28
	-	No group	12	= 12
3		**Sub-total**		**= 40**
3 to 4	Structure R	1698	1	= 1
		No group	4	= 4
3 to 4		**Sub-total**		**= 5**
3 to 5	Waterhole	7239	1	= 1
		No group	0	= 0
3 to 5		**Sub-total**		**= 1**
3 to 6	Waterhole	796	1	= 1
		No group	0	= 0
3 to 6		**Sub-total**		**= 1**
4	Structure Q	970	1	
	Structure I	7269	4	
	Structure I	7306	1	
	Structure R	1698	1	
	Waterhole	7023	10	
	-	20	1	
	-	30	3	
	-	430	1	
	-	1260	3	
	-	1680	1	
	-	1690	2	
	-	1700	1	
	-	1740	4	
	-	1755	1	
	-	7670	2	
	-	7860	4	
	-	8160	2	
	-	8270	1	
	-	8500	1	
	-	9210	1	
	-	9370	1	
	-	9390	1	
	-	9450	3	
	-	9520	1	
	-	9570	1	
	-	9580	1	
	-	10420	1	= 54
	-	No group	38	
		(Includes ctx 7127 20)		= 38
4		**Sub-total**		**= 92**

Table 5.21   (continued)

Phase	Structure	Group/Feature	No.	
4 to 5	Structure I	7269	2	
	Structure I	7306	2	
	Structure R	1760	1	
		8510	2	
		10170	1	
		10190	2	
		10250	2	= 12
		No group	4	= 4
4 to 5		**Sub-total**		**= 16**
5	Structure R	1200	14	
	Structure R	1220	2	
	Structure R	1230	1	
	Structure R	1233	2	
	Structure R	1437	1	
	waterhole	796	14	
		220	10	
		820	2	
		1675	1	
		5173	1	
		7239	1	
		7500	5	
		8500	1	
		8770	2	
		10415	4	
		10440	1	= 62
		No group	50	
		(Includes ctx 7279 40)		= 50
5		**Sub-total**		**= 112**
6	waterhole	796	18	
		5090	8	= 26
		No group	0	= 0
6		**Sub-total**		**= 26**
Ph ?		7	5	
		526	4	
		8850	1	
		9360	1	
		10260	1	= 12
		No group	21	= 21
Ph ?		**Sub-total**		**= 33**
		Total		**= 337**

weight than number, as witnessed by the Inchtuthil deposit, which probably contained as many as a million nails.

The recovery of hobnails is very much related to identified cremation graves (Table 5.22). A few stray hobnails were recovered from ditch and pit fills and a small number were found in the waterhole 796 (Phase 6), but the majority are from burials (Phase 3, groups 5220 and 9860; Phase 4, group 210; Phase 5, group 220).

The miscellaneous pieces (Table 5.23) and fragments of uncertain identification (Table 5.24) are quite few in number. The unidentified fragments are also tabulated for the sake of completeness (Table 5.25). The distributions of these small groups of material reveal no significant patterns.

Overall spatial distribution

The ironwork assemblage as a whole does show some spatial patterning. If we set aside the identified objects, many of which are from unphased contexts,

Table 5.22   Ironwork: Summary and quantification (fragment count) of hobnails by Phase, Structure and group/context.

Phase	Structure	Group	Context	Sf no	No.	Length	Description
3	-	5220	5133	554	19		hobnails, 19 complete and 3 small pieces
3	-	5220	5133	558	2	21	hobnails, two fused together
3	-	5220	5133	559	3	13	hobnails, complete
3	-	5220	5220		1	12	hobnail, complete
3	-	9860	9843		20		hobnails, mainly heads. From Sample 742
3					45		
4	Structure Q	970	1027		1	18	hobnail complete. From Sample 52
4	-	210	233		27		hobnails including 2 strips of 2, and stem fragments. From Sample 6.
4	-	1740	686		1	16	hobnail. From Sample 41
4	-	1740	686	0	1	22	hobnails, strip of 3, 2 complete. From Sample 41
4	-	9210	8857	1459	1	15	hobnail, or furniture tack, complete
4	-	-	1460		1	19	hobnail, complete. From Sample 97
4					32		
5	Waterhole	796	1359	0	1	22	possible hobnail, complete. From sample 172
5	-	220	231	0	55		hobnails, fused into strips and blocks. Found with c. 7 nail fragments. From Sample 7
5	-	220	231	34	19		Strips of hobnails, heavily mineralised. From cremation group 220.
5	-	10415	8191	1419	1	15	hobnail
5	-	-	1232	0	4		hobnails, include 2 fused together and 1 complete. From Sample 67
5					80		
6	Waterhole	796	379	0	4		hobnails, 3 complete, 1 head, 1 stem and tiny fragment. From Sample 16
6	Waterhole	796	379	0	2		hobnails, 2. From Sample 16
6					6		
All			**Total**		**163**		

the distribution of the ironwork concentrates in four main areas. First, to the north-west of the main road and particularly around structure I and to its immediate south-west; secondly, at the north-east edge of the excavation around and to the north-west of structure R; thirdly in and around the shrine enclosure (structure Q); and finally a small scatter within the enclosures to the south-west of the shrine and its adjacent open space. There are also two dump deposits – contexts 7127 and 7279 – which produced a number of iron fragments. Context 7127 produced 20 nails and three miscellaneous pieces, while context 7279 produced 40 nails, 13 miscellaneous and 1 uncertain piece, a total of 54 fragments. There are no dense concentrations.

The identified objects on the other hand display a much less patterned distribution. They are generally from the south-west part of the site, away from the concentrations of other iron finds and away from settlement features such as buildings and ditches. This probably reflects the fact that the ten unphased objects (Table 5.20) were found in topsoil (contexts 7000 and 7003) or subsoil (context 7004), or outside cut features (finds references 7009, 7083, 8014-15) and probably demonstrates that there has been some post-depositional movement of finds presumably through ploughing.

Evidence for religion and ritual

There are small concentrations of ironwork finds associated with specific structures and features, some associated with the temple and waterholes, others with the metalworking areas structures I and R.

Waterhole 796 produced the most pieces: seven identified objects, including a bucket handle and bucket handle mount, 33 nails, six hobnails, and five miscellaneous pieces and six fragments of uncertain identification - a total of 58 items (Table 5.26). Although in the context of the Westhawk Farm site, this represents a concentration of iron objects, it is not a large concentration, and has no distinctive features in its composition. The bucket fittings could simply represent the utilitarian items one would associate with a waterhole, but they could also have a ritual significance, though the two functions are not mutually exclusive. The other identified objects (Table 5.20) comprise a small cow bell fragment and unremarkable structural fixtures and fittings. The former is a common Romano-British site find. The seven objects form 22.6% of all identified objects (including post-medieval pieces), which is interesting and perhaps significant. Again it must be stressed that the numbers are small.

In contrast, waterhole 7239 produced only two identified objects (an L-shaped lift, or slide key, and an L-shaped staple fragment). It also produced two nails, one miscellaneous fragment and two fragments of uncertain identification, a total of seven pieces. Waterhole 7023 produced 14 objects (10 nails, three bar fragments and unidentifiable fragment) from its upper fills (7024, 7042 and 7043). On the evidence of the ironwork neither of these two features needs to have had any ritual significance.

Table 5.23   Ironwork: Summary and quantification (fragment count) of miscellaneous fragments by Phase, Structure and group/context.

Phase	Structure	Group	Context	SF No	Object Id	No	L (mm)	Description and Comments
2	-	8620	7535		sheet	1		sheet fragment, no original edges. From Sample 632
2					**Sub-total**	**1**		
2 to 3		5171	5030	506	bar	1	59	bar, or nail, fragment, with rounded point at one end. Could be a tool point.
2 to 3					**Sub-total**	**1**		
3	Structure Q	80	166	0	sheet	1	43	sheet, or strip, fragment
	Structure Q	80	166	15	strip	1	59	strip, or plate, with nail hole
	Structure Q	80	417	75	bar	1	70	bar fragment, possibly fragment of awl?
	Structure I	200	150	11	bar	3		bar, or nail, fragments
	-	5220	5133	552	bar	1	35	bar, or nail, fragment, square section
	-	none	1447	0	sheet	3		sheet fragments, very small. From Sample 91
3					**Sub-total**	**10**		
3 +		0	9083		plate	1	35	?plate fragment, with possible rolled-over edge.
		0	10297	1542	bar	1	48	bar fragment, curved, of ?square section
		0	10297	1544	bar	1	46	bar, or nail stem, fragment, slightly curved and tapering. Uncertain section
3 +					**Sub-total**	**3**		
3 to 4		0	9839	1528	bar	1	65	bar, or rod, fragment of ?square section
3 to 4					**Sub-total**	**1**		
4	Structure I	7306	7397	1091	bar	1	27	bar, or nail stem, fragment of square section
	Waterhole	796	1386	0	plate	1	17	plate fragment, irregular, with tiny perforation near one end. From Sample 88
	Waterhole	7023	7024	910	bar	1	26	bar, or nail stem, fragment of square section
		7023	7042	919	bar	1	42	bar, or nail stem, fragment of square section
		7023	7043	924	bar	1	c 77	bar, rod, fragment of circular section
	-	30	369	85	bar	1	28	bar, or nail stem, fragment
	-	666	956	186	bar	1	41	bar, or nail, fragment, of square section.
	-	770	749	154	bar	1	44	bar, or nail, fragment, tapering
	-	1260	578	0	bar	1	53	bar, or nail, fragment of square section
	-	1755	785	0	strip	1	50	Strip with possible rivet? Needs further investigation?
	-	1765	866	184	bar	1	56	bar, or nail, fragment, of square section.
	-	8160	8189	1445	strip	1	80	irregular strip, no nail holes.
	-	8590	7005	901	bar	1	46	bar, or nail, fragment, very heavily corroded.
	-	8680	8132	1411	bar	1	38	bar, or nail stem, fragment of square section
	-	9210	8857	1460	bar	1	51	bar fragment of ?square section
	-	9390	7562	1291	bar	1	38	bar, or nail stem fragment, of uncertain section.
	-	9390	7564	1311	bar	1	32	bar, or nail stem, fragment of square section
	-	9450	7572	1293	strip	1	47	?strip, narrow. No nail holes.
	-	9450	7572	1318	bar	1	34	bar, or nail stem, fragment of uncertain section
	-	9900	7682	1334	strip	1	63	strip, possibly thicker and narrower at one end. No nail holes
	-	none	524	94	bar	1	70	bar fragment
	-	none	524	94	bar	1	32	bar fragment
	-	none	730	0	sheet	1	47	sheet fragment of irregular shape.
	-	none	841	0	rod	1	42	rod or bar fragment. Possibly a nail shank
	-	none	7127	963	bar	1	46	bar, or nail, fragment of circular section
	-	none	7127	977	bar	1	16	bar, or rod, fragment of sub-rectangular section, small
	-	none	7127	990	bar	1	46	bar, or nail, fragment of ?square section.
	-	none	7496	1263	strip	1	41	Strip, no nail holes
	-	none	7499		bar	1	19	bar, or nail stem, fragment, of sub-rectangular section. From Sample 729
4					**Sub-total**	**29**		
4?		8160	8648	1440	strip	1		irregular strip or rod
		0	526	97	plate	1	54	plate fragment, slightly dished
		0	1142		sheet	1	50	sheet fragment with a nail hole and nail and one edge turned up. No original edges.
		0	7205	1002	bar	2	47, 36	bar fragments of well-formed square section
4?					**Sub-total**	**5**		

(Continued on next page)

Table 5.23   (continued)

Phase	Structure	Group	Context	SF No	Object Id	No	L (mm)	Description and Comments
5	Waterhole	796	302	50	strip	1	30; 17	Fragment of strip in two pieces
	Waterhole	796	344	0	bar	1	42	bar, or nail stem, fragment of square section. From Sample 14
	-	7239	7240	1186	bar	1	57	bar fragment of uncertain cross section
	-	7850	7453	1247	bar	1	51	bar fragment of ?square section
	-	10415	8192	1422	strip	1	92	Rectangular strip, or block, of thick rectangular section. No nail holes.
	-	10415	8191	1425	plate	1	63	plate fragments, flat, forming corner with possible nail hole.
	-	none	1448	0	strip	1	38	strip fragment. From Sample 92
	-	none	7237	1017	bar	1	c 48	bar, of square section, strongly curved
	-	none	7237	1501	strip	1	31	strip fragment, slightly curved, with ?corrosion lump
	-	none	7279	1030	bar	1		bar fragment of round/sub-rectangular section, small
	-	none	7279	1033	bar	1	26	bar fragment of square cross-section
	-	none	7279	1047	bar	1	c 47	bar, or nail, fragment, of square section
	-	none	7279	1051	bar	1	102	bar, or nail, fragment of square section. No taper.
	-	none	7279	1052	bar	1	35	bar, or nail, fragment of square section
	-	none	7279	1055	bar	1	31	bar, or nail stem, fragment of square section
	-	none	7279	1060	plate	1	60	strip, possibly with rounded end and nail hole. Possibly bonding or hinge strap?
	-	none	7279	1064	bar	1	c48	bar, or nail stem, fragment with square cross section.
	-	none	7279	1082	bar	1	47	bar or nail stem, fragment of uncertain section
	-	none	7279	1093	bar	1	31	bar, or nail fragment, of circular section. Curved
	-	none	7279	1094	Ring	1	44, 35	?ring fragments x 2. Sub circular section. Both fragments curving.
	-	none	7279	1032	strip	1	120	strip, rectangular with rounded edges. No nail or rivet holes.
	-	none	7279	1226	strip	1	43	strip of irregular outline.
	-	none	8855	1473	bar	1	28	bar, or strip, fragment, small
	-	none	9101		bar	1	40	bar fragment of square section.
5					**Sub-total**	**24**		
6	Waterhole	796	429	0	sheet	1	37	Disc, irregular in outline and slightly dished. From Sample 19
	Waterhole	796	739	200	bar	1	40	bar, or nail, fragment, square section
6					**Sub-total**	**2**		
Ph?		none	7001	1189	strip	1	60	Strip of rectangular section, tapers from 22 mm to 19 mm wide. No nail holes.
		none	7004	1355	strip	1	90	strip of spring steel, thin in section, with three cut-and-raised notches/holes. Modern.
		none	7084	935	bar	1	90	bar, or bolt, fragment, of tapering square section. Laminating badly.
		none	7731		bar	1	32	bar, or nail stem, fragment of square section, no taper.
		none	7761	1368	bar	1	57	bar, or rod, fragment of circular section
		none	7769	1365	bar	1	52	rod, or bar, fragment of ?circular section
		none	7945	1396	bar	1	35	bar, or nail stem, fragment of square section
Ph?					**Sub-total**	**7**		
					Total	**83**		

Structure Q - the polygonal shrine and enclosure - produced a total of 31 pieces of iron (Table 5.27); of these 24 were from the structure and only seven from the enclosure ditch. Interestingly all of the latter were from a fill (context 1027) of the later re-defined (Phase 4) north-east ditch (group 970). The absence of iron objects from the rest of shrine enclosure ditch fills is interesting, since elsewhere on the site, bound-ary ditches have been one of the main sources of iron finds, albeit the numbers of items are small.

This raises questions about how material arrives in ditches: did lost and discarded items simply collect in ditches, was material deliberately dumped during rubbish disposal or demolition, or was it ritually de-posited? Hingley has stressed the role of boundaries and ritual deposition of ironwork in ditches (Hingley

Table 5.24   Ironwork: Summary and quantification (fragment count) of pieces of uncertain identification by Phase, Structure, and group/context.

Phase	Structure	Group	Context	SF No	No	L (mm)	Description and Comments
3	Structure Q	80	166	15	1	23	Possibly broken chain link
	Structure Q	80	461	81	1	167	Spike or pointed slightly curving blade. It was found positioned with the point downwards.
	Structure Q	80	461	83	1	90	Dense block of irregular shape.
	Structure Q	80	632	114	1	50	bar of square section, with wedge-shaped flat flange, bent over at the end. Possible binding
3			**Sub-total**		**4**		
3?	-	-	696	126	1	55	Strip, of uncertain (lenticular?) section, tapering to an apparent point.
3?			**Sub-total**		**1**		
4	Structure I	-	7270	1105	1	46	Object comprising length of bar of square to rectangular section with irregular round flat end. There is no nail hole through the flat end. Incomplete.
	Waterhole	7239	7120	951	1	112; 110	Object formed from thick plate, in poor condition (laminating). Both pieces have turned up edges, suggesting the possibility that they were parts of a vessel or shovel.
	Waterhole	7239	7248	997	1	59	Bar, or rod, of circular section with a slight taper. Possibly a punch or part of a tool. Badly laminated
	-	1755	785	0	1	64	Strip with possible rivet?
	-	8160	8189	1448	1	65	Uncertain object. X-ray shows trace of a possible tang.
	-	8590	7056	926	1	70	Rectangular bar, dense, with central hole.
	-	9210	8857	1463	1	77	Strip, heavy, bent into a curve. One end is square, with a possible nail hole, the other is broken in part. Possibly part of a collar
	-	10050	8903	1484	1	152	Object formed from strip with flared end. Could be a handle. Badly preserved.
	-	10050	8903	1483	1	60	Curved fragment, could a part of a ring.
	-	-	7379		1	28	Tube formed from rolled sheet. Small, with open seam. Function uncertain
4			**Sub-total**		**10**		
4?		-	526	109	1	367	Bar, of square section that appears to taper at both ends to a blunt point. Purpose?
		none	526	102	1	65	Possibly fan-tailed object.
4?			**Sub-total**		**2**		
5	Structure R	1200	1176	205	1	81	Possible nail, incomplete, heavily encrusted
	-	-	1448	0	2	34	Objects, unidentified. From Sample 92
	-	-	7237	1020	1	77	Bar or strip of rectangular cross-section, slightly tapering.
	-	-	7279	1053	1	37	Object, fragment of uncertain function. Possibly part of a buckle
	-	-	8855	1465	1	85; 50	Handle or tang (2 pieces).
	-	-	8855	1471	1	36	Plate fragment, triangular in outline and slightly curved with a smooth convex face.
5			**Sub-total**		**7**		
5?	-	-	9088	1500	1	102	Nail, ?complete, of uncertain section with ?flat head. Poorly preserved
5?			**Sub-total**		**1**		
6	Waterhole	796	739	0	1	30	Bar fragment or broken end, of sub-triangular section
6			**Sub-total**		**1**		
8?	-	-	10077	1539	1	113	Strip, tapering and curved. ?handle.
8?			**Sub-total**		**1**		
Ph?	-	-	7003	1125	1	108	Pointed object formed from strip. The square end, which may be broken, has a deep slot. Function uncertain.
		none	7004	1325	1	76	Strip of irregular outline, with slightly curved cross section; one end is slightly bent up. Evidence for a band across the object on x-ray. Dense, could be cast iron. Fragment of bomb or shell case?
		none	7630	1324	1	84	Tapering point or spike, of square section and strongly curved. The wider end is broken. Uncertain function, possibly part of a tool.
Ph?			**Sub-total**		**3**		
			Total		**30**		

Table 5.25   Ironwork: Summary and quantification (fragment count) of unidentifiable fragments by Phase, Structure and group.

Phase	Structure	Group	Context	SF No	No	Description and Comments
2	-	8620	7535		1	amorphous lump. From sample 632
	-	-	1263	0	4	four tiny fragments from sieving. From Sample 72
	-	-	1264	0	6	amorphous fragments including pieces of mineralised iron. From Sample 74
2			**Sub-total**		**11**	
2 to 4	-	none	10166	1538	1	amorphous lump, small
2 to 4			**Sub-total**		**1**	
3					0	
3			**Sub-total**		**0**	
3 to 4	-	1720	161	0	1	amorphous lumps
3 to 4			**Sub-total**		**1**	
4	Structure Q	970	1027		5	amorphous lumps. From Sample 52
	Waterhole	7023	7042	920	1	amorphous lump
	-	770	749	153	1	amorphous lump
	-	1260	576	96	1	Unidentifiable fragment
	-	8160	8548	1442	1	irregular fragment
	-	-	7127	972	1	small amorphous lump
4			**Sub-total**		**10**	
5	Structure R	1200	1258	0	4	amorphous lumps. From Sample 71
	Structure R	1233	1232	0	1	amorphous lump. From Sample 67
	-	-	8855	1472	1	amorphous lump
	-	-	8855	1474	1	amorphous lump, small
	-	-	8855	1477	1	amorphous lump
	-	-	8855	1476	1	amorphous lump, small
5			**Sub-total**		**9**	
			Total		32	

2006). If we accept Hingley's contention that deposition in ditches and boundaries can have some meaning beyond the merely pragmatic and practical, then the absence of material from the shrine enclosure might take on added significance. Does it support Hingley's proposal, and suggest that the ditch was ritually cleansed before it was abandoned? Or does it suggest that in this particular ditch associated with a ritual setting ironwork was not deposited?

The material from the shrine structure (group 80) consists of 24 objects, including 16 nails and 8 miscellaneous or uncertain fragments. Most are derived from fills of the central pit 415 (Table 5.27) and include nails and a small dense block. The latter could have been an offering of a sample of the iron produced on the site. The evidence for ritual deposition is limited, although there is a small concentration of finds associated with the shrine; the finds themselves are mundane and apparently of little value.

Table 5.26   Ironwork: Waterhole 796: Summary quantification (fragment count) of iron finds by Phase and functional category.

Phase	Objects	Nails	Hobnails	Misc.	Uncertain	Totals
4	2	0	0	1	0	= 3
5	2	14	1	2	0	= 19
6	3	18	6	2	6	= 35
3-6	0	1	0	0	0	= 1
Total	7	33	7	5	6	= 58

Evidence for ironworking

The ironwork assemblage provides little evidence of the ironworking attested by structural evidence and the presence of substantial quantities of iron slag (see Chapter 7). The distribution of ironwork broadly coincides with known ironworking areas – structures I and R – but there are few if any specific associations and none of the finds is diagnostic.

The finds from Structure I and its associated features in Plot NW3 total 28 objects (Table 5.28), of which 18 are nails and a further 5 are nail stem or bar fragments. The only identified object is a split spike loop (no. 24) from the fill of posthole 540, which is one of the large rectangular postholes linked with gully 1790. The latter is parallel to the south-west boundary of Plot NW3. A nail or nail fragment and three bar, or nail stem, fragments were found in the fill (150) of the north boundary ditch 200 on the north side of Structure I.

Other finds came from pits and a well. A single hobnail came from pit 1461 and a nail or bar fragment from pit 7944, which were respectively east and west of structure I. More finds came from pit 7306 and well 7269, which were both east of Structure I and just south of the original plot boundary 8540. The well produced 15 pieces of iron. It is thought that the boundary of Plot NW3 was moved south. Fenceline 1698 ran parallel to and to the south of boundary 8540. Two postholes (370 and 383) in the fence line each produced a single nail.

There are 31 iron objects, including 24 nails, from structure R (Table 5.29). Most of the iron finds come

Table 5.27   Ironwork: Structure Q: Summary of iron finds from features and contexts belonging to the temple and its enclosure.

Group	Feature	Description	Context	Finds	No.	Total
80		Octagonal structure				
	192	Posthole	166	Sheet fragment	1	
				Strip fragment	1	
				Nails	6	
				Possible chain link	1	9
	115	Posthole	198	Nail	1	1
	415	Central pit	417	Nails	6	
			416	Nail	1	
				Bar fragment	1	
				Possible hinge strap	1	
			461	Nails	2	
				Spike or blade	1	
				Dense block	1	
				Possible binding	1	14
970		Ditch re-defining NE side of Temple enclosure				
	1026		1027	Nail	1	
				Hobnail	1	
				Amorphous fragments	5	7
				Total		**31**

from boundary ditches 1200, 1220/1760 and 1230. The largest number (19) come from fills of the north-west boundary ditch 1200 (Table 5.29). Pit 1233, which cut into ditch 1200, produced two nails, four hobnails, and an unidentified amorphous fragment. Ditch 1230 produced one nail. Ditches 12201760 produced three nails. Hearth 1438 within Structure R, produced a single nail.

Although the distribution of ironwork seems to favour structures I and R slightly, the surviving material gives no real clue as to the processes performed there. The iron finds comprise predominantly nails and fragments of utilitarian items. The absence from the ironwork assemblage of any tools or other items associated with the working of iron blooms or smithing is scarcely to be wondered at. The smith's tools - anvils, tongs, hammers and other the like – would not easily have been mislaid and were essential to his livelihood, as well as being valuable. Large objects such as these would not normally be expected in the archaeological record unless deliberately buried or otherwise deposited. The best evidence for ironworking, and in particular the smithing of blooms, is provided by the iron billet (no. 2), which unfortunately was not found directly associated with any ironworking area. The object has been the subject of analysis (see Chapter 7,

Table 5.28   Ironwork: Structure I: Summary of iron finds from features and contexts belonging to the iron producing workshop.

Group	Feature	Description	Context	Finds	No	Total
200	149	N boundary	150	Bar/nail fragments	3	
				Nail	1	4
1790		Gully and postholes				
	540	Posthole	542	Split spike loop	1	1
-	1461	Pit	1460	Hobnail	1	1
-	7944	Large pit	7945	Bar/nail fragment	1	1
1698		Fence line				
	370	Posthole	371	Nail	1	
	383	Posthole	383	Nail	1	2
-	7306	Large pit	7397	Bar/nail fragment	1	
				Nail	1	
			7307	Nails	2	4
-	7269	Well	7270	Nail	1	
				Bar with flattened end	1	
			7309	Nails	2	
			7327	Nail	1	
			7484	Nails	2	
			7535	Nails	6	
				Sheet fragment	1	
				Amorphous fragment	1	15
				Total		**28**

Table 5.29   Ironwork: Structure R: Summary of iron finds from features and contexts belonging to the iron producing workshop.

Group	Feature	Description	Context	Finds	No	Total
1200	1177	NW gully	1176	Nail	1	
				Possible nail	1	
	1221		1219	Nails	3	
			1222	Nails	4	
	1342		1258	Nails	6	
				Amorphous fragments	4	19
-	1233	Pit cutting 1200	1231	Nail	1	
			1232	Nail	1	
				Hobnail	4	
				Amorphous fragment	1	7
1230	1368	SW gully	1366	Nail	1	1
1220	1218	SE gully	1216	Nails	2	2
-	1438	Hearth	1437	Nail	1	1
1760	1445	NW/SE ditch	1334	Nail	1	1
					Total	**31**

below). The form of the billet is interesting: it is 0.32 m long, tapered at both ends and weighs *c* 4.46 kg.

The billet is a semi-finished product of the bloomery process. The bloom produced in the furnace was converted to usable iron by heating and smithing. It was time consuming process, but the result was a billet or bar of iron suitable for trading and transporting.

Only a comparatively small number of iron billets have been found in archaeological contexts. There are billets from Newstead (Curle 1911, 288, plate lxv, no. 9; see also Manning 1976, plate 1). These are roughly worked rectilinear blocks. A similar but smaller worked bloom comes from the Roman bloomery site at Little Farningham Farm (Cleere and Crossley 1985, fig. 16). This rough rectilinear block is only *c* 200 mm long and weighs about 2 kg. It is therefore much smaller than the Westhawk billet. Another form of worked bloom, or billet, is the trapezoid billet with a hook at the top as typified by an example from the Roman small town of Asthall, Oxfordshire (Salter 1997, 95-6, citing other examples, and fig. 4.4, no. 1; plate 4.1). The latter is an insular Iron Age form (Crew 1994, 348 and figs 1 and 2).

The Ashford billet is more akin to the northern European Iron Age tradition of trade iron in the form of pointed bars than to the British tradition of sword-shaped billets or trapezoid billets. Individual currency bars and other trade iron from the British Iron Age range in weight from as little as 145 to 165 g up to 1200 to 1640 g (ibid., fig. 3).

Comparison can be made with a number of examples of double-pointed iron base recovered from Iron Age sites in the Rhineland-Palatinate, Germany (Engels 1974). The examples published by Engels range in length from 310 mm to 563 mm, although most are between 366 mm and 455 mm. Their cross-sections vary from 71 mm by 60 mm to 54 mm by 43 mm and 55 mm by 36 mm. In weight they range from 1960 g to 5845 g, although most are between 3150 g and 5040 g. They are therefore significantly larger than anything produced during the insular Iron Age in

Britain. The only items of trade iron found in Britain that compare are the '*spitzbaren*', or double-pointed ingots of continental origin from the Isle of Portland; these weigh in excess of 6 kg each (Crew 1994, 348).

Although it would inappropriate to draw direct comparisons between La Tène double pointed bars, typified by those from the Rhineland-Palatinate, and the Westhawk Farm billet, a number of points can be made. Firstly, currency bars and other trade iron from the insular Iron Age were light in weight by comparison with continental material. This reflects the limited production of iron and its consequent value which determined its use during the British Iron Age. Secondly, no trade iron comparable in form or size to the Westhawk billet seems to have been produced during the Iron Age in Britain. These two pointers indicate that the billet from Westhawk is a Romano-British product, and furthermore one influenced by north European Iron Age practice.

Phased assemblages

A proportion of the ironwork (97 fragments or 14.5% by count) is either from unphased contexts – often isolated features – or from contexts which cannot be closely phased. This material is not discussed in considering the phase assemblages, but will be briefly discussed at the end of this section.

Phase 2 (AD 43-70)

The quantity of material from this phase is very limited and comprises only 18 pieces made up of nails (6) and unidentifiable scraps (11) and one miscellaneous piece, a fragment of sheet (see Tables 5.18 and 5.19). The nails, one of the unidentified fragments and the miscellaneous fragment are all from the primary phase of the roadside ditch (group 8620) on the south-east side of the road (see Tables 5.21, 5.23 and 5.24). The other unidentified fragments are from cremation deposits (1263 and 1264).

Phase 3 (AD 70-150)

The ironwork from this phase comprises a total of 104 pieces, most of which are nails (45) and hobnails and strips of hobnails (40). There are 14 miscellaneous objects and pieces of the ironwork of uncertain identification. There are five identifiable objects (see Tables 5.18 and 5.19).

The identified objects comprise an L-shaped lift, or slide, key (no. 11) and a possible L-shaped staple fragment (no. 26) from waterhole 7239, a looped pin or spike (no. 21) from a NW-SE boundary gully (group 8530) and a split-spike loop (no. 24) from a gully or beam slot (group 1790) of structure I. A possible hinge strap fragment came from the central pit within the polygonal temple, structure Q (no. 13). These are all structural or domestic objects.

The majority of nails come from the probable shrine enclosure, structure Q (16 nails) and from a box cremation grave in Area C (group 5220: 8 nails; see Table 5.21). The latter group also produced 25 hobnails/hobnail strips. The other 20 hobnails/hobnail strips came from another cremation group, 9860 (see Table 5.22). The remaining nails came from gullies (groups 8790 and 9990), a boundary ditch (group 200) of structure I, and from a grave cut (8002, group 8520).

Three of the miscellaneous pieces (Table 5.23) and all four objects of uncertain function (Table 5.24) are from the shrine structure (structure Q). Three miscellaneous fragments of bar were from a boundary ditch (group 200) of structure I. Another miscellaneous fragment came from cremation group 5220. Finally three small fragments of sheet came from pit 1447, which was filled in large part with roasted iron ore.

Phase 4 (AD 150-200)

There are 178 pieces of iron from Phase 4 (see Tables 5.18 and 5.19). Only Phase 5 produced more pieces. The bulk of the Phase 4 assemblage comprises nails (92 = 51.7% by count), hobnails (32 = 18.1%) and miscellaneous fragments (29 = 16.3%). There are 10 pieces of uncertain identification and 10 unidentifiable fragments. Finally, there are five identified objects.

These comprise a large fragment of a bucket handle and bucket handle mount (nos 15 and 16), both from the large waterhole 796, an awl (no. 5), which came from a grave (group 8160), a chisel-shaped object (no. 7) from a pit (group 1260) - which is cut by ditch 970 forming the re-defined north-east side of the shrine enclosure - and a looped pin (no. 21) from a plot boundary (group 9210).

The nails were found in a number of groups (see Table 5.21), but there do not seem to be any concentrations; the nails are found in small numbers only. Most nails are from contexts not assigned to groups – isolated pits and the like. The largest number (20) comes from a dumped deposit (context 7127), which was located in a shallow, possibly natural hollow and which also contained a concentration of pottery. A number of nails, together with some miscellaneous bar fragments, came from the upper fills of waterhole 7023: context 7043 produced a single nail and a bar fragment; 7042 three nails, a bar fragment and an amorphous fragment; context 7024 six nails and a bar fragment. Most of the hobnails (27 of 32) came from a cremation grave, group 210 (see Table 5.22). The remainder came from ditches or a pit.

The distributions of miscellaneous fragments (Table 5.23) and the pieces of uncertain identification (Table 5.24) do not reveal any concentrations. Most of the pieces from groups were from the fills of boundary ditches, plot divisions and roadside ditches. The exceptions were the single fragments from a grave (group 8160), from a pit (group 1260), from the large waterhole 796 and from a pit 7306, associated with structure I. The fragments from ungrouped contexts came mainly from the fills of single pits or postholes, although some pieces were from the upper fills of waterhole 7023, as noted above. Three fragments came from the dump deposit 7127, which also contained a number of nails, as noted above.

Phase 5 (AD 200-250)

This phase produced 237 objects, which is the most from any phase (see Tables 5.18 and 5.19). Again much of the material comprises nails (112 = 47.3%) and hobnails (80 = 33.8%). There are 24 miscellaneous objects and seven of uncertain identification, together with nine small unidentifiable fragments. There are a mere five identified objects.

The five identified objects comprise a possible carpenter's chisel (no. 4), a linchpin (no. 8), a chain link (no. 18), a large collar with thickened or reinforced edges (no. 19), and a T-staple (no. 25). The ring and T-staple were both recovered from the waterhole 796, and the chain link came from pit 8855, which also produced other iron fragments. The possible chisel was provided with a finds reference number only (7237), while the linchpin was from a shallow pit (7235).

There are some concentrations of nails (see Table 5.21). Single nails were recovered from ditches, gullies and isolated pits. There were 10 nails from a cremation grave (group 220), which also produced most of the hobnails from this phase, and at least 14 nails from the waterhole (796). Four nails came from a line of four postholes forming a fenceline (group 10415). Seventeen nails were recovered from enclosure ditches (1200, 1220 and 1230) bounding structure R, which is associated with metalworking (see above). The main concentration of nails came from a spread of material (context 7279), which also produced a concentration of pottery and small finds. Forty nails were from this deposit.

The majority of the hobnails (74 of 80) from this phase were recovered from a cremation, group 220 (see Table 5.22). One hobnail came from waterhole 796 and another from fenceline 10415. The four remaining hobnails came from the single fill (1232) of pit 1233 associated with structure R.

The miscellaneous finds of bar, strip, etc. and the pieces of uncertain identification formed a small part of the assemblage (see Tables 5.23 and 5.24). The only concentration was in dump deposit 7279, which produced 13 of the miscellaneous pieces and one of the uncertain fragments. One fragment was found in ditch 1200, which formed part of the enclosure around structure R, and two fragments came from fenceline 10415. Other fragments came from pit fills or given a finds reference only. Of the unidentified small fragments (Table 5.25), which totalled only nine from this phase, four were from ditch 1200 bounding the north-west side of structure R, and four from pit 8855.

Phase 6 (AD 250-350)

The ironwork from Phase 6 comprises only 38 fragments, 26 of which are nails. There are six hobnails and two miscellaneous pieces and one fragment of uncertain identification (see Tables 5.18 and 5.19).

Three identified objects – a bell fragment (no. 9), a hook (no. 20) and a binding (no. 23) - were all recovered from the waterhole 796. Eighteen of the nails (see Table 5.21) also come from the waterhole (796) and the other eight from a cremation grave (group 5090). The six hobnails are likewise from waterhole 796, which also produced the miscellaneous material and fragment of uncertain identification (see Tables 5.23 and 5.24).

Unphased material and material of uncertain phase

The material that falls into this category (see Tables 5.18 and 5.19) is of limited value for understanding the site, but does include a disproportionate number of identifiable objects (see Table 5.20). Thirteen objects were either of uncertain phase or unphased. These include four objects, which are certainly, or probably, post-Roman in date; the scissors and horseshoe are certainly post-Roman, and the two rectangular buckle frames are probably post-Roman in date (all uncatalogued). There are a number of objects, which are not typologically diagnostic: the smith's wedge (no. 1), spade shoe (no. 6), L-shaped hinge staple (no. 14), handle fragment (uncatalogued), possible hinge strap (no. 12) and broken knife (no. 17) could be Roman, but equally could be later in date and the spade shoe came from the top of a post-medieval ditch fill. The L-shaped key (no. 10) is probably Roman in date. The billet of iron (no. 2) and small dense block of iron (no. 3) are probably Roman in date and products of the main economic activity of the site.

Distribution of different types of material across the phases

Given the small size of the assemblage, few conclusions about the changing the composition of the assemblage through time can be drawn, and any conclusions are likely to be tentative and broadly drawn and therefore of limited interest. The limited number of identified objects (see Table 5.20) from the assemblage as a whole has been stressed, and little can be added with regard to the various phase assemblages. The miscellaneous material derives mainly from Phases 4 and 5, but the numbers are so small as to be of little statistical relevance (see Table 5. 23). The situation is similar with regard to the fragments of uncertain function (see Table 5.24), although they occur in Phase 3 as well as Phases 4 and 5. There are more nails (see Table 5.21), but this still a small sample of the large number that must have been needed on site. There is little that can be said regarding changes in distribution through the site phases. Overall there is a preponderance of nails in Phases 3, 4 and 5. The distribution of hobnails (see Table 5.22) is tied to the occurrence and excavation of cremations and therefore does not provide independent evidence for the use of ironwork.

Catalogue of identified and illustrated objects

Tools (Fig. 5.10: 1-2, 4-6)

1. **Smith's wedge**. Top is square and battered and lipped by hammering. The cutting edge appears slightly rounded. L: 77 mm. Context 7004, SF1256, unphased.
2. Large pointed billet. Weight 4.5 kg. L: 320 mm. Context 7009, SF905, unphased.
3. (*not illustrated*) **Block of iron**, may be production debris. L: 70 mm. Context 8014, SF1403, unphased.
4. **Carpenter's ?chisel**, blade fragment. Shank of rectangular section with flaring blade. Firmer chisel. L: 44 mm. Context 7237, SF1504, Phase 5.
5. Possible **awl**, tapering to a point at each end, square section in centre. L: 62 mm. Context 8189 (Group 8160), SF1447, Phase 4.
6. **Spade shoe**, fragment comprising corner of blade and part of one side arm. Probably straight mouthed or only slightly curved. There is slight evidence for a slot on the inside edge of the blade. The arm has a rectangular section., L: 142 mm. Context 7082 (Group 9000), SF933, Period 4.
7. (*not illustrated*) **Chisel-, or paddle-, shaped object**, chamfered on three sides. There is a stout tang or arm on the fourth side. Could be a chisel, but the identification is far from certain. Dense. L: 124 mm. Context 510 (Group 1260), SF92, Phase 4.

Transport (Fig. 5.11: 8-9)

8. **Linchpin**, with irregular spatulate head and rolled-over loop. L: 150 mm. Context 7235, SF1018, Phase 5.
9. **Bell**, part of the upper portion of an iron 'cow bell'. L: 60 mm. Context 723 (Group 796), SF147, Phase 6.

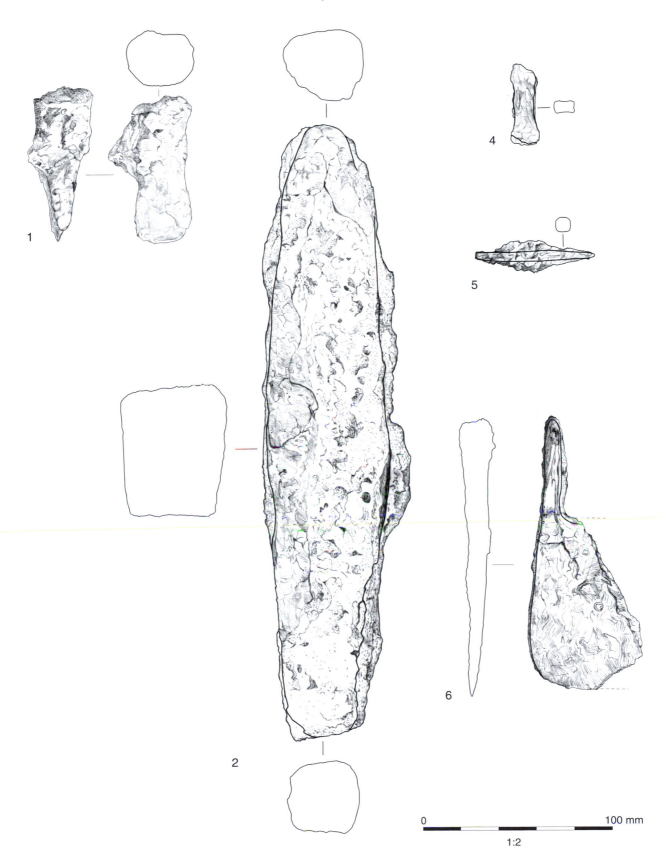

Figure 5.10   Iron objects (nos 1-2, 4-6).

Locks and keys (Fig. 5.11: 10-12, 14)

10 **L-shaped slide key**, small. No obvious teeth on the bit. The handle is pierced for suspension. L: 65 mm. Context 7083, SF934, unphased.

11 **L-shaped lift or slide key**, with rectangular handle but ?no extant bit. L: 115 mm. Context 9155 (Group 7239), SF1508, Phase 3.

12 Possible **hinge strap**, comprising tapering strip with rounded end 1 extant part nail hole. L: 100 mm. Context 8015, SF1446, unphased.

13 (*not illustrated*) Possible **hinge strap**. Comprises a strip with two nail holes. It is pinched in at each end. One end is broken but slightly curved as if rolled over to form a loop. L: 101 mm. Context 417 (Group 80), SF88, Phase 7.

14 Possible **L-shaped hinge staple**. The long arm is of flat rectangular section with a rounded end, the short arm is of ?circular section. L: 66 mm. Context 7626, SF1320, unphased.

Household objects (Fig. 5.11: 15; Fig. 5.12: 16)

15 **Bucket handle**, with one hooked end. Rectangular sectioned, with U-sectioned handgrip. L: 270 mm; Context 1547 (Group 796), SF248, Phase 4.

16 **Bucket handle mount** comprising strip with two nail holes with d-shaped loop at one end. L: 93 mm. Context 1547 (Group 796), SF253, Phase 4.

17 (*not illustrated*) **Knife fragment**, with slim rod handle, or possible whittle tang. Too little of blade is extant to identify the form, but it has a triangular section. L: 93 mm. Context 7054 (Group 8600), SF925, medieval or post-medieval.

Fixtures and fittings (Fig. 5.12: 18, 20-25)

18 **Chain links or looped junction**. L: 50 mm. Context 8855, SF1467, Phase 5.

19 (*not illustrated*) **Collar or ring** of thin rectangular section, thickened at the edges. It is too light to be a nave band or hub lining from a wheel, and its precise use is unclear. Possibly a binding or hoop fixed around a wooden post or pole. L: 205 mm. Context 367 (Group 796), SF73, Phase 6.

20 **Hook** 47 mm across, formed from rectangular strip. L: 81 mm. Context 255 (Group 796), SF28, Phase 6.

21 **Looped pin or spike** with stout circular section stem pointed at one end and rolled over into a loop at the other. L: *c* 93 mm. Context 7950 (Group 8530), SF1397, Phase 3.

22 **Loop-headed spike** fragment formed from rod of ?circular section with rolled over loop. L: 52 mm. Context 8857 (Group 9210), SF1461, Phase 4.

23 **L-shaped binding** with tear-shaped plate, ?pierced for a nail, at the end of one arm. The other arm, of rectangular section, appears broken. L: 57 mm. Context 739 (Group 796), SF263, Phase 6.

24 **Split spike loop**, highly encrusted. L: 85 mm. 5 Context 42 (Group 1790), SF104, Phase 3.

25 **T-shaped staple**, incomplete. L: 103 mm. Context 1359 (Group 796), SF259, Phase 5.

26 (*not illustrated*) Possible **L-shaped staple** fragment. L: 42 mm. Context 9155 (Group 7239), SF1507, Phase 3.

WORKED STONE
by Fiona Roe

Introduction

The worked stone assemblage consists almost entirely of quern or millstone fragments, which came from 44 contexts. The other stone objects amount to a single whetstone, a slab used as a whetstone or polisher and 33 slingstones. The quern and millstone fragments were nearly all brought to the site from outside Kent. Niedermendig lava from the Rhineland was imported in some quantity, while Millstone Grit from the Pennines was also much utilised (Table 5.30). Greensand, which was available nearer to the site, was used less frequently, although three rotary querns of Lodsworth greensand were acquired from Sussex. The local greensand from Folkestone only accounts for two rotary querns. Local Wealden sandstone was used for the whetstone and whetstone/polisher, while the slingstones are all flint pebbles from the coast.

Querns and Millstones

Niedermendig lava

Niedermendig lava seems to have been extensively used at Westhawk Farm, and this may well have been the easiest grinding material to transport, since it could have been brought nearly all the way from the Rhineland by boat. If it was delivered to *Portus Lemanis* (Lympne), which in Roman times was closer to the sea than it is now (Cunliffe 1980, 258), there would have been a direct, onward road journey of only 14 km. Much of the lava found at Westhawk Farm is very fragmentary. A large number of small pieces were found (Table 5.30), and it is difficult to estimate how many querns or millstones might be represented. Lava was recorded from 33 contexts, but in many cases mere crumbs weighing only a few grams were recovered, and the total recorded weight of some 24 kg is probably unrepresentative. Four rotary querns could be distinguished (eg SF244 and SF249, Fig 5.13: 15 and 16 respectively), together with one millstone (context 9422), which although very weathered, could be identified by its diameter of about 750 mm. The diameters of two of the querns were about 430 mm. These two querns have a typical Roman feature, a raised rim around the edge of the upper stone, providing a wide hopper into which the grain could be poured. They are both well made upper stones, with other Roman characteristics, such as

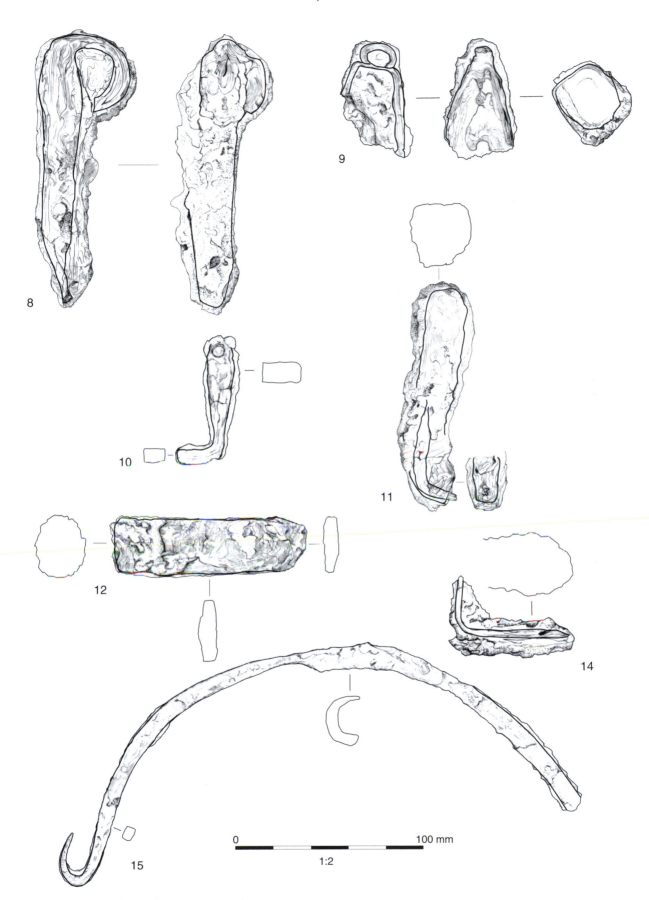

Figure 5.11   Iron objects (nos 8-12, 14-15).

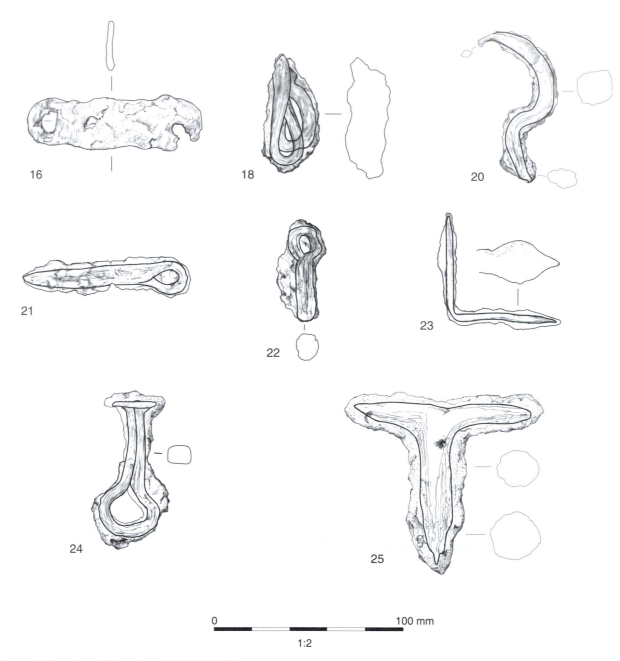

Figure 5.12   Iron objects (nos 16, 18, 20-25).

vertical striae around the rim, and, in one case, radial grooving on the grinding surface (SF249). Both also have decorative grooving on the upper surface, as illustrated.

Table 5.30   Worked stone: Quantification (weight and fragment count) of quern and mill stone by stone type.

Stone	Total weight	No of fragments
Niedermendig lava	24.219 kg	507+
Millstone Grit	12.910 kg	14
Lodsworth greensand	2.515 kg	3
Folkestone greensand	6.075 kg	51+

Lava does not always survive well, but these two better preserved quern fragments (SF244 and SF249) came from waterhole 796, while the lava millstone came from waterhole 9179 (context 9422). By contrast, a lava quern in a particularly friable state was retrieved from the upper silt (context 1433) of a ditch, where it would have had a less certain chance of survival in the acidic, silty clay of the site. Some 39% of the lava, according to the number of contexts, was found in various wells or waterholes. Another 3% came from ditches, with few pieces from pits or gullies, but the record from these other contexts could well be misleading, since they might have been expected to produce a higher proportion of the lava.

190

The finds are spread across all phases (Table 5.31), although there is only one from Phase 2 (AD 43–70). The majority are from Phases 4 and 5 (AD 150-250). All the Phase 6 pieces were from the upper fills of well/waterhole 796.

Millstone Grit

Millstone Grit may also have been transported to Kent by sea, using an east coast route from the Humber, since a cumbersome cart journey of some 300 km overland from the Pennines would have been impractical. The finds of Millstone Grit are somewhat different in character from the lava, consisting of a small number of large fragments. There are pieces from seven contexts, and while no certain rotary querns were identified, there are fragments from at least three millstones. There is a stream, the Whitewater Dyke a tributary of the Great Stour, adjacent to the site and although it cannot be certain what conditions were like in Roman times, it seems probable that this stream provided water power for the millstones. These were less carefully crafted than the lava querns, with crude pitting on the top surfaces of the upper stones (SF1449, 1521, 1523 and 1525), or, in one case, coarse grooving (SF1520).

Two small fragments of Millstone Grit were found in waterhole 796, which otherwise contained numerous fragments of lava, along with other finds. A probable millstone came from waterhole 8479 (context 8480, SF1491). However, the majority of pieces had been re-used as packing in large post holes. On a site based on clay, and in an era when little was wasted, the Millstone Grit would have been ideal for this purpose, unlike the Niedermendig lava, which was probably too friable. The finds of Millstone Grit come mainly from Phase 4 contexts (AD 150-200), with only the fragments from waterhole 796 belonging within Phase 6 (AD 250–350).

Lower Greensand, Lodsworth stone

The three finds of querns made from Lodsworth stone were somewhat unexpected, since this material has not previously been recorded in Kent, and a local source of greensand was available not far away at Folkestone. The Lodsworth stone was brought from a quarrying area in Sussex some 100 km or more to the west of Ashford (Peacock 1987). There was no known direct route by road, so deliveries by boat are once again a possibility, this time along a southern coastal route. The three pieces are all fragmentary, but one has a grooved surface (context 1068, SF195). Two of the finds are from Phase 4 contexts (AD 150–200), one (context 1068) from a pit, the other (context 7114) from a roadside ditch, while a third fragment (context 9951) came from a ?Phase 5 post-pipe.

Lower Greensand, Copt Point, Folkestone

The local greensand was used for just two rotary querns, although it was available from a known quarrying area at Copt Point, East Wear Bay, Folkestone, only 24 km south-east of Westhawk Farm (Keller 1989). Both pieces are from Phase 4 contexts (AD 150–200). One is a re-used quern fragment from a pit (context 510), the other (SF 1164, Fig 5.13: 48) a nearly complete but unevenly-shaped upper stone (finds reference 7379). The poor workmanship of this quern is in marked contrast to the skill clearly used on the lava querns. The grinding surface has been crudely pitted, as illustrated, with an area of rough grooving near the rim, and further patches that have been worn smooth. This quern was probably made from a beach boulder, and may have seen considerable wear, since it is now fairly flat and only some 39 mm in thickness, whereas the greensand boulders at Copt Point tend to be well rounded.

Other Stone Objects

Cretaceous sandstone from the Wealden Beds (Gallois 1965, 22) was not suitable for rotary querns, but was used for a whetstone from a Phase 5 feature. This is not the usual rod or slab shape, but has been worn to a triangular cross-section (Fig 5.13: 49). A slab of the same sandstone was found in a Phase 4 ditch (context 9031), and has a flat, worn surface, suggesting use as a whetstone or a smoother. The 33 slingstones are all rounded, slightly oval, flint pebbles, for which there are two possible sources. They could have come from the Clay-with-Flints capping the North Downs some 8 km north of the site (Smart *et al.* 1966, 201). More probably they were collected

Table 5.31   Worked stone: Occurrence of stone types (number of contexts) by phase.

Stone	2	3	3/4	4	4/5	5	6	0	Total
Niedermendig Lava	1	5	1	11	2	5	6	2	33
Millstone Grit				5			1	1	7
Lodsworth stone				2	1			1	3
Copt Point, Folkestone				2					2
Wealden sandstone				1		1			2
Slingstones								33	33
Total	1	5	1	21	2	7	7	36	80

from a shingle beach similar to present day Dungeness Beach (Lake and Shephard-Thorne 1987). Parts of the local coast were nearer to Westhawk Farm in Roman times than they are today, and beach pebbles could have come from near Lympne, at distances of between 7.5–14.5 km south-east of Westhawk Farm (Cunliffe 1980, 258). These slingstones came from an undated area of trample, and so it is uncertain whether they are one of the few traces of Iron Age activity at the site, or represent the continuation of older traditions during the Roman period. Similar flint slingstones were found at Oldbury hillfort (Ward-Perkins 1944, 166).

Discussion

The three main quern or millstone materials found at Westhawk Farm - lava, Millstone Grit and greensand, are typical of Roman sites in Kent (Roe nd). Of 32 Roman sites in Kent with known quern and millstone finds, some 22 are presently recorded with finds of Niedermendig lava, while Millstone Grit has occurred at 16 sites; greensand was also widely used, coming from 18 sites (Roe, report in archive). Some of the greensand querns may prove, on closer inspection, to be made of Lodsworth stone, which has not previously been noted in Kent. Other greensand querns are undoubtedly made of stone from Folkestone, which is now becoming known from a number of sites (Keller 1988, 64), including Springhead. Formerly these grinding materials have been recorded mainly from villas (Black 1987, 218, fig 21), or towns such as Canterbury (Blockley *et al.* 1995) and Springhead (Roe nd), which all cluster in the northern part of the county. What is now becoming clear is that the imported stone, particularly lava and Millstone Grit, were not restricted to these types of higher status site, but were widely distributed to all varieties of settlement, including the iron-working community at Westhawk Farm.

The importation of Niedermendig lava from the Rhineland was not necessarily a Roman innovation, although at present only one reasonably certain, earlier, find from Kent is known. A segment of lava rotary quern was incorporated into a rampart at Oldbury hillfort, thought by the excavator to have been reconstructed around AD 43 in response to the Roman invasion (Ward-Perkins 1944, 166), although it is more likely that activity here only extended into the early 1st century AD (cf Cunliffe 1991, 368; Hamilton and Manley 2001, 19). It is already known that Lodsworth stone was transported quite widely around southern England in pre-Roman times, occurring, for instance, near Portsmouth in a late Bronze Age context (Hall and Ford 1994, 29). It is not, as yet, known from a prehistoric site in Kent, and only from Westhawk Farm in a Roman context, but further finds could be expected. However the greensand from Folkestone appears to have been used in Kent both for earlier prehistoric saddle querns and for Iron Age rotary querns (Keller 1989). Only Millstone Grit remains, at

present, unknown from pre-Roman contexts in the area.

During the Roman period lava may have been used in Kent to an even greater extent than the large number of recorded instances suggests, since it fragments easily under certain soil conditions, and the resulting grey crumbs may not always have been recorded. It seems to have been in use both for rotary querns and millstones throughout the Roman period, having been retrieved from Phase 2–6 contexts at Westhawk Farm, and from a wide date range at other sites. Lava millstones are also known from Snodland (Ocock and Sydell 1967, 213), Stone-by-Faversham (Philp 1976, 63) and Fishbourne in Sussex (Cunliffe 1971, 153), while a fairly small one, *c* 570 mm in diameter, came from Springhead (Roe nd, 29). There may well have been more, either found as fragments, or else recorded as querns.

Millstones made from Millstone Grit are remarkably common in Kent. In addition to the pieces found at Westhawk Farm, there are three examples from Darenth (Philp 1973, 143), and further finds from Horton Kirby (Philp and Mills 1991, 71), Keston (Philp *et al.* 1991, 180), The Mount at Maidstone (Kelly 1992, 228), Shuart (op. cit.) and Worth (Parfitt 2000, 139). Fragments from Canterbury (Blockley *et al.* 1995, 1206), Springhead (Roe nd, 29) and the Thurnham Roman Villa (Shaffrey, forthcoming) may also come from millstones. Other fragments of Millstone Grit have frequently been reported, often re-used. No querns have been specifically identified, and it may be that this particular commodity was brought to Kent entirely in the form of millstones. It has been suggested that *Classis Britannica* ships were used to supply Wealden iron to the army military zone in northern England, transporting the goods to York by an East coast route (Cunliffe 1988, 84). The opportunity may well have been taken to load them with useful supplies of Millstone Grit for the return journey. This could have been transported as a form of ballast, which would fetch a good price at the port of return. The evidence is beginning to suggest that it was large millstones that were transported, rather than rotary querns. It is thought that the *Classis Britannica* ceased to be operational in the Kent area around AD 250 (Salway 1981, 529), and the phasing for the millstone fragments from Westhawk Farm seems to reflect this, since all the dated finds of Millstone Grit fall within an approximate time range of AD 150 to 250. Good dating evidence for this type of find is not always forthcoming, and broken millstones were in any case often re-used, as at Westhawk Farm, and also at Darenth (Philp 1973, 143), so that the date of their original use is uncertain. Finds of Millstone Grit, when dateable, do however seem to fall within the period that the *Classis Britannica* was transporting iron to the north. The site at Worth is estimated to have been occupied between AD 50 and 225 (Parfitt 2000, 142); at Horton Kirby the deposit containing the millstone is late 2nd or early 3rd century (Philp and Mills 1991, 7); the millstone at Keston has a date range that is a little later, approximately AD 200–300 (Philp *et al. 1991*, 180), which is still well within the range of possibility. In an area with such prolific finds of millstones, further dateable examples of Millstone Grit seem likely to occur.

The choice of any particular material for a quern or millstone must have been dependent to quite an extent on availability. The supply of goods arriving by sea would have been erratic at the best of times. It may have been necessary to be equipped with spare rotary querns or even saddle querns for use if left without a complete millstone, as appears to have been the practice at Ickham, where Millstone Grit fragments were extensively re-used for these items (Spain 1989, 171). If a boat from the Rhine or the Humber failed to arrive, a rotary quern of Lodsworth or Folkestone stone would also have been a serviceable alternative.

For those unable to afford imported querns of superior stone, local quernstone from Folkestone could have been used instead. Rotary querns made from this greensand were sometimes well made and finished (eg Keller 1989, 195 and fig. 3). However, one well-worn rotary quern of this stone from context 7379 (Fig 5.13: 48) shows so little skill in the making that it suggests a disadvantaged owner, maybe an ironworker accustomed to hard manual labour, but lacking finer craft skills. This unfortunate individual might even have had to walk to Folkestone to collect beach boulders and then shape them into upper and lower rotary quern stones as best he could.

Conclusion

It can be shown that the use of specific kinds of stone for querns and millstones at Westhawk Farm was part of an established pattern in Roman Kent. Most of the materials had been in use from before the conquest, although improved road and sea communications must subsequently have facilitated distribution of such essential commodities in the Roman period. The main innovation during the Roman period seems to have been the organisation of transport for millstones from the Pennines. Watermills must have been a common site in Kent by the 2nd century AD, when the first of the mills at Ickham was in operation (Spain 1989). All this activity was part of a much wider pattern, in which lava and Millstone Grit were brought to many sites in southeast England (Black 1987, 117), while their use was supplemented by local greensands. The transport of Millstone Grit may have eased off once the *Classis Britannica* was no longer sailing up and down the North Sea route, but lava was also brought into Kent and elsewhere during the Saxon period (eg Blockley *et al.* 1995, 1206). Whether this trade was part of the same operating system, or was differently organised after a break, remains a matter for future consideration.

Catalogue of worked stone (including illustrated examples)

Quern or millstone fragments

Niedermendig Lava (Fig. 5.13: 15-16)

1 Two fragments. Wt: 105 g. Context 344 (Group 796), Phase 6.
2 Four fragments. Wt: 90 g. Context 346 (Group 796) Phase 6.
3 Ten fragments. Wt: 40 g. Context 378 (Group 796) Phase 6.
4 Three fragments. Wt: 45 g. Context 502 (Group 1760) Phase 4-5.
5 Ten fragments. Wt: 87 g. Context 724 (Group 796) Phase 6.
6 Three fragments. Wt: 20 g. Context 739 (Group 796) Phase 6.
7 Thirty fragments. Wt: 435 g. Context 758 (Group 796) Phase 6.
8 One fragment. Wt: 15 g. Context 805 (Group 1740) Phase 4.
9 Thirty-one fragments. Wt: 98 g. Context 841, SF178, Phase 4.
10 Five fragments. Wt: 340 g. Context 933 (Group 1720), SF185, Phase 3-4.
11 Thirty-three fragments. Wt: Context 430 g. 956 (Group 666), SF187, Phase 4.
12 Twenty-one fragments. Wt: 143 g. Context 1236, Phase 4.
13 One fragment. Wt: 7 g. Context 1308 (Group 1040) Phase 4.
14 Eighty-seven(+) fragments. Wt: 2,360 g. Context 1433 (Group 1760) SF243, Phase 4-5.
15 (*Fig. 5.13*) Part of **rotary quern**, upper stone, with raised rim round edge on upper surface, while rest of upper surface has decorative grooving. There are vertical striae around the rim and the grinding surface appears to be slightly pecked. D: *c* 430 mm, Th at rim: 60 mm, worn to 14 mm in centre, Wt: 2,700 g. Context 1434 (Group 796) SF244, Phase 4.
16 (*Fig. 5.13*) Part of **rotary quern**, upper stone, with raised rim round the edge. Very similar to no. 15 above, but a different quern, because the grinding surface has radial grooving. Both rim and upper surface have decorative grooves, and there are vertical striae round the edge. Lava has whitish phenocrysts, probably of nepheline. D: *c* 430 mm, worn to *c* 18 mm in centre. Context 1547 (Group 796) SF249, Phase 4.
17 One fragment. Wt: 5 g. Context 5129 (Group 5210) Phase 5.
18 Twelve fragments. Wt: 370 g. Context 5175, Phase 3.
19 One fragment. Wt: 18 g. Context 5179 (Group 5280) Phase 3.
20 Seven fragments. Wt: 18 g. Context 7024 (feature 7023) Phase 4.
21 Two fragments. Wt: 20 g. Context 7087, SF938, unphased.

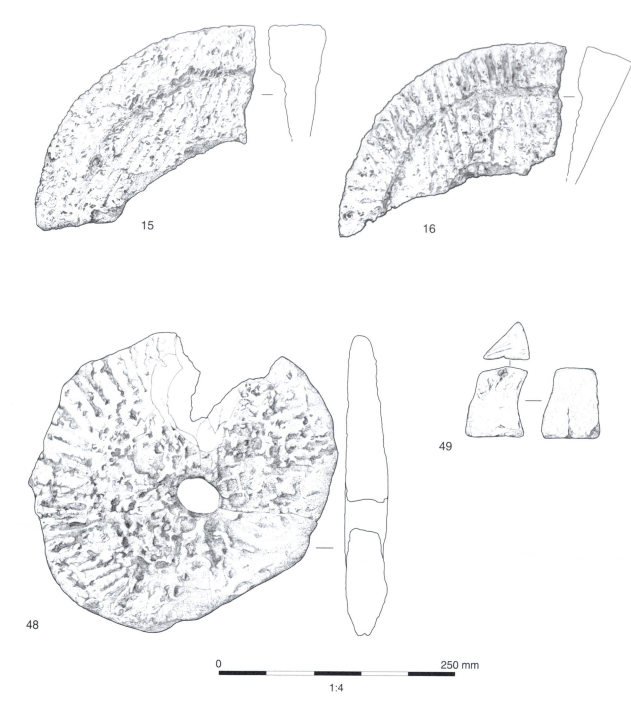

Figure 5.13   Stone objects (nos 15-16, 48-49).

22 Probable **rotary quern** fragments. Five fragments, including one large weathered piece,. Wt: 443 g. Context 7120 (feature 7239) SF960, Phase 4.
23 Sixteen fragments. Wt: 125 g. Context 7237, SF1502, Phase 5.
24 Seventeen fragments. Wt: 135 g. Context 7244 (feature 7239) SF1193, Phase 4.
25 Twenty-three(+) fragments, including one large weathered piece probably from a rotary quern. Wt: 3,700 g. Context 7274, SF947, Phase 5.
26 Eight fragments. Wt: 450 g. Context 7279, SF1078, Phase 5.

27 Five fragments. Wt: 92 g. Context 7415 (feature 7416) Phase 4.
28 Twelve fragments. Wt: 150 g. Context 7536 (Group 8620) SF1285, Phase 2.
29 Fourteen fragments. Wt: 120 g. Context 7536 (Group 8620) SF1292, Phase 2.
30 Thirteen fragments. Wt: 113 g. Context 7658 (Group 9100) SF1340, Phase 3.
31 Nine fragments. Wt: 215 g. Context 7768 (Group 7850) SF1339, Phase 3.
32 Large segment from probable **millstone**, very weathered, also worn. D: *c* 750 mm, extant Th:

c 42 mm at rim, 39 mm in centre, Wt: 8,200 kg. Context 9422 (feature 9179) SF 1518, Phase 4.

33 Four fragments. Wt: 20 g. Context 10077, Post-Roman.

34 One hundred and fourteen(+) fragments. Wt: 860 g. Context 10323 (Group 10070) SF1545, Phase 3.

Millstone Grit

35 **Quern** or **millstone**, weathered fragment with part of grinding surface. Wt: 3,000 g. Context 293, SF47, Unphased.

36 Fragments, small burnt and weathered. Two pieces. Wt: 100 g. Context 758 (Group 796) SF198, Phase 6.

37 **Rotary quern** or **millstone** fragment, burnt slightly pink, part of outer edge, traces of pitted surface. Th at rim: 59 mm, Wt: 830 g. Context 8189, SF1449, Phase 4.

38 Probable **millstone**, large weathered fragment, with one fairly smooth surface. Maximum Th: 98 mm, Wt: 2,700 g. Context 8480 (feature 8479) SF1491, Phase 4.

39 Small fragment, slightly burnt. Wt: 7 g. Context 8745, sample 683, Phase 4.

40 Probable **millstone** fragment, probably upper stone, with part of rim. Grinding surface worn into rings, upper surface has been grooved diagonally. D: *c* 750 mm, Th at rim: 58 mm, Wt: 1,665 g. Context 9488, SF1520, Phase 4.

41 Possible **millstone**, worn fragment. Very similar to millstone No. 43. Worn grinding surface with rings, upper surface pitted, part of central hole. Maximum Th now: 38 mm, Wt: 760 g. Context 9488, SF1523, Phase 4.

42 **Quern** or **millstone**. Four fragments, two fitting, probably all from the same stone. Include two fragments with part of outer edge, grinding surface worn into rings. Maximum Th at rim: 64 and 66 mm, Wt: 2218 g. Context 9488, SF1524-SF1527, Phase 4.

43 **Millstone.** Two joining fragments with part of rim, well worn grinding surface, which is now fairly smooth with traces of rings, upper surface pitted fairly crudely. D: *c* 750 mm, maximum Th at rim now: 34 mm, Wt: 830 g. Context 9636, SF1521 and SF1522, Phase 4.

Lower Greensand, Lodsworth stone

44 **Rotary quern** fragment with grooved grinding surface and part of rim. Maximum Th: 83 mm, Wt: 400 g. Context 1068, SF195, Phase 4.

45 Probable **rotary quern** fragment, weathered and slightly burnt. Extant dimensions: 122 x 122 mm, maximum Th: 70 mm, Wt: 575 g. Context 7114 (Group 8590) SF950, Phase 4.

46 **Rotary quern** fragment, burnt. D: *c* 430 mm, Th at rim: 71 mm, Wt: 1,540 g. Context 9951, SF1533, Phase 5.

Lower Greensand, Copt Point, Folkestone (Fig. 5.13: 48)

47 Probable **rotary quern** fragment, worn top and bottom with concave grinding surface, burnt. Wt: 475 g. Context 510 (Group 1260) Phase 4.

48 (*Fig. 5.13*) Fragmentary **rotary quern,** crude and unevenly shaped. Almost complete, comprises four large pieces and *c* 46 small fragments. Grinding surface is more or less flat and crudely pitted, with an area of grooving near the rim, extending about half the way round. Some evidence of wear. Other surface looks like the unmodified part of a beach boulder. D: 330 x 300 mm, oval hole *c* 45 x 35 mm, Th at hole: 39 mm, Wt: 5,600 g. Context 7379, SF1164, Phase 4.

Other stone objects

Wealden Sandstone (Fig. 5.13: 49)

49 (*Fig. 5.13*) **Whetstone**, pyramidal block, worn on three sides. Unusual shape for a whetstone, but well worn. Two narrow grooves from point sharpening. Dimensions: 72 x 60 x 57 mm, Wt: 215 g. Context 7279, SF1046, Phase 5.

50 Possible **smoother or whetstone**. Slab broken in three, worn smooth on one flat side. Dimensions: 142 x 74 x 26 mm, Wt: 360 g. Context 9031 (Group 10420) Phase 4.

Flint

51 Pebbles, all slightly oval, likely to be **slingstones**. 33 examples. Average Wt: 48.5 g. Context 10239, unphased.

WOODEN FINDS
by S J Allen

Introduction

Some 78 pieces of waterlogged wood were recovered during the excavation, deriving from fills of three waterholes: 796, 7239 and 9179, containing 12, 13 and 53 pieces of wood respectively. This material was recorded and assessed by Nick Mitchell in 2000 (records held in archive), being cleaned and checked for original surfaces, joints, toolmarks and fixings such as nails. After this a number of pieces, consisting primarily of unworked oak from waterhole 9179, were discarded. These includ ed a part of a small tree trunk (context 10117) found in an upright position against the south-west edge of the feature. A sample was taken from this timber for dendrochronological dating, but despite having a sequence of some 300 rings it was impossible to find a match (the rings were unusually closely-spaced throughout) and, consequently, a date (D Miles pers. comm.; data and notes in project archive). Some 30 pieces of worked wood were then submitted for more detailed reporting.

Methodology

The 30 pieces of wood were subject to further cleaning and washing. Notes were made on each piece as it was dealt with and these form the basis of the present report. The overall condition of the wood was poor. Although the ladder parts and withy tie (see below) were in excellent, though soft, condition, the remainder of the assemblage was much degraded.

Each piece was sampled for species identification at York. These were examined in transverse, radial longitudinal and tangential longitudinal sections under a microscope; all species identifications follow Schweingruber (1990). All identifications carried out in this way were incorporated into the database using their scientific names. A database was created using Microsoft Access to record information about each object and to allow the data to be sorted and interrogated after the completion of recording. Following examination, each piece was returned to its original packaging to await a decision on its future, with the exception of the ladder parts and withy tie, which were fully conserved.

Most of the wood can only be identified to a particular genus. For example, while there are many different species of willow, their wood cannot be differentiated. Only three species, *Fraxinus excelsior* L. (Ash), *Quercus spp.* (Oak) and *Salix spp.* (Willow) were noted in the assemblage.

Catalogue and summary of assemblages

In all cases, the wood survived through burial in waterlogged anoxic conditions, maintained from burial through to excavation. Many of the pieces exhibited shrinkage cracks which suggest that the site has been recently subjected to dewatering or that the wood had suffered some period of drying during the excavation.

Finds from Waterhole 796 (Fig. 5.14: 1-4)

1 Part of radially faced pierced wooden **board** with curved edge/ends. Broken along the grain with the break passing across a small through drilled hole in the face. Half of a pot lid, or possibly a blade from a small scraping tool. *Quercus spp.* L: 119 mm, W: 63 mm, Th: 12 mm, hole D: *c* 16 mm. Context 1456 (Group 796) Phase 4

2 Section of **roundwood stake point** with beginning of two opposing facets cut to form the (missing) tip. Faint tool signature marks. *Salix sp.* Spring cut. L: 137 mm, D: 33 mm. Context 1547 (Group 796) Phase 4

3 Butt end of **handle** cut from radially faced board. 'Pommel' is of semi circular plan with shoulders to handgrip formed by sawing. Grip and curved edge of 'pommel' formed by hewing. *Quercus sp.* L: 110 mm, W: 55 mm, Th: 28 mm. Context 1547 (Group 796) Phase 4

4 **Withy tie**. Three strands, each 'S' twisted, plaited 'Z' fashion to form a short length of rope. No

bark present. No working marks *Salix sp..* D of strands: 8 mm, 10 mm and 12 mm, rope D: 30 mm. Context 1583. SF250 (Group 796) Phase 4

Woodworking debris from waterhole 9151

5 (*not illustrated*) **Offcut**. Section of box halved worked timber, originally of rectangular cross-section with at least two of the corners chamfered. Very eroded, with deep shrinkage cracks. *Fraxinus excelsior* L. L: 88 mm, W: 61 mm, Th: 40 mm. Context 9389 (Group 9151) Phase 3

6 (*not illustrated*) **Chipping**. Radially faced and eroded section of timber with much sapwood present. Very eroded with deep shrinkage cracks. *Quercus sp.* L: 118 mm, W: 32 mm, Th: 32 mm. Context 9389 (Group 9151) Phase 3

7 (*not illustrated*) Heartwood **chipping**. Section of boxed heart timber. Very eroded with deep shrinkage cracks. *Fraxinus excelsior L.* L: 137 mm, W: 44 mm, Th: 44 mm. Context 9389 (Group 9151) Phase 3

8 (*not illustrated*) **Heartwood chipping**. Section of radially faced timber. Very eroded with deep shrinkage cracks. *Quercus sp.* L: 148 mm, W: 37 mm, Th: 30 mm. Context 9389 (Group 9151) Phase 3

9 (*not illustrated*) **Heartwood chipping**. Section of tangentially faced timber. Very eroded with deep shrinkage cracks. *Fraxinus excelsior* L. L: 87 mm, W: 33 mm, Th: 17 mm. Context 9389 (Group 9151) Phase 3

Rectangular shaft and peg from Waterhole 9151 (Fig. 5.15: 10)

10 **Shaft**. Section of radially faced wood cut to regular rectangular cross-section with one end slightly angled, other end broken. Pierced near intact end by single sub-rectangular peg hole through face. Good condition, slightly eroded surfaces. Possibly part of a ladder? *Fraxinus excelsior* L. L: 252 mm, W: 43 mm, Th: 31 mm, peg hole 9 x 10 mm. 9392 (Group 9151) SF1516, Phase 3

11 (*not illustrated*) **Peg**. Small rectangular cross-section peg fitting to pierced hole of Cat.No.10. One end broken, other slightly bifaced. *Quercus sp.* L: 29.5 mm, W: 10 mm, Th: 10 mm. Context 9392 (Group 9151) SF1516, Phase 3

Broken ladder rail and broken ladder rung from Waterhole 9151 (Fig. 5.15: 12-13)

12 **Ladder rail**. Section of box halved rectangular cross-section heartwood, with chamfered edges. One end had chamfered corner, other end broken. Complete rectangular through mortise almost halfway along length for ladder rung, with remains of a second similar mortise at the broken end. Good condition, though heavy mineral staining over much of surface. *Quercus sp.*

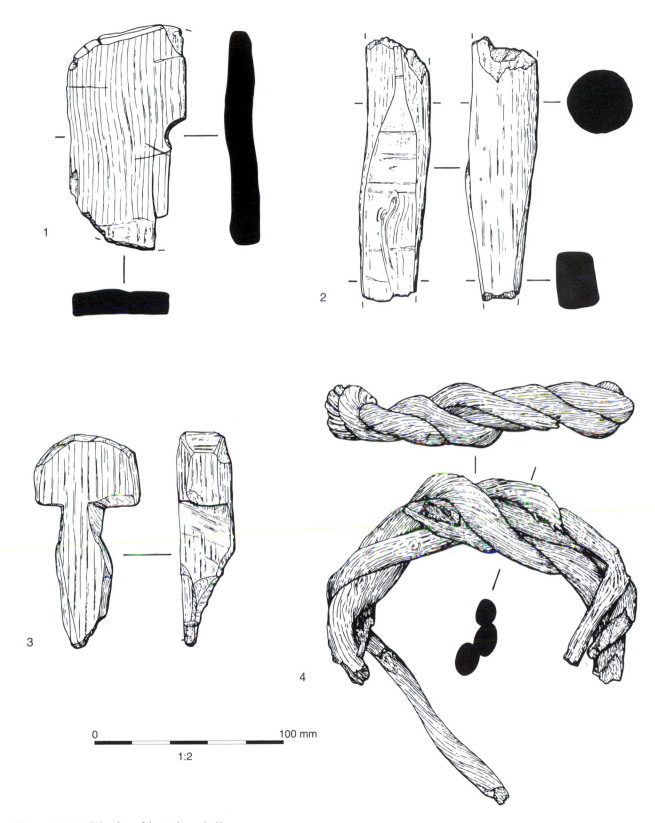

Figure 5.14   Wooden objects (nos 1-4).

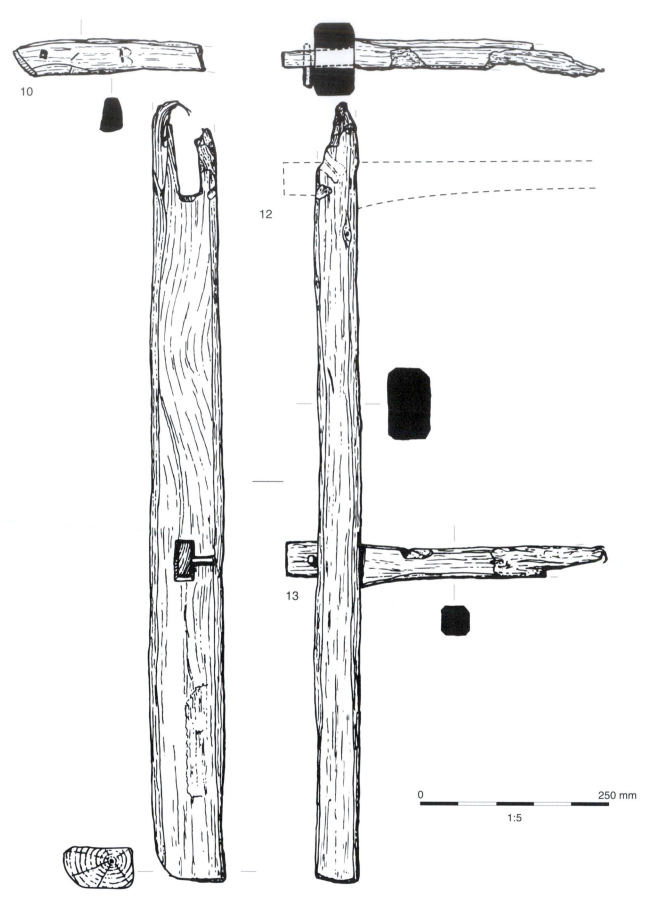

Figure 5.15   Wooden ladder (nos 10, 12-13).

L: 1016 mm, W: 93 mm, Th: 55 mm. Intact mortise 50 x 30 mm, broken mortise W: 30 mm. Context 9396 (Group 9151) SF1517, Phase 3

13 **Ladder rung**. Section of radially-faced heartwood with one end cut to form a tenon. Tenon pierced for single rounded peg, of which remains are present. From shoulder of tenon, one edge continues straight and the opposing edge is carved to a concave form before terminating at a break. Light saw marks on shoulders of tenon, worked surfaces of tenon itself are hewn. Good condition though heavy mineral staining over much of surface. *Quercus sp.* L: 421 mm, W: 51 mm, Th: 35 mm. Tenon: L: 101 mm, W: 43 mm, Th: 20 mm, hole D: 7 mm. Context 9396 (Group 9151) SF1517, Phase 3

Worked timbers or remains derived from worked timbers from waterhole 9179, (Fig. 5.16: 14, 18)

14 **Offcut**. Tangentially faced sub-rectangular cross-section timber broken into two refitting parts. Larger piece has flat based groove cut across one face with faint hewing marks in base. Very eroded with deep shrinkage cracks. Several small knots - cut from branch wood. *Quercus sp.* L: 1107 mm, W: 190 mm, Th: 104 mm. Groove 58 mm wide, 26 mm deep. Context 9422 (Group 9179) Phase 4

15 (*not illustrated*) **Offcut**. Radially faced section of sub-rectangular cross-section heartwood. Very eroded with deep shrinkage cracks. *Quercus sp.* L: 352 mm, W: 120 mm, Th: 68 mm. Context 9422 (Group 9179) Phase 4

16 (*not illustrated*) **Offcut**. Radially faced section of sub-rectangular cross-section heartwood. Possible remains of a smashed bare faced tenon at one end. Very eroded with deep shrinkage cracks. *Quercus sp.* L: 253 mm, W: 138 mm, Th: 69 mm. Context 9422 (Group 9179) Phase 4

17 (*not illustrated*) **Offcut**. Halved section of sub-rectangular cross-section heartwood/sapwood. Cut from branch wood. Very eroded with deep shrinkage cracks. *Quercus sp.* L: 194 mm, W: 110 mm, Th: 65 mm. Context 9422 (Group 9179) Phase 4

18 **Offcut**. Radially faced section of sub-rectangular cross-section heartwood. One fair face, possibly torn from a post or plank. *Quercus sp.* L: 488 mm, W: 104 mm, Th: 54 mm. Context 9422 (Group 9179) Phase 4

19 (*not illustrated*) **Stump**. Section of tree at branch or root junction, with at least four shoots springing from this bole. Very eroded. *Quercus sp.* L: 224 mm, W: 198 mm, Th: 143 mm. Context 9422 (Group 9179) Phase 4

20 (*not illustrated*) **Roundwood**. Section of roundwood with cut ends. Very eroded, deep shrinkage crack along whole length. *Quercus sp.* L: 598 mm, diameter 31 mm. Context 9422 (Group 9179) Phase 4

Worked, eroded, light timber from waterhole 9179

None of the pieces fit to make coherent structures.

21 (*not illustrated*) **Offcut**. Box halved section of irregular cross-section heartwood. Very eroded with deep shrinkage cracks. *Quercus sp.* L: 437 mm, W: 86 mm, Th: 40 mm. Context 10079 (Group 9179) Phase 3 or 4

22 (*not illustrated*) **Offcut**. Box quartered section of sub-rectangular cross-section heartwood. Very eroded. *Quercus sp.* L: 154 mm, W: 46 mm, Th: 34 mm. Context 10079 (Group 9179) Phase 3 or 4

23 (*not illustrated*) **Offcut**. Box halved section of sub-rectangular cross-section heartwood. One end broken, other tapered and cut off. Very eroded. *Quercus sp.* L: 199 mm, W: 64 mm, Th: 47 mm. Context 10079 (Group 9179) Phase 3 or 4

24 (*not illustrated*) **Offcut**. Box heart section of sub-rectangular cross-section heartwood. Possible eroded joint at one end. Very eroded with deep shrinkage cracks. *Quercus sp.* L: 184 mm, W: 42 mm, Th: 41 mm. Context 10079 (Group 9179) Phase 3 or 4

25 (*not illustrated*) **Offcut**. Box heart section of irregular cross-section heartwood. Very eroded with deep shrinkage cracks. *Quercus sp.* L: 198 mm, W: 40 mm, Th: 34 mm. Context 10079 (Group 9179) Phase 3 or 4

26 (*not illustrated*) **Offcut**. Radially faced section of irregular cross-section heartwood. Very eroded with deep shrinkage cracks. *Quercus sp.* L: 141 mm, W: 36 mm, Th: 27 mm. Context 10079 (Group 9179) Phase 3 or 4

27 (*not illustrated*) **Offcut**. Box halved section of sub-rectangular cross-section heartwood. Broken into two refitting pieces. Very eroded with deep shrinkage cracks. *Quercus sp.* L: 352 mm, W: 61 mm, Th: 34 mm. Context 10079 (Group 9179) Phase 3 or 4

28 (*not illustrated*) **Offcut**. Radially faced section of sub-rectangular cross-section heartwood. Very eroded with deep shrinkage cracks. *Quercus sp.* L: 231 mm, W: 36 mm, Th: 27 mm. Context 10079 (Group 9179) Phase 3 or 4

29 (*not illustrated*) **Offcut**. Box heart section of irregular cross-section heartwood. Broken into two refitting pieces. Possible eroded remains of half lap dovetail housing in one edge. Very eroded with deep shrinkage cracks. *Quercus sp.* L: 771 mm, W: 81 mm, Th: 45 mm. Context 10079 (Group 9179) Phase 3 or 4

30 (*not illustrated*) **Offcut**. Box heart section of irregular cross-section heartwood. Very eroded with deep shrinkage cracks. *Quercus sp.* L: 296 mm, W: 83 mm, Th: 45 mm. Context 10079 (Group 9179) Phase 3 or 4

31 (*not illustrated*) **Offcut**. Box heart section of irregular cross-section heartwood. Very eroded. *Quercus sp.* L: 358 mm, W: 84 mm, Th: 43 mm. Context 10079 (Group 9179) Phase 3 or 4

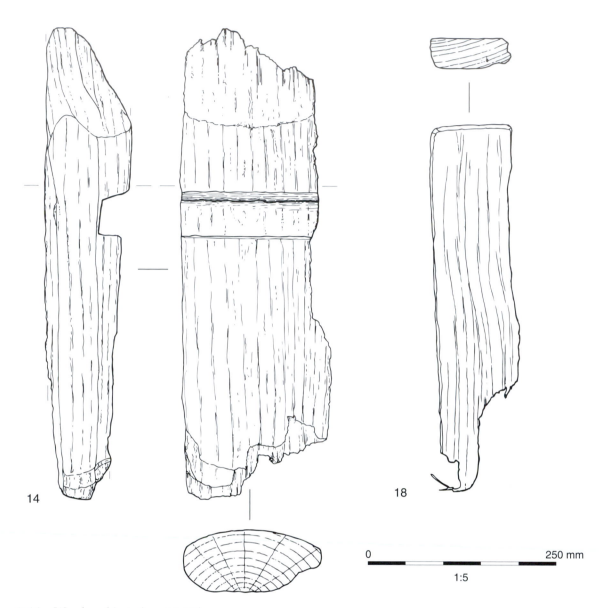

Figure 5.16   Wooden objects (nos 14, 18).

32 (*not illustrated*) **Offcut**. Radially faced section of irregular cross-section heartwood. Very eroded. *Quercus sp.* L: 171 mm, W: 53 mm, Th: 25 mm. Context 10079 (Group 9179) Phase 3 or 4

33 (*not illustrated*) **Offcut**. Box halved section of irregular cross-section heartwood. Very eroded with deep shrinkage cracks. *Quercus sp.* L: 183 mm, W: 46 mm, Th: 41 mm. Context 10079 (Group 9179) Phase 3 or 4

Discussion

All of the wood examined from this site has been worked, and has presumably formed part or parts of structures now lost. The circumstances of recovery (extraction by machine bucket in some cases) were such that careful examination of all the timbers could not be carried out *in situ*. However, it is clear from their recorded locations that the majority (at least) of the timbers did not derive from structures within the features from which they were recovered, such as shaft linings or revetments, and it is likely that in all cases they represent 'scrap' material discarded into a convenient feature. The derivation of the timbers cannot be identified.

What can be said is that a very narrow species range is represented. Both Oak and Ash are well-known as timber trees and to find them utilised to produce the objects found at Westhawk Farm is unsurprising. The three tree species represented are all native species and could have been found growing locally.

Little can be said about the working of the wood. No bark edges survive on the timbers and felling seasons cannot be identified. The few joints found are highly eroded, and it is not certain whether they are joints, or simply fortuitous erosion and breakage patterns. Only the groove on a timber (No. 14) from context 9422 exhibited any trace of tool marks. These indicated that the groove had been cut out with an axe or similar heavy bladed cutting tool.

The 'small finds' material is of much greater interest. The pierced board (No. 1) is superficially similar to offcuts of board often found as debris on Roman and medieval sites. The ends, however, show signs of working, being deliberately cut to form a curve. How extensive this curved end/edge was cannot be known owing to damage. If part of a scraping tool, it is very small. The most likely identification therefore is as a pot lid, one of those utilitarian and probably very common objects which rarely survive in an archaeological context.

The handle (No. 3) may derive from any of a number of carved wooden tools, but the closest parallels to it are the handles of wooden swords. These are usually described as toys, though in a military context such artefacts might be practice weapons, used in training. There is no military presence at this site, so far as the writer is aware, and so it is best to consider this item as indeed part of a child's toy. In form it is similar to a more complete example of Iron Age date from The Breiddin (Britnell and Earwood 1991, 164-5, no 353), though the handgrip is not so regular.

Withy ties are being found with increasing frequency on prehistoric waterlogged sites including such Iron Age examples as Goldcliff (Brunning and Bell 2000, 216) and The Breiddin (Britnell and Earwood 1991, 164). Westhawk Farm adds another example to those which have been recovered from Roman sites. These include Perry Oaks, Middlesex (Allen 2001) and New Fresh Wharf, London (Miller *et al.* 1986, 232). Unfortunately, few of the Roman examples have yet been found in a context which would shed light on their function, but an example from a well at Stonea was interpreted as a possible bucket binding (Jackson 1996, 552). These objects could have been used for a variety of purposes, such as handles, fastenings, bindings or ties. Of possible relevance to this site is an Iron Age find from Glastonbury, where one was found *in situ* employed as a replacement rung for a ladder (Bulleid 1911, 332).

The ladder rail and one rung (SF1517) are from the same ladder, while a second rung (SF1516) may be a replacement rung for the same ladder. The rail is clearly from one end of the ladder, probably the lower end. One corner of an edge/end junction has been chamfered away, suggesting that this was the right hand side of the ladder when propped in use. Each edge/face corner has been chamfered, removing any sharp angles on the rail. The sockets for the rungs were sharply cut using a chisel type of tool with a blade width of 15 mm. Each socket is at a slight angle to the axis of the rail and when propped in place, this would mean that the faces of the rungs they housed would be closer to the vertical than otherwise.

The rung associated with this rail was shaped from a rectangular cross-section radially-faced batten. The complete end is cut to form a tenon, fitting the socket in the rail. The shoulders of this tenon are sawn. The waste wood may have been removed by a small axe, or wedge, but the final trimming marks show that

a chisel or similar was used to pare away the faces of the tenon to permit a fit to the rail. The rest of the rung is carefully shaped with a straight flat upper edge and a concave-profile lower edge. The curve of this lower edge, if regular, shows that just over half of the length of the rung is present.

The tenon projected beyond the outside edge of the rail and was fastened in place by a single wooden peg. Rather than being pegged through the rail, the peg went through the projecting portion of the tenon outside the rail, locking it in place between the peg and the shoulders of the tenon. Such an arrangement would have made the rung easier to replace if broken, than if the peg had been driven through the rail as well.

If SF1516 is a replacement rung from a ladder, then it would seem to have been fastened in place in a similar fashion, that is, with a projecting end and a peg to lock the rung in place outside the rail. The entire ladder could not have been made in this fashion though, as there is nothing on the rung to prevent the rails moving closer together. It is more likely that this piece went through the sockets on both rails and was fastened outside both rails to stop it falling out of position. Rail spacing would have been maintained by the rungs above and below the replacement.

The upper edge of the rung is around 5 mm below the upper edge of the rung socket, and thus the distance from ground to the top of the first rung is 438 mm. The other rungs may have been spaced further apart, as the distance between the top of the lower socket and the bottom of the upper socket is 450 mm. If the second housing were the same size as the first, this would make a step distance of around 500 mm. Assuming that the rung was symmetrical, its overall length would have been 550 mm and the distance between the rails at this point some 348 mm.

Ladder parts are uncommon finds on Roman sites. Those which have been found, such as those from Silchester (St John Hope and Fox 1901, 244) and Queen Street, London (Weeks 1978) were, like the Westhawk Farm example, recovered from wells or waterholes. The construction and dimensions of the components of the Westhawk ladder are very similar to the Silchester and Queen Street examples. At Silchester, however, the rungs were held in place by wedges and the rails may have been cut from softwood rather than Oak. In terms of width and step distance, the three are also similar. The Silchester example is not closely dated, although that from Queen Street seems to have been buried in the late 1st century (Wilmott 1982, 47). The Westhawk ladder is from a context assigned to Period 2, Phase 3 (AD 70-150). The type may have a long history- a ladder of similar construction and size, although with more crudely fashioned rails, was recovered from the Iron Age settlement at Glastonbury (Bulleid 1911, 332), so the form of construction alone may not indicate an early date.

Where the Westhawk ladder differs is in the form of the rung. The other ladders have rungs of plain rectangular cross-section (although one of those from

Silchester may be circular). None appears to have been shaped in the same way as that described here. Although this working reduced the cross-sectional area of the rung at its midpoint, most of the weight of an occupant is placed to one side or the other of a rung when climbing or descending. A rung shaped this way would reduce the overall weight of the ladder somewhat while still retaining enough wood to give support at those parts of the rung which most needed it.

LEATHER
by Quita Mould

Methodology

The leather was washed and wet when examined. Leather species identification was made using low powered magnification.

Discussion

Four fragmentary leather objects were among the finds assemblage recovered from waterhole 796, a feature located on the north-west side of the axial road opposite the shrine enclosure. It is thought that the feature was dug sometime between AD 70-150

(within Phase 3) and may originally have been associated with a metalworking structure (Structure I) immediately to the west. The leather was found in the middle fills of the waterhole, attributed to Phase 4 and dated to AD 150-200. It has been suggested that the relatively large number of coins found in the upper (Phase 5 and 6) fills might include redeposited votive material (see Guest, above). However, there is no reason to think that the other categories of material recovered, including the leather, represent anything other than discarded domestic rubbish.

Though the group of leather is small it is of interest as it comes from a civilian settlement in the south of the country. Our knowledge of Romano-British leatherwork is principally based on large collections associated with military establishments, which have dominated the corpus of archaeological leatherwork recovered to date. Details of the leather from Westhawk Farm can be usefully added to the evidence that is slowly accumulating regarding the southern civilian population.

Context 1547 contained a length of seam torn from an unidentifiable item of goatskin (SF251, Fig. 5.17: no. 1) and the remains of two heavily worn shoes of one-piece construction (SF247.1, Fig. 5.18: 2; SF247.2, Fig. 5.18: 3). Little can be said about the simple seam (no. 1) other than it has been sewn with fine thonging in a running stitch. The two one-piece shoes (nos

1

0 _____ 100 mm

1:2

Figure 5.17   Leather shoe (no. 1).

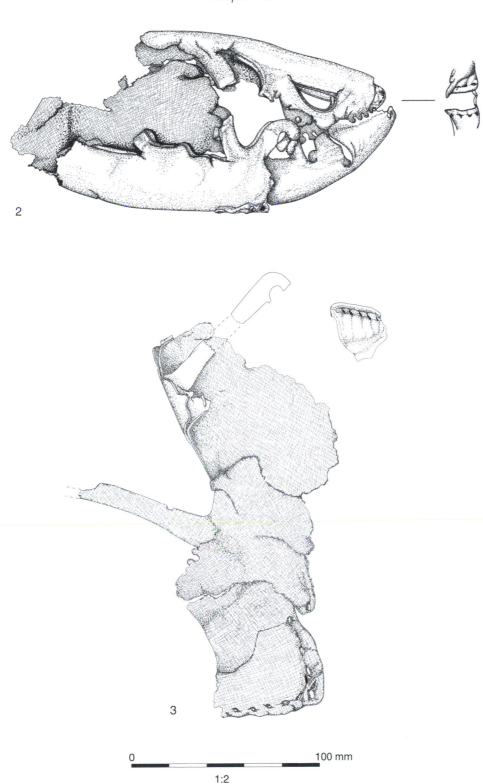

Figure 5.18   Leather shoes (nos 2-3).

2 and 3) are of similar style and it is possible, though unlikely, they may have been a pair. The shoes are fragmentary, several of their fastening loops are now missing and their exact style is uncertain (see Fig. 5.19 for a possible reconstruction). However, it is clear that they belong to a generic style of footwear worn in the mid 2nd century. Individual shoes of this gen-eral style vary greatly in the arrangement and shape of their loops and accompanying decorative features. The arrangement of the surviving fastening loops with small lobes at the base most closely resembles those seen on the uppers of shoes of nailed construction, suggesting that at this time shoes with similar styles of uppers were being made in both nailed and one-piece

Figure 5.19   Reconstruction drawing of one-piece shoe.

constructions, a feature also noted for other upper styles found elsewhere (for example at Welzheim - van Driel-Murray 2001, 191); the different constructions employed reflect the need for heavier 'outdoor' wear and lighter footwear. Nailed shoes with comparable upper styles have been found at the fort of Birdoswald, associated with mid to late 2nd century pottery (style 2 - Mould 1997, 335), and at the Antonine fort of Bar Hill (type A calceus - Robertson *et al.* 1975, fig. 22, no. 5).

Context 1456 contained the bottom unit of a shoe of nailed construction (SF245; Fig. 5.20: 4). The shoe

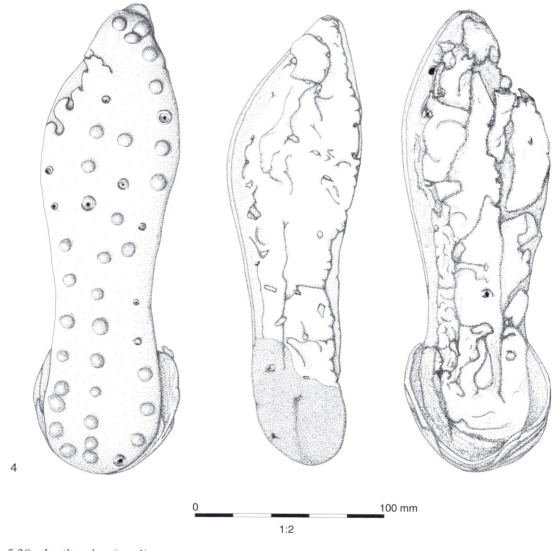

4

0   100 mm

1:2

Figure 5.20   Leather shoe (no. 4).

204

is of elegant shape with a pointed toe and was lightly nailed (type 1a - van Driel-Murray 1983, 20, fig. 3; type B3 - Mould 1997, 335, fig. 243) with an extra nail at the toe and exterior seat indicating repair. The bottom unit had no constructional thonging to join the insole to the middle laminae. Little evidence of the upper was preserved except for a small area around the heel stiffener and fragments of the upper lasting margin lying on top and to one side of the narrow middle laminae preserved beneath the insole. Slots were visible on the underside (flesh side) of the insole that appear to be tunnel stitching used to secure the upper lasting margin in place.

There is little available material with which to compare the Westhawk Farm leather. A small group of nailed shoes from Ickham, Kent (Mould in Riddler *et al.* forthcoming), though likely to be of somewhat later date, does show some similarities. Nine of the Ickham shoes had a similar nailing pattern, while a single shoe (SF1960), from a timber-lined well backfilled at the end of the 4th century, combined the same nailing pattern with a lack of constructional thonging on the bottom unit, as seen on the Westhawk Farm example.

Catalogue of illustrated items (Figs 5.17-5.18, 5.20)

1 **Leather cut down seam.** Remains of two panels joined by a simple thonged seam. The seam runs close to the edge of the upper panel (2-6 mm from the cut edge) and is sewn with a narrow, flexible thong (2 mm in width) passing through a series of small thong holes spaced 15 mm apart. The remains of an edge with a similar thonged seam is present at right angles to the long seam. At the opposite end (the bottom as illustrated) is a cut edge running parallel to the long seam with relatively closely spaced holes at right angles to the edge which appear slightly puckered, suggesting it may also have been sewn with a tightly pulled thong. All the other edges are torn and worn away. The long seam now assumes a gentle curve that may be original; the wear suggests one of the panels may have been folded close to the seam originally. Leather sheep/goatskin. L: *c* 280 mm, max W: 156 mm. Context 1547 (Group 796) SF251, Phase 4.

2 **Leather shoe of one-piece construction.** Shoe for the right foot with an asymmetrical cutting pattern. Heavily worn, worn through at the sole tread and seat, longer fastening loops torn off, back

part missing. Central toe seam with grain/flesh stitching a closed seam. D-shaped loop next to the toe seam, longer fastening loops surviving on the left side have rounded terminals, loops have decorative lobes present at the base. The edges of the loops are tooled (compressed). Leather is delaminated and the grain surface has split from the flesh in several areas. Leather calf/cattlehide. Surviving L: 207 mm, W: across tread 97 mm. Context 1547 (Group 796) SF247, Phase 4.

3 **Leather shoe of one-piece construction.** Part of left side of shoe, torn away from rest of the shoe, foot uncertain, but possibly also for right foot. Toe area missing, two long fastening loops with decorative lobes at the base. Top edge of the left quarters area present 50 mm above the seam joining the sole seat to the base of the quarters. The left side of the central back seam present with large grain/flesh stitches (stitch length 9 mm); thread/thong impression suggests it had been sewn with a whip stitch (oversewn). Surviving L: 200 mm. Also fragments from two fastening loops with rounded terminals and tooled edges, and a fragment of toe seam with grain/flesh stitches from a closed seam. Likely to come from this shoe. Context 1547 (Group 796) SF247.2, Phase 4

4 **Leather bottom unit of shoe of nailed construction for the right foot.** Complete bottom unit comprising sole, middle *laminae*, and insole, with a heel stiffener and small area of uppers preserved around the quarters, and lasting margin. Bottom unit has pointed toe, petal-shaped forepart and waist and seat of the same width. Sole is worn away at the exterior tread. Widely spaced nailing with a single row of nailing around the edge and a line down the centre with infilling at the tread (van-Driel-Murray 1a; Mould B3), with an additional nail at the toe and exterior seat from repair. Two narrow middle laminae lying along the centre of the sole. Fragments of upper lasting margin present lying between middle laminae and insole. Edge of upper lasting margin shows signs of bracing. Insole is same size as the sole; underside of the insole has suggestion of thonging running parallel to the side of the shoe to attach the upper. No constructional thonging present. Leather worn cattlehide. Insole L: 246 mm, W: tread 74 mm, waist 47 mm. Adult size 4 (no allowance for shrinkage). Context 1456 (Group 796) SF245, Phase 4

Chapter 6: Ceramic Finds

ROMAN AND MEDIEVAL POTTERY
by Malcolm Lyne

Introduction

The site produced some 73,000 sherds (*c* 850 kg), mainly of 1st- to 3rd-century Roman pottery, from stratified contexts. Area C yielded just over 3600 sherds (24 kg) of hand-retrieved pottery, but the overwhelming bulk of the material (*c* 69,000 sherds, 819 kg) came from Area B features. These included a few medieval pottery assemblages from a small occupation site at the south-west end of Area B (246 sherds, 3150 g, including 4 sherds probably of 16th-century date). Sieving of environmental samples produced a further 3092 sherds (17,586 g) of pottery.

Methodology and report format

All the context assemblages were quantified by numbers of sherds and their weights per fabric. The Roman fabrics were classified using the Canterbury Archaeological Trust's coding (those with B, BER, R and LR prefixes: see Macpherson-Grant, *et al.* 1995) with additions. The fabrics were identified using a x8 magnification lens with built-in metric scale for determining the natures, forms, sizes and frequencies of added inclusions. Finer fabrics were additionally examined using a x30 pocket microscope with built-in artificial illumination source.

Many of the assemblages are too small for more precise quantification by Estimated Vessel Equivalents (EVEs) based on rim sherds (Orton 1975), but seven of the larger ones were so quantified and the results incorporated in the report below. The sieved pottery is excluded from quantification tables because of the different methods employed to retrieve it.

The fabrics represented in the assemblage are listed and discussed first. This is followed by the listing, illustration (where appropriate) and discussion of selected groups/assemblages in chronological sequence, with material from Area C presented before that from Area B. The selection of the assemblages for discussion is based on their importance in either archaeological or ceramic terms, or both. Pottery from burials (except 8160) is catalogued and discussed separately, in association with the other evidence for those burials.

Fabrics

'Belgic'/Romanised Native wares

Handmade and tournetted grog-tempered wares constitute the largest single component of pottery assemblages from the site throughout its Roman occupation. Such wares appear to have made up more than three-quarters of the pottery in use on the site during the mid-late 1st century, dropping to just over half during the 2nd century. There was a further decline in the significance of such wares to around 40% during the period *c* AD 200-270, with the late 3rd to early 4th century assemblage from the uppermost fills of waterhole 796 suggesting the beginnings of a revival in their use. The following fabric variants are present:

B1 'Belgic' fine grog-tempered ware. One sherd only recorded.

B2 'Belgic' coarse grog-tempered ware with profuse 1 to 4 mm crushed grog. Vessels in this handmade and tournette-finished fabric tend to be fired brown to black with lumpy surfaces, although some are partially oxidised. Pots in this somewhat variable fabric come from a variety of sources, including east Kent, the Weald of Sussex and the Ouse valley in the same county. The 1st- and early 2nd-century vessels in this fabric are mainly east Kent types but are supplanted by East Sussex ware forms during the 2nd and early 3rd centuries. East Sussex Ware sometimes has small amounts of ironstone, chert grit and quartz as well as grog and where this is present the coding **B2/ESW** is used. Large storage-jars of the period *c* AD 50-150 tend to be oxidised and are frequently decorated with combing.

B2.1 'Belgic' coarse grog-tempered wares with additional sparse white siltstone grog. Wares in this fabric variant tend to be fairly uncommon over much of east Kent and their much greater frequency at Westhawk Farm may be indicative of a local or Wealden source.

B2.4 Tournette-finished grog-tempered fabric with superior polished finish, fired reddish-brown with black smudges and with frequent lid-seating on both jars and bowls. Vessels from this unknown source are absent from most sites in east Kent but have been seen by the author in assemblages from other, unpublished, sites in the Ashford area such as Waterbrook Farm (Lyne forthcoming a) and the Harville villa at Wye (J Bradshaw pers. comm.). Wares of this type appear *c* AD 120 and continue in circulation until after AD 170. They are probably of local manufacture.

B6 Soft, patchily fired fabric tempered with moderate crushed shell. Perhaps a north Kent product. One sherd only.

B8 'Belgic' fine-sanded soot-soaked wares from south-east Kent. 'Belgic' wares with sand filler are characteristic of the Folkestone area in south-east Kent, where they are common during the late Iron Age and mid to late 1st century (Thompson 1982, 14). At Ashford, however, they are surprisingly rare and represented by a mere handful of pots from 1st-century contexts.

BER1 'Stuppington Lane' (Canterbury) type coarse sandy fabric, tempered with 'black sand' - probably Glauconite. A single sherd from Westhawk Farm is tentatively assigned to this source.

Early Gallo-Belgic and Central Gaulish fine ware imports

Mid 1st-century continental fine ware imports are quite rare on the site and largely restricted to a few white ware flagon and butt-beaker fragments; there is no *terra rubra*.

B17 Hard white or cream, or occasionally pink, fabric with smooth surfaces. Rigby (1995, 648) white ware fabric 1A. Gallo-Belgic, perhaps from Picardy, and usually pre-Conquest. The butt-beaker and flagon sherds encountered here (contexts 7200 and 7575) are assigned to the immediately post-Conquest period.

BER5 Hard fine fabric with variable quantities of very fine clear quartz sand, cf. Rigby (1995, 651) fabric WW1. ?Central or North Gaul, *c* AD 10-50. Butt-beaker and flagon fragments are present and are likely to be post-Conquest.

BER7 Hard off-white fabric with very fine quartz filler and smooth surfaces. Rigby (1995, 648) fabric 1B. Gallo-Belgic. *c* AD 43-70. There is a butt-beaker fragment from the fill of hollow-way 840 and flagon fragments from the fill of pit 640.

BER10 Soft cream fabric with very fine quartz filler and smooth surfaces. Gallo-Belgic from North Gaul (?Picardy). Rigby fabric IIB (1995). Dated *c* AD 43-70. Represented by a few flagon and butt-beaker sherds. Fragments of one such vessel from a fill of waterhole 10460 (7832) have traces of resin lining indicating the flagon's use as a container for wine or some other liquid commodity (Fig. 6.2, no. 24).

BER11 Hard white to pink near sand-free fabric with soft red to black ferrous inclusions. ?Rhenish white ware. Rigby fabric WW1 (1995). 1st century. Represented by a few flagon fragments from plot division gully 10270 and elsewhere.

BER12 Gallo-Belgic *terra nigra*. A rim sherd of a platter of uncertain form in the assemblage from ditch fill context 9107 is the only fragment in this fabric, apart from the micaceous *terra nigra* platter from the late Iron Age burial, 9200.

Early Roman wares

R1 'Native coarse ware' (Pollard 1995, 704). Vessels, mainly knife-trimmed jars, in this somewhat variable handmade and tournette-finished fabric replaced 'Belgic' grog-tempered wares over much of east Kent during the third quarter of the 2nd century. The fabric is characterised by profuse, angular, up to 2 mm, grey grog filler with a little sand and rounded black ferrous inclusions and is fired to a high temperature. The very large quantities at Ickham and Monkton suggest manufacture on coastal sites in the vicinity of the Wantsum Channel during the period *c* AD 170-300; vessels in the fabric are common in early 3rd-century assemblages from sites in the Folkestone area. Such wares are, however, very rare at Westhawk Farm and there are just a handful of sherds from a few 3rd-century contexts.

R5 Canterbury sandy grey wares. Lid-seated and carinated bowls, jars and other forms were supplied to Westhawk Farm in small, but persistent quantities from *c* AD 70 to 175 or later.

R5.1 Pale grey to off-white sandy fabric with sparse brown and black ferrous inclusions, fired rough darker grey. Vessel forms associated with this fabric are similar to those in fabric R5 and it may be that fabric R5.1 is a variant Canterbury grey ware product.

R6 Canterbury oxidised sandy wares. Flagons and *lagenae* in the three colour variants - 6.1, 6.2 and 6.3 (fired orange, red and buff respectively) - were supplied to the site in significant quantities between *c* AD 70 and 200+. Mortaria in fabric R6.1 were also supplied between *c* AD 100 and 150. Other forms are rare. Fragments from a flagon in orange fabric R6.1 from boundary gully 9100 have traces of internal resin lining and may suggest that some at least of these vessels came to the site as packaging for locally-produced wine.

R8.2 Miscellaneous fine sanded red wares. Fragments from a lid-seated jar in this rare fabric of unknown origin come from ditch 1700.

R13 BB1 ware from Poole Harbour (Farrar 1973). Bowls, dishes and cooking-pots in this handmade black fabric with profuse 0.3 mm to 1 mm quartz filler and occasional shale, chert and gypsum inclusions appear in small quantities at Ashford during the late 3rd century just before the abandonment of most of the excavated part of the Roman town.

R14 Thameside BB2 ware (Monaghan 1987). Medium grey to black fabric with profuse ill-sorted fine-to-medium sub-angular grey, colourless and milky quartz filler, fired polished black with brown margins. The overwhelming predominance of undecorated 'pie-dishes' (*c* AD 170-250) and near absence of those with burnished lattice decoration (*c* AD 120-180) suggests that BB2 was a late arrival on the scene

R16 Upchurch ware (Monaghan 1987). Wheel-turned, sand-free, medium-grey fabric with soft brown and grey grog inclusions. Biconical vessels, beakers, flasks and open forms in this fabric make up the bulk of the fine wares supplied to the site during the period *c* AD 50-270.

R17 Fine orange Upchurch/Hoo fabric (Monaghan 1987). Small, but persistent quantities of flagons in this oxidised version of Upchurch ware were supplied to the site during the same period. Their rarity compared with products in reduced Upchurch ware may have been due to a preference for oxidised fabric R6 flagons (and their putative contents) from the somewhat nearer Canterbury kilns.

R25 Cologne ware. Hard, near sand-free white fabric with dark-grey to orange colour-coat. Very small quantities of roughcast beakers and hunt-cups were supplied to the site between *c* AD 130 and 200 or later.

R31 Very fine grey ware with green glaze over white barbotine decoration. A single sherd of this probable Staines-area fabric came from the fill of posthole 239 in structure J. Dated *c* AD 70-150.

R32 Argonne colour-coated ware. Two sherds from the lower part of a roughcast beaker in this sand-free orange fabric with glossy reddish-brown to black colour-coat came from pit 9817. Dated *c* AD 130-200.

R33 Colchester colour-coated ware. Small quantities of roughcast and other types of beakers in this reddish-brown fabric with matt grey to brown colour-coat were supplied to the site between *c* AD 130 and the early 3rd century.

R35 Central Gaulish fine dark colour-coated ware (Symonds 1992). A very small number of beakers and at least one Ritterling 8/Drag. 40 cup copies in this late 2nd-century fabric are present.

R36 *Moselkeramik* (Symonds 1992). A few beakers in this thin-walled, orange/grey, sandwich-fired fabric with metallic colour-coat were supplied to the site during the period *c* AD 200-275, possibly in conjunction with barrels of Moselle wine.

R37 Central Gaulish colour-coated white ware. Hard white to buff sand-free fabric with mica and dark-brown/orange/black colour-coat. A few beaker sherds come from the site, including fragments of a hairpin beaker from the primary silts of ditch 40 (Fig. 6.2, no. 17). *c* AD 70-150.

R42 La Graufesenque South Gaulish samian ware. Dated *c* AD 43-110.

R43 Central Gaulish Les Martres-de-Veyre and Lezoux samian ware. Dated *c* AD 90-200.

R46 East Gaulish samian ware. Dated *c* AD 140-260.

R50 Baetican Dressel 20 amphora fabric. Appreciable quantities of Dressel 20 amphora sherds were found in contexts across the site, ranging in date between the 1st and 3rd centuries. It may be that some of these fragments come from amphorae re-used as plunge pots in the ironworking process, rather than from examples brought in loaded with olive oil.

R56 South Gaulish Gauloise 4 amphora fabric. Quantities of sherds in this fabric are far fewer than those in fabric R50 and mostly from 1st-century contexts.

R63 Kent/Colchester cream-buff ware mortaria (Hartley 1972). A few of these *c* AD 100-150 dated mortaria in cream fabric with crushed flint trituration grits came from contexts 22, 876, 1317, 7122, 7126 and elsewhere. Believed to originate in the Rochester area.

R64 Rhenish mortarium fabric. Three wall-sided mortarium sherds in this very fine sanded buff fabric came from occupation spread 7279.

R65 Verulamium Region white ware. Small numbers of flagons and mortaria in this sandy, oxidised fabric arrived on the site during the period *c* AD 70-150. Traces of resin lining on examples from other sites suggest that the flagons may have been marketed as packaging for wine or some other liquid commodity.

R68 Patchgrove ware. Vessels in this oxidised grog-tempered fabric are rare in east Kent: all of the fragments from Westhawk Farm belong to large, two-handled *lagenae*, which come mainly from late 1st-century contexts.

R71 Miscellaneous oxidised sand-tempered wares.

R73 Miscellaneous sandy grey wares most of which are probably Thameside products. The suffix 'cse' is used for the coarse variants in this range.

R75 Miscellaneous white wares.

R81 Black Eggshell ware (Green 1980). A large part of an elaborate carinated beaker in this fabric came from the fill of pit 7530 and three further sherds from posthole 7748.

R88 General category for a number of pale flagon fabrics of uncertain origin and of late 1st to 2nd century date (Rigby 1995, Fabric WW3). A few of the Westhawk Farm flagon sherds belong in this category and include the variants: **R88A** - sand-free pale orange fabric fired creamy-yellow with grey and pink patches. Some large, fresh possible kiln waster sherds from ring-neck flagons came from pit 5176 and nearby gully 5178 in Area C (nos 1-4). Mid-late 1st century - and **R88B** - very fine-sanded orange flagon fabric with localised cream-buff slip, chiefly on the handles and necks of vessels. A number of sherds came from the 2nd-century midden 7126/7127 and waterhole fill 7314 (no. 170). Vessels in this fabric variant may also be of local manufacture.

R89 Soft powdery cream, beige or pink fabric used for flagons, honey-pots and, as Hartley's fabric

1, for mortaria (Hartley 1977). Rigby's fabric WW4 (1995). Late 1st to early 2nd century. A few *lagena* sherds are present in the pottery from the site. Probably from Picardy.

R95 — Amiens region pentice beaker fabric. Two beaker sherds are present in the large occupation spread assemblage from context 7279, dated *c* AD 170-270.

R98 — Miscellaneous amphorae.

R99 — Miscellaneous mortaria.

R110 — Miscellaneous fine wares.

R113 — Gauloise 12 amphorae.

G238 — Gillam 238 mortaria (Hartley 1977, Group II). Both undeveloped (*c* AD 60-80) and developed mortaria (*c* AD 80-150) in this cream fabric with quartz, flint and limestone trituration grits are present in very small quantities at Westhawk Farm. Bavai in Gallia Belgica appears to have been a major source.

G255 — Gillam 255 mortaria (Hartley 1978). Stubby-flanged mortaria of this type in powdery cream fabric are represented by examples from pit 1233 and ditch 1265, *c* AD 160-230

Hardham — Grey fabric with slightly 'oatmeal' appearance, produced at Hardham in East Sussex. Sherds possibly in this fabric occur in Phase 4 context 8857.

NFSE — A blanket term, as used in London (Davies, *et al.* 1994, 62), for mortaria and flagons in fine buff fabrics deriving either from south-east England or northern France/Belgium. The overall category includes mortaria of Gillam type 238, recorded here as a separate category (G238 above). Only a single sherd was noted, from a Phase 4 context.

RDBK — Buff ring-and-dot beaker fabric, as defined in London (Davies, *et al.* 1994, 142-145). Found in a single Phase 2-3 context (50), but apparently used for a bowl imitating samian form Curle 11.

Late Roman wares

LR1.1 — Late Roman coarse grog-tempered ware with off-white siltstone grog. The distribution of wares of this type (Lyne 1994) suggests that they were made somewhere in the vicinity of Lympne from *c* AD 270 to 400 or later. They are significant in the mid to late 3rd-century assemblages from Westhawk Farm and particularly in the assemblages from the fills of water-hole 796. Some earlier storage-jars were also made in this fabric.

LR2.2 — Fine-grey, sand-tempered Thameside fabric with superficial surface reddening. Cooking-pots in this distinctive fabric appeared *c* AD 180 and were distributed across Kent in large quantities until the early 4th century. A few examples are present in 3rd-century assemblages from Westhawk Farm.

LR2.4 — Coarse version of the same fabric.

LR5.1 — Alice Holt/Farnham industry type grey ware, but slightly coarser and of east Kent origin, possibly from Preston-by-Wingham. A very rare fabric at Westhawk Farm and represented by no more than three sherds from late 3rd- to early 4th-century contexts. Dated *c* AD 270-370.

LR6 — Portchester D/Overwey sandy buff/orange fabric (Fulford 1975; Lyne and Jefferies 1979). Distinctive cream-to-buff surfaced fabric with profuse coarse to very coarse multi-coloured quartz and ironstone sand filler. Two horizontally-rilled jar sherds in this mid to late 4th-century fabric came from pit 415 in the centre of the temple.

LR10 — Oxfordshire colour-coated ware, AD 240-400. Only five small sherds came from the site, one from Phase 7 context, 417, the remainder in unphased contexts.

LR11 — Lower Nene Valley colour-coat wares. A few sherds from beakers in this fabric are present in 3rd-century features on the site and a complete beaker was present in the late burial 5028.

LR13 — Hadham oxidised ware. There are two flag-on sherds from fill 9311 of the 3rd-century pit or waterhole, 8479.

LR21 — Lower Nene Valley white ware. This fabric is represented by a single mortarium from waterhole 796, fill 275.

Salt container briquetage

BER15 — Chaff-tempered fabric, fired patchy white/purple/grey. Handmade salt container sherds in this distinctive fabric are fairly frequent on Late Iron Age and Early Roman sites in Kent. Little cups or bowls in this fabric were used to transport sea-salt to Canterbury until *c* AD 70 (Macpherson-Grant 1980), but transport in similar containers seems to have continued for somewhat longer at Ashford. The largest assemblages of such container fragments come from the 1988 Channel Tunnel site at Folkestone and the latest evidence suggests a source at or near Lydd on Romney Marsh.

Medieval wares

M.1 — Wheel-turned very fine-sanded grey-black fabric fired rough reddish-brown to black. *c* AD 1250-1350.

M.2 — Similar, but with sparse additional shell filler.

Quantification

The overall quantities of pottery fabrics by phase are set out in Tables 6.1 and 6.2, expressed as percentages

Table 6.1   Pottery: Fabrics by phase: Percentage of period or phase sherd count for each fabric (Roman fabrics only) (+ = less than 0.1%).

Fabric	Period 1	0	1	2	2-3	2-4 & 2-5	3	3-4	3-5	4	4-5	5	5-6	6	7	Period 3	Period 4	Total	%
					(Period 2 — Phase)														
Prehistoric	(39)	(1)			(2)				(2)	(7)	(1)	(1)		(1)				(54)	
B1				+													13.4	1	+
B2		2.7		5.3	6.1	5.5	8.3	13.1	4.9	2.3	6.0	2.1					1	3219	4.4
B2 var				1.4	1.9		0.5	0.3		0.2	0.8	9						266	0.4
B2/2.1		0.8						3.4										169	0.2
B2/R1	4.4	46.7		61.1	54.3	66.6	44.8	49.6	33.0	48.6	36.8	37.1	31.3	3.1		20.0	41.9	32719	44.8
B2/R1 var										+	+							3	+
B2/R1/B2.1		9.6					2.5			2.5		11.3						2467	3.4
B2/R1/LR1		0.2										+						3	+
B2/ESW							0.1			0.3	0.3	2.1		11.3				612	0.8
B2.1	57.3	19.0		15.4	18.6	21.4	17.5	14.9	23.8	13.3	14.0	7.1	54.2	5.1		80.0	13.0	9900	13.6
B2.1 var					1.8									0.2				87	0.1
B2.1/R1																		4	+
B2.1/LR1.1		0.9		0.1			0.2	2.7	3.2	0.9	4.9	1.5		8.8			2.4	1009	1.4
B3																		1	+
B5							+											2	+
B6												+						1	+
B8				0.6	0.3		+	0.1		+	0.1	+						57	0.1
B8/R73					0.3													15	+
B11.ELG			100															23	+
B17		0.1		0.5														16	+
BER				0.2	+		2.2	0.1		0.3	+			2				288	0.4
BER1	1.1																	1	+
BER5					0.3		+	0.1										22	+
BER7							+	+		+								5	+
BER10				0.3	+		+					+						13	+
BER11				0.1	+		+			+								11	+
BER12				+	+		+			+								2	+
BER15		0.1			0.1		0.1	0.1		0.3	0.1	+					0.4	110	0.2
R1		0.3		+	+		+	0.2		0.2	1.0	0.3		0.8				161	0.2
R5		0.3		1.6	0.4		1.3	1.7	3.2	3.6	2.6	1.8		0.3			3.6	1659	2.3
R5/73		0.1					+			+								5	+
R6				0.3			0.1			+								22	+
R6.1	19.1	0.4		0.6	3.9		2.7	1.2	1.1	2.3	2.0	1.0	2.1	0.5			1.6	1493	2.0
R6.2							+	+		+	0.1	0.1						17	+
R6.3		0.5		0.4	0.6		2.8	0.4	1.1	0.8	0.7	1.2		0.2			0.8	802	1.1
R6.3 var							+			+								7	+
R8.1										+								4	+
R8.2					+		+			+								12	+
R13				0.1	0.1						0.1	0.1	2.1	0.6				36	+
R14		1.1		1.2	0.1		0.2	0.3	4.3	1.3	2.4	3.5		6.5	5.6		0.4	1146	1.6
R14/73							+			+								10	+

(Continued on next page)

Table 6.1 (Continued).

Fabric	Period 1	Period 2														Period 3	Period 4	Total	%
		Phase																	
		0	1	2	2-3	2-4 & 2-5	3	3-4	3-5	4	4-5	5	5-6	6	7				
R16	15.7	5.2		7.9	5.7	1.9	7.1	4.8	13.0	14.8	14.3	17.4	4.2	19.5	29.6		5.9	9025	12.4
R16 cse					+					0.1	0.3							38	0.1
R17		0.6		0.8	2.3	2.1	2.5	1.7		0.9	2.2	1.5		2.0			2.0	1112	1.5
R17 var														0.1				2	+
R22										+								1	+
R25							0.1	0.2		0.2	0.2	0.1						96	0.1
R27											+							1	+
R31										+								1	+
R32										+								2	+
R33										0.3								77	0.1
R35							+			+	+	0.1		0.2				14	+
R36										+		0.3		0.2				37	0.1
R37							0.2			+								42	0.1
R42		1.8		0.8	0.9		1.1	1.0		0.3	0.4	0.2		0.1			4.3	394	0.5
R42/43	2.2						+			+	+							5	+
R43		0.3		0.3	0.2		0.7	1.2	0.5	2.0	2.1	2.2	2.1	4.7	5.6		0.8	1189	1.6
R46										0.2	0.2	0.4	2.1	1.4				140	0.2
R46.1										+	+							4	+
R50		3.9		0.2	0.7	1.1	0.7	0.8	1.6	1.5	0.7	1.0		1.0			0.8	807	1.1
R56		0.5			+		0.3		4.3	+	+	+		0.5			2.0	82	0.1
R61							0.1			+								10	+
R62										+	+							2	+
R63		0.1					+			+								11	+
R64		1.0					0.1			+		0.1		0.2				19	+
R65		0.2			+		+			+	0.1	+					0.4	43	0.1
R68				0.2			0.1			+				0.2				24	+
R70										+								2	+
R71		0.1		0.1	0.4		+	1.2	0.5	0.1	0.7	0.1		0.4	1.4			151	0.2
R73						1.5	0.7	0.6	4.3	0.8	2.1	3.7	2.1	5.4			1.6	999	1.4
R73 cse							0.1					+			1.4			10	+
R74										0.1	+	+						21	+
R74.3										+								1	+

Fabric	1	2	3	4	5	6	7	8	9	10	11	12	13	14	15	16	Total (n)	Total (%)
R75		0.1			0.2		0.1	0.1		0.2	0.6	0.1					139	0.2
R81							+			+							9	+
R95																	2	+
R98					+		+			+	+	+					9	+
R99				0.2	+		0.1			0.2	0.1	+		0.1/0.2			90	0.1
R109												+					1	+
R110										+		+					4	+
R113										+		+					12	+
Flint												+					1	+
G238		0.1			0.1		0.1			+		+					20	+
G255											0.2	0.1					17	+
HARDHAM										0.2		0.2					68	0.1
NFSE										+							1	+
RDBK					+					+							2	+
LR1.1		1.4					+			0.1	2.2	1.2		24.8	42.3		864	1.2
LR2									1.1	0.2	0.4	0.8		0.3			180	0.2
LR2.1										+	0.1	+		0.2			21	+
LR2.2										+		+		0.5			30	+
LR2.3										+				+			2	+
LR2.4										+	+			+			2	+
LR5										+				+			3	+
LR5.1												+		+			1	+
LR6									0.5						2.8		3	+
LR10										+	+	+			1.4		5	+
LR11										+	+	+		+			11	+
LR13												+		0.1			3	+
MISC		0.2		0.2	0.4		2.5	0.1	0.5	0.6	1.1	1.0		0.5	9.9	4.0	732	1.0
MISC FINE		1.9					0.2			+	0.1			+			41	0.1
Medieval	89	(6)	23		(2)									(418)		5	(426)	
TOTAL Roman fabrics only	89	1165	23	2918	4885	476	12394	3449	187	28423	4703	11741	48	2205	71	253	73035	
%age of assemblage	0.1	1.6	+	4.0	6.7	0.7	17.0	4.7	0.3	38.9	6.4	16.1	0.1	3.0	0.1	0.3		

Table 6.2   Pottery: Fabrics by phase: Percentage of period or phase weight total for each fabric (Roman fabrics only) (+ = less than 0.1%).

Fabric	Period 1	Period 2 Phase														Period 3	Period 4	Total	%
		0	1	2	2-3	2-4 & 2-5	3	3-4	3-5	4	4-5	5	5-6	6	7				
Prehistoric	(286)	(4)		(4)	(10)				(4)	(180)		(14)		(4)				(502)	
B1				0.8														298	+
B2		2.1		4.9	8.3	5.1	4.6	13.7	2.6	3.0	6.6	1.9					18.8	34904	4.0
B2 var					1.1		0.2	0.3		0.2	0.7	0.1					0.4	2248	0.3
B2/2.1		0.4		0.4				3.1										1468	0.2
B2/R1	(26)	46.0		47.7	72.4	31.2	43.3	46.3	28.0	44.8	30.9	30.7	19.9	2.4		1.8	30.3	342417	40.4
B2/R1 var										+								36	+
B2/R1/B2.1		3.1					2.3			2.4	+	9.2						21957	2.5
B2/R1/LR1		0.2										+						38	+
B2/ESW							+			0.4	0.6	3.2		10.2				11097	1.3
B2.1	(576)	18.1		30.8	3.7	49.1	31.8	21.7	41.4	22.1	20.7	16.2	70.8	4.5		98.2	12.8	179515	21.2
B2.1 var					1.2													606	0.1
B2.1/R1														0.2				106	+
B2.1/LR1.1		1.4		0.2			0.2	3.8	2.2	1.6	9.7	2.5		13.3			2.6	23189	2.7
B3																	0.4	10	+
B5							+											16	+
B6												+						2	+
B8				0.4	0.2		+	0.1		+	0.1	+						434	0.1
B8/R73					0.2													106	+
B11.ELG			100															909	+
B17				0.3														106	+
BER	(4)	+		0.1	0.1		1.5			+	+			+				2292	0.3
BER1							+											4	+
BER5							+	+										96	+
BER7					0.1		+	+		+								26	+
BER10				0.7	0.2		+											368	+
BER11				0.2	+		+			+		+						107	+
BER12		0.1					+			+								14	+
BER15		+		+	0.1		+	+		0.1	+	+					0.1	282	+
R1		0.5		1.0	+		0.1	0.3		0.6	2.2	1.0		1.0				5319	0.6
R5		0.3			0.1		0.8	1.3	1.7	3.1	1.4	1.5		0.1			3.3	14576	1.7
R5/73		+								+								8	+
R6				0.1			+			+								124	+
R6.1	(24)	0.6		0.5	1.4		1.3	0.6	3.4	1.5	0.8	0.6	0.2	0.7			0.2	9582	1.1
R6.2										+	+	+						70	+
R6.3		0.1		0.2	0.5		0.8	0.1	0.6	0.4	0.3	0.6		0.6			0.7	4170	0.5
R6.3 var										0.1								182	+
R8.1										+								58	+
R8.2							+			+								126	+
R13				+							0.1	0.1	0.4	0.5				470	0.1
R14		2.4		0.6	0.2		0.1	0.2	1.9	1.4	3.2	4.7		4.3	1.4		0.1	15004	1.7

	(n)	1	2	3	4	5	6	7	8	9	10	11	12	13	14	Total	%
R14/73									+							148	+
R16	(50)	1.8	4.2	2.1	0.4	2.4	1.3	7.1	6.4	6.5	7.2	1.5	9.5	6.1	8.7	44769	5.2
R16 cse				0.1					+	0.3			0.9			372	+
R17		0.1	0.3	1.9	1.3	0.9	1.1		0.5	0.6	2.5		0.2		0.4	8286	1.0
R17 var																106	+
R22									+	+						1	+
R25						+	+		0.1	+	+					265	+
R27										+						6	+
R31									+							1	+
R32									+							24	+
R33									0.1	+	+					365	+
R35						=			+	+	+		0.1			89	+
R36									+		+		+			67	+
R37		1.4	1.0	+		+	0.6		0.3	0.2						145	+
R42				0.8		1.1					0.1		+		2.7	4096	0.5
R42/43						+			+							11	+
R43	(86)	0.1	0.2	0.1		0.5	1.2	0.9	2.5	1.4	2.9	0.4	3.2	5.2	1.7	15386	1.8
R46						+			0.1	0.2	1.3	5.9	2.2			3368	0.4
R46.1									+	+						21	
R50		7.9	4.4	4.3	7.1	4.0	3.3	0.5	5.6	3.0	4.6		3.3		8.0	39249	4.6
R56		0.8		+		0.4		2.6	+	0.1	0.1		0.4		5.7	1298	0.2
R61						0.3					+					430	+
R62										0.1						62	+
R63				+		+			0.2							778	0.1
R64		0.5				0.1			0.1	0.3	0.3		0.3			970	0.1
R65		6.7				0.3			+		+				0.3	1282	0.1
R68		0.4	0.6						0.1	0.1			0.3			1148	0.1
R70									+		+					12	+
R71		0.1	+	0.3	5.8	+	0.6	0.1	0.5	0.2		0.8	0.8	1.1		1343	0.2
R73						0.3	0.2	3.1		1.3	3.2		4.7		0.9	9401	1.1
R73 cse														0.5		70	+
R74											+					120	+
R74.3						+										48	+
R75		+		0.2		+	+		0.1	0.5	0.2					1142	0.1
R80.81									+							52	+
R95											+					3	+
R98			0.2	0.1		+					0.1		+			394	+
R99				+		0.1			0.2	0.5			1.1			2203	0.3
R109											+					40	+
R110											+					12	+
R113						0.3					0.1					156	+
Flint																2	+
G238		0.8		0.1		0.2			0.1		+					738	0.1
G255										0.4	0.2					418	+
HARDHAM									0.1							360	+
NFSE				0.1					+							10	+
RDBK		2.3														30	+
LR1.1									0.3	6.6	3.5		33.2	77.3		28121	3.3
LR2									0.2	0.3	0.4		0.4			1363	0.2

(Continued on next page)

Table 6.2 (Continued).

Fabric	Period 1	Period 2														Period 3	Period 4	Total	%
		Phase																	
		0	1	2	2-3	2-4 & 2-5	3	3-4	3-5	4	4-5	5	5-6	6	7				
LR2.1										0.1	0.1	+		0.2				409	0.1
LR2.2										+		0.1		0.2				302	+
LR2.3										+				0.1				79	+
LR2.4											+			+				18	+
LR5										+				+				28	+
LR5.1														+				4	+
LR6									0.4						1.6			20	+
LR10															1.4			34	+
LR11										+	+	+		0.8				451	0.1
LR13		0.1																26	+
MISC		1.8		0.3			1.3	0.3	0.1	0.2	0.2	0.5		0.1	5.4		1.9	3917	0.5
MISC FINE					+		+			+	+			+				209	+
Medieval	(38)				(56)											(5086)		(5180)	
TOTAL Roman fabrics only	766	13546	909	35738	49882	3824	150202	41121	1548	316717	58094	115254	472	54864	882	448	2343	846618	
%	0.1	1.6	0.1	4.2	5.9	0.5	17.7	4.9	0.2	37.4	6.9	13.6	0.1	6.4	0.1	0.1	0.3		

of the total material in each phase by sherd count and weight respectively. These tables represent the background against which the more specific data extracted from selected assemblages below should be viewed.

Assemblages from Area C

Note that the pottery from graves in this area is listed in the grave catalogue (see Chapter 8).

Assemblage 1 (Fig. 6.1). From the fill 5175 of pit 5176 (Period 2, Phase 3). This context produced 164 sherds (1698 g) of pottery, all of which is derived from at least four flagons in fabric R88A and includes large, fresh fragments:

1 **Ring-neck flagon** in sand-free pale orange fabric R88A fired creamy yellow with grey patches. Rim D: 90 mm. Context 5175 (feature 5176) Phase 3.
2 **Ring-neck flagon**. Similar fabric (R88A) fired grey with cream-yellow surfaces. Rim D: 90 mm. Context 5175 (feature 5176) Phase 3.
3 **Ring-neck flagon** Fabric R88A fired cream. Rim D: 100 mm. Context 5175 (feature 5176) Phase 3.
4 **Ring-neck flagon**. Fabric R88A of uncertain rim diameter. Context 5175 (feature 5176) Phase 3.

The nearby gully 5178 produced a further 64 sherds from yet another flagon in this fabric fired patchy pink-red/cream-buff. The patchy firing of the sherds suggests that they could be wasters from a nearby kiln, although this is by no means certain. This material could to at any time between AD 70 and 200 but furrowed jar sherds in association with the fragments from gully 5178 suggest a date in the late 1st century.

Assemblages from Area B

Period 1: Prehistoric

Pit 791, posthole 1130 and soil spread 8242 between them produced 46 sherds of calcined-flint tempered pottery (462 g). Some of the sherds are abraded. This material lacks diagnostic fragments, but its general character, and the thickness of many of the sherds, is consistent with a middle Bronze Age date. Posthole 1130, which produced 7 sherds (176 g) of this pottery, is assigned to Period 2, Phase 4, and the prehistoric pottery is presumably redeposited.

Period 2, Phase 2 (AD 43-70)

From building A and ?related ditches

Assemblage 2 (Fig. 6.1). From a deposit (context 9543) overlying the fills of ditch 9480, which was a component of the possible Bronze Age field system. This deposit produced 68 sherds (572 g) of early-looking material, including fragments from an Upchurch fine ware beaker and much of the following vessel:

5 **Cordoned jar** with black paint on the neck, in brown-grey grog-tempered fabric B2.1. Rim D: 180 mm. Context 9543, Phase 2.

Assemblage 3 (Table 6.3; Fig. 6.1). From the fills (contexts 8767, 8791, 8793, 8879 and 8849) of the pen-annular eaves-drip gully 8790 around circular Building A. The fills of this feature produced 495 sherds (4236 g) of pottery mostly of pre-Flavian character; suggesting that the building was contemporary with deposit 9543 which overlay prehistoric ditch 9480. The assemblage has an overwhelming predominance of grog-tempered sherds (92.2%) by sherd count including:

6 **Necked bowl** in brown-black fabric B2/R1. Rim D: 180 mm. Context 8793 (Group 8790) Phase 2.
7 **Jar with undercut bead-rim** in fabric B2/R1. Rim D: 160 mm. Context 879 (Group 8790) Phase 2.
8 **Necked and cordoned jar** in fabric B2/R1 fired black. Context 879 (Group 8790) Phase 2.
9 **Type 3 foot-ring platter** (Stead and Rigby 1989) in fabric B2/R1 fired black. Dated *c* AD 50-80. Rim D: 160 mm. Context 887 (Group 8790) Phase 2.

Imported wares include fragments from a South Gaulish samian Drag. 18 platter (*c* AD 43-90) and a Drag. 29 bowl (*c* AD 43-85), as well as a biconical vessel in grey Upchurch fine ware (*c* AD 45-130).

From boundary ditches 40/860 and 8620

Assemblage 4 (Table 6.4; Fig. 6.1). From the primary silts (contexts 9, 60, 180, 822, 836, 892 and 926) of ditch 40/860. The primary silts produced a total of 532 sherds (7938 g) of pottery, which were quantified by numbers of sherds and their weights per fabric. Table 6.4 reveals an assemblage totally dominated by 'Belgic' grog-tempered wares (82% by sherd count), with just a few fragments in the sandy soot-soaked 'Belgic' fabric B8 characteristic of the Folkestone area of Kent (Thompson 1982). The fine ware imports include the lower part of a rouletted butt-beaker in grey Upchurch fabric R16 (*c* AD 45-80), as well as fragments from a South Gaulish samian Drag. 27 cup (*c* AD 43-110) and Drag. 18 platter (*c* AD 43-90). The following pieces are also present:

10 **Bead-rim jar** of Thompson type B5-5 (1982) in patchy brown/black fabric B2.1 with traces of resin on upper half. Complete. Vessels of this type tend to be pre-Conquest in date. Rim D: 130 mm. Context 60 (Group 40) Phase 2.
11 **Slack-profiled jar** with weakly everted-rim in black fabric B2 with polished patchy black/brown exterior. Rim D: 180 mm. Contexts 892 and 926 (Group 860) Phase 2.
12 **Cordoned jar** of Thompson type B2-1 in patchy brown/black/orange fabric B2.1. Late Iron Age-AD 60. Rim D: 80 mm. Context 9 (Group 40) Phase 2.
13 **Cordoned jar**, of type C8-1 with finger-impressed cordon around shoulder, in similar fabric (B2.1), fired grey with polished black surfaces. Late Iron

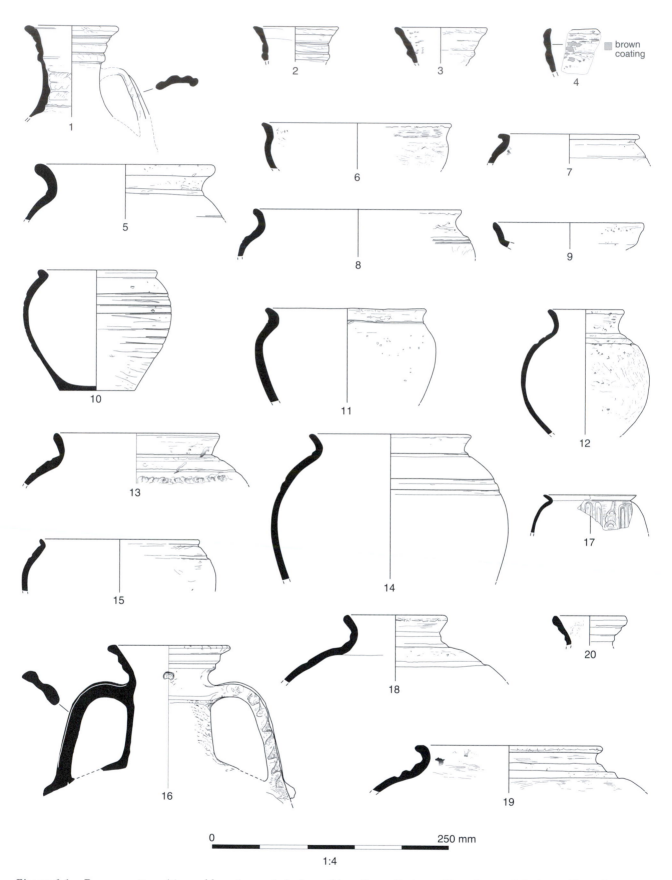

Figure 6.1   Roman pottery (Assemblage 1: nos 1-4; Assemblage 2: no. 5; Assemblage 3: nos 6-9; Assemblage 4: nos 10-17; Assemblage 5: nos 18-20).

Table 6.3   Pottery assemblage 3: Fabric quantification by sherd count and weight.

Fabric	Sherds	% sherds	Weight (g)	% weight
B2	422	85.3	3645	86.0
B2.1 Store-jar	34	6.9	388	9.1
B2.1	3	0.6	62	1.5
R16	25	5.1	61	1.4
R17	2	0.4	2	0.1
R42	7	1.4	34	0.8
R50	1	0.2	42	1.0
MISC	1	0.2	2	0.1
Total	495		4236	

Table 6.4   Pottery assemblage 4: Fabric quantification by sherd count and weight.

Fabric	Sherds	% sherds	Weight (g)	% weight
B2	331	62.2	4173	52.6
B2.1	106	19.9	2650	33.4
B8	15	2.8	106	1.3
R6.1	14	2.6	48	0.6
R16	27	5.1	260	3.3
R17	28	5.3	534	6.7
R37	4	0.8	27	0.3
R42	3	0.6	40	0.5
R50	3	0.6	96	1.2
R71	1	0.2	4	0.1
Total	532		7938	

Age-AD 50. Rim D: 180 mm. Context 9 (Group 40) Phase 2.

14   **Cordoned jar** with shoulder groove in grey-fired fabric B2, polished black. Rim D: 180 mm. Context 9 (Group 40) Phase 2.

15   **Bead-rim beaker** in similar fabric (B2), fired patchy orange/grey. Late Iron Age-AD 50. Rim D: 160 mm. Context 836 (Group 40) Phase 2.

16   **Ring-neck** *lagena* in orange fabric R17 with two finger-impressed strap-handles. The type is absent from Monaghan's corpus (1987), but the rim treatment suggests a date-range of *c* AD 70-150. Rim D: 130 mm. Context 9 (Group 40) Phase 2.

17   **Hairpin beaker** in Central Gaulish White ware fabric R37 with black colour-coat. Dated *c* AD 60-120. Rim D: 100 mm. Context 9 (Group 40) Phase 2.

The make-up of this assemblage suggests that the ditch was cut at about the time of the Roman Conquest or slightly earlier and that its primary silts were still receiving pottery until after AD 60. The primary fill (context 8569) of the continuation of this ditch - ditch 8700 - produced a further 29 sherds (438 g) of pottery, including flagon fragments in sandy buff Canterbury fabric (*c* AD 70+).

A further length of ditch passing under the later road looks in plan like a continuation of ditch 8700, but the character of its fill suggests that it was prehistoric in origin. The fill (context 7052) produced 12 sherds (76 g) of pottery, including a jar fragment in the largely late Iron Age/pre-Flavian soot-soaked sandy fabric B8 and combed grog-tempered closed form sherds. This material was presumably intrusive.

From the roadside and enclosure ditches

Assemblage 5 (Fig. 6.1). From the primary fills (contexts 7015, 7890, 7921, 8224, 8294, 8279, 8426, 8496, 8578, 8984, 9071, 9626, 10268 and 10426) of the first roadside ditch 8950. Most of the primary siltings in the sections through the fills of ditch 8950 were lacking in pottery, but a total of 216 sherds (4314 g) was recovered. The sherds include fragments from Dressel 20 olive-oil amphorae, a grey Upchurch fine ware

7A2 platter (*c* AD 43-140) and a South Gaulish samian Drag. 36 bowl (*c* AD 70-110). The nature of the fills is such that some of the later material could easily have been intrusive.

18   **Narrow-mouthed-jar** of Thompson type B3-8 in brown-black, grog-tempered ware fabric B2/R1. Much of this vessel is present. Dated *c* AD 43-100. Rim D: 100 mm. Context 8486 (feature 8950) Phase 2.

19   **Jar with corrugated neck** in black fabric B2.1, fired patchy black/buff externally. As Pollard type 29 (1988), but undecorated. Dated *c* AD 43-150. Rim D: 220 mm. Context 8578 (feature 8950) Phase 2.

20   **Ring-necked flagon** in buff Canterbury sand-tempered fabric R6.3. Dated *c* AD 70-150. Rim D: 80 mm. Context 8984 (feature 8950) Phase 2.

Assemblage 6. From the fills (contexts 7591, 7759, 7905, 7937, 7965, 8004, 8005, 8084, 8093, 8094 and 9015) of ditch 8620 south-east of the road. The various cuts across the fills of this ditch yielded 239 sherds (3544 g) of pottery of broadly similar make-up and date to that from ditch 40/860/8700 (Assemblage 4) across the road. This material includes body sherds from a barrel-beaker in sandy black Folkestone area fabric B8 (*c* late Iron Age-AD 60), a rim sherd from another example in black grog-tempered ware, bead-rim jars in similar fabric, a South Gaulish samian Drag. 29 bowl (*c* AD 50-70) and a Drag. 18 platter (*c* AD 43-90).

From the waterholes

Assemblage 7 (Fig. 6.2). From the upper fill (context 7832) of waterhole 10460. The lower fills of this feature were lacking in pottery, but the upper fill yielded 204 sherds (4464 g) of pre-Flavian pottery including the following:

21   Lower part of a **cordoned butt-beaker copy**, of King Harry Lane type 1K10 (Stead and Rigby 1989) in patchy orange/grey/black fabric B2.1. Dated *c* AD 10-50. Context 7832 (Group 10460) Phase 2.

22   **Necked-jar/bowl** of Thompson type G2-3 (1982) in black-brown fabric B2 with orange patches.

Dated *c* AD 10-50. Rim D: 130 mm. Context 7832 (Group 10460) Phase 2.

23 **Barrel jar** of Thompson type B5-3 in grey-black fabric B2.1. Dated *c* 1-AD 50. Rim D: 200 mm. Context 7832 (Group 10460) Phase 2.

24 Complete top of **ring-necked flagon** in white ware fabric R88. The presence of internal resin lining indicates that the vessel was probably traded to the site containing wine. Dated *c* AD 50-80. Rim D: 70 mm. Context 7832 (Group 10460) Phase 2.

25 **Biconical vessel** of Monaghan form 2G2-3 (1987) in grey Upchurch fine ware fabric R16. Dated *c* AD 45-100. Rim D: 100 mm. Context 7832 (Group 10460) Phase 2.

The assemblage also includes the lower three-quarters of a jar in grog-tempered ware with external scratched decoration that was probably deposited around AD 50-60.

Period 2, Phase 3 (AD 70-150)

From the roadside and enclosure ditches

Assemblage 8 (Fig. 6.2). From the upper fills (contexts 172, 740, 741, 742, 752, 753, 821, 924 and 925) of ditch 860. The upper fills of ditch 860 produced a total of 552 sherds (6773 g) of pottery with a very similar fabric breakdown to that of Assemblage 4. The grog-tempered ware fabrics B2 and B2.1 account for a virtually identical 82% of the assemblage by sherd count, with Canterbury, Upchurch and South Gaulish samian products making up most of the rest. The samian includes fragments from Drag. 29 bowls, Drag. 18 platters and a Drag. 27 cup. There are also fragments from Hoo flagons and Canterbury flagons in fabrics R6.1 and 6.3, as well as the following unusual vessel.

26 **Tiny bowl** with in-turned rim in sandy buff-orange fabric R6.1. Rim D: 100 mm. Context 172, (Group 860) Phase 3.

There is nothing that needs be later than *c* AD 80-90.

Assemblage 9 (Table 6.5; Fig. 6.2). From the upper fills of ditches 8950 and 10070. The various fill contexts produced a total of 1880 sherds (26010 g) of pottery; a large enough assemblage for quantification by Estimated Vessel Equivalents (EVE) based on rims. The quantification of Assemblage 9 (Table 6.5) is based therefore on a different methodology to that used for Assemblages 3 and 4 (Tables 6.3 and 6.4) above. The difference in quantification methodology notwithstanding, the figures suggest that grog-tempered wares have declined in the significance to less than 60% of the entire assemblage, and conversely that imported wares have increased in significance, when Assemblage 9 is compared to assemblages 3 and 4. There are very few open forms and most of these are in South Gaulish samian.

The imported wares include fragments from various vessels: South Gaulish Drag. 35 (*c* AD 70-110),

Drag. 36 (*c* AD 70-110), Drag. 18 (*c* AD 43-90) and Drag. 67 (*c* AD 70-110) forms, a Martres-de-Veyre Drag. 36 (*c* AD 90-120) platter and Central Gaulish samian Drag. 18/31 platter (*c* AD 120-150), sandy orange Canterbury flagon sherds, chaff-tempered salt-container fragments and Upchurch biconical vessels (*c* AD 45-130). The following are also present:

27 **Mortarium**, developed Gillam Type 238, in cream-buff fabric (G238). Two large fresh sherds are present. Dated *c* AD 80-150. Rim D: 300 mm. Context 8294 (Group 10070) Phase 3.

28 **Everted-rim jar** with multiple cordoned shoulder in patchy black/red, grog-tempered fabric. Fabric B2/R1. Much of this vessel is present. Rim D: 180 mm. Context 7011 (Group 8950) Phase 3.

29 **Bead-rim jar** with corrugated neck, in black grog-tempered fabric B2.1, fired brown externally. Rim D: 200 mm. Context 7920 (Group 8950) Phase 3.

30 **Necked and cordoned bowl** in black fabric B2.1 with external polish. One of several examples. Rim D: 140 mm. Context 7920 (Group 8950) Phase 3.

31 **Cordoned jar** with lid-seated rim in brown-black fabric B2.3. Most of this vessel is present. Rim D: 140 mm. Context 10115 (Group 10070) Phase 3.

32 **Pulley-rim flagon** in sandy buff Canterbury fabric R6.3. Dated *c* AD 70-150. Rim D: 60 mm. Context 7918 (Group 8950) Phase 3.

33 **Triangular-section rim flagon** in pinkish-cream sandy fabric R6.3. Rim D: 100 mm. Context 7918 (Group 8950) Phase 3.

34 **Ring-necked flagon** in black-cored red Hoo fabric R17. Rim D: 100 mm. Context 9922 (Group 10070) Phase 3.

35 **Mortarium** in sandy orange Canterbury fabric R6.1. Dated *c* AD 100-150. Rim D: 180 mm. Context 10441 (Group 10070) Phase 3.

A fragment of a grog-tempered, girth-cordoned jar from the Newhaven area of East Sussex is also present. The latest dated fragment is of a Central Gaulish samian Drag. 18/31 platter from the uppermost ditch fill (context 10115) in cut 10112 and suggests that the feature remained in use until just after AD 120.

From the structures and related features

Assemblage 10 (Figs 6.2 and 6.3). From the fills (contexts 103, 104, 111, 112, 150, 722, 1402, 1501 and 1502) of the first enclosure gully (110/200) around structure I. Enclosure gully 200 and its north-western extension 110 cutting ditch 40 produced a total of 207 sherds (3488 g) of excavated and 21 sherds (106 g) of sieved pottery. This material includes fragments from South Gaulish samian Drag. 29 and Drag. 37 bowls (*c* AD 43-85 and AD 70-110) and a Drag. 18/31 platter (*c* AD 90-110), a jar of Monaghan Type 4A1 (*c* AD 70-120) and a biconical vessel (*c* AD 50-130) in fine Upchurch grey ware, and fragments from a flagon in sandy buff Canterbury fabric R6.3. Pieces from the following vessels are also present:

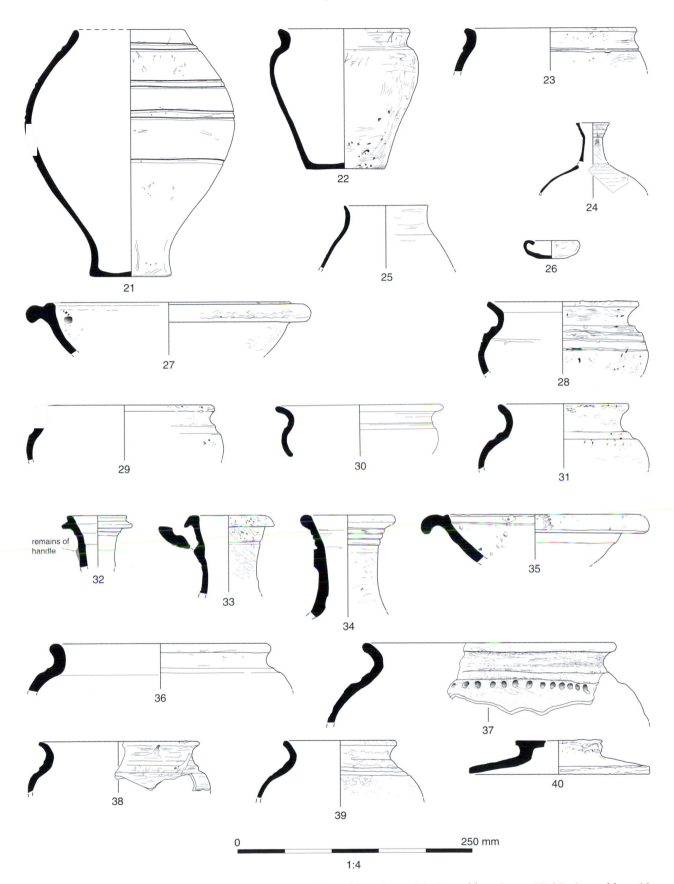

Figure 6.2   Roman pottery (Assemblage 7: nos 21-25; Assemblage 8: no. 26; Assemblage 9: nos 27-35; Assemblage 10: nos 36-40 continues).

Table 6.5   Pottery assemblage 9: Fabric and form quantification by EVEs (+ = present, though lacking rim).

Fabric	Jars	Bowls	Dishes	Beakers	Store-jars	Others	Total	%
B2	3.78	0.05	0.07		+		3.90	46.0
B2.1	0.62		0.09				0.71	8.4
B2.3	0.32						0.32	3.8
R6.1						Mortarium 0.17	0.17	2.0
R6.3						Flagon 0.61	0.61	7.2
R16	0.11	0.05	0.07	0.42			0.65	7.7
R17						Flagon 1.00	1.00	11.8
R42			0.36				0.36	4.2
R43			0.10				0.10	1.2
R71	0.12						0.12	1.4
R75						Flagon 0.54	0.54	6.3
Total	4.95	0.10	0.69	0.42	+	2.32	8.48	
%	58.4	1.2	8.1	5.0		27.3		

36 **Cordoned jar** in black fabric B2. Rim D: 220 mm. Primary silting, Context 1502 (Group 200) Phase 3.

37 **Jar with corrugated neck and stabbed shoulder** in high-fired, blue-grey fabric B2.1. Several large fresh sherds from this vessel are present. Rim D: 270 mm. Primary silting, Context 103 (Group 110) Phase 3.

38 **Jar**, smaller version in black fabric B2.4, fired polished reddish-brown. Rim D: 160 mm. Primary silting, Context 112 (Group 110) Phase 3.

39 **Cordoned-jar** in grey fabric B2.1 with black paint around its neck. Rim D: 130 mm. Context 111 (Group 110) Phase 3.

40 **Lid** in grey-brown, grog-tempered fabric B2. ?Re-fired. Rim D: 200 mm. Context 1501 (Group 200) Phase 3.

41 **Jar** in brown-black, grog-tempered fabric B2.1 with weak bead-rim flattened and polished on its upper surface for lid seating. Context 1501 (Group 200) Phase 3.

42 **Necked and cordoned jar** in patchy orange/black fabric B2. Rim D: 140 mm. Context 1501 (Group 200) Phase 3.

The pottery from this feature suggests a date of *c* AD 80-120+. A later series of enclosure gullies (300, 1400, 1610, 1620 and 8850) yielded very little pottery (46 sherds, 764 g). These fragments include a Central Gaulish Drag. 18/31 platter (*c* AD 120-150), a reeded-rim bowl in Canterbury sandy grey ware (*c* AD 120-175) and a fragment from a BB2 vessel. These sherds indicate that structure I remained in use during the second quarter of the 2nd century.

The interior of the structure I enclosure produced very little pottery indeed, perhaps indicating that it was entirely given over to industrial activity. Pit 316 contained a large truncated storage jar in patchy-fired grog-tempered fabric B2.1 (*c* AD 43-150); the 23 sherds from pit 483 included fresh fragments from the following two vessels:

43 **Lid-seated hemispherical bowl** in polished reddish-brown/black fabric B2.4. Dated *c* AD 120-170. Rim D: 220 mm. Context 482 (feature 483) Phase 3.

44 **Bead-rim beaker** in patchy grey/black polished fabric B2.1. Rim D: 120 mm. Context 480 (feature 483) Phase 3.

Assemblage 11 (Fig. 6.3). From the fills (contexts 7013, 7886, 8566, 8943 and 9627) of ditch 8960/8690. Feature 8690 was linked to the enclosure gullies around Structure I and was therefore contemporary with the life of that structure. It extended to the line of the Canterbury road. A possible continuation to the south-west, though perhaps later in date, was road-side ditch 8960, a recut of the Phase 2 roadside ditch 8950. Ditch 8960/8690 yielded 105 sherds (1380 g) of pottery, including chips of Central Gaulish samian, a Verulamium region white ware amphora rim sherd of Frere type 1948 (1984; *c* AD 105-115) and the following pieces:

45 **Mortarium** in sandy orange Canterbury fabric R6.1. Dated *c* AD 100-150. Exterior rim D: 240 mm. Context 7886 (Group 8960) Phase 3.

46 **Segmental flanged bowl** of Monaghan type 5B3 (1987) in grey Upchurch fine ware fabric R16. Two large, fresh sherds are present. Dated *c* AD 70-130. Rim D: 190 mm. Context 7886 (Group 8960) Phase 3.

47 **Necked and cordoned bowl** of Monaghan type 4B0.1 with girth carination, in fabric R16. Dated *c* AD 70-130. Rim D: 160 mm. Context 8943 (Group 8690) Phase 3.

Other Upchurch fine grey ware sherds include fragments of a beaker of Monaghan type 2H1 (c. AD 80-130) and an everted rim beaker dated to post AD 120. Amounts of pottery are rather small, but they suggest a date of *c* AD 120-150 for this ditch.

Assemblage 12. From the fills (contexts 71, 87, 90, 91, 94, 174, 185, 414, 424 and 453) of ditch 70 around the temple precinct. This ditch produced very little pottery (42 sherds, 234 g), most of which is heavily broken-up and includes nothing that needs be later than AD 100. The sherds are made up almost entirely of featureless body sherds, but include two sherds from a South Gaulish samian Drag. 18/31 platter (*c* AD 90-

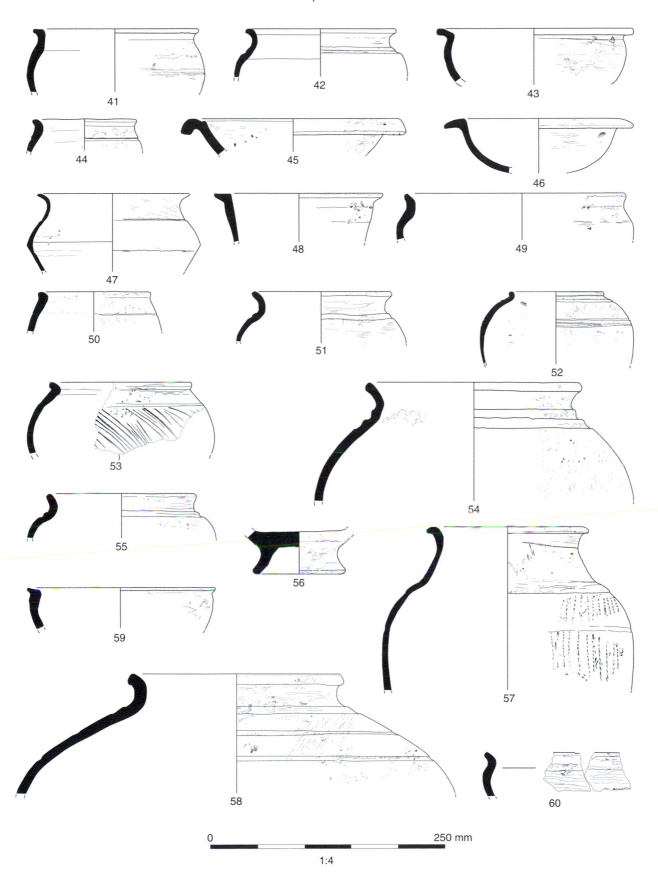

Figure 6.3   Roman pottery (Assemblage 10 (cont.): nos 41-44; Assemblage 11: nos 45-47; Assemblage 13: no. 48; Assemblage 15: no. 49; Assemblage 16: nos 50-51; Assemblage 17: nos 52-60 continues).

110). It is possible that all of this material is residual, as the only sherds in a constructional context from the temple itself are two fragments of Central Gaulish samian (*c* AD 120-200) from the packing of posthole 278 (context 279).

Assemblage 13 (Fig. 6.3). From the fills (contexts 7372, 7395 and 7406) of the eaves drip gully 8250 for structure H. The 139 sherds (1138 g) of pottery from this feature include a bead-rim jar fragment in grog-tempered 'Belgic' fabric B2.1 (*c* AD 43-100), a sherd in sandy black Folkestone region fabric B8 (*c* AD 43-100), 13 sherds from a Cologne beaker (*c* AD 130-200), a fragment from an East Gaulish samian Drag. 38 bowl (*c* AD 140-230) and a number of fresh fragments from the following vessel:

48　**Flanged bowl** in polished patchy brown-black grog-tempered fabric B2.3. Dated *c* AD 120-170. Rim D: 180 mm. Context 7372 (Group 8250) Phase 3.

Assemblage 14. From the fills (contexts 8623, 8625, 8627 and 8629) of the eaves-drip gully 9990 for structure K. The 112 sherds (1224 g) of pottery from the gully are almost entirely made up of grog-tempered sherds. The assemblage includes the greater part of a flanged bowl with chamfered base in fabric B2.3 (*c* AD 120-170), a fragment from a reeded-rim carinated bowl in Canterbury grey ware (*c* AD 130-175) and a fragment from a South Gaulish samian Drag. 18/31 platter (*c* AD 90-110), suggesting that this building was functioning during the early 2nd century.

Assemblage 15 (Fig. 6.3). From the fill (context 8235) of the central posthole 8236 for structure L. This assemblage, which comprises 46 sherds (510 g), is probably constructional in that most of the sherds come from one pot, which may have been used as packing:

49　**Slack-profiled jar** in oxidised buff-brown, grog-tempered fabric B2. This vessel is very poorly made and irregular in finish and may be pre-Flavian in date. Context 8235 (feature 8236) Phase 3.

Assemblage 16 (Fig. 6.3). From the fills (contexts 8138, 8144, 8176, 8183 and 8185) of the penannular eaves-drip gully 8270 for structure L. The six cuts across the gully produced 57 sherds (544 g) of excavated and 22 sherds (90 g) of sieved pottery, including 5 fragments from combed, grog-tempered storage jars, a polished lid-seated jar in grog-tempered fabric (*c* AD 120-150) and the following:

50　**Bead-rim jar** in brown-black fabric B2.1. Dated *c* AD 43-100. Rim D: 120 mm. Context 8176 (Group 8270) Phase 3.
51　**Necked and cordoned jar** in fabric B2.1. Rim D: 150 mm. Context 8176 (Group 8270) Phase 3.

This assemblage suggests that structure L was occupied at the same time as structure K.

From pits

Assemblage 17 (Table 6.6; Figs 6.3 and 6.4). From the fills (contexts 808, 809, 843, 865, 872, 873, 874, 943, 944 and 948) of pit 844. The 537 sherds (17,875 g) of pottery from this pit constitute an assemblage large enough for quantification by EVEs.

The assemblage includes many grog-tempered storage-jar sherds from at least three such vessels, fragments from Dressel 20 amphorae, South Gaulish Drag. 18 platters (*c* AD 43-90), a Drag. 37 bowl (*c* AD 70-110) and Drag. 27 cups (*c* AD 43-110), an Upchurch fine grey ware biconical vessel (*c* AD 43-130) and the following:

52　**Cordoned bead-rim jar** of Thompson form B5-5 (1982) in grey fabric B2.1, fired patchy black/brown. Rim D: 100 mm. Context 873 (feature 844) Phase 3.
53　**Bead-rim jar** in black fabric B2 with diagonal slashed decoration on the body. Rim D: 140 mm. Context 873 (feature 844) Phase 3.
54　**Everted rim jar with corrugated neck** in black fabric B2.1 with whitened exterior. Context 874 (feature 844) Phase 3.
55　**Cordoned jar** of Thompson type B2.1 in black fabric B2. One of several. Rim D: 160 mm. Context 843 (feature 844) Phase 3.
56　**Pedestal base** in fabric B2.1 fired black with patchy reddish-brown/black surfaces. Context 874 (feature 844) Phase 3.
57　**Butt-beaker copy** of Thompson form G5-5 in black fabric B2.1 with comb-stabbed decoration on the body in imitation of rouletting. Dated *c* AD 43-80. Rim D: 160 mm. Context 873 (feature 844) Phase 3.
58　**Large narrow-necked storage jar** in oxidised buff-brown fabric B2. Rim D: 260 mm. Context 874 (feature 844) Phase 3.
59　**Flanged bowl** of Thompson form G2-3 in black fabric B2.1. Rim D: 200 mm. Context 808 (feature 844) Phase 3.
60　**Flanged bowl**, variant of the same type in similar fabric (B2.1). Context 808.
61　**Handmade pulley-neck flagon** in hard grey-black fabric B2.1 with red patches. Dated *c* AD 43-100. Rim D: 50 mm. Context 865 (feature 844) Phase 3.
62　**Lid-seated jar** in grey Canterbury fabric R5. Dated *c* AD 70-175. Context 808 (feature 844) Phase 3.
63　**Gallo-Belgic platter imitation** in very fine-sanded pink fabric R56A with sparse soft red ferrous inclusions. Dated *c* AD 43-100. Rim D: 200 mm. Context 809 (feature 844) Phase 3.
64　**Gauloise 4 amphora rim** in fabric R56A fired pink-orange. The form indicates a date of *c* AD 70-100. Rim D: 120 mm. Context 809 (feature 844) Phase 3.

A further 340 sherds (2874 g) of pottery were retrieved through sieving of environmental samples; they include fragments from a South-Gaulish samian

Table 6.6   Pottery assemblage 17: Fabric and form quantification by EVEs (+ = present, though lacking rim).

Fabric	Jars	Bowls	Dishes	Beakers	Store-jars	Others	Total	%
B2	0.97	0.19			0.48	Lid 0.05	1.69	27.6
B2 oxid.	0.15						0.15	2.5
B2.1	1.56	0.13		0.15		Flagon 1.00	2.84	46.6
R5	0.05						0.05	0.8
R6						Flagons +	+	
R16				+			+	
R17				+			+	
R42			0.16			Cups 0.98	1.14	18.7
R50						Amphora +	+	
R56			0.06			Amphora 0.17	0.23	3.8
Total	2.73	0.32	0.22	0.15	0.48	2.20	6.10	
%	44.8	5.2	3.6	2.5	7.9	36.0		

Drag. 36 platter (*c* AD 70-110) and further bead-rim jars in grog-tempered fabric B2.

Period 2, Phase 4 (AD 150-200)

From the roadside and enclosure ditches

Assemblage 18 (Fig. 6.4). From the fills (contexts 7885, 8595 and 9410) of roadside ditch 9520. The 102 sherds (1686 g.) of pottery from the second recut of the roadside ditch include fragments from a Central Gaulish samian Drag. 31 platter (*c* AD 150-200), much of a biconical vessel in grey Upchurch fine ware fabric (*c* AD 50-130) and the following:

65 **Jar with corrugated neck** in black fabric B2/R1. Large fresh sherds. Dated *c* AD 70-150. Rim D: 160 mm. Context 7885 (Group 9520), Phase 4.

66 **Jar with corrugated neck**, example with slack profile in fabric B2/R1. Large fresh sherd. Rim D: 180 mm. Context 7885 (Group 9520), Phase 4.

67 **Deep dish** of Monaghan type 5F4 in black BB2 fabric. Much survives. Dated *c* AD 130/170-210. Rim D: 180 mm. Context 9410 (Group 9520), Phase 4.

68 **Plain poppyhead beaker** of Monaghan type 2A4 in grey fine ware fabric R16. Dated *c* AD 130-170. Rim D: 110 mm. Context 9410 (Group 9520), Phase 4.

These sherds suggest a date range of *c* AD 140-170+ for the life of this ditch.

Assemblage 19 (Fig. 6.4). From the primary fills of roadside ditch 8590 (contexts 7114, 8564 and 8594). These fills of the third recut of the roadside ditch produced a total of 92 sherds (880 g) between them. The pottery is somewhat broken up, but includes fragments from a BB2 open form and jar rims of Monaghan type 3H7.7 (*c* AD 180-250) and 3J3 (*c* AD 150-240) in fine-sanded Thameside fabric LR2. These suggest that the ditch was cut shortly before the end of the 2nd century.

The upper fills (contexts 7005, 7056, 7091, 7092, 7115, 7116, 7884, 8681 and 9630) yielded a further 695 sherds (6652 g) of pottery, including many residual sherds derived from the fills of earlier roadside ditch cuts and the following:

69 **Small necked bowl** in red-brown fabric B2.3 with polished surfaces. Large fresh sherds. Dated *c* AD 120-170. Rim D: 100 mm. Context 8681 (Group 8590) Phase 4.

70 **Convex-sided dish** in black fabric B2/ESW. One of two. Rim D: 200 mm. Context 7005 (Group 8590) Phase 4.

71 **Flanged bowl** in black fabric B2.1, fired brown internally and patchy pink/grey externally. Rim D: 180 mm. Context 7005 (Group 8590) Phase 4.

72 **Poppyhead beaker** with rectangular dot-barbotine panels of Monaghan type 2A5 in grey Upchurch fine ware fabric R16. Dated *c* AD 150-190. Rim D: 120 mm. Context 7005 (Group 8590) Phase 4.

None of this pottery needs be later than AD 200.

Assemblage 20A (Fig. 6.4). From the fills of gullies 9380 and 9910 defining plot SW1 (contexts 7605, 7678, 9215, 9216, 9279, 9281, 9550, 9915 within gully 9380 and 7680, 8852, 8971, 9147, 9156, 9492, 9614, 9676 and 9885 within gully 9910). The fills of enclosure gully 9380 were very largely free of pottery, but cut 9213 towards its north-western end produced a small 15 sherd assemblage of early 2nd century character, including fragments from both Canterbury and Hoo flagons and a Central Gaulish samian Drag. 18/31 platter (*c* AD 120-150). A further eight sherds were retrieved from sieved samples and include fragments from a fine grey Upchurch beaker of Monaghan form 2A4 (*c* AD 130-160).

The roadside ditch extension of this gully (9910) yielded a somewhat larger, but still rather small 41 sherd (850 g) assemblage, including fragments from a Central Gaulish samian Drag. 36 platter (*c* AD 120-200), an East Gaulish samian Drag. 33 cup (*c* AD 140-200+), Canterbury flagons and the greater part of the body of a barbotine-dot decorated beaker of Monaghan type 2A3 or 2A4 (*c* AD 100-160). The following pieces are also present:

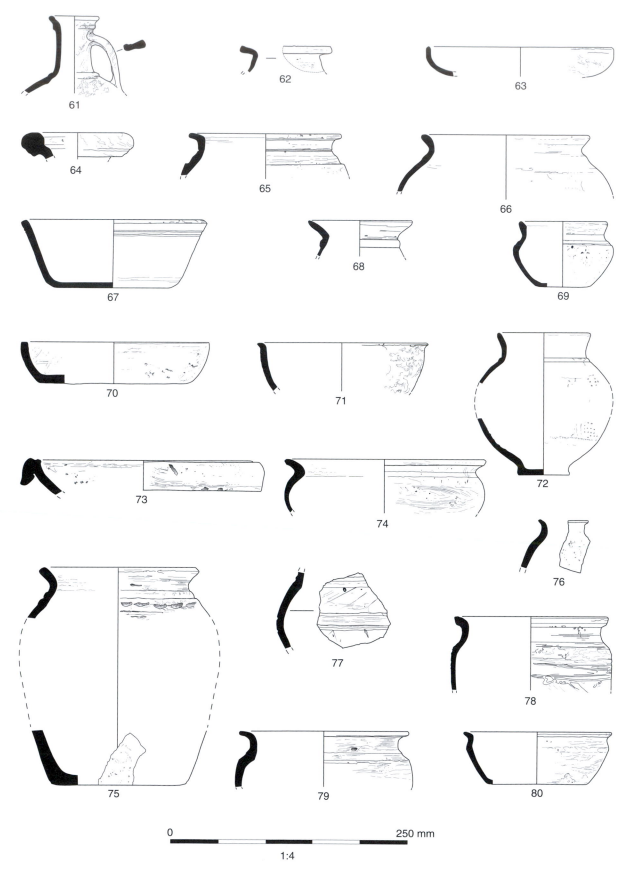

Figure 6.4   Roman pottery (Assemblage 17 (cont.): nos 61-64; Assemblage 18: nos 65-6; Assemblage 19: nos 69-72; Assemblage 20A: nos 73-75; Assemblage 20B: nos 76-80 continues).

73 **Mortarium** in very fine pale buff-brown fabric with flint trituration grits (R99). Several fresh sherds are present. Dated *c* AD 150-200. Rim D: 250 mm. Context 7680 (Group 9910) Phase 4.

74 **Necked-bowl** in black fabric B2.4 fired polished brown. Dated *c* AD 120-170. Rim D: 220 mm. Context 8971 (Group 9910) Phase 4.

75 **Jar with stabbed shoulder**, in brown-black fabric B2.1. Two large fresh sherds are present. Rim D: 160 mm. Context 9676 (Group 9910) Phase 4.

It appears that the ditch was dug during the early 2nd century and remained open until *c* AD 150/170. The biggest concentration of material in gully 9910 was fairly central to it and may be rubbish thrown out by the occupants of structure G.

Assemblage 20B (Figs 6.4 and 6.5). From the fills of gullies 9440 and 10060 defining plot SW2 (contexts 7593, 9191, 9239, 9287 and 10454 within gully 9440 and 8028, 8059, 9220, 9221, 9671, 10215 and 10245 within 10060). The five cuts across gully 9440 produced 118 sherds (2416 g) of late 1st to early 2nd century character of which the overwhelming bulk (108 sherds) came from cut 9238 at the junction with the roadside extension 10060. This large assemblage includes fragments from a biconical vessel in grey Upchurch fine ware (*c* AD 45-130), a South Gaulish samian Drag. 37 bowl repaired with lead rivets (*c* AD 90-110), Canterbury jars and flagons and, apart from 11 nondescript sherds retrieved from sieved environmental samples, the following:

76 **Slack-profiled jar** in brown-black fabric B2/R1. Context 9239 (feature 9440) Phase 4.

77 **Jar with both neck and girth cordons**, in fabric B2/R1 with burnished lattice decoration. Fresh sherds. Context 9239 (feature 9440) Phase 4.

78 **Furrowed jar** in patchy brown-black fabric B2.1. Four fresh sherds are present. Rim D: 160 mm. Context 9239 (feature 9440) Phase 4.

The roadside extension of the enclosure gully (10060) produced a further 68 sherds (1472 g) of excavated and 7 sherds (50 g) of sieved pottery distributed fairly evenly along it. This material includes an East Gaulish samian Drag. 18/31 platter repaired with lead rivets (*c* AD 130-150), fragments from a poppy-head beaker in grey Upchurch fine ware (*c* AD 130-160), a Canterbury mortarium (*c* AD 100-150) and the following:

79 **Jar with carinated shoulder** in grog-tempered fabric B2. Rim D: 180 mm. Context 9220 (Group 10060) Phase 4.

80 **'Pie-dish'** in fabric B2 fired patchy black/grey/brown. Rim D: 160 mm. Context 9220 (Group 10060) Phase 4.

81 Greater part of **jar** in polished reddish-brown fabric B2.4. Dated *c* AD 120-170. Rim D: 110 mm. Context 9671 (Group 10060) Phase 4.

The life of this enclosure can thus be dated *c* AD 90-160+.

Assemblage 20C. From the fills of gullies 9570 and 10410 defining plot SW3 (contexts 9051, 9057 and 10184 within 9570 and 9967, 10291, 10321, 10372, 10396, 10406, 10412, 10413 and 10414 within 10410). Gully 9570 produced 42 sherds (452 g) of excavated and 16 sherds (65 g) of sieved pottery, including fragments from a platter of Monaghan type 7A2 in grey Upchurch fine ware (*c* AD 43-140), a Central Gaulish samian Drag. 31 platter (*c* AD 150-200) and a corrugated grog-tempered jar neck, which should not be later than AD 150. This pottery could well have come from occupation within plot SW2 to the north-east, however, as the seven cuts across the roadside ditch extension 10410 to the south-west yielded no pottery.

Assemblage 21 (Fig. 6.5). From the primary silting (contexts 738, 783, 848 and 1081) of ditch 1740. The primary silting of this first enclosure ditch around the ironworking area on the north-eastern edge of the site produced 229 sherds (2941 g) of pottery from the eight cuts across it. These include rim sherds from a Dressel 2-4 amphora, a large part of a Gallo-Belgic white ware *lagena* (*c* AD 43-80), South Gaulish Drag. 18 platter and Drag. 27 cup sherds (*c* AD 43-90 and 43-110 respectively), fragments from a Martres-de-Veyre samian Drag. 18/31 platter (*c* AD 90-120), a platter of Monaghan type 7A2 and a beaker of ?type 2A3.4 in grey Upchurch fine ware (*c* AD 43-140 and *c* AD 100-130 respectively) and the following:

82 **Necked and cordoned jar** in grey fabric B2 with black paint around its neck. Dated *c* AD 70-150. Rim D: 160 mm. Context 738 (Group 1740) Phase 4.

83 **Necked and cordoned jar** in patchy black/brown grog-tempered fabric B2 with polished surfaces. Dated *c* AD 70-150. Rim D: 140 mm. Context 783 (Group 1740) Phase 4.

The primary silting also produced fragments from a chaff-tempered salt-container (Macpherson-Grant 1980). The pottery indicates that the ditch was dug in the late Flavian period and probably at the same time as the first roadside ditch 8950/10070.

The upper fills of the feature produced another 287 sherds (3265 g) of pottery, including more material dated *c* AD 70-150. The sherds include both South Gaulish and Central Gaulish samian and the following:

84 Greater part of **Platter** of Monaghan type 7A1.2 in grey Upchurch fine ware fabric R16. Dated *c* AD 43-120. Rim D: 220 mm. Context 746 (Group 1740) Phase 4.

85 **Disc-rimmed flagon** of Pollard type 76 (1988) in sandy orange fabric R6.1. Dated *c* AD 70-150. Rim D: 50 mm. Context 746 (Group 1740) Phase 4.

86 **Flagon rim** in oxidised Hoo fabric R17. Rim D: 80 mm. Context 746 (Group 1740) Phase 4.

Upper levelling layers 805, 806 and 1059 produced a further 190 sherds (2506 g) of pottery, including late

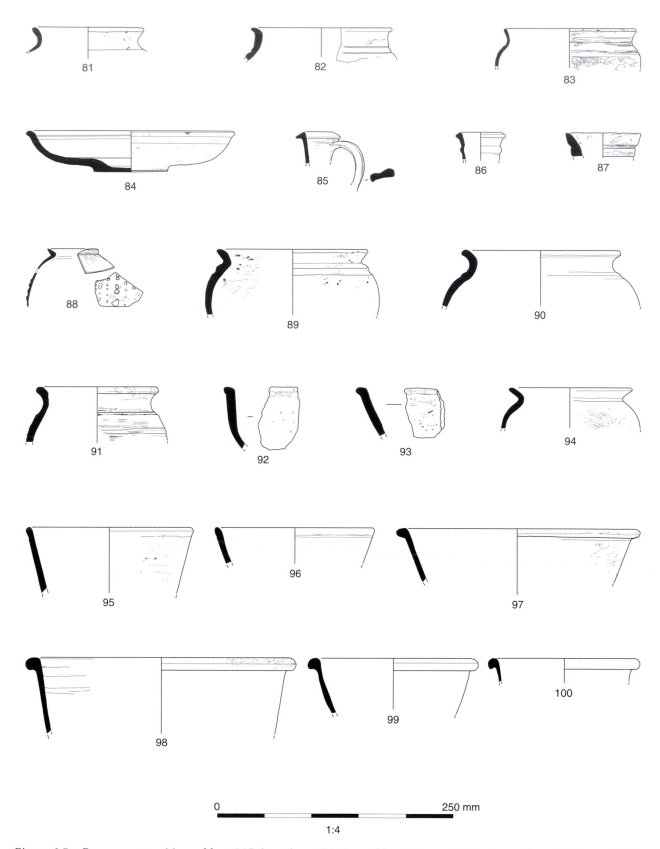

Figure 6.5   Roman pottery (Assemblage 20B (cont.): no. 81; Assemblage 21: nos 82-86; Assemblages 22B: nos 87-88; Assemblage 22C: no. 89; Assemblage 23: nos 90-100 continues).

2nd to early 3rd century BB2 dishes. It would appear that the ditch remained open until the third quarter of the 2nd century and was then levelled up and replaced by ditch 1765 (see Assemblage 23).

Assemblage 22A. From the fills of gullies 9390 and 9890 forming the north-east and south-east sides of the first rectilinear enclosure (contexts 7562, 7566, 9212, 9483, 9552, 9616, 9678 and 9827). The 431 sherds (3204 g) of pottery from gully 9390 and the 4 sherds (18 g) from its short roadside extension, 9890, include fragments from a South Gaulish samian Drag. 30 bowl (*c* AD 80-100), Central Gaulish Drag. 36 and Drag. 31 platters (*c* AD 120-200 and 150-200 respectively) as well a dish of Monaghan type 5E1.8 in BB2, fabric R14 (*c* AD 170-230) and a Colchester colour-coated beaker (*c* AD 130-200). Some material is probably derived from the fills of the earlier enclosure ditch 9380, but the rest suggests a date range of *c* AD 150-250 for the recut feature. The sherds are nearly all heavily broken up.

Assemblage 22B (Fig. 6.5). From the fills of gullies 9450 and 10040 forming the north-east and south-east sides of the second rectilinear enclosure (contexts 7568, 7570, 7572, 8845, 8847, 9125, 9175, 9189, 9217, 9224, 9241 and 9887). The 495 sherds (5364 g) of excavated and 16 sherds (66 g) of sieved pottery from the 11 cuts across these gullies include material derived from the earlier gully 9440, including fragments from the following more unusual vessels:

87 **Collared flagon** in very fine powdery-buff North Gaulish fabric (Davies, *et al.* 1994, fig. 52, 289). Dated *c* AD 43-80. Rim D: 80 mm. Context 7572 (Group 9450) Phase 4.
88 **Ring-and-dot beaker** sherds in fine orange fabric with contrasting cream barbotine dots. Uncertain rim diameter. Context 7572 (Group 9450) Phase 4.
  Similar vessels in similar bi-chrome fabrics were manufactured both at Staines, Middlesex (Lyne forthcoming b) and Cherry Hinton, Cambridgeshire (Evans 1990) during the period *c* AD 70-100. This example is probably from the putative Staines kilns.

The contemporaneous material includes fragments from a Central Gaulish samian Drag. 31 platter (*c* AD 150-200), a Cologne roughcast beaker (*c* AD 130-200), a fine Upchurch grey ware beaker of Monaghan type 2A4/5 (*c* AD 130-190), a jar in rough Thameside grey ware fabric LR2 with superficial surface reddening (*c* AD 180-300), and polished grog-tempered jars with lid-seating (*c* AD 120-170+). A similar date range to that for the recut plot SW1 ditch is implied.

Assemblage 22C (Fig. 6.5). From the fills of gully 9580 forming the north-east side of plot SW3 (contexts 8393, 9545, 9548, 10183, 10216 and 10328). Only contexts 8393 within cut 8394 and 9545 within cut 9544 produced any pottery (63 sherds, 668 g); the

other four cuts across the feature were sterile. Forty-six of the sherds were freshly broken and came from the following vessel:

89 **Jar** in brown-black grog-tempered fabric B2.1 with stubby everted rim and cordoned neck. Rim D: 160 mm. Context 8393 (Group 9580) Phase 4.

The jar is unlikely to be later than mid 2nd century in date and, coupled with the lack of other sherds within the gully, suggests a short life for the feature, terminating well before AD 200.

Assemblage 22D. From the fills (contexts 9035, 9036, 9182, 9183, 9346 and 9364) of gully 9370 forming the south-west side of plot SW4. The 490 sherds (2954 g) of pottery from this feature are heavily comminuted and include both mid-late 1st century material and sherds with a date-range of *c* AD 150-270. The earlier material may be derived from occupation associated with structures A and B to the south-west. The broken-up nature of the pottery means that none is suitable for illustration, but sherds include Central Gaulish samian and BB2.

Assemblage 23 (Figs 6.5 and 6.6). From the fills (contexts 866, 1556, 1633, 1647, 1653 and 1657) of ditch 1765. The seven segments across the fills of this feature produced 330 sherds (4093 g) of pottery. Most of the pottery came from cuts 1634 and 1648, which were sealed beneath the floor of structure R and produced 274 sherds (3683 g). This assemblage is too small for quantification by EVEs, but includes fragments from Central Gaulish samian forms Drag. 31 (*c* AD 150-200), Drag. 33 (*c* AD 120-200), Curle 23 and the related form listed by Oswald and Pryce (1920, plate lv, no. 13) as Drag. 46 (*c* AD 120-200), a rouletted Lower Nene Valley colour-coated beaker (*c* AD 180-270), a Cologne beaker (*c* AD 130-200), beakers of Monaghan types 2A4 and 2A5 (*c* AD 130-190) in fine grey Upchurch ware and the following pieces:

90 **Necked and cordoned jar** in soft buff oxidised fabric B2. Rim D: 160 mm. Context 1633 (Group 1765) Phase 4.
91 **Necked jar** with combing on its body in black fabric B2/ESW. Rim D: 130 mm. Context 1647 (Group 1765) Phase 4.
92 **Bead-rimmed dish or bowl** in handmade black fabric B2/ESW, fired patchy buff/black externally. Context 1633 (Group 1765) Phase 4.
93 **Flanged bowl** in black fabric B2.1. Rim D: 200 mm. Context 1647 (Group 1765) Phase 4.
94 **Everted-rim jar** in patchy grey/white 'Native Coarse Ware' fabric R1. Dated *c* AD 170-250. Rim D: 120 mm. Context 1653 (Group 1765) Phase 4.
95 **Dish** of Monaghan type 5F4.2 in black BB2 fabric R14. Dated *c* 130-210. Rim D: 180 mm. Context 1647 (Group 1765) Phase 4.
96 **Dish** of Monaghan type 5F4.1 in rough-grey Thameside fabric LR2.4. Dated *c* AD 130-230/300. Rim D: 180 mm. Context 1633 (Group 1765) Phase 4.

97 **'Pie-dish'** of Monaghan type 5C3.5 in grey Thameside fabric R73. Dated *c* AD 170-210. Rim D: 300 mm. Context 1633 (Group 1765) Phase 4.

98 **'Pie-dish'** of type 5C4.2, in fabric R73. Dated *c* AD 170-250. Rim D: 260 mm. Context 1633 (Group 1765) Phase 4.

99 **'Pie-dish'** of type 5C4.3, in grey Thameside fabric R73. Dated *c* AD 170-250. Rim D: 180 mm. Context 1633 (Group 1765) Phase 4.

100 **'Pie-dish'** of type 5C4.4, in fabric R73. Dated *c* AD 180-230. Rim D: 180 mm. Context 1633 (Group 1765) Phase 4.

101 **Mortarium** of Gillam 255 form in powdery greenish-cream fabric (G255). Dated *c* AD 160-230. Rim D: 260 mm. Context 1633 (Group 1765) Phase 4.

The primary silting in cut 1634 was lacking in pottery but the same layer (Context 1657) in cut 1648 yielded a fragment from a Central Gaulish samian Drag. 27 cup (*c* AD 120-150) and a rim fragment from a Colchester colour-coated cornice-rimmed beaker (*c* AD 130-200+). All this suggests that the ditch was dug during the mid 2nd century and backfilled *c* AD 200. The fills elsewhere in the ditch produced the following:

102 **Indented Colchester rough-cast beaker** with cornice rim and brown colour-coat. Fabric R33. Most of this vessel is present. Dated *c* AD 130-200. Rim D: 120 mm. Context 1556 (Group 1765) Phase 4.

103 **Jar** of Monaghan type 3H8 in grey Upchurch fine ware fabric R16. Dated *c* AD 170-230. Rim D: 180 mm. Context 1556 (Group 1765) Phase 4.

From the structures and associated features

Assemblage 24 (Table 6.7; Fig. 6.6). From the fills of the penannular gully (group 9280) around structure C (contexts 9229, 9231, 9233, 9257, 9259, 9261 and 9265). The fills of this feature produced 396 sherds (3122 g) mainly of badly broken-up pottery. This assemblage is dominated by grog-tempered wares (87%), including the following:

104 **Carinated bowl** with plain rim in oxidised grog-tempered ware fabric B2/ESW. Rim D: 180 mm. Context 9229 (Group 9280) Phase 4.
Similar in form to an East Sussex ware example from Meeching School, Newhaven dated *c* AD 60-100 (Green 1976, fig. 23, 28). The Newhaven example of this rare type was also re-fired red.

105 **Necked and carinated bowl** with flanged rim in fabric B2/ESW, fired patchy grey/black. Two large fresh sherds. Rim D: 200 mm. Context 9229 (Group 9280) Phase 4.

Fragments from several lid-seated grog-tempered jars similar to those in Assemblage 23 are also present. The fine wares include fragments from a Central Gaulish samian Drag. 18/31 platter (*c* AD 120-150), two Drag. 31 examples (*c* AD 150-200) and a Drag. 37 bowl (*c* AD 120-200), and sherds from an Upchurch fine ware poppyhead beaker of Monaghan Type 2A4 (*c* AD 130-160). The relatively high percentage of East Gaulish samian is brought about by the presence of a large number of fresh sherds from a single Curle 23 platter (*c* AD 140-200+). This assemblage suggests that occupation of the structure commenced some time during the second quarter of the 2nd century and continued well into the period *c* AD 150/170.

Assemblage 25 (Table 6.8; Figs 6.6 and 6.7). From the fills of grave 8160 within structure C. This feature yielded a very large assemblage (2065 sherds, 25,738 g) derived from a number of freshly broken vessels. The make-up of this assemblage, even allowing for differing quantification methodologies, is very different from that from the associated penannular gully around structure C. There is a far smaller percentage of grog-tempered wares (52%), a percentage more in keeping with that from the similarly quantified upper fills of the first roadside ditches (see Assemblage 9), dated 30 to 50 years earlier. There are significantly larger numbers of open forms than are present in that assemblage, including a riveted Drag. 37 bowl in the style of the Sacer-Attianus group (*c* AD 125-150; see Bird below), two Drag. 18/31 platters (*c* AD 120-150), a Drag. 27 cup (*c* AD 120-150) and a Drag. 33 cup (*c* AD 120-200), all in Central Gaulish samian ware. The samian has suffered from acidic soil conditions, but one of the Drag. 18/31 platters has a surviving stamp, CETVS.F (*c* AD 140-150). The other wares include the following:

106 **Jar with corrugated neck** in black fabric B2.1. Rim D: 140 mm. Context 8410 (grave 8160) Phase 4.
A similar vessel was present in the assemblage from context 8462.

107 **Necked and cordoned jar** in black fabric B2.1 with burnished shoulder latticing. Rim D: 140 mm. Context 8688 (grave 8160) Phase 4.

108 **Necked jar** in grey fabric B2.1 fired patchy black/brown with stabbed shoulder decoration. Rim D: 220 mm. Context 8356 (grave 8160) Phase 4.

109 **Jar with weakly-everted rim** in high-fired grey fabric B2.1, fired flecky grey/orange externally. Rim D: 160 mm. Context 8407 (grave 8160) Phase 4.

110 **Necked jar** in brown-black fabric B2.1 with knife-trimmed body. Rim D: 160 mm. Context 8352 (grave 8160) Phase 4.

111 **Necked jar** with compressed everted rim in polished brown/black fabric B2.1. Rim D: 130 mm. Context 8637 (grave 8160) Phase 4.

112 **Flanged bowl** with undercut rim in brown-black fabric B2.1. Much of this vessel is present. Rim D: 160 mm. Context 8459 (grave 8160) Phase 4.

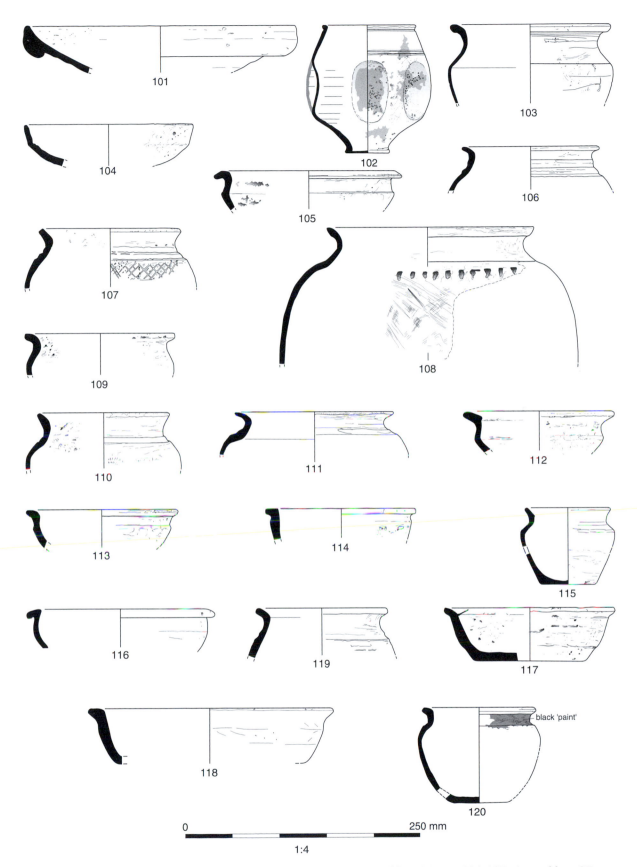

101

102

103

104

105

106

107

108

109

110

111

112

113

114

115

116

119

117

118

120

black 'paint'

0   250 mm

1:4

Figure 6.6   Roman pottery (Assemblage 23 (cont.): nos 101-103; Assemblage 24: nos 104-105; Assemblage 25: nos 106-120 continues).

Table 6.7   Pottery assemblage 24: Fabric quantification by sherd count and weight.

Fabric	Sherds	%	Weight (g)	% weight
B2	199	50.3	1204	38.6
B2.1	145	36.6	1544	49.5
R5	1	0.2	12	0.4
R5.1	1	0.2	24	0.8
R6.1	1	0.2	4	0.1
R6.3	2	0.5	18	0.6
R16	5	1.3	16	0.5
R17	2	0.5	14	0.4
R43	6	1.5	76	2.4
R46	28	7.1	46	1.5
R50	2	0.5	142	4.5
R73	3	0.8	12	0.4
MISC	1	0.2	10	0.3
Total	396		3122	

113 **Flanged bowl** in fabric B2/R1. Rim D: 160 mm. Context 8469 (grave 8160) Phase 4.

114 **Flanged bowl** in fabric B2/R1. Rim D: 140 mm. Context 8609 (grave 8160) Phase 4.

115 **Small necked bowl or jar** with girth carination in black fabric B2/R1. Rim D: 80 mm. Contexts 8585 and 8689 (grave 8160) Phase 4.

116 **Bowl with down-turned flanged rim** in brown-black fabric B2/R1. Rim D: 200 mm. Contexts 8133, 8304, 8358, 8584 and 8585 (grave 8160) Phase 4.

117 **Flanged dish** in black-brown fabric B2.1. Rim D: 200 mm. Contexts 8415 and 8734 (grave 8160) Phase 4.
Paralleled at Meeching School, Newhaven in a mid 2nd century assemblage (Green 1976, fig. 35, 253, 254).

118 **Flanged dish**, coarser example in fabric B2/R1, fired patchy grey/black. Rim D: 240 mm. Contexts 8456, 8463 and 8724 (grave 8160) Phase 4.

The following four grog-tempered ware vessels differ from the above in showing evidence for tournette-finishing and having smooth, reddish-brown to black polished surfaces. These superior-finished grog-tempered wares have not been detected on other Kent sites other than ones in the neighbourhood of Westhawk Farm, such as Waterbrook Farm, Ashford and the Harville villa at Wye and it is probable that they were made nearby. These wares are first seen in the tertiary fill of the first roadside ditch (no. 31), suggesting that they appeared *c* AD 120. Their significance in this assemblage (36% of the grog-tempered wares by EVE) indicates continued manufacture until at least AD 170 and probably later.

119 **Lid-seated jar** in polished patchy black/orange/brown fabric B2.4. Rim D: 130 mm. Contexts 8412 and 8638 (grave 8160) Phase 4.

120 **Lid-seated jar.** Another example in fabric B2.1 with black paint on its neck. Rim D: 140 mm. Context 8691 (grave 8160) Phase 4.

A similar lid-seated jar with black paint on its neck came from Context 8403.

121 **Lid-seated necked and cordoned jar** in fabric B2.4. Rim D: 140 mm. Context 8193 (grave 8160) Phase 4.
Fragments from at least three other jars of this type are present in the assemblage.

122 **Necked bowl with lid-seated rim** in black fabric B2.4. The greater part of this vessel is present. Rim D: 160 mm. Contexts 8303, 8304, 8457 and 8649 (grave 8160) Phase 4.

123 **Narrow-necked storage-jar** in black grog-tempered fabric LR1.1. Rim D: 130 mm. Context 8660 (grave 8160) Phase 4.
Possibly an Asham jar variant from an East Sussex source (Green 1980, fig. 28, 16-18).

124 **Necked and cordoned storage jar** in black fabric B2 with vertically grooved body and black paint or resin on its neck. Rim D: 260 mm. Context 8536 (grave 8160) Phase 4.

125 **Lid** in lumpy brown/black fabric B2.1. Rim D: 170 mm. Context 8635 (grave 8160) Phase 4.

126 **Necked and cordoned jar** in grey Canterbury fabric R5. Most of this vessel is present. Rim D: 180 mm. Contexts 8661, 8662 and 8693 (grave 8160) Phase 4.
Similar to an example from Rose Lane, Canterbury dated *c* AD 90-140 (Wilson 1995, fig. 303, 129).

127 **Jar** in gritty blue-grey fabric R5. Rim D: 140 mm. Context 8416 (grave 8160) Phase 4.
Similar to an example from the St. Stephen's Road kilns, Canterbury, where it was dated *c* AD 130-140 (Jenkins 1956, fig. 5.5).

128 **Reeded-rim carinated bowl** in blackened grey Canterbury fabric R5. Dated C AD 120-175. Rim D: 140 mm. Context 8461 (grave 8160) Phase 4.

129 **Reeded-rim carinated bowl.** Fabric R5. Rim D: 150 mm. Context 8414 (grave 8160) Phase 4.

130 **Biconical vessel** of Monaghan type 2G2.2 in grey Upchurch fine ware fabric R16. Much of this vessel is present. Dated *c* AD 43-100. Rim D: 180 mm. Context 8299 (grave 8160) Phase 4.

131 **Biconical vessel** of Monaghan type 2G0.4 in fabric R16. Rim D: 140 mm. Dated *c* AD 70-100. Contexts 8585, 8658, 8665 and 8739 (grave 8160) Phase 4.

132 **Poppyhead beaker** of Monaghan type 2A5 without decoration in fabric R16. Much of this vessel is present. Dated *c* AD 150-190. Rim D: 110 mm. Context 8299 (grave 8160) Phase 4.
Fragments from a similar beaker, but with rectangular dot-barbotine panels, are also present in context 8649.

133 **Carinated bowl** in fabric R16. Most is present. Rim D: 160 mm. Contexts 8149, 8163 and 8311 (grave 8160) Phase 4.

134 **Globular beaker** of Monaghan type 2H1 with stubby everted rim in fabric R16. Dated *c* AD 80-130. Rim D: 110 mm. Context 8601 (grave 8160) Phase 4.

135 Rim from *lagena* with reeded rim in coarse-sanded grey fabric (?R6.1) with orange and

brown patches. Rim D: 75 mm. Context 8740 (grave 8160) Phase 4.

All of the vessels represented in the assemblage, apart from one or two indeterminate form fragments, are illustrated or referred to above. The following are also present and not included in Table 6.8. Their function is further discussed below.

136 Complete **small pot** or **crucible** in polished brown-black grog-tempered fabric B2/R1. Rim D: 30 mm. Context 8152 (grave 8160) Phase 4.

137 Complete **small girth-cordoned pot with stubby everted rim** in grey fabric R5 with blue-black patches. Rim D: 50 mm. Context 8605 (grave 8160) Phase 4.

From the rectangular earth-fast post built structures

Assemblage 26. From the posthole packing of structure D (contexts 8399, 8743, 8745, 8803, 8935, 8973, 9008, 9027 and 9059). These constructional deposits produced 111 sherds (1275 g) of pottery between them. Most of these sherds are not closely datable, but the packing of posthole 8934 yielded two fragments from an undecorated 'pie-dish' of Monaghan Type 5C1.5 (*c* AD 150/170-240) in Black-Burnished 2 ware. BB2 seems to have arrived at Westhawk Farm at a later date than at Canterbury or Dover. Mid-late 2nd century pottery assemblages at both of those places have large quantities of the earlier lattice decorated 'pie-dishes' of *c* AD 120-180 date as well as plain forms dated *c* AD 150-250, whereas the overwhelming majority of such dishes at Westhawk Farm are plain; only two lattice decorated fragments are known from the entire site. This would suggest that BB2 open forms appeared at Westhawk Farm *c* AD 170/180 and that structure D was built around that time or later still.

Assemblage 27 (Fig. 6.7). From occupational features associated with structure D. Rectilinear gully 8510 to the south-west of structure D produced 339 sherds (3124 g) of pottery, including Central Gaulish samian Walters 79 (*c* AD 160-200), Drag. 31 (*c* AD 150-200) and Drag. 38 (*c* AD 140-200) sherds, fragments from several lid-seated and polished grog-tempered ware jars and the following:

138 **Cornice-rimmed bag-beaker** in pimply buff-brown fabric R71 with sparse up-to 0.50 mm. multi-coloured quartz filler and occasional flint inclusions. Much of this vessel is present. Rim D: 70 mm. Context 8899 (feature 8510) Phase 4.

139 **Rouletted bag-beaker** with beaded rim in grey Upchurch fine ware fabric R16. Rim D: 90 mm. Context 8968 (feature 8510) Phase 4.

The Phase 4-5 enclosure gully 10170 around two sides of the building yielded a further 231 sherds (2088 g) of pottery, much of which was badly broken-up, but included a large part of the following vessel:

140 **Shallow 'pie-dish'** with chamfered base in black BB2 fabric (R14) without decoration. Similar to Pollard type 181 (1988). Fresh fragments from another, slightly smaller, example are also present. Dated *c* AD 190-250. Rim D: 240 mm. Context 8697 (feature 10170) Phase 4.

These assemblages suggest that the building was occupied from *c* AD 170/180 to 250 or later.

Assemblage 28. From the primary fills (contexts 8994 and 9111) of penannular eavesdrip gully sectors 10250 and 10260 around structure E. The 23 sherds (256 g) of pottery from these contexts include fragments from a straight-sided dish in rough grey Thameside fabric (*c* AD 170-250) and a BB2 open form of similar date. These fragments suggest that the structure was put up after AD 170 although farmyard trample deposit 9333 overlaying it indicates abandonment by AD 200.

Assemblage 29. From the cluster of pits and postholes making up structure G. These various features produced small assemblages of late 1st to early 2nd century character. The fill (context 8217) of pit 8216 yielded eight sherds (60 g), including fragments from a biconical vessel in fine grey Upchurch fabric (*c* AD 50-130) and a sherd of South Gaulish samian (*c* AD 43-110). The 24 sherds (170 g) from the fills of pit 7961 include fragments from a mortarium in sandy orange Canterbury fabric R6.1 (*c* AD 100-150) and a reeded-rim bowl in the grey version of the same fabric (*c* AD 70-175); the 44 fragments (476 g) from pit 9907

Table 6.8   Pottery assemblage 25: Fabric and form quantification by EVEs.

Fabric	Jars	Bowls	Dishes	Beakers	Others	Total	%
B2/ESW	1.61	0.46	0.76	0.18		3.01	11.5
B2.1	3.32	1.35	0.68		Lid 0.15	5.50	21.0
B2.4	4.22	0.54				4.76	18.2
LR1.1	0.27					0.27	1.0
R5	2.62	0.87				3.49	13.3
R6.3					Lagena 1.00	1.00	3.8
R16	0.19	0.40	0.55	4.18		5.32	20.3
R43		0.38	1.10		Dr27 0.81	2.84	10.8
					Dr33 0.55		
Total	12.23	4.00	3.09	4.36	2.51	26.19	
%	46.7	15.3	11.8	16.6	9.6		

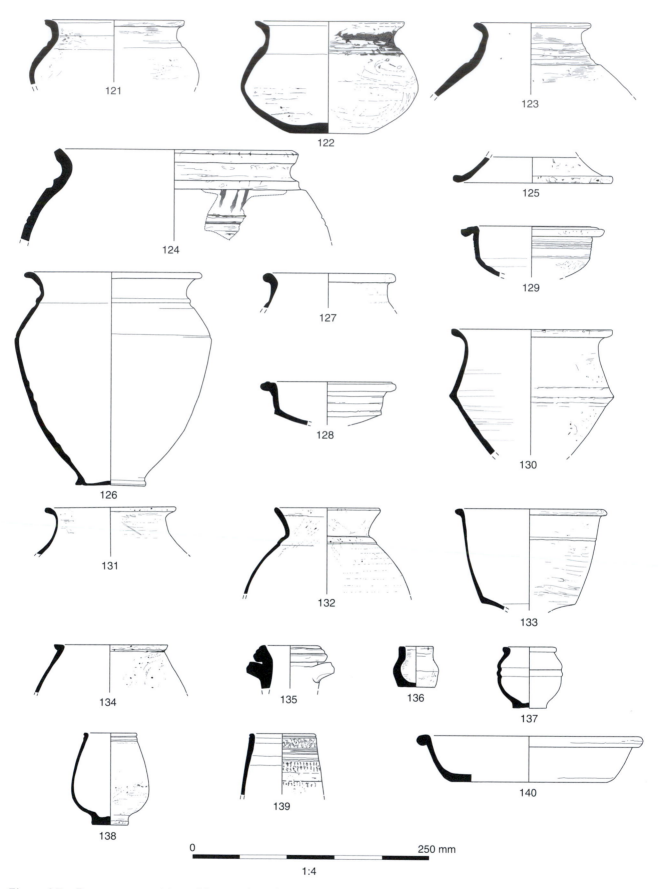

Figure 6.7   Roman pottery (Assemblage 25 (cont.): nos 121-137; Assemblages 27: nos 138-140).

include a rim sherd from one of only two 'pie-dishes' from the site with lattice decoration (*c* AD 120-200).

It seems likely that the occupation within this putative building concentrates in the period *c* AD 70-150.

Assemblage 30 (Fig. 6.8). From the posthole packing fills (contexts 268 and 283)of structure J. Most of the packing for the six postholes were lacking in pottery, but those around posts 269 and 284 produced seven and eleven sherds respectively. These fragments include a body sherd from a jar in sandy Thameside fabric LR2.2 with superficial surface reddening (context 283) and the following:

141   **Lid-seated jar** in buff sandy Canterbury fabric R6.3. Dated AD 160-200. Context 268 (feature 269) Phase 4.

The presence of the Thameside jar sherd strongly suggests that the structure was erected after *c* AD 180 and perhaps during the early 3rd century.

Assemblage 31 (Table 6.9; Fig. 6.8). From the fills (contexts 7232, 7233, 7517, 7519, 7521, 7533, 7542, 7552, 7576, 7606 and 7607) of the penannular gully 7660 around structure O. The 470 sherds (6166 g) of pottery from the nine cuts across the fills of this gully included a large enough collection of rim fragments for quantification by EVEs.

Table 6.9 shows an assemblage with a predominance of grog-tempered wares (54%); a figure only slightly down on that arrived at for the similarly quantified Assemblage 9 from the upper fills of roadside ditches 8950 and 10070, dated 50 years earlier. As with that assemblage the overwhelming bulk of such vessels are cooking-pots with just a few lids. The superior finished lid-seated cooking-pots account for as much as 46% of the grog-tempered wares. There is a predominance of jar/cooking-pots in general, with relatively small numbers of open forms and beakers. Percentages of such vessel forms are, however, higher than those in Assemblage 9. Sherds include

fragments from a Central Gaulish samian Drag. 31 platter (*c* AD 150-200), beakers of Monaghan forms 2A4 (*c* AD 130-160) and 2A5 (*c* AD 160-190), a platter of type 7A2.1 (*c* AD 43-140) in grey Upchurch fine ware, two Colchester roughcast beaker sherds (*c* AD 130-200), and one fragment from a Cologne white ware example (*c* AD 130-200).

142   **Lid-seated jar** in grey fabric B2.4 with black-paint under its rim. One of several. *c* AD 120-170. Rim D: 180 mm. Context 7542 (Group 7660) Phase 4 .

143   **Lid-seated jar** in black fabric B2.4. Dated *c* AD 120-170. Context 7606 (Group 7660) Phase 4.

144   **Necked jar** in brown-black fabric B2.1. One of two. Rim D: 220 mm. Primary silting, context 7607 (Group 7660) Phase 4.

145   **Necked bowl** in black fabric B2/ESW. Rim D: 200 mm. Primary silting, context 7607 (Group 7660) Phase 4.

146   **Lid** in brown-black fabric B2/ESW. Context 7552 (feature 7660) Phase 4.

147   **Everted jar rim** in grey Native Coarse Ware fabric R1. Dated *c* AD 170-250. Context 7232 (Group 7660) Phase 4.

148   **Lid-seated jar** in sandy grey Canterbury fabric R5. Dated *c* AD 120-175. Rim D: 180 mm. Primary silting, context 7607 (Group 7660) Phase 4.

149   **Reeded-rim bowl** in fabric R5. Dated *c* AD 120-175. Rim D: 160 mm. Primary silting, context 7607 (Group 7660) Phase 4.

150   **'Pie-dish'** of Monaghan type 5C4.3 in grey Thameside fabric R73. Dated *c* AD 170-250. Rim D: 200 mm. Context 7232 (Group 7660) Phase 4.

151   **'Pie-dish'** of type 5C1 in fabric R73. Dated *c* AD 170-240. Rim D: 240 mm. Context 7232 (Group 7660) Phase 4.

152   **'Pie-dish'** of type 5C6.1 in blackened BB2, fabric R14. Dated *c* AD 190-240. Rim D: 220 mm. Context 7521(Group 7660) Phase 4.

Table 6.9   Pottery assemblage 31: Fabric and form quantification by EVEs.

Fabric	Jars	Bowls	Dishes	Beakers	Store-jars	Others	Total	%
B2/ESW	0.71	0.06			0.05	Lid 0.15	0.97	12.3
B2.1	1.06		0.12			Lid 0.14	1.32	16.7
B2.4	1.97						1.97	24.9
R1	0.05						0.05	0.6
R5	0.32	0.15				Lid 0.07	0.54	6.8
R5.1	0.17						0.17	2.2
R6.1						Flagon 0.25	0.25	3.2
R14		0.15					0.15	1.9
R16	0.59		0.05	1.06			1.70	21.5
R17		0.09					0.09	1.1
R42			0.05				0.05	0.6
R43			0.13				0.13	1.6
R73	0.11	0.17	0.05				0.33	4.2
MISC	0.18						0.18	2.3
Total	5.16	0.62	0.40	1.06	0.05	0.61	7.90	
%	65.4	7.8	5.1	13.4	0.06	7.7		

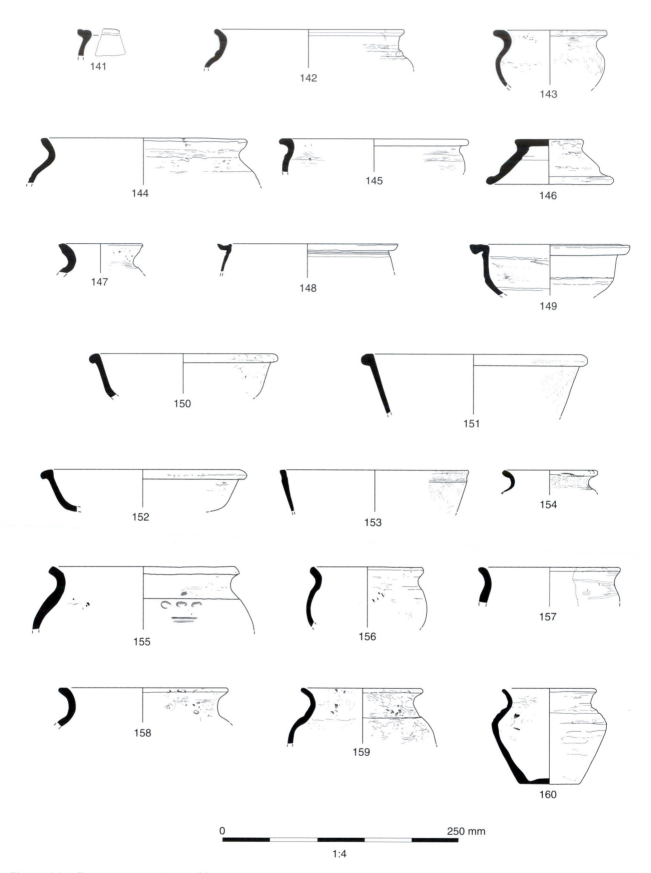

Figure 6.8   Roman pottery (Assemblage 30: no. 141; Assemblage 31: nos 142-154; Assemblage 32: nos 155-160 continues).

153 **Straight-sided dish** of Monaghan type 5F3 with beaded-rim, in grey Thameside fabric R73. Dated *c* AD 130-230. Primary silting, context 7233 (Group 7660) Phase 4.

154 Rim from **small necked jar** or **beaker** in patchily-fired Canterbury sandy fabric R6.1. Rim D: 100 mm. Context 7519 (Group 7660) Phase 4. Paralleled in the stoke-pit of kiln 1 at the St. Stephen's Road site (Jenkins 1956, fig. 5.16) in association with a developed beaded-and-flanged bowl in BB1 dated *c* AD 240-300+ and copies of early-3rd-century Thameside open forms. The excavator dated this material to *c* AD 130-140, but it must surely belong to the early-mid 3rd century.

The presence of BB2 and Thameside vessels in the primary silting of the gully suggests that structure O was built after AD 170, with no. 154 indicating that it remained in use until a least AD 200.

Pit 7582 just outside the entrance to the structure held a truncated storage-jar in oxidised grog-tempered ware with overall body combing. This may have been used as a plunge pot in ironworking, in the same manner as the that in pit 316 inside the ironworking structure I.

From the waterholes

Assemblage 32 (Table 6.10; Figs. 6.8 and 6.9). From the fills (contexts 9398, 9397, 9395/9176, 9396, 9394, 9393, 9392, 9197, 9158, 9391, 9157, 9154, 9155, 9153/7242, 7241, 9152/7314, 7120, 7243/7251, 7250, 7249, 7246, 7245, 7248, 7247, 7244 and 7240) of waterhole 7239/9151 (Group 7239). The lower fills of this feature lacked pottery, but the upper ones yielded 1031 sherds (9875 g), most of which seems to date to the last quarter of the 2nd century. The combined assemblage from these upper fills (contexts 9155, 7242, 7241, 7314, 7120, 7243, 7251, 7250, 7249, 7246, 7248, 7247, 7244 and 7240 in ascending order) is large enough for quantification by EVEs.

The breakdown of this assemblage (Table 6.10) differs from that from the contemporary penannular gully around structure O (see Assemblage 31) in several respects. The most obvious difference lies in the poor showing of handmade grog-tempered wares (27% compared with 55%) and a resultant low percentage of cooking-pots - only half of that in Assemblage 31. Such vessels are replaced by a doubling of the percentages of open forms and beakers from 26% of the structure O assemblage to 53% of this. A possible reason for this difference in form breakdown is discussed below.

The sherds include fragments from four Thameside 'pie-dishes' (*c* AD 170-250), a jar and a further 'pie-dish' in late Thameside fabric LR2 (*c* AD 180-270), Central Gaulish samian forms Drag. 30, 18/31, 31, 33 and 45, East Gaulish forms Drag. 31 and 37 and the following:

155 **Everted-rim jar** in black fabric B2.1. Rim D: 220 mm. Context 9155 (Group 7239) Phase 4.

156 **Slack-profiled jar** in black fabric B2/ESW, polished inside and outside. Rim D: 120 mm. Context 9155 (Group 7239) Phase 4.

157 **Weak-rimmed jar** in fabric B2/R1 with body combing. Rim D: 160 mm. Context 9155 (Group 7239) Phase 4.

158 **Slack-profiled**, everted-rim jar in fabric B2/R1. Rim D: 160 mm. Context 7240 (Group 7239) Phase 4.

159 **Necked jar** in oxidised fabric B2. Rim D: 130 mm. Context 7244 (Group 7239) Phase 4.

160 **Jar** with corrugated shoulder and everted rim in black fabric B2.1. Most of this vessel is present. Rim D: 100 mm. Context 7120 (Group 7239) Phase 4.

161 **Bead-rimmed dish** or **bowl** in black fabric B2.1. Context 7249 (Group 7239) Phase 4.

162 **Bowl** in black fabric B2.1. Context 7240 (Group 7239) Phase 4.

163 **Lid-seated jar** in oxidised fabric B2.3. Rim D: 200 mm. Context 7249 (Group 7239) Phase 4.

164 **Everted-rim jar** in grey fabric R5.1. Rim D: 130 mm. Context 7248 (Group 7239) Phase 4.

165 **Small jar** of Monaghan type 3J1 but without body decoration, in grey Upchurch fine ware fabric R16. Dated *c* AD 120-190. Rim D: 110 mm. Context 9155 (Group 7239) Phase 4.

166 **Flask** of Monaghan type 1B7 in fabric R16. Dated *c* AD 150-190. Rim D: 120 mm. Context 7240 (Group 7239) Phase 4.

167 **Bottle** of Monaghan type 1B6.5 in fabric R16. Rim D: 60 mm. Dated *c* AD 150-200. Context 7240 (Group 7239) Phase 4.

168 **Beaker** of Monaghan type 2A6 in fabric R16. Dated *c* AD 190-230. Rim D: 90 mm. Context 7240 (Group 7239) Phase 4.

169 **Beaker** of Monaghan type 2A6 in fabric R16. Dated *c* AD 160-190. Rim D: 120 mm. Context 7244 (Group 7239) Phase 4.

170 Upper part of **flagon** in very-fine-sanded orange fabric R88B with cream to buff slip on the neck and handle only. Context 7314 (Group 7239) Phase 4.

171 **Disc-rimmed flagon** in re-fired fabric R6, fired patchy pink/grey. Rim D: 90 mm. Context 7240 (Group 7239) Phase 4.

172 **Mortarium** in very fine-sanded white ware fabric R99. Rim D: 160 mm. Contexts 7244 and 7246 (Group 7239) Phase 4.

Fragments from a rouletted ovoid beaker of type 2A6 (*c* AD 190-230) in fabric R16 are also present in the assemblage from the uppermost waterhole fill 7240 and together with no. 172 suggest that the filling of this feature was completed at some time during the period 190-200.

Period 2, Phase 5 (AD 200-250)

Assemblage 33. From the packing (contexts 8191, 8362 and 8721) around postholes 8190, 8361 and 8720 of structure F. These various contexts produced

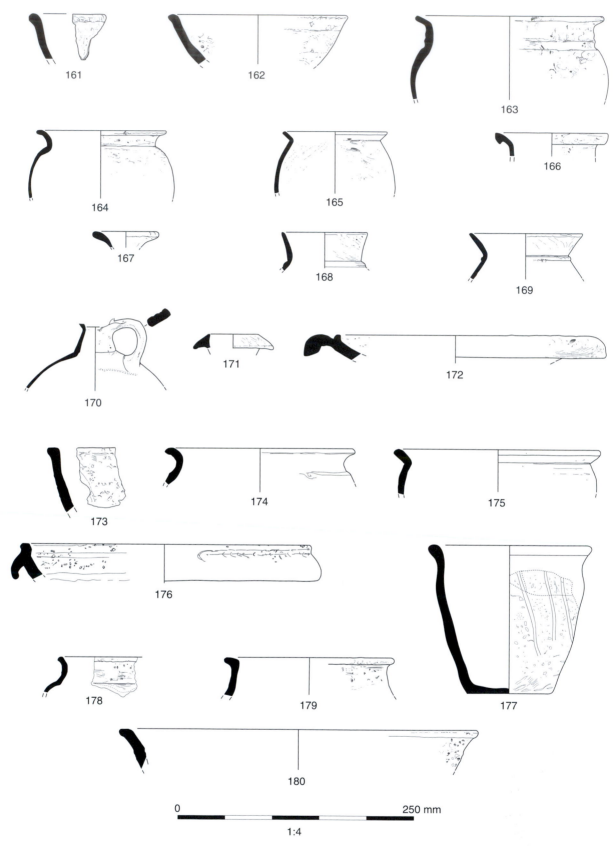

Figure 6.9   Roman pottery (Assemblage 32 (cont.): nos 161-172; Assemblage 34: nos 173-176; Assemblage 35: nos 177-180 continues).

Table 6.10   Pottery assemblage 32: Fabric and form quantification by EVES.

Fabric	Jars	Bowls	Dishes	Beakers	Store-jars	Others	Total	%
B2	1.50				0.05	Lid 0.05	1.60	17.9
B2.1	0.28		0.17			Flask 0.17	0.62	6.9
B2.4	0.19						0.19	2.1
R5	0.55	0.29					0.84	9.4
R6.1						Flagon 0.15	0.15	1.7
R6.3	0.08		0.12				0.20	2.2
R14		0.14	0.48				0.62	6.9
R16			0.06	2.49		Flasks 0.48	3.03	33.8
R43		0.17	0.34			Mortarium 0.01 Cup 0.20	0.72	8.0
R61						Mortarium 0.14	0.14	1.6
R71		0.08					0.08	0.9
R73	0.19	0.30					0.49	5.5
LR2	0.15	0.07	0.06				0.28	3.1
Total	2.94	1.05	1.23	2.49	0.05	1.20	8.96	
%	32.8	11.7	13.7	27.8	0.6	13.4		

147 sherds (1308 g) of pottery. The packing around posthole 8190 (8191) yielded fragments from Central Gaulish samian forms Drag. 31 (*c* AD 150-200) and Drag. 36 (*c* AD 120-200) and a bead-rimmed Thameside dish (*c* 170-230). The 60 sherds from the packing around posthole 8361 include a rim from a beaker of Monaghan type 2A4 (*c* AD 130-160) and the single sherd from that around posthole 8720 is from a hook-rimmed jar of Monaghan type 3H1 (*c* AD 170-250+). These fragments indicate that the structure was erected after AD 170 and possibly as late as the early years of the 3rd century.

Assemblage 34 (Fig. 6.9). From the gleyed animal trample deposit (context 9333) between structures D and F and over structure E. The 246 sherds (4282 g) of excavated and 17 sherds (112 g) of sieved pottery from this deposit probably includes residual fragments from structure E. There are fragments from a Dressel 20 amphora dated after AD 170, a Central Gaulish samian mortarium (*c* AD 170-200) and Drag. 31 dish (*c* AD 150-200), an East Sussex Ware storage-jar with finger-impressed girth cordon (*c* AD 200-270), a BB1 developed bead-and-flanged bowl (*c* AD 270-350), an ovoid Upchurch grey poppyhead beaker (*c* AD 190-230) and the following:

173   **Large handmade flanged dish** in black fabric LR1.1 with profuse white siltstone grog. ?Early 3rd century. Context 9333, Phase 5.

174   **Cavetto-rimmed jar** in brown-black East Sussex Ware (fabric B2/ESW). One of two. Rim D: 200 mm. Context 9333, Phase 5.

175   **Everted-rim jar** in orange fabric R1 fired grey. Dated *c* AD 170-250. Rim D: 200 mm. Context 9333, Phase 5.

176   **Mortarium** in cream fabric with soft red inclusions and profuse (up to 2 mm) multi-coloured quartz and white flint trituration grits (fabric 99). Dated *c* AD 150-250. Rim D: 260 mm. Context 9333, Phase 5.

From the circular structures and associated features

Assemblage 35 (Table 6.11; Figs 6.9 and 6.10). From the fills (contexts 7225, 7226, 7265, 7272, 7295, 7347, 7386, 7428, 7433 and 7296) of the penannular gully 7500 around structure P. The eight cuts across the fills of this gully yielded a substantial assemblage of 882 sherds (8624 g) of pottery.

The composition of this assemblage is superficially similar to that from the preceding circular structure O, but closer examination shows a decline in the significance of grog-tempered wares to 42% of the material (Table 6.11). There is a consequential decline in the percentage of cooking-pots and an increase in the significance of open forms from 13% of the structure O group to 22% of this assemblage. Lid-seated cooking-pots now account for less than 8% of the grog-tempered wares and are probably all residual. Further differences between this and the structure O assemblage include an increase in the significance of Thameside/BB2 industry coarse ware products from 6% to 15% of the material.

Pollard (1988, 95) thought that the export of Canterbury sandy grey wares terminated *c* AD 175 and their poor showing in both the structure O and P assemblages may merely mean that a few vessels remained in use after such wares had ceased to be available. It may be significant that the freshest Canterbury grey ware sherds from the structure O penannular gully come from a single primary silting context (7607) and make up more than half of the small amount of such wares by EVEs. Canterbury grey ware products probably ceased to be sent to Westhawk Farm soon after structure O was built.

The wares from the structure P gully include fragments from a Central Gaulish samian lion's head Drag. 45 mortarium (*c* AD 170-200), Drag. 31 and Drag. 37 sherds in the same fabric, a small cup of Symonds' Group 6 in Central Gaulish colour-coated fabric R35 (*c* AD 150-200; Symonds 1992, 19-20) as well as a rouletted ovoid beaker of Monaghan type

Table 6.11   Pottery assemblage 35: Fabric and form quantification by EVEs.

Fabric	Jars	Bowls	Dishes	Beakers	Others	Total	%
B2/ESW	1.11				Lids 0.27	1.38	15.9
B2.1	1.10	0.20		0.25	Lids 0.28	1.83	21.1
B2.4	0.26					0.26	3.0
LR1.1	0.21					0.21	2.4
R5	0.22	0.10	0.07			0.39	4.5
R6.1		0.07			Flagon 1.00	1.07	12.4
R14		0.34	0.05			0.39	4.5
R16	0.21			1.18		1.39	16.1
R35		0.16				0.16	1.8
R43			0.35		Dr33 0.14	0.63	7.3
					Mortarium 0.14		
R73	0.19	0.28	0.26			0.73	8.4
LR2	0.22					0.22	2.5
Total	3.52	1.15	0.73	1.43	1.83	8.66	
%	40.7	13.3	8.4	16.5	21.1		

2A6 (*c* AD 190-230), a jar of type 4A4 (*c* AD 70-150) and an indented beaker in grey Upchurch fine ware.

177 **Slack-profiled handmade grog-tempered jar** in black fabric LR1.1 with buff patches. Dated *c* AD 250-300+. Rim D: 180 mm. Context 7265 (Group 7500) Phase 5.

178 **Slack-profiled jar** in fabric LR1.1, but thinner-walled. Rim D: 160 mm. Context 7347 (Group 7500) Phase 5.

179 **Jar** with flanged rim in black grog-tempered fabric B2/ESW. Rim D: 180 mm. Context 7295 (Group 7500) Phase 5.

180 **Flanged bowl** in black, grog-tempered fabric B2.1. Rim D: 380 mm. Context 7295 (Group 7500) Phase 5.

181 **Bead-rim bowl** in black grog-tempered fabric B2.1. Rim D: 320 mm. Dated *c* AD 200-270. Context 7295 (Group 7500) Phase 5.

182 **Miniature jar** or **necked bowl** with carinated shoulder in fabric B2.1. Rim D: 60 mm. Context 7295 (Group 7500) Phase 5.

183 **Beaker** or **flagon** in similar fabric. Rim D: 60 mm. Context 7347 (Group 7500) Phase 5.

184 **Lid** in black grog-tempered fabric B2/ESW. Exterior rim D: 120 mm. Context 7272 (Group 7500) Phase 5.

185 Rim from **jar** of Monaghan type 3H1.9 in sandy grey Thameside fabric LR2 with superficial surface reddening. Dated *c* AD 180-250. Rim D: 160 mm. Lower fill, context 7226 (Group 7500) Phase 5.

186 Rim from **jar with rolled-over rim** in fabric LR2 with similar surface treatment. Rim D: 140 mm. Context 7295 (Group 7500) Phase 5.
A similar form in Alice Holt/Farnham grey ware is dated to the third century (Lyne and Jefferies 1979, Type 1.31).

187 Rim from **jar** of Monaghan type 3H7-6 in coarse grey Thameside fabric R73. Dated *c* AD 180-250. Rim D: 140 mm. Context 7272 (Group 7500) Phase 5.

188 **'Pie-dish'** of Monaghan type 5C1.5 in late blackened BB2 fabric (fabric R14). As Gillam form 225 this is dated *c* AD 200-250. Rim D: 240 mm. Context 7265 (Group 7500) Phase 5.
Another somewhat smaller example, in fabric R73, is present in the assemblage from context 7347.

189 **'Pie-dish'** smaller, but similar example in grey Thameside fabric R73 with patches of resin on its exterior and possibly used as packaging for some unknown product. Dated *c* AD 200-250. Rim D: 200 mm. Context 7265 (Group 7500) Phase 5.

190 **Straight-sided dish** in coarse grey Thameside fabric R73. Rim D: 200 mm. Context 7428 (Group 7500) Phase 5.
An identical form with slightly out-turned rim was present in Kiln A at Oakleigh Farm, Higham, where it was dated to the mid-3rd century (Catherall 1983, fig. 12.5).

191 Rim from **beaker** of Monaghan type 2C2 or 2C3 in grey Upchurch fine ware fabric R16. Dated *c* AD 250-280. Context 7265 (Group 7500) Phase 5.

192 **Flagon** of Pollard Type 81 (1988) with cupped and ringed neck in orange sandy Canterbury fabric R6.1. Dated *c* AD 150-250. Rim D: 30 mm. Context 7428 (Group 7500) Phase 5.
The rim form is paralleled in the Whitehall Gardens kiln 3 products at Canterbury, where it was dated *c* AD 150-180 (Jenkins 1960, fig. 5, 22).

The pottery indicates occupation during the earlier 3rd century, with an absence of BB1 and Thameside developed bead-and-flanged bowls suggesting that occupation did not continue beyond *c* AD 270.

Pit 9802 just inside the entrance to the structure produced 67 sherds (2948 g) of pottery, very largely made up of large, fresh Dressel 20 amphora sherds. Most of the rest of the pottery consists of ?residual grog-tempered body sherds (including a fragment from a bead-rim jar) and it may be that the pit originally held the amphora as a plunge-pot in the same manner as the storage-jar in pit 7582 outside the entrance to structure O.

Assemblage 36 (Figs 6.10 and 6.11). From features associated with structure R. Gullies 1200, 1220 and 1230 around rectangular structure R produced only 88 sherds (1782 g) of excavated and 40 (178 g) of sieved pottery in total, most of which are featureless body sherds. The following pieces are, however, worthy of note:

193   **Everted-rim jar** with rim-edge bead, in brown-black fabric B2.1. Dated *c* AD 200-270. Rim D: 140 mm. Context 1252 (Group 1200) Phase 5.
194   Complete rim from **flask** of Monaghan type 1B7 in grey Upchurch fine ware fabric (R16). Dated *c* AD 150-190 by Monaghan (1987), although Pollard (1988) argues for continued production through the 3rd century. Rim D: 75 mm. Context 1332 (Group 1220) Phase 5.
195   **Bead-rimmed bowl** copying Thameside original in re-fired patchy orange/grey fabric B2/ESW. Rim D: 180 mm. Context 1356 (Group 1220) Phase 5.
196   **Moselkeramik beaker** rim. Fabric R36. Dated *c* AD 200-270. Rim D: 70 mm. Context 1332 (Group 1220) Phase 5.

The posthole fills of Structure R yielded very little pottery (22 sherds, 228 g) and none at all came from the post packing contexts. The few sherds from the postpipe fills did, however, include the following:

197   **'Pie-dish'** of Monaghan type 5C1.5 in rough grey Thameside fabric R73. Dated *c* AD 200-250. Context 1464 (posthole 1465) Phase 5.
198   **Dish** of Monaghan type 5F7.3 in black BB2 fabric R14. Dated *c* AD 180-230. Rim D: 220 mm. Context 1483 (posthole 1484) Phase 5.

Pit 1636 within the building contained a large truncated jar in patchy brown/black fabric B2.1, probably used as a plunge pot in ironworking. Pit 1233, also within the building, yielded 35 sherds (524 g) of excavated and 21 (102 g) of sieved pottery, including fragments from a rouletted ovoid beaker of Monaghan type 2A6 in grey Upchurch fine ware (*c* AD 190-230) and the following pieces:

199   **Everted-rim jar** in black fabric B2.1. Rim D: 120 mm. Context 1231 (feature 1233) Phase 5.
200   **Small slack-profiled jar** in brown-black fabric B2/ESW. There are seven fresh sherds from this pot. Context 1232 (feature 1233) Phase 5.
201   **Mortarium**, Gillam 255, in powdery cream fabric (G255). Dated *c* AD 160-230. Much of this vessel is present. Rim D: 200 mm. Context 1231 (feature 1233) Phase 5.
202   **Everted-rim jar** in sandy grey fabric LR2.1 with reddened surfaces. Dated *c* AD 180-270. Rim D: 110 mm. Context 1231 (feature 1233) Phase 5.

The pottery from these various contexts suggests that structure R was in use from *c* AD 200 perhaps up to *c* AD 270.

From the waterholes

Assemblage 37 (Fig. 6.11). From the fills (contexts 7260, 7261, 7262, 9179, 10163, 10162, 10161, 10159, 10158, 10119, 10118, 9421, 9420, 9419, 9418, 9417, 9416, 9415, 9414, 9413, 9188, 9187, 9185, 7258, 9186, 7129, 9184 and 7128) of waterhole 9179. This feature produced a mere 84 sherds (2476 g) of pottery, which is unfortunate in view of its relationship with the temple to its north-east and the possibility that it might have been a focus of ritual activity. The lowest fills were, unfortunately, not excavated and those immediately above produced little or no pottery. The lowest fill to yield any sherds was the yellow clay layer 9417 which produced 59 fragments (1794 g) of mid to late 2nd century character, including the following:

203   **Slack-profiled jar** in black fabric B2/ESW. Rim D: 160 mm. Context 9417 (Feature 9179) Phase 5.
204   **Lid-seated jar** in grey fabric B2.4. Rim D: 180 mm. Dated *c* AD 120-170+. Context 9417 (Feature 9179) Phase 5.
205   **Mortarium** in sand-free grey fabric fired brown with thick pink margins and superficial surface greying (fabric R99). Rim D: 240 mm. Late 2nd century. Context 9417 (Feature 9179) Phase 5.

Two further sherds (88 g) from dark-grey clay deposit 9413 at a higher level come from a poppyhead beaker of Monaghan type 2A6 in grey Upchurch fine ware fabric (*c* AD 190-230). Grey-blue clay silt 7129 near the top of the feature produced a further 10 sherds (86 g), including fragments from Central Gaulish samian Drag. 31 and Drag. 42 dishes (*c* AD 150-200 and 120-140 respectively) and a Drag. 33 cup (*c* AD 120-200). A fragment from a dish of Monaghan Class 5F3 (*c* AD 130-230) is also present.

There is too little pottery to detect any evidence for ritual activity in the composition of the overall assemblage but the very paucity of such material within what is a very large feature may in itself be indicative of a special character. The small amounts of material are indicative of the sporadic deposition of pottery during the late 2nd and early 3rd centuries. There is nothing later than *c* AD 230.

Assemblage 38 (Fig. 6.11). From the fills of pit or waterhole 8479 (contexts 8480, 9309, 9311 and 10366). The 337 sherds (3848 g) of pottery from this feature north-west of structure G include fragments from a Central Gaulish samian Drag. 31 platter (*c* AD 150-200), a lid-seated jar in fabric B2.4 (*c* AD 120-170+), two fragments from a Hadham oxidised ware flagon (*c* AD 250-400) and the following vessels:

206   Complete **everted-rim jar** in grey-black grog-tempered fabric B2.1 with external orange-brown patches. A small hole has been punched

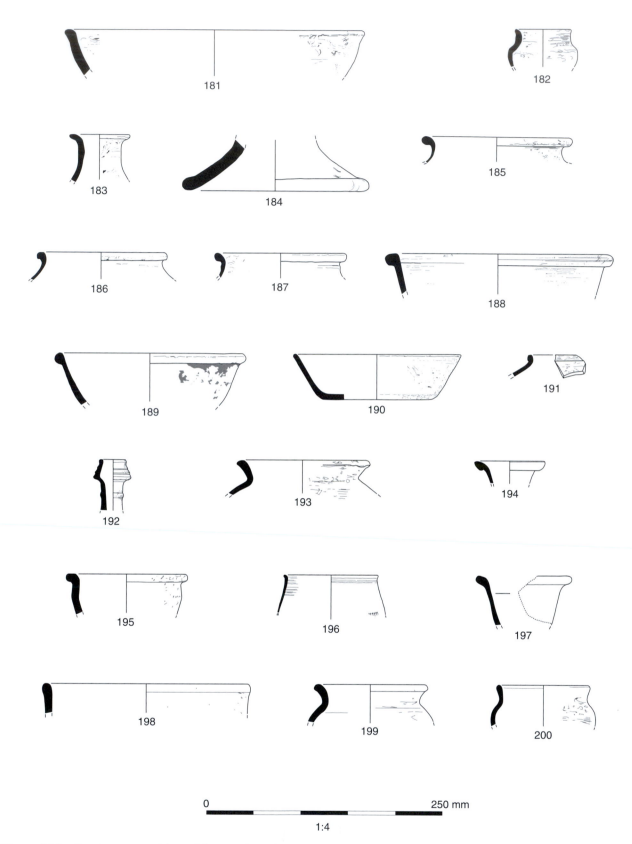

Figure 6.10   *Roman pottery (Assemblage 35 (cont.): nos 181-192; Assemblage 36: nos 192-200 continues).*

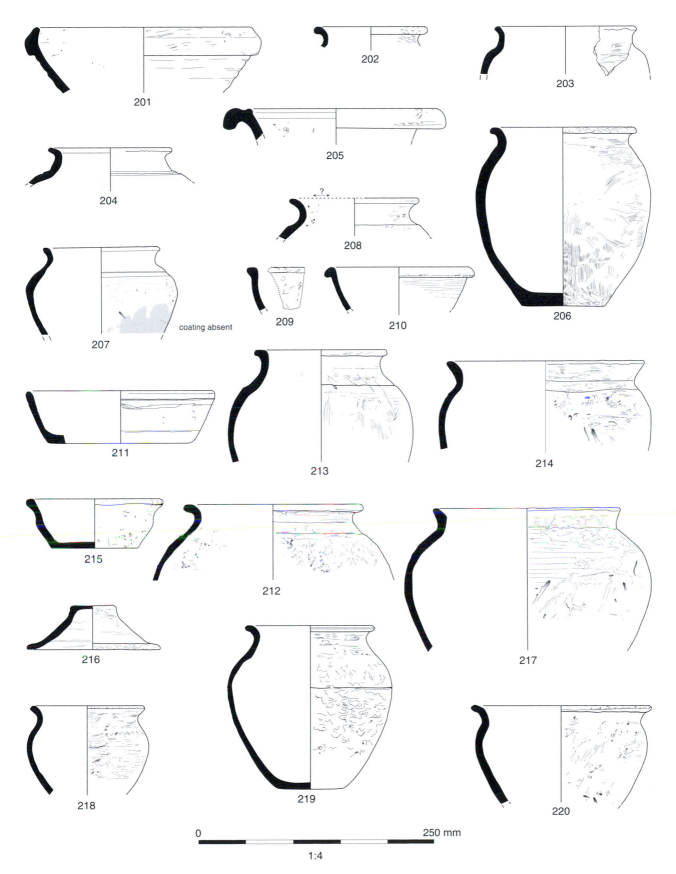

Figure 6.11   Roman pottery (Assemblage 36 (cont.): nos 201-202; Assemblage 37: nos 203 205; Assemblage 38: nos 206-211; Assemblage 39: 212-220 continues).

through the side of the vessel after firing. Dated *c* AD 200-270. Rim D: 150 mm. Context 9309.

207 **Cordoned jar** in black fabric B2.1. Context 8480 (Feature 8479) Phase 5.

208 **Jar with cavetto rim** in black, grog-tempered fabric LR1.1. Dated 3rd century. Context 9311 (Feature 8479) Phase 5.

209 **Flanged dish** in fabric LR1.1. Dated 3rd century. Context 9311 (Feature 8479) Phase 5.

210 **'Pie-dish'** of Monaghan type 5C4.2 in black BB2 fabric (R14). Dated *c* AD 170-250. Rim D: 160 mm. Context 8480 (Feature 8479) Phase 5.

211 **Dish** of Monaghan type 5F4 in black BB2 fabric R14. Dated *c* AD 130-250. Rim D: 200 mm. Context 9311 (Feature 8479) Phase 5.

Period 2, Phase 6 (AD 250-350)

Assemblage 39 (Table 6.12; Figs 6.11, 6.12 and 6.13). From the lower dumping (contexts 310, 322, 344, 345, 346, 366, 368, 379, 427, 428, 429, 437, 723, 724, 725, 739, 758, 1359, 1380, 1384 and 1554) in the top of waterhole 796. The fills in the bottom of the waterhole (contexts 1385, 1386, 1434, 1456, 1547, 1583, 1586-1604 and 1628) were largely lacking in pottery and produced a mere 50 sherds (2114 g) between them. These sherds include fragments from a Martres-de-Veyre samian Drag. 37 bowl (*c* AD 90-120), a Central Gaulish samian Drag. 18/31 platter (*c* AD 120-150) and Drag. 45 mortarium with lion-headed spout (*c* AD 170-200), Canterbury grey ware jar fragments (*c* AD 70-175) and a BB2 dish of Monaghan Type 5E1.4 (*c* AD 160-200), and may represent sherds dropped into the feature during its period of use.

The overlying deposits, within the upper part of the waterhole, produced 1129 mainly large fresh sherds (33,546g) of excavated pottery with enough rim fragments to justify quantification by EVEs. A further 317 sherds (1706 g) of pottery was recovered through the sieving of environmental samples.

Table 6.12 reveals an assemblage in which most of the kitchen wares such as cooking-pots, lids, coarse bowls and dishes were supplied by Wealden and local suppliers of handmade grog-tempered wares. The most significant suppliers of pottery to the site, however, were the Thameside industries (52%), which supplied BB2 and sandy grey kitchen wares in fabrics R14, R73 and LR.2 as well as fine grey ware beakers and other forms from the Upchurch kilns. Small amounts of both Central Gaulish and East Gaulish samian are also present, including fragments from Drag. 31, Drag. 31R, Drag. 36 and Walters 79 platters, Drag. 33 cups, Drag. 38 and 44 bowls, Drag. 45 mortaria and a Drag. 37 bowl in the style of Paternus II of Lezoux (*c* AD 160-195). Two of the Drag. 31R platters have stamps of Senator (*c* AD 150-200) and Celsianus (*c* AD 160-190). The East Gaulish fragments include those from Argonne Curle 21 and Drag. 81 bowls and an indeterminate Rheinzabern closed form.

One of the most significant features of an assemblage which otherwise has a fairly normal form breakdown is the very high percentage of beakers, largely made up of early-3rd-century Upchurch types (see below). The percentage of vessels of this form from the penannular gully around the part contemporary structure P is also fairly high at 16%, but still somewhat lower than the 24% of this assemblage. Percentages of jars and open forms from the two assemblages are remarkably similar (41%/40% and 22%/21% respectively). A dumping of material within this waterhole towards the end of the occupation of structure P may, however, be indicated by a much lower percentage of vessels in the post AD 250/270 Roman grog-tempered ware fabric LR1.1 from the latter feature (2%) compared with the 28% from the waterhole. Grog-tempered wares overall otherwise make up very similar percentages of the material from the two features (43% from Structure P and 39% from waterhole 796).

Table 6.12   Pottery assemblage 39: Fabric and form quantification by EVEs.

Fabric	Jars	Bowls	Dishes	Beakers	Store-jars	Others	Total	%
B2/ESW	1.32		1.00	0.20		Lids 0.26	2.78	8.6
R1	0.36		0.05		0.10		0.51	1.6
LR1.1	7.45	0.21	0.60			Lids 0.94	9.20	28.4
R14	0.56	0.26	2.10				2.92	9.0
R16				7.71		Flasks 1.36	9.62	29.8
						Cup 0.55		
R36						Cup 0.22	0.22	0.7
R43		0.65	0.01			Cup 0.12	0.83	2.6
						Mortaria 0.05		
R46		0.41	0.26			Mortaria 0.14	0.81	2.5
R71						Cup 0.45	0.45	1.4
R73	1.90	0.86	0.36				3.12	9.6
R99						Mortaria 0.34	0.34	1.1
LR2	1.15		0.12				1.27	3.9
LR5.1	0.24						0.24	0.7
MISC			0.03				0.03	0.1
Total	12.98	2.39	4.53	7.91	0.10	4.42	32.34	
%	40.1	7.4	14.0	24.5	0.3	13.7		

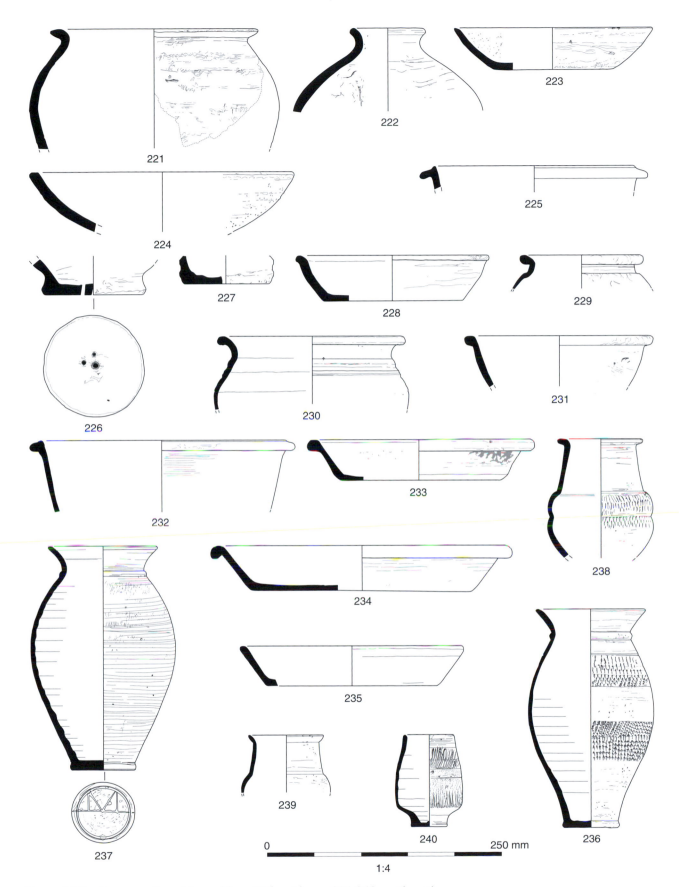

Figure 6.12   Roman pottery (Assemblage 39 (cont.): nos 221-240 continues).

212 **Necked jar** in brown-black East Sussex Ware (fabric B2/ESW) with flattened rim top. Rim D: 180 mm. Context 366 (Group 796) Phase 6.

213 **Necked jar** in fabric B2/ESW. Rim D: 140 mm. Context 758 (Group 796) Phase 6.

214 **Everted-rim jar** in fabric B2/ESW. Rim D: 200 mm. Context 758 (Group 796) Phase 6.

215 Complete **lop-sided and poorly-finished bowl** in fabric B2/ESW fired patchy black/grey/orange. Rim D: 150 mm. Context 1359 (Group 796) Phase 6.

216 **Lid** in brown-black East Sussex Ware (fabric B2/ESW). Rim D: 140 mm. Context 366 (Group 796) Phase 6.

217 **Everted-rim cooking-pot** in black fabric LR1.1 with burnished linear decoration on the body. Rim D: 200 mm. Context 1380 (Group 796) Phase 6.

218 **Everted-rim jar** in patchy grey/black/brown fabric LR1.1. Rim D: 120 mm. Context 1359 (Group 796) Phase 6.

219 **Slack-profiled jar** with girth groove in fabric LR1.1 fired black. Rim D: 140 mm. Context 758 (Group 796) Phase 6.

220 **Large necked jar** in fabric LR1.1 fired brown-black. Rim D: 200 mm. Context 758 (Group 796) Phase 6.

221 **Everted-rim jar** with flattened rim top in fabric LR1.1 fired black. Rim D: 200 mm. Context 344 (Group 796) Phase 6.

222 **Narrow-necked jar** in fabric LR1.1 fired black. Rim D: 75 mm. Context 345 (Group 796) Phase 6.

223 **Plain-rim dish** in black fabric LR1.1. One of two. Context 758 (Group 796) Phase 6.

224 **Large dish** in fabric LR1.1 fired black. Rim D: 260 mm. Contexts 310 and 758 (Group 796) Phase 6.

225 **Incipient bead-and-flanged bowl** in grey fabric LR1.1. Context 1380 (Group 796) Phase 6.

226 **Pedestal base** from jar in black fabric LR1.1 with three holes drilled through it. Context 1359 (Group 796) Phase 6.

227 **Pedestal base** from jar in fabric LR1.1 with single central perforation. Context 725 (Group 796) Phase 6.

228 **Bead-rim dish** in grey Native Coarse Ware fabric R1 fired patchy brown/black. Rim D: 220 mm. Context 427 (Group 796) Phase 6.

229 **Necked jar** of Monaghan type 3H1.8 in reddened-grey fabric LR2.1. Dated *c* AD 170-230. Rim D: 130 mm. Context 427 (Group 796) Phase 6.

230 **High-fired necked and cordoned jar** in very fine-sanded blue-grey fabric LR5.1. Possibly an early Preston-by-Wingham product. Rim D: 180 mm. Context 725 (Group 796) Phase 6.

231 **Bowl** of Monaghan class 5C1 in grey Thameside fabric R73. Dated *c* AD 170-250. Rim D: 220 mm. Context 427 (Group 796) Phase 6.

232 **Incipient bead-and-flanged bowl** of Monaghan type 5A2.2 in grey Thameside fabric R73 with

superficial reddening. Dated *c* AD 230-320. Rim D: 260 mm. Contexts 723 and 1380 (Group 796) Phase 6.

233 **Dish** of Monaghan type 5C4.1 in grey Thameside fabric R73 with traces of resin on its exterior under the rim suggesting use for packaging. Dated *c* AD 170-250. Rim D: 240 mm. Context 427 (Group 796) Phase 6.

234 **Dish** of similar proportions in fabric R73, but with a drooping bead rim. Rim D: 320 mm. Context 758 (Group 796) Phase 6.

235 **Dish** of Monaghan type 5E1.1 in black-surfaced fabric R14. Dated *c* AD 160-260. Rim D: 240 mm. Context 739 (Group 796) Phase 6.

236 **Poppyhead beaker** of Monaghan type 2A6.5 with rouletted decoration in Upchurch fabric R16. One of several. Rim D: 120 mm. Context 367 (Group 796) Phase 6.

237 Complete **plain poppyhead beaker** of Monaghan Type 2A6.2 in Upchurch fabric R16 with polished black exterior and graffito on base. Dated *c* AD 190-230. Rim D: 140 mm. Context 367 (Group 796) Phase 6.

238 **Rouletted pentice-beaker** of Monaghan type 2C1.3 in grey Upchurch fabric R16. Rim D: 85 mm. *c* AD 220-250. Context 344 (Group 796) Phase 6.

239 **Funnel-necked beaker** of ?Monaghan Type 2C8.1 in fabric R16. Dated *c* AD 170/190-210/230. Rim D: 80 mm. Context 344 (Group 796) Phase 6.

240 **Beaker**, similar to Monaghan type 2B1.1 in fabric R16 with overall rouletting. The greater part of this vessel was present. Rim D: 55 mm. Context 1554 (Group 796) Phase 6.
Monaghan (1987, 61) dates the form *c* AD 43/50-70/100, but this is clearly erroneous as he bases his dates on a somewhat dissimilar 'Belgic' grog-tempered butt-beaker copy (Thompson 1982, G5.5). A fragment from another example came from context 724.

241 **Cup** copying East Gaulish samian form (Oswald and Pryce 1920, pl. lv, no. 13) in fabric R16. Monaghan's form 6A1.1 dated by him to the early 2nd century (probably too early). Early 3rd century. Context 345 (Group 796) Phase 6.
Paralleled at the White Cliffs Experience site in Dover, in the uppermost occupation horizon of the *Classis Britannica* fort (Booth 1994, fig. 15.55).

242 **Bowl** in pink Upchurch fabric R16 variant copying samian Drag. 37 with body rouletting. Rim D: 140 mm. Context 367 (Group 796) Phase 6.

243 **Mortarium** in sand-free grey fabric R17 fired orange with discontinuous white slip and crushed-flint trituration grits. Context 367 (Group 796) Phase 6.

244 **Handled cup** in fabric R71 fired rough orange-brown with smoked patch on the handle. Rim D: 80 mm. Context 725 (Group 796) Phase 6.

245 **Flask** similar to Monaghan type 1B7.1 in grey Upchurch fabric R16 with rouletted body dec-

oration, but double neck cordon. Dated *c* AD 150-190. Rim D: 50 mm. Context 1380 (Group 796) Phase 6.

Fragments from a Rhenish white ware wall-sided mortarium (*c* AD 150-300) are also present.

Assemblage 40 (Table 6.13; Fig. 6.13). From the upper dumping (contexts 255, 275, 298, 302, 303, 378, 675, 676, 677, 707, 720 and 726) in the top of waterhole 796. The uppermost fills of this feature yielded 994 sherds (16,905 g) of excavated and 100 (442 g) of sieved pottery. This is a somewhat smaller collection than from the lower sinkage fills (see Assemblage 39), but the excavated material is still suitable for quantification by EVEs.

This assemblage is considerably more broken up than that from lower down in the waterhole and, like it, has significant quantities of handmade grog-tempered ware cooking-pots, bowls and dishes similar to those in Assemblage 35. These now form the largest single component of the assemblage: there is a decline in the significance of Thameside products (36%), brought about by the presence of far fewer fragments from beakers and other fine ware forms in grey Upchurch Fabric R16. It is probable that nearly all of the few Upchurch ware sherds are now residual in nature. Dorset BB1 is present for the first time in very small quantities and includes the following forms:

246 **Developed bead-and-flanged bowl**. Fabric R13. Dated *c* AD 270-350. Rim D: 180 mm. Context 255 (Group 796) Phase 6.
247 **Straight-sided dish with external burnished arcading**. Fabric R13. Dated *c* AD 220-350. Rim D: 200 mm. Context 675 (Group 796) Phase 6. Another example is present in the assemblage from context 677.

The sand-tempered grey wares include Thameside 'pie-dishes' and straight-sided dishes of forms dated *c* AD 170-250, similar to those from the lower fills. A large part of the following pot is also present:

248 **Necked storage vessel** in rough grey fabric R73 with polished black patches on its surface. This vessel looks like a kiln second, originally meant to be fired polished black all over. Rim D: 100 mm. Context 303 (Group 796) Phase 6.

The other wares include the following:

249 **Incipient bead-and-flanged bowl** in BB2, fabric R14. Rim D: 220 mm. Context 675 (Group 796) Phase 6.
250 **Mortarium**, Lower Nene Valley white ware, fired pale buff-brown (fabric LR11). Rim D: 300 mm. Context 275 (Group 796) Phase 6.
251 **Mortarium** with unusual concave-flanged rim in sandy orange ?Canterbury fabric R6.1 fired orange-brown with calcined-flint trituration grits. Rim D: 280 mm. Contexts 275 and 302 (Group 796) Phase 6.
252 **Mortarium**, with bead-and-flanged rim in fabric R6.1, fired buff-brown. Contexts 302 and 677 (Group 796) Phase 6.
253 **Mortarium** in fabric R6.1 fired orange-brown but with beaded rim and mixed flint, ironstone and multi-coloured quartz trituration grits. Rim D: 280 mm. Context 275 (Group 796) Phase 6.

The samian includes a Central Gaulish Drag. 33 cup with a stamp of Calvinus and a late-looking East Gaulish Drag. 36 platter (*c* AD 220-260). A few fragments from a Moselkeramik beaker (*c* AD 200-275) are also present.

Table 6.13   Pottery assemblage 40: Fabric and form quantification by EVEs.

Fabric	Jars	Bowls	Dishes	Beakers	Store-jars	Others	Total	%
B2/ESW	1.97	0.17	0.52			Lid 0.07	2.73	17.6
LR1.1	4.25	0.14	0.39			Lid 0.06	4.84	31.2
R1		0.05					0.05	0.3
R5	0.15					Lid 0.10	0.25	1.6
R6.1						Mortaria 0.20	0.20	1.3
R6.3	0.05					Mortaria 0.12	0.17	1.1
R13		0.29	0.30				0.59	3.8
R14	0.23	0.78	0.80				1.81	11.6
R16	0.33			0.28		Flask 1.00	1.61	10.3
R17						Flagon 0.10	0.10	0.6
R36				0.11			0.11	0.7
R43			0.26			Cup 0.05 Mortaria 0.05	0.36	2.3
R46			0.26			Cup 0.09	0.35	2.2
R64						Mortaria 0.10	0.10	0.6
R71			0.05				0.05	0.3
R73	0.80	0.30	0.12		0.56		1.78	11.4
LR2	0.28	0.05					0.33	2.1
LR21						Mortaria 0.15	0.15	1.0
Total	8.06	1.78	2.70	0.39	0.56	2.09	15.58	
%	51.7	11.4	17.3	2.5	3.6	13.5		

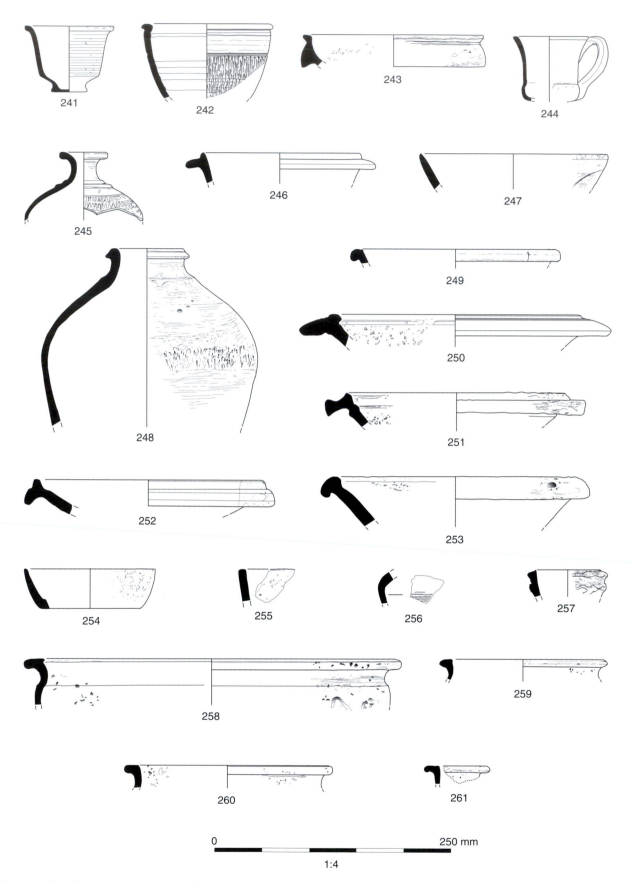

Figure 6.13   Roman pottery (Assemblage 39 (cont.): nos 241-245; Assemblage 40: nos 246-253; Assemblage 41: nos 254-257); and Medieval pottery (Assemblage 42: nos 258-261).

Period 2, Phase 7 (AD 350-400+)

Assemblage 41 (Fig. 6.13). From the fill (context 417) of pit 415 in the centre of the temple. The 71 sherds (882 g) of excavated pottery and 12 additional sherds (30 g) from sieved samples from this context is a rather unusual collection which has a wide date-range. It includes a substantial portion of a plain late poppyhead beaker of Monaghan type 2A6 (*c* AD 190-230), a sherd from a Central Gaulish samian Drag. 38 bowl (*c* AD 140-200), a sherd of Oxfordshire colour-coated ware (the only securely-stratified sherd of this ware from the entire site) and the following:

254 **Convex-sided dish** in grey-black grog-tempered ware fabric LR1.1. Dated *c* AD 350-400+. Rim D: 140 mm. Context 417 (pit 415, Group 80) Phase 7.

255 **Straight-sided dish** in fabric LR1.1. Dated *c* AD 270-370. Context 417 (pit 415, Group 80) Phase 7.

256 **Horizontally-rilled jar** fragment in oxidised Overwey/Portchester D fabric LR6. Dated *c* AD 330-420. Context 417 (pit 415, Group 80) Phase 7.

257 Top of **bottle** or **flagon** of unusual form in very-fine-sanded buff-orange fabric (R71) with finger-impressed rim and similarly-decorated cordon around the neck. Possibly from a ritual vessel. Rim D: 70 mm. Context 417 (pit 415, Group 80) Phase 7.

The presence of the rilled jar body sherds in Overwey/Portchester D fabric makes this the latest pottery assemblage from the entire excavation and indicates that the shrine remained a focus of activity after this part of the town had otherwise been abandoned.

Period 3: Medieval (c AD 1200-1350)

Assemblage 42 (Fig. 6.13). From the fill of large pit 10078 (context 10077). This feature produced 186 fresh sherds (2106 g), mainly incorporating large fragments from a small number of pots in sandy medieval fabric M.1, including the following:

258 **Bowl** with lid-seated rim fired reddish-brown to black with scribed wavy line around its exterior. Medieval fabric M1. Rim D: 400 mm+. Context 10077 (pit 10078) Period 3.

259-61 Rims from three **cooking-pots** similarly fired. Medieval fabric M1. Context 10077 (pit 10078) Period 3.

Assemblage 43 (Fig. 6.14). From the fills of pit 9987 (contexts 9988 and 9989). The 157 medieval sherds (1490 g) of pottery from this pit are all from a single vessel:

262 Sagging-base cooking-pot in reddish-brown to black fabric M.1. Rim D: 320 mm. Contexts 9988 and 9989 (pit 9987) Period 3.

The forms in these two assemblages are very similar to those illustrated by Grove and Warhurst (1952) as coming from a 13th century pottery kiln waster deposit at Potters Corner, Ashford.

Miscellaneous vessels from Roman contexts

A number of unusual vessels mostly from otherwise insignificant assemblages are catalogued below and illustrated (Fig. 6.14):

263 **Multiple cordoned barrel-shaped butt-beaker** of Thompson form G5-1 in grey fabric B2.1 fired polished black externally. Dated *c* AD 1-50. Rim D: 180 mm. Context 7997 (pit 7733).

264 Upper part of **wide-mouthed bowl** of Thompson form E1-2 with multiple cordons, in grey fabric B2.1 with white patches. Late Iron Age to AD 60. Rim D: 190 mm. Context 1058 (hollow-way cut 1107).

265 **Bead-and-flanged dish** in patchy white/black fabric LR1.1 with perforations made through the sides before firing. 4th century. Rim D: 160 mm. Context 680 (pit 681) .

266 **Jug**, (Cam 161) in grey Patchgrove ware fabric R68 fired patchy orange/brown. Dated *c* AD 43-60. Rim D: 150 mm. Context 936 (ditch 840).

267 **Jug**, almost identical vessel in fabric R68 fired smooth orange-brown. Late 1st century. Rim D: 170 mm. Context 7768 (ditch 7850).

268 **Finely-moulded beaker** in thin-walled black eggshell ware fabric R81. Rim D: 95 mm. Context 7529 (pit 7530).

269 **Small bottle** in grey Upchurch fine ware fabric R16. Rim D: 42 mm. Context 7952 (pit 7951).

270 *Tettina* in grey Upchurch fine ware fabric R16. Most of this vessel is present. Rim D: 40 mm. Context 8857 (cut 8856 Group 9210).

271 Slightly **carinated sherd** in very-fine grey ware with apple-green glaze over white barbotine decoration. Probably from the Staines area. Dated *c* AD 70-150. Context 238 (posthole 239 Group 350).

272 Foot from crudely-made salt **briquetage container** fired patchy pink/pale purple. Context 585 (surface collection).

273 **Trimmed-down flagon neck** in sandy-orange Canterbury kilns fabric R6.1. Context 8141 (pit 8143).

274 Complete **miniature handmade pot** in brown-grey fabric B2 with black internal residues. Rim D: 70 mm. Context 530 (hollow way cut 626).

275 Complete **miniature handmade pot** in soft grog-tempered ware fired orange/brown/black. Rim D: *c* 35 mm. Context 922 (ditch 923).

276 Incomplete **miniature handmade pot** in similar fabric fired grey-brown. Context 7249 (Group 7239) Phase 4.
See Assemblage 32 above.

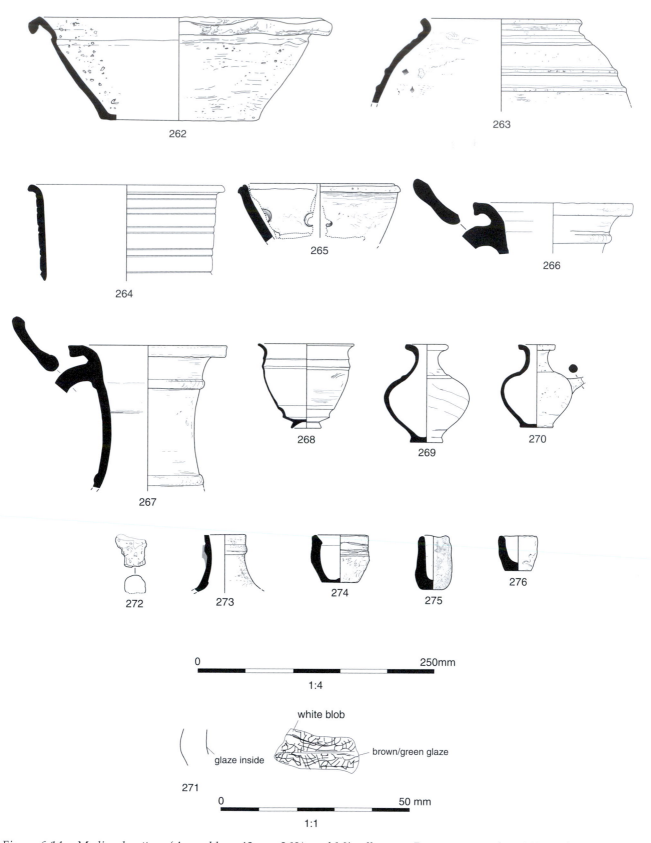

Figure 6.14   *Medieval pottery (Assemblage 43: no. 262); and Miscellaneous Roman pottery (nos 263-276).*

Ceramic evidence for site status and specialised activities

Even without any ceramic evidence, it seems likely that ironworkers living in circular structures as late as the end of the 2nd century, must have been fairly low down the social order even if they were not slaves This is born out by the samian, of which 11 vessels in a fairly small overall assemblage show evidence of riveting after breakage. These riveted vessels include one Drag. 18/31 platter, four Drag. 31 platters, a Drag. 33 cup and four Drag. 37 bowls in Central Gaulish fabric.

Dressel 20 olive oil and Gauloise 4 wine amphorae are the most common forms of this type of ceramic container on most Romano-British sites between *c* AD 70 and 250. Gauloise 4s, however, are represented by a mere 55 sherds from 17 contexts at Westhawk Farm and it seems clear that the inhabitants of the part of the town that was excavated drank little if any Gallic wine. Even the vessels which are represented may have been brought in empty for re-use as plunge pots in the iron production process. The same applies to the somewhat more common Dressel 20 sherds of which 561 were found, with concentrations in the ironworking areas.

The smelting and working of iron does not involve much use of ceramics other than tuyères and plunge-pots. Old flagon necks were sometimes used as tuyères (Lyne 1999, fig. 182) and there is one possible example of this from the site (no. 273 above). More possible evidence for the use of flagon necks as tuyères lies in the surprisingly large numbers of flagon body sherds, but comparatively few rim fragments from the site. Most context assemblages from the site seem to include some body sherds. However, it should be noted that the fired clay from the site does include possible pieces from specially made plate tuyères (see Paynter, Chapter 7).

Remains of six *in situ* plunge-pots were found on the site, in the form of large grog-tempered storage-jars, with or without body combing, set in pits 316, 600, 844, 1238, 1636 and 7581. All may have had their rims removed possibly to open them out, though the effects of post-Roman truncation of deposits should also be borne in mind. They are thus unsuitable for illustration.

Ceramic evidence for ritual and other activities is less obvious. Where assemblages have been quantified by EVE, their composition by form has been tabulated in an attempt to detect unusual patterns of vessel type usage (Table 6.14). The most obvious anomalies in this tabulation are the high percentages of beakers in late 2nd- to 3rd-century Assemblages 25 to 39 and the high flagon percentages from Assemblages 9, 17 and 35. The high flagon percentages, unfortunately, reveal one of the drawbacks in quantification by EVEs based on rim sherds in that the narrowness of flagon necks gives them extra strength and a tendency to survive intact after the breakage of the vessel. The presence of complete or reconstructable flagon rims in pottery assemblages thus distorts EVE quantification by overstating the importance of this vessel type.

The highest beaker percentages are in assemblages 32 and 39 from the sinkage fills in the tops of waterholes 7239/9151 and 796 and may have more significance. It was noted that the complete and largely-complete pot groups from the sinkages over the ritual shafts at Folly Lane, St Albans had significantly larger percentages of beakers and open forms than both the shaft fills beneath and ordinary domestic assemblages from the site (Lyne 1999, 301). This suggested ritual meals at the closing of the shafts, and it may be that the waterholes at Westhawk Farm also had a ritual element to their usage and were the focus of similar meals on being abandoned. Further support for ritual activities associated with the waterholes comes from the discovery of the complete jar with a hole drilled in the side (no. 206) in waterhole or pit 8479. Such ritually 'killed' pots were also found in the shafts at Swan Street, Southwark (Lyne forthcoming c). At both Southwark and Folly Lane, St Albans, dogs were also found in the fills of shafts and it was suspected that the worship of the Gallo-Roman hammer god Sucellos, as well as other deities, was involved (Lyne 1999, 301; Ross 1992, 423). Such a deity or local equivalent may well have been worshipped by an ironworking community such as that at Westhawk Farm. The small, complete bottle (no. 269) from pit 7951 is the only item from that feature and may also have been ritually deposited.

The site produced five miniature pots, four of which have the appearance of crucibles but no evidence of exposure to high temperature (nos 136 and 274-276). The fifth (no. 137) is a miniature wheel-turned jar. These pots may possibly have been used to burn cannabis or hallucinatory drugs for inhalation since

Table 6.14   *Pottery: Percentage of vessel classes (quantified by EVEs) in selected assemblages (+ = present, but lacking rim).*

Assemblage	Jars	Open forms	Beakers	Store-jars	Flagons	Others	Date-range
17	44.8	24.9	2.5	7.9	16.4	3.5	70-90
9	58.4	9.3	5.0	+	25.4	1.9	90-120
25	46.7	32.3	16.6		3.8	0.6	170
31	65.4	12.9	13.4	0.6	3.2	4.5	170-200
32	32.8	27.6	27.8	0.6	8.9	2.3	190-200+
35	40.7	23.3	16.5		11.5	8.0	200-270
39	40.1	25.1	24.5	0.3	4.2	5.4	200-270
40	51.7	29.6	2.5	3.6	7.1	5.5	270-300+

similar Roman examples - in handmade Alice Holt fabric - have recently been excavated at Frensham in Surrey, and were found to contain burnt cannabis residues (D Graham pers. comm.). They may thus be evidence for shamanistic practices. Two of the Westhawk pots (nos 136-137) are in the assemblage from the manifestly ritual deposit in grave 8160. Except for the presence of an abnormally high percentage of open forms, the form breakdown of this group differs little from a normal domestic assemblage. The funeral may have been accompanied by a ritual meal and perhaps by attempts to communicate with the other world by means of drug-induced trances.

Decorated Samian
by Joanna Bird

Summary

The twenty-four decorated samian bowls from Westhawk Farm, Ashford are generally in poor condition, some of the pieces having lost their slip and finer decorative detail completely (Figs 6.15 and 6.16). They range in date from the middle of the 1st century to the late 2nd. Eight of the bowls are South Gaulish, from La Graufesenque; among these are two examples of Drag. 29 which were probably made by the Neronian potter Murranus and three bowls dating from the Flavian-Trajanic period, including a Drag. 37 in the style of the later Germani. Early 2nd-century wares are absent, not surprisingly with such a small group since a general fall in the amount of samian in circulation has been observed at this date (Marsh 1981). Apart from a bowl by the Hadrianic-Early Antonine potter Cettus of Les Martres-de-Veyre, the 2nd-century wares all come from Lezoux. The Hadrianic-early Antonine bowls include single vessels by Attianus, Quintilianus and an unknown potter whose work has also been recorded at Canterbury. Later wares include at least five bowls by the mid-Antonine potter Cinnamus and later 2nd-century vessels by Paternus II (two pots) and Casurius; these are the potters who would normally dominate a group of this date.

Five of the bowls have been repaired using lead wire staples through drilled round holes; one of them is of Flavian-Trajanic date, the others Hadrianic to Antonine. Although the assemblage is too small to allow any definite conclusions, this seems an unusually high proportion. Two reasons suggest themselves: either the community was poor, and samian was treasured and repaired, or they were unable to obtain new samian in the first half of the 3rd century, when supply became more variable. The latter explanation seems the less likely, since the inhabitants of nearby Canterbury were able to obtain a range of samian dating up to the middle of the 3rd century (Bird 1995a, 774-775).

Catalogue (Figs 6.15 and 6.16)

1 (*not illustrated*) **Drag. 37, South Gaul**; the ovolo has been completely removed in the finishing.

The upper frieze is a hunting scene with vines separating the figures; these include a cupid (Hermet 1934, pl. 18, 34), a hound (ibid, pl. 26, 40) and a boar (ibid., pl. 27, 42). Below is a band of wreath festoons containing spirals. Similar designs were made by such potters as Biragillus (Mees 1995, Taf. 14.1) and the Germani; the design by the potter numbered Germanus II by Mees, has an astragalus bead row supporting the festoons (ibid., Taf. 71.1), as here, where it also forms a pendant between them. The beads used in the borders are unusually large, a feature of other Germani bowls (eg. Mees 1995, Taf. 80.1 and 9, by his Germanus III). Seven sherds; very abraded. Dated *c* AD 75-95. Context 263 (Group 1740) Phase 4.

2 **Drag. 37** in the style of Paternus II of Lezoux. The motifs are all on mould-stamped bowls: the ovolo on Stanfield and Simpson 1958, plate. 109.1, the figure on ibid., plate 104.3, and both borders, the ring and what may be the same dolphin on ibid., plate.104.4. Dated *c* AD 160-195. Context 1380 (Group 796) Phase 6.

3 (*not illustrated*) **Drag. 37** in the style of Paternus II of Lezoux. The leaf is on Stanfield and Simpson 1958, plate104.3; the small medallion motif uses a ring such as the outer one on ibid., plate 105.15, round a beaded ring (ibid., pl. 107.30). The motif above is probably the wide single festoon on ibid., plate 105.15. Dated *c* AD 160-195. Context 7042 (feature 7023) Phase 4.

4 **Drag. 37** in the distinctive style of Cettus of Les Martres-de-Veyre. The ovolo is on Stanfield and Simpson 1958, plate 143.44, the seated Apollo on ibid., plate 143.38, the naked figure on ibid., plate 143.37, the leopard on ibid., plate 144.61, and the lion on ibid., plate 144.53; the latter example also has the S-motif across the beaded border. Five sherds. Dated *c* AD 135-165. Context 7065 (feature 7023) Phase 4.

5 **Drag. 37** by the Sacer-Cinnamus group of Lezoux, with the ovolo (Rogers 1974, B144). The two riders, an amazon and a figure with a whip, were regularly used by Sacer (Stanfield and Simpson 1958, pl. 83.9-12; no. 10 also has leaf-tips in the field). The little figure, the bear and the hound were used by Cinnamus, who also used leaf-tips (ibid., pls 159.26 and 33, 160.35, and 163.71); the other animal is a small leopard (cf ibid., pl. 84.16). The ovolo is dated *c* AD 145-175; the proportions of the bowl suggest an early date in this range, so perhaps Sacer rather than Cinnamus. Nine sherds; six lead wire repairs and a hole for a seventh. Contexts 7126 and 7127 (dump) Phase 4.

6 (*not illustrated*) **Drag. 37**, Lezoux. The ovolo is lost; below is a panel design. The small naked figure and the hound were used by Cinnamus (Stanfield and Simpson 1958, pl.159.26, pl. 160.45), who also used a similar acanthus (Rogers 1974, K20), though this one is too abraded to identify certainly. The figure of Venus standing on a mask was regularly used by Divixtus, who also set small

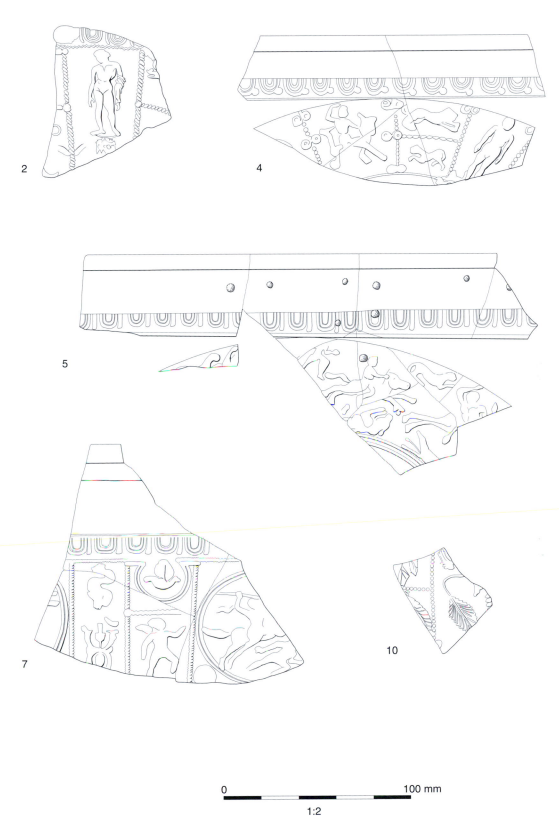

Figure 6.15   Decorated Samian ware (nos 2, 4-5, 7, 10).

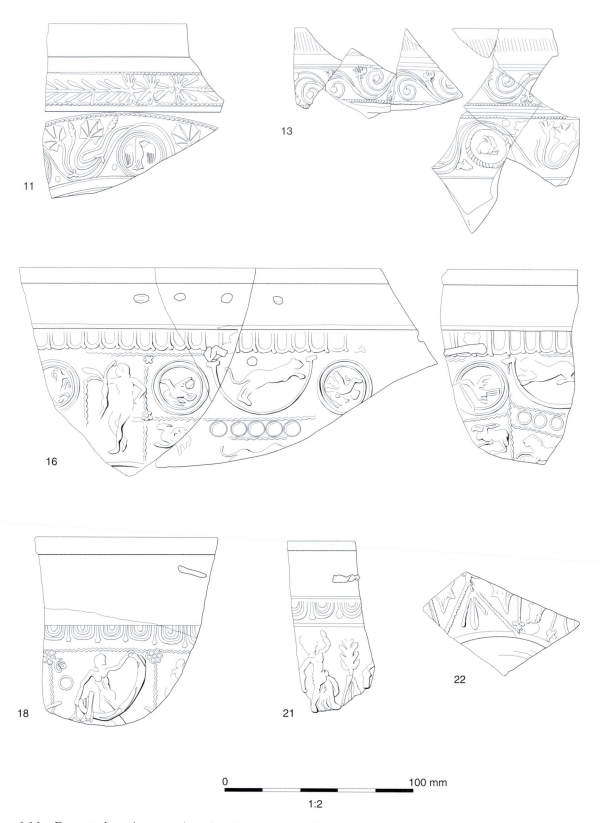

Figure 6.16   Decorated samian ware (nos 11, 13, 16, 18, 21-22).

medallions inside larger ones, though not ones of the same size as here (Stanfield and Simpson pl. 116.10 and 15). The figure inside the medallions may be a crane. Five sherds; very abraded. Antonine. Context 7127 (dump) Phase 4.

7 **Drag. 30** in the style of Cinnamus of Lezoux, with his characteristic ovoid beads and small round terminals. The ovolo and large double medallion are on Stanfield and Simpson 1958, plate 160.35, the horseman on ibid., plate 163.72, the small naked figure and the festoon on ibid., plate 159.26, the cupid on ibid., plate 158.16, the dolphin (here impressed vertically, its tail incomplete) on ibid., plate 159.24, and the bird on ibid., plate 162.60. The tall ornament (Rogers 1974, Q43) is also recorded for Cinnamus. Four sherds. Dated *c* AD 155-175. Contexts 7240 and 7241 (Group 7239) Phases 5 and 4 respectively.

8 (*not illustrated*) **Drag. 37**, Lezoux. The ovoid beads and small terminal suggest the work of Cinnamus; the motifs in the medallion are probably a draped figure and an astragalus. Antonine. Context 7244 (Group 7239) Phase 5.

9 (*not illustrated*) **Drag. 37** in the style of the Cinnamus group at Lezoux. The ovolo, fine beads and the scroll over a double medallion are on Stanfield and Simpson 1958, plate 162.59. Two holes for lead wire repairs. Dated *c* AD 145-175. Context 7327 (pit 7269) Phase 4.

10 **Drag. 37** in the style of Casurius of Lezoux. The ovolo is not previously recorded in his work; it seems to be the same as Rogers 1974, B97, which was used by the earlier Les Martres potter Cettus. The heavy beads are characteristic of Casurius, and the pinnate leaf and tendril are on Stanfield and Simpson 1958, plate 137.63, the festoon on ibid., plate 134.31, and the vine leaf and a small acanthus which is probably the motif in the curve of the tendril on ibid., plate 137.58. Two sherds. Dated *c* AD 165-200. Context 7327 (pit 7369) Phase 4.

11 **Drag. 29**, probably by Murranus of La Graufesenque. The straight wreath in the upper zone is composed of a trifid motif and a small palmette: both motifs are on Mees 1995, Taf. 148, 2, from what is probably a signed mould; a similar wreath, using a different trifid leaf, is on a stamped Murranus bowl from Southwark (Bird 1988, fig. 99, no. 347). The lower zone scroll of palmate leaves with bifid bindings is similar to another Murranus bowl which also has a small double medallion (Mees 1995, Taf. 149.1). The eagle is Hermet 1934, plate 28.9. Dated *c* AD 50-70. Context 7489 (Group 7850) Phase 3.

12 (*not illustrated*) **Drag. 30**, South Gaul. Trident-tongued ovolo above a panel design, including a large faun (Hermet 1934, pl. 19.93), a satyr (ibid., pl. 18.42) and a bird. Four sherds. Dated *c* AD 80-100. Context 7562 (Group 9390) Phase 4.

13 **Drag. 29**, probably by Murranus of La Graufesenque. A closely similar upper zone scroll, with the same palmette, is on Mees 1995, Taf. 151, 2, while the lower zone leaf scroll - here slightly blurred on removal from the mould - is similar to ibid., Taf. 149.1, which also has what may be the same hare in a medallion. The simple corded medallion is not apparently recorded in Murranus' work. Eight sherds. Dated *c* AD 50-70. Context 7694 (Group 7850) Phase 3.

14 (*not illustrated*) **Drag. 37**, South Gaul. Panel design, including a saltire with formal buds and a wreath medallion flanked by little geese which contains a hare over arrowhead motifs. The hare is Hermet 1934, plate 26.66, the goose probably ibid., plate 28.68 left. Dated *c* AD 70-90. Context 7947 (pit 7946) Phase 3-4.

15 (*not illustrated*) **Drag. 29**, South Gaul. The lower zone consists of a row of corded sticks above a basal wreath of bifid leaves, with a bead-row between. The same design is on a number of unpublished bowls in the Musée Fenaille at Rodez, associated with stamps of Albus, Lucceius and Niger. Dated *c* AD 50-70. Context 7965 (Group 8620) Phase 2.

16 **Drag. 37**, Central Gaul, by the potter who made a bowl found at Canterbury (Bird 1995b, fig. 341, no. 677). The ovolo (Rogers 1974, B77) is known from a stamped bowl of Curmillus and on other bowls in several styles, perhaps including Sissus II, who sometimes used a similar wavy-line border; unlike the Canterbury bowl, the same border is used here throughout the design. The main decoration is in the style of the Sacer-Attianus group. As well as the ovolo and border, the rosette, astragalus, row of rings, shallow festoon and both birds are on the Canterbury bowl; the additional motifs here are also found on Sacer-Attianus bowls: the hare and double medallion on Stanfield and Simpson 1958, plate 87.23, and the lion to left and at least one of the pair of leopards (cf ibid., pl. 84.16). Four sherds; five lead wire repairs and a hole for a sixth. Dated *c* AD 125-150. Context 8204 (Group 8160) Phase 4.

17 (*not illustrated*) **Drag. 37**, Central Gaul. Scroll design, including a vine scroll (Rogers 1974, M2) shared by several potters. The fabric suggests one of its earlier users, such as Drusus II. Hadrianic-early Antonine. Context 8243 (Group 10420) Phase 4.

18 **Drag. 37** in the style of Quintilianus of Lezoux. The ovolo, border, dancer and the astragalus impressed across the border are on Stanfield and Simpson 1958, plate 71.23; the rosette (Rogers 1974, C29) and trifid motif (ibid., G118) are both recorded for Quintilianus. Two sherds; two lead wire repairs. Dated *c* AD 125-150. Context 8411 (Group 8160) Phase 4.

19 (*not illustrated*) **Drag. 30**, Central Gaul. Panel design, with fine wavy line borders and a row of neat rings; the other motifs include a small double medallion. Hadrianic-Early Antonine. Context 8749 (Group 9350) Phase 4.

20 (*not illustrated*) **Drag. 37** in the style of Cinnamus of Lezoux. The ovolo is on Stanfield and Simpson

1958, plate 159.27, the herm with flute and pipes on ibid., plate 163.35; the double festoon and medallion occur regularly in his work, but the other motifs are not identifiable. Ten sherds, very abraded. Dated *c* AD 150-170. Context 8857 (Group 9210) Phase 4.

21 **Drag. 37**, South Gaul. The ovolo is recorded from Flavian-Trajanic sites, but is not associated with a known potter (Dannell, Dickinson and Vernhet 1998, ovolo TU). The other motifs are a dancer (Hermet 1934, pl. 20.120), an ornament composed of a coarse pinnate leaf and a trifid motif, and probably the dancer again. Lead wire repair. Dated *c* AD 90-110. Context 9239 (Group 9440) Phase 4.

22 **Drag. 37** in the style of Attianus of Lezoux, with his four-lobed rosette (Stanfield and Simpson 1958, pl. 86.17 and 19). He also used the motifs in the saltire, an ivy leaf and what is probably the same trifid (ibid., pl. 85.6, pl. 86.10); the motif in the narrow panel is probably the base of a caryatid. Dated *c* AD 125-150. Context 9246 (pit 9196) Phase 4.

23 (*not illustrated*) **Drag. 37** in a pale yellowish fabric and brownish slip occasionally used at Lezoux in the Antonine period. The ovolo is probably one used by Cinnamus (Stanfield and Simpson 1958, pl. 162.61); below is a freestyle scene, including a stag (ibid., pl. 163.66), a large lion (ibid., pl. 163.73) and probably a small hound (ibid., pl. 163.74). Two sherds. Dated *c* AD 145-175. Context 9273 (pit 9197) Phase 4.

24 (*not illustrated*) **Drag. 37**, South Gaul. The style is typical of Flavian form 37s, particularly those made by the group of potters associated with M.Crestio. The S-volutes and triple medallion are on Mees 1995, Taf. 38.1, in a generally similar arrangement; the bud is on ibid., Taf. 36, 1, and a similar but narrower trifid leaf tendril on ibid., Taf. 36.7. The two larger trifids used in the saltire were shared by a number of potters. *c* AD 75-95. Context 9374 (Group 10430) Phase 5.

The changing pattern of pottery supply

Introduction

The fabric percentages from the assemblages quantified by EVEs are brought together in Table 6.15 and give some idea of the changes in pottery supply to the site during its period of occupation (see also Tables 6.1 and 6.2).

The bulk of cooking-vessels and many of the lids and open-forms are in handmade or wheel-turned grog-tempered wares and form the largest single component of the pottery supplied to the Westhawk Farm settlement throughout the history of Roman occupation there. Therein lies a problem in that these grog-tempered wares all have very similar fillers, but quite clearly come from a variety of as yet unlocated sources in both east Kent and East Sussex. It has, however, proved possible to subdivide the bulk of the late 1st- and early 2nd-century grog-tempered sherds into those without a siltstone grog element (fabric B2) and those with (fabric B2.1). Close examination of the forms in these two fabric variants does, however, suggest that some of the vessels in both fabrics originate from the same source and merely indicate the variability of the clay available to the potters. What does seem likely is that these grog-tempered wares were made where ample supplies of low-temperature-fired clay were readily available. Such places include coastal brine-boiling and inland iron smelting sites, which would provide ample supplies of grog in the form of broken up furnaces and briquetage.

Period 2, Phase 2 (AD 43-70)

None of the pre-Flavian assemblages is large enough for quantification by EVEs but the sherd count quantification for the assemblages from structure A and the lower fills of ditch 40/860 suggest that 'Belgic' grog-tempered wares accounted for between 80 and 90% of the pottery supplied to the site and included bead-rim jars, imitation butt-beakers, barrel-jars and

Table 6.15   Pottery: Fabric representation in selected assemblages (% of EVEs) (+ = present, but lacking rim).

Fabric	Assemblages							
	17	9	25	31	32	35	39	40
B2/ESW	30.1	49.8	11.5	12.3	17.9	15.9	8.6	17.6
B2.1	46.6	8.4	21.0	16.7	6.9	21.1		
B2.4			18.2	24.9	2.1	3.0		
LR1.1		1.0				2.4	28.4	31.2
R1				0.6			1.6	0.3
R5	0.8	13.3	9.4	4.5	9.4	4.5		1.6
R6	+	9.2	3.8	3.2	3.9	12.4		2.4
R13								3.8
R16	+	7.7	20.3	21.5	33.8	16.1	29.8	10.3
R14				1.9	6.9	4.5	9.0	11.6
R73				4.2	5.5	8.4	9.6	11.4
LR2					3.1	2.5	3.9	2.1
R42	18.7	4.2		0.6				
R43		1.2	10.8	1.6	8.0	7.3	2.6	2.3
R46							2.5	2.2
MISC	3.8	6.2	4.0	8.0	2.5	1.9	4.0	3.2

Gallo-Belgic platter copies alongside more mundane cooking vessels and bowls. Examination of the morphology of these vessels suggests that nearly all of the grog-tempered native wares in use on the site at this time were supplied by east Kent sources. The paucity of sand-tempered 'Belgic' wares from the Folkestone area (Thompson 1982, 14) is rather surprising and may be indicative of poor communications with that area.

Small quantities of biconical vessels in fine grey Upchurch fabric and flagons in the oxidised Hoo equivalent were brought in from production sites around the Medway estuary after AD 45 and the earliest Canterbury products appeared soon afterwards. Equally small amounts of Gallo-Belgic white ware butt-beakers and flagons, Central Gaulish hairpin and roughcast beakers and La Graufesenque samian Drag. 29 bowls, Drag. 18 platters and other forms were imported from Gaul to the site. There is no *terra rubra* and fragments from just one *terra nigra* platter are present, apart from the complete vessel in the late Iron Age burial 9200.

Chaff-tempered container fragments from a number of early contexts are evidence for the importation of salt from coastal brine-boiling sites in east Kent and probably from the Lydd area in Romney Marsh (Barber 1998, 339).

Period 2, Phase 3 (AD 70-150)

The period between *c* AD 70 and 100 has produced one quantifiable assemblage, from pit 844 (Assemblage 17, Table 6.6). This reveals very little change in pottery supply during the period other than increased supply of South Gaulish samian. Only nominal amounts of sherds in Upchurch and Hoo fine ware and Canterbury fabrics are present in Assemblage 17, but assemblages from elsewhere on the site suggest that supply of pottery from these sources increased in significance during the Flavian period. Exotic imports include Patchgrove ware amphorae and jugs (Fig. 6.14, nos 265-66) and a few sherds in glazed fabric R31 (Fig. 6.14, no. 270) and of a bi-chrome orange/cream dot barbotine beaker (Fig. 6.5, no. 88); both from the Staines area of Surrey. The Patchgrove ware vessels may well have arrived on site as containers for some kind of commodity.

The first two decades of the 2nd century saw significant changes in the pattern of pottery supply to the Westhawk Farm settlement. The assemblage from the upper fills of the first roadside ditch 8950/10070 (Assemblage 9, Table 6.5) reveals a significant decline in the supply to the site of handmade grog-tempered wares to less than 60% of all the pottery. South Gaulish samian ware was replaced by smaller amounts of Central Gaulish samian from the Les Martres-de-Veyre kilns. Increased amounts of both Canterbury sandy grey lid-seated jars, carinated bowls and lids and oxidised flagons and mortaria were supplied to the site, although they still account for less than 10% of Assemblage 25. Upchurch grey fine ware biconical vessels, platters, beakers and cups now account for

nearly eight percent of the assemblage and flagons in the white-slipped oxidised Hoo version of the fabric are also present (12%), although their percentage is distorted upwards by the presence of a complete flagon rim. Although most mortaria were supplied by the Canterbury kilns, some Gillam 238 examples were imported from the Continent and there are a few white ware examples from the Rochester area of north Kent.

It is possible that some manufacture of pottery took place at the Westhawk Farm settlement during the late 1st and early 2nd centuries. The flagon fragments in cream ware fabric R88A from Area C (Assemblage 1) are patchily fired and may be wasters. The ample supplies of fired clay generated by the destruction of iron smelting furnaces and the furnace firing technology possessed by the ironworkers make it more than likely that some of the native grog-tempered wares were also produced at Westhawk Farm.

There is no meaningful quantification of assemblages from the second quarter of the 2nd century, but there were several changes in pottery supply during the period. Lid-seated cooking-pots in the superior wheel-turned and polished grog-tempered fabric B2.4 are present for the first time in the top fill of roadside ditch 8950/10070 and suggest that such wares appeared *c* AD 120. The local nature of the distribution of jars and bowls in fabric B2.4 may mean that they were made at or near Westhawk Farm. Similar, wheel-turned, grog-tempered wares, but of slightly different character, were made during the late 2nd to early 3rd century at the large Wealden iron producing settlement of Bardown near Ticehurst, 60 kilometres to the west of Westhawk Farm and linked to it by road and trackway (Lyne 1994, Industry 5A).

Colour-coated hunt-cups and roughcast beakers from Cologne were supplied to the site in very small quantities after AD 130, as were small amounts of East Gaulish samian ware. Roughcast bag-beakers from Colchester and the Argonne are also present in minute quantities from the same time.

Period 2, Phase 4 (AD 150-200)

Assemblage 25 from grave 8160, dated *c* AD 170, has lid-seated jars and bowls in the wheel-turned grog-tempered fabric B2.4 accounting for nearly one-fifth of all the pottery (18%) and similar wares make up a quarter of the pottery from structure O Assemblage 31, dated *c* AD 170-200. The increase in the significance of these wares during the Hadrianic and Antonine periods was at the expense of other native grog-tempered ware producers and overall supply of such wares seems to have remained fairly constant at around half of all the pottery in both assemblages 25 and 31.

Supply of grog-tempered wares from elsewhere in east Kent seems to have virtually dried up during the mid 2nd century and been replaced by East Sussex Ware (fabric B2/ESW) products. These include girth-cordoned storage-jars from as far away as the estuary of the Ouse valley at or near Newhaven, where there is evidence for the production of East Sussex ware on coastal brine-boiling sites (Green 1977, 155; Lyne 1994, 319).

The rest of east Kent had seen the supplanting of 'Belgic' grog-tempered wares by much higher fired, but still handmade 'Native Coarse Ware' during the third quarter of the 2nd century (Pollard 1988, 98; 1995, 704). These wares were probably made at brine-boiling sites along the western end of the Wantsum Channel and are common on most sites in east Kent between *c* AD 170 and 250. They are, however, exceedingly rare at Westhawk Farm and highlight the change in supply of grog-tempered cooking wares to the Westhawk Farm settlement from east Kent sources to local and East Sussex ones during the mid 2nd century.

Supply of grey Upchurch fine ware vessels (mainly poppyhead and other beaker forms, jars and bottles) increased markedly during the Antonine period to a point where they account for between a fifth and a quarter of the pottery in assemblages 25 and 31. They were joined by BB2 (R14) and Thameside grey wares (R73) from the same production sites around the Thames estuary during the late 2nd century. Significant quantities of BB2 open forms were already being supplied to Canterbury and the *Classis Britannica* fort at Dover by AD 130 (Willson 1981), but the lattice decorated 'pie-dishes' in this fabric, characteristic of the period *c* AD 120-200, are represented at Westhawk Farm by fragments from only two examples. Nearly all of the 'pie-dishes' from Westhawk Farm in BB2 fabric and Thameside grey ware are of undecorated types dated *c* AD 170-250 and suggest that BB2 was not supplied in any significant quantity to the site until *c* AD 170. Vessels, mainly open forms, in BB2 and Thameside grey ware are absent from Assemblage 25 dated *c* AD 170, but make up 4% of Assemblage 31 dated *c* AD 170-200.

Canterbury sandy grey ware lid-seated cooking-pots and bowls and oxidised flagons (fabric R5) continued to be supplied to Westhawk Farm during the late 2nd century, but never account for much more than 10% of all the pottery in total. Central Gaulish samian and dark colour-coated ware beakers, together with East Gaulish samian forms are also present in small quantities, but were clearly difficult to replace as witness the fact that ten of the late 2nd-century samian vessels from the site (and mostly from similarly-dated contexts) had been riveted together again after breakage.

Assemblage 32 was deposited in waterhole 7239/9151 during the last decade or so of the 2nd century. Vessel fabric percentages are very distorted by the probable ritual nature of the assemblage with an abnormal emphasis on open forms and beakers in Upchurch ware (R16), BB2 and Thameside grey ware at the expense of (mainly grog-tempered) cooking vessels. What this assemblage does tell us, however, is that the fine wheel-turned grog-tempered ware vessels in Fabric B2.4 had ceased being made by *c* AD 190 and been replaced by East Sussex wares (fabric B2/ESW).

Period 2, Phase 5 (AD 200-250)

The period after c AD 200 is characterised by the appearance of largely undecorated cooking-pots with everted rims and other forms in coarse handmade fabric LR1.1 with profuse white siltstone grog filler. These wares are believed to have been made near the shore-fort at Lympne (Lyne 1994, 419) and became quite significant during the mid 3rd century; making up 28.4% of the pottery from the lower fills of the sinkage over waterhole 796 (Assemblage 39). Overall handmade grog-tempered wares from Assemblage 39 comprised 38.6% of the assemblage, with the remaining grog-tempered ware all coming in from East Sussex (B2/ESW). The supply of handmade grog-tempered wares shows a decline from 42.4% of the pottery from the early 3rd-century structure P (Assemblage 35) to 38.6% of Assemblage 39.

Significant quantities of grey Upchurch fine wares (fabric R16) - now almost entirely rouletted and plain ovoid and pentice beakers - continued to be supplied during the early 3rd century and made up nearly 30 % of all the pottery in Assemblage 39. This figure may, however, be inflated by the probable ritual nature of the assemblage; the figure of 16 % from structure P (Assemblage 35) may be more realistic.

BB2 (fabric R14) and Thameside (fabric R73) 'pie-dishes' and straight-sided dishes certainly became more significant during the early 3rd century. They make up 12.9% of the pottery from structure P and 18.6% of that from the waterhole and were joined by small numbers of sandy grey cooking-pots with superficial 'scorching' from the same north Kent source after *c* AD 180 (fabric LR2.2). This increase in the supply of BB2 and Thameside products may have been brought about by the near termination of pottery supply from the Canterbury kilns in the last years of the 2nd century.

Very small numbers of Moselkeramik beakers from Trier and a little East Gaulish samian constitute the only Continental ceramic imports after AD 200.

Period 2, Phase 6 (AD 250-350)

The period between AD 270 and the early years of the 4th century is represented by Assemblage 40 from the uppermost fills of the sinkage in the top of waterhole 796. This assemblage indicates continued increases in the importation of jars and other forms in the siltstone grog-tempered fabric LR1.1 (31.2%) and of East Sussex Ware (fabric B2/ESW) (17.6%).

Although there are some grey Upchurch fine wares (fabric R16) in the assemblage, the broken up nature of the material suggests that they are all residual. BB2 (fabric R14) and Thameside grey (fabric R73) and 'scorched' grey wares (fabric LR2.2) do, however, seem to have continued to grow in importance (25.1%) and include developed bead-and-flanged bowls and other late 3rd-century forms.

A few cooking-pots, developed beaded and flanged bowls and straight-sided dishes in Dorset BB1 fabric also make their appearance for the first time in this assemblage. These wares are never common on rural sites in Kent but are usually associated with a final occupation phase or a downturn in the fortunes of such sites in the last quarter of the 3rd century. Significant quantities of Dorset BB1 wares were present in late 3rd-century Shore fort construction contexts at Dover (Booth 1994, 99) and the earliest occupation within the fort at Richborough (Lyne 1994, 131-2) and suggest that their appearance in Kent during the late 3rd century may coincide with external threats to the region, such as the depredations of Frankish pirates and the ensuing secession of the British provinces under Carausius and his successor Allectus.

ROMAN BRICK AND TILE
by Louise Harrison

Introduction

The Roman brick and tile retrieved from the excavation was generally in a soft, worn and fragmentary condition. Because of this it has sometimes proved difficult to positively identify the tile as a particular type or to ascertain diagnostic features. These tiles have usually been classed as miscellaneous, although they could conceivably be *tegula* body fragments.

Quantification

A total quantity of 452 identifiable Roman brick and tile fragments weighing approximately 75.4 kg were recovered from the excavation. They can be divided into eight types (Table 6.16).

Fabrics

The material was studied using a microscope to identify the different fabric types. The following fabric numbers and descriptions are based on a Roman brick and tile fabric typology which is currently being developed at Canterbury Archaeological Trust (CAT). It should be noted that it is the writer's opinion that fabrics 21, 22 and 23 are quite possibly all derived from the same Wealden clay source and may be products of the same kiln or kilns situated near the clay outcrop.

Fabric 1   Red/orange in colour; it has a fine sandy matrix with very few large quartz grains; occasional calcareous inclusions are sometimes present. It is very similar to tile excavated from two kiln sites in Canterbury situated in Whitehall Gardens and St Stephen's and probably dates up to the early 3rd century (Jenkins 1956; 1960).

Fabric 2   Red/orange in colour and very fine; it contains few, if any inclusions in the matrix. Very occasionally, calcareous inclusions are visible. This fabric may be a non-sandy variant of fabric 1.

Fabric 3   Red/orange in colour, it has a fine, sandy 'background matrix' with a moder-

Table 6.16   Roman brick and tile: Quantification (fragment count) of tile types present.

Form	Number	Weight (kg)
Brick	87	39.380
Brick/miscellaneous	5	1.080
Brick/flue	1	0.065
Imbrex	19	3.705
Tegula	22	5.075
Miscellaneous	255	14.103
Flue Tile	61	8.060
Voussoir	2	3.915

ate quantity of medium to large white and clear coloured quartz grains (up to 1 mm). This may be a sandy variant of fabric 1.

Fabric 5   Red/orange in colour and has a large quantity of iron oxide and a scatter of small (>0.5 mm) quartz grains.

Fabric 6   Red/orange in colour and contains a moderate quantity of large sized quartz grains (up to 1 mm), common iron oxide, and occasional calcareous inclusions.

Fabric 8   Varies from white/cream, to a yellow or pale orange colour. Its colour is one of its most characteristic features. It contains a scatter of usually small-sized, clear, 'rose' and white coloured quartz grains (up to 0.5mm); occasionally red clay pellets or lenses are visible. Additionally, the sanding on the back of these tiles consists of 'rose' coloured quartz. This fabric was produced at Eccles, northwest Kent from c AD 56-60 to the early 2nd century (Betts 1992).

Fabric 10   Red/orange in colour, it is a fine sandy fabric with characteristic common black oxides appearing abundantly in the matrix; occasional red clay inclusions are also present. A similar fabric has been identified in London as coming from Radlett in Herts. The Canterbury examples are less sandy and have smaller quantities of iron oxides present, suggesting that this fabric type may have been produced at a kiln closer to Canterbury, probably in east Kent. Unfortunately a date is not yet known for this fabric type.

Fabric 11   Orange/red in colour, it is fine and slightly sandy, with characteristic cream coloured 'swirls' or lenses (silty inclusions) appearing commonly in the matrix. Additionally, scattered small sized quartz grains (0.5 mm) are present. This fabric was produced in London or nearby and is dated (in London) to approximately AD 100-120 (Ian Betts pers. comm.).

Fabric 11b   A variant of fabric 11 and resembles it in every way except that it has a large quantity of iron rich inclusions in the matrix.

Fabric 21 Varies from orange to a pale red/pink colour; it has a fine sandy matrix with a moderate quantity of silty swirls and lenses; some iron rich inclusions are also present.

Fabric 21a It has the same fabric structure as fabric 21, but with fewer silty or iron rich inclusions and is therefore thought to be a variant of fabric 21.

Fabric 21b It has the same fabric structure as fabric 21, but in this variant occasional block-like silty inclusions (measuring up to 15 mm) are present.

Fabric 22 Pale orange to pink in colour and has a fine non-sandy matrix with occasional rounded red and white clay inclusions, some silty swirls and lenses and some iron rich rounded inclusions. This fabric also has fine moulding sand. It is similar to clay found in the central Weald and is presumably a product of a kiln near the clay outcrop; a tile kiln has yet to be located.

A similar fabric has been identified by Peacock (1977, 237-42, fabric 2) as being one of the two fabric types found in tiles bearing CLBR stamps. An example was found in the assemblage from Townwall Street in Dover (Parfitt, Corke and Cotter 2006, 313); it was not possible to identify the stamp type due to it being obscured by keying. This fabric is dated in Dover from the mid to late 2nd century to the early 3rd century.

Fabric 23 This fabric varies in colour from white to pink to pale orange. It has a fine, non-sandy matrix with rounded red clay and white silty inclusions. Additionally, some iron rich inclusions are sometimes present.

Table 6.17   Roman brick and tile: Quantification (fragment count and weight) of tile by fabric type.

Fabric Type	No. fragments	% fragments	Weight (kg)	% weight
1	92	20.4	15.995	21.2
1/2	2	0.4	0.555	0.7
2	3	0.7	0.580	0.8
1/3	5	1.1	0.470	0.6
3	11	2.4	4.360	5.8
5	1	0.2	0.050	0.1
7	6	1.3	1.000	1.3
8	14	3.1	0.320	0.4
10	11	2.4	1.065	1.4
11b	1	0.2	0.170	0.2
21	196	43.4	23.893	31.7
21a	73	16.1	10.625	14.1
21b	6	1.3	7.555	10.0
22	8	1.8	3.430	4.6
23	23	5.1	5.315	7.1
Total	452		75.383	

Table 6.17 indicates that fabric 21 and fabric 1 were by far the most common fabric types, representing 31.7% and 21.2% (by weight) of the assemblage respectively. Including its variants (21a and 21b) fabric 21 accounted for 55.8% (by weight) of the assemblage and 60.8% by fragment count.

Table 6.18 shows that both fabric 21 or fabric 23 were used predominantly for bricks and flue tiles; there are very few examples of other types of tile in either fabric. This suggests that the kiln or kilns exploiting these clay sources may have specialised in these tile types. A more even representation of different tile types appears in fabric 1, however, suggesting that the kiln using this clay source produced a wider variety of tile types.

Brick

The brick makes up 52 % (by weight) of the assemblage from Westhawk Farm. No complete bricks

Table 6.18   Roman brick and tile: Quantification (fragment count) by tile types and fabric.

Fabric	Brick/Tile type							
	Brick	Brick/misc	Misc.	*Tegula*	*Imbrex*	Flue Tile	Voussoir	Brick/flue?
1	23	1	39	12	11	6		
1/2	1		1	1				
2			1		2			
1/3			3			2		
3	3	1	3			4		
5			1					
7		1	3	1		1		
8			14					
10	1		8	2				
11b			1					
21	37	1	115	1	3	37	1	1
21a	5		56	2	3	5	1	
21b	6							
22	4		3	1				
23	7	1	7	2		6		
Total	87	5	255	22	19	61	2	1

were retrieved, but most bricks recorded varied from 27 mm to over 60 mm in thickness. The majority of the bricks had an average thickness of around 40-45 mm suggesting that they were probably fragments of *bessalis* and *pedalis* type bricks. The piece measuring over 60 mm is most likely to be part of a *sesquipedalis* brick. There are 14 unusually thin bricks measuring between 27 mm and 32 mm in thickness; these may have been small *bessalis* bricks or floor tiles. One brick fragment (thickness 41 mm) had a scorched surface suggesting that it may have been used as a hearth brick.

Although all dimensions are required to positively identify bricks to a particular type, three bricks provided some width/length measurements aiding identification (Table 6.19). The possible *lydion* brick has a ?width measurement that is slightly larger than the average sized *lydion* (Brodribb 1987, 37-40). The other brick is either a large *bessalis* or a small *pedalis* but as not all dimensions are present this is not clear. The other brick measuring only 142 mm in width/length is unusually small and may be either an unusually small *bessalis* or possibly a floor tile or hearth brick, although no scorching was apparent. The size of the brick suggests a late Roman date as tiles tended to decrease in size through the Roman period. The context from which it derives is of early Roman date, but was the uppermost fill of the roadside ditch at this point. As such it could have contained intrusive later material.

Four bricks (from contexts 302, 8097, 9051 and 9333) are keyed with characteristic wide, deep combing. This has been carried out using of a four-toothed comb, the stroke measuring 38-40 mm in width (Fig. 6.17, no 1). These bricks occur commonly in fabric 23 and are similar to Brodribb's type 1 (Brodribb 1979, 146). A number of examples of these combed bricks have been found at Townwall Street in Dover (Parfitt, *et al.* 2006, 313), at Beauport Park (Brodribb 1979), where they occur with material with *Classis Britannica* stamps, and 15-23 Southwark Street in London (Crowley and Betts 1992).

Flue tile

The flue tile represents 10.7% of the assemblage by weight. It was all fragmentary, but most was keyed and a number of different types (based on the Canterbury type series) could be identified (see below). Because of their fragmentary state, it is possible that some of the tiles, particularly those displaying keying on both face and side, may have been classed as flue tiles when they could conceivably be voussoirs. The most common pattern appeared to be a diagonal cross formed with a number of different sized combs,

Table 6.19   Roman brick and tile: Brick dimensions.

Fabric	Context	Dimensions	Type
21	739	w/l: 306 mm x th: 40 mm	*Lydion?*
3	1258	w/l: 225 mm x th: 45 mm	*Bessalis?*
3	8222	w: 142 mm x th: 36/40 mm	small brick

but four examples of tiles with lattice scoring (type 7) were also present. The clearest examples of keying types have been illustrated.

Three flue tiles had sooting on their interiors suggesting that they had been positioned at the base of the flue near the furnace of a hypocaust system.

Type 5   Flue tile ?face fragment combed with a diagonal cross with a vertical stroke down the centre of the cross. Teeth: 6; W of stroke: 38 mm; Ht: 163-165 mm; with no cutaway.

Type 7   Flue tile fragment with lattice scoring, carried out with a sharp pointed implement, such as a knife. (*Fig. 6.17: 2*).

Type 13?   Flue tile fragment with a combed straight stroke with a possible wavy one as well. Teeth: 8; W of stroke: 33 mm.

Type 14   Flue tile fragment with a diagonal stroke, probably forming a cross. Teeth: 6; W of stroke: 38 mm.

Type 25   Flue tile fragment, combed on both face and side with a diagonal cross. Teeth: 5; W of stroke: 18 mm (*Fig. 6.17: 3*).

Type 26   Corner flue tile fragment with wide combing on both face and side. Teeth: 4+?; W of stroke: 45+ mm. Has rectangular or square cutaway 33 mm away from the corner (*Fig. 6.17: 4*).

Type 27   Flue tile fragment with wide combing consisting of a diagonal cross. Teeth: 4; W of stroke: 44 mm. This type also has a round cutaway, D: 30 mm in example.

Type 28   Corner flue tile fragment with combing on both face and side consisting of a diagonal cross on one surface and possible vertical combing in the other. Teeth: 6; W of stroke: 40 mm. This example also has a square or rectangular cutaway 35 mm from the corner.

Type 29   Thin flue tile fragment (10 mm thickness), combed with a diagonal stroke. Teeth: 9; W of stroke: 36 mm.

Type 30   Flue tile fragment with a widely combed diagonal cross. Teeth: 12; W of stroke: 103 mm (*Fig 6.17: 5*).

Type 31   Flue tile ?face fragment combed with a diagonal cross. Teeth: 4; W of stroke: 24 mm. This tile also has a height measurement (162-164 mm) but no cutaway.

Voussoir Tile

Only one tile was sufficiently complete to provide dimensions which allowed it to be positively identified as a voussoir tile.

Type V6   A complete tile (in five fragments) with all surfaces combed and no cutaways present. The keying consists of combed diagonal crosses, teeth: 6, W of stroke: 41 mm. The tile varies in Ht: 161-170 mm, and in W: 135-152 mm (*Fig 6.18: 6*).

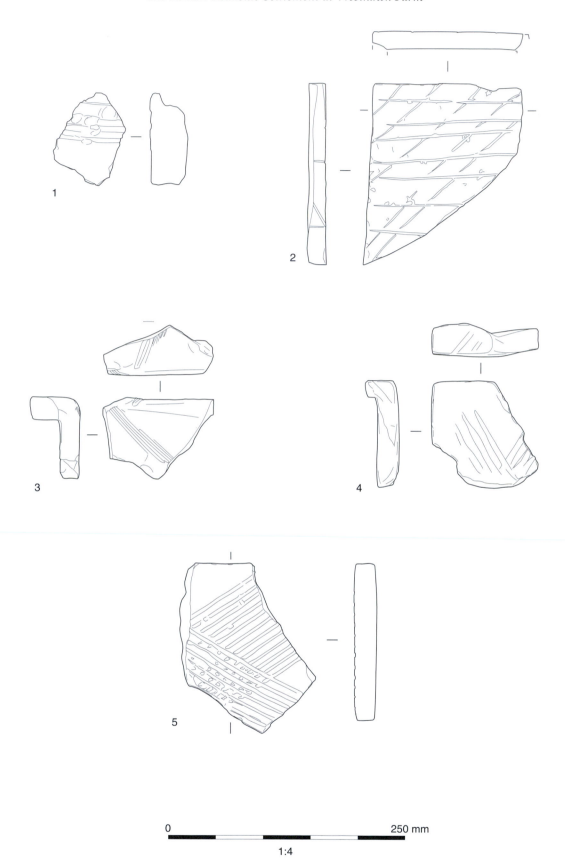

Figure 6.17   Roman tile (nos 1-5).

Roofing Tile

Imbrices

These were all fragmentary, representing roughly 4% (by weight) of the assemblage. The ratio of *imbrices* to *tegulae* (see below) is typical of the use of both types together for roofing.

Tegulae

Tiles were only recorded as *tegulae* if a distinguishing feature such as a flange or cutaway was present; these tiles represented 6.7% of the assemblage by weight. All the *tegulae* were fragmentary, but a small number had flange profiles and cutaways that were complete enough to be identified as a particular type (Table 6.20).

Table 6.20 indicates that flange types 1, 12 and 13 were the most commonly represented. One tile is very unusual because it has had its flange cut away on both sides rather than just the one side as is the normal practice. This has left a small section of flange surviving measuring 78 mm in length (Fig 6.18, no. 7). The base of the tile is rough, sanded (characteristic of a *tegula*) and is faintly burnt. It appears to have originally been made in the form of a *tegula*, rather than a half box tile, and then modified for a different purpose. If it had been originally made in the form of a half box tile the base would have been finished in some way, showing evidence of being either smoothed, trimmed or keyed. It is unclear what this tile would have been used for, but it is probable that it was made for a very specific purpose, possibly to fit between two *tegulae* where a section of tile on a roof had broken.

Signature Marks

These were recorded using the CAT ceramic building material recording system developed by the writer. Signature marks that have been previously recorded by CAT have been consecutively numbered (by type) and therefore the signature marks below conform and relate to this system.

Only nine fragments of brick and tile bore signature marks on their surfaces (Table 6.21). These were generally incomplete but consisted of two signature marks, type 2 and type 7 (see Fig 6.18, nos 8 and 9). On the basis that signature marks were probably used by different tile makers to identify their particular tiles or batches of tile, the presence of these two different signature marks from this assemblage tentatively suggests that at least two different tile makers were producing tiles for use at this site. It is notable, however, that type 2 signature marks occur on tiles in a variety of fabrics likely to derive from at least two distinct sources and it is improbable that the same individual was involved in tile production at both. The relatively simple nature of these signature marks makes it unlikely that many of them can be regarded as unique to one individual.

Phasing

The majority of the brick and tile discussed above (just over 97% by weight) was derived from Area B, while the remaining material was from Area C. The occurrence of tile per phase (in terms of weight) is shown in Table 6.22 (some very small phase groups have been merged to provide more meaningful data). Relatively small amounts of tile were present before Phase 4; it is likely that little or no tile was in use on the site in Phase 2. Approximately 22.5% (by weight) of the tile was from Phase 4 contexts, with a similar representation in the combined Phase 4-5 and 5 groups. Phase 6 contexts, however, produced the greatest quantities of tile, though much of this material was from the well/waterhole feature 796 and may therefore have been redeposited at this time.

Table 6.22 gives little clear indication of chronological patterning in the use of particular tile fabrics. Fabric 8 occurred entirely in relatively early contexts, and a similar emphasis was noted for fabric 2, but the overall quantities of these fabrics and the size of some of the phase assemblages are quite small and the significance of conclusions based on these data is therefore questionable. Fabric 1 was relatively most important in Phase 3 and occurred in declining quantities thereafter. The commonest fabric, 21, was well-represented in all the main phase groups, though with a peak in Phase 6. As already indicated, however, a particularly high proportion of the tile in this phase is likely to have been redeposited.

The assemblage was virtually all fragmentary and was derived from the fills of postholes, pits, ditches and waterholes suggesting that much of the material was residual. Spatially, there was no obvious concentration of ceramic building material, and there was no obvious pattern of particular tile types being found in one context or feature. No context contained more than twenty pieces of brick and/or tile. Because of this, it is not possible to ascertain whether the material was derived from one structure or from different structures present on the site.

The voussoir, the only virtually complete tile in the assemblage (Fig. 6.18, no. 6) was from context 9088, a posthole fill assigned to Phase 5 (AD 200-250), while the unusual *tegula* (Fig. 6.18, no. 9) was from a Phase 6 silting fill (298) of waterhole 796.

Discussion

Although a substantial quantity of brick and tile was recovered, the majority of it was in a fragmentary and abraded state and was probably residual. The material can be dated by its fabrics principally to the mid Roman period. Despite its general character the quantity of tile suggests that a substantial Roman building or buildings probably existed in or near the area of excavation, and the relatively high proportion of brick and flue tile present suggests that the building had a hypocaust system and, on the basis of the presence of at least one voussoir tile, may have had

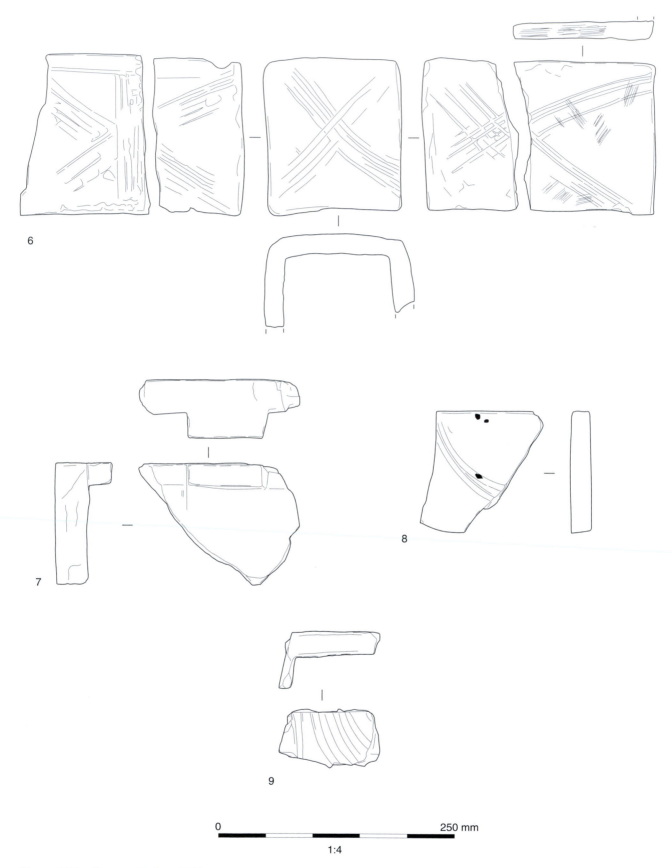

Figure 6.18   Roman tile (nos 6-9).

Table 6.20 *Roman brick and tile: Tegula flange and cutaway types by fabric.*

Flange Type	Lower Cutaway Type	Fabric Type	Quantity
1	c	1	2
1		10	1
1		21	1
4	e	1	1
7		22	1
12	c	1	4
12		1/2	1
13		23	1
13		1	1
13		10	1
15		21a	1

Table 6.21 *Roman brick and tile: Signature marks on tile by form and fabric.*

Signature mark	Form	Fabric
2	brick	1
2	brick	3
2	brick	21
2	brick	21
2	brick	22
2	miscellaneous	1
2	miscellaneous	21
2	miscellaneous	23
7	tegula	1

a vaulted roof. This suggests the existence of a bathhouse structure in close proximity to the excavation.

It is not clear, however, whether the buildings associated with ironworking or any of the other structures would have had tiled roofs. Their relatively small size might indicate that these buildings would have had another form of roofing.

There are no published detailed studies of ceramic building material from the Ashford area at the present time. Meaningful comparison with other groups of brick and tile found in the Ashford area is therefore difficult. However, the large quantity of material from Westhawk Farm appearing in fabrics 21 and 23 suggests that a tile kiln or kilns situated in the Weald near a clay outcrop was producing and supplying tiles to this area. A large proportion of the material produced in these fabrics was brick and flue tile. This suggests that one or more of the kilns may have specialised in producing these tile types. Brick and tile bearing the CLBR stamp and relatively unusual keyed bricks also appear in these fabrics and have been found in Sussex (Beauport Park) and at Dover (Townwall Street). All of this evidence suggests that the kiln or kilns situated in the Weald produced large quantities of tile and served a wide geographical area.

A wide variety of tile types from Westhawk Farm also appear in fabric 1 (similar to a Canterbury fabric) suggesting the existence of a kiln or kilns that produced large quantities of different types of tile for Canterbury and the Ashford area. This particular fabric (and its variants) occurs commonly in Kent, for example at Maidstone (Harrison 1999, 130), Ickham (Riddler, *et al.* forthcoming) and Harrietsham (Jarman, *et al.* forthcoming).

The wide variety of different clay and tile types appearing at Westhawk Farm is not surprising considering that the site lies near the junction of two Roman roads and a tributary stream of the Great Stour which would have facilitated the transport of ceramic building material to the area.

Table 6.22 *Roman brick and tile: Quantification (% weight) by fabric type and phase.*

Fabric type	Period 2							Period 4 & unphased	Total weight (g)	% weight
	Phases 2-3 & 2-4	Phase 3	Phases 3-4 & 4	Phases 4-5	Phase 5	Phases 5-6 & 6	Phase 7			
1		42.1	32.0	21.4	19.4	17.9		16.9	15,995	21.2%
1/2			2.2			0.6			555	0.7%
2		13.4		1.3	0.6				580	0.8%
1/3			0.7		1.2	0.6			470	0.6%
3	20.0		6.6		10.4	2.7			4,360	5.8%
5								8.1	50	0.1%
7			0.8		1.2	2.2			1,000	1.3%
8	0.1	9.4							320	0.4%
10			0.5		2.7	1.9			1,065	1.4%
11b								27.4	170	0.2%
21	33.9	10.6	30.6	12.8	12.8	46.0	66.1	47.6	23,893	31.7%
21a	8.4	2.5	22.2	10.6	37.8	2.5			10,625	14.1%
21b			5.1	16.2		19.5			7,555	10.0%
22	27.8	5.8	3.5		0.6	3.9			3,430	4.6%
23	9.9	16.2	1.1	37.7	13.4	2.3	33.9		5,315	7.1%
Total (weight, g per phase)	4810	3360	16986	3155	13862	31690	900	620	75,383	
% wt per phase	6.4%	4.5%	22.5%	4.2%	18.4%	42.0%	1.2%	0.8%		
Total fragments per phase	15	26	144	25	67	165	4	6	452	
% count per phase	3.3%	5.8%	31.9%	5.5%	14.8%	36.5%	0.9%	1.3%		

Catalogue of illustrated pieces (Figs 6.17-6.18)

1 **Brick** with wide combing. Fabric 23. Context 9333, Phase 4-5.
2 **Box flue**, lattice scored. Fabric 23. Context 406, Phase 6.
3 **Box flue**, combed. Fabric 21. Context 322, Phase 6.
4 **Box flue** with wide combing. Fabric 23. Context 417, Phase 7.
5 **Box flue tile** with combing, sooted on inside. Fabric 21. Context 1359, Phase 6.
6 Complete **voussoir**, combed. Fabric 21a. Context 9088, Phase 5.
7 **?*Tegula*** with flange cut away on both sides. Fabric 21. Context 298, Phase 6.
8 Uncertain type with signature type 2. Fabric 23. Context 1639, Phase 3.
9 *Tegula* with signature. Fabric 1. Context 9155, Phase 3.

BURNT CLAY
by Kayt Brown

The excavations produced a total of 6385 fragments of burnt clay, weighing 49,303 g. This includes material from both hand-excavated contexts and material retrieved during the processing of environmental samples. The assemblage was in relatively poor condition with the majority of the material comprising abraded, amorphous oxidised fragments.

The material was examined by context and identified to fabric using a binocular microscope (x10), and to form based on morphological characteristics. The material was quantified by fragment count and weight for each context. Two broad fabrics were identified within the assemblage; the most common contained varying amounts and proportions of sand, ferruginous and clay pellets, with a second fine sandy fabric occurring in lesser quantities. Occasionally daub fragments in the former fabric also displayed voids resulting from burnt out organic matter. As a result of the abraded nature of much of this material, only a small proportion could be identified as daub, that is clearly deriving from structures. Some of the assemblage showed evidence of exposure to high temperatures and in some cases had charcoal adhering to the surface and may therefore represent oven or hearth lining. Vitrified clay furnace lining was present within the slag assemblage (see Paynter, Chapter 7).

Burnt clay material can result from a number of domestic and industrial activities and is a common find on sites of this type. The assemblage at Westhawk Farm is generally very abraded, with little diagnostic material. This suggests at least a moderate amount of redeposition of the material, resulting in the fragmentation of any large pieces of fired clay. Although there is some material in the earlier phases, the majority of burnt clay occurs within Phases 3 to 5 of the Roman period, corresponding to the main period of activity at the site. Spatial analysis of this material reveals a general distribution of burnt clay across the site within these phases, although there is a notable concentration around building R in Phases 4 and 5. Given that a proportion of the burnt clay displays evidence of exposure to high temperatures, it is likely to have been connected to the metal working activity that was located within this building and much of it may have derived from the outer (generally undiagnostic) parts of furnace structures.

Chapter 7:   Metalworking Remains

by Sarah Paynter

SUMMARY

Approximately 1.65 tonnes of ironworking waste were recovered from Westhawk Farm. This comprised largely smelting debris, although some smithing slag was also present. Much of the debris was recovered from contexts surrounding two workshops, one pre-dating the other. Both smelting and primary smithing of the product took place in the workshops, and some furnaces, hearths and hammerscale deposits survived. Analysis of the different types of waste has enabled the process of formation of the different types of slag to be modelled. The scale of iron-production at Westhawk has also been estimated and discussed in the context of Wealden iron production in the Roman period.

INTRODUCTION

A large quantity of ironworking debris was recovered during the excavation of Area B. Features thought to be associated with ironworking were identified within two structures, now referred to as Structures I and R. David Starley, from English Heritage's Ancient Monuments Laboratory, visited the site and produced a report (Starley 1998) with a list of recommendations pertaining to the investigation of the metalworking features. In accordance with these recommendations, a high-resolution fluxgate gradiometer survey was conducted over the two areas of interest by Rob Vernon, from the University of Bradford (Vernon 1999).

The quantity of ironworking waste recovered during the excavation of Area B (approximately 1.65 tonnes) indicates that this industry is likely to have been important to the economy of the settlement. Although larger ironworking sites of Roman date are known from the Weald nearby, Westhawk Farm is unusual and important because of the two ironworking workshops within which some features, and in one instance an occupation surface, survived. This report aims to identify the type, location, duration and scale of the ironworking activity at the settlement. The type of activity is determined by identifying the types of ironworking waste produced. The location of the activity is determined by analysis of the spatial distribution of the waste, the geophysical survey data, the descriptions of the excavated features and the examination of occupation deposit samples. The duration of activity is determined by the dating of the deposits of ironworking waste and the workshops themselves. The scale of the activity is approximated from an estimate of the amount of waste produced for the duration of the ironworking activity. Additional information about Roman ironworking technology and the formation of the different categories of waste can be derived through examination of the raw materials, waste and products from these processes.

IRONWORKING PROCESSES AND THE WASTE PRODUCED

Ironworking processes produce characteristic waste products, which can be differentiated on the basis of their shape, colour, density, porosity, surface texture and occasionally chemical composition. A description of various ironworking processes, and the different types of waste that they produce, is given below. The waste from Westhawk Farm was categorised according to these descriptions.

Ironworking processes

Smelting

Smelting is the process of reducing iron ore to produce iron metal. Previous work has shown that iron smelting in this period and area took place in bloomery furnaces, which were typically fairly small, rounded structures with an inside diameter of about 0.3 m and probably with a height of about 1 m. These structures were constructed from clay and had walls about 0.25 m thick (Cleere and Crossley 1985; Crew 1991; Pleiner 2000). Charcoal fuel was used. Some types of ore were roasted prior to smelting to convert the ore to iron oxide and to facilitate crushing into smaller pieces. Air was blown into the furnaces using bellows, generally through one or more small holes near the base, known as blowholes. The furnace would have been lit and allowed to reach full temperature before roasted ore was fed into the top. Additional fuel and ore would have been fed into the furnace for the duration of the smelt. The area near the blowhole would have been the hottest region of the furnace but the temperatures used in the bloomery process were insufficient to melt the iron alloys produced. Therefore, when the iron ore reacted to form particles of iron, these accumulated near the blowhole to form a spongy mass, known as a bloom, which was removed through the top of the furnace or through a tapping aperture. The gangue (non-iron minerals) in the iron ore reacted with some of the iron, and potentially also with the lining of the furnace and ashes from the fuel, to form a liquid slag. The slag was tapped into a pit or down a slope through a hole - sometimes known as the tapping arch - at the base of the furnace. The chemical reactions occurring during smelting can be generalised as:

Ore roasting:

$4FeCO_3$ (siderite ore) $+ O_2 \rightarrow$ heat $\rightarrow 2Fe_2O_3 + 4CO_2$

or

$4FeO.OH$ (goethite ore) $\rightarrow$ heat $\rightarrow 2Fe_2O_3 + 2H_2O$

Metal production:

$Fe_2O_3 + CO$ (from burning of fuel) $\rightarrow 2FeO + CO_2$

$FeO + CO$ (from burning of fuel) $\rightarrow Fe$ (metal) $+ CO_2$

Slag production:

$2FeO + SiO_2 \rightarrow Fe_2SiO_4$ (fayalite slag)

Smithing

When removed from the furnace, the iron bloom contained much slag and voids and required consolidation by smithing. This is the process of hammering and shaping iron, generally at red heat, as the metal is then more malleable. The iron was heated in a charcoal-fuelled hearth, which may have been a shallow, walled structure, constructed from clay or stone, either on the floor or at waist height. Bellows blew air into the hearth through a hole in the hearth wall. During smithing the surface of the iron became oxidised and reacted with the materials with which it came into contact, such as the lining of the hearth and ashes from the fuel. When this surface covering was detached from the metal it formed small flakes and spheres of iron oxide and slag, known as hammerscale. Debris from smithing accumulated in the bed of fuel in the hearth and formed a lump of slag known as a smithing hearth bottom. Once hot, the metal was hammered into shape on an anvil, resulting in the loss of more slag and scale, which collected on the floor. Since hammerscale is magnetic it can be detected in archaeological occupation surfaces with a magnet. The smith would form the iron into a billet or bar for subsequent trading.

Primary and secondary ironworking *(Fig. 7.1)*

The processes of smelting iron ore to form metal and the subsequent smithing to form the bloom into a billet or bar are together known as 'primary ironworking'. The iron billets or bars produced by primary ironworking would then be supplied to smiths at other sites where they were used to produce iron objects by 'secondary ironworking'. In secondary ironworking, bars or billets of iron, or recycled iron, were made into useable objects by further smithing. As this also involved repeatedly heating iron in a hearth and hammering the hot metal into shape, hammerscale and smithing hearth bottom slags were again produced. However, this smithing activity was not associated with smelting. The stages involved in both primary and secondary ironworking are compared in Figure 7.1.

Ironworking waste

Categories of ironworking waste

The ironworking debris from Westhawk Farm was categorised into the classes summarised in Table 7.1 following the Centre for Archaeology *Guidelines* (Bayley *et al.* 2001). The classes and processes that produced each are as follows:

Tap slag *(smelting)*: Dense slag, with a rough lower surface and an upper surface that looks like a lava flow.

Slag-coated clay *(smelting and smithing)*: Clay that formed part of the furnace or hearth lining, with a surface that has reacted with the slag or the ash from the fuel at high temperatures and has developed a

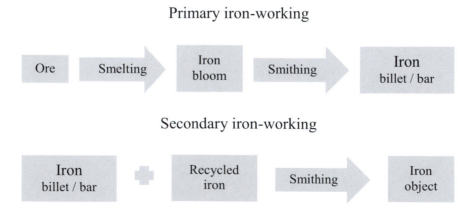

Figure 7.1 Summary of the stages involved in primary and secondary iron-working.

Table 7.1 Metalworking remains: Summary of types of waste produced by primary and secondary iron-working (√ = present, X = absent).

Iron-working Waste	Primary Iron-working	Secondary Iron-working
Tap slag	√	X
Slag-coated clay	√	√
Fired clay	√	√
Ore	√	X
Smithing hearth bottom	√	√
Furnace bottom	√	X
Iron lumps, bar or billet	√	√
Hammerscale	√	√
Runs	√	X
Undiagnostic	√	√
Fuel ash slag	√	√

dark-coloured, slag-like or glassy surface. Furnaces and hearths are hottest near the blowing hole, and pieces of vitrified clay from a furnace or hearth wall with the outline of the blowing hole are sometimes found. This debris is also often referred to as vitrified clay or hearth/furnace lining.

Fired clay (*smelting, smithing and other high temperature processes*): This can include clay that was sufficiently near the hotter regions of the furnace or hearth to be fired by its heat, but has no identifiable vitrified or slag-coated surface remaining. However, many processes involving high temperatures can result in the production of fired clay and so alone it is not diagnostic of metalworking.

Ore and iron-rich stone (*smelting*): Any iron-rich stone in the assemblage was categorised as potential ore, although not all of the different types of stone were necessarily smelted. Unroasted ironstone was grey/brown in colour. Roasted ironstone was deep red to metallic grey. Ore that has been heated can be magnetic.

Furnace bottom slag (*smelting*): If slag accumulates at the bottom of a furnace below the tapping level, a bowl-shaped slag with a level surface and a low porosity is formed. Unlike tap slag it has no flow lines on the surface and occasionally has clay adhering to the bottom. Large lumps of slag with fractured edges, sometimes with protruding flows or runs of slag and often with abundant incorporated fuel fragments, were also categorised as slag from a furnace base that had remained after tapping.

Hammerscale (*smithing*): Small flakes or spheres of slag and iron oxide, expelled or detached from the surface of iron during smithing. Hammerscale can be produced by primary smithing, during bloom consolidation, or secondary smithing. Hammerscale is magnetic.

Smithing hearth bottom (SHB) (*smithing*): Spongy lumps of slag containing many small pores with characteristic convex bottom surfaces and concave upper surfaces, produced in the smith's hearth during primary or secondary smithing.

Iron lumps (*smelting and smithing*): Lumps or fragments of iron including partially consolidated bloom fragments and partially shaped objects.

Undiagnostic slag (*smelting and smithing*): Much of the slag does not have enough diagnostic features for it to be categorised.

Slag runs (*smelting*): Slag runs of various sizes, including long slender tubes of slag often in groups or emanating from substantial lumps of slag, produced during slag tapping.

Fuel ash slag (*smelting, smithing and other high temperature processes*): This material is produced by reaction of plant ashes, for example from charcoal fuel, with siliceous material, such as clay. It is usually vesicular and is lighter-coloured and less dense than the iron-rich slag commonly produced by ironworking processes. Non-metallurgical, high temperature processes can produce fuel ash slag and so alone it is not diagnostic of ironworking. Very little fuel ash slag was found amongst this assemblage.

Charcoal fuel was found in many contexts associated with ironworking. Stores of this fuel are sometimes found in the vicinity of furnaces, and charcoal pits, or platforms, may be found near to where the charcoal was produced. However, no such deposits were identified at Westhawk Farm. Iron pan was also noted in some contexts. Iron pan forms when iron compounds precipitate from solution, forming an orange, iron-rich layer. Iron pan is common in ironworking contexts where there is a large amount of corroding iron-rich material, such as iron lumps or objects, and could also be used as ore. However, it is common geologically and so its presence is not diagnostic of ironworking.

Disposal and reuse of ironworking waste in the past

Many of the large, dense products of ironworking processes, such as tap slag and smithing hearth bottom slags, were removed from ironworking sites and dumped in pits or ditches. Therefore the presence of tap slag does not necessarily indicate that smelting took place in the immediate vicinity, although a very large deposit generally indicates that smelting took place nearby. Slag was also reused, either in antiquity, for example as road metalling, or more recently, for example as ore to be smelted in blast furnaces. Therefore assessments of the scale of metalworking at a site from the amount of waste remaining are likely to be underestimates, since an unknown proportion of the waste will have been removed. In contrast, as hammerscale consists of very small flakes and spheres, it was left to accumulate on the workshop floor where it often formed thick layers. Therefore the presence of hammerscale in an occupation surface indicates that primary or secondary smithing activity occurred in that structure (Bayley *et al.* 2001). Fired clay fragments are fragile and less likely to survive transportation and dumping so, if found, often indicate nearby ironworking activity. Blooms and billets are rarely found, as they were valuable and were processed further.

Identification of ironworking waste

Some 1.4 tonnes of ironworking waste were recovered during excavation in 1998. The waste from 229 contexts, comprising 80% by weight of the slag excavated from Area B, was examined to identify the different types of slag present. Of the ironworking waste recovered in 1999 (which included contexts 7000 to 11150), 94 kg (from 29 contexts) were examined for this report, whereas the waste from 22 boxes, estimated at 150 kg, was not examined. The total amount of ironworking waste recovered from Westhawk Farm was estimated at 1.65 tonnes. The material was sorted into the categories defined above and weighed. Some examples were removed for further analysis. In Table 7.2 the different types of slag and ironworking debris identified in contexts with more than 5 kg are listed, comprising 70% by weight of the total for the site. (A Table giving a full listing of the slag recovered, by context and type, can be found in the archive report on the ironworking debris.) The majority of the metal working waste was deposited during Phase 3 (AD 70-150), Phase 4 (AD 150-200) and Phase 5 (AD 200–250) of the site.

Figure 7.2 shows the percentages by weight of different types of slag represented in the total assemblage. Over half of the assemblage is made up of tap slag, iron-rich stone and furnace bottom slag, all exclusively associated with iron smelting, and therefore the great majority of the slag-coated clay is likely to be waste from smelting furnaces rather than smithing hearths. However, nearly 3.6% by weight of the assemblage is made up of smithing hearth bottom (SHB) slags indicating that some smithing activity took place on the site.

STRUCTURAL EVIDENCE FOR IRONWORKING ACTIVITY

Location of ironworking activity

The distribution of the ironworking waste was studied to determine whether the slag was concentrated

Table 7.2: Metalworking remains: Iron-working debris from contexts containing more than 5 kg of slag categorised by type (weights in kg) (Phase 3 = AD 70-150, Phase 4 = AD 150-200 and Phase 5 = AD 200-250)

Context	Structure	Phase	Tap slag	Ore	Furnace bottom	Slag-coated clay	Fired clay	SHB	Runs	Un-diagnostic	Totals
7773	I	2-3	7.1	0.3	0.0	1.5	0.0	0.0	0.0	0.0	8.9
7866	I	3	2.7	0.0	0.0	0.8	0.0	0.5	0.0	1.4	5.4
1510	I	3	0.1	0.1	5.5	0.0	0.0	0.0	0.0	0.0	5.7
318	I	3	4.0	0.0	0.0	1.6	0.0	0.0	0.1	0.0	6.3
7839	I	3	4.4	0.0	0.0	2.0	0.1	0.0	0.0	0.7	7.2
1156	I	3	1.8	0.0	4.0	2.4	0.0	0.3	0.0	0.5	8.9
319	I	3	3.0	0.0	0.0	1.1	0.0	0.0	0.0	5.8	9.9
481	I	3	3.3	0.0	0.0	3.9	0.0	0.0	0.0	2.8	10.1
8022	I	3	4.1	0.0	0.8	1.1	0.0	6.0	0.0	0.4	12.4
1460	I	4	1.4	0.0	0.0	2.7	0.7	2.7	0.0	0.7	8.1
1206	I	4	2.0	0.0	1.1	5.5	0.0	0.0	0.0	1.5	10.1
1522	I	4	6.7	0.1	0.0	1.4	0.1	0.2	0.2	3.8	13.2
1166	I	4	3.0	0.0	0.0	10.8	0.0	0.0	0.0	0.1	13.9
480	I	4	9.1	0.1	2.8	6.1	0.0	0.0	0.0	0.9	19.1
1126	I	4	41.7	0.1	0.4	22.8	2.1	1.6	0.0	5.8	74.4
1193=1225	I	4	50.9	0.0	4.2	47.7	5.4	6.8	0.1	5.0	120.1
1082=1106	I	5	42.8	0.3	2.1	18.6	4.2	1.0	0.0	5.5	74.5
676	I	6	0.5	0.0	1.1	1.0	0.0	3.3	0.0	0.0	5.9
7623	P	3	3.7	0.0	1.0	2.6	0.0	0.0	0.0	0.0	7.3
7471	P	4	4.5	0.0	0.0	1.3	0.0	0.0	0.0	1.5	7.3
8449	P	4	6.2	0.2	0.0	11.8	0.1	0.0	0.0	0.7	19.1
1157	R	3	0.4	0.0	0.0	6.1	1.2	0.0	0.0	0.0	7.6
1585	R	4	0.6	0.1	0.0	0.4	0.0	0.0	0.0	4.3	6.9
1222	R	4	7.0	0.2	0.0	1.5	0.2	1.0	0.0	0.8	10.6
922	R	4	11.3	1.3	0.8	13.9	0.0	0.0	0.9	0.7	29.0
1356	R	4-5	102.4	10.8	3.0	62.4	3.6	0.2	4.0	11.3	197.7
1219	R	5	1.4	0.1	0.0	1.7	0.0	0.0	0.0	1.7	5.1
1331	R	5	4.1	0.0	0.0	1.6	0.0	0.0	0.1	0.1	5.9
1231	R	5	3.0	0.1	3.1	0.5	0.0	0.0	0.1	0.8	7.7
1216	R	5	2.2	2.7	0.0	1.2	0.2	0.0	0.0	3.4	9.7
1258	R	5	5.6	0.7	1.8	7.3	0.0	0.9	0.1	2.1	18.5
1257	R	5	5.5	0.3	0.0	2.7	0.0	0.0	0.0	10.9	19.3
1332	R	5	14.8	0.4	0.6	6.3	0.0	4.1	0.0	1.1	27.5
1265	R	5	40.4	2.1	0.0	9.4	0.3	0.2	1.6	7.6	61.5
1217	R	5	57.3	2.9	0.3	24.4	1.1	6.0	2.4	10.2	104.7

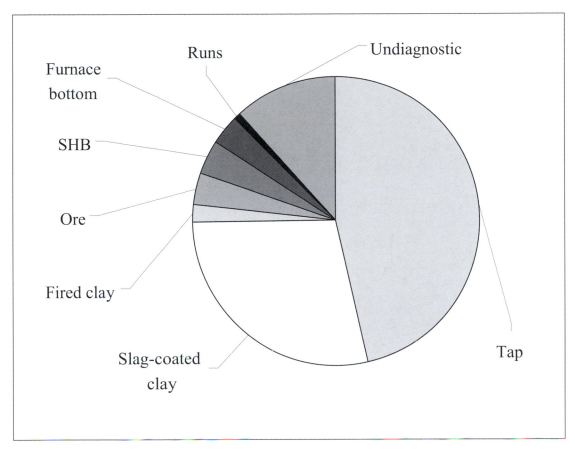

Figure 7.2   Pie chart showing the relative proportions of different types of iron-working debris for the contexts listed in Table 7.2.

in particular areas. The contexts containing in excess of 5 kg of ironworking waste (listed in Table 7.2 and marked on Figure 7.3) are largely concentrated around two structures: structure R and structure I. The remains of features associated with metalworking, such as furnaces, were identified in these structures, which were therefore interpreted as workshops. The layout of the workshops is discussed below. Some metalworking waste and a large iron billet were also found in the vicinity of structure P, but no ground-level metalworking features or metalworking occupation deposits were identified within that structure.

Structure I

Figure 7.4 shows the proportions of the different types of waste recovered from contexts containing more than 5 kg of slag in the vicinity of structure I (see Table 2). The vast majority was smelting waste, although some smithing slags were also identified.

Structure R

Figure 7.5 shows the proportions of the different types of waste recovered from contexts containing more than 5 kg of slag in the vicinity of structure R (see Table 2). As with Structure I, the vast majority

was iron smelting waste with some smithing slags also identified.

Structure P

Figure 7.6 shows the proportions of the different types of waste recovered from contexts containing more than 5 kg of slag in the vicinity of structure P (see Table 2). Again virtually all of the waste was from smelting.

Duration of ironworking activity

Many contexts, and particularly those associated with structure I, contained little pottery that could be closely dated. Consequently the contexts are dated largely by stratigraphic associations. These indicate that structure I was probably built in the early 2nd century (in Phase 3; c AD 70-150) and was used into, but not for the duration of, Phase 4 (c AD 150-200). Examination of the pattern of iron production across the Weald by Cleere and Crossley (1985, 62-63) highlighted a shift towards ironworking at sites in the High Weald between AD 120 and 140, with which this evidence is consistent. Structure R was probably in use from the early 3rd century until AD 250, which is consistent with the evidence

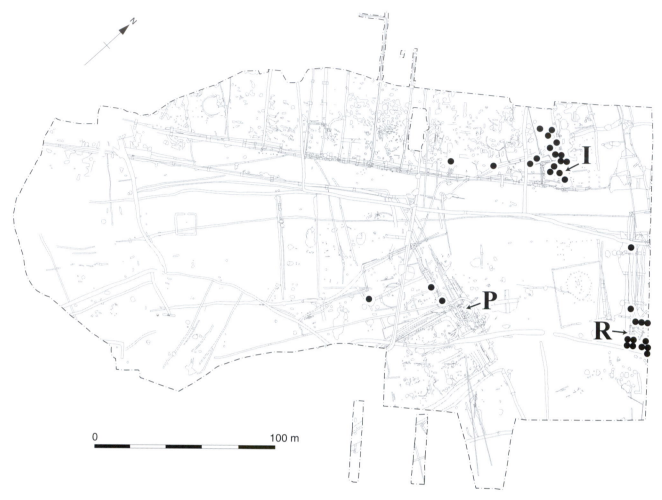

Figure 7.3   Location of contexts with more than 5 kg of iron-working waste recovered.

for the cessation at the same date of smelting activity at other Wealden sites. Other evidence, such as the almost complete absence of coins and pottery from the second half of the 3rd century at the site, suggests that the settlement itself was largely abandoned at this time. The major deposits of ironworking waste surrounding structure I are largely from Phase 4 and the waste in the vicinity of structure R is largely from Phase 5 (*c* AD 200-250). It has been assumed that the periods of iron smelting activity in both structure I (*c* AD 110-160) and structure R (*c* AD 200-250) were of approximately 50 years duration (*c* AD 110-160). This leaves a gap between the ironworking activity based in these two workshops. It is possible that some ironworking took place on the site of structure R prior to the construction of that workshop or, as is discussed later in this report, that other ironworking structures are present in the unexcavated portions of the site. The geophysical survey highlighted several areas with strong readings, potentially resulting from industrial activity, in Area A; therefore an estimate of the duration of ironworking activity for the site as a whole, based only on the activity in structures R and I, is likely to be an underestimate.

The waste in the vicinity of structure P is from contexts assigned to Phases 3 and 4, while the structure itself has been assigned to Phase 5, contemporary with structure R. Although ironworking waste and an iron billet were found in the vicinity of structure P, no smelting furnaces, hearths or occupation deposits associated with ironworking activity were identified in that area. It is likely that the waste deposited at structure P was produced in a workshop elsewhere on the site. However, the concentration of slag in the vicinity of the structure suggests that there is a link of some kind between structure P and the ironworking activity at the site.

Features associated with ironworking activity

Structure I (Fig 7.7)

Structure I lay within a rectangular enclosure defined by ditches and gullies, and beam slots aligned with the ditches. Internal features included eight postholes. The enclosure is at the top of a gradual incline, which slopes towards the south-east. The occupation spreads survive less well than in structure R. At the top of the slope there was no post-medieval subsoil

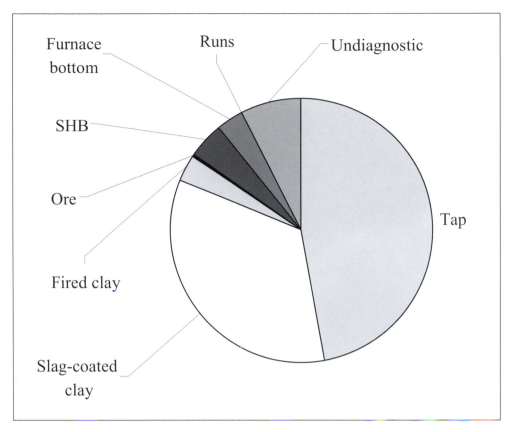

Figure 7.4   Pie chart showing relative proportions of different types of iron-working debris from contexts in the vicinity of Structure I (total 350 kg).

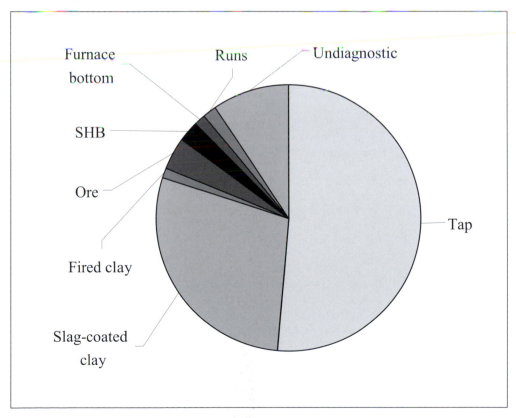

Figure 7.5   Pie chart showing relative proportions of different types of iron-working debris from contexts in the vicinity of Structure R (total 490 kg).

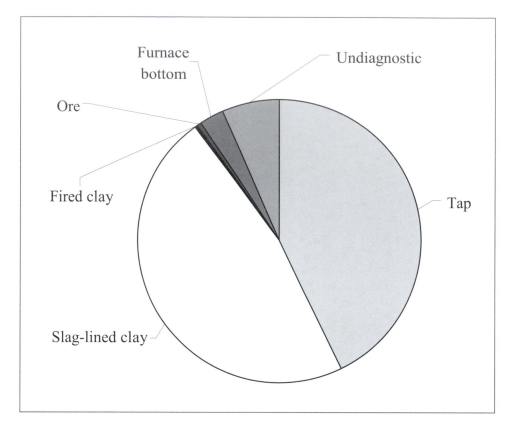

Figure 7.6   Pie chart showing relative proportions of different types of iron-working debris from contexts in the vicinity of Structure P (total 34 kg).

and the modern topsoil directly overlay the natural Wealden clay.

The structure appears to have been partitioned into two working areas. In the north-west working area were two rounded features, 1525 and 1511, with fired clay linings, likely to be the bases of bloomery furnaces. Feature 1525 was 0.46 m in diameter and 0.14 m in depth, with moderate to steeply sloping sides. It was heavily truncated and contained a very charcoal-rich fill. Feature 1511 had similar dimensions (0.7 m diameter) and contained a complete furnace bottom slag (1510) weighing 5.5 kg. This was 0.26 m in diameter and 80 mm deep at its thickest point and bowl-shaped, with a very thin layer of reduced-fired, grey clay adhering to the bottom. The average overall diameter of these furnaces at the base is 0.6 m and the internal diameter, indicated by the furnace bottom slags (a second complete furnace bottom was found in context 1225 nearby) is about 0.26 m. Therefore, the walls of these furnaces were about 0.17 m thick. Experiments by Crew (1991) have indicated that this wall thickness ensures adequate heat retention in the furnace. The furnaces were to the west of the building, side by side and approximately perpendicular to the slope of the land. The slag tapped from the furnaces may have flowed downhill in a south-easterly direction, though no evidence for this survives. Also in this area was a crescent-shaped feature, 1523, which was 1.2 m in diameter and 0.3 m deep with moderate 45° sloping sides. Although this

feature contained ironworking debris there were no signs that the debris was *in situ* or that the feature had been fired to high temperatures.

Several features in and around structure I were identified as possible ore roasting pits at the time of excavation. Pit 1549, which was 0.4 m long and 0.14 m deep, and nearby pit 1551, which was 0.3 m long and 0.1 m deep, both contained roasted iron-rich stone, deep red in colour. The fill of pit 1581, which was oval, 0.64 m long and 0.08 m deep, was also described as deep red, but no iron-rich stone from the fill was found amongst the assemblage and neither was any unworked or burnt stone listed for this feature. All of these pits are on the north-west edge of the enclosure, near to each other and to the furnaces. Feature 1494, a posthole situated to the south of the structure, also contained entirely iron-rich stone. Although one or more of these features may have been used for ore roasting, no evidence of heating was observed in the features themselves. Therefore the roasted ore may have been dumped or stored in these areas and not necessarily roasted there. Rounded features interpreted as ore roasting areas have been found at early Wealden sites (Cleere and Crossley 1985, 35) and large elongated roasting pits, 2.5 m long by 0.8 m wide, were found at Bardown in the Weald.

In the south-east working area of structure I was pit 316, which had a diameter of 0.46 m and depth of 0.4 m and contained a large, upright, 0.4 m diameter storage jar. This is one of several large pots of 'Belgic'

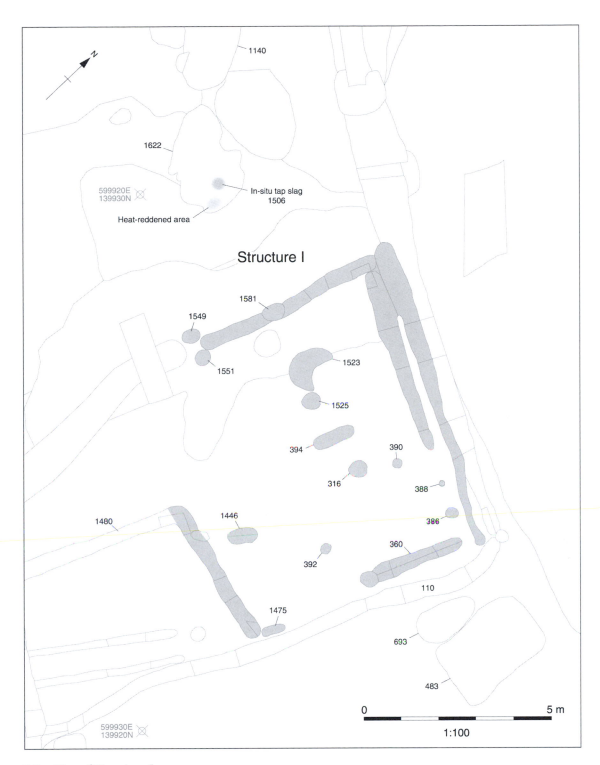

Figure 7.7   Plan of Structure I.

tradition decorated with combing found across the site. The pit contained some consolidated hammerscale, indicating that smithing probably took place in structure I. Although only a small amount of hammerscale was found within the structure, and always in cut features, this was not unexpected given the poor survival of occupation spreads in this area. A shallow oval feature (1446) 0.88 m long and 0.08 m deep in this

working area was described as another ore roasting pit. However, no iron-rich stone was found amongst waste from this feature, although there were many rusty agglomerates containing small flecks of charcoal and a small amount of hammerscale, typical of smithing debris. There were also small dribbles of slag.

Features outside the enclosure to the east included two large pits, 483 and 1226, and two smaller pits,

693 and 1461, which were full of ironworking debris. To the west of the structure, there was a feature (1622) within the base of which was an unexcavated, thin deposit of silt (1516). An area approximately 0.5 m by 0.7 m at the south-east end of the silt was fire-reddened with a large piece of tap slag adjacent to it. The tap slag (1506) weighed 4.5 kg and had a flow direction away from the fired clay patch. A photograph of this area gives the impression that this slag was *in situ*. However, this feature is at a distance from structure I, where the two probable furnaces were located, while the direction of flow of the tap slag was up the slope from the fired clay. These factors suggest that this slag may have been dumped rather than created *in situ*. Furthermore, the burnt area differs in size and shape from the furnaces and it seems unlikely that the burnt patch constituted the remains of a furnace. However, this cannot be conclusively established with the evidence available.

Structure R *(Figs 7.8-7.9)*

Structure R lies at the north-east edge of the excavated Area B and continued into the unexcavated Area A. Fortunately the majority of the structure appears to have been included in the excavated area. However, the geophysical survey detected strong readings in Area A at the north-east side of structure R, which probably correspond to pits and gullies full of ironworking debris. As exposed structure R had at least six posts, and again appears to have been partitioned into north-east and south-west sections where different ironworking activities took place. The boundary between the two areas lay on the line between postholes 1465 and 1484.

At the south-west end of structure R there were a series of rounded features, in intercutting groups, arranged in a row, the majority of which were the basal remains of bloomery furnaces (Fig. 7.8). The first group consisted of feature 1455 (sides slope at 70°, 0.6 m by 0.5 m by 0.15 m deep), which was cut by 1451 (sides slope at 45°, 0.55 m by 0.55 m by 0.1 m deep), which in turn was cut by 1449 (sides slope at 60°, 0.8 m by 0.6 m by 0.11 m deep) (see Fig. 3.45, section 310). In feature 1455, reduced-fired, grey clay was found with 80 mm of oxidised-fired, reddened clay beneath and feature 1451 also had a layer of red, oxidised-fired clay at the base. Feature 1449 had a charcoal-rich fill but there were no signs that the clay had been fired.

The second group consisted of feature 1443 (sides slope at 80°, 0.7 m by 0.5 m by 0.24 m deep), which was cut by 1438 (sides slope at 70°, 0.9 m by 0.8 m by 0.25 m deep) (see Fig. 3.45, section 309). In feature 1443, 60 mm of red, oxidised-fired clay was found, followed by a layer of fill and another 50 mm thick layer of oxidised-fired clay. Feature 1438 had not been fired and contained a very charcoal-rich fill.

The third group consisted of feature 1425 (sides slope at 70°, 0.6 m by 0.4 m by 0.15 m deep), which was cut by 1428 (sides slope at 60°, 0.65 m by 0.65 m

by 0.18 m deep) which in turn was overlain by feature 1423 (sides slope at 60°, 0.5 m by 0.5 m by 0.1 m deep) (see Fig. 3.45, section 306). Feature 1425 had a fire-reddened base, 1428 had a greyish-red base and 1423 had a grey, reduced-fired base with a layer of red, oxidised-fired clay beneath. Feature 1383 was fourth in the row (sides slope at 60°, 0.6 m by 0.4 m by 0.05 m deep) and had oxidised-fired, reddened edges (see Fig. 3.45, section 298).

Cuts 1455, 1451, 1443, 1428, 1425, 1423 and 1383 are likely to be the remains of repeatedly reconstructed bloomery furnaces. The layer of oxidised-fired, reddened clay with a layer of reduced-fired, grey clay above, in features 1455, 1428 and 1423 is very characteristic of furnaces, where high temperatures are combined with reducing conditions inside, and oxidising conditions increase with distance from the interior. In features 1383, 1425, 1443 and 1451 only the oxidised-fired, reddened clay layer was identified; presumably the reduced-fired, grey zone has not survived. The furnace remains are all rounded with diameters of approximately 0.6 m. An internal diameter of 0.2-0.3 m was estimated for these structures at the time of excavation (Starley 1998), so a wall thickness of 0.15 to 0.2 m is again indicated. The furnaces are aligned across the slope of the land at the south-west end of the building and slag from the furnaces may have flowed downhill in a south-westerly direction. Features 1449 and 1438 are shallow, fairly large pits with charcoal-rich fills, but there is no evidence that the pits were exposed to high temperatures. Although in close proximity to the furnaces, and therefore likely to be related to smelting activity, these pits cut the first and second furnace groups, and so must post-date them. There were no similar pits cutting the third and fourth furnace groups. This may indicate that the furnaces were constructed and used one at a time or in pairs rather than all at once, and that the third and fourth furnace groups were in operation after the first and second groups. There is little indication as to the purpose of the shallow pits, although if they are assumed to cut older furnaces, their function may be associated with the construction or operation of the newer ones.

A large oval pit, 1233, 1 m in diameter, situated at the north-east edge of the enclosure alongside the row of furnaces, contained a high concentration of charcoal and several kilos of waste including 0.75 kg of iron-rich stone (plus unworked stone). Pit 1233 occupied a similar position to feature 1581 in structure I at the edge of the enclosure next to the furnaces and, given the similarities between the layouts of workshops R and I, may have had a similar function, perhaps for ore preparation.

The north-east working area within the structure contained an occupation layer, 1585, with an extremely high concentration of hammerscale, so thickly deposited that in areas it had become consolidated into large lumps of smithing pan (Fig. 7.9). The south-west edge of the hammerscale deposit 1585 was more or less straight and coincided with postholes 1465 and 1484. Within the north-east area

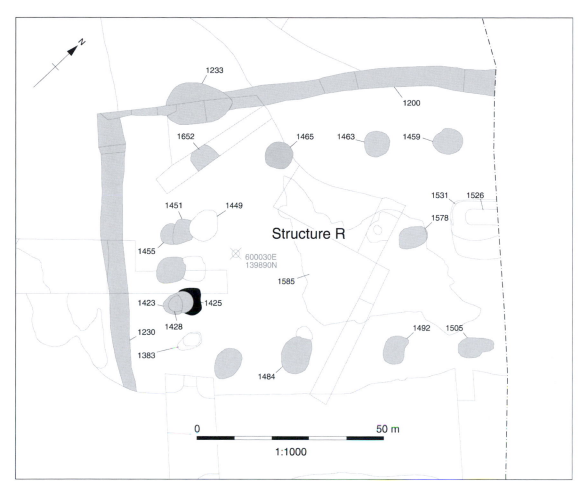

Figure 7.8   Plan of Structure R.

were a small pit 1636 containing a large upright jar and a sub-rectangular feature 1578 with a flat base and almost vertical sides, measuring 0.5 m by 0.7 m by 0.18 m deep. Although the latter feature had fire-reddened edges and a charcoal-rich fill, the base was not reddened. The occupation spread within this working area was sampled at 0.5 m intervals across a grid, although feature 1578 was excavated prior to the sampling. Only the area of the floor visibly rich in hammerscale was sampled, rather than the entire occupation surface of the structure plus a small area outside, that is generally recommended. However, the results (Fig. 7.9) show that the limits of the deposit were estimated accurately and so it is likely that little data has been lost. The samples were sieved to remove particles greater than 3 mm in size, and then processed using a magnet to separate the magnetic hammerscale and heavily fired clay fragments from the remaining residue (Mills and McDonnell 1992). The magnetic fraction present was expressed as a weight percent of the total. A plot of hammerscale concentration across the sampling grid shows the change in concentration from low levels (light) to high concentrations (dark) (Fig. 7.9).

Very high concentrations of hammerscale were detected (up to 90% by weight) indicating that smith-

ing took place in this section of the structure. The highest concentrations were in the north-west half of the workshop near to the large pot and feature 1578, which strongly suggests that an anvil was situated in this area and that a hearth was also nearby. The sharp decrease in concentration of hammerscale to the right of the spread coincides with feature 1578 (labelled H in Figure 7.9) which was excavated prior to sampling. The trough in the hammerscale deposit, extending towards the east and west, is likely to be a result of individuals treading the deposit across the floor as they left the area towards the eastern corner. The proximity of the large pot and feature 1578 suggest that both were involved in the smithing process. The large pot may have held water for use by the smith, for example for cooling tools. Feature 1578 may be the remains of a ground-level smithing hearth. The internal dimensions of the feature (0.5 m by 0.7 m) are comparable to smithing hearths of the period identified elsewhere (Pleiner 2000, 218-227; Tylecote 1990; Salter 1997). The feature would also have been big enough to take the large billets potentially produced at Westhawk (the billet recovered on the site was 0.32 m long), and to have produced the large smithing hearth bottom slags found near structure R, the biggest of which was 0.19 m in diameter.

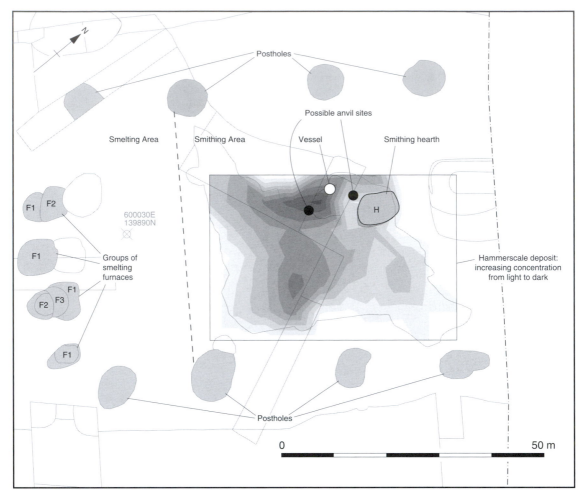

Figure 7.9   Plot of hammerscale distribution in Structure R, in relation to other features, including the furnaces and potential hearth. (Darkest tone shows highest concentration).

The anvil, possibly set on a tree stump, appears to have left no diagnostic mark.

A further series of fired features were identified at the north-east edge of the excavated area within the structure (see Fig. 3.45 section 331). Feature 1526 was subrectangular, with near vertical sides and a flat base, and measured 0.7 m by 0.33 m and 0.48 m deep. It had a slightly fired, reddened base and cut feature 1531, which had a flat base, a diameter of 1.1 m and was 0.2 m deep, with sides sloping at 60°. The base of this feature was slightly fire-reddened. Feature 1531 cut feature 1530, which was oval-shaped, vertical-sided and flat-based and measured 0.6 m by 0.4 m and 0.2 m deep. The base and sides of this feature were heavily fired and reddened. These features were filled with clay and some charcoal, but little slag. Interpretation of these features is difficult as they lay at the edge of the excavated area. They had been used for high temperature processes, but little indication remains as to what these processes may have been. These might be the remains of additional primary smithing hearths and elongated features similar to these have been interpreted as such elsewhere (Pleiner 2000, 223). However, the features are

2 m distant from the area with the highest concentrations of hammerscale and therefore the anvil. Hearths are generally situated near to the anvil for convenience and also to ensure that the object looses the minimum of heat between hearth and anvil (Schmidt 1997, 198-208). Elongated ore roasting hearths have been identified at Roman sites, as mentioned previously, but no ore was found in these features.

Parallels between Structures I and R

Structures R and I are both thought to have been in use for similar periods of up to 50 years and therefore the intensity of ironworking activity for each structure might be anticipated to be roughly equivalent. Structure R contained four probable furnace bases, some with evidence of repeated reconstruction. It is likely that there were furnaces other than the two identified in structure I but that the features have not survived. Like the structure R furnaces these would have been used and repeatedly relined. Approximately 44% of the total ironworking waste by weight from the site was from contexts near structure I.

There are similarities in the layouts of structures I and R, in that both were partitioned with the probable remains of furnaces in one area and a large sunken pot in the other. Although no occupation spread survived in structure I, some smithing pan (consolidated hammerscale) was found in the cut for the pot. Therefore it appears that in both enclosures smelting took place in one area and smithing of the products in the other. This workshop layout can be compared with that of other Roman smelting workshops. The workshop discovered at Woolaston, Gloucestershire (Fulford and Allen 1992, 173, fig. 10) was a post-built structure, with two parallel rows of padstones. It measured 16.5 by 8.2 m and therefore much larger than the post-built structure R at Westhawk Farm. Four groups of heavily-fired, rounded features were identified as furnaces, two groups at each end of the building (F24, F324, F311 and F312: ibid., figs 11 and 12). In the south-east half of this structure, there were three stone settings (F30, F316 and F317: ibid., figs 16 and 15) with evidence of *in situ* breaking of the stones interpreted as ore crushing units. Features F30 and F317 were lined with quartz-rich stone, such as sandstone, which would have been resistant to high temperatures. A fourth feature, a shallow pit (F325: ibid., fig. 14) may originally have been a similar stone setting. The entire lower part of an upright pot (F26) was found near to feature F30, and feature F317 yielded joining sherds of a pot. At Westhawk Farm large ceramic vessels have been found in the workshop areas used for smithing. If features F317 and F30 at Woolaston were the remains of stone-lined hearths used for primary smithing this would be consistent with the presence of the large pots, the surrounding concentrations of charcoal, the proximity to the furnaces and the fracturing of the stones themselves. However, this interpretation of the Woolaston features is tentative since no hammerscale was found in the vicinity of these settings, although it was sought.

Another Roman ironworking structure was excavated at Lenham, Kent, very near to Westhawk Farm (Philp 1994). Postholes were identified forming three sides of a building, within which were three fire-reddened features identified as hearths, a number of features full of ironworking slag and the lower half of a large pot (0.45 m diameter), sunken into the floor. By analogy with Westhawk, it is likely that smithing and possibly smelting took place in this workshop. The finds from the area were dated from AD 50-200 with the majority being of 2nd-century date. The well-preserved bases of two repeatedly reconstructed smelting furnaces, containing *in situ* furnace bottom slag of identical dimensions to those from Westhawk, were also found, some 20 m from the posted structure in an area otherwise reduced by ploughing. Over 30,000 pieces of slag were recorded from the site, but these were not investigated further.

MATERIALS AND THEIR ANALYSIS

The ironworking waste from Westhawk Farm included fragments of furnace lining, quantities of iron-rich stone and charcoal, large amounts of tap slag and smithing slag and some furnace bottom slag. Examples of the end products, in the form of fragments of unrefined iron blooms and a complete refined iron billet, were also recovered. This assemblage provides an opportunity to investigate the compositional relationships between the raw materials, waste products and products of iron smelting and smithing. Detailed examination of the ironworking waste has also provided information on how the different types of by-product may have formed.

Samples were analysed using X-ray fluorescence spectrometry (XRF), energy dispersive spectrometry (EDS) or X-ray diffraction (XRD). Both XRF and EDS determine the elemental composition of a sample while XRD identifies the compounds present. The XRF spectrometer analyses an area of just under 0.5 mm in diameter. Using EDS, areas as large as several millimetres (mm) in width or as small as tens of microns (μm) could be selected for analysis. For bulk analyses, larger areas were analysed to obtain a more generalised result.

Raw Materials

Clay

The furnaces and parts of the smithing hearths were constructed from very quartz-rich clay, which is ideally suited to these high temperature applications because of the refractory properties of quartz. The clay was either selected because of its high quartz content or was quartz-tempered before use and is likely to derive from sand formations in the Lower Greensand or from sandy deposits on the crest of the North Downs, near to the site. The ore smelted at Westhawk Farm probably also derives from the latter deposits (see below). Heavily quartz-tempered clay was also used for lining or constructing furnaces at other Roman smelting sites (Fulford and Allen 1992; Crew 1998). The quartz grains in the furnace clay are angular and are generally less than 150 μm in diameter, although some grains up to 0.5 mm in size were observed. The fabric has a friable, sandy texture. As a result of its iron oxide content the clay has a grey colour when reduced-fired and a red colour when oxidised-fired. All of the vitrified or slag-coated clay, regardless of thickness, colour, phase or origin (structures R, I or P) had a similar appearance and composition. Samples of slag-coated clay from contexts near structures I and R were analysed and the results are compared in Table 7.3.

The heavily vitrified, black surfaces of the fired clay pieces probably originally formed part of the internal walls of furnaces and were subjected to very high temperatures. The fragments were dumped when the furnaces were destroyed, relined as part of a repair, or rebuilt altogether. Many of the pieces are likely to derive from areas near a blowing-hole, where the temperature would have reached its maximum. At high magnifications the black vitreous surface of the lining can be seen to consist of quartz

Table 7.3   Metalworking remains: Composition of quartz-rich, slag-coated clay used for furnace construction, analysed by EDS, average of 3 analyses, normalised (see Table 7.15).

Context	Na_2O	MgO	Al_2O_3	SiO_2	P_2O_5	SO_3	K_2O	CaO	TiO_2	MnO	FeO
1332	0.05	0.43	9.08	83.81	0.79	0.10	1.35	0.50	0.81	0.03	3.06
1225	0.00	0.54	10.07	83.48	0.20	0.22	1.13	0.32	0.94	0.05	3.06

grains and some crystallising silica polymorphs (all mid-grey) surrounded by an iron-rich glassy matrix (lighter grey) with some bubbles (black). In many areas, dispersions of sub-micron, spherical droplets (white) in an iron-rich, glassy matrix were observed (Fig. 7.10). Those large enough to be analysed were found to be iron, often containing several weight percent of phosphorus.

Samples of slag-coated clay lining from contexts near to structures R and I were analysed (Table 7.4). The vitrified surface was formed by the reaction of the clay with ashes from the charcoal fuel and the slag in the furnace and was enriched in iron, calcium, potassium and phosphorus oxides and depleted in titanium, aluminium and silicon oxides relative to the original clay composition. The slag provided the majority of the iron and manganese oxides and some of the phosphorus oxide while the clay provided the majority of the silica, alumina, titania and some of the potash. Larger amounts of potash, lime, magnesia and phosphortus oxide relative to iron oxide were detected in the clay lining compared to the tap slag. This suggests that the contribution of the fuel ashes

to the formation of the vitrified lining was significant relative to the small contribution that the ashes made to the formation of by-products such as tap slag.

Furnace and hearth construction

Some pieces of furnace lining had delaminated into parallel-sided slabs. This may be an indication of successive relining of the furnaces, resulting in weak bonding between linings where previous vitrified surfaces were overlain. Alternatively the lamination could have been as a result of the reactions occurring during furnace use. A concentration gradient of different elements was observed through the thickness of the lining fragments, caused by the reaction zone at the lining surface extending inwards during the temperature cycling of the furnace with each smelt. This resulted in the formation of successive layers within the lining, each with different compositions and microstructures, some of which may have been weaker than others.

Some Roman bloomery furnaces were constructed from clay blocks (Crew 1998) with layers of increas-

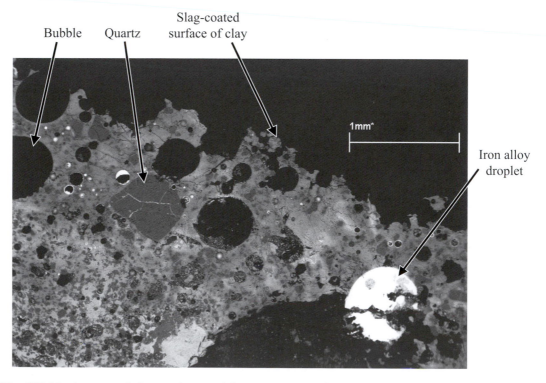

Figure 7.10   SEM back-scattered electron image of the cross section of a piece of furnace lining from context 480.

Table 7.4   Metalworking remains: Composition of different regions of the vitrified surface of slag-coated clay from context 480, analysed by EDS, normalised.

Area	Na_2O	MgO	Al_2O_3	SiO_2	P_2O_5	SO_3	K_2O	CaO	TiO_2	MnO	FeO
Surface (bulk)	0.20	0.54	5.60	74.54	0.90	0.04	4.79	1.93	0.48	0.17	10.81
5.5mm from surface (bulk)	0.38	0.30	6.31	79.16	0.44	0.00	1.24	0.40	1.07	0.08	10.62
Glassy matrix, near surface	0.64	0.58	7.53	66.39	1.29	0.00	7.47	3.01	0.85	0.26	11.98
Dispersion near surface	0.37	0.66	7.28	69.22	1.24	0.11	6.17	3.72	0.72	0.29	10.21
Dispersion second area	0.57	0.85	8.05	57.87	1.97	0.11	3.23	2.49	1.02	0.18	23.65
Matrix of dispersion area	0.66	0.75	8.38	61.52	1.21	0.23	3.37	2.38	0.97	0.17	20.35

ingly siliceous clay used to line the furnace internally. By contrast, the majority of the furnace lining fragments from Westhawk Farm, including very large ones, had no shaped edges and it is therefore probable that the clay was moulded directly to form the basic furnace structures. However, many shaped fragments of slag-coated clay with one or two original edges were also found among the assemblage. All of these had formed part of the inner furnace or hearth wall because they had vitrified and blackened surfaces. Interpretation of these shaped, slag-coated clay fragments is complicated by the fact that debris from both smelting and smithing structures is likely to be included in the waste from the site. Although debris from smithing hearths is generally found to be less blackened and vitrified by slag than debris from smelting furnaces (McDonnell 1986), the hearths at Westhawk Farm would have been used for refining slag-rich iron blooms and so it cannot be assumed that this distinction would apply. For this reason hearth and furnace debris could not be confidently differentiated. Examples of the shaped fragments were found in contexts near workshops R and I and also near to structure P (particularly in context 8449), indicating that, whatever their function, it was common to all of the workshops. The form of the surviving edges indicated that the fragments derived from several groups of differently shaped clay pieces, which may have been used for different applications, and these are described below.

The first group of fragments had two perpendicular (but rounded and uneven) edges, with a varyingly rounded corner. One piece had finger impressions along the edge where it had been pushed into position while plastic. The pieces were generally more than 50 mm thick although none survived to full thickness or sufficiently intact to conclusively establish their function. Possibilities include that they are fragments from near the blowing-hole of a furnace or hearth as the area near the blowing hole was the hottest zone and therefore required frequent repairs. Sometimes replaceable blowing-hole plates were used, consisting of a block of clay with one or more holes through which the bellows blast entered the furnace or hearth. The use of a replaceable plate enabled damaged blowing-holes to be replaced in their entirety by inserting a fresh plate with little disruption to the rest of the furnace or hearth. However, no surviving blowing-hole fragments were found

among the assemblage and so this possibility could not be investigated further.

The second group of clay fragments also had one, or more rarely two, original edges. These differed from the previously described blocks because some of the edges were sharp and extremely straight with a glassy green surface. From the flow of the vitrified surfaces on these fragments, it appeared that the very straight edges had frequently formed the base, but occasionally the side, of the piece when in use. Some of the fragments with two original sides were wedge-shaped with a straight, glassy edge forming the base although the second edge was generally less defined and blackened with slag (Plate 7.1). These fragments may have been set against a temperature-resistant flat surface, such as a slab of stone or a tile to produce the straight bases observed. Alternatively the flat edges may have been necessary in order to ensure that a number of blocks could be fitted together. The fragments examined were flat, rather than curved, and one small-angled wedge survived to its full thickness of about 50 mm. These observations suggest that the flat-edged clay fragments, including the wedge-shaped pieces, may have been used to form smithing hearth structures since the hearth was probably not rounded (the possible hearth feature in structure R is sub-rectangular) and the wall thickness could have been less than that of the furnaces. However, there are other alternatives, including that a number of the shaped clay fragments may have formed a furnace-tapping aperture. Fragments of shaped clay blocks with one glazed surface and occasional finger marks have also been found on other Wealden smelting sites (Cleere and Crossley 1985, 50), and were tentatively interpreted as having been used to block the tapping aperture when this was not in use.

Charcoal

Oak was the main species of charcoal from ironworking contexts (see Challinor, Chapter 9 below), but no evidence was found of coppicing. Oak constituted a large proportion of the hardwoods of the Wealden forest and also provided good quality charcoal (Tylecote 1990, 225; Cleere and Crossley 1985, 37). At the Roman ironworking site at Woolaston (Fulford and Allen 1992, 190-91) the identified charcoal consisted mostly of oak and hazel. There, small branches between 7 and 18 years old had been cut, probably in

0 10 20 mm

Plate 7.1   Wedge-shaped fragment of slag-coated clay, with a flat edge at the bottom of the picture, a reasonably flat edge at the top of the picture and the point of the wedge in the foreground.

the autumn and/or winter, and left to dry for some time before being burnt. Similarly, studies of charcoal production practices found that charcoal producers using traditional forest kilns (Kelley 1986) generally burnt wood between April and November. However, although ironworking was dependent on the availability of charcoal, the seasonality of charcoal production does not necessarily mean that ironworking was also a seasonal activity, as charcoal could have been stockpiled until it was required. Compositional data for the ashes of oak are given in Table 7.5. However, these data can only be used as a guide since the compositions of plant ashes vary with many factors including the geology of the region where the plant grew, the season and the part of the plant ashed. Ashes from charcoal are likely to have made a varying contribution - predominantly of lime, potash and some phosphorus oxide - to the composition of the different types of ironworking waste discussed in this report.

Ore

Iron-rich stone, potentially intended for use as ore, was recovered from contexts in and around the ironworking structures at Westhawk. Some of the material had been heated in an oxidising atmosphere,

suggesting that the ore was roasted prior to smelting. Samples were analysed using XRD, EDS and XRF spectrometry to determine the compounds present and the compositions of the stone. The samples ranged from more silica-rich ferruginous sandstone to iron-rich ironstone, although it appears that these two extremes are end-members of a continuous series and that all of the stone may have derived from the same source. The unroasted examples were orange/brown/grey in colour, either nodular or tabular in form, and the minerals present were hydrous iron oxides (goethite and lepidocrocite) and quartz. The quartz grains were present in widely varying amounts and were angular and generally small (less than 200 µm in diameter), although some coarser-grained examples were also observed. Roasted examples were red to metallic grey in colour and consisted of haematite and varying amounts of quartz in the coarser sandstone examples and haematite plus magnetite in the iron-rich, fine-grained examples. Some of the concretionary nodules were found in association with flint nodules or small flint chips (Plate 7.2). Flint nodules had been used along with ironworking slag for metalling the road through Westhawk (see above).

The compositions of some potential ore samples from Westhawk are given in Table 7.6. The analyses have been presented in two groups: ferruginous

Table 7.5   Metalworking remains: Composition of ashed oak, from Wolff (1871).

Sample	Na$_2$O	MgO	Cl	SiO$_2$	P$_2$O$_3$	SO$_3$	K$_2$O	CaO	FeO
Oak bark	0.0	1.4	0.1	2.0	0.0	0.7	8.0	87.8	0.0
Oak bark	2.3	6.9	0.5	0.5	4.8	0.6	8.3	75.6	0.4
Oak wood	5.7	4.5	0.0	0.8	3.5	1.2	8.4	75.4	0.5

sandstone, which contained a considerable proportion of quartz grains (SiO$_2$); and ironstone, which contained little or no quartz. The varying quartz content between samples is illustrated by the change in silica content of the analyses; some ironstone contained virtually no silica or alumina. The heterogeneity of the stone, in particular the coarse sandstone, made it necessary to conduct relatively large numbers of analyses in order to obtain representative compositions. In addition to the tabulated analyses, four other samples from each category were screened to ensure that the analyses were representative. EDS analyses of fragments of ironstone from contexts 1548 and 1356 detected on average 91% iron oxide (FeO) by weight, 0.6% phosphorus oxide (P$_2$O$_5$), 4.5% silica (SiO$_2$) and 0.6% manganese oxide (MnO).

There are a number of possible sources of ore at varying distances from Westhawk Farm. The site is situated on an outcrop of the Weald clay and the main form of ore utilised in the Weald was clay ironstone, which generally occurs as nodules between 0.05 and 0.25 m in diameter, but also in layers in the Wealden beds. The predominant constituent of the ironstone nodules is siderite (iron carbonate). At Shadoxhurst, 3 km south-west of the site, thin nodular ironstone beds have been noted. Siderite seams, up to 0.13 m thick, have also been mapped on British Geological Survey Sheet 304 (Tenterden) near High Halden, Woodchurch and Bethersden, all about 8 km from Westhawk Farm (Worssam 1985). However, although siderite could have been obtained locally, no siderite was identified in the site assemblage.

A second potential source of ore is a concretionary form of iron-rich stone, which is also found in the Weald, formed by weathering of iron-rich minerals such as siderite. The siderite is oxidised in successive layers, broken off and dispersed in the soils or incorporated in river gravels. In the Weald the greater permeability to water of river terrace gravels than of clays can also lead to the formation of large, thick masses of concretionary iron pan (Worssam 1985, 13-14). Hydrous iron oxides, goethite or lepidocrocite, are the most common alteration products of siderite (Deer *et al.* 1992). However, no conclusive evidence for the utilisation of this type of ore was found at Westhawk.

Two other possible sources of ore, which could both be described as ferruginous sandstone, have been mentioned in past studies of the Wealden iron industry (Worssam 1985, 9-10, 14-15). These are the Lower Greensand ironstone and the ironstone of the Lenham Beds and the 'Sand in Clay-with-flints'.

The sandy ironstone that occurs in the Folkestone Beds within the Lower Greensand is known as carstone and contains a significant quantity of silica in the form of quartz grains. The Lower Greensand was deposited when the area became a shallow sea; some beds contain phosphatic nodules (Gallois 1965), which may have been formed by replacement of the original matter by calcium phosphate during a long exposure on the sea floor (Chatwin 1961). Although the carstone may have been smelted elsewhere in the region, this stone is unlikely to have been exploited at Westhawk since little carstone is found in the vicinity of the site (B Worssam, pers. comm.).

The ironstone of the Lenham Beds and the 'Sand in Clay-with-flints' is found along the North Downs between Detling and Folkestone. These sands are the remains of a Pliocene deposit that was laid down on the floor of a sea. Little is known about the sands or whether ironstone derived from them may have a significant phosphorus content. However the discovery

Plate 7.2   *Roasted ferruginous sandstone nodules and pieces, one (top centre) with associated flint (the white areas).*

Table 7.6   Metalworking remains: Composition of ironstone samples measured by XRF, the number of analyses is given in brackets (see Table 7.16).

Type: Context: Description:	*Ferruginous Sandstone* **1332** (average 9) Orange nodule, fine	*Ironstone* **1548** (average 4) Red nodule, fine	**1356** (average 2) Red nodule, fine
FeO	57.5	89.3	95.7
Al_2O_3	6.6	3.0	0.9
SiO_2	33.6	5.9	1.9
P_2O_5	0.9	0.7	0.5
K_2O	0.2	0.1	0.0
CaO	0.2	0.2	0.2
MnO	0.5	0.6	0.5
SO_3	0.3	0.2	0.4
TiO_2	0.4	0.1	0.0

of bloomery slag on the summit of the Downs above Hollingbourne suggests that Lenham Beds sandstone may nonetheless have been smelted in bloomery furnaces (Worssam 1985, 15). A Roman smelting site has also been identified at Lower Runhams Farm, Lenham (Philp 1994) and a bloomery smelting site has been identified at Chapel Farm, Lenham Heath (Worssam 1985, 14). Dr Worssam has kindly identified the iron-rich stone from Westhawk as being derived from the Lenham Beds of British Geological Survey Sheet 288 (Maidstone) or from the 'Sand in the Clay-with-flints' of Sheets 289 (Canterbury) and 305/6 (Folkestone and Dover). The presence of flint in some of the samples proves that they are post-Cretaceous and is consistent with the stone being from these Pliocene deposits.

In summary, although all of the ore used at Westhawk probably derived from two deposits - the Lenham Beds or the 'Sand in Clay-with-flints' - it ranged from ferruginous sandstone, containing about 50% silica by weight, to ironstone, containing about 85% iron oxide. The lower and higher iron content stone were probably intentionally combined in each ore batch to ensure that the batch had an intermediate iron content overall and would produce a reasonable yield of iron metal. The sandstone would also contribute a large proportion of the silica required to produce fluid iron silicate slag during smelting. Although the slag is a waste product, its formation influences the progression of other reactions in the furnace and fluid slag separates more easily from the iron bloom (Pleiner 2000). The ore was roasted prior to smelting.

Smelting slags

Tap slag

Samples of tap slag from three contexts, 1332, 319 and 480, were analysed. The tap slag from contexts 1332 (near structure R) and 319 (near structure I) consisted predominantly of fayalite laths in a glassy matrix. Some wustite (FeO) was also present but these dendrites were scarce and very fine. The iron content of the slag from context 480 was found to be higher and this slag consequently contained more wustite. The microstructure of each flow of slag was coarser towards the base, as a result of slower cooling, and successive flows of slag could therefore be distinguished. Although the tap slag was relatively homogeneous (Table 7.7) some compositional variation was observed; for example, the base of one slag cake (319, see Table 7.17) was richer in alumina, silica and potash but depleted in iron oxide.

The smelting slag from Westhawk was found to have a high phosphorus content, suggesting that the ore smelted at Westhawk was phosphorus-rich. Variable but significant levels of phosphorus oxide were detected in samples of potential ore (Table 7.16), the highest being 3.4% by weight in ferruginous sandstone. Examination of data on the composition of bloomery smelting slag from other sites in England has revealed five with phosphorus-rich bloomery slag, three of which are in Norfolk and two in North Yorkshire (Tylecote 1962a; Chirikure and Paynter forthcoming; McDonnell 1986). Additional sites are likely to be found in the future as more material is analysed, particularly from these areas. Two Roman

Table 7.7   Metalworking remains: Composition of tap slag, measured by EDS, average of 6 analyses for each sample, normalised (see Table 7.17).

Context	Sample	Na_2O	MgO	Al_2O_3	SiO_2	P_2O_5	SO_3	K_2O	CaO	TiO_2	MnO	FeO
1332	Tap (R)	0.6	0.4	6.6	26.5	1.9	0.1	0.7	2.6	0.3	0.6	59.5
319	Tap (I)	0.1	0.5	6.8	24.7	1.6	0.1	0.9	2.1	0.3	0.5	62.6
480	Tap (I)	0.1	0.4	6.3	21.8	2.0	0.2	0.4	1.9	0.2	0.3	66.5

Table 7.8   Metalworking remains: Composition of phosphorus-rich tap slag from Ashwicken and West Runton, Norfolk and Baysdale and Ouse Gill, Yorkshire, compared with the composition of low-phosphorus Roman tap slag from selected other sites.

Site	Na_2O	MgO	Al_2O_3	SiO_2	P_2O_5	SO_3	K_2O	CaO	TiO_2	MnO	FeO	Ref
Ashwicken	nm	1.4	3.3	21.8	1.8	nm	0.0	0.4	nm	0.5	70.8	A
West Runton	nm	0.5	9.6	26.3	1.8	0.1	0.0	1.5	nm	3.1	57.3	B
Baysdale	0.3	4.1	9.7	27.4	2.5	0.5	2.2	10.4	0.6	1.3	41.1	C
Ouse Gill	0.4	4.2	9.6	30.9	1.8	0.5	2.4	11.3	0.6	1.2	36.2	
Snettisham	0.1	0.2	1.98	24.1	1.4	0.2	0.3	1.3	0.1	0.5	69.8	D
Camerton	nm	0.3	6.9	13.0	0.6	0.4	nm	2.3	0.4	nm	76.2	E
Wilderspool	nm	0.0	2.1	29.6	0.3	nm	nm	1.7	nm	nm	66.2	
Sharpley Pool	nm	1.1	6.0	32.8	0.0	0.0	nm	1.9	nm	trace	58.2	F
Worcester	nm	1.3	6.0	16.5	0.0	0.0	nm	3.1	nm	0.2	72.8	
Woolaston	nm	1.8	4.6	23.5	0.2	nm	1.8	2.2	0.3	0.2	65.5	G

nm = not measured.
References: A: Tylecote 1962a, B: Tylecote 1962b, C: McDonnell 1986, D: Chirikure and Paynter forthcoming, E: Tylecote 1990, F: Morton and Wingrove 1969, and G: Fulford and Allen 1992.

sites, Snettisham and Ashwicken, are situated on the Lower Greensand in Norfolk. Ferruginous sandstone nodules derived from the Lower Greensand carstone were probably smelted at these sites (Chatwin 1961; Tylecote 1962a; Chirikure and Paynter forthcoming). The third Norfolk smelting site, West Runton, is on the coast near Cromer. Tylecote (1962b) describes a sandy, ferruginous conglomerate in that area, sometimes containing flint or shells as well as nodules of hydrated iron oxides. This stone may be derived from Pliocene and Pleistocene Crag deposits, which extend over the eastern part of Norfolk. Therefore types of ore similar to that from Westhawk (nodules of hydrous iron oxides with varying quartz grain contents derived from sandy deposits) were probably smelted at the Norfolk sites. However, ironworkers at the North Yorkshire sites are likely to have utilised ore composed of the mineral siderite, for example Jurassic ironstone or ironstone from the Coal Measures. The slag from these sites can be further distinguished by the increased concentrations of lime and magnesia resulting from the substitution of Fe^{2+} by Ca and Mg in the ore. Phosphorus-rich smelting slag could

also be produced when bog iron ore was smelted, as demonstrated by research at the Iron Age settlement of Snorup in Denmark (Høst-Madsen and Buchwald 1999). The compositions of phosphorus-rich tap slag from these sites are given in Table 7.8, where they are compared to the lower phosphorus compositions of tap slag from some other Roman sites.

Furnace bottom slag

Samples from bowl-shaped furnace bottom slags from contexts 1510 and 1225 near structure I were examined (Plate 7.3). The microstructure consisted of fayalite laths and wustite in a glass matrix. The composition of the slags varied from surface to base resulting in microstructural variations. There was a relatively sharp boundary in the microstructure between the lower and upper halves of the slag. Towards the top of the slag the concentration of iron oxide was higher and the concentration of the other components was correspondingly lower. Large fayalite laths and wustite were plentiful and the upper half of the slag also had the greatest porosity. The

0 10 20 mm

Plate 7.3   Furnace bottom slag from the side (circular in plan).

Table 7.9   Metalworking remains: Composition of furnace bottom slags, measured by EDS, average of 7 (1510) and 5 (1225) analyses, normalised (see Table 7.18).

Sample	Na_2O	MgO	Al_2O_3	SiO_2	P_2O_5	SO_3	K_2O	CaO	TiO_2	MnO	FeO
Furnace Bottom (1510)	0.13	0.42	3.84	20.31	0.91	0.20	0.57	1.57	0.17	0.08	71.52
Furnace Bottom (1225)	0.14	0.16	4.41	23.66	0.80	0.05	0.82	1.66	0.23	0.20	67.64

lower half contained less wustite (and finer dendrites), but more glass, with very little wustite present at the base of the slag.

These samples were analysed (Table 7.9) and were found to have a higher ratio of iron oxide to silica (SiO_2) and of silica to alumina (Al_2O_3) overall than the tap slags. The furnace slags also contained slightly less phosphorus oxide (P_2O_5) than the tap slags, but still more than the equivalent slag from bloomery sites producing low-phosphorus smelting slags (cf Fulford and Allen 1992, table 9). These compositional variations indicate that the tap slag and furnace slag formed in slightly different environments. For example, differences may be a result of changes in the atmospheric conditions between regions of the furnace. Fulford and Allen (1992, 194) noted that 'massive slags', which they often found attached to tap slag, were also noticeably richer in iron oxide and depleted in other constituents. They also detected magnetite in these slags, indicative of a relatively oxidising atmosphere. These massive slags are likely to have been the equivalent of the Westhawk furnace bottom slags. The Westhawk furnace slags had also reacted to some extent with the siliceous lining at the furnace base, as a result of prolonged contact at high temperatures, and this was reflected in the decreased iron oxide content and scarcity of wustite dendrites towards the slag base.

Products

Unrefined blooms

Two fragments of blooms from the slag assemblage were sectioned and examined. The first (1333) was predominantly ferritic with occasional small patches of pearlite, indicating a low overall carbon content. The average of eleven EDS analyses showed that the bloom contained 0.3% phosphorus oxide (P_2O_5) by weight. The detection of phosphorus in the metal is to be expected as there are very high levels in the slag within the bloom and analysis of the slag within this bloom showed 7.32% of phosphorus oxide by weight (Table 7.10). The slag remaining in the bloom is the remains of smelting slag, and it would be expected that the composition of the bloom slag and the smelt-

ing slag would be broadly similar. This is so with the exception of the increased phosphorus content of the slag in this bloom fragment. In addition, the iron content of the bloom slag is slightly higher, and the alumina and silica contents consequently lower, than that of the smelting slag. Høst-Madsen and Buchwald (1999) also noted phosphorus oxide enrichment of the slag in a bloom relative to the tap slag from the same site. They attributed this to phosphorus dissolving in the metal and then later partitioning between the metal and the slag with which it was closely associated, resulting in phosphorus enrichment of the slag in the bloom.

The second bloom fragment (1259) was probably rejected because it still contained particles of ore, fuel and regions with a high proportion of partially reacted quartz grains (less than 100 μm and angular) as well as slag and ferritic iron. The particles of ore were interpreted as such, rather than as corrosion products formed in voids, because of the presence of tiny crystals nucleating around the perimeter of each particle, indicating that the particles were present when the bloom was hot (Fig. 7.11). As a result of the smelting process, and corrosion of the bloom since it was discarded, the ore fragments are likely to have been converted to iron oxide (haematite or magnetite) or hydrous ferric oxide (goethite) regardless of their original composition. Consequently a total of *c* 74% iron oxide (FeO) by weight was detected by analysis (the data in Table 7.11 are normalised). The ore fragments were up to about 1 mm in diameter with a plate-like appearance and the outline of euhedral crystals, probably goethite, could be seen in some. No quartz grains were observed in the ore fragments, suggesting that the quartz has already reacted to form the surrounding iron silicate slag or that little was originally present.

The slag comprised dendrites of wustite, fayalite laths and a glassy matrix, with occasional crystals of hercynite ($FeAl_2O_4$). The regions containing large concentrations of quartz grains may derive from detached furnace lining or from ferruginous sandstone added as part of the ore batch. The iron metal within the bloom fragment contained less than 0.05% phosphorus oxide by weight (four EDS analyses) and the associated slag contained correspondingly less phos-

Table 7.10   Metalworking remains: Composition of slag within a partially refined bloom from context 1333, measured by EDS, average of 6 analyses, normalised (see Table 7.19).

Na_2O	MgO	Al_2O_3	SiO_2	P_2O_5	SO_3	K_2O	CaO	TiO_2	MnO	FeO
0.09	0.51	2.09	12.84	7.32	0.38	0.77	1.46	0.09	0.35	74.10

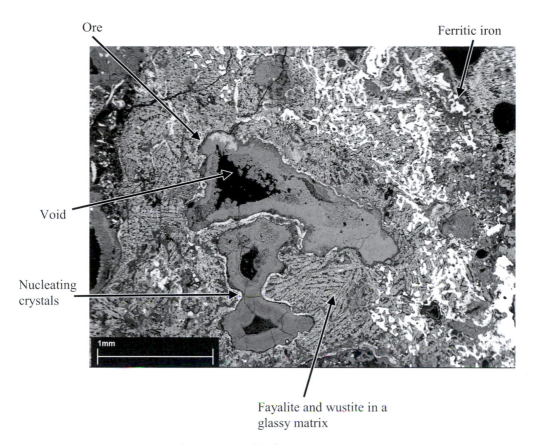

Ore

Ferritic iron

Void

Nucleating
crystals

1mm

Fayalite and wustite in a
glassy matrix

Figure 7.11   SEM back-scattered electron image of unrefined bloom, showing areas of ferritic iron (white), ore (mid-grey) and central voids (black) surrounded by nucleating crystals (white) and slag comprised of wustite (light grey) and fayalite (mid-grey laths) in a glass matrix (dark grey).

phorus (Table 7.11) than the previously described bloom fragment (Table 7.10).

Refined billet

A refined billet (SF905; see Scott, Chapter 5, cat. no. 2; Fig. 5.10) was found in context 7009, during cleaning of a layer above structure P, a circular structure that probably dates to *c* AD 200-250. The billet weighed 4.46 kg and was 0.32 m long, with a maximum width of 75 mm and a thickness of 55 mm. The longitudinal section of the billet (both parallel and perpendicular to the base of the billet) was trapezoid shaped with rounded vertices. A sample of the billet was examined metallographically and analysed using EDS (Table 7.12). A value of 0.11% of phosphorus by weight was detected in analyses of approximately 4 mm² areas of the billet selected as they contained

very little slag (standard deviation 0.04%, average of four analyses). This level of phosphorus is intermediate between the levels detected in the bloom fragments, suggesting that the phosphorus content of the iron produced at Westhawk was variable. The variation in phosphorus content within the billet sample demonstrates the heterogeneity of the iron. This amount of phosphorus would slightly increase the hardness of the iron (Tylecote 1990, 145).

The billet appeared to be very well consolidated and the few slag inclusions remaining were analysed (Table 7.12). The majority of the larger slag inclusions consisted only of glass or of glass with fayalite. The fayalitic slag inclusions were very iron-rich and consequently contained little phosphorus oxide. The smaller inclusions contained wustite dendrites in addition to fayalite and glass and also contained the highest concentration of phosphorus oxide. The

Table 7.11   Metalworking remains: Compositions of different regions within theterogeneous discarded bloom fragment, measured by EDS and normalised.

Area	Na₂O	MgO	Al₂O₃	SiO₂	P₂O₅	SO₃	K₂O	CaO	TiO₂	MnO	FeO
Quartz-rich region	0.81	0.28	2.96	33.23	1.44	0.18	0.46	0.09	0.13	0.00	60.42
Fuel-rich region	0.63	0.09	1.73	13.41	1.32	0.24	0.22	0.12	0.09	0.00	82.15
Slag (average of 3)	0.26	0.49	7.81	21.63	2.02	0.15	1.22	1.78	0.28	0.65	63.71
Ore (average of 3)	0.56	0.14	0.27	0.36	0.21	0.52	0.01	0.39	0.05	0.12	97.36

Table 7.12   Metalworking remains: Compositions of slag inclusions sampled from billet (SF905, context 7009), measured by EDS and normalised (see Table 7.20).

Slag	MgO	Al$_2$O$_3$	SiO$_2$	P$_2$O$_5$	SO$_3$	K$_2$O	CaO	TiO$_2$	MnO	FeO
Fayalite and glass (average of 3)	0.35	1.71	8.45	0.38	0.11	0.31	0.91	0.11	0.29	87.38
Wustite, fayalite, glass (average of 5)	0.73	4.49	24.01	1.14	0.56	1.12	3.28	0.28	0.92	63.48
Glass (average of 3)	0.88	5.30	30.59	0.81	0.42	1.48	4.22	0.45	1.26	54.60
Overall average	0.67 ± 0.22	3.95 ± 1.5	21.56 ± 9.4	0.84 ± 0.4	0.40 ± 0.3	1.00 ± 0.5	2.89 ± 1.4	0.28 ± 0.1	0.84 ± 0.4	67.58 ± 14.0

compositions of the slag inclusions and the smelting slag from Westhawk were approximately similar although the concentration of phosphorus oxide in the inclusions was slightly less than that detected in the tap slag analysed from the site.

The compositions of the Westhawk billet and the slag inclusions it contains are consistent with the billet having been produced at Westhawk, although the slag contained slightly less phosphorus than the smelting slag from the site. The varying phosphorus contents of the billet and bloom fragments suggest that the products of Westhawk ranged from ferritic to phosphoric iron.

Smelting summary

The ore used at Westhawk was probably concretionary ironstone with a varying quartz content, ranging from silica-rich ferruginous sandstone to ironstone with a low silica content. The ore was derived largely from the Lenham Beds or from the 'Sand in the Clay-with-flints' no more than 10 miles from the site. If the more iron-rich stone was combined with the more silica-rich stone in appropriate proportions the ore batch would have had a sufficiently high iron content overall for a good yield of iron metal. The gangue from the ore is likely to have provided a large proportion of the silica from which the tap slag formed. The ore was roasted before being smelted. Analyses of the ore detected widely varying levels of phosphorus oxide of up to 3.4% by weight.

As a result of the phosphorus content of the ore, the tap slag from Westhawk was phosphorus-rich (containing several weight percent) relative to slag from other bloomery smelting sites (Table 7.8). On the basis of the analyses in Table 7.7 the tap slag composition appears to have been consistent between the two workshops suggesting that the smelting conditions and raw materials were similar. The large, bowl-shaped furnace bottom slags formed in the base of the furnaces in a depression below the level of the tapping aperture. The furnace bottom slags had different compositions to the tap slag from the same workshops, containing higher proportions of iron oxide and less phosphorus oxide overall. The form of the tap and furnace slags suggests that slag was tapped through a hole 40 mm to 90 mm wide and up to 60 mm deep, slightly below the level of the furnace base.

The slag in the bloom fragments from Westhawk was enriched to varying degrees with phosphorus relative to the tap slag from the site and some phosphoric as well as ferritic iron was identified. The billet recovered from Westhawk contained an amount of phosphorus intermediate between the amounts in the two bloom fragments. Tylecote (1990, 174) states that 'two types of metal were used in Roman tools: moderate to high phosphorus iron, such as that from the Weald, and carburised iron such as that from the Forest of Dean'. Work-hardened phosphoric iron is considerably harder than ferritic iron (ibid., 145) and therefore suitable for applications where a hard metal is required.

Silica-rich clay was used to construct the furnaces. The furnace lining was subjected to high temperatures, and the inner lining reacted with ashes from the fuel and slag to form a vitrified surface. No intact blowing holes were found, although fragments of clay blocks were recovered that may have formed parts of blowing-hole plates. Wedge-shaped clay fragments with very flat, green-glazed edges, found amongst the ironworking waste, may have been used, in conjunction with another temperature resistant material such as stone, to form smithing hearth structures, although these fragments did not survive sufficiently well to investigate this further.

Smithing Slags

Hammerscale

A sample of hammerscale, a by-product of smithing, from the occupation deposit of structure R was examined. A magnet was used to separate the magnetic fraction, including the hammerscale, from the rest of the material in the sample. The magnetic fraction was found to contain small particles of slag and heavily-fired quartz-rich material (Fig. 7.12) in addition to hammerscale flakes and spheres. Examination of the magnetic fraction using an electron microscope showed charcoal fuel fragments and fired quartz-rich material frequently adhering to the hammerscale flakes. The presence of a thin reaction zone between the quartz-rich material and the hammerscale indicated that they had been in contact while at high temperatures and therefore that the hammerscale, slag and fired quartz-rich particles were all by-products of the smithing process.

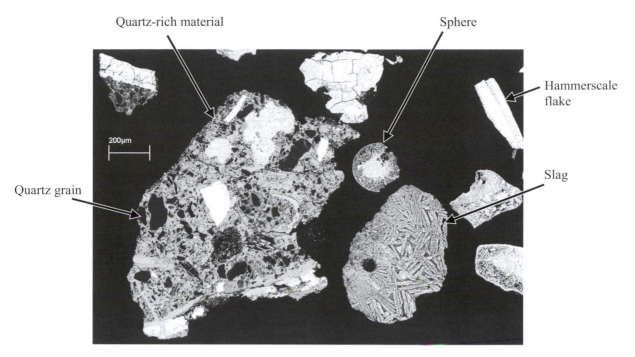

Figure 7.12   SEM back-scattered electron image of a hammerscale sample, which includes lumps of slag, spheres of hammerscale and hammerscale flakes with quartz-rich material adhering.

The quartz-rich particles consisted of angular quartz grains, the majority less than 130 μm in diameter, in an iron-rich matrix. Hammerscale flakes and spheres were analysed using XRD and found to consist predominantly of the iron oxides wustite (FeO) and magnetite (Fe_3O_4) (Fig. 7.13). The compositions of the different components of the magnetic fraction were also determined, using EDS analysis. The results are given in Table 7.21 and discussed further below.

It has already been suggested that the smithing hearths used for bloom refining were constructed, at least in part, from silica-rich clay (see 'Smithing hearth bottom slags' below, and also 'Clay' above), as were the smelting furnaces. The quartz grains in the material adhering to the hammerscale are similar

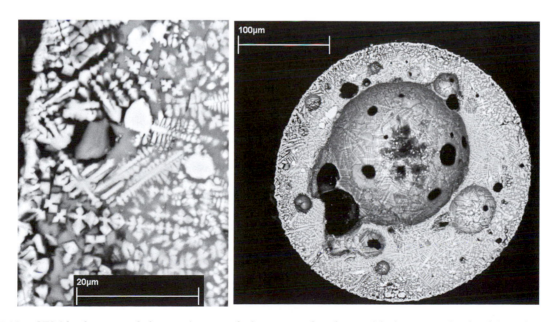

Figure 7.13   SEM back-scattered electron images of a hammerscale sphere, with the magnetite dendrites shown at high magnification on the left.

in size and angularity to the grains in the fragments of furnace lining from the site. Therefore the fired quartz-rich material amongst the hammerscale may be hearth lining that has been heavily fired and has partially reacted with slag. An alternative is that the smith may have used sand as a flux during smithing, which could result in the formation of fired, quartz-rich particles. Sand would react with the oxides on the surface of the iron to form molten slag that was easily removed to leave a clean metal surface (McDonnell 1991). However, the composition of some of the quartz-rich inclusions in the smithing hearth bottom slags, discussed in the next section of this report, suggests that the former hypothesis is more likely.

Mills and McDonnell (1992) have shown that there is a correlation between the amount of hammerscale in soil samples from smithing deposits and the weight of the magnetic fraction of the sample, even though other types of magnetic material are present. Therefore the inclusion of highly-fired, quartz-rich particles in the magnetic fraction of the Westhawk samples will not distort the hammerscale distribution plot (Fig. 7.16) as all samples are affected equally.

Smithing hearth bottom slags

The smithing slags recovered from Westhawk varied widely in form and size, from very small, low porosity slags (0.2 to 0.3 kg) to medium-sized slags (1 kg) to extremely large, unusually shaped slags (2 to 3 kg). Small, medium and large smithing slags were recovered from contexts 1257 and 1332 around structure R (Table 7.12). The large smithing hearth bottom slag from context 1332 is shown in cross-section in Figure 7.20. A medium-sized smithing slag from context 1225, near structure I, was also examined. All these slags were heterogeneous and are described in terms of a succession of layers, although a continuous gradation between the different regions was generally observed, rather than distinct boundaries. The average compositions of the smithing slags are given in Table 7.13. These are useful for comparison with other types of slag from Westhawk as well as with the average compositions of smithing slags from other sites. Only compositional data on bulk regions of the slags, rather than analyses of particular phases or inclusions, were used to generate the averages. Despite this the heterogeneity of this slag type is demonstrated by the large standard deviation of the

results (Table 7.13) and therefore caution must be exercised when using the data. The full analytical data are given in Tables 7.22-7.26.

The top layer of each of the slags consisted of a corroded, iron-rich, amorphous matrix surrounding angular grains of quartz. The majority of the quartz grains were less than 150 μm in diameter although occasionally grains of up to 0.05 mm were observed. The grains were similar in size and shape to those in the quartz-rich material found in the magnetic fraction of the hammerscale samples and also to the quartz grains in samples of furnace lining (see above). Particles of entrained, quartz-rich material were observed in the upper halves of the medium-sized smithing slags from contexts 1225 and 1332. The particles nearer the middle of the slag were surrounded by reaction products, confirming that the particles were incorporated into the slag while it was forming, rather than being post-depositional material. These areas had compositions similar to the furnace lining samples discussed above. Charcoal fragments were also observed. Characteristically-shaped, iron-rich hammerscale particles, either spheres or parallel-sided flakes up to 0.4 mm in length, were occasionally observed in this top layer, and were particularly abundant in the small slag from context 1257 (Fig. 7.14).

The second layer of the smithing hearth slags sometimes contained a high proportion of charcoal. In this layer, and in the region immediately below, a large number of voids were consistently observed. The slag in these regions consisted of varying proportions of wustite dendrites and fayalite in a glassy matrix. The remainder of the slag also consisted largely of wustite dendrites and fayalite in a glassy matrix, although there were large variations in porosity and localised changes in composition led to variations in the relative proportions of the different phases and to the formation of other phases. For example an increased concentration of alumina led to the formation of very fine crystals of hercynite spinel and a pyroxene phase in the glass matrix surrounding the wustite and fayalite in some areas of the large smithing hearth bottom slag. A gradation to a coarser microstructure was quite frequently observed in the lower half of the slags suggesting that they had cooled more slowly. The base of the smithing slags was often found to contain a slightly lower proportion of wustite and have lower porosity. The medium-sized smithing hearth slag from context 1332 was particularly porous throughout with only small regions of crystalline slag having formed amongst the voids.

Table 7.13   Metalworking remains: Average compositions (and standard deviations) of smithing hearth bottom slags (SHB) (see Tables 7.22-7.26).

Ctx	SHB size	Na_2O	MgO	Al_2O_3	SiO_2	P_2O_5	SO_3	K_2O	CaO	TiO_2	MnO	FeO
1257	small	0.3 ± 0.1	0.9 ± 0.5	3.6 ± 0.8	23.3 ± 4.4	1.2 ± 0.3	0.2 ± 0.2	1.4 ± 1.0	3.5 ± 2.2	0.2 ± 0.1	0.2 ± 0.2	65.0 ± 7.4
1332	large	0.2 ± 0.2	0.5 ± 0.1	6.3 ± 1.3	27.7 ± 3.0	1.3 ± 0.3	0.3 ± 0.2	1.0 ± 0.7	3.5 ± 1.9	0.3 ± 0.0	0.2 ± 0.1	58.8 ± 4.8
1332	medium	0.0 ± 0.1	0.4 ± 0.3	4.2 ± 2.6	17.4 ± 10.0	0.8 ± 0.5	0.2 ± 0.1	0.7 ± 0.6	2.1 ± 1.5	0.2 ± 0.1	0.2 ± 0.1	73.7 ± 15.1
1225	medium	0.0 ± 0.1	0.5 ± 0.1	8.2 ± 4.3	27.0 ± 12.0	2.0 ± 0.4	0.4 ± 0.6	0.4 ± 0.3	1.9 ± 0.5	0.4 ± 0.4	0.3 ± 0.1	59.0 ± 17.1

Quartz grain

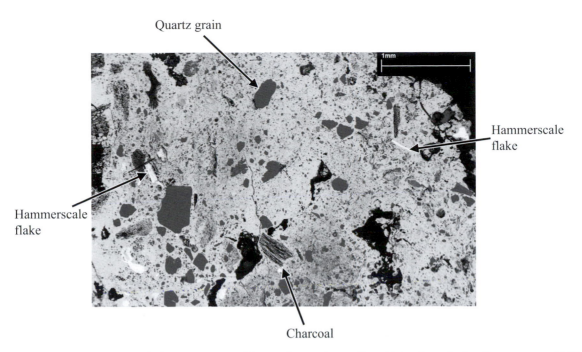

Hammerscale flake

Hammerscale flake

Charcoal

Figure 7.14   SEM back-scattered electron image of the top layer of a small smithing hearth slag from context 1257, consisting of an iron-rich matrix with fuel fragments surrounding angular quartz grains and hammerscale flakes and spheres (no spheres in this image).

A distinct boundary with a scalloped edge (Fig. 7.15) was observed in the large slag from context 1332 towards the base of the thicker end (to the right in Plate 7.4). The slag immediately beneath the boundary had a very low porosity and a coarser microstructure. The boundary may have formed when a smithing hearth bottom slag was displaced in the hearth, rather than being removed completely, and slag from a subsequent smithing operation was then deposited on top. The uneven shape and large size of this slag relative to others from the site also suggest that it may be the product of more than one smithing operation. The thicker end of this large slag was positioned near to the hearth wall as a thin layer of hearth lining adheres to it at this point. The hearth lining was analysed and found to be siliceous clay similar to that used in the furnace construction, containing approximately 75% silica by weight, 11% alumina and 7% iron oxide.

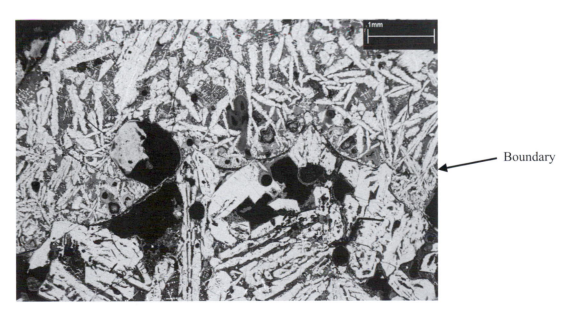

Boundary

Figure 7.15   SEM back-scattered electron image of the microstructurural boundary in a large smithing slag, with a coarser fayalitic microstructure below the boundary.

0 10 20 mm

Plate 7.4   Cross section of large smithing hearth slag.

Smithing slag summary

On average 0.2% manganese oxide by weight (up to 0.4%) and 1.3% phosphorus oxide (up to 3.3%) were detected in the Westhawk smithing slags. This compares with an average of 0.1wt% manganese oxide and 0.8wt% phosphorus oxide in smithing slags that have been studied from other sites (McDonnell 1986). The smithing slags at Westhawk Farm were found largely in contexts near workshops where waste from both smelting and smithing activity was found and is likely to be waste from primary smithing, during which the iron blooms produced by smelting were consolidated. The tap slag from Westhawk Farm contained high levels of phosphorus oxide and intermediate levels of manganese and the slag incorporated in some bloom fragments was particularly rich in phosphorus. The elevated levels of phosphorus and manganese oxides in the smithing slags from Westhawk Farm are likely to be the result of the incorporation of slag from the bloom and are consistent with the interpretation of these slags as by-products of primary smithing. Substantial inclusions of very fluid slag runs, resembling tap slag, were observed in the large smithing hearth slags examined. However, it should be noted that McDonnell (1986) found one or two secondary smithing slags with phosphorus oxide contents over 1wt% from an Anglo-Saxon smithy at Wharram Percy, Yorkshire, and in three analysed slags from a Roman smithy at Heybridge, Essex. The reasons for the compositional variation between smithing slags recovered from different sites are as yet poorly understood but these data demonstrate that elevated phosphorus (and manganese) contents in smithing slags do not necessarily indicate that the slags are by-products of primary smithing.

Although the smithing slags from Westhawk Farm were of different sizes, they were compositionally similar and this confirms that they are all by-products from smithing metal produced at the site.

However, the different-sized slags may have been produced by different stages of a smithing process or hearth conditions, by multiple smithing operations or by different smiths using different techniques. For example, medium sized slags may be typical of one period of hearth use whereas larger slags may have been formed by multiple periods of hearth use. The smaller slags, which were less porous and more iron-rich, may have been formed in a shorter period of hearth use, for example when producing smaller objects or during the final stages of billet production.

The microstructure of the smithing slags suggests that they were formed through the accumulation and reaction of slag from the bloom, hammerscale, particles of fired quartz-rich material and charcoal fuel. All of these components were observed amongst the hammerscale samples examined. The quartz-rich material may derive from the hearth lining, which was, at least in part, siliceous clay. The lining would react with fuel ash and slag, becoming gradually vitrified during hearth use, until fragments were dislodged. Alternatively the quartz-rich material may derive from siliceous fluxes used by the smith. The hammerscale, slag, quartz-rich material and fuel ash reacted to form slags within which fuel fragments and gases became trapped. However, with increasing time in the hearth at high temperatures, the porosity was reduced and the fuel fragments burnt away except in the more recently formed, upper layers.

The microstructural changes observed through the thickness of each smithing slag may have resulted from variations in the smithing activity or hearth conditions during the period of hearth use. The less porous, coarser microstructure observed in the lower half of many of the slags is probably because this slag has been heated for longer, and because the lower regions of the hearth cooled more slowly once the fire was allowed to die down. The incomplete reaction of the components in the top layer of the smithing slags is consistent with the fairly rapid cooling of the slag after this final layer was deposited and the smithing operation completed. Compositional variations may similarly result from changes in the smithing activity or hearth conditions. For example, an iron-poor region might result from the deposition of vitrified hearth lining while the hearth was heated prior to smithing commencing. Iron-rich areas could result from large quantities of bloom slag being expelled or large amounts of hammerscale being dislodged.

The top layer of each smithing slag, comprised of quartz grains and hammerscale, contained slightly lower concentrations of phosphorus and manganese oxides relative to the rest of the slag. Manganese and phosphorus are likely to have been derived largely from the slag expelled from the bloom, the majority of which might be incorporated into the lower layers of the smithing slag during the early stages of smithing. Experimental replication of the primary smithing process and examination of the by-products it produces might help to explain these observations on the composition and structure of Roman slags.

The relative contributions of slag and hammerscale (from the bloom), quartz-rich material (from the hearth lining or flux) and ashes (from the charcoal) to the formation of the smithing hearth slags can be estimated from the compositions of each of these materials. For example if the slag from the bloom contributed the majority of the phosphorus and manganese detected in the smithing hearth bottom slag then approximately 70w% of each smithing hearth bottom by weight would derive from bloom slag, 10% from the hearth lining, about 20% from hammerscale and a small amount (around 2%) from the charcoal. (In this calculation it is assumed that the bloom slag contains approximately 2% phosphorus oxide and 24wt% silica.)

Secondary Smithing

The ferrous metalwork recovered from the site was largely in the form of nails (50% by number) and hobnails (24%) but the presence of 83 miscellaneous pieces of strip, rod and sheet suggests that some secondary smithing activity, producing objects other than billets, took place (see Scott, Chapter 5 above). As the ironwork is concentrated around structures R and I the same smith was probably responsible for both primary and secondary smithing. To determine whether any additional secondary smithing activity took place on site, the slag assemblage was examined to identify any contexts containing a particularly high proportion of smithing slag, relative to smelting slag and to see if these were concentrated in one area or assigned to a particular phase.

In Table 7.14, the contexts with more than 10% of smithing slag by weight (as a proportion of the total amount of slag recovered from that context) are listed. Nearly all of the contexts listed in Table 7.14 were near structure I and six (676, 739, 675, 720 and 707) were from one waterhole. However the vast majority of these contexts also contained some tap slag or furnace bottom slag. The remaining contexts contained only a small quantity of waste and so the proportion of smithing slag in the context was heavily weighted by the presence of one piece. Therefore the vast majority of the smithing slags from Westhawk Farm are likely to be by-products of primary, rather than secondary, smithing derived from workshops I and R. The chemical analyses of a small selection of the smithing slags, discussed previously, support this conclusion.

Other workshops

It appears that there was a break between the cessation of ironworking in structure I and the beginning of activity in structure R. However, the similarities between the layouts of the workshops, and the materials and technologies utilised in them, suggest that ironworking at the site was continuous until the settlement was largely abandoned in the mid 3rd century AD. There is a possibility that an earlier structure, possibly used for ironworking, was situated on the site of structure R (see above). Alternatively there

Table 7.14   Metalworking remains: Summary of iron-working waste from contexts containing a large proportion of smithing hearth bottom slags.

Context	Phase	Area	Tap (kg)	SHB (kg)	Furnace bottom (kg)	Slag-coated clay (kg)	Total (kg)	% SHB
565	3	I	0.0	2.3	0.0	0.4	2.7	83.7
8022	3	I	4.1	6.0	0.8	1.1	12.5	48.0
8569	3	I	0.0	1.6	0.0	0.0	1.6	98.9
1193	4	I	10.5	4.6	2.5	16.4	42.4	10.7
1460	4	I	1.4	2.7	0.0	2.7	8.1	32.9
707	5	I	0.0	0.3	0.0	0.0	0.3	92.3
720	5	I	0.0	0.8	0.8	0.2	2.0	41.4
725	5-6	I	0.0	1.0	0.0	0.0	1.0	100.0
275	6	I	0.7	0.5	0.0	1.9	3.4	14.5
675	6	I	0.4	0.5	0.0	0.3	3.5	13.2
676	6	I	0.5	3.3	1.1	1.0	5.9	55.9
739	6	I	0.8	1.3	0.0	1.4	4.4	29.2
1086	2	Nr P	0.0	0.3	0.0	0.0	0.3	100.0
1332	5	R	14.8	4.1	0.6	6.3	27.5	14.8
510	4	Nr R	0.4	0.4	0.9	0.0	1.7	23.5

may have been additional workshops in the unexcavated area of the site.

Ironworking hearths, furnaces and waste give rise to very strong responses in gradiometer surveys. While such responses can result from many different types of industrial activity as well as from features that are in no way related to industrial activity - and differentiation between these is not possible on the basis of the readings alone - at Westhawk Farm data interpretation is aided by the fact that the location of two iron smelting and smithing workshops is known. Both workshops gave rise to strong geophysical readings against which data from other areas of the settlement can be compared.

Geophysical Surveys of Bradford highlighted magnetically strong readings that might indicate regions of industrial activity in survey areas G (structure R), B (structure I), C, F, E, L (the slag deposits near structure P), M, Q and P (Fig. 7.16). The strong readings in areas P and E are not necessarily the result of industrial activity as the concentration of archaeological features suggests that these may be intensively occupied areas. The strong responses in areas F and Q appear to be slightly more scattered and/or less strong than those observed in the known workshop areas. The readings from Area M, and to a lesser extent Area C, appear to be the most similar to those from the ironworking workshops R and I. Areas M and C, like structures R and I, are also in the southwest half of settlement, with Area M on the same side of the road as structure R and Area C on the north-west side of the road near structure I. In Area C there appears to be an enclosure with quite strong, although slightly scattered, readings on both sides of the road. In Area M there is a large, dense cluster of very strong readings, the strongest of these forming a crescent shape, and a number of broad pit-type features were also identified. A high-resolution survey of these regions, particularly Area M, could be used to investigate the existence of additional workshops in the unexcavated area and to resolve features if a workshop is located.

Geophysics anomalies - archaeological

Geophysics anomalies - ferrous

0   200 m

1:5000

Figure 7.16   Geophysical survey areas where strong readings were detected, from the report by Geophysical Surveys of Bradford.

DISCUSSION

Scale of ironworking activity

Estimating the scale of the ironworking activity at Westhawk Farm involves many approximations as only a fraction of the ironworking waste was recovered and less than half of the site was excavated. The amount of slag in the excavated Areas B and C was estimated by extrapolating the amount of slag recovered from the volume of the feature sampled to approximate the amount in the feature as a whole. For example, since half of each pit was excavated, the ironworking waste recovered constitutes half of that likely to be present in the entire feature, and therefore the recorded figure was doubled to give an approximate value for the total ironworking debris in the pit. Similarly 10% of each linear feature was excavated, therefore the quantity of ironworking waste recovered from each linear feature was multiplied by 10 to give an estimate of the total present in the feature as a whole. However, this assumes an even concentration of waste along the length of the feature, which is unlikely. This process was completed for all of the contexts listed in Table 7.2, which gave an estimated total of ironworking debris in these features of 6300 kg, whereas 960 kg was actually recovered from the excavated sections. Across Areas B and C approximately 1650 kg (1.65 tonnes) of ironworking waste were recovered. Assuming a similar ratio of recovered waste to the total present for the whole assemblage, the amount of waste across Areas B and C can be estimated at (6300 / 960) by 1650 kg = 10830 kg.

Although the geophysical survey covered both the excavated and unexcavated areas of the site, it is not possible to differentiate between areas of high positive data caused by metalworking processes and those resulting from other types of activity or features, as mentioned previously. Therefore the amount of slag in Area A was estimated by assuming a similar density of debris across Area A (10 ha) as across Areas B and C (in total approximately 6 ha). Thus the quantity of ironworking waste in area A is assumed to be approximately (10 / 6) by 10830 kg = 18050 kg and the total quantity of slag across the whole site (areas A, B and C) is estimated at 18050 + 10830 kg = 28880 kg (about 29 tonnes).

This figure is likely to be an underestimate of the amount of ironworking waste produced over the lifetime of the site, since some of the slag has almost certainly been moved and reused. The road through the settlement (Margary's route 130) was metalled with slag and flint nodules within the site, although this only survived in small areas, and was also metalled with slag further west (Cleere and Crossley 1985). Some of this slag may have come from the Westhawk site since to date few other smelting sites of Roman date have been identified in the area. Hodgkinson (1999) estimates that 540 m³ (roughly equivalent to 540 tonnes of slag) may have been used to metal each kilometre of a Roman road. If it were known that slag from Westhawk had been used to metal just one kilometre of road, the estimate of the site's slag

output and hence iron production would increase by more than 30 times. Therefore in this discussion the estimate of the scale of the iron production at Westhawk is referred to as a minimum, since it is based on the quantity of slag recovered from the site and it is likely that some was removed in the past.

The Westhawk billet weighs approximately 4.5 kg. From experimental work Crew (1991) has estimated that about 50% of the bloom remains by weight after primary smithing, when the iron bloom is refined into a billet or bar. Assuming that the Westhawk billet was produced from one bloom, then the bloom in its unrefined state would have weighed about 9 kg. This estimate was compared to the weights of other blooms and billets of Roman date, although caution is required since the distinction between refined billets, or lumps of iron, and unrefined blooms is inconsistent in the literature. The Roman bloom recovered from Elms Farm, Heybridge weighed 12.2 kg (Dungworth 2001), another from Lower Slaughter, Gloucestershire weighed about 11 kg (O'Neil and Brown 1966) and one from Forewood Crowhurst, Sussex weighed 12.4 kg. A billet from Cranbrook, Kent weighed 7.1 kg and another from Strageath, Tayside weighed 5.7 kg (Tylecote 1990). Estimates of the size of refined blooms have also been obtained by examining large iron beams from Catterick and Corbridge, determining the number of refined iron masses that they contain, and calculating that each weighs approximately 7.5 kg (Bell 1912; Wright 1972; Starley 1997). Hooked billets of the period range in weight from 1.1 kg to 2.9 kg (Salter 1997, 96). These data raise the possibility that the unrefined blooms produced at Westhawk Farm may have been larger than 9 kg on average and that the production of the large (4.5 kg) billet may not have required the use of a complete bloom. However, for the purposes of these calculations, it has been assumed that a 9 kg unrefined bloom was produced in each smelt at the site.

Investigation has shown that the ore utilised by smelters at Westhawk Farm had a variable iron content. However, the three tap slag samples analysed had similar compositions suggesting that the ore batch may have varied very little between smelts. For the purposes of these calculations, a value of 70% of iron oxide (Fe_2O_3) by weight in the roasted ore has been used, which is an appropriate value if a mixture of ferruginous sandstone and more iron-rich concretionary ironstone were smelted together in each batch. The results of experimental smelting in bloomery furnaces have indicated that approximately 40% of the iron (as Fe) available in the ore will form the bloom whereas the rest is lost as slag (Crew 1991, 29). The quantity of ore required in each smelt, to produce a 9 kg bloom, can be approximated as follows (atomic weight iron Fe = 55.85; molecular weight FeO = 71.9; molecular weight Fe_2O_3 = 159.7):

The amount of iron (Fe) in the ore = 9000 / 0.4 = 22500 g Fe

Moles of iron (Fe) in the ore = 22500 / 55.85 = 402.9

In the roasted ore, the iron is in the form of Fe_2O_3, therefore the amount of roasted ore per smelt = 402.9 by 159.7 = 64.3 kg

Approximately 60% of the iron (Fe) available in the ore will form the waste slag = 0.6 by 22500 = 13500 g

Moles of iron in slag = 13500 / 55.85 = 241.7

Amount of iron oxide (FeO) in slag = 241.7 by 71.9 = 17378 g

The slag produced contains approximately 60wt% of iron oxide (FeO). Therefore the approximate quantity of slag produced per smelt = 17378 / 0.60 = 29 kg

From experimental work it has been estimated that approximately 100 kg of charcoal are required per 100 kg of ore (Crew 1991, 27). Therefore 64 kg charcoal are likely to have been required for each smelt and approximately 416 kg of wood might be required to produce this amount (Kelley 1986). Additional charcoal would be used for smithing the bloom, which has not been taken into account here:

Ore (64 kg) + Charcoal (64 kg) → Iron bloom (9 kg) + Smelting slag (29 kg)

The total estimated quantity of ironworking waste on the site is 29 tonnes. About 60% of the waste from Westhawk Farm by weight is tap slag, furnace bottom slag and undiagnostic slag (likely to derive from smelting). Therefore, assuming that 29 kg of slag were generated per smelt, the number of smelts at the site can be approximated at a minimum (as some slag may have been removed from the site) of 29000 by 0.6 / 29 = 600. The amount of refined iron produced can be estimated at a minimum of 600 by 4.5 = 2.7 tonnes (equivalent to 600 billets of 4.5 kg each). A minimum of approximately 38.4 tonnes of ore would have been consumed with a minimum of 250 tonnes of wood (38.4 tonnes of charcoal).

The duration of occupation of structures I and R has been estimated at 100 years in total, although it is possible that smelting activity also took place elsewhere on the site, particularly during the period between the ironworking ceasing in structure I and starting in structure R. However, if the smelting activity were spread evenly over the estimated period of occupation of structures I and R, it would equate to a minimum of six smelts a year. As some of the waste slag is likely to be unaccounted for (for example, if slag was removed for road metalling) six smelts a year is an underestimate.

Although the ironworking waste was fairly equally divided between Structures R and I, the geophysical survey suggests that there may be large deposits of ironworking waste associated with structure R that were not excavated. However survival of features in and around structure I was poorer than at structure R. Therefore it is difficult to draw any meaningful conclusions about the relative intensity of ironworking activity between the two structures. However, assuming that smelting activity was comparable in structures R and I, then a minimum of 300 smelts

would have been completed in structure R during its occupation. From observations on furnace re-use from experimental smelting (Crew 1991, 22) it is likely that at least 40 smelts could be completed before furnace reconstruction was necessary. As the basal remains of seven furnace structures were identified in structure R, this would equate to at least 280 smelts over the period of occupation. In addition, since only very shallow remains of these furnaces survived, it is probable that additional furnaces were constructed and used but the evidence of these has not survived. If the scale of ironworking activity in Structures R and I was similar, then a similar number of furnaces would have operated in Structure I, although only two survive in this workshop.

Impact of ironworking activity on the settlement

The assemblage of ironwork at Westhawk has been described as 'remarkable only because of the limited number and range of objects found' (Scott, Chapter 5 above). As it has been estimated that in excess of 27 kg of refined iron was produced at the site each year, the vast majority was probably traded, perhaps in the form of billets like the one recovered from the site. The situation of the site, at the intersection of two roads leading to ports and major towns, would facilitate transport of the iron produced. Cleere has attempted to calculate the consumption of the military and civilian populations of Roman Britain and concluded that a considerable proportion was probably traded outside Britain. Gaul and the army of the Rhine have been suggested as possible markets. The abandonment of the Westhawk settlement, and many others in the Weald, coincides with the upheaval in Gaul in the second half of the 3rd century AD and the disappearance of the Roman fleet in Britain, the *Classis Britannica*, from the record (Cleere and Crossley 1985; Salway, 1981 639).

Iron was a valuable commodity and the ironworking at Westhawk Farm is likely to have contributed to the prosperity of the settlement and that of the area as a whole (Cleere and Crossley 1985, 79-84). Previous research has suggested that the *Classis Britannica* supported the iron industry in the south of Britain and this is further evidence of the strategic importance of the Wealden iron industry (Cleere and Crossley 1985; Salway 1981, 637). However, although large quantities of iron were produced in the Weald, the ironworking activity would not necessarily have involved a large number of people or have occupied all of their time.

Examination of the slag heaps at Beauport Park, Holbeanwood and Bardown in the Weald has suggested that ore collection, timber felling, charcoal production, smelting, forging and furnace reconstruction, may have been performed consecutively on an annual cycle (Cleere and Crossley 1985, 50-51). Ethnographic studies of ironworking have also observed seasonality in the operations associated with iron smelting (Schmidt 1996, 64). This may be particularly true of sites with a smaller smelting operation and greater dependence on other activities, for example agriculture, where ironworkers have been observed to work the fields during part of the year, smelt in the dry season and smith intermittently (Childs and Killick 1993, 329). It has been estimated from ethnographic studies and smelting experiments that three individuals can comfortably operate a furnace and smithing hearth. If the gathering of raw materials, smelting and smithing took place seasonally, spanning a long period, and if only one or two furnaces were operated at a time, then a small number of individuals could have undertaken the entire process.

Ironworking in the Weald

Westhawk Farm is at the north-east edge of the Weald and examination of the chronological patterns of iron production in the area (Cleere and Crossley 1985) has suggested that there was a shift towards more northern sites, in the High Weald, around AD 120-140. Where sites were already established in the High Weald it appears that satellite sites developed in their vicinity. However, there appears to have been a cessation of smelting activity across the Weald around the mid 3rd century AD, save at some of the larger sites. Therefore the estimated duration of smelting activity at Westhawk is entirely consistent with evidence from other sites in the region.

Some of the Wealden Roman sites are estimated to have produced iron on a vast scale (Hodgkinson 1999). For example, there is estimated to have been 30,000 tonnes of ironworking waste of Roman date at Beauport Park (~AD 120-250). The ironworking at Westhawk Farm, on the basis of the quantity of slag remaining, was on a much smaller scale. However, it is probable that some slag was removed from the site and that the scale of iron production has therefore been underestimated.

CONCLUSIONS

Approximately 1.65 tonnes of ironworking waste was recovered during the excavation. Two structures, R and I, where ironworking took place, were located within the excavated area. The waste, more than half of which was diagnostically iron-smelting waste, was concentrated around these two structures. A small proportion of smithing slag was identified and a deposit of hammerscale was found in a workshop context indicating that some primary smithing also took place at the site. No conclusive evidence of secondary smithing activity was found, although the recovery of a number of fragments of bar and sheet from around the workshops suggests that some secondary smithing may have taken place there. Ironworking activity in structure I (~AD 110-160) preceded that in structure R (~AD 200-250). There were strong similarities between the organisation of the workshops and the technologies and materials used in each, suggesting that ironworking continued uninterrupted from the early 2nd to the mid 3rd centuries. If this is so, at least one additional workshop must be located in the

preserved region of the settlement. The duration of smelting activity is consistent with the overall pattern observed for the Weald during this period, with activity ceasing in the mid 3rd century.

Smelting and smithing both took place in the same ironworking enclosures at Westhawk Farm, although the areas for each activity were distinct. Groups of bloomery-tapping furnaces were arranged at the edge of the workshop structure in each enclosure. They were round in plan, constructed from quartz-rich clay (in excess of 80% silica by weight), with an internal diameter of about 0.26 m and a wall thickness of about 0.17 m. The tapping apertures of the furnaces probably faced away from the workshops and downhill, although no evidence of tapping apertures or tapping pits survived. The shape of some of the tap slag flows indicates that the tapping aperture was probably up to 90 mm wide and up to 60 mm deep. The furnaces are likely to have been operated one at a time or in pairs. No surviving examples of blowing-holes (or tuyères) were found, although fragments of slag-coated clay blocks were recovered, which may have been parts of blowing-hole plates or repairs. The workshops may have been open along one or more sides, but the roofs are likely to have extended over the furnaces to provide overhead cover for bellows operators, the people charging the furnaces and the furnaces themselves.

Primary smithing took place in another area of each workshop. A ground level, sub-rectangular hearth, 0.6 m in diameter, appears to have been used in workshop R, although the entire hearth construction may have been larger than the fired area that survives. The hearth was probably constructed from blocks of siliceous clay, and possibly another material such as sandstone or tile. A large, consolidated hammerscale deposit covered the floor in workshop R. The distribution of the hammerscale indicates that the hearth and anvil are likely to have been situated near to each other and to a large, sunken ceramic vessel; examples of the latter were found in both workshops. No trace of the anvil remains.

The ore used was probably concretionary ironstone containing varying amounts of quartz, ranging from very iron-rich stone to more silica-rich ferruginous sandstone. The majority of the ore was obtained locally from the Lenham Beds or the 'Sand in Clay-with-flints', less than 10 miles from Ashford. The ore was roasted before smelting, possibly in the shallow, rounded features near the furnaces at the perimeters of the workshops. Charcoal, predominantly oak, was used as a fuel. The waste produced was largely tap slag with some furnace slag, including fuel-rich lumps and large, bowl-shaped furnace bottom slags. The ore contained variable, but significant quantities of phosphorus, which led to the production of smelting slag with a characteristically high phosphorus content. The products of smelting were probably blooms of iron containing varying amounts of phosphorus, from ferritic (low-phosphorus) to phosphoric iron (high-phosphorus). The potentially greater hardness of the latter meant that it was selectively utilised for certain objects, such as tools, in this period, in much the same way as steel was used.

The blooms of iron produced were probably smithed into large billets for trade, since a billet of 4.5 kg was found at the site. Very few iron objects were recovered, other than nails. The by-products of the smithing operation were hammerscale and smithing hearth bottom slags. Quartz-rich material, likely to be vitrified, siliceous hearth lining, adhered to many of the hammerscale flakes and spheres, although another possibility is that this quartz-rich material is a siliceous flux that was used by the smith. Fuel fragments and larger droplets of fayalitic slag were also observed amongst the hammerscale. The smithing hearth bottom slags probably formed from the reaction of these components: hammerscale, quartz-rich material, fuel ash and slag. They had slightly higher phosphorus and manganese contents than most smithing slags from other sites for which data was available. This is consistent with the conclusion that the Westhawk smithing slags were by-products of primary smithing and therefore contained a proportion of slag from the bloom, containing elevated levels of phosphorus and manganese. The size of the smithing hearth bottom slags varied greatly, even when comparing material from one workshop, from 0.2 kg up to 4 kg. The different sizes and shapes may have resulted from different stages and types of smithing operation and possibly multiple periods of hearth use.

The total quantity of ironworking waste on the site was estimated at 29 tonnes. The amount of refined iron produced over the lifetime of the site was estimated as a minimum of 2.7 tonnes (equivalent to 600 billets of 4.5 kg each). A minimum of approximately 38 tonnes of ore would have been consumed with a minimum of 250 tonnes of wood (38 tonnes of charcoal). These figures are likely to be underestimates as some slag was probably removed from the site in the past for reuse, for example for road metalling, and the efficiency of the smelting and smithing processes, based on the results of experimental archaeology, may have been underestimated.

Unlike other types of metal ore, which are found only in certain regions, sources of iron ore can be found across the country. However, the intensity of iron production in the Weald, with a large number of smelting sites, some of them operating on a vast scale, is unparalleled elsewhere in Britain during this period. Cleere concludes that the scale of the Wealden iron production in this period exceeded the iron consumption of the military and civilian markets in Britain and suggests that a considerable proportion of the iron produced was traded outside Britain, for example to Gaul and the army of the Rhine (Cleere and Crossley 1985). Iron was traded widely both within the province of Britannia and in adjacent provinces of the Roman Empire. Therefore the proximity of the Wealden smelting sites to ports and the proposed involvement of the *Classis Britannica*, in facilitating transport of the iron produced, may have been very important to the development of the Wealden iron industry.

FUTURE WORK

Despite the Weald being a major producer of iron in this country in the Roman period, virtually no analyses of bloomery smelting slag from the region could be found in the literature. Siderite, a carbonate of iron, was not smelted at Westhawk Farm, but it is likely to have been smelted at sites across much of the region and some compositional data on this ore were available. These data indicated that the roasted ore generally contains significant levels of lime, phosphorus oxide and some magnesia and may therefore have resulted in slag by-products with characteristic compositions also rich in lime, phosphorus oxide and magnesia. To date, the author has analysed bloomery slag samples, thought to be Roman, from only two additional locations in the Weald; a smelting site at Far Blacklands (TQ45153810) and a road at Holtye (TQ46253884), both near East Grinstead, Sussex. The slag from the former site contained about 6% lime by weight, 2.5% magnesia and 0.9% phosphorus oxide, suggesting that siderite was smelted at Far Blacklands. The slag samples from the road at Holtye contained about 1% magnesia, 1.2% lime and 1.1% phosphorus oxide, which suggests that an alternative ore to siderite may have been smelted to produce this slag. A programme of analyses of bloomery slag from smelting sites across the Weald would enable regional variations in slag compositions to be established and potentially liked to the local geology and ore sources.

TABLES OF RESULTS OF ANALYSES

Table 7.15   Composition of furnace linings, measured by EDS, normalised (see also Fig. 7.3 above).

Context	Na$_2$O	MgO	Al$_2$O$_3$	SiO$_2$	P$_2$O$_5$	SO$_3$	K$_2$O	CaO	TiO$_2$	MnO	FeO
1332	0.00	0.28	8.54	83.07	0.94	0.11	1.35	0.53	0.89	0.04	4.03
	0.16	0.65	11.35	80.65	0.77	0.06	1.52	0.44	0.77	0.03	3.31
	0.00	0.33	7.14	86.13	0.64	0.12	1.16	0.52	0.74	0.01	2.95
1225	0.00	0.55	10.74	82.39	0.25	0.22	1.09	0.27	0.95	0.07	3.43
	0.00	0.48	9.89	83.14	0.13	0.14	1.12	0.34	0.93	0.03	3.51
	0.00	0.58	9.36	83.49	0.22	0.30	1.16	0.34	0.92	0.03	3.36

Table 7.16   Composition of ore samples, measured by XRF, normalised (see also Fig. 7.6 above).

Context	Al$_2$O$_3$	SiO$_2$	P$_2$O$_5$	SO$_3$	K$_2$O	CaO	TiO$_2$	MnO	FeO
1332	7.98	32.83	0.41	0.36	0.28	0.16	0.28	0.55	57.16
	3.69	62.37	0.28	0.24	0.06	0.09	0.10	0.22	32.94
	18.24	6.10	3.43	0.36	0.20	0.45	0.27	1.77	69.18
	7.76	43.06	0.44	0.24	0.49	0.13	1.37	0.24	46.25
	8.49	31.62	1.46	0.24	0.26	0.24	0.32	.45	56.92
	6.78	21.38	0.63	0.60	0.10	0.17	0.28	0.64	69.40
	2.41	29.49	0.49	0.00	0.00	0.12	0.00	0.27	67.22
	2.26	28.54	0.51	0.00	0.00	0.10	0.00	0.32	68.27
	2.03	47.37	0.33	0.00	0.00	0.07	0.00	0.40	49.79
841	3.47	7.81	1.67	0.00	0.00	0.20	0.00	0.29	86.56
17	5.35	24.66	0.22	0.00	0.11	0.22	0.00	0.33	69.13
502	2.50	45.35	1.00	0.00	0.00	0.26	0.00	2.68	48.20
1460	13.03	22.69	0.50	0.00	0.00	0.59	0.00	3.15	60.04
198	2.15	32.46	0.28	0.00	0.00	0.05	0.00	0.27	64.78
802	2.44	5.17	0.43	0.00	0.00	0.13	0.00	0.49	91.34
1548	1.58	2.19	0.91	0.33	0.01	0.20	0.00	0.57	94.21
	6.63	14.23	0.26	0.30	0.23	0.15	0.00	0.46	77.73
	2.04	3.72	0.75	0.00	0.00	0.24	0.19	0.83	92.24
	1.94	3.32	0.94	0.00	0.00	0.17	0.20	0.49	92.94
1356	1.33	2.85	0.17	0.44	0.03	0.10	0.00	0.26	94.82
	0.47	0.86	0.80	0.30	0.00	0.21	0.00	0.74	96.61
1265	4.35	34.01	0.97	0.00	0.11	0.30	0.29	0.53	59.44

Table 7.17   Composition of tap slags, measured by EDS, normalised (see also Fig. 7.7 above).

Context	Na$_2$O	MgO	Al$_2$O$_3$	SiO$_2$	P$_2$O$_5$	SO$_3$	K$_2$O	CaO	TiO$_2$	MnO	FeO
1332	0.90	0.47	5.95	25.65	1.72	0.00	0.31	2.83	0.08	0.58	61.22
	0.56	0.39	6.15	25.31	2.18	0.19	0.48	2.53	0.38	0.54	61.20
	0.46	0.47	6.80	26.15	1.87	0.15	0.33	2.37	0.38	0.73	60.29
	0.19	0.22	7.23	27.23	2.07	0.00	1.37	2.78	0.39	0.57	57.66
	0.72	0.45	6.74	27.97	1.84	0.12	1.14	2.59	0.42	0.50	56.94
319	0.00	0.42	5.62	23.92	1.34	0.07	0.68	1.49	0.34	0.52	65.60
	0.85	0.02	13.76	28.51	6.05	0.55	6.05	8.94	0.41	0.16	34.69
	0.13	0.48	7.41	24.73	1.69	0.14	1.20	2.25	0.23	0.43	61.31
	0.00	0.49	7.21	24.61	1.83	0.06	1.35	2.36	0.22	0.52	61.35
	0.33	0.43	7.12	24.98	1.77	0.17	0.18	2.27	0.28	0.45	62.02
	0.00	0.55	6.36	25.33	1.51	0.08	0.97	1.93	0.31	0.47	62.48
480	0.24	0.33	5.35	24.64	2.73	0.12	0.15	2.70	0.30	0.31	63.12
	0.15	0.33	5.98	23.53	3.10	0.29	0.38	2.79	0.19	0.27	63.00
	0.00	0.41	5.64	22.25	1.59	0.34	0.41	1.51	0.08	0.35	67.43
	0.09	0.52	5.53	19.93	1.04	0.02	0.08	0.97	0.20	0.36	71.26
	0.00	0.35	9.32	19.88	1.90	0.15	0.83	1.97	0.15	0.34	65.11
	0.00	0.39	5.75	20.62	1.39	0.10	0.49	1.45	0.12	0.38	69.31

Table 7.18   Composition of furnace bottom slags, measured by EDS, normalised (see also Fig. 7.9 above).

Context	Na$_2$O	MgO	Al$_2$O$_3$	SiO$_2$	P$_2$O$_5$	SO$_3$	K$_2$O	CaO	TiO$_2$	MnO	FeO
1225	0.08	0.25	4.03	21.79	0.61	0.06	0.73	1.54	0.24	0.23	70.42
	0.34	0.15	5.21	23.59	1.07	0.00	1.09	1.93	0.29	0.24	65.74
	0.05	0.13	4.16	23.02	0.76	0.00	0.80	1.57	0.19	0.16	68.91
	0.25	0.00	3.70	22.67	0.82	0.14	0.82	1.72	0.23	0.14	69.25
	0.00	0.26	4.95	27.22	0.74	0.05	0.66	1.55	0.17	0.20	63.85
1510	0.30	0.28	5.34	27.13	0.91	0.21	0.93	2.04	0.29	0.10	62.14
	0.11	0.40	4.17	20.19	1.05	0.15	0.81	1.99	0.28	0.12	70.38
	0.23	0.25	4.71	18.23	1.17	0.34	0.78	2.15	0.29	0.11	71.66
	0.05	0.40	3.73	19.61	0.91	0.18	0.32	1.02	0.05	0.03	73.55
	0.00	0.47	2.84	17.14	0.90	0.21	0.44	1.22	0.06	0.01	76.33
	0.06	0.58	2.74	18.95	0.68	0.00	0.27	1.15	0.10	0.04	75.12
	0.17	0.53	3.38	20.93	0.73	0.29	0.46	1.41	0.13	0.14	71.46

Table 7.19   Composition of slags within the bloom fragment from context 1333, measured by EDS, normalised (see also Fig. 7.10 above).

Na$_2$O	MgO	Al$_2$O$_3$	SiO$_2$	P$_2$O$_5$	SO$_3$	K$_2$O	CaO	TiO$_2$	MnO	FeO
0.24	0.42	2.11	11.71	3.53	0.17	0.86	1.29	0.05	0.24	79.38
0.20	0.49	1.82	7.01	7.25	0.45	0.52	1.20	0.09	0.25	80.72
0.00	0.30	1.40	6.61	5.02	0.27	0.12	0.86	0.13	0.28	85.02
0.00	0.79	1.79	20.99	10.44	0.25	1.19	1.60	0.04	0.49	62.41
0.00	0.51	2.72	15.01	8.62	0.45	0.85	1.88	0.12	0.42	69.40
0.11	0.54	2.68	15.72	9.08	0.66	1.09	1.90	0.11	0.42	67.68

Table 7.20   Compositions of slag inclusions sampled from billet (SF905, context 7009), measured by EDS and normalised (see also Fig. 7.12 above).

Area (μm^2)	Type	MgO	Al$_2$O$_3$	SiO$_2$	P$_2$O$_5$	SO$_3$	K$_2$O	CaO	TiO$_2$	MnO	FeO
22494	Fayalite	0.32	1.07	4.07	0.16	0.06	0.12	0.46	0.08	0.25	93.41
14276	and glass	0.31	1.50	6.69	0.31	0.06	0.25	0.74	0.11	0.30	89.74
28500		0.42	2.56	14.60	0.67	0.20	0.56	1.53	0.14	0.31	79.00
1666	Wustite,	0.82	4.59	25.73	1.39	0.63	1.22	3.53	0.34	0.99	60.77
1980	fayalite	0.77	4.83	26.61	1.32	0.67	1.35	3.69	0.20	1.00	59.55
7548	and glass	0.66	3.86	19.96	0.50	0.21	1.01	2.78	0.33	0.81	69.88
1360		0.69	4.31	21.46	1.43	0.81	0.75	2.72	0.29	0.80	66.73
1218		0.73	4.86	26.28	1.06	0.47	1.25	3.68	0.25	0.97	60.46
68400	Glass only	0.84	5.30	30.13	0.70	0.32	1.44	4.12	0.46	1.23	55.46
31740		0.89	5.34	30.50	0.87	0.48	1.49	4.25	0.47	1.26	54.45
15755		0.92	5.26	31.14	0.84	0.45	1.50	4.30	0.43	1.28	53.88

Table 7.21   Composition of various components of the hammerscale deposit from structure R, measured by EDS, normalised.

Area	MgO	Al$_2$O$_3$	SiO$_2$	P$_2$O$_5$	SO$_3$	K$_2$O	CaO	TiO$_2$	MnO	FeO
Flake plus adhered quartz-rich region	0.3	4.7	24.6	2.0	0.3	0.4	1.5	0.1	0.0	66.0
Flake (bulk)	0.1	0.6	1.2	0.1	0.0	0.0	0.1	0.1	0.0	97.8
Flake matrix (point analysis)	0.3	2.5	6.0	2.6	0.3	0.2	0.5	0.0	0.0	87.6
Sphere (bulk)	0.3	2.0	11.4	2.7	0.2	0.4	1.0	0.1	0.1	81.8
Adhered quartz-rich region (bulk)	0.3	3.9	32.1	2.4	0.6	0.3	1.3	0.3	0.2	58.6
	0.2	2.8	41.8	3.3	0.3	0.3	1.5	0.2	0.2	49.3

Table 7.22 Composition of various areas of the small smithing hearth slag from context 1257, measured by EDS, normalised (see also Fig. 7.13 above).

Mini SHB	Na$_2$O	MgO	Al$_2$O$_3$	SiO$_2$	P$_2$O$_5$	SO$_3$	K$_2$O	CaO	TiO$_2$	MnO	FeO
Top layer (bulk)	0.22	0.22	3.21	25.39	1.02	0.45	0.31	0.76	0.10	0.00	67.89
Top layer matrix (spot analysis)	0.39	0.35	4.14	11.66	0.24	0.44	0.26	0.47	0.09	0.29	79.86
3rd layer – high wustite (bulk)	0.17	1.03	2.56	16.64	0.95	0.00	0.77	2.71	0.27	0.36	74.13
4th layer (bulk)	0.37	1.29	4.23	25.53	1.56	0.15	2.29	5.43	0.24	0.32	58.41
	0.36	1.14	4.33	25.62	1.14	0.00	2.17	5.16	0.30	0.27	59.40

Table 7.23 Composition of different regions of the thicker end of the large smithing hearth bottom slag from context 1332, measured by EDS, normalised (see also Fig. 7.13 above).

1332 Large SHB	Na$_2$O	MgO	Al$_2$O$_3$	SiO$_2$	P$_2$O$_5$	SO$_3$	K$_2$O	CaO	TiO$_2$	FeO
Top layer	0.00	0.51	7.31	28.70	1.19	0.33	0.00	2.72	0.24	59.01
Porous 2nd layer	0.23	0.49	7.02	24.54	1.46	0.29	1.32	4.41	0.36	59.78
Different areas above	0.00	0.40	6.11	23.84	1.09	0.67	1.07	2.57	0.27	63.72
boundary	0.29	0.61	7.02	28.94	1.72	0.13	1.65	6.51	0.35	52.34
	0.00	0.00	15.28	34.65	3.34	0.13	12.03	4.17	0.46	29.43
Below boundary	0.34	0.41	7.30	30.08	1.64	0.16	1.84	4.78	0.37	53.09
Base	0.52	0.85	3.91	29.74	0.92	0.16	1.14	2.84	0.33	59.56

Table 7.24 Composition of different regions of the thinner end of the large smithing hearth bottom slag from context 1332, measured by EDS, normalised (see also Fig. 7.13 above).

1332 Large SHB	Na$_2$O	MgO	Al$_2$O$_3$	SiO$_2$	P$_2$O$_5$	SO$_3$	K$_2$O	CaO	TiO$_2$	MnO	FeO
Top layer	0.22	0.48	5.12	32.66	0.93	0.12	0.72	0.66	0.29	0.11	58.62
Upper half	0.23	0.51	7.68	26.48	1.41	0.06	1.86	6.08	0.28	0.20	55.10
Lower half	0.04	0.49	6.88	28.35	1.33	0.52	0.69	2.99	0.38	0.06	58.24
Base	0.15	0.38	4.59	23.39	0.87	0.37	0.02	1.22	0.34	0.27	68.24

Table 7.25 Composition of different regions of medium-sized smithing hearth bottom slag from context 1225, analysed by EDS, normalised (see also Fig. 7.13 above).

1225 SHB	Na$_2$O	MgO	Al$_2$O$_3$	SiO$_2$	P$_2$O$_5$	SO$_3$	K$_2$O	CaO	TiO$_2$	MnO	FeO
Top quartz-rich layer	0.00	0.43	15.94	50.56	1.44	1.64	0.26	2.46	1.25	0.04	25.98
2nd layer	0.22	0.48	6.81	24.52	2.20	0.16	0.88	2.40	0.16	0.33	61.83
2nd layer	0.01	0.50	7.29	23.63	2.17	0.28	0.50	2.06	0.13	0.30	63.13
2nd layer	0.00	0.33	9.76	26.61	2.59	0.20	0.00	1.27	0.25	0.29	58.69
Quartz-rich area	0.00	0.27	7.42	77.60	0.91	0.32	1.17	0.47	0.47	0.02	11.34
3rd layer	0.00	0.48	4.18	17.85	1.52	0.07	0.28	1.37	0.13	0.40	73.73
Final layer	0.01	0.50	4.97	18.85	1.91	0.12	0.60	1.97	0.21	0.29	70.58

Table 7.26 Composition of different regions of medium-sized smithing hearth bottom slag from context 1332, analysed by EDS, normalised (see also Fig. 7.13 above).

1332 SHB	Na$_2$O	MgO	Al$_2$O$_3$	SiO$_2$	P$_2$O$_5$	SO$_3$	K$_2$O	CaO	TiO$_2$	MnO	FeO
Quartz-rich top layer	0.00	0.36	3.93	22.08	0.78	0.29	0.46	0.81	0.22	0.10	70.97
2nd layer fayalitic region	0.00	0.78	5.97	24.20	1.13	0.09	0.81	2.90	0.33	0.29	63.50
2nd layer porous region	0.00	0.19	0.61	2.95	0.24	0.27	0.05	0.56	0.05	0.02	95.05
3rd layer quartz-rich clay	0.01	0.53	7.02	52.14	0.13	0.61	0.94	0.45	2.39	0.00	35.78
3rd layer fayalitic region	0.23	0.74	6.04	24.47	1.11	0.09	1.52	3.78	0.32	0.21	61.47
4th layer porous	0.00	0.11	1.73	6.48	0.24	0.43	0.06	0.82	0.04	0.09	90.00
Base bulk fayalitic	0.00	0.47	6.86	24.47	1.42	0.17	1.18	3.57	0.35	0.22	61.31

Chapter 8:   Grave Catalogue and Human Remains

GRAVE CATALOGUE

The grave catalogue collates the evidence for graves from all parts of the site. The evidence from the late Iron Age cremation group 9200 is presented first, followed by that from the Area C cemetery and then the more scattered burials from various parts of Area B. In both these cases cremation graves are listed first, followed by inhumation graves.

Late Iron Age Grave group 9200 (Fig. 8.1)

Cut 9201, ?rectangular and approximately 0.55 m x 0.50 m x 0.30 m, with steep sides and a flat base. Containing wooden box 9203 (itself containing cremated remains and unburnt animal bone, pottery and copper alloy vessels) and bucket 9207, packed around by yellow silt-clay 9208, partly overlain by light grey clay silt 9205, up to 0.3 m deep. See Chapter 3 for detailed description.

Copper alloy catalogue
by H E M Cool

This catalogue describes the principal recognisable pieces. No attempt has been made to catalogue the small unrecognisable fragments. To make the AML numbers more easily comprehensible where several have to be quoted as part of the catalogue entry for a single item, the convention will be used where '~' replaces number 2001914; thus '~23.7' will be used instead of '200191423.7'. The finds from the grave are discussed in Chapter 3 above.

1   **Jug**. Cast copper alloy. Curved handle with sloping upper surfaces forming slight ridge centrally accentuated by beaded decoration, groove parallel to each edge. Upper end expands to form curved upper attachment to (missing) jug rim with wide angular rebate below and female bust above; one arm of this attachment broken. Many collapsed fragments of back of neck found corroded to the handle (not shown in Fig. 8.1). Profile not reconstructable, but upper thickened edge of this mass clearly fits into rebate on the upper attachment. Majority of face and upper part of head of bust destroyed by corrosion with only one eye and part of finely grooved eyebrow remaining. Hair shown as a roll down either side of face, gathered at nape of neck in loose chignon, at back of head hair shown parted centrally. Three concentric channels below neck indicate necklaces on breast. Lower handle attachment shown as male mask with luxuriant curling beard and moustache with hair parted centrally and swept

down either side of forehead, eyebrows shown as finely grooved bands. Cast ridges forming the hair on both figures often accentuated by fine diagonal grooving. Traces of wood internally on mass. Total length of handle 145 mm, diameter of back of neck of jug *c* 80 mm, handle section 18 x 7 mm, thickness of wall 1.5 mm. (200191409).

2   *Patera* **handle**. Copper alloy; cast. Hollow cylindrical spout or handle with part of 'wall' (~ 11) - this the piece identified on site as the possible strainer bowl spout. Two loose fragments (~23.15) collected separately on site joined ~11 to complete the circuit of the base of the cylinder. A fragment of unknown provenance collected separately on site (~23.9) joined the edge of the 'wall'. Wall is asymmetrically curved with the junction with cylinder being *c* 120° at the 'top' and more gently curved *c* 150-160° at bottom. The lower edge of the more gentle slope has a straight finished edge with an angular moulding immediately above. ~23.9 also has a straight finished edge which would have met the other edge at an angle of approximately 60°. The base of the cylinder had two horizontal mouldings, traces of the ends of the vertical fluting running along the length of the cylinder. Additional fluted fragments were planned separately *in situ* (~23.7, ~ 23.9, ~23.14) or were excavated from soil Block C2. This complex of fragments was part of the area excavated as Block C2. ~12 was found during the excavation of that block. It consisted of many small fragments, many of which had clearly originally joined and which had been fragmented *in situ*. The fragments are consistent with being one side of the fluted cylinder. Fragments of the terminal of the cylinder were found (~12.5, ~12.27, ~12 unnumbered). A fourth fragment of the terminal had been collected on site (~23.9). The terminal had a straight edge with two narrow horizontal mouldings immediately behind with the vertical fluting running up to these mouldings. As excavated, these fragments were face down suggesting that they formed the underside of the cylinder and the ones collected on site the upper side. The extant length suggests the cylinder was at least 85 mm long. Including the base of the cylinder on ~11, this indicates a cylinder length of at least 100 mm. The junction of the cylinder and the 'wall' is smooth and well-finished on the exterior but ridged on the interior.

3   *Patera* **foot**. Cast copper alloy. Delta-shaped with central projection forked and small projection internally before pointed terminals.

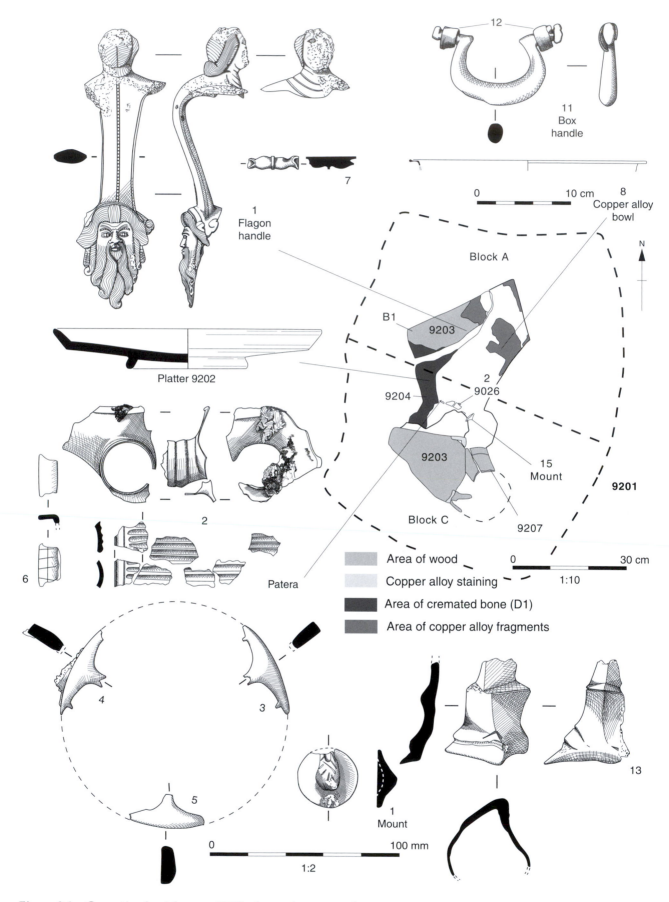

Figure 8.1   Cremation burial group 9200, plan and grave goods.

Rectangular-sectioned with outer edge sloping in towards base. Traces of solder on upper surface. Length 50 mm, thickness 7 mm, outer diameter *c* 120 mm. (200191419).

4   *Patera* **foot**. Cast copper alloy. Description as no. 3 with one terminal broken. Retains part of base of vessel including small area projection beyond the curved edge of the base. Present length 47 mm, thickness 6 mm, outer diameter 120 mm. (200191420).

5   *Patera* **foot**. Cast copper alloy. Description as no. 3 with terminals and central projection broken. Present length 38 mm, thickness 8 mm, outer diameter *c* 120 mm. (200191418).

6   **?*Patera* rim fragment**. Cast copper alloy. Horizontally out-turned rim broken at junction with body. Lightly incised decoration on underside of rim in cross-hatch pattern. Fragment insufficient to obtain accurate rim diameter, but greater than 170 mm. (200191423.15).

7   **Mount**. Cast copper alloy. D-sectioned bar, centrally two oval mouldings separated by a transverse rib; cupped ends. Length 27 mm, section 7 mm. (200191423.9).

8   **Bowl**. Copper alloy; probably raised. Three rim fragments, horizontal out-turned rim with thickened edge; side bent over to vertical side. Approximately one-quarter of circumference extant. Rim diameter 250 mm. (200191423.2; 200191423.4; 200191423.8).

9   **Bowl**. Copper alloy; probably raised. Rim fragment as 8 from the surface of Block B.

10   **Bowl**. Copper alloy. Found in Block B. Now extant as a curve of much corroded sheet and corrosion products held together by fill showing a straight side sloping in and an apparently concave base. One area suggests a base diameter of *c* 200 mm, but it may not have been circular and that diameter may relate to the narrow end of an ellipse. Wood preserved on underside of the base. (200191424).

11   **Drop handle**. Cast copper alloy. Omega-shaped with oval cross-section and circular-sectioned drum terminals, one chipped. Width 66 mm, depth 43 mm, maximum cross-section 12 x 10 mm. (200191416).

12   **Handle attachments**. Copper alloy. Fragments of two rectangular curved strips of same width and internal diameter as attachment bars of omega mount. Width 8 mm, section 7.5 x 2 mm. (200191423.16).

13   **Stand**. Cast copper alloy. Excavated from Block C2 below cylinder and cremated bone. Approximately half circumference of hollow casting; minerally preserved organics internally. Part of 'rim' extant with beaked outline; intermediate angular moulding with possibly square-sectioned leg above. Present height 50 mm. (200191414).

14   **Bar**. Copper alloy. Much corroded solid bar which includes to one side a fragment of the fluted cylinder. The bar is currently *c* 18 mm wide and *c* 15 mm deep. (200191413).

15   **Mount**. Cast copper alloy. Flat circular disc, chipped at one point of circumference; slightly dished on underside with asymmetrical knob on upper side, central part damaged. Knob decorated with diagonal grooving on either side, with two ear-like features on upper margin. Possibly representing feline. Slight scar centrally on underside, but no evidence of any shank. Small lump with copper alloy corrosion products on face that fits into underside of mount; lump retains layer of wood. Diameter 31 mm, thickness of backing disc 2.5 mm. (200191417: Block C3).

Textiles
by Penelope Walton Rogers

There are fragmentary remains of a textile adhering to one of the pieces of *patera* (9206). The textile lies both inside and outside the hollow handle and clearly passes over the broken edges of the metal-work, indicating that it must have come into contact with the object after it had been broken. The textile is crumpled and folded, but in the best preserved areas it appears to be a torn strip of fabric, 16-20 mm wide, folded in half lengthways. It has been woven in tabby (plain weave) from yarn spun Z in warp and weft. There are 18-20 threads per cm in one direction and 12-14 per cm in the other.

Examination of a sample of fibres under a high-power microscope (x100-x640 magnification) revealed the raw material to be a plant stem fibre ('bast'), processed down to its finest possible elements (the 'ultimates'). The fibres were 10-18 microns diameter, had a fine lumen (central channel) and well-spaced cross-markings, and when dried under a hot lamp, they consistently rotated clockwise. This indicates that the fibres come from the flax plant, *Linum usitatissimum* L. Individual fibres have the kind of frayed ends seen in heavily distressed linens and the textile as a whole has crown damage and fibrillation at the interstices of the weave (for different types of fibre damage in textiles, see Cooke and Lomas 1989). This textile evidently saw heavy wear before burial.

Cultivated flax has been recorded in the form of seeds and pollen from a number of Bronze Age and Iron Age sites in Great Britain (A R Hall, pers. comm.), but this is the first example of a textile from the British Iron Age to be confidently identified as flax. Textiles have been recovered from a number of other Iron Age sites, the largest collection being from the Arras Culture cemeteries of Yorkshire (Crowfoot 1991), where they were mostly too heavily mineralised to allow fibre identification. The textiles from late Iron Age cremation graves at Verulam Hills Field, St Albans (J P Wild in Anthony 1968, 14-16), and Westhampnett, Sussex (Walton Rogers 1997), were almost certainly wool. Only two textiles, both from a late Iron Age warrior's burial at St Peter's Port, Guernsey, have been firmly identified as plant fibre, although whether the plant was flax, hemp or nettle was impossible to tell (Watkins and Cameron 1987).

By the Roman period, linen production was well established in Britain and there is evidence for flax processing at Ickham, East Kent (Riddler *et al.* forthcoming), as well as linen textiles from other sites (Wild 1970, 91-4). The Ashford example of linen suggests that this industry may have been in existence before the Roman invasions.

Note: since this report was written one other certain example of linen cloth is now known from a late Iron Age context. This material was used to wrap the sword from the warrior burial at Kelvedon, Essex (Walton Rogers 2007).

Bucket

The bucket was of yew wood, perhaps with metal binding and mounts (see above). Measurements for nine staves identified in post-excavation assessment are presented in Table 8.1. Fragments of seven 'additional' staves are likely to have derived from the staves tabulated, and are not listed separately. The estimated diameter is c 150 mm and the height may have been similar. The sides were presumably, but not demonstrably, vertical. The base was c 22 mm thick with the staves projecting c 5 mm below it. Context 9207.

Pottery

The grave contained only one pottery vessel, a platter of *Camulodunum* form 1 in a fine micaceous *terra nigra* fabric. Some 23 fragments were recovered, forming seven sherds reflecting fractures predating the discovery of the burial, but not necessarily present at the time that the burial was put in place. Allowing for erosion of the already broken sherds and loss of a few tiny chips in the process of recovery by the building contractors, the vessel was complete, with a total weight of 909 g. Rim diameter 280 mm. Context 9202.

Human bone

Some 703 g of cremated bone were recovered from context 9204, the number assigned to the spread of cremated bone as recovered, but possibly consisting of more than one distinct deposit. The individual

Table 8.1   Burial 9200: The wooden bucket stave measurements.

Stave no.	Length (mm)	Width (mm)	Thickness (mm)
1	137.3	76.8	3.4
2	101.4	49.9	8.2
3	22.8	15.2	-
4	55.3	11.7	6.3
5	13.4	-	-
6	66.8	12.5	10
7	92.5	5.9	9.7
8	79	5.3	9.5
9	108.1	22	10.1

represented was adult and probably male (see further below). Context 9204.

Animal bone

A total of 314 fragments of animal bone (34 cremated, 280 unburnt) was recovered from contexts 9200, 9202, 9204 and 9205. Context 9200 (a general number for unstratified material associated with the burial) contained elements from a very young/neonatal sheep, including 26 fragments of vertebrae including the atlas and axis. Also identified were five pig teeth which had been stained green, almost certainly from contamination by associated material. The only burnt bone from this context was a single fragment of a radius, probably of sheep, which was completely burnt white. None of the 150 fragments of bone from context 9202 (in or above the *terra nigra* platter) had been burnt. These again consisted of the remains of a neonatal sheep including both the right and left femur and the unfused proximal articulation of a left tibia, in addition to more vertebral fragments. Many of the fragments were broken and could not be positively identified, but they included fragments of ribs which may have been associated with the neonatal sheep skeleton.

Sixty-three fragments of bone from context 9204 included 31 unburnt fragments, many of unidentified bone stained green, along with a stained fragment of pig molar. The remaining material was cremated and included three fragments of undiagnositic bird. Identifiable elements included three fragments of pig molar teeth and a small part of an innominate (pelvis) acetabulum, probably of sheep, though not positively identified. The remaining pieces were too fragmented for positive identification.

Twenty-nine fragments of bone came from context 9205. The only cremated fragments were most of a sheep astragalus and a fragmented pig molar. Other identified elements consisted of a pig's premolar tooth stained green and part of the lower shaft of a juvenile sheep's tibia. The remaining elements were not burnt and appeared to be from a juvenile animal consisting of fragments of the vertebral column and other broken and unidentifiable elements.

In summary, cremated material from 9204 and 9205 suggests the presence of sheep/lamb (possibly more than one animal), pig and bird on the cremation pyre. The unburnt remains were again of (neonatal) sheep and pig, but it is unclear if more than one animal of each kind was represented.

Area C Cemetery

Cremation graves

Group 5050 (Fig. 8.2)

Cut 5010, sub-circular measuring 0.65 m x 0.4 m x 0.15 m deep, sides sloping steeply at approximately 70°, and rounded slightly to a flat base. Filled by 5011, yellow-brown silt clay.

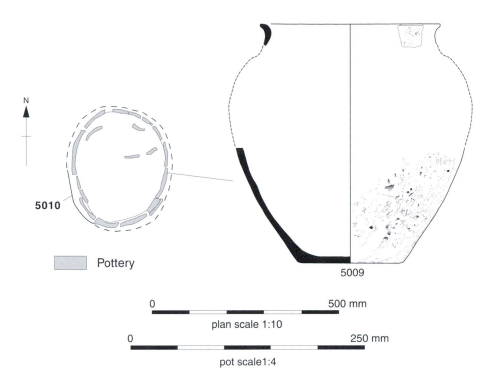

Figure 8.2 Cremation burial group 5050 (cut 5010).

Urned cremation burial, 814 g cremated bone in vessel 5009. Adult.

Non ceramic finds:

1 **Intaglio**, 3rd-century (see Cool, Chapter 5, cat. no. 22; Fig. 5.4). Fill of vessel 5009, SF508.

Ceramic finds:

1 **Jar**, in Native Coarse Ware fabric R1; high-fired grey with reddened patches externally, truncated. Vessel 5009.

Date: AD 200-250 (ceramics and intaglio); Period 2 Phase 5.

Group 5060 (Fig. 8.3)

Cut 5016, sub-circular measuring 0.5 m x 0.6 m x 0.12 m deep, with steeply-sloping to vertical sides and flat base. Filled by 5012, greyish yellow-brown silty clay.
  Possible cremation burial, but no cremated bone associated.

Non ceramic finds: None.

Ceramic finds:

1 **Flagon**, disc-rimmed in orange-red oxidised Up-church fabric R17 with slightly more sand than is usual, incomplete and fragmented. Vessel 5013.
2 **Beaker** or **jar** of uncertain form, fine grey Up-church fabric R16, only fragments. Vessel 5014.

Date: ?3rd-century (ceramics); Period 2 Phase 5.

Group 5070 (Fig. 8.3)

Cut 5061, sub-circular measuring 0.7 m x 0.6 m x 0.15 m deep, gradually sloping sides and a rounded base. Filled by 5062, brownish-grey clay silt.
  Urned cremation burial, 31 g cremated bone in vessel 5063. Adult.

Non ceramic finds: None.

Ceramic finds:

1 **Jar**, fine oxidised Upchurch fabric R17, truncated ?*c* AD 150-250. Vessel 5063.
2 **Beaker**, fine grey Upchurch fabric R16, truncated, ?early 3rd century type. Vessel 5065.

Date: *c* AD 200-250 (ceramics); Period 2 Phase 5.

Group 5080 (Fig. 8.4)

Cut 5021, circular measuring 0.6 m diameter x 0.15 m deep, steeply-sloping sides and slightly rounded base. Filled by 5017, greyish yellow-brown silty clay.
  Urned cremation burial, 706 g cremated bone in vessel 5019. Young adult male.

Non ceramic finds: None.

Ceramic finds:

1 **Jar** in patchy grog-tempered ?East Sussex Ware, truncated. Vessel 5019.
2 **Flagon** of uncertain form in reddish-brown Up-church fabric R17, only a small fraction of this vessel is present. Vessel 5020.

Date: ?Mid 2nd century or later; Period 2 Phase 4 or 5.

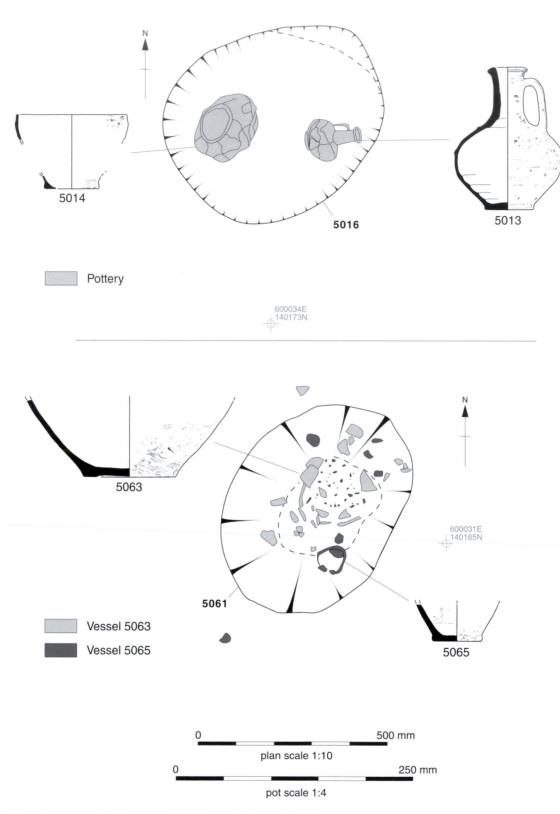

5014

5016

5013

Pottery

600034E
140173N

5063

5061

600031E
140165N

5065

Vessel 5063

Vessel 5065

0   500 mm

plan scale 1:10

0   250 mm

pot scale 1:4

Figure 8.3   Cremation burial groups 5060 (cut 5016) and 5070 (cut 5061).

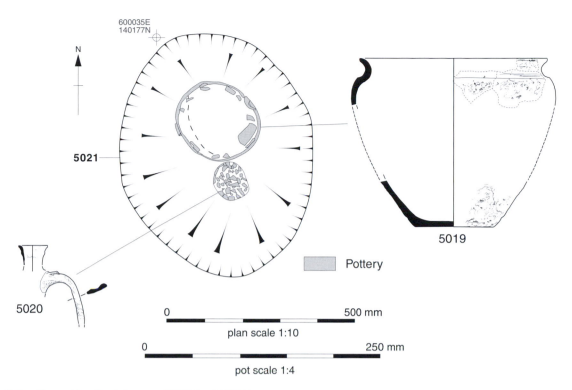

600035E
140177N

N

5021

Pottery

5019

5020

0   500 mm
plan scale 1:10

0   250 mm
pot scale 1:4

Figure 8.4   Cremation burial group 5080 (cut 5021).

Group 5090 (Fig. 8.5)

Cut 5028, sub-rectangular measuring *c* 1 m x 0.7 m x 0.25 m deep, with fairly steeply sloping sides and flat base. Only the south-east edge of the feature was well defined. Fill 5024, greyish yellow-brown silty clay.

Urned cremation burial, 1310 g cremated bone in fill 5025 of vessel 5026. Young adult male.

Non ceramic finds:

1   **Burnt animal bone** (x 22 fragments), includes juvenile sheep and bird. Fill 5025, of vessel 5026.
2   **Copper alloy armlet** (see Cool, Chapter 5, cat. no. 21; Fig. 5.4). Context 5025, SF563.
3   **Armlet** of jet and lignite beads. Formed from three large, oval, ridge-backed beads, on which traces of gold leaf were found, and 24 flat elliptical beads (see Allason-Jones, Chapter 5; Figs 5.8: 6-31, and 5.9). Context 5025, SF511, SF520, SF564, SF567-SF578, SF580-SF584, SF654-SF656, SF657-SF658.
4   **Necklace** comprising 183 jet cylinder beads (see Allason-Jones, Chapter 5; Fig.5.8: 1-5). Context 5025, SF504, SF512-SF519, SF521-SF539, SF541-SF549, SF586, SF589-SF610, SF643-SF653, SF659-SF738.

Ceramic finds:

1   **Jar** in grog-tempered ware fabric LR1.1; fired black with profuse white siltstone grog, complete. *c* AD 270-370. Vessel 5026.
2   **Lid** in patchy brown/black grog-tempered East Sussex Ware, complete. Within jar 5026.

3   **Beaker** in cream Lower Nene Valley fabric with white-painted scroll decoration over brown-black colour-coat, complete. *c* AD 270-350. Vessel 5003.
4   **Flagon** (under)fired orange with black core, heavily truncated. Vessel 5027.

Date: AD 270-370 (all finds), but probably late 3rd- to early 4th-century; Period 2 Phase 6.

Group 5110 (Fig. 8.6)

Cut 5036, circular measuring 0.35 m diameter x 0.15 m deep, with steep sloping sides rounding to a flat base. Filled by 5033, redeposited natural silt clay.

Urned cremation burial, 411 g cremated bone in vessel 5035. Adult.

Non ceramic finds: None.

Ceramic finds:

1   **Beaker** in fine grey Upchurch fabric R16 with a large hole ?deliberately made in the base, truncated. The basal pedestal suggests an early date of *c* AD 43-100. Vessel 5035.

Date: Period 2 Phase 2 or 3.

Group 5120 (Fig. 8.7)

Cut 5043, circular measuring 0.6 m diameter x 0.15 m deep, with shallow sloping sides and a rounded base. Filled by 5040, yellow-brown silt clay.

Urned cremation burial, 343 g cremated bone in vessel 5042. Adult male.

309

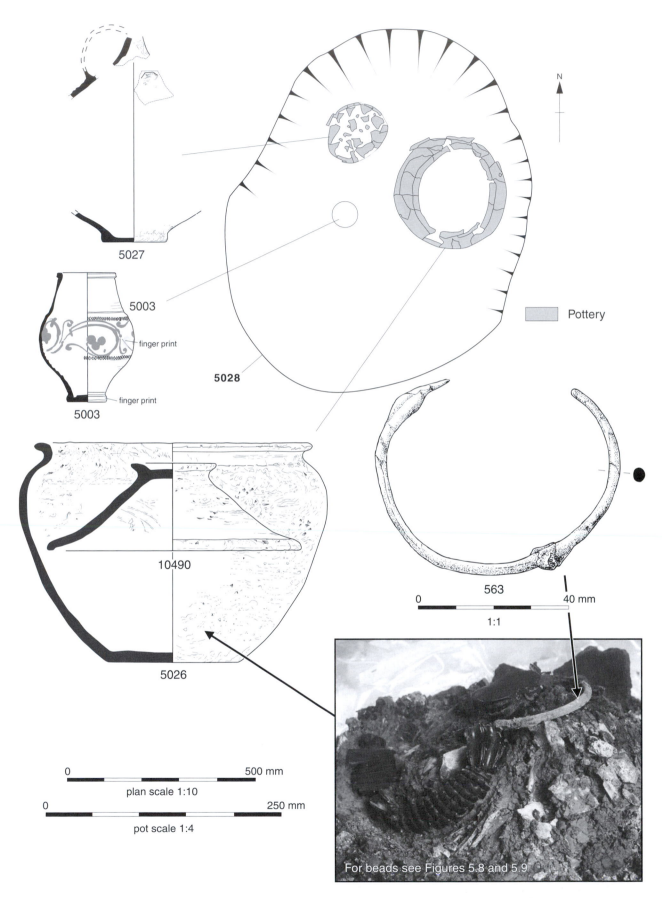

5027

5003

5003

finger print

finger print

5028

N

Pottery

10490

5026

563

0   40 mm

1:1

For beads see Figures 5.8 and 5.9

0   500 mm

plan scale 1:10

0   250 mm

pot scale 1:4

Figure 8.5   Cremation burial group 5090 (cut 5028).

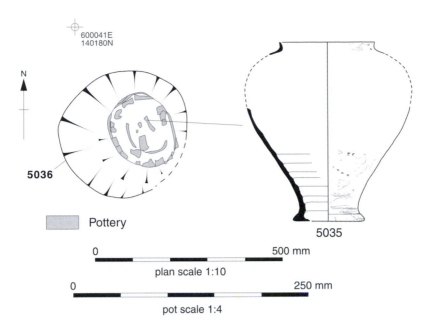

600041E
140180N

N

5036

Pottery

0   500 mm

plan scale 1:10

0   250 mm

pot scale 1:4

5035

Figure 8.6   Cremation burial group 5110 (cut 5036).

Non ceramic finds: None.

Ceramic finds:

1   Large **jar** in grog-tempered fabric B2.1; fired black, truncated. Vessel 5042.

Date: ?1st- to 2nd-century; Period 2 Phase 2 to 5.

Group 5210 *(Fig. 8.8)*

Cut 5128, sub-rectangular measuring 0.94 m x 0.52 m x 0.05 m deep. The remaining edges were shallow and sloped gradually to an irregular base. Filled by 5127, grey brown clay silt.

Unurned cremation burial, 478 g cremated bone in pit 5128. Adult.

Non ceramic finds: None.

Ceramic finds:

1   **Beaker** in fine grey Upchurch fabric R16, badly truncated. The plain base suggests a late 2nd- to 3rd-century date. Vessel 5125.

Date: Late 2nd- to 3rd-century (ceramics); Period 2 Phase 5.

Note: Beaker 5125 lay on its side at the northern edge of the pit, and a spread of cremated bone lay to the south of this. The bone may have originally been within the beaker and displaced by post-Roman ploughing. Alternatively, the cremated bone could have been held within an organic container.

Group 5220 *(Fig. 8.9)*

Cut 5131, sub-circular measuring 1.7 m x 1.1 m x 0.2 m deep, with steeply-sloping sides and flat base. Filled by 5132, grey-orange silt clay. Cremated bone

and ancillary vessels in box *c* 0.70 m x 0.85 m (depth unknown) indicated by soil stain and 5 nails along the northern edge of the pit.

Urned cremation burial, 756 g cremated bone in vessel 5134 and 119 g in backfill of pit 5133. Adult male.

Non ceramic finds:

1   Cremated **animal bone,** 6 fragments including sheep and bird. Fill 5135 of jar 5134.
2   **Nails** (x 9). Fe. Context 5133, SF550-SF553, SF555-SF558, SF560.
3   **Hobnails** (x3). Fe. Context 5133, SF554 and SF558-SF559.

Ceramic finds:

1   **Cordoned jar**   in polished reddish-brown grog-tempered fabric with black patches. *c* AD 100-160. Vessel 5134.
2   **Flagon** in buff-brown Canterbury fabric R6.3, truncated. *c* AD 70-150. Vessel 5136.
3   **Beaker** of uncertain form, in fine grey Upchurch fabric R16, badly truncated. Vessel 5138.
4   **Platter,** Drag. 18/31, Central Gaulish samian. The stamp has been eroded away. *c* AD 120-150. Vessel 5141.

Date: AD 120-150 (ceramics); Period 2 Phase 3.

Group 5230 *(Fig. 8.10)*

Cut 5146, circular measuring 0.33 m diameter and 0.07 m deep, with gently sloping sides and a rounded base. Filled by 5143, grey-brown silt clay.

Urned cremation burial, 3 g cremated bone in vessel 5145. Tiny flecks of cremated bone were seen on the surface of 5143.

Non ceramic finds: None.

Ceramic finds:

1   Base of **jar** in grog-tempered fabric B2.1, fragmentary. Vessel 5145.

Date: 1st- to 2nd-century (ceramics); Period 2 Phase 2 to 4.

Group 5240 (Fig. 8.11)

Cut 5166, roughly square measuring 0.51 m x 0.54 m x 0.07 m deep, sides slope at *c* 45° to a flattish base. Filled by 5163, grey-brown silt clay.

Urned cremation burial, 55 g cremated bone in vessel 5165. Adult.

Non ceramic finds: None.

Ceramic finds:

1   Necked **jar** in fine grog-tempered grey fabric fired polished reddish-brown, fragmentary. *c* AD 100-160. Vessel 5165.

Date: AD 100-160 (ceramics); Period 2 Phase 3.

Note: The shape of the grave suggested that the burial had originally been within a box. No nails or

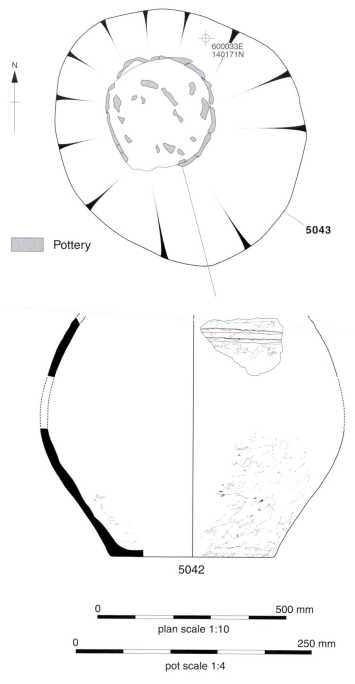

Figure 8.7   Cremation burial group 5120 (cut 5036).

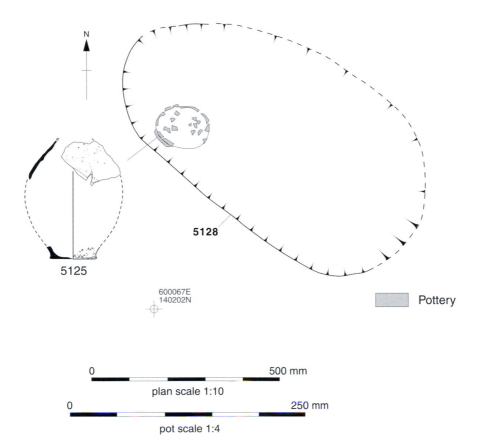

N

5128

5125

600067E
140202N

Pottery

0   500 mm
plan scale 1:10

0   250 mm
pot scale 1:4

Figure 8.8   Cremation burial group 5210 (cut 5128).

other fittings were recovered, but these could easily have been lost to the plough.

Inhumation graves

Group 5100 (Fig. 8.12)

Cut 5032, E-W, sub-rectangular measuring 2.8 m x 1.0 m x 0.15 m deep, with moderate to steep edges and an irregular base. Filled by 5031, grey brown clay silt.
   No human bone preservation.

Non ceramic finds: None.

Ceramic finds:

1   **Pottery sherds** (x 34) mostly abraded, in various fabrics and only datable within a 1st- to 3rd-century range. Wt: 150 g. Context 5031.

Date: Uncertain; Period 2 Phase 3 to 5.

Group 5130 (Fig. 8.13)

Cut 5047, E-W, sub-rectangular measuring 1.8 m x 0.9 m x 0.12 m deep, with steep sloping sides and an irregular base. Filled by 5046, dark grey silt clay.
   No human bone preservation. Small amount of burnt animal bone.

Non ceramic finds: None.

Ceramic finds:

1   **Beaker** of Monaghan form 2I7.1 in dull reddish-brown Upchurch fabric R17 variant with a little mica and occasional iron-stained quartz (up to 0.2 mm), badly shattered. Vessel 5044.

Date: AD 43-60 (ceramics); Period 2 Phase 2.

Group 5140 (Fig. 8.14)

Cut 5052, NW-SE, sub-rectangular measuring 3.0 m x 1.2 m x 0.2 m deep, with steep but irregular sides and an uneven base. Filled by 5051, mid grey silt clay.
   No human bone preservation.

Non ceramic finds: Iron slag.

Ceramic finds:

1   **Pottery sherds** (x 6). Wt: 48 g. Context 5051.

Date: After AD 270 (ceramics); Period 2 Phase 6.

Group 5150 (Fig. 8.15)

Cut 5054, E-W, sub-rectangular measuring 2.5 m x 0.6-1.1 m x 0.18 m deep, steeply sloping sides and flat base. Filled by 5053, greyish-brown silty clay.

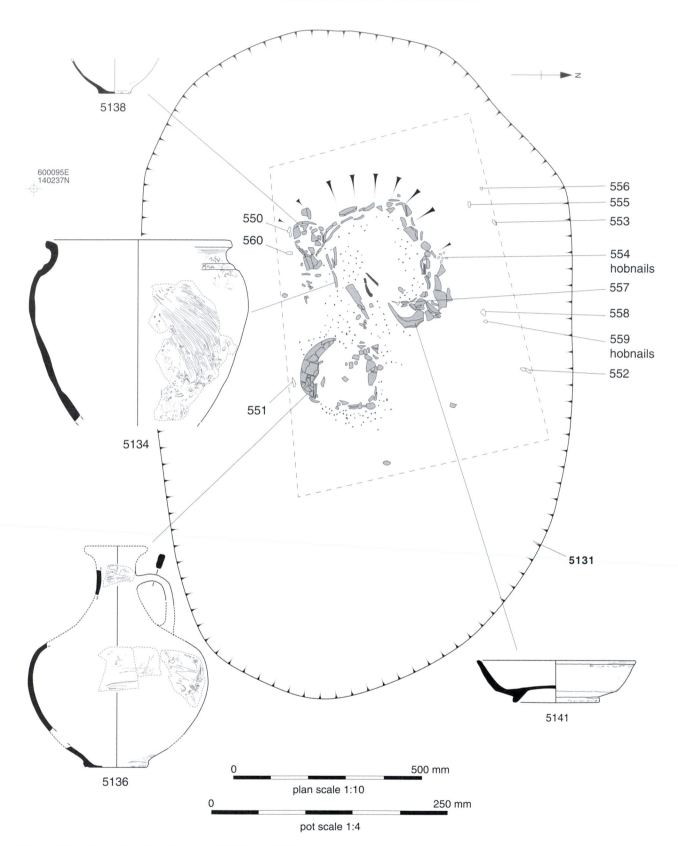

600095E
140237N

5138

5134

550
560

551

5136

556
555
553

554
hobnails

557
558

559
hobnails

552

5131

5141

0   500 mm
plan scale 1:10

0   250 mm
pot scale 1:4

Figure 8.9   Cremation burial group 5220 (cut 5131).

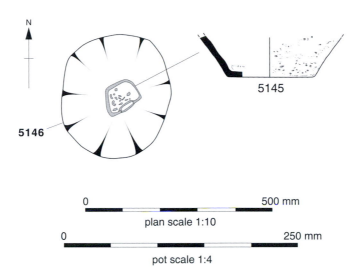

Figure 8.10   Cremation burial group 5230 (cut 5146).

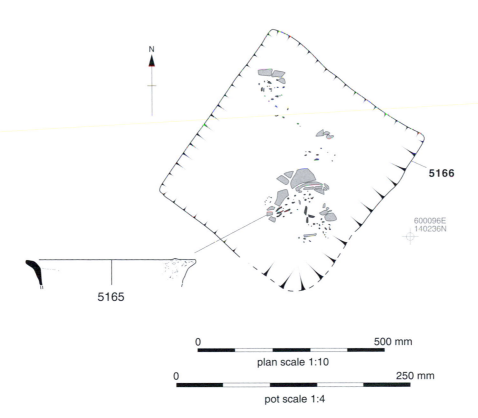

Figure 8.11   Cremation burial group 5240 (cut 5166).

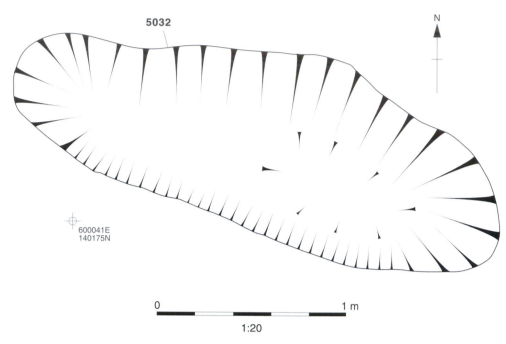

5032

N

600041E
140175N

0   1 m

1:20

Figure 8.12   Inhumation burial group 5100 (cut 5032).

No human bone preservation.

Non ceramic finds: None.

Ceramic finds:

1   **Pottery sherds** (x 11). Wt: 86 g. Context 5053.

Date   Early 2nd-century or (probably) later (ceramics); Period 2 Phase 5.

Group 5160 (Fig. 8.16)

Cut 5072, north-west to south-east, irregular measuring up to 2.3 m x 1.1 m x 0.19 m deep, but the width of the base averaged 0.8 m. The sides were near vertical apart from the south-east edge which sloped at approximately 30° to a flat base. Filled by 5071, grey silt-clay.
   No human bone preservation.

Non ceramic finds: None.

Ceramic finds:

1   **Pottery sherds** (x 9). Wt: 32 g. Context 5071.
2   **Tile fragment** (x 1). Wt: 4 g. Context 5071.

Date   ?1st- to 2nd-century (ceramics); Period 2 Phase 2 to 4.

Group 5170 (Fig. 8.17)

Cut 5023, E-W, sub-rectangular measuring 1.9 m x 1.0 m width x 0.1 m deep, with near vertical sides and a generally flat base. Filled by 5022, grey-brown silt clay.
   No human bone preservation.

Non ceramic finds: None.

Ceramic finds:

1   **Pottery sherds** (x 15). Wt: 92 g. Context 5022.

Date   ?Late 1st- to 2nd-century (ceramics); Period 2 Phase 3.

Group 5180 (Fig. 8.18)

Cut 5099, N-S, sub-rectangular measuring 2.1 m x 1.0 m width x 0.12 m deep, steeply sloping sides and flat base. Filled by 5098, dark greyish yellow-brown silty clay.
   No human bone preservation.

Non ceramic finds:

1   **Pillar-moulded-bowl.** Two body fragments (see Cool, Chapter 5, cat. no. 35). Context 5098, SF504.

Ceramic finds:

1   **Pottery sherds** (x 12). Wt: 46 g. Context 5098.

Date   ?1st- to 2nd-century (ceramics); Period 2 Phase 2 to 4.

Group 5190 (Fig. 8.19)

Cut 5085, NW-SE, irregular measuring *c* 3.0 m x, 1.0 m x 0.2 m deep, sides slope up to 50° to flattish base. Filled by 5084, grey silt clay.
   No human bone preservation.

Non ceramic finds:

1   **Pillar-moulded-bowl.** Single body fragment (see Cool, Chapter 5, cat. no. 36). Context 5084, SF503.

N

5047

600066E
140201N

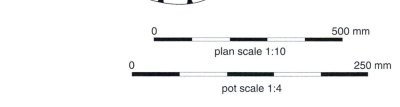

5044

0   500 mm
plan scale 1:10

0   250 mm
pot scale 1:4

Figure 8.13   Inhumation burial group 5130 (cut 5047).

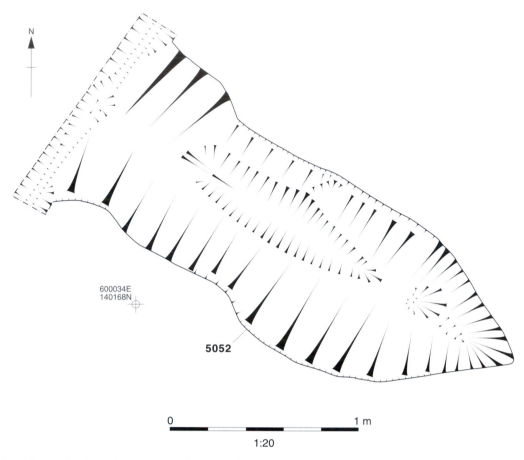

600034E
140168N

5052

0   1 m
1:20

Figure 8.14   Inhumation burial group 5140 (cut 5052).

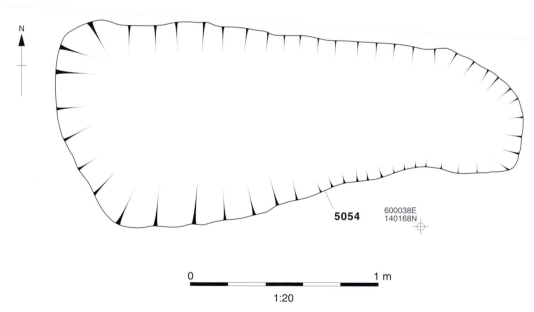

5054

600038E
140168N

0   1 m
1:20

Figure 8.15   Inhumation burial group 5150 (cut 5054).

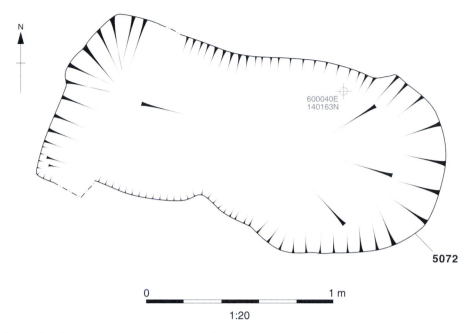

5072

0   1 m

1:20

Figure 8.16   Inhumation burial group 5160 (cut 5072).

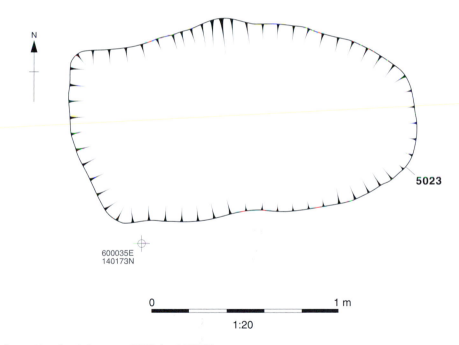

5023

600035E
140173N

0   1 m

1:20

Figure 8.17   Inhumation burial group 5170 (cut 5023).

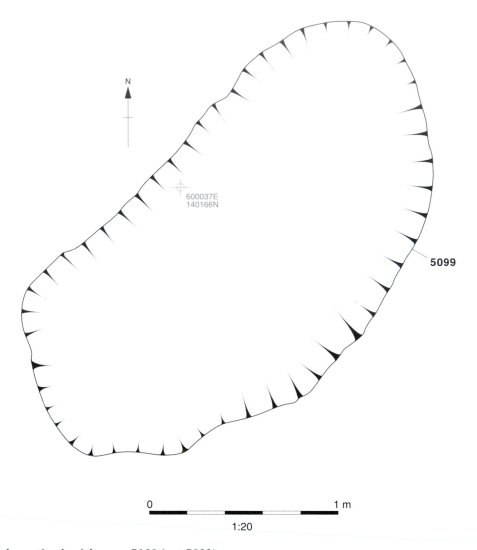

N

600037E
140166N

5099

0 _____ 1 m

1:20

Figure 8.18   Inhumation burial group 5180 (cut 5099).

Ceramic finds:

1   **Pottery sherds** (x 24). Wt: 102 g. Context 5084.

Date   ?1st-century (ceramics and glass); Period 2 Phase 2.

Burials in Area B

Cremation graves

Group 210 (Fig. 8.20)

Cut 232, sub-oval measuring 0.9 m x 0.75 m x 0.2 m deep, near vertical sided with a slightly uneven base. Filled by 233.

Urned cremation burial, 386 g cremated bone partly in vessel 205 but also scattered through grave fill. Adult female.

Non ceramic finds:

1   **Needle**, cu alloy (see Cool, Chapter 5, cat. no. 34; Fig.5.4). Context 233, SF32.
2   **Hobnails** (x 27). **Fe.** Context 233, sample 6.

Ceramic finds:

1   **Jar** with shoulder cordon, in grey Native Coarse Ware fabric R1, truncated. *c* AD 170-250. Vessel 205.
2   Small **beaker** in fine grey Upchurch fabric R16; unusual form with a high shoulder and stubby everted rim. Vessel 207.
3   Ovoid **poppyhead beaker** of Monaghan form 2A5.5 in similar fabric without decoration. *c* AD 160-190. Vessel 209.
4   **Cup** Drag. 33, Central Gaulish samian. No stamp. Date *c* AD 120-200. Vessel 249.
5   **Flanged bowl** in brown-black grog-tempered ware fabric B2.1. Vessel 212.
6   **Bowl** of Monaghan form 5C2, polished black BB2. Date *c* AD 150-210. Vessel 216.
7   **Platter** Drag. 31 Central Gaulish samian. Stamp completely eroded away. The vessel has been broken and riveted together in antiquity. *c* AD 150-200. Vessel 214.

Date   AD 170-200 (ceramics); Period 2 Phase 4.

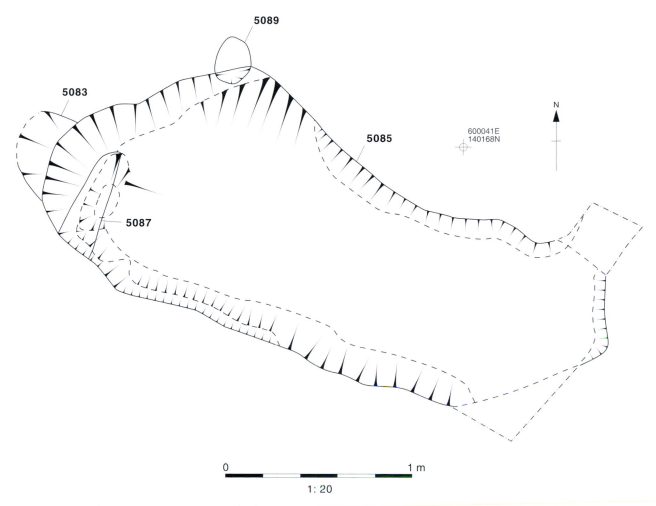

Figure 8.19   Inhumation burial group 5190 (cut 5085).

Group 220 (Fig. 8.21)

Cut 251, sub-rectangular measuring 0.88 m x 0.72 m x 0.12 m deep, with near-vertical edges and a flat base. Filled by 231. Possible box burial (?*c* 0.60 x 0.60 m, height unknown) suggested by arrangement of vessels and iron nails.

Urned cremation burial, 1364 g cremated bone in vessel 218. Young adult female.

Non ceramic finds:

1   **Burnt animal bone** (not identifiable to species) (x 12 fragments). Fill 219, of jar 218.
2   **Nails** (x 3). Fe. Context 231, SF29-SF31.
3   **Hobnails** (x 74). Fe. Context 231, SF34 (x 19 hobnails) and sample 7 (x 55 hobnails).

Ceramic finds:

1   Large **jar** in brown-black grog-tempered fabric B2.1, truncated. Vessel 218.
2   **Ovoid beaker** of Monaghan form 2A6 in fine grey Upchurch fabric R16 without decoration, truncated. Date *c* AD 190-230. Vessel 223.

3   **Cup**, Drag. 33, Central Gaulish samian. The stamp has been obliterated by acidic soil conditions. Date *c* AD 120-200. Vessel 227.
4   **Cup**, Drag. 33, Central Gaulish samian in similar condition to above. Date *c* AD 120-200. Vessel 240.
5   **Platter** of Monaghan Form 5C3 in smooth black BB2 fabric. Date *c* AD170-250. Vessel 244.
6   **Platter**, Drag. 31, Central Gaulish samian, stamped. '. . . AZI.M'. Date *c* AD 150-200. Vessel 229.
7   **Platter**, Drag. 31, Central Gaulish samian stamped 'OFNONV...'. Date *c* AD 150-200, below 246. Vessel 10491.
8   **Platter**, Drag. 31, Central Gaulish samian, of similar size to 10491 but with the stamp obliterated by acidic soil conditions. Date *c* AD 150-200. Vessel 246.
9   Large **platter**, Drag. 31/Sb, East Gaulish samian. Surface and stamp eroded by acidic soil conditions. Date *c* AD 200-250. Vessel 221.
10   Small **platter**, Drag. 31/Sa, East Gaulish samian. Condition as Vessel 221. Date *c* AD 200-250. Vessel 225.

Date   AD 200-250 (ceramics); Period 2 Phase 5.

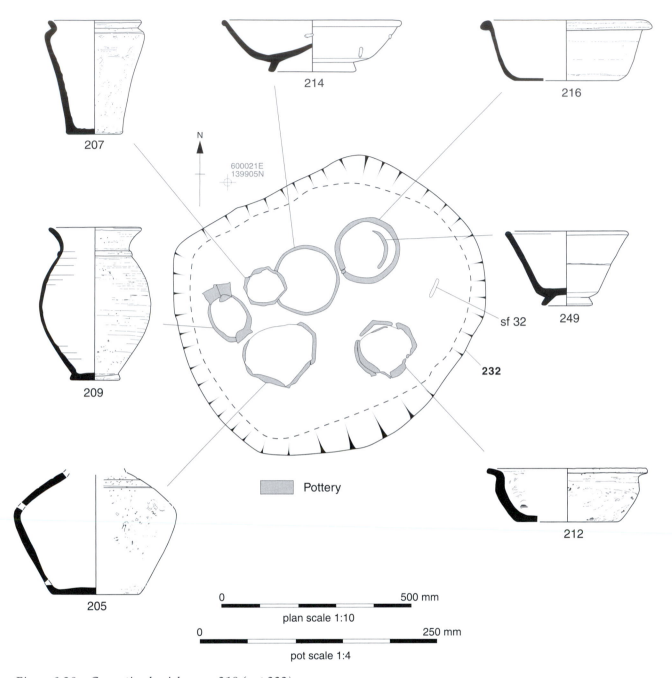

Figure 8.20   Cremation burial group 210 (cut 232).

Group 1007 (Fig. 8.22)

Cut 1007, circular measuring 0.36 m diameter x 0.15 m deep. Filled by 1006.

Urned cremation burial,1225 g cremated bone in vessel 1004. Adult male.

Non ceramic finds: None.

Ceramic finds:

1   **Storage jar** in fabric B2.1, truncated. Vessel 1004.

Date   AD 43-100 (ceramics); Period 2 Phase 2 to 3.

Group 1261 (Fig. 8.22)

Cut 1261, sub-rectangular measuring 0.46 m x 0.2 m x 0.12 m deep. Filled by 1263, mid-grey clay silt.

Unurned cremation burial, 125 g cremated bone in pit backfill 1263. Adult.

Non ceramic finds: None.

Ceramic finds:

1   **Cordoned jar** in fabric B1, fragmented. Vessel 1262.

Date   ?Late Iron Age-AD 50 (ceramics); Period 2 Phase 2.

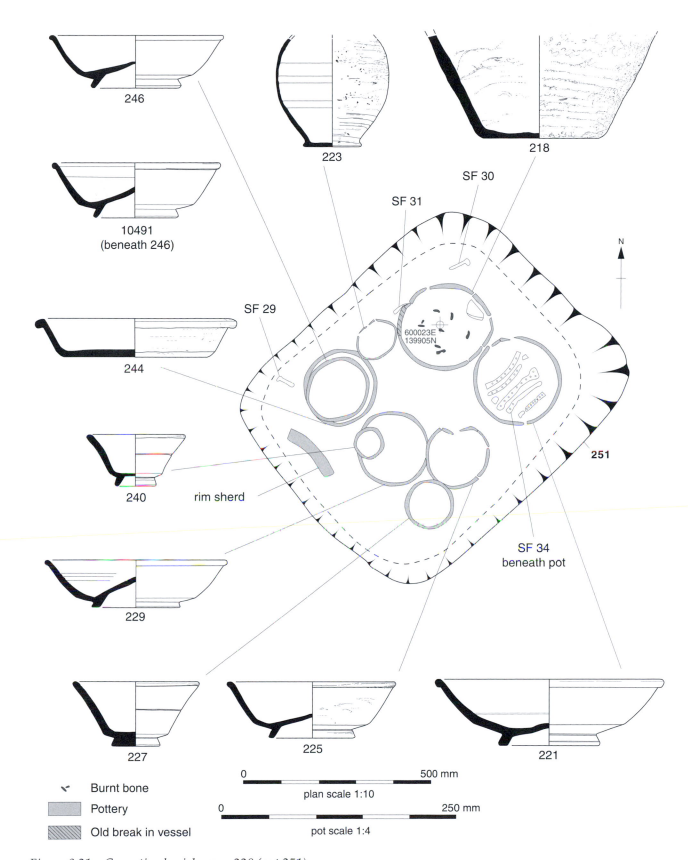

246

10491
(beneath 246)

223

218

SF 30

SF 31

244

SF 29

600023E
139905N

251

SF 34
beneath pot

240

rim sherd

229

227

225

221

Burnt bone

Pottery

Old break in vessel

0   500 mm
plan scale 1:10

0   250 mm
pot scale 1:4

Figure 8.21   Cremation burial group 220 (cut 251).

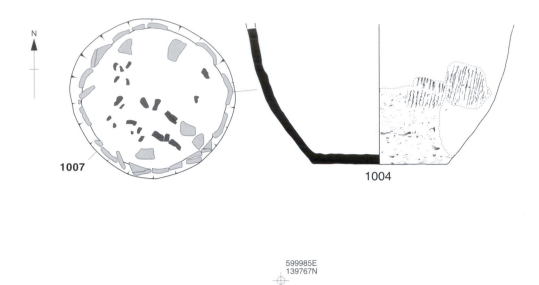

599985E
139767N

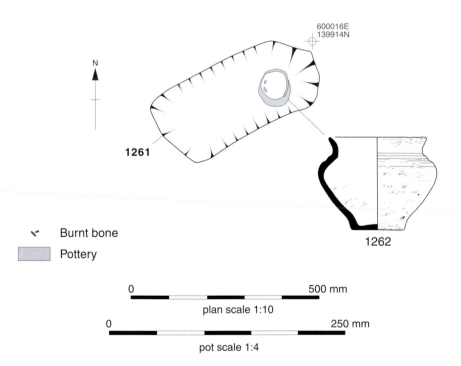

600016E
139914N

ᕝ Burnt bone

▨ Pottery

0 ━━━━━━━ 500 mm

plan scale 1:10

0 ━━━━━━━ 250 mm

pot scale 1:4

Figure 8.22   Cremation burial groups 1007 (cut 1007) and 1261 (cut 1261).

Group 8956 (Fig. 8.23)

Cut 8956, sub-rectangular measuring 0.5 x 0.35 x 0.19 m deep. Filled by 8955.

Unurned cremation burial, 53 g cremated bone in pit 8956. Adult.

Non ceramic finds: None.

Ceramic finds:

1 **Pottery sherds** (x 4). Wt: 32 g. Context 8955.

Date   ?AD 70-175 (ceramics); Period 2 Phase 4.

Group 9860 (Fig. 8.24)

Cut 9840, rectangular measuring 0.6 x 0.7 x 0.03 m deep. Filled by 9841, redeposited natural silt clay.

Unurned cremation burial, 283 g cremated bone in pit 9840. Adult.

Non ceramic finds: None.

Ceramic finds:

1 **Cordoned jar**, everted-rim, in brown-black fabric B2.1 with resin on shoulder, shattered. Vessel 10488 (SF1530).

324

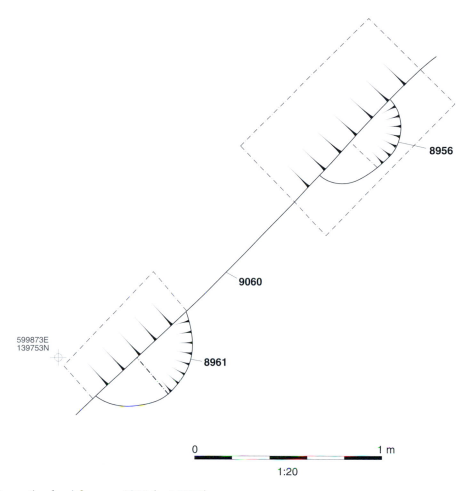

599873E
139753N

8956

9060

8961

0   1 m

1:20

Figure 8.23   Cremation burial group 8956 (cut 8956).

2 **Flagon** in sandy orange Canterbury fabric R6.1, shattered. Vessel 10487 (SF1529).

Date   AD 70-150 (ceramics); Period 2 Phase 3.

Note: The majority of the cremated bone was within a shallow bowl-shaped depression in the centre of the grave and does not seem to have been placed within the jar. It may originally have been held in a bag or some other organic container.

Group 9940 (Fig. 8.25)

Cut 9468, circular measuring 0.6 m diameter x 0.32 m deep with steep sides and a rounded base. Filled by 9469, redeposited natural silt clay.
   Urned cremation burial, 837 g cremated bone in vessel 9523. Mature adult.

Non ceramic finds: None.

Ceramic finds:

1 **Jar**, plain narrow-necked in grog-tempered black fabric B2.1. Date c AD 43-100. Vessel 9523.
2 **Flagon** in fabric R6.3, comminuted. Vessel 10489.
3 **Cup**, Drag. 46, South Gaulish samian, inverted. Date c AD 70-110. Vessel 9521.

Date   c AD 70-100 (ceramics); Period 2 Phase 3.

Group 10337 (Fig. 8.26)

Cut 10337, circular measuring 0.3 m diameter x 0.06 m deep, with steep near vertical sides. Filled by 10338, dark brown silt clay.
   Unurned cremation burial, 268 g cremated bone in fill 10338. Adult.

Non ceramic finds: None.

Ceramic finds: None.

Date: Uncertain; Period 2 Phase 4?

Inhumation graves

Group 8160 (see Fig. 3.36)

Cut 8188, NE-SW, rectangular measuring 1.94 m x 0.76 m x 0.54 m deep, with near-vertical sides and a flattish base. Filled by backfill 8189 and 8547, light grey silt clay and coffin stain 8548 of dark grey clay.
   No human bone preservation, 1 g unidentified cremated (animal?) bone in backfill 8189.

Non ceramic finds:

1   Possible **awl**. Fe. (See Scott, Chapter 5, cat. no. 5; Fig. 5.10). Context 8189, SF 1447.
2   **(Coffin) nails** (x 2). Fe. Context 8548, SF1440, Context 8606, SF1442.

Ceramic finds:

The remains of some 30 near complete pottery vessels were found within the backfill. Many appeared to have been deliberately broken before being placed into the grave, the only exception being a small but complete crucible (see Assemblage 25, Chapter 6; Figs 6.6 and 6.7).

Date   *c* AD 170, Period 2 Phase 4 (ceramics).

Group 8520 (Fig. 8.27)

Cut 8002, NE-SW, sub-rectangular measuring 2.46 m x 0.75 m x 0.14 m deep, with irregular, near vertical edges and a very uneven base. Filled by 8026.

Human bone: only incomplete parts of the right and left tibia and the right femur survive.

Non ceramic finds:

1   **(Coffin?) nail** (x 1). Fe. Context 8026, SF1406.

Ceramic finds:

1   **Flagon** in Hoo fabric R17, shattered. Late 1st century. Vessel 8051.

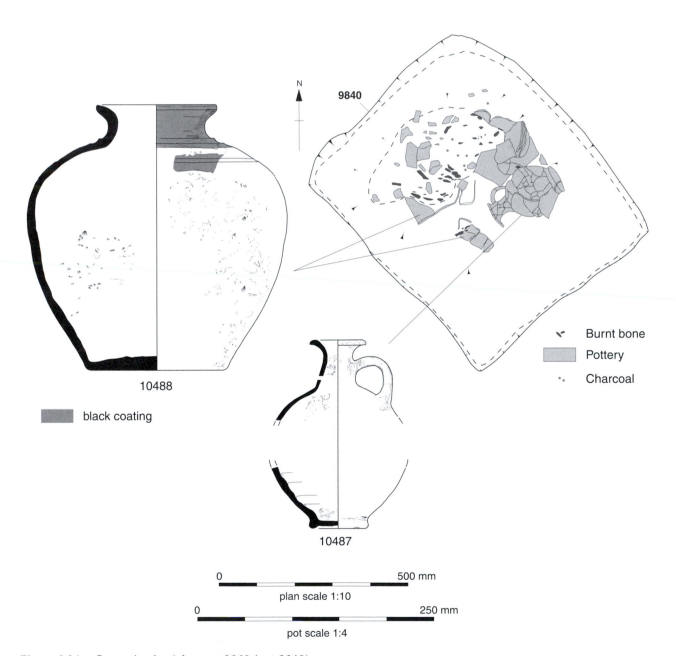

Figure 8.24   Cremation burial group 9860 (cut 9840).

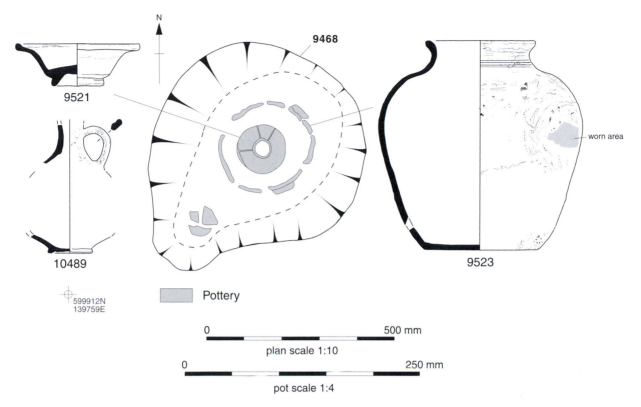

Figure 8.25   *Cremation burial group 9940 (cut 9468).*

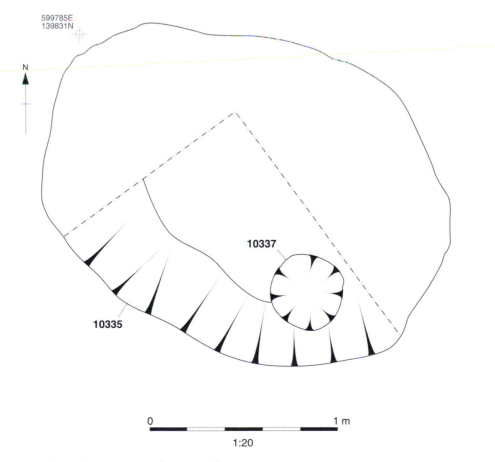

Figure 8.26   Cremation burial group 10337 (cut 10335).

327

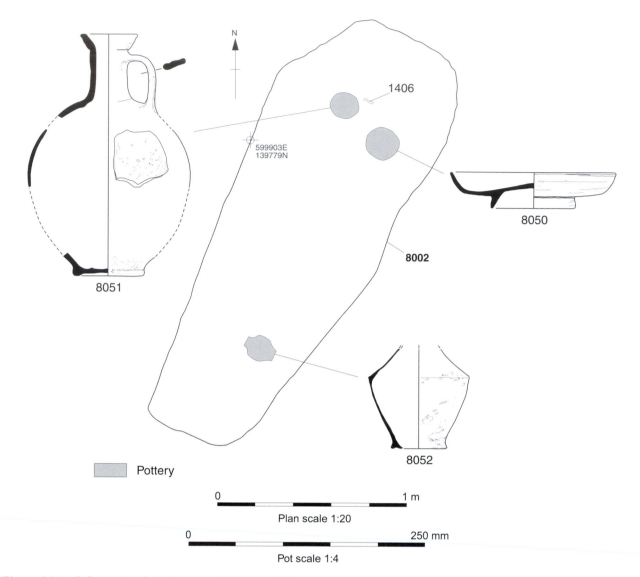

Figure 8.27   Inhumation burial group 8520 (cut 8002).

2   **Biconical beaker** of Monaghan type 2G1-9 in grey Upchurch fine ware, fabric R16, shattered. Date *c* AD 70-110. Vessel 8052.

3   **Platter**, Drag. 18, South Gaulish samian, stamp illegible, complete. Date *c* AD 43-90. Vessel 8050.

4   Abraded **sherd** in grog-tempered fabric B2.1. Context 8026.

Date   AD 70-90 (ceramics); Period 2 Phase 3.

Uncertain

Unstratified complete vessel (Fig. 8.28)

Complete pottery vessel, suggestive of grave context, an unstratified find from a service trench north-west of Area B.

1   **Platter**, Drag. 18/31, South Gaulish samian, stamp illegible, complete but very eroded. Date *c* AD 90-110. An eight-pointed 'star' has been incised on the underside of the vessel within the footring. Vessel 8068.

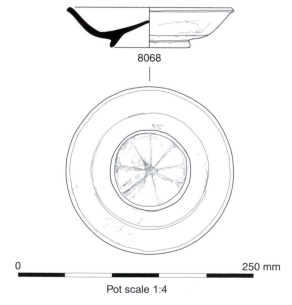

Figure 8.28   Samian Drag. 18/31 platter, unstratified find, probably derived from a grave.

HUMAN REMAINS
by Annsofie Witkin

Introduction

A total of twenty probable or possible cremation burials and ten possible inhumation graves were excavated: eleven cremations and eight inhumation graves in the Area C cemetery, eight cremations and two inhumation graves at various locations in Area B, and one cremation grave (9200) located outside of the area of investigation. Fragmentary bone survived from only one inhumation grave (8058 in grave group 8520) as a consequence of the acidic nature of the soils on the site, while burnt bone was recovered from nineteen cremation graves. Sixteen cremation graves (seven from Area B, eight from the Area C cemetery and the late Iron Age burial 9200) produced sufficiently large amounts of cremated bone to merit full osteological and palaeopathological analysis. These comprised six male, two female and eight unsexed adult individuals. Fragments from a further seven deposits (5046, 5144, 5164, 8189, 8955, 9469 and 9841) were thought to be from primary cremation burials, the first three from within the Area C cemetery. These burials produced between 1 and 55 grams of cremated bone each, groups which were too small to warrant full analysis. The investigation of the burial ritual concluded that there had been no preference in the selection of bone included in the burials. Three cremation burials were excavated in 20 mm spits to investigate the order of deposition, but the placement of the bone in the urns appears to have been random. Cremated animal bone was also found in four burials indicating that these had been present on the pyre.

Methods

Recovery

In excavation, most of the cremation burials were subjected to 100% recovery as whole-earth samples and subsequently wet sieved. Three urns, 218, 5025 and 5034 were compete enough to be lifted and excavated in 20 mm spits. A plan of each spit was produced to illustrate the distribution of the bones and any grave-goods within the urn. Material from the >2 mm fraction was retained *en masse*.

Osteological procedures

The cremated bone from each context was passed through a sieve stack of 10, 5 and 2 mm mesh size. The bones from each sieve were weighed and calculated as a percentage of the total weight of the burial. This allowed the degree of fragmentation to be calculated for each burial. The degree of fragmentation may indicate if the cremated bones have been further processed after the body had been burnt.

In each of the sieved groups, the bones were examined in detail and sorted into identifiable bone groups, which were defined as skull (including mandible and dentition), axial (clavicle, scapula, ribs, vertebra and pelvic elements), upper limb and lower limb. This may elucidate any deliberate bias in the skeletal elements collected for burial. Each sample was weighed on digital scales and details of colour and largest fragment were recorded. Where possible, the presence of individual bones within the defined bone groups was noted.

In any cremation burial, the majority of the bones are unidentifiable fragments of long bone shafts and spongy bones. The quantity of the unidentified bone is dependent upon the degree of fragmentation. It is of course easier to identify larger fragments than smaller. Some areas of the skeleton, for example the skull, are also easier to identify than other bones. This is a factor which needs to be considered when analysing cremation burials.

The estimation of age of a cremated individual is dependent upon the survival of particular skeletal elements indicative of age. In cremations of adult individuals, cranial suture closure (Meindl and Lovejoy 1985), degenerative changes to the auricular surface (Lovejoy *et al.* 1985) and pubic symphysis (Suchey and Brooks 1990) may be used as a general guide. The age categories used are:

Young Adult (YA)	19-25 years
Mature Adult (MA)	26-45 years
Older Adult (OA)	45 years +
Adult (A)	19-45 years +

Sex of the individual was obtained from the sexual dimorphic traits visible on the skeleton. A combination of traits are usually used to securely ascribe the sex of an individual. However, when dealing with fragmented material, the sexing of cremated remains is usually based on isolated features. Assessment of sex should therefore be viewed as tentative.

Condition of the bone and disturbance

Most of the cremated bone was in good condition. However, fragments from a few contexts were abraded. This may be due to erosion from acid solution passing through the burial medium. All but one (10338) of the cremation burials had been placed in urns. These were in turn positioned in graves. The graves were generally between 0.05 m and 0.25 m deep and had all been truncated by post-Roman ploughing which had usually also damaged the urns and the ancillary vessels. The urns recovered from the shallowest graves (between 0.05 and 0.07 m, group numbers 210, 5210, 5230 and 5240) were all broken with the cremated bone spread out around the fragmented vessel. This disturbance may also have contributed to the abrasion of bone fragments. Three burials were complete or near complete. Burial 5025 was situated within the Area C cemetery and was deposited at a depth of 0.25 m which had protected it from plough damage. The burial from group 220 and burial 1005, both in Area B, were also located at a slightly greater depth which favoured greater survival of the urns and their contents.

The burial found outside the area of excavation (9204) had been badly disturbed by the machine stripping approximately 75 mm into the natural and the subsequent investigation made by the workmen. Approximately half of the deposit of cremated bone remained *in situ* and the rest was relocated by the archaeologists, but due to the circumstances involving the discovery and recovery of the cremated deposit, it has been treated as incomplete. The bone was, however, in good condition and none of the fragments was abraded.

Quantification

A summary of the deposits that underwent full osteological and palaeopathological analysis is given in Table 8.2. This table also includes the material from seven context groups thought to derive from primary burials, but which were too small for full analysis (these are indicated by an asterisk in the table) The cremation burials ranged considerably in date (ex-cluding the single late Iron Age example), from perhaps as early as *c* mid 1st century AD (1263) to late 3rd-mid 4th century (group 5090).

Age and sex

Of the 16 fully recorded cremation burials, none represented an immature individual. Three (18.75%) were aged between 19 and 25 (young adult). Two (12.5%) were estimated to be aged between 26 and 45 years (mature adult) and eleven individuals (68.75%) could not be aged any closer than adult. Eight (50%) of the 16 individuals could be tentatively sexed. Of these, two were female and six male.

Pathology

Pathological lesions may be present on cremated bone, although the lesions seen may be fewer than one would expect from inhumation burials. The cremated bones present in a burial do not necessarily represent a complete individual and this may hamper the diagnosis of a specific disease.

Table 8.2   Human remains: Summary of cremated bones (Contexts that produced too little bone for analysis are marked with an asterisk).

Context	Group	Period	Weight (Total)	NI	Age	Sex	Pathology/identifiable fragments of small groups
206	210	AD 170-200	116 g	1	A	?	
208	210		57 g		A	?	
211	210		99 g		MA?	F?	Degenerative spinal joint disease
213	210		1 g		?	?	
215	210		29 g		A	?	
233	210		47 g		A	?	
217/250	210		37 g		A	?	
			386 g				
219	220	AD 200-250	1362 g	1	YA	F?	
231	220		2 g		?	?	
			1364 g				
1005	1007	AD 43-150	1225 g	1	A	M?	
1263	1261	AD 0-50	125 g	1	A	?	
5008	5050	AD 170-250	814 g	1	A	?	
5018	5080	AD 150-250	706 g	1	YA	M	
5025	5090	AD 270-350	1310 g	1	YA	M?	
5034	5110	AD 43-100	411 g	1	A	?	
5041	5120	AD 43-200+	343 g	1	A	M?	
5046*	5130		1 g	1	?	?	
5062	5070		31 g	1	A	?	
5064	5070	AD 200-250	575 g		A	?	
			606 g				
5129	5210	AD 170-250	478 g	1	A	?	
5133	5220		119 g	1	A	?	
5134	5220		206 g	1	A	?	
5135	5220	AD 120-150	550 g	1	A	M?	
			875 g				
5144*	5230		3 g	1	?	?	(long bone)
5164*	5240		55 g	1	A		(skull vault, humerus)
8189*	8160		1 g	1	?	?	
8955*	8956		53 g	1	A?	?	(humerus)
9204	9200	Late Iron Age	703 g	1	A	M?	
9469*	9940		7 g	1	?	?	(skull vault, long bone shaft)
9524	9940	AD 70-100	837 g	1	MA?	?	
9841*	9860		1 g	1	?	?	
9843	9860	AD 70-150	283 g	1	A	?	
10338	10337		268 g	1	A	?	Maxillary dental abscess

Two (12.5%) of the individuals had pathological lesions present. Cremation deposit 211 had one vertebral body fragment with new bone formation along the rim. This osteophyte formation is a compensatory reaction to the degenerative changes of the intervertebral disc (Roberts and Manchester 1995, 106). The condition would have caused stiffness and intermittent back ache.

Cremation deposit 10338 had a maxillary apical abscess. These are commonly caused by the introduction of bacteria to the pulp cavity through a carious lesion. The pus collected may track to the apex of the root. As the pus accumulates, a hole is formed which drains it. An abscess may also occur when an individual develops periodontal disease and a periodontal pocket (Roberts and Manchester 1995, 50).

Pyre technology and ritual

Efficiency of cremation

The efficiency of a cremation is dependent upon the construction of the pyre, position of the body, tending of the pyre, duration of the cremation and the temperature of the pyre (McKinley 1994, 82-84). The process of cremation is one of oxidisation of the organic components of the body and dehydration. If there is poor oxidisation, the bones will be grey, black, blue or even brown in colour.

When colouration and cracking is variable, the skeleton is likely to have been exposed to a variety of temperatures on the pyre. This may be caused by the movement of the body on the pyre during the cremation process, such as during the collapse of the pyre. When the bones are mainly charred black or blue-grey, this might indicate insufficient time for the completion of the cremation process. It may also signify that the pyre was not tended properly. Poorly oxidised small bones and fragments may be those which fell to the lower, cooler part of the pyre during the initial stages of the process. Large fragments may also indicate a lack of pyre-tending which may serve to break up the bone (Boyle 1999, 178).

The colour of the bone fragments from the Westhawk Farm cremation burials was predominantly white. Only a very small amount of small fragments was black or grey coloured. This indicates a high degree of efficiency in the cremation process and that the process was complete. Moreover, since it was only small fragments which were coloured, it is likely that the pyres were well tended.

Weight of bone

Observations at modern crematoria have shown that collectable fragments (<2 mm fraction) from an adult cremation burial weigh between 1000-2400 g with an average of 1650 g. Weights between 1600-3000 g have also been cited, but it is unclear whether this also includes the weight of bone dust (McKinley 1997a, 68).

The weights of the Westhawk Farm deposits are variable ranging from 118 g to 1364 g (see Tables 8.2 and 8.3). Of the sixteen burials, three appeared to be undisturbed: 220 (1362 g), 1005 (1225 g) and 5025, (1310 g). The weight of these complete burials are lower than the average weight values quoted above. It therefore appears that all bones were not collected from the pyre for burial. It was observed during analysis that there was very little spongy bone present - including the small bones of the hands and feet, articular surfaces of long bones and vertebral body fragments. This suggests poor bone survival which could equally account for the lower bone weight. Alternatively, a combination of the two aforementioned explanations may account for the lower than average weight of the cremation burials.

Six cremation burials weighed between 500 and 1000 grams. These were burials 5008, 5018, 5070, 5220, 9204 and 9524. Seven weighed between 1 and 500 grams and these were burials 1263, 5034, 5041, 5129, 9843 and 10338 and from cremation group 210. The weights of these burials are relatively low. This may signify selection of bones for a token deposit. However, the most likely explanation is that the low weight is due to significant post-Roman disturbance, which took place in the form of ploughing.

Fragmentation

The factors governing fragmentation of cremated bones are cremation, collection, burial, excavation and post-excavation treatment (McKinley 1997a, 69). These processes do not involve deliberate breakage of the bone. Since larger bones are easier to identify, the level of fragmentation is reflected in the percentage of identifiable bones.

Of all the Westhawk Farm cremation burials, 44.5% of the bone fragments were in the 10 mm fraction. The average maximum fragment size was 49.4 mm. Within the category of undisturbed burials, 56.9% of the bone fragments were in the 10 mm group and the average maximum fragment size measured 56.5 mm.

The fragmentation rates were compared with those from a late Iron Age cremation cemetery (90-50 BC) and a Romano-British cremation cemetery (AD 70-150) from the A27 Westhampnett Bypass site, West Sussex (McKinley 1997a and b). The late Iron Age burials were unurned. The Romano-British burials were mostly dated c AD 70-150 and thus fall in the central part of the date range of the Westhawk Farm assemblage (see Table 8.3).

It is apparent that the maximum fragment size in both the undisturbed category and the total assemblage at Westhawk Farm is slightly larger than both the Iron Age and Romano-British assemblages at Westhampnett. However, the percentages of fragments present in the 10 mm group (all cremation burials) is more comparable with the figure given for all late Iron Age burials at Westhampnett. This probably reflects the level of disturbance amongst the Westhawk Farm burials since unurned burials are more prone to fragmentation than urned burials. The proportion of fragments present in the 10 mm

Table 8.3   Human remains: Comparison of fragmentation data from Westhawk Farm and Westhampnett Bypass Late Iron Age and Romano-British periods.

Fragments	Westhawk Farm		Westhampnett Late Iron-Age		Westhampnett Romano-British	
	All	Undisturbed	All	Undisturbed	All	Undisturbed
Max size	49.4 mm	56.5 mm	41.1 mm	43.0 mm	42.0 mm	50.0 mm
10 mm group	44.5%	56.9%	42.7%	68.4%	55.7%	69.8%

fraction in the undisturbed burials is lower than in both the Iron Age and Romano-British groups at Westhampnett. Although the total burnt bone present in the Westhawk Farm undisturbed burials suggest that the burials were intact, the lower percentage represented in the 10 mm fraction may again reflect the level of ground disturbance present on site.

The level of fragmentation and fragment size of the Westhawk Farm burials are within the normal ranges observed (McKinley 1994). There is nothing to suggest that any deliberate fragmentation of the burnt bone took place prior to burial.

Skeletal elements within the burials

Fragments from all body part groups were present amongst all the burials (see Table 8.4). In general, fewer fragments from the upper limb were identified than any other body group. This was related to the fragment size. Moreover, humeri, ulnae and radii can be easily confused with femora and fibulae. When fragments are generally small, fewer fragments may therefore identified. The relatively high proportion of cranial fragments is due to the ease of identification since the bone morphology displayed is unique to this part of the skeleton. Since bone from all areas of the skeleton was included in the burials this suggests that there was no preference in the selection of bones included in the burials.

Deposition of bone

Three urns were excavated in 20 mm spits in order to investigate the sequence of deposition. The proportions of bone fragments within each spit are presented in Figure 8.29. Comparatively, the pattern of deposition of bone in the urns is very similar in cremation burials 5025 and 5034, in which the majority of all fragments are situated in the middling spits and there is very little bone in the top of the urn or in the bottom. In cremation group 220, however, the bone fragments are more evenly distributed throughout the different levels of fill of the urn. There is also a slightly higher proportion of bone in spit 5, at the base of the urn.

Since this is a very small sample, it is very difficult to speculate as to the reasons why there is a difference in the deposition of the bone fragments. It is also impossible to discern which one of the two patterns may have been the norm. There is, however, a difference in the burial location. Cremation burials 5025 and 5034 were located in the cemetery in Area C while 220 was situated in Area B. The different location of the burials may hint at a difference in the burial practice which may be reflected in the deposition of the bone within the urns.

When comparing the distribution of identified fragments per body group, the pattern of deposition is broadly similar in all three burials. Skull and lower limb bones are found throughout the different levels

Table 8.4   Human remains: Weights of cremated bone within anatomical groups and size ranges.

Context	10 mm					5 mm					2 mm					Total Weight
	Skull	Axial	Upper Limb	Lower Limb	Uniden-tified	Skull	Axial	Upper Limb	Lower Limb	Uniden-tified	Skull	Axial	Upper Limb	Lower Limb	Uniden-tified	
210	10 g	19 g	12 g	7 g	80 g	4 g	6 g	2 g	2 g	153 g	1 g	1 g	0 g	0 g	89 g	386 g
220	72 g	106 g	23 g	125 g	295 g	19 g	14 g	14 g	9 g	436 g	2 g	2 g	0 g	0 g	245 g	1362 g
1005	111 g	74 g	76 g	98 g	595 g	12 g	12 g	6 g	6 g	130 g	0 g	1 g	0 g	0 g	104 g	1225g
1263	2 g	9 g	4 g	11 g	16 g	3 g	1 g	0 g	0 g	52 g	0 g	0 g	0 g	0 g	27 g	125 g
5008	92 g	30 g	12 g	43 g	137 g	28 g	22 g	12 g	8 g	296 g	1 g	2 g	1 g	0 g	130 g	814 g
5018	59 g	3 g	25 g	76 g	132 g	17 g	9 g	0 g	7 g	269 g	1 g	0 g	0 g	0 g	108 g	706 g
5025	147 g	92 g	26 g	73 g	306 g	21 g	20 g	4 g	6 g	397 g	1 g	2 g	0 g	0 g	215 g	1310 g
5034	70 g	44 g	7 g	54 g	55 g	9 g	11 g	3 g	3 g	123 g	0 g	1 g	1 g	0 g	30 g	411 g
5041	22 g	12 g	7 g	32 g	64 g	1 g	7 g	1 g	3 g	140 g	0 g	1 g	0 g	1 g	52 g	343 g
5070	16 g	28 g	29 g	54 g	109 g	6 g	13 g	3 g	3 g	211 g	0 g	1 g	0 g	0 g	102 g	575 g
5129	22 g	16 g	6 g	14 g	117 g	6 g	9 g	3 g	5 g	204 g	0 g	1 g	0 g	0 g	75 g	478 g
5220	61 g	11 g	26 g	60 g	187 g	31 g	18 g	4 g	11 g	334 g	2 g	2 g	0 g	0 g	138 g	875 g
9204	14 g	7 g	4 g	45 g	89 g	10 g	4 g	5 g	7 g	274 g	5 g	0 g	0 g	0 g	239 g	703 g
9524	13 g	16 g	19 g	58 g	256 g	6 g	7 g	1 g	6 g	266 g	1 g	2 g	0 g	0 g	186 g	837 g
9843	11 g	5 g	7 g	10 g	34 g	13 g	8 g	4 g	3 g	101 g	0 g	2 g	1 g	1 g	83 g	283 g
10338	13 g	2 g	12 g	12 g	16 g	9 g	5 g	3 g	3 g	149 g	1 g	1 g	1 g	1 g	40 g	268 g

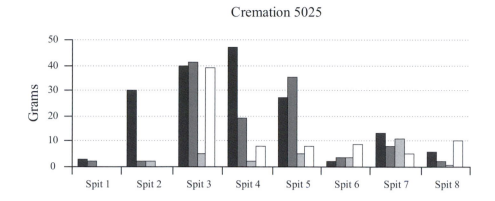

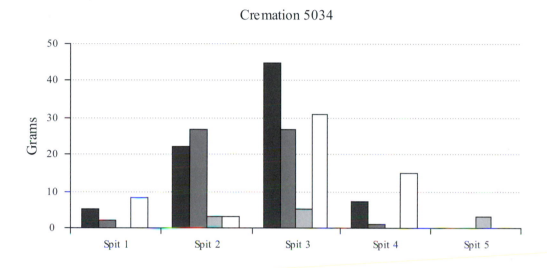

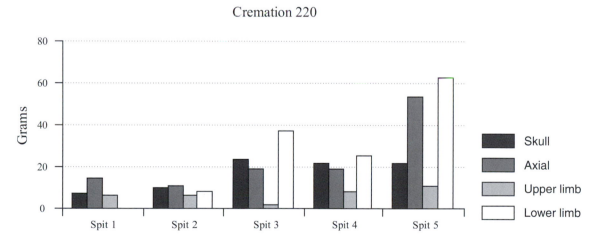

Figure 8.29   Quantities of bone fragments within each spit, cremations 5025, 5034 and 220.

of the urns. This pattern of deposited bone in the urns does not suggest a systematic order of deposition with, for example, collection beginning at one end of the pyre and progressing to the other. There are various possible explanations for the random deposition of the bone. It may be that the bone was raked together off the pyre prior to collection and mixed in the process; several people may have taken part in the collection of the bone and deposited the bone at random, or the urn may not have been the original receptacle used during collection (McKinley 1997b, 252).

Animal bone and grave goods

Cremated animal bone was found with four cremation burials: 5025, 5135, 9204 and group 220, with bird, pig and sheep bones identified (see Charles, Chapter 9 below). The quantities were in general very small, a few grams in each burial. However, cremation deposit 9204 contained a substantial amount of bone from bird, sheep and pig. The presence of animal bone is dependent upon a) it being collected from the pyre along with the human remains and b) the fragments being recognised as animal and not human. Since the surviving sample sizes show that not all human bone was collected from the pyre, it is likely that not all animal bone was collected. Moreover, some fragments of unidentifiable animal long bone are also likely to have been overlooked in analysis. It may be noted that while cremation deposit 5025 contained jet beads and a copper alloy bracelet these objects were, unlike the bird bones present, unburnt and had therefore been deposited in the urn after the cremated bone had been collected from the pyre.

Cremated remains from non-burial contexts

Small quantities of cremated bone were recovered from a variety of non-burial contexts and are listed below (Table 8.5). The bones derived from fills of pits, ditches, post holes and gullies as well as from various layers. These cremated bone deposits listed here weighed between 1 and 18 grams and were too small to warrant full analysis. They occurred sporadically in all phases up to the middle of the 3rd century AD, with no particular concentration in any one phase. In no case was the material sufficiently diagnostic to provide an indication of age or sex.

Table 8.5   Human remains: Small groups of cremated bone from non-burial deposits.

Context	Context type	Phase	Weight	Identifiable fragments
414	Fill of ditch 413	3	1 g	
461	Fill of pit 415	3	1 g	
530	Fill of hollow way 626	3-4	2 g	Skull vault
538	Fill of pit 539	4	3 g	
687	Layer	5	1 g	
873	Fill of pit 844	3	4 g	
971	Fill of ditch 975	4	2 g	
1092	Fill of pit 1093	5	1 g	
1156	Layer	3	18 g	Long bone shaft
5154	Fill of ?waterhole 5153	3	3 g	Long bone shaft
7126	Layer	4	7 g	Long bone shaft
7127	Layer	4	3 g	Long bone shaft
7212	Fill of gully 7211	4	15 g	
7240	Fill of waterhole 7239	5	2 g	Long bone shaft
7255	Fill of ditch 7254	5	1 g	
7265	Fill of ditch 7266	5	1 g	
7282	Fill of gully 7280	4	1 g	
7309	Fill of pit 7269	4-5	1 g	Long bone shaft
7313	Fill of pit 7312	3-4	7 g	Long bone shaft
7732	Fill of pit 7733	4	2 g	Long bone shaft
8128	Fill of ditch 8127	4-5	1 g	Long bone shaft
8191	Fill of posthole 8190	5	1 g	Long bone shaft
8366	Fill of ditch 8240	2-3	2 g	Long bone shaft
8697	Fill of gully 8696	4-5	1 g	
8793	Fill of gully 8792	2	4 g	
8879	Fill of gully 8880	2	3 g	Skull vault, long bone shaft
9504	Fill of gully 9503	2-4	2 g	
9823	Layer	?	2 g	
10336	Fill of hollow 10335	2-4	2 g	

Chapter 9:   Environmental Evidence

ANIMAL BONES
by Bethan Charles

Introduction

A total of 1376 fragments of bone was recovered by hand in the course of the excavation. A further 1045 fragments of bone were recovered from environmental samples, sieved through meshes of >10 mm, 10-4 mm and 4-2 mm where necessary.

In addition to the bones recovered from environmental sieving, 40 fragments of burnt animal bone were recovered from sieving of human cremation burials 219, 5025 and 5135 and further material, both burnt and unburnt, came from grave 9200. These elements have not been included in the tables and are discussed below. A further 36 fragments of burnt animal bone were recovered from non-burial contexts across the site. These are included in the overall totals given above.

Condition

Animal bone did not survive in most excavated contexts, owing to the acidic nature of soils across the site. Occasional survival of bone is attributable to localised variations in soil acidity levels, with waterlogged or semi-waterlogged contexts offering the best chance of bone survival. Even so, the large majority of the bone recovered from the site was in poor condition with signs of root damage and chemical etching, characteristics which contributed to the difficulties in identifying many bones. Almost 70% of the bulk bone had fresh breaks, again indicating the fragile condition of many of the elements. It is certain that many signs of butchery, carnivore damage or pathological changes in the bone were obscured because of the attritional damage on many of the bones.

Methodology

Numbers of fragments were recorded along with an estimation of the number of individuals in each context and in total. All elements were recorded, including vertebrae, ribs and teeth. Insufficient bones were identified to species for the Minimum Number of Individuals (MNI) to be calculated.

For the Caprine sub-family an attempt was made to separate sheep and goat bones, the similarity of which often pose difficulties in identification, using the criteria of Boessneck (1969) and Prummel and Frisch (1986), in addition to the use of the reference material housed at Oxford. However, since no goat bones were positively identified in the collection all caprine bones are referred to as sheep in the text.

Ageing was based on tooth eruption and wear as well as on epiphyseal fusion. Tooth eruption and wear was measured using a combination of Payne (1973), Grant (1982) and Halstead's (1985) tables for cattle and sheep. Silver's tables (1969) were used to give the timing of epiphyseal closure for cattle and pig, again due to lack of other indicative elements from other species. However, there were insufficient elements to provide meaningful information for this report. All data can be found in the archive. No elements were complete enough to allow measurement.

Results

Tables 9.1 and 9.2 show that only a small number of bones were identified to species, principally because of the poor condition of the bone as mentioned above. The majority of elements identified to species were teeth. All of the elements identified to species from Phase 5 deposits were recovered from a waterhole (796) and represent the majority of identified fragments of bone from the site.

Cattle were the dominant species through all phases of occupation. However, it is very likely that they have been over-represented in the assemblage since their bones are larger and more robust than those of pig and sheep, which may not have survived as well as a result of the soil conditions on the site.

Two cattle mandibles from ditches assigned to Phases 3 and 4 were aged. Both were between 30 and 36 months old at death. Two further cattle mandibles from waterhole 796 were aged at 18-30 months and 30-36 months old at death. This may indicate that the majority of cattle killed were animals that had been bred for their meat, rather than animals kept for dairy products or for traction purposes. It is possible that beef made up the majority of the meat diet of the inhabitants during this phase, but the numbers are too small for certainty.

Only two sheep mandibles were complete enough for ageing. One from a Phase 6 layer (context 7279) was between 2 and 3 years of age and the other from a Phase 4 ditch (context 10373) was 4 to 6 years of age at death. Individually, these do not tell us very much about the general age of the animals at death. However, most sheep in Britain during the Roman period were primarily kept for wool (Grant 1975) and would have been older animals.

A small number of horse bones were recovered, including two mandibles from contexts 7279 and 7346 as well as a few fragments of feet bones and teeth. None of the elements had signs of butchery. One fragment of red deer antler was found within each of contexts 1381, 366 and 298 (298 is in waterhole 796).

Table 9.1   Animal bones: Total number of hand collected bone fragments by species and phase (all Period 2).

Phase	Sheep	Cattle	Pig	Horse	Red Deer	Unidentified	Total
2	3	4	1	0	0	45	53
3	1	5	0	1	0	15	22
4	9	40	7	1	0	258	315
5	3	28	1	2	3	402	439
6	3	14	0	7	0	355	379
Unphased	3	13	0	0	0	149	165
Total	22	104	9	11	3	1224	1373

Table 9.2   Animal bones: Total number of bones from sieved environmental samples by species and phase (all Period 2).

Phase	Sheep	Cattle	Pig	Bird	Fish	Unidentified	Total
2	0	0	0	0	0	1	1
3	1	0	0	0	0	8	9
4	2	5	1	1	0	94	104
5	2	7	1	1	1	878	889
6	0	0	0	0	0	31	31
Unphased	0	0	0	0	0	11	11
Total	5	12	2	2	1	1023	1045

None of the antlers had signs of working, but all were in poor condition and fragmented which may have obscured cut marks. It is not clear if deer were eaten, since at least one of the antlers had been shed. A small quantity of bird and fish bone was recovered, all from contexts in waterhole 796. Neither of the bird bones could be identified to species. A single vertebra belonging to a flatfish was recovered from context 310.

The majority of the 36 fragments of burnt bone recovered were from Phase 4 and 5 contexts. There is, however, no evidence for spatial concentrations of burnt refuse from the site.

Animal bone from burials

A total of 354 fragments of bone were recovered from contexts 219, 5025, 5134, 5135, 9200, 9202, 9204 and 9205 among the remains of human cremated bone. The majority of the material from grave 9200 (contexts 9200, 9202, 9204 and 9205) was unburnt, however.

Twelve fragments were recovered from context 219, but none could be identified to species. A further 22 fragments of bone were recovered from context 5025 and included fragments of juvenile sheep bone (one intermediate phalanx and the unfused distal articulation of tibia) and two bird bones (ulna and coracoid, both too fragmentary to be identified to species). A single unfused proximal section of a sheep proximal phalanx was recovered from context 5134. Five fragments including fragments of bird bone shaft were recovered from context 5135.

The majority of the material (314 fragments) came from burial 9200 contexts (9200, 9202, 9204 and 9205). Context 9200 contained elements from a very young/neonatal sheep, including 26 fragments of vertebrae including the atlas and axis. Also identified were five pig teeth which had been stained green, almost cer-

tainly from contamination by associated material. The only burnt bone from this context was a single fragment of a cremated radius, probably of sheep, which was completely burnt white. None of the 150 fragments of bone from context 9202 had been burnt. These again consisted of the remains of a neonatal sheep including both the right and left femur and the unfused proximal articulation of a left tibia, in addition to more vertebral fragments. Many of the fragments were broken and could not be positively identified, but they included fragments of ribs which may have been associated with the neonatal sheep skeleton.

Sixty-three fragments of bone from context 9204 included 31 unburnt fragments, many of unidentified bone stained green, along with a stained fragment of pig molar. The remaining material was all cremated. It included three fragments of undiagnositic bird. Identifiable elements included three fragments of pig molar teeth and a small part of an innominate (pelvis) acetabulum, probably of sheep, though not positively identified. The remaining pieces were too fragmented for positive identification.

Twenty-nine fragments of bone were extracted from context 9205. The only cremated fragments included most of a sheep astragalus and the remains of a pig molar in pieces. Other identified elements consisted of a pig's premolar tooth stained green and part of the lower shaft of a juvenile sheep's tibia. The remaining elements were not burnt and appeared to be from a juvenile animal consisting of fragments of the vertebral column and other broken and unidentifiable elements.

It is likely that these bones are the remains of burial gifts placed with the human remains. The majority of the material was not burnt indicating that the gifts were placed with the human remains after the cremation process

Discussion and summary

The small quantity of bone identified from the site does not provide much information regarding the diet and the animal husbandry practices of the inhabitants of Westhawk Farm. It is clear that the main domestic species, cattle, sheep and pig, were present at the site; beef may have been the main source of meat for the inhabitants, the minimal amount of age data for cattle suggesting that these animals were exploited for meat rather than other purposes. It has been shown that many of the more Romanised sites in Britain tended to have higher levels of consumption of beef than mutton or lamb (King 1978). However, as previously mentioned the small, poorly-preserved assemblage does not provide enough reliable information to allow further interpretation.

Small amounts of fish, bird and possibly deer also may have contributed to the diet. Bird, along with sheep/lamb, was also placed on cremation pyres in two cases. In the late Iron Age cremation grave 9200 bird and sheep/lamb were joined by pig, and unburnt remains of pig and sheep/lamb were also present in this burial.

PALYNOLOGICAL ANALYSIS OF SEDIMENTS FROM ROMAN WATERHOLES
by Patricia E J Wiltshire

Introduction

Assessment of sediments from three Roman waterholes at Westhawk Farm showed that only one (feature 796, samples 110 and 111) was sufficiently polleniferous to warrant full analysis. However, useful information was obtained from the assessment data from feature 9179 (sample 778) and will be used to supplement data yielded by feature 796. The sediments analysed from feature 796 accumulated mostly in the 2nd century, although the upper part of the core probably represents the early 3rd century. The sediments in feature 9179 are thought to be mostly 1st–2nd century in date so the two features are contemporaneous to some extent. Full details of the initial assessment are given in the post-excavation assessment report produced by Oxford Archaeology (OAU 2001), and the methodology for feature 9179 is given in that document. Palynological interpretation was also outlined in that report and will only be referred to here where it complements that of the fully analysed material, or where there are obvious differences which might reflect spatial or temporal differences in the palynological record.

Methods
Processing

Standard preparation procedures were used (Dimbleby 1985). Every sample was acetolysed and treated with hydrofluoric acid. Samples were lightly stained with 0.5% safranine and mounted in glycerol jelly.

Counting and expression of data

Pollen counting was carried out with a Zeiss phase contrast microscope at x400 and x1000 magnification. Counts for pollen and plant spores ranged between 350 and 495, depending on pollen concentration in each sample. These were expressed as percentages of total land pollen and spores (tlp/s). Microscopic charcoal (charred fragments >5.0 micrometres) was expressed as the number of fragments for a count of 100 palynomorphs. Fungal hyphal fragments were expressed as a percentage of total palynomorphs (including fungal hyphal fragments and fungal spores but excluding algae). Fungal spores were expressed in the same way as for hyphae. Algae were expressed as percentage of the palynomorph sum plus algae (but excluding fungi).

Nomenclature

Palynological nomenclature follows that of Bennett *et al.* (1994) and Moore *et al.* (1991). Cereal-type pollen refers to all Poaceae grains >40 μm with annulus diameters >8 μm (Anderson 1979; Edwards 1989). Botanical nomenclature follows that of Stace (1997).

Pollen diagrams

Diagrams were drawn with Tilia and Tiliagraph (Grimm 1992). Figure 9.1 is a summary diagram while Figures 9.2 and 9.3 show all taxa. For convenience of description, the diagrams were zoned subjectively and designated WHF1-3 respectively.

Results

The results for feature 796 are given in standard pollen diagrams Figures 9.1 to 9.3. The results for feature 9179 are given in the post-excavation assessment report (OAU 2001) and will not be repeated in detail here.

Waterhole 796

This feature has been interpreted as a waterhole with fills having accumulated between approximately AD 70 and AD 350 or a little earlier. If the chronology provided by artefactual evidence is correct, the sequence of sediments collected for palynological analysis might represent a period of about 100 years (just before AD 150 to just after AD 250). The sequences cut across three phases of sediment accumulation (Phases 3-5) with most of the sequence representing about 50 years from AD 150 to AD 200 (Phase 4). The upper 100 mm or so (Phase 5) represents the 50 years up to AD 250. This suggests that sediments accumulated relatively quickly in Phase 4 and rather slowly in Phase 5. It must be stressed, however, that the chronology presented here is dependent upon artefactual evidence rather than absolute dating and so must be viewed with some caution.

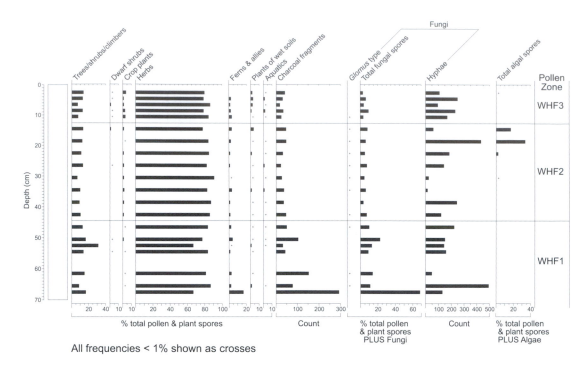

Figure 9.1   Waterhole 796: summary pollen diagram.

So few palynomorphs were found in the basal sample that the results here can only be indicative of plant taxa present rather than their relative abundance in the pollen record. The percentage values for this level must be viewed with care. However, counts adequate for reliable statistical representation were achieved for the rest of the core. The relative smoothness of the pollen curves indicate the integrity of sediment accretion and there is no evidence for any marked discontinuity or hiatus, nor anything to suggest that significant amounts of allochthonous material were dumped into the feature. Such effects would generally be reflected in erratic pollen curves.

Fungal hyphae and spores were well represented throughout the sequence. It is difficult to understand the origin of these remains although it is possible that they represent active fungal growth on organic debris falling into the feature. If this were the case, it is likely that this was during periods when water levels in the feature were relatively low, and concentrations of free oxygen were high. The relatively high percentages of unidentified palynomorphs might also reflect a fluctuating redox potential. The curve represents grains that were so badly decomposed or damaged that they could not be identified with confidence. This effect can be due to high levels of bioactivity within the sediment and this is, in turn, can be a function of availability of free oxygen.

The presence of iron pyrite framboids throughout the core shows that there were certainly periods when there was stagnant standing water in the feature. These are formed under conditions of (a) exceedingly low redox potential, (b) where there is rotting organic matter, and (c) where there is a source

of detrital iron (Wiltshire *et al.* 1994). They usually develop under conditions of waterlogging where redox potential drops to the level at which fermentation and anaerobic respiratory pathways are engaged rather than aerobic ones. The byproducts of fermentation then provide substrates for the iron-reducing and sulphur-reducing bacteria. The source of sulphur might be the fermenting organic material, but the iron is usually derived from eroding soil. It is probable that soil was, indeed, eroding into the feature since *Glomus*-type fungal vesicles were present. These fungi always grow in association with living plant roots in aerated soils, so their presence in an archaeological feature might indicate that soil erosion was contributing to the accumulating deposits.

The feature seems to have been colonised and fringed by emergents, aquatics, and plants of wet soil such as Batrachium type *Ranunculus* (e.g. water crowfoot), *Sparganium* type (eg bur-reed), *Typha latifolia* (greater reedmace), *Alisma* (water plantain), *Apium* type (e.g. fool's watercress), *Mentha* (water mint), *Lythrum salicaria* (purple loosestrife), and *Filipendula* (meadowsweet). The muddy and sodden areas in the environs of the waterhole were colonised by *Lythrum portula* (water purslane), *Sphagnum* moss, *Equisetum* (horsetail), and Cyperaceae (sedges). All these attest further to the presence of standing water and wet soils in and around the feature throughout the period of sediment accumulation.

Microscopic charcoal was present throughout the sequence, but was most abundant in the earlier period of accumulation. This might mean that some activity involving wood burning was centred near the feature early in its history, but that it moved away from the immediate environs later.

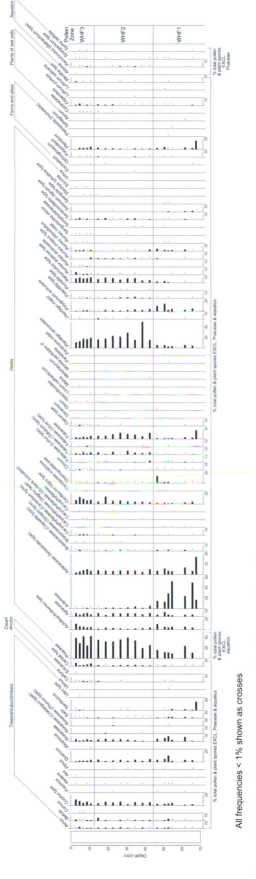

All frequencies < 1% shown as crosses

Figure 9.2   Waterhole 796: detailed pollen diagram, trees etc.

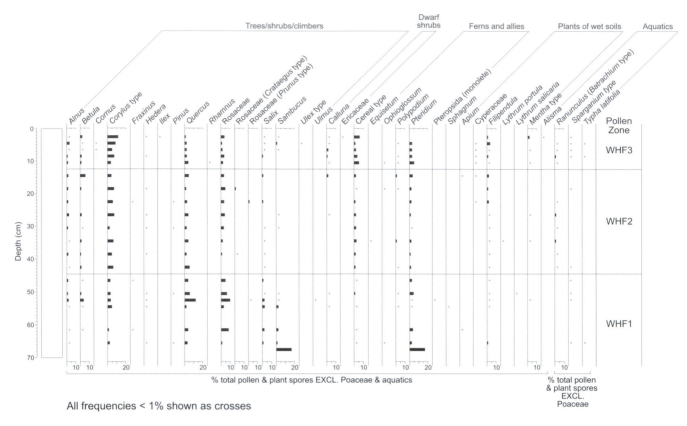

Figure 9.3   Waterhole 796: detailed pollen diagram, herbs.

Zone WHF1

Figure 9.1 suggests that this zone represents a time when the feature was set in a largely open landscape. However, a wide range of woody plants was growing in the catchment. The most abundant trees and shrubs seem to have been *Quercus* (oak), *Corylus* (hazel), and *Salix* (willow), although *Alnus* (alder), *Betula* (birch), *Pinus* (pine), Ulmus (elm), and *Fraxinus* (ash) were also growing in the area. However, the low pollen percentages of most woody plants imply that they were either growing some distance away from the feature, present in very small numbers, or heavily managed so that pollen production was much reduced.

When the low pollen production and poor dispersal of rosaceous pollen is considered, the percentages of this taxon in zone WHF1 are very high indeed. Unfortunately, preservation was such that it was not possible to identify the plants contributing this pollen with great precision; it may have been derived from *Rubus fruticosus* agg. (bramble), *Rosa* spp. (rose), or *Crataegus* type (eg hawthorn). However, it is much more likely to represent hawthorn or bramble since pollen of *Rosa* (rose) is very rare in the pollen rain (Wiltshire 1996). Other woody plants include *Prunus* type (e.g. sloe), *Sambucus* (elder), and *Hedera* (ivy). In each case, the representation was very low, but it must be remembered that all these taxa are insect-pollinated and even a single pollen grain can represent a significant biomass of the plant involved (personal observation).

There is little doubt that, although the landscape immediately around the feature was open, a diverse range of trees and shrubs was growing in its environs. Some, such as pine, birch, alder, ash, and elm were probably growing some distance away from the feature or, in the case of the deciduous trees, being managed so intensively that pollen production was low. Oak, hazel, and willow were possibly more abundant, the latter probably growing very close indeed to the waterhole. The wide range of insect-pollinated woody taxa represented in the sediments indicates that they were growing close by and, when the assemblage of shrubs is considered, it is reasonable to suggest that they formed a hedge and/or an area of scrubby vegetation close to the feature.

If the rosaceous plant(s) so well represented in the pollen spectra were *Rubus* (bramble), it is possible to imagine that the ground around the feature was either neglected or that the base of the hedge was dominated by dense growths of blackberry bushes. Not only would they add to the effectiveness of a hedge as a barrier or boundary, but could also have provided an important seasonal source of fruit.

There is little doubt that the area around the waterhole was open ground with abundant herbs and weeds. Poaceae (grasses) were relatively poorly represented and the most abundant herbs seem to have been ruderals typical of trampled waste and rough ground and 'back yards'. These include *Artemisia* (mugwort/wormwood), *Achillea/Anthemis* type (eg yarrow/scentless mayweed), Chenopodiaceae (eg goosefoots), Lactuceae (dandelion-like plants), *Polygonum aviculare* (knotweed), *Solanum nigrum* (black bindweed), and *Rumex* (docks). In particular, the values reached by *Artemisia* are remarkably high.

This herbaceous assemblage could have resulted from various kinds of pressure, including that of human trampling and compaction of local soils. However, it might also have been the result of animals poaching the ground around the waterhole, with intense and selective grazing affecting the nature of the local herbaceous communities. Certainly, low values for grasses and high values for unpalatable plants such as mugwort, and those adapted for trampling and grazing such as knotweed and dandelion-type plants, are suggestive of high grazing pressure. Cereals were also being grown and/processed in the environs of the waterhole and many of the herbaceous plants listed above are also common weeds of arable land but their pollen might even have found their way into the feature from straw or animal dung.

Zone WHF2

The zone boundary appears to mark significant changes in local land use. Apart from hazel, which had slightly higher percentage values in this zone, trees and shrubs in the catchment seem to have suffered some impact which resulted in their lower representation in the pollen rain. The most markedly affected tree seems to have been oak, but Rosaceae, willow, elder also declined. Considering the low pollen production and poor dispersal of these latter pollen taxa, their decline might be considered to be significant.

There were also marked changed in the local herbaceous flora, including a remarkable decline in ruderals such as mugwort, yarrow/scentless mayweed, goosefoot, knotweed, and docks. Small ruderals that are rarely represented in the pollen rain, such as black bindweed, also disappeared from the record while bracken, an aggressive invader of open areas was less represented than in zone 1. The levels of microscopic charcoal also fell in this zone and this might suggest that activities associated with burning had moved some distance away from the feature.

Other herbs seem to have increased and flowered more prolifically than before. In particular, grasses gradually increased to maximum levels of about 40% of the pollen sum while there was a very marked increase in *Plantago lanceolata* (ribwort plantain). There were also significantly increased representations of other plants characteristic of grassy places and pasture, such as Fabaceae (eg clover and bird's foot trefoil), *Centaurea nigra* (knapweed), *Ranunculus* type (buttercups), and *Senecio/Bellis* type (ragwort/daisy). All these plants have low representation in the pollen rain today, even when they are relatively abundant in a sward (Wiltshire 2001). This suggests that these herbs were all growing very prolifically indeed in the environs of the waterhole and/or that their pollen was being concentrated in the dung of animals grazing the local grassy areas. Cereal type pollen also increased

over the previous zone. This might suggest increased arable activity locally although, again, it could have been derived from straw or animal dung.

There does seem to have been a genuine change in the vegetation around the feature during the period represented by this zone (the latter part of the 2nd century). The decline in trees and shrubs might reflect a more intensive exploitation of local sources of wood although it could also be an indicator of a slow recovery from earlier impact. After severe coppicing and pollarding, many woody plants take much longer to recover than might be expected, often up to 20 years (Alice Holt Forestry Commission, pers. comm.). Hazel and birch are exceptions to this and can flower within a year or two of drastic cutting (personal observation based on long term garden experiment).

It is rather difficult to envisage what the vegetation changes mean in terms of land management changes in this zone, but it does appear that the surroundings of the feature become dominated by plants characteristic of rich pasture. The high values for grasses, Plantago lanceolata (ribwort plantain), and enhanced values for other pasture herbs implies that there was actually less pressure from grazing and trampling than in zone 1. Intense grazing would have the effect of removing the flowering heads of these herbs so that pastoral indicators could, actually, be reduced.

The lower values for microscopic charcoal and the increased flowering of grassland herbs might suggest that the centre of activity had moved slightly away from the site and that pasture was allowed to recover. This would also explain the demise of ruderals such as mugwort, goosefoot, and knotweed which need open ground and are poor competitors.

Zone WHF3

This zone probably represents the 50 years from AD 200 to AD 250. The local landscape seems to have changed very little indeed and land use was probably similar to that in the previous zone. However, there is some indication that the surroundings became wetter with sedges, meadowsweet, water mint, and bur-reed becoming more frequent.

Cereal pollen was also more abundant and this could mean that crop fields were located slightly closer to the waterhole, or that processing was being carried out nearby. It is even possible that cereal waste was finding its way into the feature. The better representation of elder and willow, and the appearance of *Cornus* (dogwood), *Rhamnus* (purging buckthorn), and *Ilex* (holly) might suggest that the hedgerow was less intensively managed, or that shrubs were encroaching into the area very close to the waterhole.

Plants characteristic of acidic soils such as *Calluna* (common heather), Ericaceae (other heathers), and bracken all increased in both frequency and abundance slightly in this zone. They were probably invading grassland on the more acid soils in the catchment and this could suggest less grazing and trampling pressure since none of these plants thrives under such conditions (Gimingham 1972).

Summary

In the latter half of the 2nd century, the site around the waterhole seems to have been the focus of quite intense activity. The ground appears to have had bare, trampled soils dominated by coarse ruderals plants and many other weeds. A wide range of woody plants was growing in the catchment with oak being the most important species. There seems to have been a hedge growing quite close to the waterhole but it was probably being managed quite extensively. The woodland resources were also managed by coppicing or pollarding, or else only very few trees were growing in the catchment. Later in the 2nd century, impact on the hedge and woodland resources was even greater, but human and possibly animal impact on the open ground near to the site seems to have lessened, and there was a recovery of pasture and meadow plants. Later on (possibly between AD 200 and AD 250) the site became wetter and heath plants started to encroach into the grassland. On the other hand, as heathland plants are useful domestic resources (thatching, bedding and fodder), they could have been brought from elsewhere and fortuitously found their way into the waterhole deposits. Cereal growing and/or processing also seemed to be carried out closer to the feature than in previous times although, again, the cereal pollen could have been derived from cereal waste or even dung. However, there does seem to have been some degree of recovery of the hedgerow (or scrub).

The wider picture

It is unfortunate that although, at the time of writing, a great number of studies in the environmental archaeology of sites has been completed in southern England, many have not been published. Much information is contained within unpublished assessment reports, and even comprehensive analytical reports, but the data are inaccessible and cannot be used for comparison. However, analysis of peat deposits immediately beneath Watling Street in Durovernum (Canterbury) can be quoted (Wiltshire 1989).

In spite of the accepted interpretation of the Latin name as 'a walled town by an alder marsh' (Rivet and Smith 1979, 354), palynological analysis at Canterbury showed that there was no evidence for either a marsh or abundant alder. In fact, in the late Iron Age and early Roman period in the area, the landscape was very open indeed. The area around modern Stour Street was dominated by weedy grassland with bracken being an important component of the plant community. Trees were growing in the catchment, and the most abundant were probably oak and hazel but, even here, their representation was at less than 1% of the total pollen sum at any level in the sediment sequence. It is possible that alder trees were quite abundant in the wetter areas but, if so, they

must have been severely pollarded and rarely had the opportunity to flower. Indeed, no woody plant had a continuous record in the sequence and, where they were represented, they invariably achieved less than 1% of the total pollen sum.

There was a tradition of cereal production at the site and cereal-type pollen was remarkably abundant throughout the sequence. After an horizon interpreted as representing Roman influence, the major changes were a lowering of watertable (presumably through planned drainage) and the marked reduction in the abundance of the weeds of cornfield (segetals) and waste ground (ruderals). Pastoral herbs and grasses were very abundant indeed throughout the period represented by the peat deposits.

The palynological records, therefore, indicate that the area around Westhawk Farm supported a more abundant and more diverse woodland than the environs of Iron Age and Roman Canterbury. Whether this reflects more intense management of woody resources at Canterbury cannot be determined. The deposits at Canterbury and Westhawk Farm are not strictly contemporaneous, but it is interesting that the former appears to have had fewer (or more intensively exploited) woody resources than the latter.

Discussion

The data obtained from waterholes 796 and 9179 at Westhawk Farm were similar. Both features were set in, or located close to, herb-rich pasture and areas of 'waste ground'. Cereals were also being cultivated and/or processed in, or close to, the settlement. The palynological data match those of the waterlogged plant remains very well, and the higher level of taxonomic resolution provided by the seed analysis enhances the value of the palynological results. The results from charcoal and insect analyses also complement the palynological data. All the trees and shrubs identified in the charcoal report were recorded in the pollen spectra although, as expected, plants such as *Sambucus* (elder), *Betula* (birch), *Hedera* (ivy), *Ilex* (holly), *Rhamnus* (purging buckthorn), *Rubus*-type (e.g. bramble) were not found in the charcoal remains as presumably these would not be considered for fuel if other sources were plentiful. *Pinus* (pine) was not found in the charcoal record either, but it is possible that it was growing a considerable distance away from the site and at low density. Other woody taxa such as *Solanum dulcamara* (woody nightshade) and *Prunus* (cherry/sloe) were recorded in the waterlogged remains. It is gratifying, therefore, that the various analyses are mutually supportive.

The charcoal indicates that oak provided the most abundant fuel although the pollen results suggest that hazel was possibly more frequent in the immediate vicinity of the waterholes. If oak were being managed for fuel by coppicing and/or pollarding, it is not surprising that its representation in the pollen record was proportionately lower. The relative pollen frequencies could be a function of management of various species as well as proximity to the accumulating sediments. The palynological data also support both the entomological results and those of the water-logged remains. There is little doubt that the features contained water but the pollen record indicates that the levels fluctuated considerably.

The presence of *Picea* (spruce) trees in waterhole 9179, located quite close to the shrine, was detected only by its pollen. The absence of macrofossil evidence, and the presence of spruce pollen throughout at least 100 cm of sediment of feature 9179, suggests that rather than important debris being dumped in the waterhole, one or more trees were growing in the vicinity. Furthermore, the tree must have been there for some considerable time since pollen-producing cones only occur on older trees (Mitchell 1974). The absence of spruce pollen in the other features is enigmatic since they, like feature 9179, contain sediments deemed to have accumulated in 2nd century. However, modern pollen studies have shown (Wiltshire, personal observation) that conifer pollen dispersal can be very localised indeed.

From recent, though as yet unpublished data, there is little doubt that spruce was being grown in Romano-British settlements in eastern England. Convincing evidence has been obtained for its presence in East Anglia (Cartwright 1996; Murphy 1999; Wiltshire 1998a; Wiltshire 1998b; Wiltshire 1999a) and in Hampshire (Wiltshire 1999b). Both macrofossil and palynological evidence has been obtained, and although the presence of cones and leaves does not necessarily imply that the tree was being grown, continuous record of pollen throughout sediment sequences certainly does. It is reasonable to imply a ritualistic or aesthetic reason for its cultivation since its timber is very inferior to that of most native British trees (Hyde and Harrison 1977). It was certainly being grown in the vicinity of a garden and temple at Godmanchester (Murphy 1999; Wiltshire 1999a).

Conclusions

There is little doubt that there were quite marked changes in human impact around the waterhole (feature 796) in the 100 years or so represented by the pollen sequence. After AD 150, there seems to have been a hedge near to the feature and large trees and shrubs were either growing some considerable distance away, or were being heavily exploited for fuel and other needs. The environs of the feature were dominated by open ground with ruderals (weeds characteristic of waste ground and 'back yards'). Later, the activity that encouraged these plants seems to have moved away from the area and herb-rich grassland spread into the area. Cereals were being grown or processed at the site throughout this period, but were more abundant after about AD 200. The sediments and margins of the feature were wet throughout the period represented by the pollen sequence, but the water table fluctuated. It seems to have become wetter after about AD 200 when cereals seem to have been more important at the site, and heathland plants were either starting to encroach the

grassland, or were being brought into the settlement from elsewhere. There was also some recovery of the woody plants making up the hedge.

There seems to have been a greater abundance of trees and shrubs at Westhawk Farm in the 2nd and 3rd centuries than there was at Canterbury during the very early Roman period. Whether this variation in the record was due to exploitation by coppicing and pollarding, or actual abundance of trees and shrubs, cannot be determined.

WOOD CHARCOAL
by Dana Challinor

Introduction

A total of fifteen samples were chosen for charcoal analysis. The samples were selected from a range of deposits from several structures and other feature types, such as a cremation grave and a waterhole. Since one of the main uses of the site was industrial, the aims of the charcoal analysis were to determine the taxonomic composition of deposits relating to metalworking activities and investigate the evidence for woodland management practices. The wide range of features sampled also offered the potential to look at context-related variation in the use of fuelwood.

Methodology

The samples were processed by flotation in a modified Siraf-type machine, with sample sizes mostly 20-30 litres in volume. The resultant flots were air-dried and sub-sampled using a riffle box. Some of the flots were so rich in charcoal that only a small percentage of the flot was actually examined (Table 9.3). The sub-samples were then divided into fractions using a set of sieves, and fragments > 2 mm were identified. The charcoal was fractured and sorted into groups based on the anatomical features observed in transverse section at x10 and x20 magnification. Representative fragments from each group were then selected for further examination using a Meiji incident-light microscope at up to x400 magnification. Identifications were made with reference to Schweingruber (1990), Hather (2000) and modern reference material. A total of 2653 fragments were examined.

In addition to species identification, the maturity of the wood was assessed where the condition of the wood permitted it, and the number of growth rings recorded. A total of 61 roundwood fragments were examined where the complete radius or diameter of the stems were preserved. These fragments were selected from the whole flot, not just from the sub-sample. Combined methods of ubiquity or presence analysis and quantification by fragment count have been used in this report. It is acknowledged that there are differential rates of fragmentation in charcoal and that quantification by fragment count is not always reliable, but this method has been used in this report to demonstrate relationships between individual taxa. Classification and nomenclature follow Stace (1997).

Results

The results by fragment count are given in Table 9.3 and the roundwood data is given in Table 9.4. Eight taxa were positively identified. The taxonomic level of identification varied according to the biogeography and anatomy of the taxa:

> **Fagaceae**: *Quercus* sp. (oak), tree, two native species not distinguishable anatomically.
> **Betulaceae**: *Corylus avellana* (hazel), shrub or small tree, sole native species. *Corylus* and *Alnus glutinosa* (alder) have a very similar anatomical structure and can be difficult to distinguish, hence the category *Corylus/Alnus*. However, since no *Alnus* was positively identified, it is assumed that only *Corylus* is represented here.
> **Salicaceae**: the genera *Salix* sp. (willow) and *Populus* sp. (poplar) are not distinguishable anatomically. However, given the evidence of *Salix* in the pollen record (Wiltshire, above) it is likely to be this taxon represented in the charcoal.
> **Rosaceae**: *Prunus* spp., includes *P. spinosa* (blackthorn), *P. avium* (wild cherry) and *P. padus* (bird cherry); can be difficult to distinguish anatomically, although the charcoal from Westhawk Farm was characteristic of *P. avium*. The native status of *P. avium* is uncertain and it may be a Roman introduction to Britain (see discussion in Moffet *et al.* 1989).
> **Maloideae**: subfamily of various shrubs/small trees including *Pyrus* sp. (pear), *Malus* sp. (apple), *Crataegus* sp. (hawthorn), rarely distinguishable by anatomical characteristics.
> **Buxaceae**: *Buxus sempervirens* (box), shrub/small tree, native status discussed below.
> **Rhamnaceae**: *Rhamnus cathartica* (purging buckthorn), shrub, sole native species.
> **Oleaceae**: *Fraxinus excelsior* (ash), tree, sole native species.

Several of the samples produced small quantities of oak heartwood as well as sapwood, though in some cases preservation was not good enough to determine the maturity. The preservation of the charcoal was generally very good, with large fragments preserved. Nevertheless, there were fragments in all samples categorised as indeterminate, which were not identifiable because of poor preservation or an unusual cellular structure. In several samples the charcoal was highly vitrified, having a glassy appearance indicative of high temperatures. It is likely that these indeterminate fragments represent additional specimens of taxa positively identified at the site.

Discussion

Woodland resources

The taxa identified from the Westhawk Farm charcoal are likely to have come from local woodland, on the assumption that fuelwood is usually collected from the immediate vicinity of a settlement (eg Salisbury and Jane 1940; Western 1971; Miller 1985; Neumann 1989; Thompson 1996). Consequently, the charcoal taxa will be represented in the local environment, but will not provide an adequate reconstruction of that environment. The relatively limited range of taxa identified at Westhawk Farm indicates selection of specific wood species. Certainly, the results from the pollen analysis (Wiltshire, above) reveals that a wider range of species would have been available in the region. Nevertheless, the charcoal assemblage indicates the presence of mixed deciduous woodland, dominated by *Quercus* with *Fraxinus* and a shrubby understorey of *Corylus*, *Prunus* and Maloideae. *Salix* and *Rhamnus* favour damp soil conditions and may have grown in the valley (Fig. 9.4).

Only one species found in the charcoal assemblage was not evident in the pollen - *Buxus sempervirens* (box). The native status of *Buxus* is uncertain. While it is accepted by some as 'unquestionably native in scrub and open woodland on calcareous soils in southern England' (Mabey 1997, 254; Stace 1997, 457), the earliest identification of the species from a Neolithic context is thought to be tentative (Smith, forthcoming; Gale and Cutler 2000, 54) and others maintain that it is a Roman introduction (Farrar 1998, 143). Boxwood has been identified from Roman artefacts from excavations in London (Smith forthcoming) and occasionally as charcoal (eg Price 2000, 258) so the presence of the species in Roman Kent is acceptable. Without evidence for it in the pollen record, however, it is not possible to determine whether box was growing in the region and entered the archaeological record as fuelwood or whether the few fragments found at this site were from discarded artefacts. The use of box trees as ornamental garden features is mentioned by several classical authors (eg Pliny the Younger, *Ep.*, ii, 17, 14 (Radice 1969); Pliny the Elder, *NH*, xvi, 60, 140). Since most of the boxwood fragments found at Westhawk Farm were from structure R, associated with metalworking, it is most likely that box was growing locally and was accidentally included with the main fuelwood. It is plausible that they represent trimmings from hedges; the proximity of structure R to the shrine structure may be significant.

The key issue concerning woodland resources in the Roman period is that of woodland management - were the Romans merely exploiting available resources or was there a management strategy controlling timber supply? It is very difficult to infer woodland management from charcoal, but clues to coppicing or pollarding cycles may be gained from examining patterns of similarity in ages of trees and examining patterns in growth ring widths (Morgan 1988). Figure 9.5 presents the results from all of the complete roundwood fragments from the charcoal assemblage. All species have been included in this graph as there was found to be no patterning within individual taxa groups. It is apparent from this graph that there is great variation in age and diameter be-

Table 9.3 Wood charcoal: Results of the analysis by fragment count.

Structure		-	-	Structure D	Structure I			Structure P	Structure R				-	
Feature type		Cremation	Ditch	Gully	Pit 9817	Post-hole	Pit	Hearth	Pot Fill	Ditch	Pit	Pit	Pit	Hearth	Waterhole 796	Waterhole 796
Sample number		692	671	600	749	683	53	103	213	628	66	67	89	102	15	19
Context number		8955	8366	7108	9818	8745	1082	1522	319	7347	1231	1232	1437	1529	346	429
Date		150-200	43-150	150-200	150-200	150-200	200-250	70-150	70-150	200-250	200-250	200-250	200-250	200-250	200-250	250-350
Volume of soil (litres)		15	18	20	18	20	30	25	5	20	30	30	30	30	40	10
% identified		25.0%	12.5%	1.6%	50.0%	25.0%	3.1%	25.0%	3.1%	50.0%	3.1%	3.1%	3.1%	6.3%	3.1%	12.5%
Quercus sp.	oak	130	136	201	95	162	132	129	107	115	176	126	125	180	164	149
Corylus avellana	hazel			2	10	9					6	4	9	6		7
Corylus/Alnus	hazel/alder									3						
Salicaceae	willow, poplar			6			1	1		1		3	2		3	1
Prunus sp.	blackthorn, cherry				2		2				6					
Maloideae	apple, pear, hawthorn			1	29	1			2		2	5	13	3	6	7
Buxus sempervirens	box		3								1	2	1	3		
Rhamnus cathartica	buckthorn				1							1				
Fraxinus excelsior	ash											2		1		
Indeterminate		14	19	12	16	43	24	58	28	7	27	17	20	22	19	32
Total number of fragments		144	158	222	153	215	159	188	137	126	218	160	170	215	192	196

Table 9.4   Wood charcoal: Results of the roundwood analysis. (ARW = average ring width).

Sample	Species	Ring count	Diameter (mm)	Radius (mm)	ARW
15	*Quercus* sp.	17	0	10	1.2
15	*Quercus* sp.	11	19	0	1.7
19	*Quercus* sp.	6	0	8	2.7
19	*Quercus* sp.	5	13	0	2.6
19	*Quercus* sp.	6	17	0	2.8
19	*Quercus* sp.	5	11	0	2.2
53	Salicaceae	5	0	6	2.4
66	*Quercus* sp.	14	0	15	2.1
66	*Quercus* sp.	8	12	0	1.5
66	*Quercus* sp.	7	6	0	0.9
66	*Corylus avellana*	8	0	6	1.5
66	*Quercus* sp.	14	11	0	0.8
66	*Quercus* sp.	13	0	11	1.7
66	*Quercus* sp.	13	0	7	1.1
66	*Quercus* sp.	7	13	0	1.9
66	*Quercus* sp.	10	5	0	0.5
67	Maloideae	20	22	0	1.1
67	*Quercus* sp.	15	0	13	1.7
67	Maloideae	19	0	14	1.5
67	*Quercus* sp.	14	0	6	0.9
67	*Quercus* sp.	13	11	0	0.8
67	Maloideae	23	21	0	0.9
89	*Quercus* sp.	4	0	5	2.5
89	*Quercus* sp.	5	12	0	2.4
89	*Quercus* sp.	16	0	14	1.8
89	*Quercus* sp.	12	0	10	1.7
89	*Quercus* sp.	6	0	7	2.3
89	*Corylus avellana*	11	17	0	1.5
89	*Corylus avellana*	8	16	0	2
89	*Corylus avellana*	7	8	0	1.1
89	Maloideae	10	0	8	1.6
89	*Quercus* sp.	9	0	5	1.1
89	*Corylus avellana*	11	17	0	1.5
89	*Quercus* sp.	7	0	6	1.7
89	*Quercus* sp.	8	11	0	1.4
102	*Quercus* sp.	28	20	0	0.7
102	*Quercus* sp.	29	22	0	0.8
102	*Quercus* sp.	27	20	0	0.7
102	*Quercus* sp.	28	19	0	0.7
102	*Quercus* sp.	28	0	10	0.7
102	*Quercus* sp.	27	0	10	0.7
102	*Quercus* sp.	28	18	0	0.6
102	Maloideae	12	15	0	1.3
102	*Corylus avellana*	13	0	11	1.7
102	*Quercus* sp.	31	0	12	0.8
628	*Quercus* sp.	12	0	16	2.7
628	*Quercus* sp.	13	0	18	2.8
628	*Quercus* sp.	13	0	16	2.5
628	*Quercus* sp.	12	0	15	2.5
671	*Quercus* sp.	5	5	0	1
683	*Quercus* sp.	14	0	10	1.4
683	*Quercus* sp.	9	16	0	1.8
683	*Quercus* sp.	15	0	10	1.3
683	*Quercus* sp.	23	0	10	0.9
683	*Quercus* sp.	19	0	9	0.9
683	*Quercus* sp.	18	0	9	1
683	*Quercus* sp.	17	0	7	0.8
683	*Quercus* sp.	20	0	9	0.9
683	*Quercus* sp.	23	0	11	1
683	*Quercus* sp.	10	12	0	1.2
683	*Quercus* sp.	16	0	12	1.5

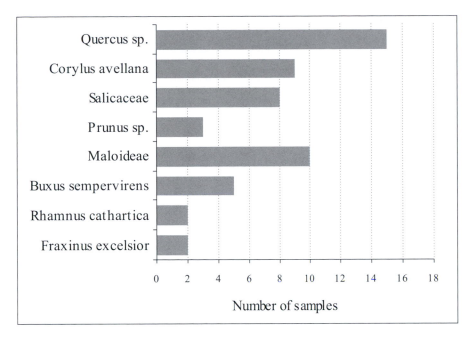

Figure 9.4   Charcoal: taxa presence by number of samples.

tween the roundwood fragments and no discernible patterns. If the wood were being regularly coppiced, a pattern of similar age/diameter would be expected (Murphy 2001, box 1) and/or wide early growth rings. At Westhawk Farm there were no indications of woodland management from the charcoal.

However, this may not be taken as conclusive evidence of lack of woodland management practices, since the roundwood fragments came from a range of deposit types which may represent several episodes of burning and deposition. It is also possible that the woodland was being managed for structural timber, not for firewood. If woodland management

was not being practised at Westhawk Farm, yet fuel requirements were high to satisfy the metalworking industry, one might expect the pressure on local woodlands to have been considerable and that this would be reflected in the selection of species.

Selection of species

The collection of firewood is influenced by a number of criteria - species availability, physical properties, potential value of the wood for other uses, function of the fire and cultural values. The results from the analysis confirm the pattern noted in the assessment

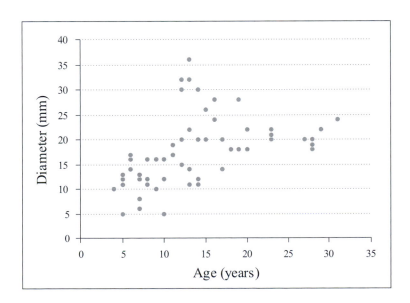

Figure 9.5   Charcoal: Age and diameter of charcoal roundwood fragments.

that oak is dominant in the samples - comprising 80% of the total assemblage (Figure 9.6) and present in all 15 samples. It is striking that the next most frequent taxa (Maloideae and *Corylus*) make up less than 3% of the total assemblage and the combined other taxa represent a mere 2%. The 'indeterminate' category is likely to be made up of some oak, but mostly non-oak/diffuse porous species which are less distinctive anatomically.

As mentioned above, all of the species in the assemblage could have grown locally. Oak is commonly found as a fuelwood in archaeological assemblages, since it makes a high energy wood fuel and its predominance in these samples suggest that the supply of this species was plentiful. Certainly, there is nothing in these results to suggest that wood supplies were limited. Given the overall dominance of oak at Westhawk Farm, the opportunity to discuss context-related variation is limited. However, there are a few interesting points worth highlighting.

Industrial activities

Several of the samples analysed came from features associated with iron-working debris, specifically structures R and I (see Chapter 7). Although there is no method for determining from archaeological material whether it was used as charcoal or as wood fuel, the processes of iron smelting and smithing would both have required charcoal as fuel (Edlin

1949, 160; Cleere and Crossley 1985, 37). At least oak would have provided good quality charcoal, capable of achieving the high temperatures necessary for iron-working. Indeed, the probable *Salix* sp. (willow) may also have entered the assemblage in this way, as it makes a better charcoal than wood fuel. It is possible that the presence of small quantities of other non-oak species (which are typical of scrub/hedgerows) may be explained by their use as an aid to ignition in charcoal burners or as an accidental inclusion. Traditional methods for making charcoal utilise shallow pits with layers of straw, grass or bracken to shut out the air (Edlin 1949, 160). There is no evidence for the process of charcoal-making at Westhawk Farm, but this is not unusual as it is rarely represented in the archaeological record for the Roman period (Cleere and Crossley 1985, 37); indeed, shallow pits or surface-level features would all have been removed by post-Roman ploughing.

The industrial samples from Westhawk Farm have produced similar charcoal assemblages to other Roman metalworking sites, although there are few examples from Kent. Nevertheless, the evidence from other sites suggests a dominance of oak, with a range of other, variable, taxa (eg Campbell 2000, 37; Cleere and Crossley 1985, 37; Figueiral 1992, 189; Gale 1999, 378). Even where there is evidence of alternative fuels being used, indicating pressure on woodland resources, oak remains a component of the assemblage (eg Murphy 2000, 220). The range of species

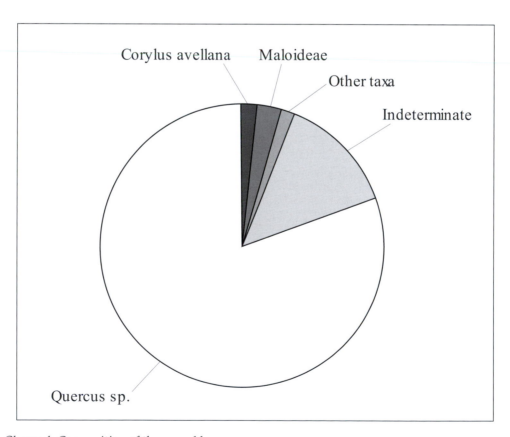

Figure 9.6   Charcoal: Composition of the assemblage.

identified at Roman metalworking sites suggests an overall picture in which there was little selection of wood for charcoal burning - oak is probably dominant because it was the most widely available wood. Certainly, there are other taxa which make better charcoal, such as *Frangula alnus* (alder buckthorn) and *Alnus glutinosa* (alder) (Edlin 1949, 165). There are also similarities between Westhawk Farm and other sites in the quantity of narrow roundwood charcoal recovered (eg Cartwright 1986, 222; Gale 1999, 382). This may relate to the intense heat produced by the use of roundwood in a fire or to collection practices; at Chesters Villa, Woolaston, the roundwood is thought to relate to coppicing (Figueiral 1992, 191), although there is no direct evidence for this here.

Domestic activities

The charcoal was interpreted as domestic refuse when it occurred as dumps in ditches and pits in association with other dumped rubbish or in association with clear settlement structures. The deposits from waterhole 796 are included in this category, although there is the slight possibility that these were ritual deposits. The significance of the assemblages from these domestic contexts lies in their similarity to those from the metalworking areas. All of the assemblages were dominated by oak, with smaller quantities of Maloideae, *Corylus*, *Prunus*, *Rhamnus* and Salicaceae. Clearly, there was no differentiation between the domestic and the industrial in terms of fuel selection. So if the fuel used for metalworking was charcoal, was this also used for domestic purposes? While it is not necessary to use charcoal for cooking and heating, it does provide a smokeless heat, which was used for some types of domestic ovens in Roman Britain (Allason-Jones 1989b, 96). However, the effort involved in charcoal-making and the resource implications of this make it unlikely to have been worthwhile for activities where standard wood fuel would suffice (Gale 1999, 383) and the size of the settlement at Westhawk Farm is unlikely to have necessitated such use of resources.

Ritual activities

Only one of the cremation burials from Westhawk Farm produced a good assemblage of charcoal (grave 8956). This is the only sample to produce a single taxon - again, oak was dominant. The predominance of a single taxon in prehistoric cremation assemblages has been noted at various sites and taken as evidence of deliberate ritual selection (eg Thompson 1999; Straker 1988). Moreover, recent assessment work on sites from the Channel Tunnel Rail Link project indicates similar predominance of a single taxon (Challinor 2000; forthcoming). However, the charcoal analysis at Westhawk Farm suggests that the predominance of oak in the cremation sample at this site is unlikely to be of ritual significance. True, the cremation sample contained only one taxon, but

since oak is abundant in all of the samples, there is no convincing indication of wood selection. The abundance of oak in this cremation is more likely to relate to the abundance of oak in the locality.

Conclusions

The clear predominance of oak in all samples, regardless of feature type, suggests plentiful resources. Yet it is generally thought that the Romans must have been managing the woodland in the Weald to cope with the wood requirements of the metalworking industry (Rackham 1997, 74-5). Of course, this assumption depends upon the scale of the industry, which was quite modest at Westhawk Farm (Paynter, Chapter 7). According to Paynter's calculations, each smelt would consume roughly 64 kg of charcoal which, at a ratio of 6.5:1, would require 416 kg of wood. On this basis, and assuming a conservative 6 smelts per year, the annual wood consumption at Westhawk Farm would have been about 2.5 tonnes (*c* 2496 kg) - hardly a vast undertaking. Of course, these calculations are likely to be underestimates given the limitations of the excavations and the fact that this does not account for non-metalworking timber requirements.

Nonetheless, it must be concluded that the iron-working industry at Westhawk Farm was probably not on a large enough scale to necessitate the use of managed wood for fuel consumption. Certainly, there is nothing in the charcoal record to indicate coppicing or to suggest limited wood resources. There was no differentiation between fuelwood utilised for industrial, domestic or ritual activities - whether charcoal or wood fuel. In fact, it is apparent that the character and type of fuel used remains the same throughout all phases, from the 1st to 4th century. At least one other Wealden site (Bardown; see discussion in Cleere and Crossley 1985, 37) shows a lack of evidence for systematic woodland management or wood selection. Apparently, the iron-working industry was placed in this location because plentiful wood supplies were available.

CHARRED AND WATERLOGGED PLANT REMAINS
by Ruth Pelling

Introduction

Features at Westhawk Farm were routinely sampled for the recovery of charred plant remains. Samples of 6 to 40 litres were processed using a modified Siraf type machine. Flots were collected onto a 250 μm mesh and allowed to dry. Residues were retained on 1 mm meshes and any charred items greater than 2 mm were added to the flots. Provisional assessment of some 215 samples demonstrated that charred seeds and chaff were present in 20 samples. In addition, one of the excavated waterholes, feature 796, was found to contain waterlogged plant remains. Following assessment of 200 g sub-samples from this waterhole to establish the quantity and quality of waterlogged plant remains, five larger samples of 1 kg were processed as for charred remains, but the flots were kept wet.

Methodology

Samples selected for analysis of charred plant remains either contained sufficient charred items to warrant analysis (generally over 100 items of grain, chaff, and/or weeds), or, in the case of sample 21, contained an unusual item noted during assessment, *Pinus pinea* (stone pine). Time limitations prevented every sample selected being examined in full, although it was felt that the full range of assemblage types was examined. Samples were sorted under a binocular microscope for seeds and chaff. Identifications were made under a binocular microscope at x10 to x20 magnification and were based on morphological characteristics and by comparison with modern reference material held at the Oxford University Museum of Natural History. Taxonomic order of weeds and nomenclature follows Clapham *et al.* (1989).

Assessment of waterlogged deposits was originally conducted by scanning the flots from 200 g sub-samples under a binocular microscope at x10 to x20 magnification. The range of species identified during the assessment was quite limited, but was felt to characterise the deposits sufficiently well that detailed sorting was not necessary. However, the identification of possible Roman introductions was deemed sufficiently significant that some investigation of larger deposits was merited. The flots from 1 kg sub-samples were therefore scanned thoroughly under the binocular microscope in order to obtain a more exhaustive species list, although abundance was estimated on a relative scale (present, common or abundant) rather than absolute counts being recorded. Nomenclature and taxonomic order follows Clapham *et al.* (1989) as for charred remains.

Results

Charred plant remains

The results are shown in Tables 9.5 and 9.6. Table 9.5 includes all the samples analysed for charred remains. Six samples were taken from one large charred deposit in a Phase 2 ditch, feature 9060/8171. A seventh sample, 37, was taken from a Phase 4 pit cutting a Phase 4 ditch in the northernmost corner of the site. This sample produced iron pan encrusted remains, and hence it was not possible to produced accurate counts for seeds and chaff. Minimum counts or approximate abundance (present, common, abundant) have therefore been entered in the table. The eighth sample, 21, was taken from a Phase 3 (AD 70-150) pit within the centre of the shrine. The ratios of grain, chaff and weed seeds from the sample are shown in Figure 9.7. Table 9.6 shows the results of assessment of the samples not examined further.

Cereal remains

Cereal remains were identified as large quantities of both grain and chaff. *Triticum spelta* (spelt wheat) dominates all the cereal rich samples, as is generally true on sites of Roman date. *Triticum dicoccum* (emmer) is also recorded, but in low numbers. A hulled six-row variety of *Hordeum vulgare* (barley) is indicated by the presence of asymmetrical grain and occasional well preserved rachis. The *Avena* sp. (oats) present is likely to be wild given that the only florets with sufficient diagnostic parts were all of *A. fatua*, the wild species. However, this does not mean that the oats were not regarded as a useful grain and they may have been deliberately collected or at least tolerated within cultivated crops.

Germinated grain of *Triticum spelta* and *Hordeum vulgare* were noted in most samples with occasional germinated *T. dicoccum*. The percentage of germinated to total grain was generally low (10% or less) with a slightly higher percentage in sample 808. Sprouted embryos were also recorded in all but samples 806 and 37, although in low numbers in each sample, particularly in relation to the number of glume base.

While grain and glume bases dominated the samples all parts of the cereal ear are represented, including terminal grain and rachis fragments. Both hexaploid (*T. aestivum* type or *T. spelta*) and tetraploid (*T. turgidum* or *T. dicoccum*) wheat rachis is represented. While some rachis may be from free-threshing wheat, most is thought to be the lower tougher parts of the *T. spelta* and *T. dicoccum* ear. Basal rachis is also recorded. Rachis of *Hordeum vulgare* is present and is particularly numerous in samples 807, 808 and 809. In addition occasional large cereal sized culm nodes may be from wheat or barley straw, and awn fragments of wheat and oats are present. The combination of all these elements suggests that whole ears of wheat and barley are represented.

Weed species

A relatively mature and varied weed flora is represented which includes two species which only became widespread during the Roman period, *Agrostemma githago* (corn cockle) and *Anthemis cotula* (stinking mayweed). Most of the taxa identified are commonly regarded as arable weeds, some of which will also grow on any nitrogen-rich disturbed ground (particularly the Chenopodiaceae and Polygonaceae). The large grasses are very prominent, notably *Bromus* subsect *Eubromus*, many of which show signs of having germinated. Also significant in terms of number are two small-seeded Compositae, *Anthemis cotula* and *Tripleurospermum inodorum* (scentless mayweed), although as these species produce composite seed heads it is possible that the seeds are from only a limited number of plants. If the small Compositae are seen as representative of seed heads, then the majority of the weed seeds can be regarded as large-seeded species, which often remain with the cereal grain until the late stages of processing (see below).

Table 9.5   Charred plant remains: Data from fully-analyses samples.

		Sample	656	806	807	808	809	810	21	37
		Context	8175	10334	10334	10334	10334	10348	416	629
		Feature	8171	9060	9060	9060	9060	9060	415	630
		Fraction	1/4	100%	1/32	1/64	1/16	100%	100%	1/16
		Volume (litres)	20	6	9	9	8	10	40	30
Grain											
Triticum spelta	Spelt wheat, germinated		32	13	3	2	4	7	-	-
Triticum spelta	Spelt wheat		32	32	13	7	1	14	-	-
Triticum spelta	Spelt wheat, terminal grain		1	-	-	-	-	-	-	-
Triticum dicoccum	Emmer wheat		1	-	-	-	-	4	-	-
Triticum cf. *dicoccum*	cf. Emmer wheat, germinated		-	-	1	-	-	-	-	-
Triticum cf. *dicoccum*	cf. Emmer wheat		1	-	-	-	1	1	-	-
Triticum spelta/dicoccum	Spelt/Emmer wheat, germinated		1	9	4	1	-	7	-	3
Triticum spelta/dicoccum	Spelt/Emmer wheat		13	-	7	-	4	29	1	2
Triticum sp.	Wheat, germinated		5	-	6	14	1	-	-	-
Triticum sp.	Wheat		146	113	38	-	15	188	-	11
Hordeum vulgare	Barley, hulled asymmetric germinated		4	-	-	-	-	-	-	-
Hordeum vulgare	Barley, hulled asymmetric		3	2	1	-	-	-	-	-
Hordeum vulgare	Barley, hulled straight, germinated		5	-	2	-	-	-	-	-
Hordeum vulgare	Barley, hulled straight		4	-	-	-	-	-	-	-
Hordeum vulgare	Barley, hulled germinated		13	5	7	1	2	-	-	-
Hordeum vulgare	Barley, hulled		21	16	9	7	4	-	-	-
Hordeum vulgare	Barley, germinated		3	1	-	-	-	-	-	-
Hordeum vulgare	Barley		92	12	18	5	5	3	-	1
Avena sp.	Oats		1	-	21	19	7	29	-	-
Avena fatua	Wild Oats		-	1	-	-	1	2	-	6
Cerealia indet	Indeterminate		299	193	88	25	20	364	-	97
Chaff											
Triticum spelta	Spelt wheat glume base		22	3	1282	434	463	707	-	285
Triticum cf. *spelta*	cf. Spelt wheat glume base		6	-	-	11	58	22	-	-
Triticum spelta	Spelt wheat rachis		-	-	1	-	-	-	-	-
Triticum dicoccum	Emmer wheat glume base		1	2	10	18	15	46	-	-
Triticum cf. *dicoccum*	cf. Emmer wheat glume base		-		40		10	37	-	-
Triticum spelta/dicoccum	Spelt/Emmer wheat glume base		40	4	1891	840	711	1254	-	649
Triticum sp. Hexaploid	Spelt/bread type wheat rachis		-	1	-	9	-	3	-	-
Triticum sp. Hexaploid	Spelt/bread type wheat basal rachis		-	-	-	-	45	8	-	+
Triticum sp. Tetraploid	Emmer/Rivet wheat rachis		-	-	4	-	-	-	-	-
Triticum sp.	Wheat, cf. free-threshing rachis		-	-	-	3	-	-	-	-
Triticum sp.	Wheat rachis		-	-	34	-	-	8	-	-
Triticum sp.	Wheat, basal rachis		3	-	18	11	18	4	-	-
Triticum sp.	Wheat awns		+	+	++	+	+	..	-	-
Avena fatua	Wild oat floret base		1	-	5	2	1	-	-	+
Avena sp. hexaploid	Oat floret base		-	-	5	-	2	-	-	-
Avena sp.	Oat floret base		-	-	4	-	8	-	-	-
Avena sp.	Oats, awn		+	+	++	++	++	++	1	++
Hordeum vulgare	Barley rachis		1	2	98	33	35	6	-	-
Hordeum vulgare	Six-row Barley rachis		-	-	18	7	6	-	-	1
cf. *Hordeum vulgare*	cf. Barley rachis		-	-	10	-	-	-	-	-
Cerealia indet	Sprouted embryo		2	-	38	24	16	12	-	-
Cerealia indet	Detached embryo		4	17	27	15	9	-	-	+
Cerealia indet	Indeterminate rachis		2	-	-	17	10	-	-	-
Cerealia indet	Indeterminate basal rachis		-	1	12	-	9	27	-	-
Cereal size	Cereal sized culm nodes		1	-	1	3	-	1	-	-
Other Cultivated Specis											
Pinus pinea	Sone pine kernel stone		-	-	-	-	-	-	1	-
Weeds											
Ranunculus subgen *Ranunculus*	Buttercup		3	-	1	-	1	-	-	-
Brassica/Sinapis sp.	Cabbage/Turnip etc.		-	-	1	-	-	-	-	-
Raphanus raphanistrum	Wild Raddish		-	-	1	1	-	-	-	3

(Continued on next page)

Table 9.5   (continued)

		Sample	656	806	807	808	809	810	21	37
		Context	8175	10334	10334	10334	10334	10348	416	629
		Feature	8171	9060	9060	9060	9060	9060	415	630
		Fraction	1/4	100%	1/32	1/64	1/16	100%	100%	1/16
		Volume (litres)	20	6	9	9	8	10	40	30
Cruciferae			14	4	2	-	-	-	-	-
Viola sp.	Violet/Pansy etc.		-	-	1	-	-	-	-	-
Silene dioica	White Campion		-	-	-	-	-	-	-	1
Agrostemma githago	Corn Cockle		1	-	-	-	-	-	-	-
Montia fontana subsp. chondroperma	Blinks		2	-	-	-	-	2	-	-
Chenopodium album	Fat Hen		14	-	9	7	5	3	-	-
Chenopodium sp.	Goosefoot/Fat Hen		-	-	-	-	-	1	-	1
Atriplex sp.	Orache		8	2	1	1	-	-	-	-
Chenopodiaceae			4	43	6	-	2	-	-	1
Vicia/Lathyrus sp.	Vetch/Vetchling/Tare			1	7	1	2	1	-	-
Aphanus arvensis	Parsley-piert		1	-	-	-	-	-	-	-
Rosa sp.	Rose		1	-	-	-	-	-	-	-
Umbelliferae			-	-	1	-	-	-	-	-
Polygonum aviculare	Knotgrass		3	-	2	-	1	5	-	-
Polygonum lapathifolium/persicaria	Pale Persicaria/Red Shank		20	6	5	2	-	52	-	-
Polygonum sp.	Knotgrass/Persicaria etc.		-	-	-	-	-	1	-	-
Fallopia convolvulus	Black Bindweed		7	3	1	-	-	1	-	1
Rumex sp.	Docks		54	9	19	2	12	68	-	59
Polygonaceae			6	-	3	1	1	2	-	-
Odontites verna/Euphrasia sp.	Red Barstia/Eyebright		1	-	-	-	-	-	-	-
Galeopsis sp.	Hemp Nettle		9	8	-	-	-	-	-	-
Labiatea, large			-	-	-	1	-	-	-	-
Plantago media/lanceolata	Plantain		-	-	-	-	-	1	1	-
Anthemis cotula	Stinking Mayweed		270	63	116	43	35	-	-	-
Tripleurospermum inordorum	Scentless Mayweed		531	166	407	126	159	15	-	1
Carduus/Cirsium sp.	Thistle		-	-	1	-	-	-	-	-
Centaurea nigra	Lesser Knapweed		-	1	-	-	-	-	-	-
Centaurea cf. *nigra*	cf. Lesser Knapweed		3	-	-	-	-	-	-	-
Centaurea sp.	Cornflower/Knapweed		-	1	-	-	-	-	-	-
Lapsana communis	Nipplewort		8	1	1	1	-	2	-	-
Leontodon sp.	Hawkbit		1	-	-	-	-	-	-	-
Compositae	Composit, large seeded		-	2	-	-	-	2	-	-
Compositae	Composit, small seeded		78	46	6	1	15	-	-	-
Juncus sp.	Rush, seed head		-	-	1	-	-	-	-	-
Bromus subsect *Eubromus*	Brome grass, germinated		290	46	22	17	33	-	-	-
Bromus subsect *Eubromus*	Brome grass		219	81	139	42	48	95	-	4
Danthonia decumbens	Heath Grass		1	-	-	-	-	-	-	-
Gramineae	Grass, large seeded		141	56	64	28	23	97	-	39
Gramineae	Grass, small seeded		45	4	31	8	10	-	-	-
Indet	seed		22	8	8	6	15	4	-	4
Indet	tree bud		-	-	2	-	-	-	-	-

Table 9.6   Charred plant remains: Data from assessed samples not subject to detailed analysis.

Sample	Context	Fill of	Feature type	Phase	Sample volume (l)	Grain	Chaff	Weeds	Species Present
34	71	68	Ditch	3	40			+	
42	808	844	Pit	3	32	+			*T.spelta T.sp*
49	942	844	Pit	3	10	+		+	Indet
56	1120	1119	Gully	4	40	+		+	T.spelta
657	8173	8171	Ditch	2	18	1000+	1000+	++++	*T.spelta T.dicoccum*
									T.sp. short grain
659	8262	8261	Ditch	?	19	+	+	+	T.spelta
660	8246	8244	Ditch	3	14	++			*T.spelta T.sp Avena*
738	9596	9593	Ditch	4-5	20	+++	+++	++	T.spelta
									Hordeum vulgare
746	7678	7563	Ditch	4	10	++++	++++	++++	T.spelta
780	10133	10131	Pit	Med	18	+		+	*T.sp.* short grain

+ = 1-10.
++ = 11-50.
+++ = 51-100.
++++ = >100.

While most of the taxa present will occur on a range of cultivated soils, a few do have more specific requirements. *Raphanus raphanistrum* (wild radish) is an annual/biennial species normally associated with slightly acidic soils. *Odontites verna* (red barstia) and *Anthemis cotula* have a preference for heavy calcareous soils. The dominance of *Tripleurospermum inodorum* over *Anthemis cotula* would suggest the soil conditions are more suited to this species, however, possibly with lighter, better drained conditions. *Montia fontana* subsp. *Chondrosperma* tends to occupy seasonally flooded ground, although given the absence of other wet ground species it is possible that its requirements could be met by a seasonally flooded ditch, or localised hollow.

A few of the species identified are unlikely to be arable weeds. *Ranunculus* subgen. *Ranunculus* (buttercup) are more generally grassland or damp ground plants, but could occupy field margins or be growing within the site. *Rosa* (rose) species are scrubby climbing or scrambling plants which again may have been growing around the site or on the field margins, over walls, trees and so on, or could have entered deposits with fire wood. *Danthonia decumbens* (heath grass) is a tufted perennial of acid grassland. The *Juncus* sp. seed head is also likely to have originated in grass-

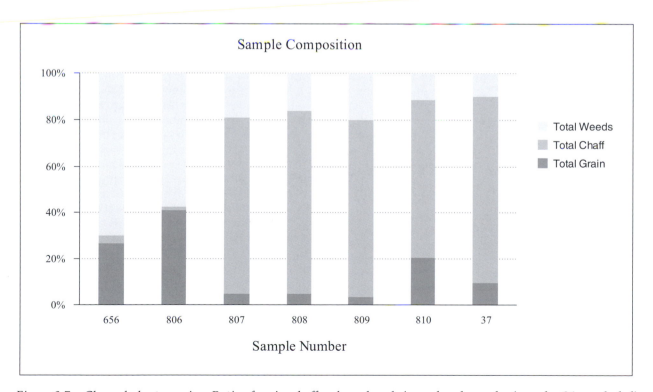

Figure 9.7   Charred plant remains: Ratio of grain, chaff and weed seeds in analysed samples (sample <21> excluded).

land or marshland. These non-arable species might have entered the site by any number of routes and given their small number this could include on clothing, in sheep's wool and so on.

The grasses form a very significant proportion of the weed assemblages, generally forming in the region of 30% of weeds and in sample 810 they form 54.5%, or 63.4% if oats are included in the weeds. Many of the *Bromus* subsect *Eubromus* seeds had germinated, particularly in sample 656. Grain of *Bromus* spp. and of wild oats are the size of cereal grains and do have some nutritional value. They are also common weeds of cereal crops and are particularly characteristic of Iron Age and Roman assemblages such that they are often regarded as potential field crops. Jones (1988, 86), however, pointed out that the question of whether *Bromus* should be regarded as a crop or a weed is meaningless as the distinction is a modern western concept. The same should be said of wild oat. If harvested with the spelt or barley crop the seeds would stay with the grain through the early stages of winnowing and sieving. They might then be separated from the cereal grain in the final stages of processing by hand picking, but could equally be left with the grain to bulk out the harvest, particularly if the harvest was poor or if it was destined for animal fodder. If the deposits represent the waste from a process involving germinating the grain, then the *Bromus* has clearly been through that process with the crop. The fact that a much higher proportion of the *Bromus* grain than the cereal grain has germinated might be due to some inherent differences in the grain (eg germinating at different temperature, moisture level etc.), or might indicate that what is represented is the waste, that is, the spelt and barley that did not germinate properly, plus the weeds and chaff.

Remains from sample 21

One sample was taken from a pit fill (context 416) of Phase 3 date (AD 70-150), located in the centre of the probable shrine. While the assemblage was very small it is significant due to the presence of a single *Pinus pinea* (stone pine) kernel shell. No seed or pine scale were recovered and no other evidence of *Pinus pinea* was found anywhere else on the site. The location of *Pinus pinea* within a shrine raises the possibility that it has derived from ritual use (possibly burning a pine cone or kernels as an altar offering) rather than as food waste. This is discussed further below.

Waterlogged plant remains

The waterlogged deposits in the waterhole (796) produced evidence for both the immediate environment around the feature and evidence for some economic species of Roman introduction. The detailed species list is shown in Table 9.7. All the deposits were dominated by large quantities of *Quercus* sp (oak) and non-*Quercus* wood fragments. The lower deposits (samples 87, 161-2, 164, 166-67) produced seeds of ru-

deral species including *Conium maculatum* (hemlock), *Stellaria media* (chickweed), *Urtica dioica* (stinging nettle) and *Solanum* sp. (nightshade), and wet ground or marshy species such as *Eleocharis palustris* (common spikerush), *Rorippa palustris* (common marsh yellowcress), *Lycopus europeus* (gipsywort) and *Juncus* sp. (rush). These species presumably derived from the wet muddy ground and disturbed soils around the waterhole. The upper deposits (samples 88, 158-59) similarly produced wet/marshy ground and ruderal species, with a slight increase in ruderal plants. In addition these deposits produced some drier grassland species such as *Prunella vulgaris* (selfheal) and *Stellaria graminea* (lesser stitchwort). *Ranunculus sceleratus* (celery leaved crowfoot) suggests the presence of shallow mineral-rich water in the waterhole.

Evidence of economic species included cereal waste in the form of *Triticum spelta* and *T. spelta/dicoccum* glume bases suggesting that activities relating to food processing were taking place in this area, possibly associated with activity represented by sample 37. Such material was more common in the upper deposits, but was also noted in sample 161 lower in the sequence. Two economic species likely to be Roman introductions into Great Britain were recovered: *Prunus avium* (cherry) and *Anethum graveolens* (dill).

Discussion

Sample composition and cereal processing activities

A cereal crop must pass through certain stages of processing from harvesting to consumption (be it as food, fodder or in some other fashion such as thatch), which are defined by the type of cereal, the tools available, and by its final desired destination. The processing stages of cereals, based on ethnographic data, have been described by Hillman (1981; 1984) and, for free-threshing cereals, by G Jones (1984), with models for interpreting archaeological data. While there are limitations in the use of ethnographic models in interpreting archaeological data, particularly the absence of data due to preservation, and geographical location, it is possible by examining the composition of archaeological assemblages to speculate which crop processing stages are represented and to reconstruct harvesting techniques.

Figure 9.7 displays the ratio of grain, chaff and weed seeds in the samples analysed other than sample 21. In all cases grain forms only a minor component and either weeds or chaff dominate. Samples 656 and 806 produced high proportions of weeds with only very small quantities of chaff. The remaining samples produced approximately 70 to 80% chaff with weeds only minor elements. Grain was always limited, but was more significant in samples 656 and 806, forming up to approximately 30 to 40%.

The grain includes tail, or terminal, grain and germinated grain of both the wheat and barley. The proportion of germinated grain was always low. Sprouted embryos were also present, but in very low numbers in relation to glume bases. The chaff was dominated

Table 9.7   *Waterlogged plant remains from waterhole 796.*

		87	88	158	159	161	162	164	166	167
	Sample	87	88	158	159	161	162	164	166	167
	Context	1386	1385	1554	1554	1386	1589	1456	1456	1456
	Weight	1kg	200g	200g	200g	200g	1kg	200g	1kg	200g
Seeds/Leaves										
Bryophyta	Moss	-	-	-	-	-	-	+	-	-
Pteridium sp.	Bracken fronds	-	+	-	-	+	+	-	-	-
Ranunculus acris/repens/bulbosus	Buttercup	++	+	-	+	+	+	-	+	-
R. sceleratus	Celery-leaved Crowfoot	+	-	+	+++	+	-	-	-	-
R. subgen *Batrachium*	Crowfoot	-	-	+	-	-	-	-	-	-
Rorippa palustris	Common Marsh Yellow-cress	-	-	-	-	-	+	-	++	-
Stellaria media	Chickweed	+	-	-	-	-	-	-	+	-
Stellaria graminae	Lesser Stitchwort	+	+	-	-	-	+	-	-	-
Cerastium sp.	Mouse-ear Chickweed	+	-	-	-	-	-	-	+	-
Chenopodium album	Fat Hen	-	-	-	-	-	-	-	+	+
Atriplex sp.	Orache	-	-	-	-	-	-	-	+	-
Malva sylvestris	Mallow	-	-	+	-	-	-	-	+	-
Potentilla	Cinquefoil	-	-	-	-	-	+	-	-	-
cf. *Prunus avium*	cf. Cherry	+	-	-	-	-	+	-	-	-
Rubus fruticosus	Blackberry/Bramble	-	-	-	-	-	+	-	-	-
Anethum graveolens	Dill	-	-	-	-	-	-	-	+	-
Conium maculatum	Hemlock	+	-	-	-	-	+	-	+	-
Polygonum persicaria/lapathifolium	Willow Shank/Pale Persicaria	+	-	-	-	-	-	-	-	-
Polygonum aviculare	Knotgrass	+	-	-	+	+	+	-	+	+
Rumex cf. *conglomeratus*	Sharp Dock	+	-	-	-	-	-	+	-	-
Rumex sp.	Dock	+	-	+	+	+	-	-	+	-
Urtica dioica	Stinging/Common Nettle	++	-	-	-	-	+	-	+	+
Corylus avellana	Hazel nut shell	+	-	-	-	-	-	+	-	-
Solanum sp.	Nightshade	-	-	-	-	-	+	-	+	-
Lycopus europaeus	Gipsywort	-	-	++	-	+	+	-	-	+
Prunella vulgaris	Selfheal	-	+	+	+	-	-	-	-	-
Ballota nigra	Black Horehound	-	-	-	-	-	+	-	+	-
Plantago media/lanceolata	Plantain	+	-	-	-	-	+	-	-	-
Plantago major	Plantain	+	-	-	-	-	+	-	-	-
Galium aparine	Goosegrass	-	-	-	-	-	+	-	-	-
Sonchus asper	Spiny Milk-Thistle	-	-	-	-	-	-	-	+	-
Centaurea sp.	Knapweed	-	-	-	-	-	+	-	-	-
Compositae		+	-	-	-	-	-	-	-	-
Juncus sp.	Rushes	+	-	-	-	-	-	-	+	-
Eleocharis palustris	Common Spike Rush	+	+	+	+	-	+	-	-	+
Carex sp.	Sedge	-	+	+	-	-	+	-	-	+
Triticum spelta	Spelt wheat glume	-	-	-	+	-	-	-	-	-
Triticum spelta/dicoccum	Spelt/Emmer glume	++	+	+	+	-	+	-	-	-
Indet	Tree bud scale	-	-	-	-	+	-	-	-	-
Indet	Leaf	-	-	-	-	-	-	+	-	-
Indet	Bud scale	-	-	-	-	-	+	-	-	-
Wood/Charcoal										
Quercus sp.	Oak, wood	-	+	++	+	+	-	-	+	-
Quercus sp.	Oak, charcoal	+	+	+	+	-	-	-	-	-
Non-*Quercus* sp.	Non-Oak wood	++	++	-	-	++	-	++	-	+++

by glume bases, but included basal rachis, awns, and occasional cereal sized culm nodes. Rachis of barley was also present. As discussed above the weeds were generally large seeded, including large numbers of grasses, or were from composite seed heads. Sample 656 in particular produced very large numbers of grasses and Compositae.

The composition of all samples would suggest the cereal processing waste is represented (the chaff and weeds) rather than the product (the clean grain). Samples 807, 808, 810 and 37 are characteristic of the by-products of Hillman's stages 11 and 12 for glumed wheats (Hillman 1981); the chaff, tail grain and weed seeds separated from the grain by sieving with me-

dium coarse and fine sieves. Some grain and cereal sized weed seeds may also be derived from hand sorting (stage 14). The fact that the material is charred would suggest that it has been burnt as waste or as fuel.

Samples 656 and 806 are not so characteristic of the 'sievings', but could represent hand-sorted weed seeds and spoilt grain. It must also be considered that these samples contain deliberately collected grasses, perhaps as hay or fodder, although traditional hay meadow species are not present. It must also be considered that preservation may have affected the composition of these samples, as chaff will be more readily destroyed than grain or weed seeds at higher temperatures (Boardman and Jones 1990). It is likely, however, that at least two separate stages or even events of cereal processing are represented in ditch group 9060, with another separate episode represented by sample 37.

The presence of germinated grain raises the possibility that germination was deliberate, which would tend to imply malting activities. Malting involves forcing the grain to germinate by steeping in water and then turning out on to a floor in a heap or 'couch' to 'chit'. Once the modification of the endosperm is sufficient the germination process is stopped by roasting the grain in hot air, which produces the malt, which in turn is used for brewing beer (Brown 1983; Corran 1975). Evidence for large scale malt production has been recovered from 'corndriers' from the 2nd century AD onwards (van der Veen 1991). The percentage of germinated grain in the deposits is low, however, as might be expected in an ordinary crop which has been allowed to spoil slightly. The very large number of germinated *Bromus* seeds is unusual. Charred remains, particularly when derived from secondary deposits such as the backfill of ditches or pits generally represent the waste or by-product rather than the product itself. It is therefore reasonable to assume that if malting were taking place it would be the waste assemblages that would be represented archaeologically, that is, the grain which had not germinated along with the chaff, weeds and coleoptiles (sprouted embryos). The deposits in ditch group 9060 might then represent malting waste, where the grains which failed to germinate are disposed of with weeds, including weedy grasses that had germinated. In the absence of the actual sprouts, however, this remains speculative.

Sample distribution

Across the site as a whole the bulk sampling tended to produce charcoal but few samples with seeds and chaff. Samples which did produce grain and cereal processing waste were concentrated in three substantial deposits and one more moderate deposit. Ditch group 9060, which includes ditch section 8171, produced the largest deposit from which multiple samples were taken (samples 656, 657, 806, 807, 808, 809 and 810). Large deposits were also recovered from ditch 7563 (sample 746), pit fill 629 (sample 37) and a slightly smaller deposit from ditch 9596 (sample 738). It is possible that much of the other charred seeds and chaff derive from these large deposits, scatted about the site by later activity including plough action. Such limited numbers of substantial deposits might suggest that cereal processing was operated on a large community scale in restricted areas rather than that individual family groups processed their own cereals as and when they needed.

In terms of area it seems that cereal processing shifted location between Period 2 Phase 2 and Phase 4. In Phase 2 the activity is located within the eastern or south-eastern area of the site, an area suggested to be concerned with agriculture. Trackways seem to lead from this area away from the settlement, possibly to adjacent fields. The later cereal processing deposits are from the area to the north or north-west of the main road, possibly representing processing activity within the separate building plots, which might indicate greater fragmentation of processing activity in the later period. No cereal processing waste was recorded from the area around the shrine in any phase.

The internal distribution of material from group 9060 provides evidence for multiple phases of deposition. One long deposit was identified, given feature number 9060, into which cut 8171 was made. Sample 810 was taken from the extreme south-west of the linear deposits, while samples 806-809 were from the north-eastern part of the deposit, sample 806 the closest to cut 8171. Samples 657 (not analysed) and 656 were taken from cut 8171. The composition of the samples suggests all those from cut 9060 might be from the same deposit with the exception of sample 806, which is more similar to sample 656, with a large proportion of weeds, little chaff and more barley than the other samples. This would suggest that 806 actually represented spill from 656 and that at least two episodes of dumping are represented. It is possible therefore that this feature received successive dumps of material over some time.

Sample 37 was taken from a feature in the northernmost corner of the site, and again is characteristic of cereal processing debris. The deposit was also characterised by iron pan encrustation of the material, suggesting a fluctuating water table in this area. Two waterholes are situated fairly close to the feature, thus it is possible that the watertable was higher here than elsewhere on the site.

Species cultivated

Spelt wheat is the principal wheat recovered across Roman Britain. In Kent it has been recorded from the middle Bronze Age (Pelling 2003, 71). In other parts of southern Britain spelt tended to replace emmer during the Late Bronze Age or Iron Age (Grieg 1991). Recent evidence from the Channel Tunnel Rail Link scheme (eg Pelling 2001) suggests, however, that both hulled wheats were cultivated alongside each other or even together in the south-east region throughout the Iron Age and into the Roman period. The paucity of emmer in the Westhawk Farm samples is therefore of some interest. Van der Veen and O'Connor (1998) suggest that in north-east England the Iron Age cultivation of emmer is linked to extensive farming systems, while the cultivation of spelt is linked to a more intensive mode of production. While insufficient detailed work has been conducted in Kent it is important to note that there do appear to be spelt producing sites and spelt/emmer producing sites, although as yet no purely emmer producing sites.

While the cereal remains generally appear to represent a continuation of Iron Age agricultural traditions, there is evidence for Roman introductions into

Westhawk Farm. *Prunus avium* appears to have been introduced into Britain by the Romans along with other cultivated *Prunus* species including *P. domestica* (plum). Pre-Roman records have been suspect, being old identifications based on charcoal. Roman examples have been recorded from several sites including Upper Thames Street in London (Willcox 1977) and Silchester, Hampshire (M Robinson, pers. comm.). *Anethum graveolens* is an aromatic umbellifer, wild forms of which are known in the Mediterranean, the probable origin of its domestication. As with other spices, such as coriander and cumin, it formed part of the diet of the Roman world and was possibly spread originally by the army. It is recorded from military sites on the frontiers of Roman Britain, such as the 2nd century AD fort at Bearsden in southern Scotland (Dickson and Dickson 2000) where it presumably formed part of the military diet. It has also been recovered from later Roman settlements, in 4th century AD deposits at Barton Court Farm (Robinson 1986) and Farmoor (Robinson 1979), both in Oxfordshire. It is interesting that it was present in rural sites in Kent as early as the 1st or 2nd century.

The other significant introduction is *Pinus pinea*, now recorded at several sites in Britain during the Roman period. Locally, seed coats have been recorded from Monkton-Mount Pleasant on the Isle of Thanet (Pelling unpublished) and a mid 2nd century site at Springhead, Northfleet (Campbell 1998) and pine cone scales from a well at Lullingstone Roman villa (Doherty 1987). Similar finds have been recorded from several sites in London in the City and Southwark (Willcox 1977; Kislev 1988; Giorgi 2000) and from York (Hall and Kenward 1990). All of these finds have been interpreted as the residue of food consumption, as they included the waste products but not the seed and were recovered from refuse contexts. As food waste the remains presumably indicate high-status food and relatively affluent residents. The Westhawk Farm example was recovered from a ritual context and must therefore raise the possibility that it was a religious offering. A growing number of sites have produced evidence for the use of stone pine in religious contexts such as temples of Mithras at Carrawburgh on the Antonine Wall (Richmond *et al.* 1951) and in London (Grimes 1968), the triangular temple at Verulamium (Wheeler and Wheeler 1936, 118-119), from Chew Park, Somerset (Rahtz and Greenfield 1977), from a shrine in Rocester, Staffordshire (Monckton 2000) and most recently the grave of the 'female gladiator' at Great Dover Street, Southwark (Giorgi 2000). Most of the ritual finds therefore are from military or urban sites. The Westhawk Farm deposit indicates that other Romano-British sites were also witnessing Roman style or influenced rituals, although the location of the site on a major road suggests that it could be visited by travelling Roman soldiers or high status visitors.

Stone pine therefore appears to be a Mediterranean food of some significance in terms of 'ritual' and value as a food. Other Mediterranean fruits or foods found on British sites are also likely to have been of some value and this is possibly reflected in their use within ritual contexts, such as grapes burnt on the funeral pyre, then placed within a grave at Pepper Hill in Kent (Davis forthcoming), and charred lentils (*Len culinaris*) from the same grave at Pepper Hill, and from cremation graves in Hopper Street, East London (de Moulins, pers. comm.). Other fruits found associated with the 'female gladiator' were dates, figs, and almonds. These finds may reflect the requirements of Mediterranean gods to receive Mediterranean fruits or may simply reflect the value of these imported goods.

While cherry and dill could have been easily cultivated locally, producing fruit/seed quickly (particularly in the case of dill). Stone pine, if cultivated locally would not have produced cones for several years. The number of finds from rural sites in Kent may be associated with its successful cultivation on suitably calcium-rich soils, although evidence of the overseas trade in Italian cones is known from a Roman ship wreck near Toulon, France (Kislev 1988). It is equally possible therefore that in Kent Roman traditions were particularly readily adopted, or that proximity to trading ports and roads was influential.

Conclusions

The plant remains recovered from the Roman roadside settlement of Westhawk Farm are in some respects typical of the pattern emerging for Roman sites in Kent. Spelt wheat is the major cereal cultivated, while emmer wheat is also recorded. At present detailed investigation of sites in Kent is too limited to speculate on the significant of spelt versus emmer cultivation. Cereal processing appears to have been taking place within the site possibly within restricted areas or zones. Germinated grain and a large number of germinated *Bromus* seeds may have derived from malting activities.

Associated weed seeds provide little evidence for soils types or cultivating conditions, but do suggest that waste from several stages of cereal processing was dumped together.

The location of the site on a major road may explain why at least three imported or newly introduced food plants were deposited. Cherry and dill may represent food debris while a find of stone pine within a shrine may represent a religious offering, perhaps by travellers or by wealthy inhabitants of the settlement.

INSECT REMAINS FROM ROMAN WATERHOLES
by Mark Robinson

Introduction

Samples from three substantial waterholes were assessed to determine their potential for insect analysis. Two of these features were considered to have good potential to provide useful palaeoenvironmental information about the site (Table 9.8).

Table 9.8   Insect remains from waterholes: Samples examined.

Sample	Context	Feature	Date	Sample weight
722	9414	Waterhole 9179	?2nd century AD (Phase 3)	4.0kg
166	1456	Waterhole 796	mid-late 2nd century AD (Phase 4)	1.0kg
165	1456	Waterhole 796	mid-late 2nd century AD (Phase 4)	1.0kg
164	1456	Waterhole 796	mid-late 2nd century AD (Phase 4)	1.0kg

Methods and results

Each sample was washed over onto a 0.25 mm mesh to separate the organic material from the inorganic fraction. The organic material was then subjected to paraffin flotation to extract insect remains from plant debris. The flot was washed in detergent then sorted in water under a binocular microscope for insect fragments. The insects were identified and the results listed in Tables 9.9 and 9.10. Nomenclature for Coleoptera follows Kloet and Hincks (1977).

Interpretation (Fig. 9.8)

Waterhole 9179

The majority of the insects from waterhole 9179 were aquatic individuals. The small water beetle *Helophorus* cf. *brevipalpis* outnumbered all the other beetles in the sample. It flourishes in small bodies of stagnant water. Other beetles of this habitat from the waterhole included *Hydrobius fuscipes*, *Ochthebius minimus* and *Hydraena testacea*. The occurrence of several individuals of *Tanysphyrus lemnae* suggested that its host plant, *Lemna* sp. (duckweed) carpeted the surface of the water. The splashed sides of the waterhole or the muddy margins around the top perhaps provided a habitat for *Platystethus cornutus* gp.

The remainder of the insects probably fell in from the surrounding landscape. There was no evidence that any had been amongst refuse dumped in the waterhole. The environment of the site in the 2nd century AD was relatively open. There were only two members of Species Group 4, beetles of wood and trees. One of them, *Scolytus rugulosus*, is a bark beetle of the family Rosaceae, particularly *Prunus* spp. (sloe, plum, cherry etc.) in hedges and orchards. The other, *Phymatodes alni*, is a cerambycid beetle that bores into more substantial dead hardwood with the bark on, such as *Quercus* sp. (oak). While it is possible that there were some oak trees on the site it is also very plausible that this beetle emerged from wood brought as fuel for the iron working that was occurring on the site.

Insects of open habitats including grassland were relatively well represented. Species of Scarabaeidae and Elateridae which have larvae that feed on the roots of grassland plants, such as *Phyllopertha horticola* and *Agriotes* sp. (Species Group 11) comprised 3.4% of the terrestrial Coleoptera. Scarabaeoid dung beetles (Species Group 2), mostly members of the genus *Aphodius*, comprised 11.9% of the terrestrial Coleoptera. This is sufficiently high a percentage to suggest that domestic animals were grazing in the vicinity of the waterhole, although an even higher value would have been expected if the waterhole had been used to water large numbers of stock corralled around it.

There was also evidence for areas of weedy disturbed ground or bare ground with clumps of vegetation, as might be expected in a settlement. Some of the Carabidae (ground beetles) from the sample, for example *Amara apricaria* and *Harpalus rufipes*, favour such habitats. They also occur in arable fields. The phytophagous Coleoptera included *Brachypterus* sp., which feeds on *Urtica dioica* (stinging nettle) and *Gastrophysa polygoni*, which feeds on *Rumex* spp. (docks) and *Polygonum* spp. (knotgrass etc.).

The insects, however, gave no evidence for structures or human habitation in the settlement. The beetles of Species Group 7, which occur in general foul organic material habitats, were not, at 5.1% of the terrestrial Coleoptera, particularly abundant. The various synanthropic beetles and woodworm beetles of Species Group 9a, 9b and 10 were absent.

Waterhole 796

The samples from waterhole 796, which were all from the same context, are considered together. The same beetles of stagnant water were again abundant and *Helophorus* cf. *brevipalpis* was likewise by far the most numerous. There was, however, less evidence for *Lemna* sp. (duckweed) growing on the surface of the water, with only a single individual of *Tanysphyrus lemnae*.

As for the previous waterhole, there were many insects which probably fell in from the surrounding landscape. However, there were also some which had perhaps been amongst refuse. The landscape of the later 2nd century AD seems to have remained relatively open. The only wood and tree-feeding beetles of Species Group 2 were *Scolytus rugulosus* again and *Chalcoides* sp. The latter feeds on the leaves of *Salix* and *Populus* spp. (willow and poplar).

Various insects gave evidence of grassland. Members of Species Group 11, such as *Agriotes lineatus*, which feeds on the roots of grassland herbs, were, at 1.9% of the terrestrial Coleoptera, not very abundant, but other grassland species were present. They included the weevil *Gymnetron pascuorum* which feeds on *Plantago lanceolata* (ribwort plantain) and the members of Species Group 3 such as *Sitona* sp. which feed on *Trifolium* spp. (clovers) and *Vicia* and *Lathyrus* spp. (vetches). Workers of a grassland ant, *Lasius flavus* gp. were also present. It is the ant which builds anthills. The scarabaeoid dung beetles of Species Group

358

Table 9.9   Insect remains from waterholes: Coleoptera.

	Minimum No. of Individuals				Species Group
Water hole	9179	796/256			
Sample	722	166	165	164	
Sample weight (kg)	4.0	1.0	1.0	1.0	
Trechus micros (Hbst.)	2	-	-	-	
Bembidion lampros (Hbst.) or *properans* Step.	1	1	-	-	
B. doris (Pz.)	1	-	-	-	
B. biguttatum (F.)	1	-	-	-	
B. guttula (F.)	1	-	-	-	
Bembidion sp.	-	-	-	1	
Pterostichus strenuus (Pz.)	-	-	-	1	
P. vernalis (Pz.)	1	-	-	-	
Tachys sp.	1	1	-	-	
Agonum viduum (Pz.)	-	-	-	1	
Amara apricaria (Pk.)	1	1	1	-	6b
Amara sp. (not *apricaria*)	2	1	-	-	
Harpalus rufipes (Deg.)	2	-	1	-	6a
H. S. Ophonus sp.	1	-	-	1	
H. affinis (Schr.)	1	1	-	-	
Acupalpus cf. *meridianus* (L.)	1	-	-	1	
Dromius linearis (Ol.)	1	-	-	-	
Haliplus sp.	1	-	1	-	1
Hygrotus inaequalis (F.)	1	-	-	-	1
Hydroporus sp.	2	1	-	-	1
Agabus bipustulatus (L.)	1	-	1	-	1
Colymbetes fuscus (L.)	1	-	-	1	1
Helophorus aquaticus (L.)	1	-	-	-	1
H. grandis Ill.	1	-	-	1	1
H. aquaticus (L.) or *grandis* (Ill.)	2	1	1	-	1
Helophorus spp. (*brevipalpis* size)	103	32	8	11	1
Cercyon haemorrhoidalis (F.)	-	-	-	1	7
Cercyon sp.	1	-	1	-	7
Megasternum obscurum (Marsh.)	2	1	1	-	7
Hydrobius fuscipes (L.)	2	1	1	1	1
Anacaena globulus (Pk.)	1	-	-	-	1
Helochares or *Enochrus* sp.	1	-	1	1	1
Histerinae indet.	-	-	1	-	
Ochthebius bicolon Germ.	-	-	-	1	1
O. cf. *bicolon* Germ.	2	-	2	-	1
O. minimus (F.)	4	-	2	-	1
O. cf. *minimus* (F.)	6	2	-	-	1
Hydraena testacea Curt.	4	-	-	-	1
Limnebius papposus Muls.	2	-	-	-	1
Carpelimus bilineatus Step.	-	-	-	1	
Platystethus cornutus gp.	4	2	2	1	
P. nitens (Sahl.)	1	-	1	2	
Anotylus rugosus (F.)	-	2	-	1	7
Stenus sp.	-	-	-	1	
Rugilus sp.	-	1	-	-	
Gyrohypnus angustatus Step.	-	-	1	-	
G. fracticornis (Müll.) or *punctulatus* (Pk.)	1	-	-	-	
Xantholinus longiventris Heer	1	-	-	-	
X. linearis (Ol.) or *longiventris* Heer	-	-	1	-	
Philonthus sp.	1	1	-	-	
Aleocharinae indet.	3	2	1	1	
Geotrupes sp.	1	1	1	1	2
Aphodius depressus (Kug.)	1	-	-	-	2
A. foetidus (Hbst.)	1	-	-	-	2
A. granarius (L.)	1	5	3	2	2
A. pusillus (Hbst.)	2	-	1	-	2

(Continued on next page)

Table 9.9   (continued)

	Minimum No. of Individuals				Species Group
Water hole	9179	796/256			
Sample	722	166	165	164	
Sample weight (kg)	4.0	1.0	1.0	1.0	
A. rufipes (L.)	-	1	-	-	2
A. cf. sphacelatus (Pz.)	1	-	1	-	2
Onthophagus ovatus (L.)	-	1	-	1	2
O. taurus (Schreb.)	-	-	1	-	2
Onthophagus sp. (not ovatus)	-	1	-	-	2
Phyllopertha horticola (L.)	1	-	-	-	11
Agriotes lineatus (L.)	-	1	-	-	11
Agriotes sp.	1	-	-	1	11
Cantharis sp.	-	-	2	-	
Cantharis or Rhagonycha sp.	1	1	-	-	
Anobium punctatum (Deg.)	-	1	2	2	10
Tenebrioides mauritanicus (L.)	-	-	-	1	9b
Brachypterus sp.	2	-	-	-	
Atomaria sp.	1	2	2	-	8
Lathridius minutus gp.	-	-	2	3	8
Enicmus transversus (Ol.)	-	-	1	1	8
Corticaria punctulata Marsh.	-	-	-	1	8
Corticariinae indet.	1	1	2	2	8
Phymatodes alni (L.)	1	-	-	-	4
Oulema lichenis Voet	1	-	-	-	
Gastrophysa polygoni (L.)	1	1	-	-	
Phyllotreta nigripes (F.)	-	-	-	1	
Longitarsus sp.	2	-	1	2	
Chalcoides sp.	-	-	-	1	4
Epitrix pubescens (Koch)	-	1	-	-	
Podagrica fuscicornis (L.)	-	1	-	-	
Chaetocnema concinna (Marsh.)	1	-	1	2	
Apion radiolus (Marsh.)	-	1	-	-	
Apion sp. (not radiolus)	1	-	1	-	3
Sitona sp.	-	2	-	-	3
Tanysphyrus lemnae (Pk.)	3	1	-	-	5
Bagous sp.	1	-	-	-	5
Ceutorhynchus erysimi (F.)	1	-	-	-	
Ceuthorhynchinae indet.	1	-	1	-	
Gymnetron pascuorum (Gyl.)	-	-	1	-	
Scolytus rugulosus (Müll.)	1	1	-	1	4
Total	194	74	51	51	

Key to species group:
1. Aquatic
2. Pasture/Dung
3. ?Meadowland
4. Wood and Trees
5. Marsh/Aquatic Plants
6a. General Distbd Grnd/Arable
6b. Sandy/Dry Distbd Grnd/Arable
7. Dung / Foul Organic Material
8. Lathridiidae
9a. General Synanthropic
9b. Serious Stored Grain Pests
10. Esp. Structural Timbers
11. On Roots in Grassland
12. Heathland and Moorland

Table 9.10   Insect remains from waterholes: Other insects (+ = present).

		Minimum No. of Individuals			
Water hole		9179	796/256		
Sample		722	166	165	164
Sample weight (kg.)		4.0	1.0	1.0	1.0
Philaenus or *Neophilaenus* sp.		-	-	1	-
Aphidoidea indet.		-	2	-	1
Saldula S. *Saldula* sp.		1	-	-	-
Lasius flavus gp.	- worker	-	-	2	-
Lasius flavus or *niger* gp.	- female	1	-	1	-
Hymenoptera indet. (not (Formicidae)		-	1	2	1
Chironomidae indet.	- larva	-	-	-	+
Bibionidae indet.	- adult	-	-	-	2
Diptera indet.	- puparium	-	261	-	-

2 were particularly abundant, comprising 18.9% of the terrestrial Coleoptera. The most numerous members of this group were again species of *Aphodius*, in this instance *Aphodius granarius*. However, there was also an example of *Onthophagus taurus*, represented by a left elytron from Sample 165. This beetle is now extinct in Britain although it still occurs in Northern France and Belgium (Allen 1976, 205-6; Paulian 1959, 88-9). The high value for Species Group 2 strongly suggested that domestic animals were concentrated in the vicinity of the waterhole.

The same species of Carabidae that favour weedy, cultivated or sparsely vegetated ground (Species Groups 6a and 6b) that occurred in waterhole 9179 were also identified from waterhole 796. One weed which commonly occurs around settlements, *Malva sylvatica* (common mallow) was the likely host of two mallow-feeding beetles, *Podagrica fuscicornis* and *Apion radiolus*. Mallows are very susceptible to grazing, so they presumably grew in an area separate from where the domestic animals were enclosed. *Epitrix pubescens*, which feeds on *Solanum* spp. (nightshades), was also present.

Unlike waterhole 9179, there was good evidence for settlement activity and structures in the vicinity of waterhole 796. *Anobium punctatum* (woodworm beetle), a member of Species Group 10, comprised 4.7% of the terrestrial Coleoptera from waterhole 796. It usually attacks structural timbers. Members of the Lathridiidae (Species Group 8), which are fungal feeders on plant material such as hay, thatch and straw, comprised 12.3% of the terrestrial Coleoptera. Most numerous was *Lathridius minutus* gp. but *Enicmus transversus* and *Corticaria punctulata* were also present. It is possible that these beetles had been among plant debris dumped in the well.

The general synanthropic beetles of Species Group 9a were absent. However, there was a single beetle from Species Group 9b, the serious pest of stored grain, *Tenebroides mauritanicus*. It is almost certainly a Roman introduction to Britain and is restricted to indoor habitats. The adults of *T. mauritanicus* are predominantly carnivorous, feeding on other pests in stored grain such as *Oryzaephilus surinamensis* (Ken-ward and Williams 1979, 94). However, the larvae chiefly feed on grain and are very destructive. A single individual does not demonstrate large scale grain storage near the waterhole, but does at least show the use of grain from a major store.

The beetles of Species Group 7 such as *Megasternum obscurum* and *Anotylus rugosus*, which occur in a wide range of foul organic debris, were, at 6.6% of the terrestrial Coleoptera, no more abundant than might be expected given the presence of scarabaeoid dung beetles. No other habitats were suggested by the insects. However, the numerous Diptera (fly) puparia in Sample 166 were likely to have been from larvae that developed and pupated in an item incorporated into the deposit. Unfortunately, it was not possible to identify the puparia.

Discussion

The insect evidence from the two waterholes at Westhawk Farm suggested that the settlement was not of fully urban character. There were open grazed areas and there was by no means a full synanthropic fauna of beetles that occur in various indoor habitats as have been found in towns such as York (eg Hall and Kenward 1990). Indeed, insects indicative of a settlement were entirely absent from one of the waterholes. However, rather similar results have been obtained from some other Roman small unwalled towns such as Scole, Norfolk and Elms Farm, Heybridge, Essex (Robinson forthcoming b). These towns probably had large open areas between buildings.

The discovery of *Tenebroides mauritanicus* in the absence of any other pests of stored grain was surprising. Its partly carnivorous habit makes it dependent on other grain beetles and there have been few finds of it from Roman Britain. The other records are from major Roman towns where there was large scale grain storage, for example York (Kenward and Williams 1979) and Lincoln (Kenward, pers. comm.). Perhaps it had been imported to Westhawk Farm amongst grain rather than living in stored grain on the site.

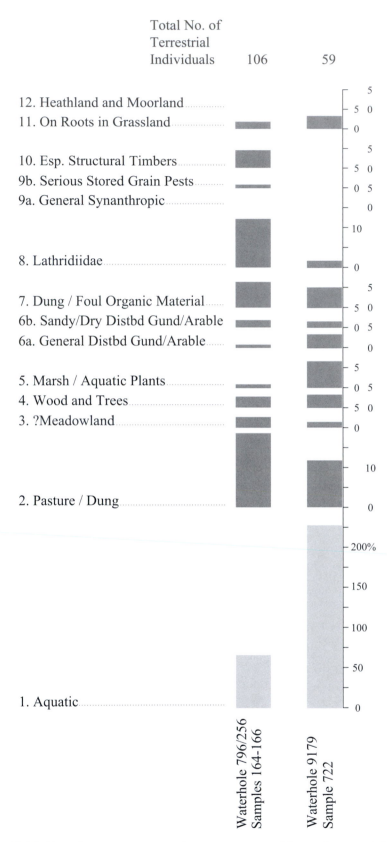

Figure 9.8 Coleoptera: Habitat/species groups expressed as a percentage of the total terrestrial Coleoptera. (Not all the terrestrial Coleoptera have been classified into groups).

The record of *Onthophagus taurus* is also of interest. This dung beetle has been recorded from several Neolithic and Bronze Age sites, but is now extinct in Britain (Robinson 1991, 320). It probably survived as a very rare member of the British fauna until the early 19th century AD (Allen 1976, 205-6, 220-21). It is possible that this beetle, which still occurs across the Channel, declined later in Kent than elsewhere in England because climatic conditions are more similar to those of north-east France.

Chapter 10: Synthesis and Discussion

TOPOGRAPHICAL AND ENVIRONMENTAL SETTING

The Roman settlement seems to have been sited to take best advantage of the local topography by being positioned at the top and on the upper slopes of a south-east facing valley side. The soils of the area, mostly clay silts, are not particularly well-drained, and the ridge top position offered the best location in relation to this problem. Moreover, a localised patch of better-draining third terrace gravel was also available for use and was exploited for the focal road junction area of the Roman settlement. It may have been these characteristics that had recommended the area for use as part of a system of fields, perhaps as early as the middle Bronze Age (see below). Little is known of the wider environmental setting at that time though analogous activity at nearby Brisley Farm may have been fairly closely preceded by tree clearance. There is no direct evidence for the physical character of the Westhawk Farm area in the Iron Age. By the early Roman period the site seems to have been set in a largely open landscape. Pollen evidence from water-hole 796 indicated that a wide range of woody plants was growing in the catchment, of which the most abundant trees and shrubs were oak, hazel and willow, but the representation even of these was at a fairly low level. By the mid to late 2nd century levels of woodland pollen, and particularly oak, had declined further, emphasizing the impression of an (at least locally) open landscape.

MORPHOLOGICAL ASPECTS

Pre-road features

The only archaeological features which demonstrably predated the Roman road alignment in Area B were a group of linear features assigned to the prehistoric Period 1 on the basis of the distinctive character of their fills, which were of a light colour and contrasted markedly with the fills of all later features. Put together, the features with these characteristics formed a pattern with its slightly irregular long axis aligned NE-SW, indicated most clearly by feature 1640/10100, which with related features was traced for a distance of at least 330 m down the axis of Area B – following the topographical trend of the site. Lesser lengths of ditch were aligned parallel and at right-angles to this feature, the only exception to this pattern being a fairly short length of ditch underlying the later road and aligned almost exactly north-south. While this alignment was anomalous the fill of the feature was consistent with those of the rest of this group and so it is included with them.

No dating evidence was recovered from any of the component features of this group. A number of potentially pre-Roman discrete features included a shallow pit, 8241, which produced flint-tempered pottery lacking diagnostic sherds but assigned on the basis of its general characteristics to the middle Bronze Age. It is not clear if this feature was associated with the ditches, but the character of its main fill was comparable with the fills of these features. Their extent and the lack of associated finds and settlement-related features support their interpretation as part of a field system. This comprised parts of three parallel alignments, of which the central was the most clearly defined, with lesser ditches, mostly at right-angles, running between these lines. Two ditches extended in a north-westerly direction beyond the observed NE-SW alignments, but no such features were seen extending downslope on the south-east side of the system.

The boundaries presumably belonged to a coaxial field system comparable to those which are being increasingly recognised both in the Thames Valley and in north Kent (Yates 1999; 2001). These systems originate in the middle Bronze Age but become more common in the later Bronze Age, though it is not certain that they are exclusively of this date. On this basis the Westhawk Farm field system could have been as early as the middle Bronze Age. This is not demonstrable conclusively on present evidence, though the ceramic material from a small number of features perhaps associated with the field system is consistent with such a date. A later Bronze Age or even later date is possible. The presence of the field system indicates extensive exploitation of the Weald Clay rather earlier than might have been anticipated, and further evidence of this is seen at Brisley Farm, only c 750 m distant, where features forming part of an extensive field system were laid out following woodland clearance (Johnson 2002). A middle Bronze Age date is likely for that system, component features of which had similar leached fills and a similar alignment to their counterparts at Westhawk Farm (Casper Johnson, pers. comm.; for the comparability of the alignments see Champion 2007, 101). At Westhawk Farm only a small number of features were positively identified as tree-holes, and it is possible that this area was relatively clear of trees rather before the field system was put in place. Whatever the precise date of the Westhawk Farm and Brisley Farm features, however, the analogies with the Thames Valley systems suggest an association with animal husbandry rather than arable agriculture (Yates 2001, 65-66). It is possible, on the basis of their alignments, that the features at these two sites were part of the same system of land division, but this is not demonstrable on present evidence.

Road network

There is no direct evidence to demonstrate how long the Period 1 field system remained in use. The subsequent Roman road followed the general trend of the field system alignment, but this may have been simply because both reflected the underlying topography. At one point, on the north-west side of the Canterbury road towards the south-west end of the settlement, the line of one of the field system ditches was perpetuated in the early Roman period, but only from the point at which it was cut by the earliest roadside ditch. In detail, the alignment of the Canterbury road disregarded the underlying features, and it is likely that at least some components of the field system were no longer significant elements in the early Roman landscape. Equally, the survival of *any* such components after a millennium or perhaps even longer argues for continued maintenance of the system over an extended period, and perhaps particularly the survival of hedgerows.

It is clear that the line of the Canterbury road was established in Phase 2 of Period 2, that is, in the pre-Flavian period, even if it was not necessarily surfaced at that time. It is possible that the route was of pre-Roman origin, forming a logical south-westerly extension of the 'natural' route up the Stour valley from Canterbury providing access to the resources of the Weald. Be that as it may, the early Roman date contradicts the view of Cleere and Crossley (1985, 62-64), who followed Margary (1947; cf. 1948, 208) in seeing the Weald-Canterbury road (his (1973) route 130) and route 13 (Weald-Rochester via Maidstone) as late additions to the scheme of Roman roads in the eastern Weald (see Fig. 1.2). Whether or not route 130 reached its full westerly extent (as far as Benenden) in the early Roman period is unclear. Its completion should, however, have post-dated the construction of the north-south route 13 at that point, on the basis of the relationship between the two.

The same argument applies to the relationship between route 130 and Margary route 131, from Lympne to Maidstone. The latter is clearly the later of the two main roads at Westhawk Farm, now that the absence of a straightforward crossroads here has been established. Why the southerly section of this route, from Lympne, should have been aligned directly on the settlement at Westhawk Farm while the northerly section, from Maidstone, was not, is unclear. It is just possible that the northerly section could have predated the establishment of significant settlement at Westhawk Farm, but this would make it a very early road indeed given the likelihood that settlement was well-established here before the Flavian period. Such an early date for the northern part of the Maidstone-Lympne road seems unlikely.

The date of the southern section of route 131 is also uncertain, but the evidence of the geophysical survey reveals a fairly clearly-defined road line with only slight indications of features not respecting its position. This parallels the situation for route 130, the early date of which is not now in doubt. The apparently coherent plan of the central part of the settlement at Westhawk Farm (see below) suggests that the two roads may have been fairly closely contemporary.

Junction zone

It is unfortunate that knowledge of the area surrounding the junction of routes 130 and 131, which seems likely to have been the focus of the settlement, is based almost exclusively on the results of the geophysical survey and therefore has no chronological dimension. The junction area was enclosed by linear boundaries which in places are very well-defined on the geophysical survey, particularly at the points where the area is entered from the south-east by the road from Lympne and from the south-west by the road from the Weald. Including the widths of the two roads, this defined area was up to *c* 70 m across and at least *c* 190 m NE-SW. Several minor enclosures of uncertain function were located within the northern part of this defined area, and a number of significant discrete magnetic anomalies were more widely distributed, principally in the south-eastern half of the area. Some of these may represent significant structural and other activity, but even so there is a strong impression of a well-defined focal space, not all of which is likely to have been occupied by buildings. Relatively few such spaces have been identified in the 'small towns' of Roman Britain, though they have been claimed for Dorchester-on-Thames (Frere 1985, 98-100), Godmanchester (Green 1975, 204), Alcester, Warwicks (Booth 1994, 173-174), Heybridge, adjacent to the temple complex (Atkinson and Preston 1998, 107) and Catterick (Wilson 2002a, 76). They are likely to have been more common than appears at present, given that they probably served (among other functions) as market places (cf Burnham 1987, 180). The Westhawk Farm space, if correctly identified, is, however, the largest known example in a 'small town' or similar context.

Although the presence of defining ditches helps to identify the focal junction area on the geophysical survey plan the degree of definition of this area seems a little unusual. The apparent scale of the ditches hints that access to the area may have been constrained, particularly given the emphasis on the enclosing features in the vicinity of the roads entering them. This may have implications for the overall nature of the settlement (see below). There is no particular indication from the geophysical survey that the boundary defining the junction area was superimposed on an earlier settlement layout - the configuration of the detectable features is such that they could all have related to the junction area layout after its main boundary was established.

Major boundaries north-west of the Canterbury Road

The geophysical survey demonstrates that the north-western side of the Canterbury road was defined by a ditch or ditches along its entire length. Excavation in Area B, however, revealed that these ditches were not continuous throughout the life of the settlement. In particular, there was no north-west roadside ditch at the northern end of Area B in Phases 2 or 3 of Period 2 (though further south-west the earliest roadside ditches were of Phase 2). The principal early ditch alignment north-west of the road at this point diverged from the road edge some 95 m from the edge of the excavation and ran in a more northerly direction. This alignment then almost certainly formed the north-western boundary of the settlement proper, set back roughly 40-45 m from the road edge on a line followed by the recent hedge and treeline. The date of the earliest north-west roadside ditches evident in the geophysical survey of Area A is therefore unknown since they could not be correlated with excavated features in Area B.

The early settlement boundary as seen at the north-west corner of Area B originated in Phase 2 and was modified in Phase 3, but was out of use at the latest by Phase 4, when it was cut by boundaries roughly at right-angles to the road - though features associated with plot NW3 already cut the boundary in Phase 3. Further north, however, in the vicinity of Area C, for example, this boundary was probably never superseded and is likely to have remained in use, probably with repeated redefinition, as the main settlement boundary up to the late Roman period, although insufficient of the ditch sequence was seen next to excavation Area C for this to be certain.

Major boundaries south-east of the Canterbury Road

South-east of the Canterbury road the arrangement of boundaries was much less coherent. At the south-western end of the site the presence of an early post-conquest ditch line, corresponding to the one on the other side of the road, is assumed, but over most of its length this feature had been removed by later cuts in the roadside ditch sequence. This earliest ditch stopped about 145 m short of the north-east margin of Area B and turned south-eastwards towards the first of a complex and long-lived sequence of roughly rectilinear enclosures which lay at the southern margin of the shrine area (see below). There was no discernible definition of the road margin in the latter area until the early 3rd century.

At the north-east margin of Area B a further complex sequence of ditches appears to have formed the south-western side of a large sub-rectangular enclosure which the geophysical survey suggests fronted the Canterbury road for a distance of just over 100 m. This enclosure was probably double ditched, though the evidence is only reasonably clear for the excavated south-west side and on the road-fronting north-west side. The geophysical survey evidence for the north-east side is obscured by a modern field boundary, and the south-eastern side of the putative enclosure does not appear on the geophysical survey at all, though the existence of this side is strongly indicated by the ditches of the south-west side turning sharply to the north-east beneath building R at the north-east margin of Area B. The maximum dimensions of the enclosure can thus be estimated at roughly 110 m by 65 m. A single boundary perpendicular to the road line appears to bisect the enclosure, but the significance of this is unclear and the relative chronology of the features is of course unknown.

The southern margin of the defined road junction area lay between c 40 m and 55 m north-east of the probable north-east side of this enclosure. This boundary was not at right-angles to the line of the Canterbury road, but was parallel to two linear features (or in one case possibly an alignment of discrete features) lying between it and the probable double-ditched enclosure to the south. The reason for this change of alignment is unclear. The easterly extent of these alignments is also uncertain. Outside (ie east of) the enclosed junction area the geophysical survey reveals a variety of features, some fairly clearly related to the Lympne road and others less clearly associated and less readily interpreted. There is no indication of a single settlement boundary defining the south-east side of the site to correspond with that seen to the north-west. A fairly substantial linear feature aligned roughly NNE-SSW can be traced for a length of some 80 m towards the bottom of the slope close to the Whitewater Dyke, but this appears to be too isolated from other features to have served as a major boundary for the settlement as a whole.

Plot divisions

A particular feature of the site plan as revealed by the geophysical survey and amplified in places by excavation is the occurrence of property units or plots defined by ditches laid out, for the most part, at right-angles to the alignment of roadside ditches. Such plots are of course a common characteristic of roadside settlements or 'small towns'. The geophysical survey hints at the existence of plots established at right-angles to the line of the Lympne road, particularly on its northern side, but their detailed layout is unclear. The best evidence is found on the north-west side of the Canterbury road, though in the vicinity of the focal road junction area of the settlement the definition of plot boundaries was variable. Plots identifiable with reasonable confidence here ranged from c 27-34 m in width at the road frontage, and a hypothetical block of six plots covering a distance of some 170 m just north of the bend in the Canterbury road alignment had a notional average plot width of c 28 m (allowing for the reconstruction of one boundary where the geophysical survey is obscured by a modern hedge-line). North of here the plot boundary spacing was less consistent. Two larger plots were located opposite the point where the Lympne road entered the junction area, the first apparently almost 50 m wide and the one to the north of it some 34 m wide. A hypothetical subdivision of the first of these would produce two plots much nearer to the notional average plot width of *c* 28 m, but there is no clear evidence for such a division on the geophysical survey. There is a suggestion of a slight offset in the alignment of the north-west roadside ditch at the junction of these two larger plots, and it may be that the more regular arrangement seen further south changed here.

Further south still, evidence for systematic roadside plot divisions in Area B is again confined to the north-west side of the Canterbury road. There were two distinct groups of plots here, defined as north-west and south-west groups. At the north-west corner of Area B at least three rather irregular plots were defined by ditches by Phase 4. The two northernmost plots of this group (NW1 and NW2) were both *c* 20 m wide, but in neither case did the boundary ditches extend straightforwardly to meet the roadside ditch. Plot NW2 adjoined ironworking structure I in plot NW3, so its south-west boundary, associated directly with structure I, was therefore already in existence in Phase 3. Plot NW3 was in turn defined on its south-west side by a slighter linear feature which did reach to the road frontage and extended back from it to the limit of the excavated area, a distance of some 45 m. The plots in this part of the site were therefore all relatively deep - at least 45 m - and narrow; that containing structure I being only 11-12 m wide (although a later redefinition of this boundary with a fenceline increased the width to *c* 15-16 m). Their boundaries disregarded the earlier major settlement boundary, which they overlay.

It is not clear that the north-west plot group formed part of a continuous block with the plots seen further north in Area A. The distance between the northern boundary of Plot NW1 and the most southerly of the group of six '28 m unit' plots discussed above is just over 40 m. This would allow for two plots of *c* 20 m width, but there is no indication of a boundary defining such units on the geophysical survey and its existence is at best speculative.

South-west of the plots in the vicinity of structure I there is no indication of formal planning for some 60-70 m, at which point a block of six south-west plots, of which the northern four were particularly well-defined, is encountered. The most southerly plot (SW6) was a unit that had been in existence from Phase 2. Curiously, the redefinition of the north-east side of this plot in Phase 4, approximately contemporary with the layout of the other five, was at a marked angle to the line of the associated roadside ditch, contrasting not only with the precisely perpendicular layout of the other plot boundaries, but also with the original definition of the plot, which had been at right-angles to the roadside ditch alignment. This is the exact reverse of the development sequence which might have been expected, but there is no doubt about the stratigraphic sequence upon which the present interpretation is based.

Despite the broad regularity of appearance of these plots their frontage widths were slightly variable, being (from the north) *c* 16 m, 17 m, 18 m, 22 m, 18 m and 20 m (the last figure assumes that the south-west 'boundary' of plot SW6, not certainly redefined after Phase 2, was in some way still in use). Plot SW3 seems to have been subdivided lengthways, giving two very narrow blocks, and it is possible that this subdivision was in place from the initial establishment of the plots, though it seems improbable that these were intended to be two separate units. The depth of the plots is also unclear and may have been equally variable. Their north-west ends lay outside the limit of the excavation area, and while limited additional work was permitted by the developers it was not possible to provide conclusive evidence for all the plots. Plot SW2 was shown to be some 80 m deep, but there was no continuation of a rear boundary for plot SW1 from the north-east corner of SW2. Indeed the north-east boundary ditch of plot SW1 was seen to terminate some 67 m from the roadside ditch, but with no apparent trace of a return south-westwards from this point to mark the rear boundary of the plot. It is thus possible that the degree of definition of the rear boundaries of these plots was very variable and a uniform depth cannot be assumed for all of them (a similar lack of uniformity was observed amongst the admittedly less regular plots of the south-central group). This and the variation in width may suggest that despite being quite closely contemporary the plots were not laid out as a single operation.

Analysis of the relationships of the SW plot group boundaries, albeit hampered by truncation of the evidence by later features, allows a tentative reconstruction of part of the sequence of layout. Plots SW3 and SW4 may have lain at the heart of the scheme, assuming that the longitudinal division of plot SW3 was a secondary feature. The layout of the primary boundaries of plots SW2 and SW1 suggests that these were additions to the series of plots, though it is most likely that they will have followed in quick succession (see above). This argument is based on the termination of boundary ditches in relation to (presumably) already established plot corners. It is curious that the ditches/gullies were not apparently dug in such a way as to achieve a consistent flow of water for drainage purposes, but a similar discontinuity of drainage ditches in line with plot boundaries has been noted elsewhere, for example at Alchester (Oxfordshire), where it was interpreted as indicating that responsibility for boundary maintenance lay with individual plot owners or tenants (Booth *et al.* 2001, 430).

The relationship of the south-west plot boundaries to associated structures may shed further light on the nature of land tenure within this part of the settlement. It seems fairly clear that structures A and B at the south-western end of the site were extant before the establishment of the south-west plots. They may indeed have been out of use by Phase 4, which would help to explain why the somewhat notional plot SW6 was not apparently defined on its south-west side except by a relict prehistoric feature. Further circular structures are indicated in plots SW4 (structure C) and SW3 (structure E). If it is assumed that the component gullies of the latter did relate to a complete circular building (see discussion of structures below) then it must have been removed to make way for the plot SW2/SW3 boundary, if it was not already out of use when the boundaries were established. The latter alternative is perhaps more likely. The almost total absence of traces of structure E within plot SW2 can be accounted for by the nature of Phase 4-5 use of that part of the plot, as mentioned above. The pottery from the gully fills of structure E, while consistent in date with the use of the area after the establishment of the plot boundaries in Phase 4, may consist of intrusive material.

The status of structure C in relation to the establishment of the plots is less certain. It is notable that it was centrally placed within plot SW4 and may therefore have post-dated the establishment of the boundaries, though given a terminal date of *c* AD 170 for the associated or later grave 8160 this would imply a fairly (but not impossibly) short life for the structure. Another possibility, however, is that the structure was already standing when the plots were laid out and that this process respected the position of the structure. It is even possible, given the suggestion that plots SW3 and SW4 may have been primary components in the scheme, that structure C acted in effect as the starting point for the layout of the entire block of south-west plots.

Plots SW1-SW4 certainly or probably contained buildings, though the nature of any structure in plot SW1 remains obscure. The majority of the dating evidence associated with components of the putative structure G was assigned to Phase 3, and it is possible that this, like structure E to the south-west, predated the establishment of the south-west plots. There was no clear evidence of any structural features in plot SW5, and a relatively low level of activity here (and even more so in the area of the putative plot SW6 after Phase 3) is suggested by a lack of evidence for reworking of the roadside boundaries after the beginning of Phase 4, in contrast with the situation from plot SW4 north-eastwards.

Opposite the block of south-west plots, parallel ditches on the south-east side of the Canterbury road defined a single plot some 20 m wide and *c* 65 m deep, perhaps originating as early as Phase 3 but continuing into Phase 5 (plot SE1). These ditches (including a probable secondary phase of the south-western one) did not extend right up to the contemporary south-east roadside ditch(es), but in Phase 5 the latter feature terminated fairly close to the point where the north-east corner of the plot would have been had the features met. There were few significant features within the 'plot', however, so the purpose of its establishment is unclear.

The block of south-central (SC) plots was considerably less coherent in its layout than those discussed already, but nevertheless was far from being completely random in plan. Throughout the Roman pe-

riod these plots had a common boundary with the southern margin of the shrine area (see below), effectively equivalent to the road frontage alignments of the other plot groups, though less rigidly constrained in their position. Indeed it is possible to interpret some of the duplicated gullies, particularly in Phase 3, as defining a trackway running east-west along the northern margin of these plots and therefore separating them from the shrine area, although an interpretation of these features as marking successive stages of the plot boundaries is preferred here.

In the early phases of Period 2 the ditches defining parts of these plots were directly continuous with the south-east roadside ditches. The Phase 2 south-east roadside ditch, in particular, doubled right back on itself, in the process defining three (rather irregular) sides of an early version of plot SC1. From as early as Phase 3, however, the curvilinear plot SC1 boundaries were replaced by a rectilinear layout, setting the tone for the development of these plots through the rest of the Roman period. Despite the heterogeneous nature of the definition of these enclosures, and their differing chronological development, from Phase 3 onwards they can be seen as occupying a fairly consistently-defined, slightly wedge-shaped block of land extending up to 140-150 m west to east from the line of the Canterbury road. At the western end of this block plot SC1 was from *c* 31 m to 35 m deep in Phase 3, while at the eastern end in Phase 4 plot SC6 was *c* 50 m deep. Irregular and discontinuous but nevertheless relatively consistently-aligned ditches and gullies at the southern margin of the 'wedge' indicate that it had a maximum depth of *c* 60 m.

Boundaries at the northern margin of this area showed a slow, but steady northward progression through Period 2. More importantly, perhaps, the lateral boundaries between plots were also fluid in a manner that contrasts markedly, for example, with the definition of boundaries in the SW plot series. It is not clear, however, that this arises from any major difference in the use of the two plot groups, though the particular concentration of circular structures in the SC plots might be a slight hint of such a distinction (see further below). Another possibility, however, relates to ownership, with the implication that changing patterns of ownership or tenancy of the SC plots resulted in frequent adjustments to plot sizes, whereas the arrangement of the SW plots, in contrast, was much more stable, for example possibly suggesting that these plots remained in single ownership over a sustained period. Other interpretations of this variation may be possible, however.

Shrine/Temple area

A preliminary discussion of the shrine area has already been published (Booth 2001). The most significant characteristic of this area seems to be the way in which it was kept clear of unrelated features. The fact that waterhole 9179 always lay within the area strengthens the case for seeing this feature as having a functional link with the shrine enclosure, though there was nothing in the range or (generally small) quantities of finds from the waterhole to indicate any specific association with religious activity. Nevertheless, as noted previously (ibid., 20), a water source within a temple complex could have been important for a variety of ritual and other purposes, even if it was not in itself a focus of devotion (Derks 1998, 207-208). The lack of closely dated material from the early fills is unfortunate, as it does not clarify the question of whether the waterhole was a secondary feature or if it was already in place by the time the shrine complex was constructed.

The southern extent of the shrine area was defined at least in part as early as Phase 2 and while there was subsequent encroachment on this side this was on a relatively modest scale. The original location of its north-east boundary is not known, but may have lain in the same area as, and have been truncated by, the earliest stage of the double ditched enclosure at the north-east margin of Area B, which is assigned to Phase 3. At this time there was apparently no formal demarcation of the Canterbury road adjacent to the shrine area and the south-easterly limit of the area, probably (if defined at all) lying beyond the edge of the excavation, is not known.

The shrine could have been accessed from the Canterbury road, though this would have been the least satisfactory approach in terms of the formal layout of the complex with its south-east facing emphasis (cf Smith 2001, 7). A well-defined trackway leading into the shrine area from the south was probably in existence as early as Phase 3 and its alignment was then maintained carefully for the duration of activity in this part of the site. The trackway was aligned approximately on the south corner of the shrine enclosure and would have been a suitable access to the shrine area. The south-eastern alignment of the shrine complex, while conforming to a widely observed pattern (cf Booth 2001, 19), also provides a clue about the layout of the settlement in this area. The geophysical survey shows a (discontinuous) projection of the line of the redefined (Phase 4) northern side of the shrine enclosure running south-eastwards almost as far as the Whitewater Dyke. Two other extensive linear features converge on the same point from slightly further north within the Roman settlement, one of these having the appearance of another north-south aligned trackway. The point of convergence might very likely have been a ford, perhaps of pre-Roman origin, across the Whitewater Dyke. The projected position of this feature would have been very close to the central axis of the shrine complex and it is arguable that this location was a key factor in the precise siting of the shrine and its enclosure, given that a south-east facing vista would have been available from almost any point within the overall settlement area. Moreover, access to the shrine area from this direction would follow the main axis of its layout, a principle that is observed in many classical and Roman provincial contexts (cf Smith 2001, 25). There are two further possible inferences from this hint of an axial approach to the shrine complex from

the Whitewater Dyke. One is that access to it from the Canterbury road may have been restricted in some way that did not leave any archaeologically detectable trace, given that a major concern with demarcation is such a common feature of cult complexes (eg ibid., 17). The second is that the shrine served a wider community than just that of the Westhawk Farm settlement, and that some of these people reached it from the other side of the valley.

Cemeteries and other burial areas

Eight cremation burials and two inhumations were found at various locations with the Area B excavation. These fall broadly into three groups. The first, comprising cremation graves 8955, 9940, 9860 and 1007 and inhumation grave 8520, were spread across a distance of *c* 100 m in marginal locations at the southern extremity of the settlement. The second 'group' comprised inhumation grave 8160, associated with structure C in plot SW4 and a possible cremation 10337 in plot SW5 to the south-west. The third group of three cremation graves (210, 220 and 1261) lay close together within the large double-ditched north-eastern enclosure, on its south-west side. The last of these was assigned to Phase 2 on the basis of the likely date of the cremation urn, while the nearby burials were assigned to Phases 4 and 5, though they were probably quite close in date, falling a little before and a little after AD 200. Whether the double-ditched enclosure had a specific funerary function is unknown, but from its size (as suggested by the geophysical survey) and its position in relation to the overall settlement plan this seems unlikely. The remaining burials were all certainly or probably of Phase 3 or 4 date.

The excavation of Area C revealed a more concentrated area of burials, interpreted as a small cemetery. The late Iron Age rich burial 9200 lay little more than 40 m away, but because the immediate context of that feature is unknown it is unclear if the location of the Area C cemetery reflected an already established tradition of burial in the area, or if the association was fortuitous. At nearby Brisley Farm, for example, the late Iron Age high status burials formed a focus for ritual (but not apparently burial) activity into the Flavian period (Casper Johnson, pers. comm.). The majority of the eleven cremation and eight inhumation graves in Area C were contained within a well-defined enclosure, but two cremation graves, 5220 and 5240, lay to the north-east, outside the cemetery enclosure. Five successive phases of burial, based on the dating of associated (principally ceramic) material, have been identified within the cemetery giving a broad date range of mid 1st to early-mid 4th century. There was no concentration of burials in any particular phase. It should be noted that the description of these features has been based on the premise that deposits containing cremated human remains represented cremation burials. This cannot be assumed automatically, however, particularly since the quantities of bone recovered are in some cases very small. It is quite possible that some of these deposits were of pyre debris rather than formal cremation burials. The poor preservation of some of these deposits makes interpretation more difficult, so any attempt to quantify burials and pyre debris deposits is of limited value. For present purposes those deposits which contain evidence for the presence of substantial parts of one or more pottery vessels, for example, have been considered to be burials, regardless of the quantity of cremated bone surviving.

Layout of cemetery enclosure

The principal boundary of the cemetery was that on its south-east side, represented by NE-SW boundary ditch 5174, most likely a continuation of ditch 840 which originated in the north-east corner of Area B. Ditch 5174 was dated to Phase 3 and cut - and was therefore later than - 5270, a SE-NW aligned gully (see below). It is most likely, however, that the principal north-east to south-west boundary was initially defined earlier, before the creation of the cemetery, by a ditch which lay parallel to the Canterbury road, but just beyond the south-east limit of Area C. Gully 5270 was not itself dated, though it was at right-angles to this putative early NE-SW ditch and presumably linked to it. As such it may have formed the primary north-east boundary of the cemetery area, but it may also have predated the cemetery and been (initially) unrelated to it. Gully 5270 was succeeded by a more formal enclosure, still assigned to Phase 2 of the settlement sequence. This consisted of gullies 5250, 5171, 5172 (and re-cut 5173) and 5168. Gullies 5250 and 5171 did not respect the alignment dictated by the main NE-SW boundary ditch, but the remaining gullies, originating at the northern terminus of 5171, did reflect the alignment of the ditch, turning at right-angles to enclose the north-east area of the cemetery.

This configuration produced a distinctive plan that has a striking parallel at Pepper Hill, a cemetery associated with the small town of Springhead. The boundaries of both cemeteries have a marked dog-leg of very similar proportions in their outer sides - that is those furthest away from the nearby road lines (Biddulph forthcoming). The significance of this is uncertain, but the similarity seems too marked to be purely fortuitous. At Pepper Hill the area of the re-entrant boundary was partly occupied by a cobbled surface overlying probable pre-Roman features (ibid.) and the possibility that some kind of shrine or other religious focus was located here was considered (eg OAU 2000, 458), but the detailed interpretation of the area is uncertain. No features of any kind were located in the equivalent area at Westhawk Farm, but it should be remembered that post-Roman truncation of the whole of Area C was particularly severe, so surfaces here would probably have been completely removed. An absence of deep-cut features at this point seems likely, however.

No defined entrance to the cemetery area was identified within Area C, and even though the junction between gullies 5250 and 5171 lay just beyond the excavation area, it is unlikely to have afforded sufficient space to have formed a practical entrance. The profiles of all of the gullies suggest that they acted as drainage channels as well as defining the cemetery. It would have been impractical therefore to create a break for access. It is possible that there was a form of walkway that spanned a section of gully. Gully 5173, which was re-cut into the top of 5172 as it extended to the north-east, was most likely dug because this part of the enclosure silted up before other areas. All other areas of the gully enclosure ran downslope towards the main boundary ditch (there was a drop of 0.3 m in base level from gully 5171 to the ditch 5174). Gully 5172 running to the north-east, was, however, dug in a flat area and was therefore more prone to silting from standing water within its base.

Orientation and spatial organisation of burials

The majority of the inhumations were aligned east-west apart from Phase 2 inhumation 5130, aligned north-south, and Phase 6 inhumation 5140 on a NW-SE alignment. Within the cemetery enclosure there were two distinct rows of burials. Inhumation groups 5160, 5190 and 5100 formed a north-south row parallel to enclosure gully 5171, but to the west of these a row of seven cremations was noticeably not quite parallel to the axis of the gully but was aligned instead NNE/SSW.

All the graves were well spaced with no intercutting of burials, even between those of different phases. It would seem therefore that while the cemetery was in infrequent use throughout the life of the settlement, with graves ranging in date from Phase 2 to Phase 6, the graves were sufficiently clearly marked that intercutting did not occur.

Chronology

The row of inhumations respecting the alignment of gully 5171 suggest that the enclosure was already established before any burials were placed within the area, that is, during Phase 2. Of these, only grave 5190 is securely dated to Phase 2, with 5160 and 5100 dated broadly to Phases 2-4 and 3-5 respectively. Apart from this row of possible early phase graves, the other burials form no discernible chronological pattern of interment. The lack of pottery vessels in the majority of the inhumations makes refined phasing impossible. Seven inhumation burials had no complete ceramic vessels, but produced between 32 g and 150 g of pottery sherds within the backfill, only giving a broad *terminus post quem* for each. There is no evidence to suggest that the pottery fragments come from earlier truncated features, but nevertheless they may represent residual material.

The cremation graves within the cemetery range in date from possibly as early as Phase 2 (cremation groups 5110, 5120 and 5230) to Phase 6 (group 5090), with all phases in between represented by at least two examples. The contemporary practice of cremation and inhumation from the early Roman period onwards is paralleled quite widely in the region, most particularly at the major cemeteries of Pepper Hill and Ospringe (Biddulph forthcoming; Whiting *et al.* 1931).

The small number of burials suggests little more than intermittent use of the cemetery. Their density in relation to the space available contrasts markedly with the situation observed at Pepper Hill, in which burials were very densely packed (although the density of burials there may have been exceptional). A possible explanation is that the Area C cemetery was exclusive to a particular family group or groups or (perhaps less likely) to people of a specific social status within the settlement. It cannot have been the only established cemetery area associated with the settlement. The wider use of the area north-west of the settlement for burials is indicated by the 1960s find of a cremation at Westhawk Farm itself, as well as by the find of a complete samian Drag 18/31 dish (see Fig. 8.28) from a point only *c* 50 m south of the Farm and *c* 20 m from the edge of Area B and presumably outside the line of the north-west settlement boundary, recovered from a service trench during the recent housing construction. This vessel is most likely to have derived from a burial.

No infant or immature burials were identified, which could be a reflection of religious practice or an indication of alternative burial sites for infants within a different area of the settlement (for example within domestic features such as ditches and pits), or its environs. Alternatively, preservation factors need to be borne in mind since the cemetery area had suffered severe truncation due to post-Roman ploughing. This could have removed archaeological features which were not cut as deeply as the surviving burials. Since infant burials are typically shallower than those of older individuals they would have been particularly prone to truncation. The whole of the cemetery area had also been disturbed by root action, modern drainage channels and animal burrows. In some cases this meant that the true shape of features had been lost. The cut for cremation grave 5090, for example, had been heavily disturbed on its south-eastern edge making identification of its original profile impossible in excavation. A further preservation factor of particular relevance to infant burials relates to the survival of bone, however. The 'inhumations graves' within the cemetery area were defined principally on the basis of the grave-like form of cut features. The small features required to contain infant burials (if present) could, without bone or grave goods, have been indistinguishable from any one of several other feature types. On this basis it is quite possible that burial group 5060, a small pit identified as a possible cremation grave on the basis of associated pottery, but containing no burnt bone, was in fact an infant inhumation burial. Alternatively, features containing no bone but otherwise identical to cremation graves can be interpreted as cenotaphs, which represented the graves of individuals whose remains were unavailable for burial (McKinley 2004, 306-7).

Marginal Areas

The margins of the settlement of Westhawk Farm are variously defined. North-west of the focal road junction area a major boundary was probably maintained throughout the Roman period, its line surviving into modern times. The original south-west end of this boundary, as revealed in Area B, was superseded in the course of Phase 3, however (see above), and it is unclear how, if at all, it was replaced in this part of the settlement. Further south-west, but still north-west of the axial Canterbury road, there may never have been any formal definition of the settlement area. The block of south-west plots, possibly established as a single operation in the second half of the 2nd century, nevertheless did not have a single, coherent rear boundary and was not clearly linked into any other systems of boundary definition.

South-east of the Canterbury road at the southern edge of the settlement there was again no clear definition of its margins. Several ditch alignments in Area B tailed off into apparently open space and scattered burials (see above) suggest the marginal nature of this area without defining it closely. The most southerly feature in this part of the site was an isolated, small *c* 12 m square enclosure with an opening on its north-west side, dated, very tentatively, to the 2nd century (on the basis of a small and scrappy pottery assemblage from the ditch fill). This feature had the appearance of a funerary monument, with comparisons in sites ranging from the late Iron Age - such as King Harry Lane (Stead and Rigby 1989) and Westhampnett (Fitzpatrick 1997, 16-17) - to the late Roman period - for example at Lankhills (Clarke 1979, 97), but the only internal feature was a small central cut interpreted as a probable posthole. A possible parallel for this situation can be found in a recently-excavated cemetery at Wall, Staffordshire, where only one of four square funerary enclosures contained a central burial (excavation in advance of M6 Toll construction; OWA 2003), the others having less well-defined central features. It is notable, however, that the square ditched enclosures surrounding the two late Iron Age inhumations at nearby Brisley Farm were continuous and considerably smaller in size than the Westhawk Farm feature. If the Westhawk Farm feature had been a mortuary enclosure this interpretation might have interesting implications for the understanding of the site, but the absence of any other significant features in the vicinity makes assessment of its real significance very difficult. A 'domestic' interpretation remains possible, and has been suggested for very similar enclosures, such as a late 2nd century BC example at Soupir Le Parc, near Soissons, with an equal lack of identifiable internal features (Haselgrove 1996, 144-5).

The whole of the south-east side of the settlement appears to have been without formal coherent definition, unless the ditch seen in the geophysical survey running parallel to the Whitewater Dyke (see Chapter 3) was a boundary feature, which seems unlikely. Southward running trackways, one south and one north-east of the shrine area, appear to have provided access to the surrounding fields and perhaps to other specific settlements, potentially, in the case of the more northerly track, by way of a ford across the Whitewater Dyke. The geophysical survey data do not permit detailed interpretation of marginal activities in the area between this trackway and the Lympne road.

This area relatively close to the Whitewater Dyke might have been suitable for structures such as a bathhouse, the presence of which is suspected on the basis of tile and the less conclusive, but still suggestive, window glass evidence. There is no particular indication of the presence of such a structure in the geophysical survey results, however, so while its existence seems very likely, its location remains unknown.

STRUCTURAL ASPECTS

A substantial number of structural elements were revealed by the excavation. All related to buildings in timber, many of which were poorly preserved as a result of plough truncation. Some 21 'structures' were labelled by letters. The structures were of a variety of forms and not all such groups of features formed coherent plans. In addition, further structures may have remained unnoticed among the more ephemeral features on the site; small groups of two and three postholes which may have had structural significance but could not be interpreted beyond this were not assigned structure numbers, nor were several probable or possible fencelines.

The 21 'structures' comprise ten certain or probable circular or subcircular buildings, the polygonal shrine, eight rectilinear buildings and two 'uncertain' groups of postholes, one perhaps from a rectilinear structure and the other of uncertain form.

'Circular' structures (A, C, E, H, K, L, N, O, P and T)

The 'circular' buildings were all identified entirely or in part by gullies. Judging from their profiles and the character of their fills most if not all of these features are likely to have been for drainage around the structure rather than being wall trenches. Only in two cases (L and P) were the gullies more or less entirely present. Structure O was surrounded by an unusually substantial gully of sub-square plan, but this contained no certainly identifiable internal features, so while it is very likely that it enclosed a structure the form of this structure, whether circular or (sub)-rectangular, is unknown. On the basis of the character of other structures in this part of the site, however, a circular plan seems more likely, although the arrangement of component features associated with structure T, both closely adjacent and approximately contemporaneous, may also hint at a slightly more rectilinear plan.

The internal diameters of identified circular gullies, or diameters extrapolated from surviving gully

segments, varied widely from c 7 m to c 12 m (Table 10.1). There was no clear chronological patterning with relation to variation in gully diameter (eg an increase in size through time), nor in terms of a preference for circular rather than other building plans. Such variations were therefore presumably functionally or socially determined.

Structure P was the best defined and preserved circular structure, as well as the latest in date, being the only one whose construction (rather than possible continued use) was assigned to Phase 5. Arcs of stakeholes survived at three points around the perimeter of the structure. It is assumed that these indicate the position of the wall line, which thus suggests a building of c 10 m diameter, with the wall set very close to the associated drainage gully. There was inconclusive evidence for a central post. A construction based on stakes (presumably supporting a wattle and daub wall) might nevertheless have been sufficiently substantial to carry the roof span of this building. It is unlikely that the building was of double-ring type (cf Guilbert 1981) since given the survival of (part of) the outer stake wall the inner posts should certainly have been present. It is uncertain if stake walled construction was standard in the round structures of Westhawk Farm since the evidence elsewhere does not survive at all well. This very characteristic might, however, be indicative of stake wall construction on the basis that some evidence should have survived had buildings been based routinely upon larger upright posts, although an alternative interpretation of the circular and penannular gullies is that they could have surrounded buildings of mass wall construction (eg of cob). These, having no substantial sub-surface component, would have left no trace in the archaeological record of the site.

A probable stake-supported wall construction, 7.8 m in diameter probably with a central post was assigned to the late Iron Age-early Roman Period 1 at the Marlowe Car Park, Canterbury (Blockley *et al.* 1995, 33-34). The evidence for two probable late Iron Age circular or sub-circular buildings underlying the villa at Thurnham varied somewhat, in ways at least superficially similar to the situation at Westhawk Farm. One was clearly defined by a gully with an internal diameter of c 12.0-12.5 m, while a second was only partly defined by a gully. In neither case were other structural components evident, however (Lawrence forthcoming).

The general characteristics of the mostly poorly preserved circular structures of Westhawk Farm are thus paralleled in the late Iron Age of the region, as would be expected. The occurrence of circular structures in Lowland Britain well into the Roman period (in the present context throughout the period of occupation, though this did not extend into the 4th century here) and in the setting of a major nucleated settlement, whatever its precise status, is no longer remarkable (see, for example, Burnham 1988, 38; Mahany 1994, 148; Booth *et al.* 2001, 435-6), such structures even occurring in early Roman London and other major cities (Perring *et al.* 1991, 101). In Es-

Table 10.1   'Circular' structures: Summary information.

Structure	Group nos.	General location	General type	Dimensions (internal diameter of gullies)	Components	Phase	Comments
A	8790	Plot SW6	Circular	Dia c 9.5 m	Penannular gully	3	Entrance to N
C	9280	Plot SW4	Circular	Dia c 12 m	Gully segments	3	Burial within area of structure
E	10250 10260	Plot SW3 (and SW2)	Circular	Dia c 12 m	Gully segments	3	About half survives, adjacent to D
H	8250	NW undivided roadside area	?Circular	Dia c 9 m	Gully fragments	3	Only southern half survives, gully slightly angular in plan. Not certainly a structure
K	9990	Plot SC1	Circular	Dia c 12 m	Gully	3	
L	8270	Plot SC2/SC3	Circular	Dia c 11-12 m	Gully, central post	3	Truncated
N	9970	Plot SC5	Circular	Dia c 7 m	Gully	3	Truncated
O	7660	Plot SC4	?Circular	Dia c 10 m	Penannular gully, pits posthole and hearth	4	SE entrance
P	7500	Plot SC4	Circular	Dia c 10 m	Gully, postholes, stakeholes	5	SW entrance, succeeds O
T		Plot SC5	?Circular	?Dia c 7-8 m	Gully, postholes	4	

sex, a number of Roman-period circular structures of post or slot construction have been recorded, including at Orsett 'Cock' (Carter 1998, 33), Stansted (Havis and Brooks 2004, 273) and Strood Hall on the route of the A120 Trunk Road, where structures continued to occur well into the 2nd century AD (Biddulph 2007, 87). Circular structures were numerous at Heybridge in the late Iron Age-early Roman phase, where it was noted that, as in most cases at Westhawk Farm, they were generally set back from the road frontages of the plots in which they lay (Atkinson and Preston 1998, 94). While the chronology of this early phase of settlement at Heybridge remains a little unclear some of the circular buildings were certainly of Roman date (ibid., 105) and the temple structure remained of this form throughout the Roman period (ibid., 98-101). In Kent, however, the relative lack of knowledge of 'small towns' (except Springhead) means that such evidence has not been encountered previously here.

The incomplete nature of many of the curvilinear gullies and the general absence of evidence for identifiable internal features makes discussion of aspects of the probable circular structures such as their function effectively impossible. Even simple questions such as the orientation of entrances can only be addressed in a limited number of cases. It is assumed that the curvilinear gullies were penannular, but this is only reasonably certain for structures L, O and P. In these cases entrance positions, as defined by the break in the gully, were approximately east-facing (structure O) and roughly south-west facing for structures L and P, although this is not absolutely certain in the former example. Structure T, if correctly interpreted, also had a roughly south-facing entrance. Elsewhere a north-east or NNE direction can be suggested for structure A, but there is no certainty in relation to any of the other structures. Only in the case of structure O, therefore, is there a clear correlation with a well-established preference for Iron Age roundhouses to face east or south-east (cf Oswald 1997, 87). The Westhawk Farm data are insufficient to demonstrate any clear pattern, but they might suggest at least a partial breakdown of a culturally determined pattern. It is just possible, however, that the apparent doorway orientations of structures L, P and T, in particular, were significant in facing away from the shrine area to which they were adjacent. Their doorway alignments may have been affected by the same underlying reasoning which required the continued demarcation of the shrine area on its south side (but not, for example, to the north-west). In this respect it is not clear that structures fronting onto the northeast and north-west sides of the shrine area were affected by the same possible taboo. A similar variety of house orientations in relation to a shrine location can be seen for example in the late Iron Age settlement at Stansted (Airport Catering Site), where there was considerable variety of entrance alignment, with some structures facing the possible shrine and others facing away from it (Brooks and Bedwin 1989, 9-11; Havis and Brooks 2004).

A number of the 'circular' structures remain problematic. Not all the curving gullies can be proved to have defined such structures, though this is generally thought likely. The gully lengths defining 'structure H', however, were particularly irregular in plan. This and the presence of a possible clay lining to these gullies, an unparalleled occurrence on the site, may suggest that they were not associated directly with a structure. Further south-west the gullies associated with 'structure E' were more regularly curvilinear in plan, but if contemporary with the adjacent plot boundary to the north-east (group 9570/9580 - see discussion of this relationship under 'South-west roadside plots', Chapter 3 above) can only have defined a semicircular structure. It is more likely, however, that this structure originated in Phase 3 and predated the plot boundaries (and the immediately adjacent structure D to the south-west). There are slight hints from plot SW2 that the structure did continue into that area, its north-easterly extension being almost completely truncated or obscured by the activity associated with the extensive hollow which occupied the south-western side of that plot. A problem is caused by the fact that the dating evidence associated with structure E was fairly consistently of Phases 4 to 5, suggesting use contemporary with the plots rather than earlier. The surviving components of the structure were very shallow, however, and it is quite possible that they were contaminated by material derived from immediately adjacent intensive activity in and around structure D.

Rectangular Structures

The rectangular structures identified on the site were mostly of relatively simple plan and construction, the latter being based generally on upright posts set in the ground. One such building, however, was in what may have been a distinct regional structural tradition. Probable and possible rectilinear structures located in the northern corner of Area B were potentially less straightforward in construction and one of these, Structure I, incorporated slots amongst its structural features.

Small four- and six-post structures

A single four-post structure (structure S) was identified in one of the plots on the south side of the shrine area. The structure, roughly 2.5 m square, was assigned to Phase 2. Such structures occur in late Iron Age settlements such as that preceding the villa at Keston, where ten four-post structures were assigned to the pre-Roman farmstead, with the possibility that one of them was of the subsequent early Roman phase. They were square or rectangular in plan and ranged from *c* 1.5-2.95 m across (Philp *et al.* 1991, 25-29). Two four post structures were found in the corresponding late Iron Age phase at Thurnham (Glass 1999, 201; Lawrence forthcoming). Two more examples, from a probable farmstead at Queen Elizabeth Square, Maidstone, were either late Iron Age or possibly (on the basis of associated pottery) early Roman in date (Booth and Howard-Davis 2003) and are thus comparable with the Westhawk Farm structure. The continued use of these structures into the early Roman period thus seems clear. There is no evidence to indicate the function of the Westhawk Farm example, but there is no particular reason to doubt the generally accepted interpretation as a granary.

A similar interpretation may apply to the six post structure M, located in a comparable position to that of structure S, that is, towards the 'rear' of a plot (SC5) fronting on to the south side of the shrine area. The structure, which was not excavated, was *c* 3 m square and was assigned, on the basis of its spatial relationship with adjacent features, to Phase 3. The type is comparable to that of structure S (above), while a fairly precise parallel in terms of plan and dimensions is known from Keston. Like the four-post structures from that site the latter was assigned to the late Iron Age (Philp *et al.* 1991, 29). A more local example is from Waterbrook Farm, Ashford, where a six-post structure roughly 3 m by 4 m was either free standing or (less likely) formed a component of a larger structure with associated gullies and postholes. This was of late Iron Age or early Roman date (Rady 1996).

Larger post-built structures

A rather larger simple six-post structure (structure J) was found in a very different location, fronting the Canterbury road in the north-west corner of Area B. This structure, *c* 6.3 m square, was based on substantial posts (on average *c* 0.3 m across). No related features or deposits survived to evidence its function or details of construction. With regard to the latter, however, it appears comparable to the slightly larger ironworking building structure R. This was identical in width, and was at least 6 m long (if of three bays) or possibly longer, its north-east end lying outside the excavated area. In both buildings it is likely that the two post-rows not only carried the principal structural members, but also marked the position of the external walls, rather than forming 'arcades' as in an aisled building. In the case of structure J this interpretation is suggested by the alignment of the structure in relation to adjacent boundaries and drainage gullies - so, for example, a plot boundary ditch was aligned precisely upon the proposed north-east wall of the structure and must have been determined by it. In the case of structure R the edge of a contemporaneous gully on the north-west side (1200) varied from 1.0-1.4 m from the centre-line of the probable wall. This gully and a comparable feature set rather further from the south-west wall of the building seem certain to have been for drainage rather than carrying structural elements. It is possible that there was some sort of extension of the structure to the south-west side of building R in order to provide some protection for the smelting furnaces positioned there. The south-west end bay of structure R was approximately 2.2 m deep (based on centre to centre measurements of the post-pits), while the next bay was some 2.6 m deep.

(Only part of the third bay lay within the excavated area). It is not known if this variation was significant. It is assumed however, that each pair of posts carried a simple roof truss and that the posts were also linked longitudinally with wall plates. There is no evidence for the nature of the walling. The internal arrangements of this building have been discussed in detail by Paynter (Chapter 7 above).

The largest excavated structure on the site, structure D, appears to be of a slightly different type of timber building. Essentially it was based on paired posts like structures J and R, but in addition had two substantial uprights in each of the short axes. This characteristic is shared by several other Roman buildings in Kent which have either one or two such uprights. The known examples are generally very consistent in their dimensions, the Keston north timber building being the largest (Table 10.2). This was the only example to have a significant addition to the basic plan, in the form of (secondary) 'corridors' on two sides. It was also one of the latest in use, though again there was considerable homogeneity in the group; three buildings fall entirely within a date range from *c* mid 2nd century to early-mid 3rd, the Keston north building was constructed within this range but continued in use perhaps up to the beginning of the 4th century (Philp *et al.* 1991, 90), while the Smeeth building, also constructed in the later 2nd century, may have remained in use even later (Diez forthcoming).

The precise significance of this distinctive ground plan is uncertain. The spacing of the posts in all cases makes it clear that the opposed posts in the long walls carried roof trusses in the same way as in other posthole structures discussed above, or as in aisled buildings (which these were not, as is demonstrable from the occurrence of closely adjacent surrounding drainage gullies in the Westhawk Farm and Smeeth examples, and down one side of the Thurnham building (Glass 1999, 204; Lawrence forthcoming)). The additional short axis posts therefore appear to be structurally redundant. They are generally of the same size as the other posts and are thus unlikely to have simply carried door frames. It is possible that they provided some additional support for the ridge (presumably via a collar and further members in the cases with two intermediate posts in the short axis), but it is hard to see why this was required, and none of the buildings has evidence for such supports in any of the 'internal' roof trusses. The extra posts may hint at a hipped roof construction in which there was a perceived need for reinforcement of the end walls against the outward (as opposed to vertical) thrust imposed by the hipped ends of the roof, but this is far from certain. It is even possible that the feature was simply intended to achieve a visual effect. Its relatively localised occurrence seems to hint at a distinct regional tradition, though the distance between the Ashford area examples and Thurnham and Keston (overall some 70 km) is such as to suggest that this was quite widespread in Kent. With the exception of Westhawk Farm the known examples all occur in

Table 10.2   *Post-built structures: Examples from Kent with intermediate posts in short axis wall lines.*

Site	Structure	Dimensions (m)	Posts in long axis	'Inner' posts in short axis	Date	Reference	Comment
Westhawk Farm	Structure D	c 14 x 7	5	2	AD 150-250	Lawrence forthcoming	
Thurnham		c 15 x 7	6	1	2 C - ?early 3 C	Diez forthcoming	
Bower Road, Smeeth	Building group 550	c 20 x 7.5	8	2	late 2 C		2 additional posts in NE side
Keston	Centre timber building	c 14.6 x 6.8	6	1	Period Va c mid 1 C - 2 C	Philp *et al* 1991, 59-61	
Keston	North timber building	c 21.4 x 7.5 without additions	10	2	Period VI end 2 C - early 4 C	Philp *et al* 1991, 81-90	'corridors' added to N and W sides

rural settlement contexts, but the Westhawk building shows that the type was also appropriate to nucleated settlement, although the functional distinction between rural and many aspects of nucleated settlements is largely meaningless. At Westhawk Farm the building was presumably at least in part domestic in function, as was probably also the case at Smeeth. At Thurnham and Keston the emphasis seems to have been principally agricultural, but there is no reason why these structures, like aisled buildings, should not have been multifunctional.

It is possible that the Phase 2 posthole structure B also belongs to this group, but it appears to be distinct from the structures discussed above on criteria of size, scale of component features (the postholes were very small) and chronology, being assigned, albeit tentatively, to the pre-Flavian Phase 2. This structure had approximate dimensions of 5 m by 10 m, though the plan was not complete. It did have a central post in its one certainly identified short axis (and a possible corresponding feature in the other short wall was also identified tentatively), and in this sense may have been related to the other structures. A further possible example of the type was located at the southern end of plot SC5, probably in Phase 3. The component features, which were mostly unexcavated, were interpreted primarily as linear arrangements of small pits and postholes and a six-post structure (structure M). This is possible, but an alternative, if rather speculative, interpretation of these features as elements of a larger structure was also considered. This would have given a structure *c* 13.5 m east-west by 5.5 m north-south, with projected post spacings of 1-2 m centre to centre (typically *c* 1.5 m) and two additional posts in each short wall. Of this arrangement four posts out of a hypothetical nine survived in each long side, while all four additional short axis posts were represented. Comparison with the data in Table 10.2 above shows that this hypothetical structure is narrower and has more closely spaced posts than the other buildings in this group. There was no sign of the stone post-pit packing seen in Building D. These considerations need not invalidate the interpretation, but they may support the alternative view that the identified features constituted fortuitous alignments of pits and a smaller structure.

The enigmatic structure F in plot SW2 may also be considered here. This consisted of a single row of four substantial post-pits, in scale and general character reminiscent of those of the broadly contemporaneous structure D in the adjacent plot. The post-pits were up to 1.28 m across and 0.36 m deep while the diameter of the post voids was on average 0.4 m. No associated structural features whatsoever were identified. It seems highly improbable that such features simply carried a line of freestanding posts. The most likely explanation of this evidence, therefore, is that they supported the ridge of a structure whose other components were relatively shallow and had been completely removed by post-Roman ploughing. The general dimensions of such a structure may be suggested by its positioning in relation to the prob-

ably contemporaneous plot SW1/SW2 boundary and the roadside gully 10040 to the south-east. The latter extended some 8 m from the north-east corner of plot SW2 up to a probable entrance into the plot. A structure some 9-10 m long (the centre to centre spacing of the end posts was *c* 9.2 m) and 6 m wide with the post-row down the centre would have fitted comfortably into the north-east corner of the plot, in a mirror image position to that of building D in plot SW3. Why the structural type varied from that of the remaining rectilinear post-built buildings is not known. It is emphasised that this interpretation is speculative, but it seems to make the best use of the available evidence.

Sill-beam structures

This structural category is probably the least well understood on the site since structures based on horizontal timbers set in shallow slots were most vulnerable to erosion by ploughing (with the obvious exception of putative, entirely 'above ground' mass wall structures). Possible structures within this group, including structure U (see below) and two small square or sub-square groups of features in plots SC2 and SC5 respectively, were characteristically also associated with postholes, but in the absence of stratigraphic sequences which would have enabled the relationships of these different types of features to be determined, the significance of this association is uncertain. The two feature types might, for example, have represented structures (or other features such as fence-lines) of quite different phases, but the incorporation of vertical earth-fast posts in the sill beam structures remains a distinct possibility, though the identified post spacing does not imply closely-spaced studs set into the sill beams, as seen for example in a 2nd century structure at Canterbury (Blockley *et al.* 1995, 130-131). The only fairly certainly identified structure in the sill beam structure category, therefore, was the ironworking building I, although aspects of it remain problematic. The principal difficulty is to distinguish between those linear features which held or probably held horizontal timbers and those which served other functions, particularly as drainage gullies. Parts of three sides (NW, NE and SE) were defined by slots, apparently supplemented by vertical timbers in postholes. The maximum length of the structure (NW-SE) was probably *c* 7 m and it was probably no more than *c* 5 m wide and could have been as narrow as 3 m across. In view of the evidence for iron smelting and smithing within the structure (for discussion of the internal layout see Paynter, Chapter 7 above) it is quite likely that the south-west side was partly open, as in building R, which may explain the paucity of structural evidence, and particularly the lack of a timber slot, at this point.

The somewhat speculative structure U was based on three certain or probable beam slots. These were notably regularly spaced, but not exactly parallel, nor did they in combination form a completely regular rectangle, although the plan had none of the 'extravagant irregularity' of buildings such as the well-known barrack I at Longthorpe (Frere and St Joseph 1974, 30). The nature of any structure based on these slots, if the features are to be seen as belonging to a single structure, is quite unknown, however. Their spacing, approximately 11 m from centre to centre, would seem to be excessively wide for the horizontals in the slots to have supported the ends of longitudinal joists, unless there were intermediate supporting components which left no trace. The measurement is, however, a recognisable module; for example it is exactly twice the width of the posthole structures J and R, perhaps suggesting the availability of a stock of timber of standardised sizes, though it is possible that this correspondence was only coincidental. As indicated above, the relationship of the slots to rows of postholes on the same general alignment, but not so evenly spaced, is unknown.

Shrine

The 'shrine' structure (structure Q) has been discussed at some length elsewhere (Booth 2001) and this will not all be repeated here. Further analysis has not resolved the major questions relating to its structure or internal phasing. These remain intractable in the absence of basic evidence for stratigraphic relationships between discrete cut features, the paucity of dating material and the lack of close and better-preserved structural parallels. Interpretation of the structure as a shrine is based almost entirely on morphological criteria, although there are additional scraps of evidence which could be complementary but do not amount to a conclusive case in their own right (see below).

The structure itself had three main components, a polygonal outer wall, a group of inner posts (not all obviously related in a single scheme) and a central feature probably containing a very large post. In summary the careful axial arrangement of the central post, the polygonal structure and the surrounding enclosure ditch argue for, but do not prove, their contemporaneity as a single complex (Booth 2001, 12). The problem of the relative (and absolute) chronology of the structural components is shared by some analogous sites such as Heathrow (Grimes and Close-Brooks 1993). An alternative approach is to see the shrine consisting of successive structural phases, potentially of increasing complexity, perhaps on the model of sites such as Gournay-sur-Aronde (Brunaux et al. 1985; see Derks 1998, 170-175 for reassessment of the sequence and Woolf 2000, 622 for emphasis of the rarity of such sequences, even with recent work). The precise function and chronological placing of some of the 'internal' postholes at Westhawk Farm is particularly unclear and it is accepted that not all of these need have belonged to the original scheme. Within this broad framework there is clearly scope for much minor variation in phasing and therefore of understanding of the physical appearance of the structure. In this context the major outstanding question is whether or not it was roofed. The answer to

this question is in turn partly dependent upon interpretation of the large central post - was this intended to be a massive feature at the heart of the structure or was its principal visual and symbolic significance in its height? On most sites in which large posts occur these seem to have been freestanding rather than incorporated in structures (Booth 2001, 14), a characteristic which suggests an emphasis on height rather than bulk. Sites with free-standing posts include Ivy Chimneys, Witham (Turner 1999, 40), Chelmsford (Wickenden 1992, 19-20), both in Essex, Wood Lane End, Hemel Hempstead, Hertfordshire (Neal 1984, 205-6) and, in less certainly 'ritual' contexts, Alcester, Warwickshire (Cracknell 1989, 30), Wavendon Gate, Milton Keynes (Williams et al. 1996, 68-70), Heybridge, Essex (Atkinson and Preston 1998, 99, 105) and Thurnham, Kent (Lawrence forthcoming). At Heybridge proximity to the temple (although the post did not lie within the temple enclosure) may still suggest a 'ritual' association, and a similar association, though not demonstrable on present evidence, is possible for the Alcester example as well. A ritual association is very likely at Wavendon Gate and while interpretation of the Thurnham example is less clear, a symbolic function of some kind seems likely. Despite its location within a 'structure' the Westhawk Farm post should presumably be seen as of considerable height, suggesting that it is more likely to have been surrounded by screens, or possibly just by freestanding posts, than by a roofed building. Similarly the 1st century circular 'cella' and axially aligned square enclosure at Heybridge have been interpreted as functioning as screening walls rather than roofed structures (Atkinson and Preston 1998, 96).

The slightly irregular polygonal plan may be another factor militating against an interpretation of the structure as being roofed, but this is far from conclusive. It seems likely that all the known examples of stone built polygonal shrines and temples in Roman Britain were roofed. These were usually more regular in their plans than the Westhawk Farm structure, and the latter remains without precise parallels for its form, whether in timber or stone. The closest comparable example may be the polygonal shrine (Temple 2) at Chanctonbury, Sussex, now more clearly understood from recent work (Rudling 2001). This building is most readily interpreted as having nine sides (there is still some uncertainty about this). At c 11.4 m across it is a little smaller than Westhawk Farm (c 13 m by 16 m) but a broad similarity of plan is evident. However, the Chanctonbury structure was stone-founded and had a rectangular 'porch' attached to its east-facing side. A date around the middle of the 2nd century AD is possible for its construction, and use may have continued through the 3rd century, but not certainly thereafter.

Relative sequence, chronology and function of structural types

The relatively poor preservation of many of the structures at Westhawk Farm does not permit de-

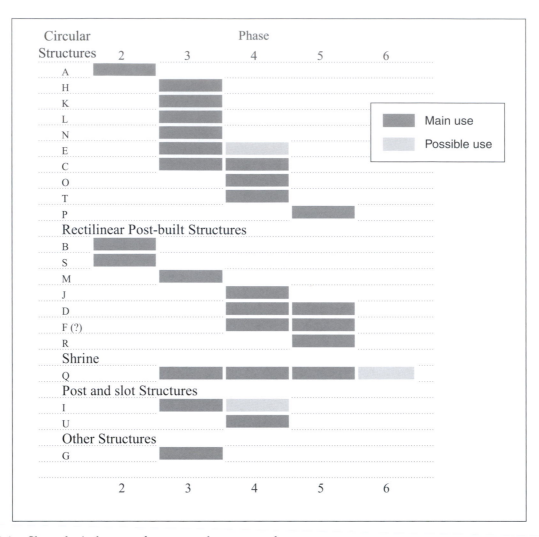

Figure 10.1   Chronological range of structures by structural type.

tailed analysis of their characteristics, but a number of broad conclusions can be drawn (Fig. 10.1). The most significant is that a pre-Roman circular building tradition, which possibly encompassed a fairly wide range of detailed structural variation, was in use throughout the period of occupation of the excavated part of the settlement, up to about the middle of the 3rd century AD. Moreover, new buildings in this tradition continued to be erected as late as those of other types. Roughly speaking, circular structures, which amounted to 50% of the 'identified' structures in Area B, accounted for about half the buildings thought to be in use in any one phase. This is most clearly demonstrable in Phases 3 and 4, when the numbers are highest and therefore most reliable. In terms of cumulative frequency over time, however, 70% of all the circular buildings were in existence before the end of Phase 3, whereas only 43% of the rectilinear post-built structures were so. This suggests, as far as the figures will allow, a slight increase in the importance of post-built structures from the middle of the 2nd century onwards, but this was far from overwhelming.

The less easily categorised buildings (in terms of their structural type), such as the shrine and the post

and slot structure I, are both assigned to Phase 3. Overall there was more new construction within this than in any other phase, which is unsurprising as this was the time at which relatively intensive development was really getting under way in this part of the settlement, after a modest start in the early post-conquest Phase 2. It was at this time, therefore, that the widest variety of structural types and construction techniques was in evidence. Subsequent development, as seen particularly in Phase 4, served principally to underline the importance of the two main structural traditions present, circular building and rectilinear posthole construction.

Direct evidence for structural function is almost non-existent in most cases. It can be demonstrated most reliably for the ironworking buildings I and R and inferred for the shrine structure Q and for the 'granary' structures S and M on the basis of morphological parallels with other sites. For the other rectilinear post-built structures it has been suggested that building D, a distinct sub-type, was probably at least part domestic in function. It is no more than an assumption that structure F, contemporary with building D and in a comparable roadside location, was similarly multifunctional, though this is plausible. This leaves structures B and J. Structure J occupied a road-frontage location close to an area associated with metalworking, although it may have been built after that activity (in structure I) had ceased. At just over 6 m square it would have been small for a domestic unit, though perhaps not impossibly so, but in an area not obviously associated with domestic activity some other function may be just as likely. Structure B seems to have been associated with the closely adjacent circular structure A, although the precise relative and absolute chronology of these buildings is uncertain. Their relative functions are equally uncertain, but the juxtaposition of circular structure N (albeit poorly defined) and the probably contemporary six post granary structure M suggests an analogy. On this basis structure A might have been a domestic unit with structure B an associated agricultural building.

Generally, therefore, the evidence tends to suggest that several of the rectilinear post-built structures were not primarily domestic in function, with building D (and possibly structure F) perhaps the main exceptions to this generalisation. The corollary of this is that the round structures probably formed the domestic component in most of the settlement units defined in Area B. Such a conclusion is simplistic and contains the risk of a circular argument, but is nevertheless attractive, though the evidence to prove it is inadequate. If it is accepted even as a rough guide, however, it is clear that there are insufficient buildings to house a significant population in this part of the site; indeed this is true even on the most optimistic assessment of the number of domestic structures present. One possible explanation of this is that the relatively marginal location of Area B resulted in a fairly thinly spread and intermittent pattern of domestic activity. An alternative view is that truncation of the archaeological deposits has resulted in the complete removal of some structural traces and the reduction of others to a point at which their original significance is unrecognisable. This may apply particularly in the case of small rectilinear buildings. Some groups of probable postholes or short lengths of slot or gully may originally have supported or related to buildings, particularly in the area of the south-central plots, and such evidence has been interpreted in this way at Neatham, for example (cf Millett and Graham 1986, 13-19), but at Westhawk Farm the surviving evidence is inadequate to sustain a confident interpretation in individual cases. The scale of the project did not allow for the very detailed examination of some feature groups which might have helped to enhance the identification of structures.

ECONOMY

Agriculture

The site was utilised for stock raising, as suggested by the presence of a field system, perhaps as early as the middle Bronze Age. Currently there are no data to indicate the nature of any local environmental changes between the Bronze Age and the Roman period. Presumably the area was still suitable for pastoral farming at the time that the Roman settlement was established. Unfortunately the soil conditions resulted in the almost total loss of faunal remains which would have informed discussion of this aspect of the agricultural economy. However, the pollen and insect remains from both waterholes 9179 and 796 indicate the presence of pasture in the near vicinity, and the pollen evidence suggests that this was herb-rich in character. The principal domestic animal species identified on the site could therefore have been pastured close to it, if not actually within the margins of the settlement.

Arable agriculture is also indicated by a range of plant and other remains. The pollen evidence shows that cereals were being cultivated and/or processed in, or close to, the settlement. This picture is amplified by the evidence of charred plant remains, which indicate relatively widespread crop processing. This activity was underway from as early as Phase 2 of Period 2, particularly south of the shrine area, though rich deposits of crop processing debris were also encountered in plot NW2 in Phase 4. The principal cereal crop was spelt wheat, represented both by grain and chaff. Emmer wheat and barley were also present, but in much smaller quantities, and occasional (probably wild) oats may have been deliberately collected or at least tolerated within cultivated crops. The combination of elements present suggested that whole ears of wheat and barley were represented amongst the material recovered.

These crops were associated with 'a relatively mature and varied weed flora', consisting principally of characteristic arable weeds, including species such as corn cockle that are generally regarded as Roman introductions to Britain. Overall, however, the cereal remains are regarded as representing a continuation of Iron Age agricultural traditions into the Roman period and there is no reason to suppose that cereal production was not part of the range of agricultural activities carried out by inhabitants of the settlement. This continuation of tradition can be seen also in the structural record, with structures M and S, probably small granaries, essentially of pre-Roman type. Interestingly the insect remains from waterhole 796 included an example of *Tenebroides mauritanicus*, a significant grain store pest, which was almost certainly a Roman introduction to Britain and is interpreted as showing the use of grain from a major store. This presumably represented a development in grain storage provision from that indicated by structures M and S. Alternatively, had the insect been imported to Westhawk Farm in a consignment of grain rather than living in stored grain on the site, as is possible, this might have implications for the ability or need of the settlement to be completely self-supporting in cereals.

Apart from cereals there was evidence for other edible plant species. With Roman introductions such as cherry and dill it is perhaps less easy to be certain that they were grown at or near the site, though there is no reason why this should not have been the case.

The physical processes of agriculture or horticulture are directly represented in the artefactual record only by part of a spade iron which, while recovered from a post-medieval context, was very likely of Roman date. Conversion of grain to flour is indicated by a range of querns, and fragments of four millstones are noteworthy. They hint at the presence of a mill, perhaps on the Whitewater Dyke, though the use of animal powered mills is also a possibility.

Other activities

There is very little evidence for craft activities within the excavated part of the settlement, with the clear exception of ironworking, discussed separately below. A couple of fragments of copper alloy hint at working of that material, and possible carpenter's tools of iron included a chisel and an awl. The presence in grave 5090 of beads of lignite, probably from a relatively local source, raises the possibility that this material was worked by a craftsman within the settlement.

Trade and market functions would normally be expected to have been located within major settlements. The excavated evidence sheds light on this in two ways. An unusually high representation of weighing equipment may have been related to marketing or perhaps, as suggested by Hilary Cool (see Chapter 5 above), to a more official aspect of such activity such as the collection and recording of goods for the *annona militaris*. Trade and other connections are identified most readily in a range of artefacts that can be assigned to sources with varying degrees of accuracy. The material ranges from the locally available, though extremely important, commodity of salt, indicated by the presence of very small quantities of briquetage possibly deriving from the Lydd area in Romney Marsh, up to imported pottery. A relatively wide range of connections is indicated by the querns and millstones, which were drawn from sources as far afield as the Pennines and the Rhineland, though both Millstone Grit and Niedermendig lava are found quite widely in Kent and do not constitute particularly exotic materials. More striking, perhaps, is the preference (in terms of the numbers of stones represented) for Lodsworth stone over the more locally available Folkestone Greensand. This may reflect a trading connection with Sussex also evident in aspects of the pottery supply (and a relative absence of communication with the Folkestone area indicated also by a lack of sand-tempered 'Belgic' wares from that area), and it may be no coincidence that East Sussex ware products were apparently replacing East Kent ones from about the mid 2nd century while the first Lodsworth querns appear in Phase 4 (AD 150-200) contexts.

The great majority of the pottery from the site was in handmade or wheel-turned grog-tempered wares. The majority of these cannot be assigned with confidence to known sources, which probably ranged from East Kent to East Sussex and can therefore be described as local to regional in distribution. There are slight hints that some of this production could have been very locally based, however, and a small group of flagons from Area C may have derived from another local production in a very different tradition. Finer 'Romanised' wares were drawn from north Kent and the Canterbury area in the early Roman period, supplemented by a range of continental imports: Gallo-Belgic white wares, Central Gaulish beakers and South Gaulish samian, but always in small quantities. South Spanish olive oil amphorae and southern Gaulish wine amphorae were also present. At a slightly later date Patchgrove ware vessels may have arrived on site as containers for some kind of commodity; this function was not unique to vessels imported from across the English Channel.

The range of imported pottery expanded slightly in the first half of the 2nd century to include Central and East Gaulish samian ware and Cologne and Argonne beakers. The last of these, together with beakers from Colchester, were only present in minute quantities, however, as were North Gaulish grey wares and mortaria from several different sources. After *c* AD 200 imported material consisted only of very small numbers of Moselkeramik beakers, a little East Gaulish samian and probably some Dressel 20 amphorae.

Coarse wares continued to be drawn from across Kent and East Sussex. North Kent remained a major source of reduced wares, but Canterbury declined in importance as a source after the 2nd century. Later Roman coarse wares from outside the region consisted of small quantities of Dorset BB1 and a few sherds of Portchester D/Overwey sandy buff/orange fabric from Surrey. Occasional sherds of Nene Valley colour-coated ware, a mortarium from the same source and two sherds of Hadham oxidised ware complete the range of non-local later Roman fabrics. The general scarcity of such fabrics, and the absence of others such as Oxford products, significant in view of the ubiquity of these wares from the late 3rd century, is a consequence of the lack of late Roman activity on the site.

The pottery was therefore drawn from a fairly wide range of sources but, for the most part, those lying outside the region were only represented by small quantities of material, which does not suggest sustained contact at an intensive level. The principal standard imported ceramics, samian ware and Dressel 20 olive oil amphorae, occurred more consistently, as might be expected. The presence of the latter in some quantity is one characteristic which distinguishes Westhawk Farm from contemporary lower status rural settlements, such as Bower Road, Smeeth (Diez forthcoming) or Runhams Farm, Lenham (Philp 1994) and even from some villa assemblages, such as Thurnham (Lawrence forthcoming). Overall, however, the range of pottery found at the site is unremarkable, particularly considering the size of the assemblage.

Iron industry

There are two main questions relating to the evidence for iron production at Westhawk Farm. The first is to assess the importance of iron production in the economy of the settlement as a whole; the second is to determine the framework within which iron production took place. Neither question can be answered simply.

An attempt has already been made to calculate the approximate volume of iron production represented by the quantities of slag recovered in the excavation of Area B. This is hampered by two principal unknown factors; the extent of removal of slag from the site in the Roman period for such purposes as road surfacing, a well-known characteristic of many roads in the Weald (Margary 1973, 21), and the extent to which on-site slag heaps may have been reduced, dispersed and removed by post-Roman activity, ranging from deliberate recycling to fortuitous attrition by agricultural processes. Neither of these unknowns can be quantified with any degree of certainty. It is clear that the Canterbury road within the settlement originally incorporated slag in its construction and the quantity of this may have been substantial, but the extent to which this material was used as metalling beyond the confines of the settlement is less certain. The use of slag has been noted at a number of points along the line of the road, for example some 16 km west of Westhawk Farm near Benenden (Aldridge 2002). While that material must have derived from iron producing sites in the vicinity, Margary notes 'scattered flint and slag metalling' around Harlakenden Farm and Criol Farm, only *c* 4-5 km west of Westhawk (Margary 1973, 48). In the absence of evidence for other iron producing sites in that immediate area it is possible that this material derived from Westhawk Farm, in which case a rather more substantial level of output than demonstrated by the excavated material may be implied. The extent of post-Roman loss of slag deposits is simply unknowable.

It is possible, however, to attempt to understand the spatial extent of iron production within the settlement. With regard to this it is worth noting that had the 1998 excavation of Area B – in which both workshop structures (I and R) were examined – constituted the entire sample of this area a significantly different conclusion might have been reached about the importance of iron production at the site. As it is, a tripling of the excavated extent of Area B in the 1999 excavation produced no further significant iron production debris and certainly no further structural evidence for such production. Examination of the structural evidence and iron slag distribution across the whole of the excavated area can now be compared with the site wide coverage of the geophysical survey to allow identification of potential foci of further ironworking.

Overall, the evidence of the geophysical survey suggests that there may have been up to six locations which can be interpreted as suggesting significant ironworking, although a more realistic estimate is that perhaps only two of these are likely to have been comparable to the concentrations of activity seen around structures I and R. If this is accepted,

and it is of course speculative, it may be admissible to multiply the known volume of production by a factor of two, or at most by a factor of four if all six possible 'hot spots' had in fact represented ironworking foci. On any calculation or estimate (and Paynter's estimate of total slag volume across the site is problematic because it assumes an even distribution of ironworking which seems, both on general grounds and on the basis of the geophysical survey data just discussed, improbable (see Chapter 7)) it must be admitted that compared with the volume of production that can be demonstrated for a number of Wealden sites (cf Hodgkinson 1999, 70-71) the likely output of Westhawk Farm was low, and indeed minimal in comparison with that of the major centres.

The excavated plan of Area B shows that a significant part of the area contained no evidence for iron production. It is unclear how far this evidence is necessarily representative – the peripheral location of much of Area B should be borne in mind here – but it is of interest that on the basis of the geophysical survey evidence the two most likely candidates for ironworking foci comparable to those of structures I and R both lay south-west of the focal junction area of the settlement and that all but two of the possible concentrations of marked magnetic anomalies lay outside that area. It may be purely coincidental that both the known ironworking areas and many of the possible ones are centred very roughly 100 m apart, but this spacing may have some implication for understanding the layout of the settlement, especially along its south-eastern margin, where the fairly regular spacing appears to be particularly marked. The absence of a chronological dimension to most parts of the distribution makes further speculation meaningless, however.

In sum, the evidence indicates that while ironworking may have been relatively widespread across parts of the settlement there were no more concentrated locations of such activity than that around structure R. Extrapolating from the data gathered there a basic level of iron production can be suggested – on the (unproven) assumptions that the nature, intensity and chronological range of ironworking activity in each likely area was similar. The numbers of workers involved in these workshops need only have been relatively small in total, as demonstrated by Paynter (Chapter 7 above) and even allowing for the involvement of other members of the settlement's population in related activities such as ore gathering and charcoal burning (again unproven assumptions) it is hard to see how Westhawk Farm can be characterised as an iron producing site, rather than a site in which iron producing was one of a number of important activities. Inclusion of the site in Burnham and Wacher's (1990) category of 'specialized sites: industrial', for example, would probably be a mistake, and indeed the adequacy of the evidence for some of the sites thus categorised by Burnham and Wacher may be questioned. In particular there are no criteria for defining a threshold beyond which the industrial capacity of a particular settlement can be identified as providing the *basis* for the existence of the settlement, rather than comprising a normal level of craft or service activity to be found in most 'small towns' (cf Booth 1998, 617). This important question is certainly relevant to Westhawk Farm.

A further aspect of iron production activity relates to its impact on the woodland environment. As noted above there seems to have been a consistent decline in tree cover in the area through the early Roman period. Use of the resource for charcoal burning prior to iron production presumably played a part in this process, but is unlikely to have been the only factor at work, others being requirements for domestic fuel and perhaps clearance for expanding arable agriculture related to the needs of the burgeoning settlement. The charcoal from Westhawk provides no evidence that the needs of the site were such that woodland management practices were required to accommodate them, although this does not exclude the possibility that such practices were used (Challinor above). The preferential use of oak is clear. These trends are in line with the wider picture from the Weald (Sim and Ridge 2002, 38-42).

Despite the suggestion that iron production may not have been the primary economic activity of the site it is still important to establish the basis on which this production was carried on and its relationship, if any, to the larger scale production of the Weald to the west. The latter has been discussed at length elsewhere, for example by Cleere and Crossley (1985) who have characterised the Weald as divided into two geographical groups, of which the eastern, centred on an area roughly 30 km south-west of Westhawk Farm, is thought to have operated under the direct control of the *Classis Britannica* (ibid., 68-70). The view that the fleet was directly involved in Wealden iron production has been widely accepted (eg Salway 1981, 637-9; Jones and Mattingly 1990, 192; Hingley and Miles 2002, 164) and with some reservation by Frere (1987, 210, 287) and Schrüfer-Kolb (2004, 127-8), though other scholars have been less certain (eg Millett 2007, 178-9).

It is true that iron production was not normally an imperial monopoly and that state involvement in mineral extraction concentrated principally on precious metals (Healy 1978). Nevertheless it is clear that there were exceptions to this, for example in central Noricum, where much of the area occupied by the most important iron mines formed part of a large imperial estate (Alföldy 1974, 115). This was administratively separated from the rest of the province and, whatever the details of the mode of exploitation, the state mines in this area are likely to have belonged to the *fiscus* (imperial treasury) (Dušanić 1977, 81). The *ferriariae Noricae* were managed by large lease holders (*conductores*) whose staff included procurators, but by the early 3rd century a system of direct (state) management had probably been adopted (ibid., 82).

There is much less direct evidence for the status of the iron production sites in the Weald, but a case has been made that this area, too, may have been an imperial estate (Cleere and Crossley 1985, 67-69). The only

(civilian) official directly attested on a Wealden site, at Beauport Park (Brodribb and Cleere 1988, 261-2), has a title (*vilicus* – the only recorded instance in Roman Britain) encountered several times in the context of iron production in Pannonia both before and after this came under direct imperial administration (Dušanić 1977, 84). The role of the *Classis Britannica* in such a scenario remains less clear, however, even though it has been argued that 'all large-scale mining operations in the early Empire required a substantial military presence' (Edmondson 1989, 97). It need not be supposed that fleet personnel provided the labour force at the Wealden production sites, though the evidence of barrack-like structures at Bardown might suggest this (Cleere and Crossley 1985, 74). Equally, the suggestion that the fleet was primarily responsible for the distribution of Wealden iron, much of it as direct export to the continent (ibid., 83) is not proven, even though this is possible. That the fleet had some role in supporting and perhaps administering the industry seems certain, however. This is most clearly demonstrated by the occurrence of stamped tiles at a small number of potentially key sites in the eastern Weald. The overall distribution of these tiles (Peacock 1977; Crowley and Betts 1992) is sufficiently restricted to suggest that it is far from random and may have been quite carefully controlled. Although *Classis Britannica* stamped tiles are absent at Westhawk Farm, the fabric typical of them is represented there, as is another unusual fabric/form combination also noted at sites such as Beauport Park, the site with the largest collection of CLBR stamped tiles (see Harrison, Chapter 6 above). The excavated ceramic building material assemblage suggests a low level of use of tile within Area B of the site, but it contains components strongly suggestive of the presence of a bath-house somewhere within the confines of the settlement, a suggestion supported by the occurrence of window glass. Such structures, of which the Beauport Park one is the best-known, are of course characteristic of the major Wealden sites at which stamped CLBR tiles have been found. A bath-house at Westhawk Farm need not have been associated specifically with the ironworking establishments there, but such an association is certainly possible.

BURIAL RITES

Burial 9200

A striking contrast is formed by burial 9200 and the two sword burials at nearby Brisley Farm. As far as the limitations of the dating evidence will allow these three high status burials were exactly contemporaneous (one and possibly both of the warrior burials being provisionally dated AD 30-50), but greater differences in burial rite between the two sites would be hard to imagine. The Brisley Farm burials have themselves been characterised by their excavator as remarkably different from each other (Stevenson and Johnson 2004; Casper Johnson pers. comm.), but from the perspective of Westhawk Farm these differences seem much less significant than the similarities. Nevertheless there are points of similarity even between the Brisley Farm and Westhawk Farm burials, the most obvious being the inclusion of a pig's head, although it is impossible to be certain if the Westhawk example was complete, or only half, like that from the smaller (and possibly later) of the two Brisley Farm graves.Burial 9200 was originally seen as lying broadly within the regional late Iron Age 'Aylesford Culture' tradition of burial (cf Whimster 1981, 147-166) on the basis of the presence of the bucket and other object types found in some burials in that tradition, but there are problems with accommodating it precisely within the scheme set out by Whimster. These are compounded by the fact that understanding of the Westhawk burial is compromised by poor preservation, exacerbated by the circumstances of recovery, but it is clear that the range of objects placed in the grave was wide. In particular, some of the extremely fragmentary copper alloy pieces are likely to have derived from objects which do not have straightforward domestic functions but might have been associated with ceremonial and status display.

One aspect of the question of the associations of the burial relates to the location of the cremated remains. These, and indeed most of the other objects in the grave, seem to have been in a box; the container was not, as so often, a ceramic vessel. Since 9200 cannot be associated either with the simplest unurned Aylesford burials or, probably, with the 'group of very much more wealthy burials in which the unenclosed ashes lie surrounded by their accompanying grave goods' (ibid., 157) – essentially those of Stead's 'Welwyn' phase of the Aylesford culture (Stead 1967) – it may perhaps be linked with a more nebulous group of 'unurned cremations associated with a more restricted group of material' (Whimster 1981, 158), exemplified by burials at King Harry Lane, where 66 out of 455 cremations were 'separate' (that is, with ashes uncontained) but with one or more pots in the grave. These included the most elaborate burials from the site (Stead and Rigby 1989, 83), but none of these was contained in a box in the fashion of the Westhawk burial.

The wooden box, estimated at 350 mm wide by 450 mm long, falls outside the size range of caskets permitted by Borrill (1981, 304). However, it was small compared with other boxes - averaging 625 mm wide and 758 mm long as calculated from a list of 20 boxes (Philpott 1991, table 2) - and was similar to caskets in other respects. Like many, the box was decorated, albeit somewhat plainly with copper alloy sheeting. A possible lion-headed mount (no. 15) may have adorned the box, but this is not certain. Boxes of any kind, and certainly boxes containing the majority of grave goods and cremated remains – as opposed, perhaps, to timber lined and/or roofed chambers as at King Harry Lane (Stead and Rigby 1989, 81) – were at best extremely rare in Aylesford culture graves. A 'warrior burial' (of Aylesford culture type in contrast to those from Brisley Farm) from Colches-ter and dated AD 43-60 contained at least one box and is among the earliest examples (Crummy 1993, 495). Philpott (1991, 17) sees the rite as introduced to Britain in the wake of the Roman conquest, though with no clear indication of its origin, and growing in popularity from the late 1st century AD. This developed Roman-period tradition was particularly common in Essex and Hertfordshire, but was also found in Sussex and Kent, not least at Westhawk Farm itself, where there were examples in the adjacent Area C cemetery and in at least one of the late 2nd century cremations in Area B.

The Westhawk burial is also anomalous with regard to pottery. The presence of multiple vessels in cremation burials is a regular feature of the Aylesford tradition, whereas here only a single vessel was present. Moreover this was a platter, rather than one of the closed forms (jar or beaker) that seem to have been most characteristic of Aylesford type burials. The particular fabric represented, micaceous *terra nigra*, is in fact relatively uncommon in grave assemblages, with certainly attested examples only at King Harry Lane, Baldock and Hurstbourne Tarrant, Hampshire (Jane Timby, pers. comm.). In general terms, however, it is notable that Ashford lies very close to a focal area for the distribution of Gallo-Belgic wares in Britain (Fitzpatrick and Timby 2002, 168, fig. 14.4). It is also notable that the tradition of burials incorporating a jug and patera set as seen at Westhawk Farm continued into the Roman period (Philpott 1991, 123-124), principally associated with cremation burials, and was well-established in Kent, for example in two of the three very rich cremation burials from the recent A2 excavations near Springhead, probably dating to the period *c* AD 50-60 (Allen 2007).

The state of many of the objects makes assessment of their condition at the time of burial difficult. In general there is little reason to suppose that the objects placed in the burial were not complete, but there are hints that this may have been true of the patera; these are the presence of a piece of fabric inside the handle and overlapping the edge of its point of attachment to the side of the vessel, and the absence of the (usually decorated) end of the handle, normally a substantial casting that would have been expected to have survived the processes of decay which had affected other parts of the copper alloy vessels.

Despite the problems of preservation the animal remains provide useful information about aspects of the burial. Sheep or lamb, pig and bird were all placed on the pyre. Sheep and bird also occurred as pyre goods in some of the Roman-period cremations, but pig did not. Pig and lamb were also included with the goods placed in grave 9200. The only identifiable fragments of pig were teeth, and although this may simply relate to preservation factors it is likely that only the pig's head was placed in the grave – the size of the grave would certainly have been insufficient to accommodate an adult pig (see also above). At the King Harry Lane cemetery, Verulamium, pig skulls were found exclusively with male burials (Pearce 1997, 177), though it should be noted that the material in question there consisted of pyre goods as the evidence for unburnt animal bones was lost (ibid., 176). This association supports the identification of the occupant of grave 9200 – slightly uncertain on the basis of the surviving cremated bone – as a male.

Area B and C cemeteries

Inhumation and cremation graves were placed within the cemetery throughout the life of the settlement, both traditions therefore coexisting. The only distinction made between the two here was that the majority of inhumation graves were concentrated in the central area of the enclosure, while the cremation graves were generally located around the north-western edge. No such clear spatial distinction between cremation and inhumation graves was noticed at Pepper Hill, although there cremation graves were more commonly located adjacent to the cemetery boundary than elsewhere. This is reminiscent of the situation at Westhawk Farm, though not so starkly demonstrated.

At least three inhumation graves (groups 5130, 5190 and 8520) date to the 1st century AD. Evidence in south-eastern Britain of early Roman inhumation graves remains unusual compared with cremation burials, but Westhawk Farm adds to a expanding list of sites. Pepper Hill is exceptional in that inhumation formed the majority rite during the early Roman period; over 130 such graves were encountered, compared with 60 cremation graves (Biddulph forthcoming). Further inhumation graves, observed as isolated graves or small groups are known at Monkton (Perkins 1985, 54-9), Mill Hill, Deal (Parfitt 1995, 156), and Chilham (Ashbee 1996). Philpott (1991, 57) regards early Roman inhumation as a continuation of Iron Age 'native' tradition, and in view of the Brisley Farm warrior graves and large late Iron Age inhumation cemeteries at Deal and Sittingbourne (Parfitt 1995), this conclusion is difficult to avoid. However, the individuals buried at Westhawk Farm, or their mourners, did not reject Roman funerary custom altogether, as the flagon and samian platter in grave 8520 appear to indicate.

Boxes found in graves were typically larger than caskets - and the box from grave 9200 - and tended to be undecorated (Borrill 1981, 304). At Westhawk Farm, Area C produced one certain box burial (5220), while a probable box burial (220) came from Area B. The soil stain in the former measured 0.85 m by 0.7 m, while the size of the suspected box in the latter is estimated at 0.60 m by 0.60 m. A further two graves, 5240 and 9860, were square in plan and may also have contained boxes. Box burials are concentrated in Hertfordshire and Essex; Philpott (1991, 16-21) records few from Kent, and then largely from Canterbury, although examples outside urban centres have begun to emerge since that survey. The cemetery at Each End, Ash produced a box burial (Hicks 1998, 113). At least three were buried at Pepper Hill; the furniture associated with a further seven cremation graves at that site was much smaller and better identified as caskets (Biddulph forthcoming).

Pottery in cremation burials

The bone from the Area C cremation burials was placed within urns, except in Group 5210. Five cremation graves, groups 5050, 5110, 5120, 5230 and 5240, contained a cinerary urn only, and three graves, groups 5060, 5070, and 5080, had a cinerary urn and a single ancillary vessel. Group 5210, as already mentioned, had no cinerary urn but did have an associated ceramic vessel. Grave 5090 contained the cinerary urn and lid with two further vessels, and grave 5220 contained the urn and three ancillary vessels (Table 10.3).

The paucity of pottery grave goods in inhumation burials - just two groups (5130 and 8520) contained vessels - appears to reflect a tradition in which formal grave goods were not essential, unlike the cremation burials of the Aylesford tradition, which were characterised by ceramic vessels. The mass of broken pottery incorporated into the backfill of group 8160, however, suggests that ceramics were required at a different stage of the funeral. The assemblage consisted of over 2000 sherds (from an absolute minimum of 37 vessels) and included a strong dining and drinking element. Like similarly broken pottery from graves at Alton, Hampshire (Millett 1986, 82), Colchester (Crummy 1993, 493) and Pepper Hill (Biddulph forthcoming), the pottery from group 8160 may represent the remains of a funerary feast. It was this stage of the funeral, in which the deceased was remembered and new social memories were created (cf Williams 2004), that pottery played an essential role.

The range of pottery from the burials overall is consistent with the types of pottery selected at most cemeteries in Kent. Some 60% of Westhawk Farm's ceramic grave goods were drinking-related (flagons, beakers and cups). Eating-related vessels - platters and dishes in this case - accounted for a further 31% of the assemblage. Jars and lids made up the remaining vessels. The composition, compared by broad functional category, is near-identical to the assemblages from Each End, Ash (Savage 1998), and Pepper Hill. The assemblages from Ospringe (Whiting *et al.* 1931) and Monkton (Perkins 1985) are close to Westhawk, although both have a stronger drinking element. The similarity across these assemblages reveals that pottery selection was standardised to a large extent; chronology and local variations in ceramic supply probably accounted for most of the differences. The absence of certain pottery at Westhawk Farm, in particular lamps, which appear most frequently at major urban centres, including London, Colchester and Chichester, provides an obvious indication that funerary assemblages can be differentiated to some degree in terms of status. However, the Westhawk Farm assemblage also contained a relatively high proportion of samian vessels. Although samian is by no means unusual in graves of any status, it was the preferentially selected ceramic in relatively high-status burials (cf Biddulph 2005). The

Table 10.3   Summary of finds assemblages from graves (Excludes graves with no finds or with small assemblages of miscellaneous potsherds).

Group	Phase	Pottery					Other 'grave goods'		Comment
		'Urn'	Flagon	Drinking vessel	Dish	Other	Pyre	Grave	
AREA C									
Cremations									
5110	2-3	1							
5120	2-5	1							
5230	2-5	1							
5220	3	1	1	1	1		sheep, bird	hobnails	box burial
5240	3	1							
5080	4-5	1	1						
5050	5	1					intaglio		
5060	5		1	1					possibly infant inhumation
5070	5	1		1					
5210	5	none		1					
5090	6	1	1	1		lid	sheep, bird	cu armlet, 'jet' bead armlet & necklace	
Inhumations									
5130	2	N/A		1					
AREA B									
Cremations									
1261	2	none				jar			
1007	2-3	1							
9860	3	none	1			jar			
9940	3	1	1	1					
210	4	1		3	3			cu needle, hobnails	possible box burial
220	5	1		3	6		animal bone	hobnails	probable box burial
Inhumations									
8520	3	N/A	1	1	1				
8160	4	N/A	numerous					fe awl	coffin (stain)

over-representation of the ware at Westhawk Farm hints at a special status for the site, possibly deriving from its religious or industrial role (see below). Malcolm Lyne and Joanna Bird (see Chapter 6) note the presence of an unusually large number of repaired samian vessels, all from non-funerary deposits. The pottery deposited in graves was, in contrast, whole, though often worn. These vessels, which probably saw household use first, were therefore in relatively good condition - perhaps the finest that mourners had to offer - and might well have been specially reserved for funerary use.

Personal possessions within cremation burials

Only three cremation graves in the Area C cemetery, 5220, 5050 and 5090, produced non-ceramic finds. Grave 5220 had been placed within a box which measured 0.7 m by 0.85 m, and two clusters of hobnails from a pair of shoes were placed at the northernmost edge of the box, beside the cremation urn. Soil conditions precluded any survival of leather and the distribution of nails was not sufficiently secure to allow the nailing pattern or the size of the shoes to be determined. The distribution of hobnails in cremation graves represents a common tradition in small towns and rural settlements in the south-east of England during the late 1st to early 2nd century (Philpott 1991). Nailed shoes were also placed beneath one of the pottery vessels in box burial 220 in Area B.

Cremation 5090 produced personal ornaments from within the funerary urn, placed above the cremated remains, consisting largely of jet, and occasional lignite beads. An armlet was made from three large, oval, ridge-backed beads, on which traces of gold leaf remained, and a further twenty-four flat elliptical beads. A necklace made from 183 cylinder beads, and a copper-alloy armlet had also been placed with the cremated remains. None of the items had been present on the pyre. In contrast, the single non-ceramic object from cremation 5050, a small intaglio, appears (unusually) to have been a pyre good.

None of the burials, apart from box cremation 5220 which produced nine nails, contained any coffin or box fittings, suggesting (but not proving) that burial within a coffin was not a common practice here. A coffin was present in grave 8160 (Fig. 8.36) in Area B, but was evidenced by a stain rather than by the presence of nails.

Distribution of burials

The distribution of burials across the excavated part of the site is characteristic of Romano-British nucleated settlements in suggesting a combination of relatively informal alongside more closely defined practices. The spread of burials at the southern fringes of the settlement indicates the marginal nature of this area. It is more difficult to account for the group of three cremation graves just north-east of the shrine area, but without evidence on the nature of the enclosure within which they lay (almost entirely outside the excavated area) little can be said. In no sense, however, should any of these burials necessarily be regarded as 'randomly placed' or of low status. Both in the context of rural settlement and in relation to nucleated sites of all types careful consideration of burial location seems increasingly likely, even if the factors determining these locations are not always clear (Pearce 1999, 157-159; Esmonde Cleary 2000). At Westhawk Farm this is most clearly shown by the apparent association of inhumation 8160 with structure C, but can be suggested for the others. The potential importance of burial 8160 is emphasised by the substantial pottery assemblage contained within the grave fill. Such assemblages can indicate the holding of a funerary feast in part reflecting the esteem in which the deceased was held, but while eating and drinking vessels were well-represented, jars were still the dominant vessel type, suggesting that the group was more typical of general domestic material. If so its interpretation is more problematical, but it is possible that its character, combined with the location of the burial within the house site, indicates some kind of ritual of termination of use of the building, perhaps involving a large part of the pottery assemblage associated with it.

The majority of the burials encountered lay within a small, defined cemetery located characteristically, just beyond the formal boundary of the settlement. On present evidence, however, this was clearly not a major cemetery for the Westhawk Farm community, but one used by an individual family or other social grouping over a sustained period. A fairly close parallel can be seen in a small cemetery of some 30 individuals lying immediately outside a major settlement boundary at Alchester, though that cemetery was not clearly defined by further boundaries (Booth *et al.* 2001, 152-158). Chance finds outside the excavated area indicate the wider use of the zone north-west of the settlement boundary for burials, although whether these formed part of a larger formal cemetery is unknown. Despite its small size, however, the defined group of burials seems, both on the basis of its enclosure and its location beyond the principal settlement boundary, to justify definition as a formal cemetery rather than as a group of 'backland' burials, of a type noted by Esmonde Cleary (2000, 129) as being particularly characteristic of small towns.

Chronology

The dated excavated burials span almost the entire period of the known life of the settlement, from Phase 2 to Phase 6 of Period 2. As far as possible, burials were assigned to a single phase, but 8 of the 19 burials in the Area C cemetery could not be so closely defined. There was no chronological distinction between inhumation and cremation graves, both rites being found together throughout Period 2, both within Area C and elsewhere. The main discernible chronological pattern relates to the use of different parts of the site for burial. No burials within the southern part of the settlement or at its margins occurred later than the early 3rd century. Cremation grave 220 adjacent to building R was assigned to Phase 5, but is probably to be dated within the early years of that phase. Otherwise, Phase 5 and later burials were only encountered in the Area C cemetery. This distinction may reflect a reduction in the level of occupation of the southern end of the site after the end of the 2nd century, though a closer correlation with the occupation sequence would have shown burials here ceasing *after* the end of Phase 5 (but the total number of burials involved may be too small to sustain detailed analysis of their chronological trends). A more interesting possibility is that the distinction between the two parts of the site indicates a move towards formalisation of the location of burial, a trend which on this evidence would start in the early 3rd century. Without evidence for further cemeteries associated with the settlement, however, this must remain speculative.

GENERAL DISCUSSION

Chronological summary of development

In outline the development of the settlement may be summarised as follows. It was established within a generation of the Roman conquest in an area which was already widely if not densely settled. The role of an immediately adjacent late Iron Age settlement focus, probably of high status (on the basis of a single surviving burial), in determining the location of the Roman settlement is unknown. The burial (9200) is the clearest single indicator of the presence of such a settlement at Westhawk Farm. Another indicator is the quarter-stater of Eppillus. The evidence for intensive activity at Brisley Farm and at other sites in the immediate area may, however, indicate the existence of a concentration of population in the area sufficiently large to influence the general alignment of roads (see below) regardless of the extent of settlement at Westhawk Farm itself.

The pottery assemblage from Area B included material which could be of pre-conquest date, but the case for occupation of that date in Area B remains unproven since none of this pottery was from contexts demonstrably earlier than the main components of the Roman settlement plan. The most important of those components, which determined the enduring form of the settlement layout, were the two major road alignments, both of which were probably established in Phase 2 (that is, before *c* AD 70). The Canterbury road was partly defined by roadside ditches at this time, but a feature diverging from this alignment formed an early boundary on the north-west side of the settlement in the vicinity of the road junction area. The way in which the latter area was defined in the earliest phase of the settlement, and the extent of settlement or other activity within or adjacent to it, is unknown. At the south-west margin of the settlement, however, two structures (A and B) were in use in an area subsequently incorporated in a block of plots on the north-west side of the Canterbury road, while on the south-east side of the road at least one settlement unit, probably of agricultural character, was also of pre-Flavian date. This lay at the southern edge of what already seems to have been a partly-defined open space, later occupied by a shrine. A small cemetery was established outside the main north-west settlement boundary very early in the life of the site.

Phase 3, dated *c* AD 70-150, saw most of the main features of the settlement in place. These included the shrine structure, set in a small enclosure within a much wider space, the north-east side of which was defined by a substantial double-ditched enclosure that fronted onto the Canterbury road. Trackways leading from beyond the settlement up to the shrine area, or relating to a crossing of the Whitewater Dyke which may have assumed added importance through having the axis of the shrine complex aligned upon it, were almost certainly (in one case) or probably (in ?two others) in place at this time. Domestic/agricultural activity continued in the complex on the south side of the shrine area. On the opposite side of the road from the latter, overlying the early settlement boundary, an iron-producing workshop (structure I) was established. This housed both smelting and related smithing activities. There was relatively little clear evidence of intensive activity further south-west of this building, but two circular structures (C and E) may already have been in existence in the area later occupied by the south-west block of roadside plots. Parallel boundaries, forming a single plot (plot SE1), were perhaps laid out opposite these structures at this time, though the dating is less secure (a later date is possible), but did not apparently enclose structures or other major features.

Phase 4 saw a number of developments in the northern corner of Area B. The iron-working building continued in use in the early part of this phase, but was then apparently abandoned, while the surrounding area was incorporated within a series of plots laid out approximately at right-angles to the line of the Canterbury road. Further south-west the establishment of a block of five or six further plots, mostly of very regular layout, is also dated to this phase. These contained timber structures of a variety of types, one of which, a circular structure possibly in use from the previous phase, was then abandoned and a burial inserted within its outline. On the south-east side of the road, however, there is less evidence for significant new development, though occupation continued in the settlement area south of the shrine complex (at least one new circular structure was attributable to this phase) and the north-east and north-west sides of the shrine enclosure were redefined.

In Phase 5, the last phase of large-scale occupation of this part of the settlement (*c* AD 200-250), intensive activity continued in some of the south-west roadside plots next to the Canterbury road. Opposite this area plot SE1 also remained in use, containing a number of pits dated to this phase. On the south side of the shrine area the latest building (structure P), still of circular plan, overlay earlier boundaries defining the edge of that area while to the north-east, on the opposite side of the shrine area, a new iron-working structure (R) overlay the south corner of the Phase 3 and later double ditched enclosure. Like the Phase 3-4 establishment (structure I), structure R accommodated both smelting and smithing activities. The occurrence of an iron billet in the area of structure P, if not certainly derived from it, hints that the two structures may have been associated in some way.

Subsequent activity in Area B was at a very low level. No new structures can be assigned to the later 3rd or 4th centuries, and even finds of this date were very localised, occurring principally in a small number of upper fills of features which had originated in earlier phases. The most important of these was a waterhole adjacent to the north-west side of the Canterbury road on the axis of the shrine structure opposite. Fourth century deposits in its upper fills contained large numbers of redeposited 2nd century coins suggested to be derived from the nearby shrine. The only activity attributable to the latest Roman phase (7) in Area B was the apparent removal of the large post which had been a focal feature within the shrine complex. Elsewhere, metal-detected finds of 4th century coins suggested continuing activity within the focal part of the settlement (Area A), but even there such material was scarce and none of the identifiable coins was later than the mid 4th century. The cemetery in Area C remained in use into Phase 6 but probably not thereafter; the latest burials, including a cremation burial of an adult male associated with black jewellery, being most likely of early 4th century date.

The character of early and later post-Roman activity is unknown. Limited activity of 13th century date, possibly indicating adjacent settlement, was located at the extreme southern end of Area B. Extant and earlier patterns of post-medieval field boundaries may have related to the pattern of land use established at that time, although the principal Roman boundary on the north-west side of the settlement survived in part as a modern alignment. The lasting significance of the Canterbury road is less clear, however. One post-medieval field boundary followed its south-east edge for some distance within Area B, but it is arguable that the general trend of the post-medieval boundaries was determined as much by the topographical logic of the site as by surviving Roman features.

Settlement character, size and morphology

The principal characteristics used to assess the broad nature of the settlement include its size, layout, structural density and diversity and economic character (cf Booth 1998, 613-615). The settlement was substantial, perhaps covering up to *c* 15 ha (see below) and, while comprising areas of contrasting morphology, contained significant zones of systematic layout, most particularly in the form of rows of fairly regular plots laid out along the north-west side of the Canterbury road. The evidence from the south-westernmost block of these plots indicates that most of them probably contained a structure or structures, but that the road frontage was not necessarily densely built-up here. There may have been more intensive use of the frontage closer to the focal area of the settlement, but it is clear that in the relatively marginal part of the site represented by Area B there were always open spaces between structures, and that these spaces were not always intensively used. The insect evidence from the two water holes indicated not only the presence of open grazed areas but, in the case of waterhole 9179, a complete absence of species indicative of settlement, though Robinson (Chapter 9 above) notes that comparable evidence comes from some other Roman nucleated settlements such as Scole, Norfolk and Elms Farm, Heybridge, Essex.

The range of structures included specialist buildings such as the shrine, a possible bathhouse (outside the excavated area) and iron producing workshops, as well as domestic and agricultural buildings and buildings which may have combined several functions. The economic character of the settlement reflected this structural diversity, with evidence for agricultural production, for iron production and, to a lesser extent, for trade. Overall these characteristics reveal a large and complex nucleated settlement which, notwithstanding the 'rural' character of some of its marginal areas, can reasonably be placed within the broad 'small town' category, albeit in the middle or lower order settlement categories as used by Burnham in his 1993 review (Burnham 1993, 103). The excavators of the comparable (though larger) site of Heybridge have chosen to characterise this as a 'market village' rather than a 'small town' (Atkinson and Preston 1998, 109), but the distinction is more one of terminology than substance. It is notable that at both sites the shrine or temple constitutes the principal, if not the only, 'public' building. At Westhawk Farm the lack of evidence for the focal area of the settlement means that this was not certainly the case here, but this phenomenon is also seen in some other 'small town' contexts (Burnham 1988) and may be considered a characteristic of them.

The Canterbury road was traced over a distance of some 700 m through the proposed development area, and on its north-west side was bounded by settlement evidence for almost the whole of this length. A fairly conservative estimate, based on the excavated and geophysical survey data, suggests a settlement area of *c* 12 ha within the original development proposal area (Areas A and B). This excludes the cemetery in Area C and takes no account of the extent of further possible cemeteries at the north-west margin of the settlement.

The settlement extended beyond Area A north-eastwards along the line of the Canterbury road into Ashford, but for how far is unclear. The narrow projection from the south-west side of Ashford parish as defined in the 19th century, which has been shown to be broadly coincident with the extent of the Roman settlement to the south-west, may be taken as a hint of its possible extent to the north-east. On this basis the settlement may have stretched at least another 250 m north-eastwards beyond Area A and a minimum site area of some 15 ha can be proposed.

Comparative settlement sizes in Kent are not easily calculated. The defences of Rochester enclosed approximately 9.5 ha (Burnham and Wacher 1990, 78), but there is little clear indication of extramural settlement there. On the basis of recent work (Boyle and Early nd; Davies 2001; Glass 1999; Philp and Chenery 1997; Smith 1997 and recent unpublished work by Wessex Archaeology) the extent of the 'small town' of Springhead may have been similar to that of Westhawk Farm (the well-known focal area covers some 3-4 ha) and is unlikely to have been larger. The roadside settlement near Syndale Park, Ospringe, possibly the *Durolevum* of the *Antonine Itinerary*, may have extended some 400 m along the line of Watling Street (its east and west limits defined by cemeteries) and at most *c* 100 m south of that road line (Sibun 2001, 191). The areas of seven 'small towns' in Essex, calculated from mapping by Wickenden (1996, 78-79) range from roughly 48 ha to 12 ha. The three smallest sites, Braintree, Great Dunmow and Kelvedon, are all between *c* 12 and 16 ha in extent and are thus closely comparable to Westhawk Farm in this regard at least.

The three Essex sites are all located at road junctions and in this respect, too, are comparable with Westhawk Farm. While the existence of the road junction seems to have been fundamental to the establishment of settlement at Westhawk Farm there is no clear indication of further development or elaboration of the road network around the junction area. In this sense the site belongs rather to Group I (simple road junction frontages) in Burnham's categorisation of 'small town' settlement plans (Burnham 1987, 159-162), rather than the 'developed' sites of Group III, while containing some hints of development. The existence in the southern part of the settlement of a number of trackways, identified principally from the geophysical survey, may be seen to support the latter view, but none of these appears to be of more than very local significance, nor do they link directly to the major road axes.

Political/military connections

Direct evidence for military or civil official links is slight, but there are a few hints of such links amongst the artefactual record. In view of its position on the regional road network, the relative proximity of Lympne (assumed, on the basis of *RIB* 66, to be a base of the *Classis Britannica*; see also Peacock 1977, 246), the clear evidence for ironworking and the known association of the British fleet with ironworking sites (in some cases), the question of official involvement at Westhawk Farm has remained a subject of lively speculation throughout the excavation and more recently. The most clearly demonstrable connection is through the occurrence of tiles in a fabric (fabric 22) found elsewhere bearing the CLBR stamp of the *Classis Britannica*. The quantity of this material at Westhawk Farm was small, although slightly larger amounts of tile fabric 23, including distinctive combed bricks of a type found at Beauport Park in association with stamped *Classis Britannica* tiles, also occurred. While suggestive, the presence of this material does not demonstrate an official connection as it cannot be certain how far bricks and tiles produced from the Fairlight Clays were exclusively intended for use in an official context. Nevertheless, such a connection would commonly be assumed (cf Brodribb 1979, 141) and has been emphasised by Peacock (1982, 144-5), and the known distribution of CLBR stamps is still consistent with this connection, even allowing for the presence of examples from London, since these might have derived from a small number of military-related construction projects (Crowley and Betts 1992, 222).

The artefacts from the site include no items with direct military associations. They do include, however, a knee brooch, a type thought perhaps to have been worn particularly by soldiers, or officials of some other kind (see Cool, Chapter 5). A 3rd century intaglio from a cremation grave in Area C forms another unusual object/context combination possibly indicative of a military association. Additionally, analysis of the metal objects from the site indicates a strikingly high concentration of weighing equipment, and finally the coin assemblage has an overall profile which is most closely comparable with a number of sites which are either demonstrably military (such as the *Classis Britannica* fort at Dover) or have close military associations.

The evidence of individual objects need not indicate more than the presence of one or two possible military personnel at best. Such a presence is increasingly recognised as a characteristic of major centres in the middle part of the Roman period in Britain (Bishop 1991; cf. Booth *et al.* 2001, 442-3) and is not in itself remarkable. Taken in combination with the other evidence, however, it is suggestive of an aspect of the life of the settlement which is perhaps most apparent from the coin loss evidence. The pattern that this displays is completely at odds with that from other civilian settlements in the region. It suggests either that the whole community had a military cast to it or, perhaps rather more likely in view of the lack of other evidence, that those elements of the population (of what has, on other criteria including aspects of the finds evidence, been characterised as a 'rural' settlement) who were using coin in the 1st and 2nd centuries were dependent on a characteristically 'military' pattern of supply.

The conflicting strands of evidence are hard to interpret, but some characteristics of the finds assemblages are so unusual when compared with 'normal' nucleated settlements that they cannot be ignored. There is nevertheless no justification for seeing Westhawk Farm as a 'military' settlement, but perhaps rather as a site containing amongst others a (probably relatively small) community of military or official personnel with an important role in regulating certain aspects of activity within the settlement. The unusually pronounced definition of the focal area of the settlement, and in particular the possible emphasis on the entrances into this area, may be a reflection of such regulatory activities. On present evidence it is most likely that this would have related principally to the production of iron. Given that the overall evidence for the scale of such production at Westhawk Farm remains quite modest, however, it is suggested that these personnel had a wider remit in relation to the administration of iron production across the region. Exactly how this may have linked with possible administrative functions at sites in the Weald such as Beauport Park is, of course, quite unknown. It is equally speculative to suggest that such activity could be seen in the context of the administration of an imperial estate, but this remains a possibility for consideration. Despite the efforts of Taylor (2000) and others (cf Millett 1990, 120-121) to deconstruct the imperial estate interpretation of the Fenland, for example, and in particular Stonea as an imperial estate centre, the real point is that we do not have any meaningful model for the archaeological manifestation of imperial estates, particularly in the north-west provinces, and indeed it is likely that many different patterns of settlement and structure type could occur in such a context, given the variety of forms of land tenure attested within imperial estates in other parts of the empire (Crawford 1976). The suggestion (see Cool, Chapter 5 above) that the quantities of weighing equipment present might indicate a special function such as involvement in the *annona militaris* would not be incompatible with other administrative functions related to the procurement of materials such as iron.

Socio-economic status

The possible military connections and administrative functions discussed above will have had some impact on wider aspects of the status of the site, but apart from specific characteristics, such as the coin loss pattern, the evidence for such impacts is relatively slight. The absence of evidence for any local administrative function of the sort sometimes associated with major nucleated settlements is unsurprising since any such evidence, even if archaeologically recoverable, is likely to have been located in the focal area of the settlement not examined. The central open space, suggesting a significant market function, may be such an indicator, but need not have been a direct reflection of any formal administrative status enjoyed by the settlement.

The three main aspects of the excavated evidence that shed light on the wider socio-economic status of the inhabitants of Westhawk Farm are the structures, the burials and other artefactual evidence, all of which have been discussed above. The structures are all simple in plan and the majority are of a conservative (approximately circular) form reflecting pre-Roman traditions. Rectilinear buildings were all of modest size. The floor area of the largest of these, structure D, is almost exactly equivalent to that of an 11 m diameter circular building (c 95-100 sq. m). A number of the circular structures from Westhawk were of this order of size. Therefore, unless structure D had an upper storey, which seems unlikely, it did not offer any significant increase in accommodation, despite its radically different plan form. It did, of course, have significantly different possibilities for the organisation of its internal space, but no evidence for this (or of internal organisation in the other structures, except for those associated with ironworking) survived. Overall, therefore, the buildings do not suggest a radical change in character from regional pre-Roman traditions. Exceptions to this generalisation may have been located in the focal area of the settlement, but apart from that consist only of the putative bath building. This might have been intended for the general use of the inhabitants of the site, but it is possible that it was specifically associated with that section of the community involved in ironworking.

The sample of burials is too small to allow extensive generalisation about the overall population of Westhawk Farm. Nevertheless, and despite the fact that funerary rites and assemblages were often manipulated by the living to suggest that the status of the deceased was different from that which he or she actually held, the surviving evidence indicates some variety of status and reflects the range of burial types seen in much larger assemblages, such as that from Pepper Hill, Springhead. This range extends from burials with no associated grave goods to those with significant numbers of vessels (7 and 10 respectively in graves 210 and 220 in Area B) and the exceptional deposit in grave 8160. The presence of an intaglio (placed on the pyre) and jet and lignite beads in burials in the Area C cemetery are indicative of some degree of personal wealth. There is, however, no Roman equivalent to the immediately adjacent high status late Iron Age burial; it is perhaps unlikely that people of this character were resident at Westhawk Farm rather than in rural estate centres in the surrounding countryside.

The remaining artefactual material from the site provides, if anything, less evidence for socio-economic variety than seen in the burial assemblages. Most groups of material are relatively small, but the non-ferrous objects suggest an interesting picture of a mixed community with some conservative, rural characteristics (which appear consistent with, for example, the structural evidence) and other more urban characteristics, suggested by the toilet and weighing equipment, for example. One of the best indicators of general site character, however, is the pottery, principally because the size of the assemblage allows fairly secure conclusions to be drawn. As already discussed,

the assemblage indicates a reasonably wide range of trading connections, but the volume of much of this trade was not significant. The material can, however, be compared with assemblages from some fifteen Channel Tunnel Rail Link Section 1 sites which have been recorded to a similar standard (Booth forthcoming). Examination of these assemblages in terms of their 'fine and specialist' ware component, potentially a useful indicator of status (cf Booth 1991; 2004) reveals that with the exception of the cemetery at Pepper Hill, Springhead, these wares (samian ware, fine wares, white and white-slipped wares, amphora and mortarium fabrics) comprise between 0.4% and 11.3% of the total sherds of all but the smallest (and therefore statistically invalid) assemblages. Chronological factors result in sites with only very early Roman occupation having very low fine and specialist ware levels, while late Roman assemblages generally have a higher baseline level of these wares regardless of status. The extremes of the CTRL fine and specialist ware representation range are readily interpreted in these terms.

Westhawk Farm, with 5.1% of fine and specialist wares (by sherd count) lies right in the middle of the CTRL range. Sites in the geographical vicinity include the villa at Thurnham (5.9%), early Roman rural settlements, apparently of low status, at Snarkhurst Wood and Beechbrook Wood (2.7% and 1.3% respectively) and two other rural settlements with rather longer date ranges, at Leda Cottages and Bower Road, Smeeth (5.0% and 4.4% respectively). Overall these figures indicate relatively little inter-site variation based on status, as far as this can be determined from morphological characteristics. The distinction in ceramic terms between Thurnham and other, nearby, contemporary rural settlements, for example, is slight, and is demonstrable more in terms of the presence of a wider range of non-local fabrics than a notable quantitative increase in fine and specialist wares. The Westhawk data fit this pattern. In detail Westhawk has a higher proportion of samian ware (2.4% of the site sherd total) than all but one of the CTRL sites (and the exception, Leda Cottages, with 2.7%, may be anomalous) and amphorae (1.2% of sherds) are also comparatively well-represented (they are indeed totally absent from 8 of the 14 CTRL sites), but in other respects the fine and specialist ware component of the Westhawk Farm assemblage is unremarkable. Only with respect to samian ware and amphorae (principally olive oil containers of Dressel 20 form) could it be argued that the potential market function and perhaps other aspects of the Westhawk Farm settlement resulted in the presence of above-average quantities, and these quantities are not themselves noteworthy in absolute terms. There is thus little indication that the pottery assemblage of the settlement had a distinct character. Pottery supply seems to have operated within a general regional framework rather than being modified in any notable way at the behest of the site's inhabitants. The requirements of the latter seem to have been in line with those of other parts of the spectrum of regional rural society. If there were groups within the population of Westhawk Farm who had rather different and distinctive ceramic preferences, the archaeological evidence for them is submerged in the general mass of the material; such groups were clearly either of small size or their rubbish disposal activities were not located in or near the excavated parts of the site.

Other social aspects

The evidence discussed so far suggests a mixed community. Some of the more readily identified elements within it, such as ironworkers and probable military/administrative personnel, were probably quite few in number, the latter perhaps particularly so. It is likely that the community retained a significant agricultural component. While the evidence for this is not as good as could be wished the general proposition is supported by aspects of the site such as the long-term survival of a native housing tradition (circular buildings) and also by the wider picture that suggests the disappearance of some local settlements (particularly Brisley Farm), with the presumption that their inhabitants may have relocated themselves to Westhawk Farm. Such relocation could have involved a change in individuals' basic livelihood, but there is no particular reason to think that this was the case. Some (but not all) aspects of the small finds assemblages have also been characterised as indicating a 'conservative' community, consistent with the evidence of building traditions. The survival of circular buildings into the Roman period has many parallels, as discussed above. However, there are as yet few sites from Kent that show the continuation of the tradition so late into the Roman period (that is, into the 3rd century) even in a rural context, let alone in the context of a substantial nucleated settlement. It is uncertain whether this simply reflects a paucity of comparable excavated evidence, or whether Westhawk Farm is genuinely unusual in this way. Here the pre-conquest building tradition survived the imposition of rectilinear building types and co-existed with them over an extended period. The extent to which the rectangular buildings can be regarded as 'Romanised' and alien is probably relatively limited, however, and it has already been suggested that one building type, represented by (almost) the largest structure on the site, was of a form that may have been a regional development within the Roman period.

The largest excavated 'structure' in terms of ground area was, however, the polygonal shrine, although it is doubtful that this was completely (if at all) roofed (see above). The importance of the location of this structure, and the extent and the long-term (relative) integrity of the associated open area, discussed above, indicate the significance of this feature for the settlement as a whole. Understanding the associated cult is, however, extremely problematic, since there is no obvious votive material associated with the structure and the unfortunate absence of faunal remains removes another possible line of enquiry into the nature of activities associated with it. The remarkable concentration of coins in waterhole 796, quite close to the shrine on the opposite side of the Canterbury road and (perhaps fortuitously) on the central axis of the shrine and its enclosure, is strongly suggestive of votive material, albeit with some indications of re-deposition. It is not clear, however, if the waterhole was a focus for votive deposition in its own right, or was used as a final resting place for material that had originally been deposited in and around the polygonal shrine. If the former, the coins shed no further light on the nature of the cult of the shrine. It is possible that, as has been suggested at Heybridge (Atkinson and Preston 1998, 98-100), the cult did not involve extensive votive deposition (Booth 2001, 18), but this would be quite unusual for a shrine which is clearly of much more than domestic significance (G Woolf, pers. comm.). The relatively poor preservation of this part of the site may be the principal factor in significant loss of the relevant material. The presence of nuts of *pinus pinea* in the central feature, discussed previously (Booth 2001, 18-19) is, however, a pointer to the nature of religious practice. While there is increasingly widespread evidence for finds from potential domestic as well as religious and funerary contexts it would be perverse to interpret the only find of *pinus pinea* from Westhawk in this way. The associations with known temples and shrines do not allow the use of cones of *pinus pinea* to be linked with a specific deity, but the fact that the cones were at least initially imported into Roman Britain argues for a more cosmopolitan aspect to the cult than might have been guessed from the form of the shrine. The integration of other aspects of religious practice into wider north-west European norms is also indicated in a small way by the presence within the settlement of a fragment from a pipeclay figurine.

Hilary Cool (Chapter 5 above) has discussed the unusual character of the grave goods associated with the adult male cremation grave 5090, and parallels for the association of male burials with 'jet' jewellery and (sometimes) other objects. In one case the individual has been interpreted possibly as a castrated devotee of Cybele (Cool 2002, 41-2). It is not completely impossible that the Westhawk Farm individual should be seen in a similar way, although it would be mischievous to make too much of the association of the pine with the worship of Cybele (Kislev 1988, 77). Whatever his religious affiliations, this person is a reminder that some of the inhabitants of Westhawk Farm may have been rather more colourful than our evidence generally suggests.

The place of the site in the regional settlement pattern

The roadside settlement of Westhawk Farm is the first site of its type to be identified in Kent south of the Downs. Its location in relation to the major road pattern is entirely logical in terms of the sort of distribution of such settlements that can be seen for example in East Anglia (eg Gurney 1995, 54; Plouviez 1995, 65-70; Millett 1995, 31-34; Going 1996, 96) or in the midlands, but in Kent the distribution of such sites is essentially confined to the line of Watling Street in the north of the county (Smith 1987, 132-9), with another possible roadside settlement at Hersden some 6 km north-east of Canterbury (*Archaeologia Cantiana* **122** (2002), 346-7) and a further probable example at Dover, though the true scale of civilian settlement there is not easy to judge. The existence of additional major settlements in the region may be predicted, perhaps for example at Lympne or Folkestone (Rigold 1972; Burnham 1989, 16) and at Maidstone (see above), but whether such sites existed further west in the Weald is perhaps questionable. On this basis Westhawk Farm may have been sited at an interface between a distinctly 'Wealden' settlement pattern and the heartland of the Cantiaci to the east. The character of settlement in the latter area, however, was by no means uniform, for while the Medway valley and parts of the northern coastal belt contained a number of villas the Chartland and the Downs to the northeast of Ashford were not characterised by such sites. On present evidence, settlement of any kind on the clay with flints of the Downs does not seem to have been very common.

As for the settlement pattern of the Weald itself, far too little is known in detail for its characteristics to be clear and again there may have been considerable local diversity. The extent to which the settlement pattern was dominated by sites devoted to iron production is unknown, but an admixture of agricultural settlements must be likely (eg Aldridge 1998). With regard to the iron producing sites, these varied considerably in size, but how this translates into structure density and morphology is simply not known. It remains possible, therefore, that a further site or sites of similar character to Westhawk Farm could have been located in this area serving as a local centre at a communications node – on which basis sites at Bodiam (Lemmon and Hill 1966) or Little Farningham Farm, Cranbrook (Aldridge 2001) might be amongst the best contenders – but it is equally possible that the nature of activity in this area did not require such centralised facilities. Even more speculative is the question of whether the apparent lack of focal settlements in the area was a consequence of its possible status as an imperial estate, or whether the character of the settlement pattern was determined simply by the nature of the economic basis of its component sites.

Whatever its status in terms of land ownership, however, the evidence of size, settlement morphology and functional diversity, both from structures and artefacts, indicate that Westhawk Farm served some if not most of the roles normally associated with a small town or local centre. These would have included provision of services by craftsmen providing for the surrounding communities, which may have been largely agricultural in character but possibly included other sites at which iron production was a major concern. The range of craftsmen conceivably included a specialist producing black jewellery from locally available lignite. The existence of a market

centre may be implied by the definition of the focal road junction area. It is also possible that local administrative functions were performed here, perhaps alongside specialised administration specifically related to iron production in the area. The shrine complex, a significant feature of the south-western part of the settlement throughout its life and, interestingly, perhaps surviving as late as any activity within the settlement as a whole, may have been an important focus not only for the people of Westhawk Farm itself but for a wider community.

While serving as a local or regional service centre for a range of agricultural and perhaps other communities it should not be forgotten that the establishment and development of the Westhawk Farm settlement would have had a more direct effect on some of these sites. This can be seen at Brisley Farm, where occupation was in decline in the later 1st century AD and did not continue after the early 2nd century (Casper Johnson, pers. comm.). At Waterbrook Farm, east of Westhawk Farm, settlement of late Iron Age-early Roman date similarly ceased in the early 2nd century at the latest (Rady 1996, 39). This was the time of major expansion at Westhawk Farm, and while it is impossible to prove it is quite likely that at least some of the population of these sites were drawn to the developing centre. The consequences of such a move for the continued agricultural exploitation of these site are unclear. Another consequence of the development of Westhawk Farm, however, might have been to provide an impetus to increased agricultural production elsewhere in the area. This assumes that the settlement was not entirely self sufficient in agricultural produce, an assumption which cannot be proved from evidence within the site itself, but can perhaps be suggested retrospectively from the decline of some rural settlements in the region contemporary with or consequent upon the major decline of the site from the mid 3rd century (see below).

The end of the settlement and its implications for the region

The early end of occupation at Westhawk Farm has been noted several times already. Although (as again already indicated) the evidence is strongest for the peripheral area of the settlement, it still seems clear that by the middle of the 4th century at the latest the site as a whole was a mere shadow of its former self. As far as the main excavated area is concerned, occupation had effectively ceased by the middle of the 3rd century. This characteristic is very striking. Does it conform to a wider pattern or is it peculiar to this site?

There is increasing evidence for differences in the broad character of settlements in eastern and western Britain with regard to questions such as patterns of coin loss (eg Reece 1995b). Such evidence can be taken to suggest a decline in the level of activity in a number of major settlements in eastern England before the end of the 4th century, in contrast to the situation observed further west (eg Reece 1998, 421;

Moorhead 2001, 95-6). In Norfolk, however, this is not particularly apparent before the last quarter of the 4th century at the earliest (Davies and Gregory 1991, 91) and a similar pattern can be observed for Suffolk (Plouviez 1995, 74-5 and 78). At Heybridge, Essex, in contrast, peripheral areas of the settlement were largely abandoned by *c* AD 200 (Atkinson and Preston 1998, 100). Occupation of the central area continued right through to the end of the Roman period, however, and coin loss seems generally to have followed a fairly 'normal' pattern (ibid., 105). Interestingly, the temple at Heybridge was seen as 'perhaps the only building which survived through the whole of this later period' (ibid., 101).

With the possible exception of Heybridge none of this evidence indicates settlement decline as early as it appears at Westhawk Farm. Within Kent most of the evidence from a range of sites, particularly in the northern part of the county, seems to follow a fairly 'normal' chronology, with structural sequences and coin loss patterns indicating occupation as far as the well-known limitations of the dating evidence allow it to be traced. Thus late Roman sequences can be observed at Canterbury and at Springhead (Burnham and Wacher 1990, 198), although certain late Roman activity at the latter site may have been localised (OWA 2006) and the suggestion that parts of the settlement may have been in decline is mirrored precisely by the scarcity of late Roman burials in the associated Pepper Hill cemetery. Meanwhile at Rochester the structural evidence for late Roman activity is unclear, but there are substantial numbers of late coins (Flight and Harrison 1978, 37, 44-54). A similar situation prevails at a variety of villas (Detsicas 1983, 181-2) including Lullingstone, where the coins cover the full range of the Roman period up to and including the House of Theodosius (Reece 1987).

Further south, however, the situation appears to be rather different. The evidence for significant decline in the level of activity at Westhawk Farm is notably coincident with the demise of a number of iron-producing sites in the Weald to the west and south-west. These include the important sites of Bardown and Beauport Park, the 'closure' of which is dated between AD 220 and AD 240 (Cleere and Crossley 1985, 84-5), while at Little Farningham Farm, Cranbrook, occupation may have ceased 'by the second half of the second century' (Aldridge 2001, 155). It is well known that the *Classis Britannica* fort at Dover had ceased to be occupied by the early 3rd century, a date of *c* AD 210 for its abandonment being favoured by the excavator and subsequent commentators (Philp 1981, 94-7). The very striking similarity between the profile of coin loss there and that at Westhawk Farm has been noted above (coins from the *Classis Britannica* fort of the period *c* 218-259 (12 out of 86 coins from the site) were all from deposits post-dating the demolition of the Period III fort or were unstratified (ibid.)). It is possible that the fleet retained an existing base at Lympne, or transferred its base there (Detsicas 1983, 176) up until its disappearance from records about AD 250 (Cleere

1989, 22). At the Dover 'Painted House' site the *mansio* buildings outlived the *Classis Britannica* fort but were superseded by the construction of the Saxon Shore fort, perhaps about AD 270 (Philp 1989, 282-3) or possibly a little later (Wilkinson 1994, 71-2).

Closer to Westhawk Farm, three rural settlement sites recently examined in Headcorn and Ulcombe parishes are dated between the mid 1st and the early 3rd centuries (Aldridge 1998, 7) and at Runhams Farm, Lenham, the occupation was essentially of 1st-2nd century date, with only limited evidence of later activity (Philp 1994, 42-44). The best evidence, however, now comes from Channel Tunnel Rail Link (CTRL) Section 1, which contained a significant number of rural settlement sites. At Bower Road, Smeeth, occupation was on a much reduced scale after about AD 270 (Diez forthcoming), while the main villa building at Thurnham seems not to have been occupied after the later 3rd century, although there was some occupation of the site into the late 4th century (Lawrence forthcoming). Many of the sites with less substantial structural evidence had more restricted chronological ranges, however. Consideration of the pottery evidence from the 15 principal CTRL assemblages (see above) shows that of the 6 assemblages in which late Roman material was present at all only one (Hazells Road, in north Kent near Springhead) consisted principally of pottery of this date. In all other cases, including Thurnham and Bower Road mentioned above, late Roman material was much less common than earlier pottery. In other words, out of 15 sites, 9 had no occupation at all after the 2nd century and a further 5 had activity at a significantly reduced level by the 4th century if not earlier. This evidence complements and expands that of Pollard's study of Roman pottery in Kent (1988), which included relatively few assemblages from this area, of which only Lympne, Dover and a group of sites at Wye contained significant 4th century components. It can now be seen that the dearth of specifically 4th century sites is indeed as significant as it initially appeared. A number of other rural settlement sites in the area east of Westhawk Farm saw either a cessation or a significant change in the character of activity in the later Roman period (K Parfitt, pers. comm.), although this cannot as yet be quantified.

The later part of the chronological range of Westhawk Farm thus appears to be closely (though not necessarily exactly) correlated with that of a number of major iron producing sites in the Weald, with the (possibly related) *Classis Britannica* fort at Dover, other non-Wealden iron-producing sites such as Lenham and Wye (Detsicas 1983, 176), and also with a number of other rural settlements, such as Smeeth, in the immediate area, although yet others, including many of the CTRL sites and further sites in the Maidstone area such as Queen Elizabeth Square (Booth and Howard-Davis 2004) had already ceased to be occupied by the end of the 2nd century (at the very latest). It is less clear if the development sequence of other sites a little further east is comparable, but this is possible. The pattern, therefore, appears to be a sub-regional one. It cannot be certain, however, that a single explanation will account for what must, within this sub-region, have amounted to a significant disruption of the settlement pattern, probably in two distinct phases, roughly of mid 2nd and mid 3rd century date. The broad synchronicity of the abandonment of a large part of the Westhawk Farm settlement and a number of the most important iron producing sites in the eastern Weald, subsequent to (though not necessarily consequent upon) the abandonment of the *Classis Britannica* fort at Dover, certainly suggests that some reorganisation of the iron industry might be invoked as a contributory factor to the 3rd century phase of site contraction and/or abandonment. In the case of Westhawk Farm it is unclear if it was the iron production itself or, perhaps more likely, this in conjunction with a range of associated support services, whose removal precipitated a significant decline in the scale of activity in the settlement. Its effective demise as a major local centre, however, inevitably had a consequence for components of the surrounding settlement pattern, perhaps including sites such as Smeeth, for whose agricultural surplus Westhawk Farm likely served as a major market.

Whether the effects of this development were sufficient to provoke the sort of changes seen a little further afield at sites like Thurnham, is unclear, but this is possible. There, and presumably elsewhere in the vicinity of Westhawk Farm and in the eastern Weald, though the evidence is largely lacking at present, some occupation continued. The countryside cannot have been totally abandoned; nevertheless the scale of disruption of the settlement pattern is such that there is likely to have been some localised depopulation, at least. This raises a wide range of questions about the mechanisms of such an operation. Was this a gradual trend or a well-defined, sharp change? Were people impelled or induced to relocate and, if so, how and how far? Was this simply a local phenomenon or did, for example, specialist ironworkers and their dependants move out of the region altogether to other centres for their trade? Was the motive force behind these developments provided by free-market economics, local elite control, state control or some other mechanism? The evidence from Westhawk Farm cannot itself answer these questions, but in combination with other new data for the region it does at least allow them to be framed more clearly.

Bibliography

Aldhouse-Green, M, 2002 Any old iron! Symbolism and ironworking in Iron Age Europe, in *Artefacts and Archaeology. Aspects of the Celtic and Roman Worlds* (eds M Aldhouse-Green and P V Webster), University of Wales Press, Cardiff, 8–19

Aldridge, N, 1995 Recent fieldwork relating to the Roman road from Sutton Valence to Ashford (Margary road no. 131), *Archaeol Cantiana* **115**, 464–465

Aldridge, N, 1998 The impenetrable forest? Pre-historic and Romano-British settlement in the Weald, an account of some recent fieldwork, *Kent Archaeol Soc Newsletter* **37**, 6–7

Aldridge, N, 2001 Little Farningham Farm, Cranbrook, revisited, *Archaeol Cantiana* **121**, 135–156

Aldridge, N, 2002 Sections of Roman road: Benenden, *Archaeol Cantiana* **122**, 413–4

Aldridge, N, 2006 The Roman road from Sutton Valence to Ashford: evidence for an alternative route to that proposed by Margary, *Archaeol Cantiana* **126**, 171–183

Alföldy, G, 1974 *Noricum*, London

Allason-Jones, L, 1985 Bell-shaped studs?, in *The production and distribution of Roman military equipment: proceedings of the Second Roman Military Equipment Research Seminar* (ed. M C Bishop), BAR Int Ser **275**, Oxford, 95–108

Allason-Jones, L, 1989a *Ear-rings in Roman Britain*, BAR Brit Ser **201**, Oxford

Allason-Jones, L, 1989b *Women in Roman Britain*, London

Allason-Jones, L, 1996 *Roman jet in the Yorkshire Museum*, York

Allason-Jones, L, 1999 Gilding the black lily, *Roman Finds Group Newsletter* **18**, 11–12

Allason-Jones, L, and Jones, J M, 2001 Identification of 'jet' artefacts by reflected light microscopy, *European J Archaeol* **4 (2)**, 233–251

Allason-Jones, L, and McKay, B, 1985 *Coventina's Well: A shrine on Hadrian's Wall*, Chesters Museum

Allason-Jones, L, and Miket, R F, 1984 *Catalogue of small finds from South Shields Roman Fort*, Newcastle upon Tyne

Allen, A A, 1976 A review of the status of certain Scarabaeoidea (Col.) in the British fauna; with the addition to our list of *Onthophagus similis* Scriba, *Entomologist's Record and Journal of Variation* **79**, 201–90

Allen, S J, 2001 *The wooden finds from Perry Oaks Sludge Works (WPR98)*, YAT Conservation Laboratory Report for Framework Archaeology, 1/10/2001

Allen, T, 2007 Archaeological discoveries on the A2 Pepperhill to Cobham widening scheme, *Kent Archaeol Soc Newsletter* **73**, 2–4

Anderson, S Th, 1979 Identification of wild grasses and cereal pollen, *Danmarks Geologiske Undersogelse Årbog 1978*, 69–92

Angus, N S, Brown, G T, and Cleere, H F, 1962 The iron nails from the Roman legionary fortress at Inchtuthil, Perthshire, *Journal of the Iron and Steel Institute* **200**, 956–968

Anthony, I E, 1968 Excavations in Verulam Hills Field, St Albans, 1963–4, *Hertfordshire Archaeol* **1**, 9–50

Ashbee, P, 1996 Julliberrie's Grave, Chilham: retrospection and perception, *Archaeol Cantiana* **116**, 1–34

Ashton, N, Dean, P, and McNabb, J, 1991 Flaked flakes: what, where, when and why?, *Lithics* **12**, 1–11

Ashton, N, and McNabb, J, 1996 The Flint Industries from the Waechter Excavations, in Conway, J McNabb and N Ashton (eds), *Excavations at Barnfield Pit, Swanscombe, 1968–72*, British Museum Occ Paper **94**, 201–236.

Atkinson, M, and Preston, S J, 1998 The late Iron Age and Roman settlement at Elms Farm, Heybridge, Essex, excavations 1993–5: an interim report, *Britannia* **29**, 85–110

Baratte, F, 1986 *Le Trésor d'orfèvrerie romaine de Boscoreale*, Paris

Barber, B, and Bowsher, D, 2000 *The eastern cemetery of Roman London Excavations 1983–1990*, MoLAS Monogr **4**, London

Barber, L, 1998 An early Romano-British salt-working site at Scotney Court, *Archaeol Cantiana* **118**, 327–353

Barton, N, 1997 *Stone Age Britain*, London

Barton, R N E, 1992 *Hengistbury Head: the late Upper Palaeolithic and early Mesolithic sites*, OUCA Monogr **34**, Oxford

Baume, P la, 1971 Das Achatgefässe von Köln, *Kölner Jahrbuch* **12**, 80–93

Bayley, J, Dungworth, D, and Paynter, S, 2001 *Centre for Archaeology Guidelines: Archaeometallurgy*, English Heritage

Bell, H, 1912 Notes on a bloom of Roman Iron found at Corstopitum (Corbridge), *J Iron and Steel Institute* **85 (1)**, 118–33

Bennett, K D, Whittington, G, and Edwards, K J, 1994 Recent plant nomenclatural changes and pollen morphology in the British Isles, *Quaternary Newsletter* **73**, 1–6

Betts, I M, 1992 Roman tile from Eccles, Kent found at Colchester, in P Crummy 1992, 259–260

Biddulph, E, 2005 Last orders: choosing pottery for funerals in Roman Essex, *Oxford J Archaeol* **24 (1)**, 23–45

Biddulph, E, 2007 Conquest and change? The Roman period, in *A slice of rural Essex: archaeological discoveries from the A120 between Stansted Airport and Braintree* (J Timby, R Brown, E Biddulph, A Hardy and A Powell), Oxford Wessex Archaeol Monogr No. **1**, 81–147

Biddulph, E, forthcoming *The Roman cemetery at Pepper Hill, Southfleet, Kent*, CTRL Integrated Site Report Series

Bird, J., 1988 Decorated samian ware, in *Excavations in Southwark 1973–76, Lambeth 1973–79* (ed. P Hinton), London Middlesex Archaeol Soc/Surrey Archaeol Soc Joint Publication **3**, 249–263

Bird, J, 1995a Summary, in Blockley *et al.* 1995, 772–775

Bird, J, 1995b Illustrated plain and decorated samian, in Blockley *et al.* 1995, 780–793

Bishop, M C, 1991 Soldiers and military equipment in the towns of Roman Britain, in *Roman Frontier Studies 1989: Proceedings of the XVth international conference of Roman frontier studies* (eds V A Maxfield and M J Dobson), Exeter, 21–27

Black, E W, 1987 *The Roman villas of south east England*, BAR Brit Ser **177**, Oxford

Blockley, K, Blockley, M, Blockley, P, Frere, S S, and Stow, S, 1995 *Excavations in the Marlowe car park and surrounding areas*, Archaeology of Canterbury **5**, Canterbury

Boardman, S, and Jones, G, 1990 Experiments on the effects of charring on cereal components, *Journal of Archaeol Sci* **17**, 1–11

Boekel, G M E C van, 1993 Terres cuites du Centre dans les Pays-Bas, le Luxembourg et la Grande-Bretagne, in *Les figurines en terre cuite gallo-romaines* (eds C Bémont, M Jeanlin and C Lahanier), Paris, 240–52

Boessneck, J A, 1969 Osteological differences between sheep (*Ovis aries* Linné) and goat (*Capra hircus* Linné), in *Science in Archaeology* (eds D R Brothwell and E S Higgs), London, 331–358

Boesterd, M H P den, 1956 *Description of the collections in the Rijksmuseum G M Kam at Nijmegen 5: The bronze vessels*, Nijmegen

Boon, G C, 1961 Roman antiquities at Welshpool, *Antiq J* **41**, 13–31

Booth, P, 1991 Inter-site comparisons between pottery assemblages in Roman Warwickshire: ceramic indicators of social status, *J Roman Pottery Stud* **4**, 1–10

Booth, P, 1994 The excavations in the context of the Roman town, in *Roman Alcester: Southern extramural area 1964–1966 excavations, part 1*, (ed. C Mahany), CBA Res Rep **96**, 164–175

Booth, P, 1994 The Roman pottery, in Excavations on the White Cliffs Experience Site, Dover, 1988–91 (D R P Wilkinson), *Archaeol Cantiana* **114**, 91–114

Booth, P, 1998 Defining small towns in Roman Britain, *J Roman Archaeol* **11**, 613–623

Booth, P, 2001 The Roman shrine at Westhawk Farm, Ashford: a preliminary account, *Archaeol Cantiana* **121**, 1–23

Booth, P, 2004 Quantifying status: some pottery data from the Upper Thames Valley, *J Roman Pottery Stud* **11**, 39–52

Booth, P (ed.), forthcoming *Ceramics from Section 1 of the Channel Tunnel Rail Link, Kent*, CTRL Scheme-wide Specialist Report Series

Booth, P, Evans, J, and Hiller, J, 2001 *Excavations in the extramural settlement of Roman Alchester, Oxfordshire, 1991*, Oxford Archaeology Monogr **1**, Oxford

Booth, P, and Everson, P, 1994 Earthwork survey and excavation at Boys Hall Moat, Sevington, Ashford, *Archaeol Cantiana* **114**, 411–434

Booth, P, and Howard-Davis, C, 2003 *Prehistoric and Romano-British settlement at Queen Elizabeth Square, Maidstone*, Oxford Archaeology Occas Paper **11**

Borrill, H, 1981 Casket burials, in *Skeleton Green: a late Iron Age and Romano-British site* (C Partridge), Britannia Monogr **2**, London, 304–21

Bowman, A K, and Thomas, J D, 1994 *The Vindolanda writing tablets (Tabulae Vindolandenses II)*, British Museum, London

Boyle, A, 1999 Human remains, in *Excavations at Barrow Hills, Radley, Oxfordshire. Vol. 1: The Neolithic and Bronze Age monument complex* (A Barclay and C Halpin), OAU Thames Valley Landscapes Monogr **11**, Oxford, 171–183

Boyle, A, and Early, R, nd *Excavations at Springhead Roman Town, Southfleet, Kent*, OAU Occas Paper **1**, Oxford

Bradshaw, J, 1970 Investigations and excavations during the year. II: Reports from local secretaries and groups. Ashford area, *Archaeol Cantiana* **85**, 177–180

Brailsford, J W, 1958 *Guide to the antiquities of Roman Britain*, London

Brent, J, 1879 *Canterbury in the olden times: from the municipal archives and other sources*, Canterbury

Brewer, R, 1986a The beads and glass counters, in Zienkiewicz 1986, 146–56

Brewer, R, 1986b Other objects of bronze, in Zienkiewicz 1986, 172–89

Britnell, J E, Cool, H E M, Davies, J L, Manning, W H, and Walters, M J, 1999 Recent discoveries in the vicinity of Castell Collen Roman fort, Radnorshire, *Studia Celtica* **33**, 33–90

Britnell, W, and Earwood, C, 1991 Wooden artefacts and other worked wood from Buckbean Pond, in *The Breiddin Hillfort: a later prehistoric settlement in the Welsh Marches* (C R Musson), CBA Res Rep **76**, York 161–172

Brodribb, G, 1979 A survey of tile from the Roman bath house at Beauport Park, Battle, East Sussex, *Britannia* **10**, 139–156

Brodribb, G, 1987 *Roman brick and tile*, Gloucester

Brodribb, G, and Cleere, H, 1988 The *Classis Britannia* bath-house at Beauport Park, East Sussex, *Britannia* **19**, 217–274

Brooks, H, and Bedwin, O, 1989 *Archaeology at the airport: the Stansted archaeological project 1985–89*, Chelmsford

Brown, A E (ed.), 1995 *Roman small towns in eastern England and beyond*, Oxford

Brown, J, 1983 *Steeped in tradition: the malting industry in England since the railway age*, Reading

Brunaux, J-L, Méniel, P, and Poplin, F, 1985 *Gournay I. Les fouilles sur la sanctuaire et l'oppidum*, Revue Archéologique de Picardie, numéro special

Brunning, R, and Bell, M, 2000 Wood artefacts, in *Prehistoric intertidal archaeology in the Welsh Severn Estuary* (M Bell, A Castledine and H Neumann), CBA Res Rep **120**, 116–118

Bulleid, A, 1911 Objects of wood and worked timber, in *The Glastonbury Lake Village* (A Bulleid and H St George Gray), Glastonbury, 310–351

Burnham, B C, 1987 The morphology of Romano-British 'small towns', *Archaeol J* **144**, 156–190

Burnham, B C, 1988 A survey of building types in Romano-British 'small towns', *J Brit Archaeol Ass* **141**, 35–59

Burnham, B C, 1993 The 'small towns' of Roman Britain - the last fifty years, in *Roman towns: the Wheeler inheritance* (ed. S J Greep), CBA Res Rep **93**, York, 99–110

Burnham, B C, and Wacher, J S, 1990 *The 'small towns' of Roman Britain*, London

Burnham, C P, 1989 The coast of south-east England in Roman times, in Maxfield 1989, 12–17

Campbell, G, 1998 The charred plant remains, in Boyle and Early nd, 36–39

Campbell, G, 2000 Plant Utilization: the evidence from charred plant remains, in *The Danebury Environs Programme: The prehistory of a Wessex landscape, vol. 1* (B Cunliffe), OUCA Monogr **48**, Oxford, 45–59

Carter, G A, 1998 *Excavations at the Orsett 'Cock' enclosure, Essex, 1976*, E Anglian Archaeol **86**, Chelmsford

Cartwright, C, 1986 Charcoal, in The Excavation of a Roman tilery on Great Cansiron Farm, Hartfield, East Sussex (D R Rudling), *Britannia* **17**, 191–230

Cartwright, C, 1996 Waterlogged wood from the sump, in Jackson and Potter 1996, 552–571

Catherall, P D, 1983 A Romano-British pottery manufacturing site at Oakleigh Farm, Higham, Kent, *Britannia* **14**, 103–142

Challinor, D, 2000 Assessment of the charcoal, in *Boys Hall Balancing Pond, Sevington, Kent, ARCBHB 98: strip, map and sample excavation assessment report*, prepared by OAU for Union Railways South (004-EZR-SOXAR-00054-AA)

Challinor, D, forthcoming The wood charcoal (Pepper Hill), in Robinson forthcoming a

Champion, T, 2007 Prehistoric Kent, in *The archaeology of Kent to AD 800* (J H Williams ed.), Kent County Council, Woodbridge, 67–132

Chatwin, C P, 1961 *British regional geology: East Anglia and adjoining areas*, London

Childs, S T, and Killick, D, 1993 Indigenous African metallurgy: nature and culture, *Annual Review of Anthropology* **22**, 317–37

Chirikure S, and Paynter, S, forthcoming *A metallurgical investigation of metalworking remains from Snettisham, Norfolk*, English Heritage

Clapham, A R, Tutin, T G, and Moore, M, 1989 *Flora of the British Isles*, 3 edn, Cambridge

Clark, J G D, 1934 The classification of a microlithic culture: the Tardenoisian of Horsham, *Archaeol J* **90**, 52–77

Clark, P, 1996 Park Farm, Ashford, *Canterbury's Archaeology 1994–1995*, Canterbury Archaeological Trust Annual Report **19**, 37

Clarke, G, 1979 *The Roman cemetery at Lankhills*, Winchester Studies 3: Pre Roman and Roman Winchester Part II, Oxford

Cleere, H, 1989 The *Classis Britannica*, in Maxfield 1989, 18–22

Cleere, H, and Crossley, D, 1985 *The iron industry of the Weald*, Leicester

Cooke, B, and Lomas, B, 1989 The evidence of wear and damage in ancient textiles, in *NESAT III: Textiles in Northern Archaeology (Textilsymposium in York)*, (eds P Walton and J P Wild), London, 215–226

Cool, H E M, 1991 Roman metal hair pins from southern Britain, *Archaeol J* **147**, 148–82

Cool, H E M, 2001 *The Iron Age and Roman finds in the Portable Antiquities Database*, unpublished assessment prepared for the Portable Antiquities Scheme

Cool, H E M, 2002 An overview of the small finds from Catterick, in Wilson 2002b, 24–43

Cool, H E M, 2004 *The Roman cemetery at Brougham, Cumbria. Excavations 1966–67*, Britannia Monogr **21**, London

Cool, H E M, forthcoming The small finds, in *Ariconium* (R Jackson), CBA Res Rep

Cool, H E M, and Baxter, M J, 1999 Peeling the onion: an approach to comparing vessel glass assemblages, *J Roman Archaeol* **12**, 72–100

Cool, H E M, Lloyd-Morgan, G, and Hooley, A D, 1995 *Finds from the fortress*, Archaeology of York **17/10**, York

Cool, H E M, and Philo, C (ed.), 1998 *Roman Castleford Excavations 1974–85. Vol. I: the small finds*, Yorkshire Archaeology **4**, Wakefield

Cool, H E M, and Price, J, 1995 *Roman vessel glass from excavations in Colchester, 1971–85*, Colchester Archaeol Rep **8**, Colchester

Corran, H S, 1975 *A History of Brewing*, London

Cotton, M A, 1947 Excavations at Silchester 1938–9, *Archaeologia* **92**, 121–68

Cotton, M A, and Wheeler, R E M, 1953 Verulamium 1949, *Trans St Albans and Hertfordshire Architectural and Archaeol Soc for 1953*, 13–97

Cracknell, S, 1989 Roman Alcester: recent excavations, *Trans Birmingham Warwickshire Archaeol Soc* **94** (for 1985–6), 1–64.

Crawford, D J, 1976 Imperial estates, in *Studies in Roman property* (ed. M I Finley), Cambridge, 35–70

Crew, P, 1991 The experimental production of prehistoric bar iron, *Historical Metallurgy* **25 (1)**, 21–36

Crew, P, 1994 Currency bars in Great Britain: typology and function, in *La sidérurgie ancienne de l'Est de la France dans son contexte européen* (ed. M Mangin), Besançon, 345–50

Crowfoot, E, 1991 The textiles, in, *Iron Age cemeteries in East Yorkshire: excavations at Burton Fleming, Rudston, Garton-on-the-Wolds and Kirkburn* (I Stead), English Heritage Archaeol Rep **22**, London, 119–125

Crowley, N, and Betts, I M, 1992 Three *Classis Britannica* stamps from London, *Britannia* **23**, 220

Crummy, N, 1983 *The Roman small finds from excavations in Colchester, 1971–9*, Colchester Archaeol Rep **2**, Colchester

Crummy, N, 1992 The Roman small finds from the Culver Street site, in P Crummy 1992, 140–205

Crummy, P (ed), 1992 *Excavations at Culver Street, the Gilberd School, and other sites in Colchester 1971–85*, Colchester Archaeol Rep **6**, Colchester

Crummy, P, 1993 Aristocratic graves at Colchester, *Current Archaeology* **132**, 492–497

Cunliffe, B, 1971 *Excavations at Fishbourne 1961–1969, vol. II: The Finds*, Rep Res Comm Soc Antiqs London **27**, London

Cunliffe, B (ed), 1975, *Excavations at Portchester Castle. I Roman*, Rep Res Comm Soc Antiqs London **32**, London

Cunliffe, B, 1980 Excavations at the Roman Fort at Lympne, Kent 1976–78, *Britannia* **11**, 227–288

Cunliffe, B, 1988 Romney Marsh in the Roman period, in *Romney Marsh: evolution, occupation, reclamation* (eds J Eddison and C Green), OUCA Monogr **24**, 83–87, Oxford

Cunliffe, B, 1991 *Iron Age communities in Britain*, 3 edn, London

Curle, J, 1911 *A Roman frontier post and its people: the fort of Newstead in the parish of Melrose*, Edinburgh

Dannell, G, Dickinson, B, and Vernhet, A, 1998 Ovolos on Dragendorff form 30 from the collections of F. Hermet and D. Rey, in *Form and fabric: studies in Rome's material past in honour of B. R. Hartley* (ed. J. Bird), Oxbow Monograph **80**, Oxford 69–109

Davies, B, Richardson, B, and Tomber, R, 1994 *The archaeology of Roman London vol. 5: a dated corpus of early Roman pottery from the City of London*, CBA Res Rep **98**, York

Davies, J A, and Gregory, T, 1991 Coinage from a *civitas*: a survey of the Roman coins found in Norfolk and their contribution to the archaeology of the *civitas Icenorum*, *Britannia* **22**, 65-101

Davies, M, 2001 Death and social division at Roman Springhead, *Archaeol Cantiana* **121**, 157–169

Davis, A, forthcoming The charred plant remains (Pepper Hill), in Robinson forthcoming a

DCMS, 2000 *Portable antiquities, annual report 1998–99*, Department for Culture, Media and Sport: Buildings, Monuments and Sites Division

Deer, W A, Howie, R A, and Zussman, J, 1992 *An introduction to the rock-forming minerals*, Harlow

Derks, T, 1998 *Gods, temples and ritual practices: the transformation of religious ideas and values in Roman Gaul*, Amsterdam

Detsicas, A, 1983 *The Cantiaci*, Gloucester

Deyber, A, 1989 Plaquettes semi circulaires biforées, in *Actes du XIIe Colloque de l'A.F.E.A.F*, 105–7

Dickson C, and J Dickson, 2000 *Plants and people in ancient Scotland*, Stroud

Diez, V, forthcoming The Roman settlement at Bower Road, Smeeth, Kent, *CTRL Integrated Site Report Series*, Archaeology Data Service

Dimbleby, G W, 1985 *The palynology of archaeological sites*, London

Doherty, G, 1987 The pine-scales, in Meates 1987, 318

Draper, J, 1985 *Excavations by Mr H P Cooper on the Roman site at Hill Farm, Gestingthorpe, Essex*, E Anglian Archaeol **25**, Chelmsford

Driel-Murray, C van, 1983 The leatherwork, in Funde aus der fabrica der legio I Minervia am Bonner Berg (C van Driel-Murray and M Gechter), *Rheinische Ausgrabungen* **23**, 1–83

Driel-Murray, C van, 2001 Vindolanda and the dating of Roman footwear, *Britannia* **32**, 185–197

Dungworth, D, 1998 Mystifying Roman nails: *clavus annalis, defixiones* and *minkisi*, in *TRAC 97: Proceedings of the Seventh annual Theoretical Roman Archaeology Conference, Nottingham 1997* (eds C Forcey, J Hawthorne and R Witcher), Oxford, 148–59

Dungworth, D, 2001 Metal working debris from Elms Farm, Heybridge, Essex, *Centre for Archaeology Report* **69/2001**

Dušanić, S, 1977 Aspects of Roman mining in Noricum, Pannonia, Dalmatia and Moesia Superior, in *Aufstieg und Niedergang der Römischen Welt* **II.6** (ed. H Temporini), 52–94

Eburacum, 1962 *An inventory of the historical monuments in the city of York. Vol. I Eburacum Roman York*, Royal Commission on Historical Monuments England, London

Edlin, H L, 1949 *Woodland crafts in Britain: an account of the traditional uses of trees and timbers in the British countryside*, London

Edmondson, J, C, 1989 Mining in the later Roman Empire and beyond: continuity or disruption?, *J Roman Stud* **79**, 84–102

Edwards, K J, 1989 The cereal pollen record and early agriculture, in *The beginnings of agriculture: symposia of the Association for Environmental Archaeology 8*, BAR Int Ser **496**, Oxford, 113–35

Engels, H-J, 1974 *Funde der Latènekultur I. Materialhefte zur Vor- und Frühgeschichte der Pfalz 1*, Veröffentlichung der Pfälzischen Gesellschaft zur Förderung der Wissenschaften in Speyer, Bd **63**, Speyer

Esmonde Cleary, S, 2000 Putting the dead in their place: burial location in Roman Britain, in *Burial, Society and Context in the Roman World* (eds J Pearce, M Millett and M Struck), Oxford, 127–142

Evans, A J, 1890 On a late celtic urn-field at Aylesford, Kent and on the Gaullish, Illyro-Italic and classical connections of the forms of pottery and bronzework there discovered, *Archaeologia* **52**, 315–88

Evans, J, 1990 The Cherry Hinton finewares, *J Roman Pottery Stud* **3**, 18–29

Everitt, A, 1986 *Continuity and colonization: the evolution of Kentish settlement*, Leicester

Farrar, L, 1998 *Ancient Roman gardens*, Stroud

Farrar, R A H, 1973 The techniques and sources of Romano-British black-burnished wares, in *Current research in Romano-British coarse pottery*, (ed. A P Detsicas), CBA Res Rep **10**, London, 67–103

Figueiral, I, 1992 The charcoals, in Fulford and Allen 1992, 188–191

Fitzpatrick, A P, 1997 *Archaeological excavations on the route of the A27 Westhampnett bypass, West Sussex, 1992. Vol. 2: the late Iron Age, Romano-British and Anglo-Saxon cemeteries*, Wessex Archaeology Rep **12**, Salisbury

Fitzpatrick, A, and Timby, J, 2002 Roman pottery in Iron Age Britain, in *Prehistoric Britain: the ceramic basis* (eds A Woodward and J D Hill), Prehistoric Ceramics Research Group Occas Pub **3**, Oxford, 161–172

Flight, C, and Harrison, A C, 1978 Rochester Castle, 1976, *Archaeol Cantiana* **94**, 27–60

Fox, A, 1940 The legionary fortress at Caerleon, Monmouthshire: excavations in Myrtle Cottage Orchard 1939, *Archaeol Cambrensis* **95**, 102–52

Frere, S S, 1970 The Roman theatre at Canterbury, *Britannia* **1**, 83–113

Frere, S S, 1984 *Verulamium excavations, vol. 3*, OUCA Monogr **1**, Oxford

Frere, S S, 1985 Excavations at Dorchester-on-Thames, 1963, *Archaeol J* **141**, 91–174

Frere, S S, 1987 *Britannia: a history of Roman Britain*, 3 edn, London

Frere, S S, and St Joseph, J K, 1974 The Roman fortress at Longthorpe, *Britannia* **5**, 1–129

Fulford, M G, 1975 The pottery, in Cunliffe (ed.) 1975, 270–367

Fulford, M G, and Allen, J R L, 1992 Iron-making at the Chesters Villa, Woolaston, Gloucestershire: survey and excavation, 1987–91, *Britannia* **23**, 159–216

Gale, R, 1999 Charcoal, in *Prehistoric and Roman sites in east Devon: the A30 Honiton to Exeter Improvement DBFO, 1996–2000. Vol. 2: Romano-British sites* (eds A P Fitzpatrick, C A Butterworth, and J Grove), Salisbury, 372–382

Gale, R, and Cutler, D, 2000 *Plants in archaeology: identification manual of vegetative plant materials used in Europe and the southern Mediterranean to c 1500*, Kew

Gallois, R W, 1965 *The Wealden district*, 4 edn, London

Gimingham, C H, 1972 *Ecology of heathlands*, London

Giorgi, J, 2000 The plant remains - a summary, in *A Romano-British cemetery on Watling Street* (A Mackinder), MoLAS Archaeol Stud Ser **4**, London, 65–66

Glass, H J (ed.), 1999 Archaeology of the Channel Tunnel Rail Link, *Archaeol Cantiana* **119**, 189–220

Going, C J, 1996 The Roman countryside, in *The archaeology of Essex; Proceedings of the Writtle conference* (ed. O Bedwin), Chelmsford, 95–107

Goodburn, R, 1984 The non-ferrous metal objects, in Frere 1984, 17–67

Grant, A, 1975 The animal bones, in Cunliffe (ed) 1975, 378–408

Grant, A, 1982 The use of tooth wear as a guide to the age of domestic ungulates, in *Ageing and Sexing Animal Bones from Archaeological Sites* (eds B Wilson, C Grigson and S Payne), BAR Brit Ser **109**, Oxford, 91–108

Graser, E R, 1940 The edict of Diocletian on maximum prices, in *An economic survey of ancient Rome. Vol. V: Rome and Italy of the Empire* (T Frank), Baltimore, 307–421

Greig, J R A, 1991 The British Isles, in *Progress in Old World Palaeoethnobotany* (eds W Van Zeist, K Wasylikowa and K-E Behre), Rotterdam, 299–334

Green, C M, 1976 The coarse pottery, in The excavation of an early Romano-British site and Pleistocene landforms at Newhaven, Sussex (M Bell), *Sussex Archaeol Collect* **114**, 256–287

Green, C M, 1977 The Roman pottery, in Excavations at Bishopstone (M Bell), *Sussex Archaeol Collect* **115**, 152–178

Green, C M, 1980 Handmade pottery and society in late Iron Age and Roman East Sussex, *Sussex Archaeol Collect* **118**, 69–86

Green, H J M, 1975 Roman Godmanchester, in Rodwell and Rowley 1975, 183–210

Grimes, W, 1968 *The excavation of Roman and medieval London*, London

Grimes, W F, and Close-Brooks J, 1993 The excavation of Caesar's Camp, Heathrow, Harmondsworth, Middlesex, 1944, *Proc Prehist Soc* **59**, 303–360

Grimm, E C, 1992 Tilia and Tilia-graph: Pollen spread-sheet and graphics programs, *Programs and abstracts, 8th International Palynological Congress, Aix-en-Provence, September 6–12, 1992*, 56

Grove, L R A, and Warhurst, A, 1952 A thirteenth-century kiln site at Ashford, *Archaeol Cantiana* **65**, 183–187

GSB, 1996 *Report on geophysical survey, Westhawk Farm, Ashford*, Geophysical Surveys of Bradford unpublished client report **96/115**

GSB, 1997 *Report on geophysical survey, Westhawk Farm, Ashford II*, Geophysical Surveys of Bradford unpublished client report **97/39**

GSB, 1998 *Report on geophysical survey, Westhawk Farm, Ashford III*, Geophysical Surveys of Bradford unpublished client report **98/20**

Guido, M, 1978 *The glass beads of the prehistoric and Roman periods in Britain and Ireland*, Rep Res Comm Soc Antiqs London **35**, London

Guilbert, G, 1981 Double-ring roundhouses, probable and possible, in prehistoric Britain, *Proc Prehist Soc* **47**, 299–317

Gurney, D, 1995 Small towns and villages of Roman Norfolk: the evidence of surface and metal-detector finds, in Brown (ed.) 1995, 53–67

Gwilt, A, and Haselgrove, C (eds), 1997 *Reconstructing Iron Age societies*, Oxbow Monogr **71**, Oxford

Hagen, W, 1937 Kaiserzeitliche Gagatarbeiten aus dem rheinsichen Germanien, *Bonner Jahrbücher* **142**, 77–144

Hall, A R, and Kenward, H K, 1990 *Environmental evidence from the Colonia: General Accident and Rougier Street*, Archaeology of York **14/6**, York

Hall, M, and Ford, S, 1994 Archaeological excavations at Grange Road, Gosport, 1992, *Proc Hampshire Fld Club Archaeol Soc* **50**, 5–34

Halstead, P, 1985 A study of mandibular teeth from Romano-British contexts at Maxey, in *Archaeology and environment in the Lower Welland Valley, vol 1* (F Pryor, C French, D Crowther, D Gurney, G Simpson, and M Taylor), E Anglian Archaeol **27**, Cambridge, 219–224

Hamilton, S, and Manley, J, 2001 Hillforts, monumentality and place: a chronological and topographic review of first millennium BC hillforts of south-east England, *European J Archaeol* **4 (1)**, 7–42

Harley, J B, and O'Donoghue, Y, 1975 *The old series Ordnance Survey maps of England and Wales, Scale 1 inch to 1 mile, vol. I: Kent, Essex, E Sussex and S Suffolk*, Lympne

Harrison, L, 1999 Building materials, in Houliston 1999,130–136

Hartley, K F, 1972 Mortaria, in Rochester East Gate, 1969 (A C Harrison), *Archaeol Cantiana* **87**, 134–9

Hartley, K F, 1977 Two major potteries producing mortaria in the first century AD, in *Roman pottery studies in Britain and beyond: papers presented to John Gillam, July 1977* (eds J Dore and K Greene), BAR Int Ser **30**, Oxford, 5–17

Hartley, K F, 1978 The Roman mortaria, in *Chichester Excavations* **3** (A Down), Chichester, 245–253

Haselgrove, C, 1996 Roman impact on rural settlement and society in southern Picardy, in *From the sword to the plough: three studies on the earliest Romanisation of northern Gaul* (ed. N Roymans), Amsterdam Archaeological Studies **1**, Amsterdam, 127–187

Hasted, E, 1797–1801 *The history and topographical survey of the county of Kent. Vol. VII: Canterbury*, 2 edn (1972), Wakefield

Hather, J G, 2000 *The identification of northern European woods: a guide for archaeologists and conservators*, London

Havis, R, and Brooks, H, 2004 *Excavations at Stansted Airport, 1986–91*, E Anglian Archaeol **107**, Chelmsford

Healy, J F, 1978 *Mining and metallurgy in the Greek and Roman world*, London

Henderson, A M, 1949 Small objects in metal, bone, glass etc, in *Fourth report on the excavations of the Roman fort at Richborough, Kent* (J P Bushe-Fox), Rep Res Comm Soc Antiqs London **16**, 106–60

Henderson, J, 2000 *The science and archaeology of materials*, London and New York

Henig, M, 1974 *A corpus of Roman engraved gemstones from British sites*, BAR Brit Ser **8**, Oxford

Henig, M, 1995 The Roman finger rings, in Blockley et al. 1995, 1000–5

Hermet, F, 1934 *La Graufesenque (Condatomago)*, Paris

Herrmann, F-R, 1969 Der Eisenhortfund aus dem Kastell Künzing: Vorbericht, *Saalburg-Jahrbuch* **26**, 129–141

Hicks, A, 1998 Excavations at Each End, Ash, 1992, *Archaeol Cantiana* **118**, 91–172

Hillman, G, 1981 Reconstructing crop husbandry practices from the charred remains of crops, in *Farming practice in British prehistory* (ed. R J Mercer), Edinburgh, 123–162

Hillman, G, 1984 Interpretation of archaeological plant remains: the application of ethnographic models from Turkey, in van Zeist and Casparie (eds) 1984, 1–41

Hingley, R, 1997 Iron, ironworking and regeneration: a study of the symbolic meaning of metalworking in Iron Age Britain, in *Reconstructing Iron Age Societies. New approaches to the British Iron Age* (eds A Gwilt and C Haselgrove), Oxbow Monograph 71, Oxford, 9–18

Hingley, R, 2006 The deposition of iron objects in Britain during the later prehistoric and Roman periods: contextual analysis and the significance of iron, *Britannia*, **37**, 213–257

Hingley, R, and Miles, D, 2002 The human impact on the landscape: agriculture, settlement, industry and infrastructure, in *The Roman era. The British Isles: 55 BC-AD 410* (P Salway), Oxford, 141–171

Hobbs, R, 1998 *Voluntary scheme for the recording of archaeological objects in Kent, annual report 1997–8*, Kent County Council, Appendix 3

Hodgkinson, J S, 1999 Romano-British iron production in the Sussex and Kent Weald: a review of current data, *Historical Metallurgy* **33 (2)**, 68–72

Høst-Madsen, L, and Bouchwald, V F, 1999 The characterization and provenancing of ore, slag and iron from the Iron Age settlement at Snorup, *Historical Metallurgy* **33 (2)**, 57–67

Houliston, M, 1999 Excavations at the Mount Villa, Maidstone 1994, *Archaeol Cantiana* **119**, 71–172

Hull, M R, 1959 The fibulae, in The Romano-British settlement at Springhead: excavations of Temple I, site C 1 (W S Penn), *Archaeol Cantiana* **73**, 48–9

Hull, M R, 1963 The brooches, in The Romano-British farmstead at Eastwood, Fawkham (B J Philp), *Archaeol Cantiana* **78**, 69–70

Hull, M R, 1968 The brooches, in *Fifth Report on the excavations of the Roman fort at Richborough, Kent* (ed. B Cunliffe), Rep Res Comm Soc Antiqs London **23**, Oxford, 74–93

Hyde, H A, and Harrison, S G, 1977 *Welsh timber trees native and introduced*, 4 edn revised by S G Harrison, Cardiff

Jackson, R, 1986 A set of Roman medical instruments from Italy, *Britannia* **17**, 119–67

Jackson, R, 1996 Wooden artefacts, in Jackson and Potter 1996, 544–552

Jackson, R, and Leahy, K, 1990 A Roman surgical forceps from near Littleborough and a note on the type, *Britannia* **21**, 271–4

Jackson, R P J, and Potter, T W, 1996 *Excavations at Stonea, Cambridgeshire 1980–85*, London

Jarman, C et al. forthcoming *Glebeland Iron Age and Romano-British settlement, Harrietsham, Kent*, Canterbury Archaeological Trust Occas Paper

Jenkins, F, 1956 A Roman tilery and two pottery kilns at Durovernum, *Antiq J* **36**, 40–56

Jenkins, F, 1958 The cult of the 'pseudo-Venus' in Kent, *Archaeol Cantiana* **72**, 60–76

Jenkins, F, 1960 Two pottery kilns and a tilery of the Roman period at Canterbury (Durovernum Cantiacorum), *Archaeol Cantiana* **74**, 151–161

Johnson, C, 2002 The excavation of a late Iron Age and early Roman site at Brisley, Farm, Chilmington Green, Ashford, Kent, *Kent Archaeol Soc Newsletter* **52**, 1–2

Jones, B, and Mattingly, D, 1990 *An atlas of Roman Britain*, Oxford

Jones, G, 1984 Interpretation of archaeological plant remains: Ethnographic models from Greece, in van Zeist and Casparie (eds) 1984, 43–61

Jones, M K, 1988 The arable field: a botanical battleground, in *Archaeology and the Flora of the British Isles* (ed. M K Jones), OUCA Monogr **14**, Oxford, 86–92

Keller, P T, 1988 The evidence for ancient quern production at Folkestone, *Kent Archaeol Rev* **93**, 59–68

Keller, P T, 1989 Quern production at Folkestone, south-east Kent: an interim note, *Britannia* **20**, 193–200

Kelley, D W, 1986 *Charcoal and charcoal burning*, Princes Risborough

Kelly, D B, 1992 The Mount Roman Villa, Maidstone, *Archaeol Cantiana* **110**, 177–237

Kenward, H K, and Williams, D, 1979 *Biological evidence from the Roman warehouses in Coney Street*, Archaeology of York **14/2**, London

King, A, 1978 A comparative survey of bone assemblages from Roman sites in Britain, *Bull Inst Archaeol* **15**, 207–232

Kislev, M E, 1988 *Pinus pinea* in agriculture, culture and cult, in *Der prähistorische Mensche und seine Umwelt* (ed. H Küster), Stuttgart, 73–79

Kloet, G S, and Hincks, W D, 1977 *A check list of British insects, 2nd edition (revised): Coleoptera and Strepsiptera*, Royal Entomological Society of London handbook for the identification of British insects **11**, part 3, London

Koster, A, 1997 The bronze vessels 2, *Description of the collections in the Rijksmuseum G M Kam at Nijmegen* **13**, Nijmegen

Lake, R D, and Shephard-Thorn, E R, 1987 *Geology of the country around Hastings and Dungeness*, London

Lawrence, S, forthcoming The Roman villa at Thurnham, Kent, *CTRL Integrated Site Report Series*, Archaeology Data Service

Lawson, A J, 1975 Shale and jet objects from Silchester, *Archaeologia* **105**, 241–75

Lemmon, C H, and Hill, J D, 1966 The Romano-British site at Bodiam, *Sussex Archaeol Collect* **104**, 88–102

Lethbridge, T C, 1952 Burial of an Iron Age warrior at Snailwell, *Proc Cambridge Antiq Soc* **46**, 25–37

Lloyd-Morgan, G., 1981. *Description of the Collections in the Rijksmuseum G.M. Kam at Nijmegen IX: the Mirrors* (Nijmegen).

Lloyd-Morgan, G, 1983 Mirror, in Excavations at Towcester, Northamptonshire: the Alchester road Suburb (A E Brown and C Woodfield), *Northamptonshire Archaeol* **18**, 106–8

Lovejoy, C O, Meindl, R S, Pryzbeck, T R, and Mensforth, R P, 1985 Chronological metamorphosis of the auricular surface of the ilium: a new method for determination of adult skeletal age-at-death, *American Journal of Physical Anthropology* **68**, 15–28

Lyne, M A B, 1994 *Late Roman handmade wares in southeast Britain*, Unpublished PhD thesis, University of Reading

Lyne, M A B, 1999 The evidence from assemblage quantifications for types of activity at Folly Lane, in *The excavation of a ceremonial site at Folly Lane, Verulamium* (R Niblett), Britannia Monogr Ser **14**, 299–307

Lyne, M A B, forthcoming a The pottery, in *Excavations at Waterbrook Farm, Ashford*

Lyne, M A B, forthcoming b The pottery, in *Excavations at 4 High Street, Staines* (A Richmond)

Lyne, M A B, forthcoming c The Roman pottery, in *Excavations at Swan Street, Southwark*

Lyne, M A B, and Jefferies, R S, 1979 *The Alice Holt/Farnham Roman pottery industry*, CBA Res Rep **30**, London

Mabey, R, 1997 *Flora Britannica*, London

Mackreth, D F, 1995 Pre-Roman and Roman brooches, in Blockley *et al.* 1995, 955–82

Mackreth, D F, 1996 Brooches, in Jackson and Potter 1996, 296–327

Mackreth, D F, 2002 Brooches from Catterick bypass and Catterick 1972 (Sites 433 and 434), in Wilson 2002b, 149–157

Macpherson-Grant, N, 1980 Chaff-tempered ware - an unusual ?Belgic -25BC - AD70 early Roman product from Canterbury, *Kent Archaeol Rev* **61**, 2–4

Macpherson-Grant, N, Savage, A, Cotter, J, Davey, M, and Riddler, I, 1995 *Canterbury ceramics 2. The processing and study of excavated pottery*, Canterbury Archaeol Trust unpublished report

Mahany, C (ed.), 1994 *Roman Alcester: southern extramural area, 1964–1966 excavations part 1: stratigraphy and structures*, CBA Res Rep **96**, York

Major, H J, and Eddy, M R, 1986 Four lead objects of possible Christian significance in East Anglia, *Britannia* **17**, 355–8

Manning, W H, 1976 *Catalogue of the Romano-British ironwork in the Museum of Antiquities, Newcastle upon Tyne*, Newcastle-upon-Tyne

Manning, W H, Price, J, and Webster, J, 1995 *Report on the excavations at Usk 1965–1976. The Roman small finds*, Cardiff

Margary, I D, 1947 Roman communications between Kent and the East Sussex ironworks, *Sussex Archaeol Collect* **86**, 22–41

Margary, I D, 1948 *Roman ways in the Weald*, London

Margary, I D, 1973 *Roman roads in Britain*, 3 edn, London

Marsh, G, 1981 London's samian supply and its relationship to the development of the Gallic samian industry, in *Roman pottery research in Britain and north-west Europe. Papers presented to Graham Webster* (eds A C Anderson and A S Anderson), BAR Int Ser **123**, 173–238

Maxfield, V A (ed.), 1989 *The Saxon shore: A handbook*, Exeter Studies in History **25**, Exeter

May, J, 1996 *Dragonby: report on excavations at an Iron Age and Romano-British settlement in north Lincolnshire*, Oxford

McAvoy, F, 1999 *Rectory Farm, Godmanchester: assessment and updated project design: Part 1*, Centre for Archaeology unpublished assessment report, English Heritage

McDonnell, J G, 1986 *The classification of early iron-working slags*, unpublished PhD thesis, University of Aston in Birmingham

McDonnell, J G, 1991 A model for the formation of smithing slags, *Materiały Archeologiczne* **26**, 23–28

McKinley, J, 1994 *The Anglo-Saxon cemetery at Spong Hill, North Elmham, part VIII: the cremations*, E Anglian Archaeol **69**, Dereham

McKinley, J, 1997a The cremated human bone from burial and cremation related contexts, in Fitzpatrick 1997, 55–73

McKinley, J, 1997b The cremated human bone from burial and pyre-related contexts, in Fitzpatrick 1997, 244–252

McKinley, J, 2004 The human remains and aspects of pyre technology and cremation rituals, in Cool 2004, 283–309

Meates, G W, 1987 *The Roman villa at Lullingstone, Kent. Volume II: the wall paintings and finds*, Kent Archaeol Soc Monogr **3**, Maidstone

Mees, A W, 1995 *Modelsignierte Dekorationen auf südgallischer Terra Sigillata*, Forschungen und Berichte zur Vor- und Frühgeschichte in Baden-Württemberg **54**, Stuttgart

Meindl, R S, and Lovejoy, C O, 1985 Ectocranial suture closure: a revised method for the determination of skeletal age at death based on the lateral-anterior sutures. *American Journal of Physical Anthropology* **68**, 29–45

Merrifield, R, 1962 Coins from the bed of the Walbrook and their significance, *Antiq J* **42**, 38–52

Merrifield, R, 1965 *The Roman City of London*, London

Miller, L, Schofield, J, and Rhodes, M, 1986 *The Roman quay at St Magnus House, London: excavation at New Fresh Wharf, Lower Thames Street, London, 1974–78*, LAMAS Special Paper **8**, London

Miller, N, 1985 Palaeoethnobotanical evidence for deforestation in ancient Iran: a case study of urban Malyan, *Journal of Ethnobiology* **5**, 1–19

Millett, M, 1986 An early Roman cemetery at Alton, Hampshire, *Proc Hampshire Fld Club Archaeol Soc* **42**, 43–88

Millett, M, 1990 *The Romanization of Britain*, Cambridge

Millett, M, 1995 Strategies for Roman small towns, in Brown 1995, 29–37

Millett, M, 2007 Roman Kent, in *The archaeology of Kent to AD 800* (J H Williams ed.), Kent County Council, Woodbridge, 135–184

Millett, M, and Graham, D, 1986 *Excavations on the Romano-British small town at Neatham, Hampshire 1969–1979*, Hampshire Fld Club Monogr **3**, Gloucester

Mills, A, and McDonnell, J G, 1992 The identification and analysis of the hammerscale from Burton Dassett, Warwickshire, *Ancient Monuments Laboratory Report* **47/92**, London

Mitchell, A, 1974 *A field guide to trees*, Glasgow

Moffet, L, Robinson, M, and Straker, V, 1989 Cereals, fruits and nuts: charred plant remains from Neolithic sites in England and Wales and the Neolithic economy, in *The beginning of agriculture* (eds A Milles, D Williams and N Gardiner), BARep Int Ser **496**, Oxford, 243–261

Moorhead, T S N, 2001 Roman coin finds from Wiltshire, in *Roman Wiltshire and after: papers in honour of Ken Annable* (ed. P Ellis), Devizes, 85–105

Monaghan, J, 1987 *Upchurch and Thameside Roman pottery. A ceramic typology for northern Kent, first to third centuries AD*, BAR Brit Ser **173**, Oxford

Monckton, A, 2000 The charred plant remains, in *The*

excavation of a Romano-British shrine at Orton's Pasture, Rocester, Staffordshire (I M Ferris, L Bevan and R Cuttler), BAR Brit Ser **314**, Oxford, 67–69

Moore, P D, Webb, J A, and Collinson, M E, 1991 *Pollen analysis*, 2 edn, Oxford

Morgan, R A, 1988 The case for wattling - what tree rings could reveal, in *The exploitation of the wetlands* (eds P Murphy and C French), BAR Brit Ser **186**, Oxford, 77–91

Morris, C A, 1990 Wooden finds, in Wrathmell, S, and Nicholson, A, 1990, 206–30

Morton, G R, and Wingrove, J, 1969 Constitution of bloomery slags: Part I: Roman. *Journal of the Iron and Steel Institute* **207**, 1556–64

Mould, Q, 1997 Leather, in *Birdoswald. Excavations of a Roman fort on Hadrian's Wall and its successor settlements: 1987–92* (T Wilmott), English Heritage Archaeol Rep **14**, London, 326–341

Mould, Q, 1998 The lead-alloy artefacts, in Cool and Philo 1998, 121–8

Murphy, P L, 1999 [Environmental assessment report] in McAvoy 1999

Murphy, P, 2000 Environmental and botanical evidence, in *Excavations on the Norwich southern bypass. Part 1: excavations at Bixley, Caistor St Edmund, Trowse, Cringleford and Little Melton* (T Ashwin and S Bates), E Anglian Archaeol **91**, Dereham, 217–227

Murphy, P, 2001 *Review of wood and macroscopic wood charcoal from archaeological sites in the west and east Midlands regions and the east of England*, Centre for Archaeology Report **23/2001**, English Heritage

Neal, D S, 1984 A sanctuary at Wood Lane End, Hemel Hempstead, *Britannia* **15**, 193–215

Neumann, K, 1989 Holocene vegetation of the eastern Sahara: charcoal from prehistoric sites, *The African Archaeol Rev* **7**, 97–116

Nuber, H-U, 1972 Kanne und Griffschale. Ihr Gebrauch im täglichen Leben und die Beigabe in Gräbern der römischen Kaiserzeit, *Bericht der Römisch-germanischen Kommission* **53**, 1–232

OAU, 2001 *Westhawk Farm, Kingsnorth, Ashford, Kent: archaeological post-excavation assesment report*, Oxford Archaeological Unit unpublished report for KCC

OWA, 2003 *M6 Toll 2000–2: proposals for archaeological post-excavation analysis and publication of results*, Oxford Wessex Archaeology Joint Venture, unpublished report

Ocock, M A, and Sydell, M J E, 1967 The Romano-British buildings in Church Field, Snodland, *Archaeol Cantiana* **82**, 192–217

O'Neil, H E, and Brown, G T, 1966 Metallurgical investigation of an iron object of Roman origin from Lower Slaughter, Glos, *Bulletin of the Historical Metallurgy Group*, **1 (7)**, 30–4

Orton, C J, 1975 Quantitative pottery studies: some progress, problems and prospects, *Sci & Archaeol* **16**, 30–35

Oswald, A, 1997 A doorway on the past: practical and mystic concerns in the orientation of roundhouse doorways, in Gwilt and Haselgrove (eds) 1997, 87–95

Oswald, F, and Pryce, T D, 1920 *An introduction to the study of terra sigillata*, London

OWA, 2006 CTRL Section 2 post-excavation archaeological works; Springhead and Northfleet updated project design, unpublished report Ref no. OWA-SPNO-DSGN-PGSG-FIN-v2.0 for London and Continental Railways

Padley, T G, 1991 Fascicule 2. The metalwork, glass and stone objects, in *The Roman waterlogged remains and later features at Castle St., Carlisle: excavations 1981–2* (M McCarthy), Cumberland and Westmorland Antiquarian and Archaeol Soc Research Ser **5**, Carlisle

Parfitt, K, 1995 *Iron Age burials from Mill Hill, Deal*, London

Parfitt, K, 2000 A Roman occupation site at Dickson's Corner, Worth, *Archaeol Cantiana* **120**, 107–148

Parfitt, K, Corke, B, and Cotter, J, 2006 *Excavations at Townwall Street, Dover, 1996*, The Archaeology of Canterbury, New Series Vol. 3, Canterbury Archaeol Trust, Canterbury

Paulian, R, 1959 Faune de France 63, *Coléoptères Scarabéides*, 2 edn, Paris

Payne, S, 1973 Kill-off patterns in sheep and goats: the mandibles from Asvan Kale, *Anatolian Studies* **23**, 281–303

Peacock, D P S, 1977 Brick and tiles of the *Classis Britannica*: petrology and origin, *Britannia* **8**, 235–248

Peacock, D P S, 1982 *Pottery in the Roman world: an ethnoarchaeological approach*, London

Peacock. D P S, 1987 Iron Age and Roman quern production at Lodsworth, West Sussex, *Antiq J* **68**, 61–85

Pearce, J, 1997 Death and time: the structure of late Iron Age mortuary ritual, in Gwilt and Haselgrove (eds) 1997, 174–180

Pearce, J, 1999 The dispersed dead: preliminary observations on burial and settlement space in rural Roman Britain, in *TRAC 98: Proceedings of the eighth annual theoretical Roman archaeology conference, Leicester 1998* (eds P Baker, C Forcey, S Jundi and R Witcher), Oxford, 151–162

Pelling, R, 2003 Charred plant remains, in Ritual and riverside settlement: A multi-period site at Princes Road, Dartford (P Hutchings), *Archaeol Cantiana* **123**, 71

Pelling, R, unpublished Monkton Mount Pleasant: the charred plant remains. Unpublished report for Canterbury Archaeological Trust

Pelling, R, 2001 Assessment of the charred plant remains, in *Waterloo Connection, Southfleet, Kent. ARC PHL 97, ARC NBR 98. Detailed archaeological works assessment report*, Oxford Archaeological Unit report for URS

Perkins, D R J, 1985 The Monkton gas pipeline: phases III and IV, 1983–84, *Archaeol Cantiana* **102**, 43–40

Perring, D, Roskams, S, and Allen, P, 1991 *Early development of Roman London west of the Walbrook*, CBA Res Rep **70**, London

Petch, J A, 1927 Excavations at Benwell (Condercum). First interim report (1926), *Archaeol Aeliana* (4th ser) **4**, 135–92

Philp, B, 1973 *Excavations in west Kent 1960–1970*, Kent Res Rep **2**, Dover

Philp, B, 1976 The probable site of *Durolevum*, *Kent Archaeol Rev* **43**, 62–64

Philp, B, 1981 *The excavation of the Roman forts of the Classis Britannica at Dover, 1970–1977*, Dover

Philp, B, 1989 *The Roman house with Bacchic murals at Dover*, Dover

Philp, B, 1994 *The Iron Age and Romano-British site at Lenham, Kent*, Kent Special Subjects Ser **7**, West Wickham

Philp, B, 1997 *Report on a programme of archaeological work at Westhawk Farm, Kingsnorth, Ashford*, Kent Archaeological Rescue Unit unpublished report

Philp, B, 1998 Roman town discovered at Ashford, *Kent Archaeol Rev* **133**, 57–65

Philp, B, and Chenery, M, 1997 *A Roman site at Vagniacae (Springhead) near Gravesend*, Kent Special Subjects Ser **9**, Canterbury

Philp, B, and Mills, R, 1991 *The Roman villa at Horton Kirby, Kent*, Kent Special Subjects Ser **5**, Dover

Philp, B, Parfitt, K, Willson, J, Dutto, M, and Williams, W, 1991 *The Roman villa site at Keston, Kent. First report (excavations 1968–1978)*, Kent Monogr **6**, Dover

Philp, B, Parfitt, K, Willson, J, and Williams, W, 1999 *The Roman villa site at Keston, Kent. Second Report (excavations 1967 and 1978–1990)*, Kent Monogr **8**, Dover

Philpott, R, 1991 *Burial practices in Roman Britain*, BAR Brit Ser **219**, Oxford

Pirling, R, 1997 *Das Römisch-Fränkische Graberfeld von Krefeld-Gellep 1975–1982*, GDV Ser B **17**, Stuttgart

Pitts, L F, and St Joseph, J K, 1985 *Inchtuthil: the Roman legionary fortress*, Britannia Monogr **6**, London

Pleiner, R, 2000 *Iron in archaeology: the European bloomery smelters*, Archeologický Ústav Avčr, Praha

Pliny the Elder, *Naturalis Historiae*, trans. H Rackham, Cambridge, Mass., 1952

Plouviez, J, 1995 A hole in the distribution map: the characteristics of small towns in Suffolk, in Brown 1995, 69–80

Pollard, R J, 1988 *The Roman pottery of Kent*, Kent Archaeol Soc Monogr **5**, Maidstone

Pollard, R J, 1995 The pottery: A. The Belgic and early Roman periods, in Blockley *et al.* 1995, 585–624

Price, E, 2000 *Frocester: A Romano-British settlement, its antecedents and successors. Vol 2: the finds*, Stonehouse

Price, J, and Cottam, S, 1998 *Romano-British glass vessels: a handbook*, CBA Practical Handbook in Archaeology **14**, York

Prummel, W, and Frisch, H-J, 1986 A guide for the distinction of species, sex and body size in bones of sheep and goat, *J Archaeol Sci* **13**, 567–577

Rackham, O, 1997 *The history of the countryside*, London

Radice, B (trans.), 1969 *The letters of the Younger Pliny*, Harmondsworth

Rady, J, 1992 Waterbrook Farm, Ashford, *Canterbury's Archaeology 1991–1992*, Canterbury, 32–34

Rady, J, 1996 Waterbrook Farm, Ashford, *Canterbury's Archaeology 1994–1995*, Canterbury, 38–39

Rahtz, P A, and Greenfield, E, 1977 *Excavations at Chew Valley Lake, Somerset,* DoE Archaeol Rep **8**, London

Reece, R, 1987 Commentary, in Meates 1987, 48–51

Reece, R,1995a Site-finds in Roman Britain, *Britannia* **26**, 179–206

Reece, R, 1995b Models in collision: east and west in Roman Britain, *Oxford J Archaeol* **14**, 113–115

Reece, R, 1998 Discussion: the Roman coins, in *Excavations at Kingscote and Wycomb, Gloucestershire: a Roman estate centre and small town in the Gloucestershire Cotswolds with Notes on related settlements* (J R Timby), Cirencester, 400–421

RIB, 1991 *The Roman Inscriptions of Britain Vol. II: Instrumentum Domesticum (personal belongings and the like). Fascicule 2: weights, gold vessel, silver vessels, bronze vessels, lead vessels, pewter vessels, shale vessels, glass vessels, spoons,* (eds S S Frere and R S O Tomlin), Stroud

Richmond, I A, Gillam, J P, and Birley, E, 1951 The temple of Mithras at Carrawburgh, *Archaeol Aeliana* (4th ser) **29**, 1–29

Riddler, I, Mould, Q, and Lyne, M, forthcoming *The Roman watermills at Ickham, Kent. Salvage excavations of a Roman industrial complex by Jim Bradshaw and Christopher Young, 1972–1979,* Canterbury Archaeological Trust

Rigby, V, 1995 Early Gaulish and Rhenish imports, in Blockley *et al.* 1995, 640–663

Rigold, S E, 1972 Roman Folkestone reconsidered, *Archaeol Cantiana* **87**, 31–42

Rigold, S E, 1977 Two common species of medieval seal-matrix, *Antiq J* **57**, 324–9

Rivet, A L F, and Smith, C, 1979 *The place–names of Roman Britain,* London

Roberts, C, and Manchester, R, 1995 *The archaeology of disease,* New York

Robertson, A, Scott, M, and Keppie, L, 1975 *Bar Hill: a Roman fort and its finds,* BAR Brit Ser **16**, Oxford

Robinson, M R, 1979 Plants and invertebrates in *Iron Age and Roman riverside settlements at Farmoor, Oxfordshire* (G Lambrick and M Robinson), CBA Res Rep **32**, London, 77–128

Robinson, M R, 1986 Waterlogged plant and invertebrate evidence, in *Archaeology at Barton Court Farm, Abingdon, Oxon* (D Miles), CBA Res Rep **50**, London, Microfiche 9.C1

Robinson, M, 1991 The Neolithic and late Bronze Age insect assemblages, in *Excavation and salvage at Runnymede Bridge, 1978: the late Bronze Age waterfront site* (S P Needham), London, 277–326

Robinson, M (ed.), forthcoming a Palaeoenvironmental evidence from section 1 of the Channel Tunnel Rail Link, Kent (ed.), *CTRL Scheme-wide Specialist Report Series,* Archaeology Data Service

Robinson, M, forthcoming b Insect remains from Roman wells, in *Elms Farm: excavations at the late Iron Age and Roman settlement at Heybridge, Essex, 1993–5* (M Atkinson and S J Preston), E Anglian Archaeol

Rodwell, W and Rowley, T (eds), 1975 *Small towns of Roman Britain,* BAR Brit Ser **15**, Oxford

Roe, D, 1968 *A gazetteer of British lower and middle Palaeolithic sites,* CBA Res Rep **8**, London

Roe, D, 1980 *A lower Palaeolithic handaxe from a Roman context at Woolbury,* unpublished manuscript

Roe, D A, 1981 *The lower and middle Palaeolithic periods in Britain,* London

Roe, F, nd The worked stone, in Boyle and Early nd, 29–30

Rogers, G B, 1974 *Poteries sigillées de la Gaule Centrale. I - les motifs non figurés,* Gallia Supplement **28**, Paris

Ross, A, 1992 *Pagan Celtic Britain,* London

Roth, J P, 1999 *The logistics of the Roman army at war (264 B.C.-A.D. 235),* Leiden

Rudling, D, 2001 Chanctonbury Ring revisited: the excavations of 1988–1991, *Sussex Archaeol Collect* **139**, 75–121

Salisbury, E J, and Jane, F W, 1940 Charcoals from Maiden Castle and their significance in relation to the vegetation and climatic conditions in prehistoric times, *Journal of Ecology* **28**, 310–325

Salter, C, 1997 Metallurgical debris, in *Asthall, Oxfordshire: excavations in a Roman 'Small Town'* (P M Booth), Thames Valley Landscapes Monogr **9**, Oxford, 89–98

Salway, P, 1981 *Roman Britain,* Oxford

Savage, A, 1998 The Roman pottery, in Hicks 1998, 132–150

Schmidt, P R, 1996 *The culture and technology of African iron production,* Gainesville

Schmidt, P R, 1997 *Iron technology in East Africa: symbolism, science and archaeology,* Bloomington

Schrüfer-Kolb, I, 2004 *Roman iron production in Britain: technological and socio-economic landscape development along the Jurassic ridge,* BAR Brit Ser **380**, Oxford

Schweingruber, F H, 1990 *Microscopic wood anatomy,* 3 edn, Zurich

Scott, P R, 1977 Piercebridge notes - 1975, *Trans Architect Archaeol Soc Durham Northumberland* **4**, 43–54

Shaffrey, R L, forthcoming The worked stone (Thurnham), in Small finds from Section 1 of the Channel Tunnel Rail Link, Kent (ed. L Allen), *CTRL Scheme-wide Specialist Report Series,* Archaeology Data Service

Shepherd, J, 1998 *The temple of Mithras, London,* English Heritage Archaeol Rep **12**, London

Shepherd, J, 1996 Glass, in Early Roman development at Leadenhall Court, London and related research (G Milne and A Wardle), *Trans London Middlesex Archaeol Soc* **44** (for 1993), 99–114

Sibun, L, 2001 Excavation at Syndale Park, Ospringe, *Archaeol Cantiana* **121**, 171–196

Silver, I A, 1969 The ageing of domestic animals, in *Science in Archaeology* (eds D R Brothwell and E S Higgs), London, 283–302

Sim, D, and Ridge, I, 2002 *Iron for the eagles: the iron industry of Roman Britain,* Stroud

Smart, J G O, Bisson, G, and Worssam, B C, 1966 *Geology of the country around Canterbury and Folkestone,* Memoir of the Geological Survey for Sheets 289, 305 and 306, London

Smith, A, 2001 *The differential use of constructed sacred space in southern Britain from the late Iron Age to the 4th century AD*, BAR Brit Ser **318**, Oxford

Smith, R A, 1912 On late-celtic antiquities discovered at Welwyn, Herts, *Archaeologia* **63**, 1–30

Smith, R F, 1987 *Roadside settlements in lowland Roman Britain*, BAR Brit Ser **157**, Oxford

Smith, V T C, 1997 The Roman road at Springhead Nurseries, *Archaeol Cantiana* **117**, 51–67

Smith, W, 2002 A *Review of archaeological wood analyses in Southern England*, English Heritage Centre for Archaeology Report 75/ 2002. Portsmouth

Snape, M E, 1993 *Roman brooches from north Britain*, BAR Brit Ser **235**, Oxford

Spain, R J, 1989 The second century Romano-British watermill at Ickham, Kent, *History of Technology* **9**, 143–180

Sparey-Green, C, 1999 Roman building material: Wye, *Archaeol Cantiana* **119**, 392–393

SSEW, 1983 *Soils of England and Wales. Sheet 6, South East England*, Soil Survey of England and Wales

Stace, C, 1997 *New flora of the British Isles*, 2 edn, Cambridge

Stanfield, J A, and Simpson, G, 1958 *Central Gaulish potters*, London

Starley, D, 1997 Metallurgical study of a Roman iron beam from the 1959 by-pass excavations, Catterick, North Yorkshire, *Ancient Monuments Laboratory Report* **89/97**, London

Starley, D, 1998 Westhawk Farm near Ashford, Kent: site visit report, Ancient *Monuments Laboratory report*

Stead, I M, 1967 A La Tène III burial at Welwyn Garden City, *Archaeologia* **101**, 1–62

Stead, I M, and Rigby, V, 1986 *Baldock: the excavation of a Roman and pre-Roman settlement, 1968–72*, Britannia Monogr **7**, London

Stead, I M, and Rigby, V, 1989 *Verulamium: the King Harry Lane site*, English Heritage Archaeol Rep **12**, London

Stevenson, J, and Johnson, C, 2004 Brisley Farm; The last Iron Age warriors of Kent?, *Current Archaeol* **191**, 490–494

St John Hope, W H, and Fox, G E, 1901 Excavations on the site of the Roman city at Silchester, Hants, in 1900, *Archaeologia* **57**, 229–256

Straker, V, 1988 The charcoal, in *The Rollright Stones: megaliths, monuments and settlements in the prehistoric landscape* (G Lambrick), English Heritage Archaeol Rep **6**, London, 102–103

Suchey, J M, and Brooks, S, 1990 Skeletal age determination based on the *os pubis*: a comparison of the Acsádi-Nemeskéri and Suchey-Brooks method, *Human Evolution* **5**, 227–238

Swift, E, 2000 *Regionality in dress accessories in the late Roman west*, Monographies Instrumentum **11**, Millau

Symonds, R P, 1992 *Rhenish wares. Fine dark coloured pottery from Gaul and Germany*, OUCA Monogr **23**, Oxford

Tassinari, S, 1993 *Il vassellame bronzeo di Pompei*, Ministero per i beni culturali ed ambientali soprintendenza archeologica di Pompei Cataloghi **5**, Rome

Taylor, J, 2000 Stonea in its Fenland context: moving beyond an imperial estate, *J Roman Archaeol* **13**, 647–658

Thompson, G B, 1996 *The excavation of Khok Phanom Di. Vol 4: subsistence and environment – the botanical evidence*, London

Thompson, G B, 1999 The analysis of wood charcoals from selected pits and funerary contexts, in A Barclay and C Halpin, *Excavations at Barrow Hills, Radley, Oxfordshire. Vol 1: the Neolithic and Bronze Age monument complex*, Thames Valley Landscapes, **11**, Oxford, 247–253

Thompson, I, 1982 *Grog-tempered 'Belgic' pottery of south-eastern England*, BAR Brit Ser **108**, Oxford

Toynbee, J M C, 1963 *Art in Roman Britain*, London

Toynbee, J M C, 1967 The bronze jug, in Two Flavian burials from Grange Road, Winchester (M Biddle), *Antiq J* **47**, 240–42

Turner, R, 1999 *Excavations of an Iron Age settlement and Roman religious complex at Ivy Chimneys, Witham, Essex, 1979–83*, E Anglian Archaeol **88**, Chelmsford

Turner, R, and Wymer, J, 1987 An assemblage of Palaeolithic Hand-axes from the Roman religious complex at Ivy Chimneys, Witham, Essex, *Antiq J* **67**, 43–60

Tylecote, R F, 1962a Roman shaft furnaces in Norfolk, *Journal of the Iron and Steel Institute* **200**, 19–23

Tylecote, R F, 1962b The bloomery site at West Runton, *Norfolk Archaeol* **34**, 187–214

Tylecote, R F, 1990 *The prehistory of metallurgy in the British Isles*, London

Lawrence, S, forthcoming The Roman villa at Thurnham, Kent, *CTRL Integrated Site Report Series*, Archaeology Data Service

VCH, 1932 *The Victoria History of the county of Kent* **3**, London

Veen, M van der, 1991 Charred grain assemblages from Roman-period corndriers in Britain, *Archaeol J* **146**, 302–319

Veen, M van der, and O'Connor, T, 1998 The expansion of agricultural production in the late Iron Age and Roman Britain, in *Science in archaeology: an agenda for the future* (ed. J Bayley), 127–44

Vernon, R W, 1999 *Report on a fluxgate gradiometer survey on a Romano-British settlement at Westhawk Farm, Ashford, Kent*, Project on the investigation of ironworking sites by Geophysical Survey, Project Report No. 12, Department of Archaeological Science, University of Bradford

Walker, D R, 1988 The Roman coins, in *The temple of Sulis Minerva at Bath. Vol. 2: the finds from the sacred spring* (ed. B Cunliffe), OUCA Mongr **16**, 281–358

Walton Rogers, P, 1997 Late Iron Age textile and fibre remains, in Fitzpatrick 1997, 110–1

Walton Rogers, P, 2007 Textile remains, in Sealey, P R, A late Iron Age warrior burial from Kelvedon, Essex, East Anglian Archaeol Rep No. **118**, Colchester, 26

Ward-Perkins, J B, 1944 Excavations on the Iron Age Hill-fort of Oldbury, near Ightham, Kent, *Archaeologia* **40**, 127–176

Ward-Perkins, J, and Claridge, A, 1976 *Pompeii AD79*, Bristol

Watkins, S, and Cameron, E, 1987 An Iron Age warrior's grave from Guernsey: the excavation, conservation and interpretation of its contents, in *Recent advances in the conservation and analysis of artifacts* (ed. J Black), London, 51–7

Waugh, H, and Goodburn, R, 1972 The non-ferrous objects, in Frere, S. S., *Verulamium Excavations Vol. I*, Rep. Res. Comm. Soc. Antiq. Lon. 27, (Oxford), 114–62

Webster, G, 1975 Small towns without defences, in Rodwell and Rowley 1975, 53–66

Webster, J, 1981 The bronzes, in *Whitton: an Iron Age Roman farmstead in south Glamorgan* (M G Jarrett and S Wrathmell), Cardiff, 163–88

Webster, J, 1992 The objects of bronze, in *Roman Gates, Caerleon* (D R Evans and V M Metcalf), Oxbow Monogr **15**, Oxford, 103–61

Wedlake, W J, 1982 *The excavation of the shrine of Apollo at Nettleton, Wiltshire, 1956–1971*, Rep Res Comm Soc Antiqs London **50**, London

Weeks, J, 1978 A Roman ladder from Queen Street, City of London, *Trans London Middlesex Archaeol Soc* **29**, 104–111

Western, C, 1971 The ecological interpretation of ancient charcoals from Jericho, *Levant* **3**, 31–40

Wheeler, R E M, 1930 *London in Roman times*, Museum of London Catalogue **3**, London

Wheeler, R E M (ed.), 1932 Romano-British remains, in *VCH Kent*, Vol 3, 1932 1–176

Wheeler, R E M, and Wheeler, T V, 1928 The Roman amphitheatre at Caerleon, Monmouthshire, *Archaeologia* **78**, 111–218

Wheeler, R E M, and Wheeler, T V, 1936 *Verulamium: a Belgic and two Roman cities*, Rep Res Comm Soc Antiqs London **11**, London

Whimster, R, 1981 *Burial practices in Iron Age Britain: a discussion and gazetteer of the evidence c 700 BC to AD 43*, BAR Brit Ser **90**, Oxford

Whiting, W, 1926 The Roman cemeteries at Ospringe. Description of the finds continued, *Archaeol Cantiana* **38**, 123–51

Whiting, W, Hawley, W, and May, T, 1931 *Report on the excavation of the Roman cemetery at Ospringe, Kent*. Rep Res Comm Soc Antiqs London **8**, Oxford

Whytehead, R, 1986 The excavation of an area within a Roman cemetery at West Tenter St., London E1, *Trans London Middlesex Archaeol Soc* **37**, 23–124

Wickenden, N P, 1992 *The temple and other sites in the north-eastern sector of Caesaromagus*, CBA Res Rep **75**, London

Wickenden, N P, 1996 The Roman towns of Essex, in *The archaeology of Essex: proceedings of the 1993 Writtle conference* (ed. O Bedwin), Chelmsford, 76–94

Wild, J P, 1970 *Textile manufacture in the northern Roman provinces*, Cambridge

Wilkinson, D R P, 1994 Excavations on the White Cliffs Experience site, Dover, 1988–91, *Archaeol Cantiana* **114**, 51–148

Willcox, G H, 1977 Exotic plants from Roman waterlogged sites in London, *J Archaeol Sci* **4**, 267–282

Williams, H, 2004 Potted histories - cremation, ceramics and social memory in early Roman Britain, *Oxford J Archaeol* **23 (4)**, 417–427

Williams, R J, Hart, P J, and Williams, A T L, 1996 *Wavendon Gate: a late Iron Age and Roman settlement in Milton Keynes*, Buckinghamshire Archaeol Soc Monogr Ser No. **10**, Aylesbury

Willson, J, 1981 Catalogue of the coarse pottery, in Philp 1981, 207–249

Wilmott, T, 1982 Excavations at Queen Street, City of London, 1953 and 1960, and Roman timber lined wells in London, *Trans London Middlesex Archaeol Soc* **33**, 1–78

Wilmott, T, Cool, H E M, and Evans, J, forthcoming Excavation and survey at Birdoswald 1996–2000, in *Research by English Heritage on Hadrian's Wall* (ed. T Wilmott), English Heritage

Wilson, M, 1995 The pottery from CEC sites, in Blockley *et al.* 1995, 755–771

Wilson, P R, 2002a *Cataractonium: Roman Catterick and its hinterland. Excavations and research, 1958–1977. Part I*, CBA Res Rep **128**, York

Wilson, P R, 2002b *Cataractonium: Roman Catterick and its hinterland. Excavations and research, 1958–1977. Part II*, CBA Res Rep **129**, York

Wiltshire, P E J, 1989 *A palynological study of organic silts from Iron Age and Roman Canterbury, Kent*, English Heritage Ancient Monuments Laboratory Report **67/89**

Wiltshire, P E J, 1996 *Palynological analysis of exhibits associated with alleged rape in Stevenage, Hertfordshire*, unpublished report for Hertfordshire Constabulary

Wiltshire, P E J, 1998a *Glinton – palynological assessment of feature fills*, unpublished report for Cambridgeshire County Council

Wiltshire, P E J, 1998b *Palynological assessment of organic deposits, Carbrooke Commandery, Norfolk*, unpublished report for Norfolk Archaeological Unit

Wiltshire, P E J, 1999a Palynological assessment of sediments from prehistoric and Roman features, in McAvoy 1999

Wiltshire, P E J, 1999b *Palynological assessment of ditch sediments at Zion Hill Copse*, unpublished report for Berkshire Archaeological Services

Wiltshire, P E J, 2001 *Palynological analysis Operation Maple*, unpublished report for Sussex Police

Wiltshire, P E J, Edwards, K J, and Bond, S, 1994 Microbially-derived metallic sulphide spherules, pollen and the waterlogging of archaeological sites, in *Aspects of archaeological palynology: methodology and applications* (ed. O K Davis), American Assoc of Stratigraphic Palynologists Contributions Ser **29**, 206–221

Wolff, E T von, 1871, *Aschen-analysen von landwirthschaftlichten Producten, Fabrik-Abfällen und. wildwachsenden Pflanzen*, Weigandt and Hempel Verlag, Berlin.

Woolf, G, 2000 The religious history of the northwest provinces, *J Roman Archaeol* **13**, 613–630

Worssam, B, 1985 The geology of Wealden iron, in Cleere and Crossley 1985, 1–30

Wrathmell, S, and Nicholson, A, 1990 *Dalton Parlours: Iron Age settlement and Roman villa*, Yorkshire Archaeology **3**, Wakefield

Wright J H, 1972 Metallurgical examination of a Roman iron beam from Catterick Bridge, Yorkshire, *Historical Metallurgy* **6**, 24–7

Wymer, J, 1968 *Lower Palaeolithic archaeology in Britain as represented by the Thames Valley*, London

Wymer, J, 1993 *The Southern Rivers Palaeolithic Project, Report 2, 1992–1993: the south west and south of the Thames*, Salisbury

Wymer, J, 1999 *The lower Palaeolithic occupation of Britain. Vol 1: Text*, Salisbury

Yates, D T, 1999 Bronze Age field systems in the Thames Valley, *Oxford J Archaeol* **18 (2)**, 157–170

Yates, D, 2001 Bronze Age agricultural intensification in the Thames Valley and Estuary, in *Bronze Age landscapes: tradition and transformation* (ed. J Brück) Oxford, 65–82

Zeist, W van, and Casparie, W A (eds), 1984 *Plants and ancient man: studies in Palaeoethnobotany*, Rotterdam

Zienkiewicz, J D, 1986 *The legionary fortress baths at Caerleon: II the finds*, Cardiff

Index

CREATED BY PAUL BACKHOUSE AND PAUL BOOTH

K

L

M

N

O

419